Issues in Indian Public Finance

Issues in Indian Public Finance

D.K. Srivastava

New Century Publications
New Delhi, India

NEW CENTURY PUBLICATIONS
4800/24, Bharat Ram Road,
Ansari Road, Daryaganj,
New Delhi-110 002
Tel.: 23247798, 55396605
Telefax: 011-51017798
E-mail: indiatax@vsnl.com
www.newcenturypublications.com

Editorial office:
34, Gujranwala Town, Part-2,
Delhi - 110 009
Tel.: 27247805, 27464774

First Published July 2005

ISBN: 81-7708-096-2

Published by New Century Publications and printed at Singhal Print Media, Delhi -110 007

PRINTED IN INDIA

About the Book

In spite of extensive fiscal reforms undertaken during the nineties, India's public finances face numerous problems. While the taxation system remains distortionary and fragmented, government expenditures remain inefficient in providing public and merit goods to the desired extent. Vertical imbalance and horizontal disparities characterise the federal fiscal system. The fiscal reform years have witnessed a sharp rise in the fiscal imbalance and deterioration in state finances.

This book undertakes a comprehensive review of the contemporary issues in India's public finances within a long-term perspective tracing its evolution since 1950-51. It critically analyses the causes of fiscal imbalance, the tensions that prevail in centre-state financial relations, the progress of decentralization, and issues related with the structure of taxation as well as government expenditures. It examines the impact of public finances on the macro economy and looks at fiscal policy options for growth, stability and poverty alleviation.

The book is divided into six parts providing in the first part an overview followed by analysis of issues in taxation, expenditure, fiscal imbalance, government debt, fiscal federalism, and fiscal policy.

Author's Profile

Dr. D.K. Srivastava is presently Director, Madras School of Economics, Chennai. He was a Member of the Twelfth Finance Commission, Principal Consultant to the Eleventh Finance Commission, and Economic Advisor to the Tenth Finance Commission. He has had a long association with the National Institute of Public Finance and Policy, New Delhi where he worked as Senior Economist, Fellow, and Senior Fellow. He was a Professor of Economics at Banaras Hindu University during 1984-1996. He has also taught at the University of Allahabad and at the University of the West Indies, Jamaica. He was a Stanley Smith Fellow at the University of St. Andrews, United Kingdom during 1978-80.

Dr. Srivastava studied at Allahabad University, and later at the University of St. Andrews, United Kingdom for M.Litt. and Ph.D. He was a National Merit Scholar and a Commonwealth Scholar in the United Kingdom. He was honoured by the award of the Tassie Medallion of Adam Smith at the University of St. Andrews, United Kingdom.

Dr. Srivastava's teaching and research interests are in the fields of Public Finance and Macroeconomics. He is the author of a number of books, reports, and articles. Dr. Srivastava has written extensively on Budgetary Subsidies and edited a volume on Fiscal Federalism in India: Contemporary Challenges.

Preface

India's public finances have charted a course during the period since 1950-51 that is exciting to study and challenging to address. This book explores the turns and twists that the Indian fiscal system went through over these years in its various dimensions covering government revenues, public expenditures, fiscal imbalance and mounting debt relative to GDP. There has been a major policy shift in the early nineties affecting the economy and public finances. For a period of nearly forty years, the Indian economy had operated with an inward looking, plan centric strategy that relied on extensive regimes of licenses, administered prices, tariff walls and controlled interest rates. Economic and fiscal reforms undertaken from the early nineties brought fresh air and released clogged up economic energies. Growth rates accelerated and the economy went through a major structural shift in the composition of output. The poverty ratio fell tangibly in the high growth years. If there is one vulnerable part of these otherwise sound developments, it is the disarray in the fiscal scenario.

The reform years witnessed one of the sharpest fiscal crises since 1950-51. The central and state governments in their combined as well as individual accounts witnessed first a transformation of revenue surplus into revenue deficit that rose in magnitude. This was linked to high levels of fiscal deficits, which resulted in persistently rising levels of debt relative to GDP and GSDPs. This book examines India's public finances through its different phases, tracing the course of its evolution, examining the causes of structural fiscal imbalance, and reviewing the scope and shape of fiscal reforms. It covers all major dimensions of public finance in a developing economy encompassing issues in taxation, government expenditures, and fiscal imbalance. It deals with issues in fiscal federalism, particularly the role of the finance commission and the planning commission. Issues in running fiscal policy and its impact on growth and macro-economic stability, requires detailed consideration of options that emanate from different theoretical perspectives. This book examines the evolution of fiscal policy in India in the context of initial growth and subsequent stagnation in the volume of government expenditures relative to GDP.

This book is meant for the undergraduate honours and postgraduate students of Indian Public Finance. It should also prove to be useful in providing an empirical context in studies of macroeconomics.

The analytical perspectives detailed in the book have developed over a long period of time that I spent at the National Institute of Public Finance and Policy, New Delhi. It provided not only a rich library but also scope for lively discussions with leading authorities in Public Finance including Dr. Raja J. Chelliah, Dr. C. Rangarajan, and Dr. Amaresh Bagchi. Working and interacting with the present Director, Dr. M.G. Rao and former Directors Dr. Partho Shome and Dr. Ashok Lahiri has proved to be immensely rewarding. The presence of colleagues like Professor Om Mathur, Dr. Indira Rajaraman, and Dr. Tapas K. Sen was exciting and enlightening. In many studies that I undertook at the NIPFP, many colleagues joined hand. I am happy to acknowledge the steady and reliable help that I received from colleagues like Dr. Bhujang C. Rao, Dr. Pinaki Chakraborty, and Shri T.S. Rangamnnar. Much of what I have written here has its roots in the numerous works that we did together. In equal measure, I have benefited from colleagues in the Tenth, Eleventh, and Twelfth Finance Commissions where we worked with close cooperation under tremendous pressure of time.

At home, I must thank my wife, Veena, who put up with both my absence from home and my presence in it with equal degree of patience and understanding. My mother, my son-in-law, Amit and my daughter, Mrinmayee have supported me with encouragement from a distance. My son, Mrinal Kanti has offered a more hands-on help.

I would also like to put on record my appreciation and gratefulness for my publisher Mr. Sandeep Sury, who not only encouraged me persistently for completing the book but did an outstanding job of production in a very limited time.

Much of the organization of my office at NIPFP and production of various studies was adeptly done by Shri R.S. Tyagi. I am thankful to him for all his help.

While I acknowledge the help of my friends, colleagues and family, the responsibility of any remaining errors fall squarely on me.

July 8, 2005

D.K. Srivastava

Contents

Part III: Issues in Government Expenditure

Part IV: Fiscal Imbalance in India and Issues in Debt Management

Part VI: Fiscal Policy and Macroeconomic Management

To
My Father

who told me Economics is worth pursuing

Part I: Introduction

1

Introduction: Role of Government

> "Fiscal resources are needed to execute state functions, and the way in which they are tendered shapes how individuals and the state are related...I think of a state as an association of individuals, engaged in a cooperative venture, formed to resolve problems of social co-existence and do so in a democratic and fair fashion."
>
> Musgrave (1999): *The Nature of the Fiscal State*

A study of public finance of a country needs to encompass five main areas: taxation, expenditures, budget balance and public debt, inter-governmental financial relations, and fiscal policy. The evolution of public finance in India since 1950-51 provides a fascinating landscape for studying the role of government finances in a developing country. This book analyses the contemporary issues of India's public finances in the background of its evolution since 1950-51. All the core issues are discussed within the context of the theoretical principles of public finance.

The first thirty-seven years from 1950-51 to 1986-87 were years of expansion of the size of government in India based on an expanding tax-GDP ratio. The size of government measured by the ratio of government expenditure to GDP is still small compared to the comparable shares of many other countries particularly in the west. Since 1987-88, not only the volume of government expenditure stagnated, Indian public finance has witnessed serious problems of mounting debt and deficit in relation to the gross domestic product at current market prices (GDP), tensions in the inter-governmental fiscal relations, and deficiencies in the provision of public goods like general administration and merit goods like education and health.

1.1 Role of Government

The rationale for government lies in market failures. Markets fail for a variety of reasons including the existence of public goods and externalities. Public goods are goods meant for collective consumption and, as discussed below, are characterized by two special features: non-excludability and non-rivalry. Other important sources of market failure are existence of increasing returns to scale, incomplete information, and chronic unemployment of available resources.

Modern day governments participate in providing public and merit goods. They are also routinely engaged in providing many private goods. Public goods are those that are characterized by two characteristics: non-rivalry and non-excludability. Examples are defence, maintenance of law and order, and general administration. Merit goods are essentially private goods, but they are characterized by positive externalities. In their case, the benefit extends beyond the individual consumer. Often, merit goods are provided on account of 'paternalistic' motives, as goods and services considered 'good' for people at large whether they themselves want it or not. Examples are health and education. In a federal structure of government, there is the additional question as to which level of government may be best suited to provide a certain service. This choice is usually made on two considerations:

- economies of scale in providing the service, and
- differences in regional preferences.

If a good or service is to be provided by the central government, its standards are likely to be uniform across the country. However, if the central government itself is dominated by people of one region, they may like to impose their own preferences in the rest of the country. Depending on the nature of the service, it is sometimes possible to divide them into national public goods, and regional and local public goods. In the case of a local public good, ideally the financing should come from local taxes paid by people living in the given jurisdiction, who would enjoy the benefit of the local public good. However, often benefits spill over to the neighbouring regions and the rest of the country. For example, education in one state can benefit another state because of the mobility of the skilled human resources. Some transfers or subsidies by the higher tier of governments may be justified in the case of benefit spill overs.

1.2 Rationale and Scope of Public Expenditure

The structure of public expenditure needs to be decided consistent with the objectives and role of public intervention in the economy. Public intervention is required because, as mentioned earlier, market fails in certain respects. At the same time, excessive public intervention is not efficient because like market failures there are government failures.

1.3 Public Goods

As mentioned earlier, public goods are distinguished from private goods due to two characteristics: non-excludability and non-rivalry. In contrast, private goods are excludable meaning that individual consumers can be separated and charged according to the extent of their consumption. Also, their consumption is rival in the sense that what is consumed by one is not available to another. There can be goods in the intermediate range having the characteristics of excludability but not rivalry and vice versa. Cases may also be cited when initially there is no rivalry in consumption, but it develops as more consumers join. This is the case of congestible goods.

1.4 Merit Goods

Externalities arise in the case of some private goods whose consumption may be excludable and rival, but the benefits of an individual's consumption extend beyond the immediate consumer. Those benefits reach out to the society at large. Examples are education and health, particularly elementary education and primary health. In these cases, the benefit to society is larger than the sum of individual benefits and the social demand is higher than private demand. Public intervention is required to reach the social optimum by subsidizing these goods.

Merit goods are often characterized by large externalities. But merit goods may be justified on grounds that go beyond externalities. Musgrave considers the demand for merit goods by the society as exogenously determined by the government due to their intrinsically 'meritorious' nature. In the financing of merit goods, one has to consider the appropriate level of subsidization. From a resource management perspective, it should be recognized that all subsidies need to be financed from taxation or borrowing, both of which entail some cost.

The required degree of subsidization may also differ across services. For example, elementary education or primary health may require a larger degree of subsidization compared to higher education or curative health. The volume of subsidies can be reduced by proper targeting. Governments have to decide the extent to which they want to provide private goods that are in the nature of merit goods as also the extent to which they want to subsidize this provision. The volume of subsidies is often very high in many economies and is justified on grounds of externalities or merit goods. In public resource management, rationalization of subsidies often holds considerable promise. In each case, the grounds of justification often require re-examination to establish whether the original justification holds.

1.5 Public Provision of Private Goods

In addition to public and merit goods, governments often also participate in the provision of a vast array of purely private goods. Examples are power, transport, industries, agriculture, petroleum, and other minerals. Such participation has been justified sometimes on account of existence of natural monopolies, sometimes due to the requirement of lumpy and large investments, and sometimes due to protection of common pool resources. Not so long ago, the motivation in India came through the objective of controlling the 'commanding heights' of the economy. Many public sector enterprises are generally set up for handling these sectors. There are no clear dividing lines, and the levels of interventions are often historically determined or are governed by ideological considerations. Many public enterprises in India have turned out to be loss-making entities while considerable amount of country's capital may be locked in them. This is an area where substantial restructuring of government expenditures can be done. Restructuring public intervention in the provision of purely private goods is one of the main current issues in the context of India's public finances.

1.6 Club or Congestible Goods

The characteristics of rivalry and excludability are matters of degree, and often there are some goods, which can be seen as characterised by different degrees of *publicness*. These goods fall in an intermediate category between pure public and pure private goods. A conceptual category is that of *club* goods or congestible goods like roads or swimming pools which relate to goods that are non-rival for small groups but become rival when the group of users becomes large. In the case of congestible goods, user charges are leviable, although these may be varied according to groups of consumers rather than individual consumers.

1.7 Transfers and Social Sector Programmes

Apart from the provision of public and private goods, public expenditures are also devoted to income transfers to individuals and for a variety of social sector programs. Some of these are aimed at providing safety nets against cyclical performance of the economy, and others are aimed at reducing chronic poverty. In most western economies, social security payments claim a high percentage of their budgets. For example, general government income transfers as percentage of GDP are in the range at 17-18.5 per cent in countries like Austria, Denmark, France, Germany, and Sweden. In developing countries, direct income transfers are less but they rely heavily on supporting income through indirect price subsidies, particularly in food and agriculture. Indirect support policies are less efficient but direct income transfers have significant incentive problems. This is also an area where designing an effective and well targeted transfer programme is a contemporary issue of some importance in the context of the increasing market orientation of the Indian economy.

In India, the responsibilities of the different tiers of governments are specified in the constitution in the three lists in the seventh schedule to the constitution.

These lists include the respective revenue sources also. These lists are: Union List, State List, and Concurrent List. The Concurrent List mentions responsibilities where both central and state governments can participate in service provision. The assignments to local bodies must be decided by the state governments from among items specified under the 73rd and 74th constitutional amendments.

1.8 Government and the Public Sector

Government and the public sector are closely related but not the same entities. The public sector may be said to consist of the government, the public sector enterprises and quasi-government bodies. The government itself consists of administrative departments and departmental enterprises. The public sector comprises autonomous enterprises but owned by the government by virtue of the investment that the government may have done in these enterprises. Government invests in these through equity as well as loans. The public enterprises are often not free to run according to commercial lines and are required to fulfil the mandate for which they might have been set up in the first place. Governments often set up public enterprises where there are natural monopolies as in the case of petroleum or telecommunications. Two other natural monopolies, namely, Railways and Posts are run in India as departmental enterprises.

1.9 Fiscal Tasks of a State: Allocation, Stabilization, and Redistribution

It goes to the credit of one of the most well known analyst of Public Finance, Musgrave, to enunciate the three basic functions of a state, namely, allocation, stabilization, and redistribution. The question of allocation leads one to the address the question of financing the provision of public goods and merit goods by the governments through taxation. Taxation in a sense determines the allocation of resources between public, merit, and private goods. The government may, however, also tax for purposes of redistribution through transfers and subsidies.

In a developing economy, the government may have to directly take up the role of stimulating growth. This may be in the form of strategies to stimulate savings, invest in human development, facilitate technology transfers, or participate directly in building-up infrastructure. In a developing economy, the government may also have to go beyond redistribution, and combat poverty by direct intervention.

In the context of defining government's role in the context of economic development, Stiglitz (1996) provides a list of six important functions:

1. Promoting education

2. Promoting technology
3. Supporting the financial sector
4. Investing in infrastructure
5. Preventing environmental degradation
6. Creating and maintaining a social safety net

Stiglitz (1996) observes that in a developing economy, the government may also have to act as an entrepreneur making investments in areas where private sector in not willing to participate.

1.10 Size of Government in India: Trends

Alternative theoretical perspectives have argued for a small or a large size of the government relative to some measure of output as desirable. Those who argue for a minimalist government would prefer a small size of the government, where its responsibility may be limited to ensuring law and order and minimal public goods. The socialists would however want a large size of government, where the government takes upon the responsibility of owning virtually all resources and producing a vast array of private goods. Such an extreme view would argue for a maximalist government. In actual practice, governments of different sizes have emerged in western market economies, socialist or communist countries, and developing economies following a mixed economy strategy through a process of evolution.

Government is one of the largest players in the economic activities of a country. It works as a consumer and a producer. It plays the role of the regulator. The government sets and oversees the rules of the game in the working of the markets and in the management of relations with the rest of the world. The government has the responsibility of managing the currency of the country in coordination with its central bank. In a functional sense, the government consists of administrative departments and departmental enterprises.

In India's federal structure, the size of the government can be measured by the combined expenditure of central and state governments relative to GDP. In adding these, care should be taken that these expenditure do not double count by eliminating any inter-governmental expenditures. Thus grants given by the central to the state governments should be eliminated. Similarly interest payments made by the state governments to the central government should also be taken out. In effect, what should be added up is what different levels of governments spend on the rest of the economy. Since the role of the government is to provide public, merit, and private goods, its role is measured by expenditure that is used for the current purchases of goods and services. To get a measure of this, transfer payments from the total expenditures should be taken out. The most important of these transfer payments is interest payments. Taking these out, one is left with primary expenditure. Table 1.1 shows that whether one looks at total expenditure or primary expenditure, there is steady expansion from 1950-51 to the late eighties, after which it appears to have stabilized or even fallen relative to GDP.

Table 1.1: Total and Primary Government Expenditure in India Relative to GDP (Per cent to GDP)

Year	Total expenditure	Interest payments	Primary expenditure	Year	Total expenditure	Interest payments	Primary expenditure
1950-51	9.060	0.664	8.395	1977-78	20.789	1.723	19.066
1951-52	10.070	0.644	9.426	1978-79	22.472	1.990	20.482
1952-53	9.290	0.724	8.566	1979-80	23.679	2.212	21.467
1953-54	9.395	0.736	8.660	1980-81	24.238	2.065	22.173
1954-55	11.538	1.040	10.498	1981-82	23.512	2.228	21.285
1955-56	13.225	1.140	12.085	1982-83	24.486	2.464	22.023
1956-57	13.034	0.957	12.076	1983-84	24.536	2.531	22.005
1957-58	15.454	0.989	14.466	1984-85	26.599	2.925	23.674
1958-59	14.670	0.988	13.682	1985-86	27.144	3.144	24.000
1959-60	15.177	1.142	14.035	1986-87	29.016	3.443	25.573
1960-61	15.576	1.270	14.307	1987-88	28.292	3.666	24.625
1961-62	15.762	1.341	14.421	1988-89	27.168	3.901	23.267
1962-63	17.888	1.467	16.421	1989-90	27.996	4.217	23.780
1963-64	18.820	1.348	17.472	1990-91	26.931	4.397	22.534
1964-65	18.322	1.350	16.972	1991-92	26.383	4.746	21.637
1965-66	19.748	1.525	18.223	1992-93	26.196	4.792	21.404
1966-67	18.812	1.677	17.135	1993-94	25.977	4.953	21.024
1967-68	17.084	1.558	15.526	1994-95	25.116	5.128	19.989
1968-69	16.557	1.551	15.007	1995-96	24.289	4.962	19.328
1969-70	16.065	1.530	14.536	1996-97	23.473	5.111	18.362
1970-71	17.175	1.635	15.540	1997-98	24.248	5.159	19.089
1971-72	19.135	1.700	17.434	1998-99	25.532	5.318	20.214
1972-73	19.343	1.546	17.797	1999-00	26.696	5.682	21.014
1973-74	17.486	1.532	15.954	2000-01	26.424	5.877	20.547
1974-75	18.113	1.508	16.606	2001-02	26.887	6.174	20.713
1975-76	20.782	1.394	19.388	2002-03	28.628	6.468	22.160
1976-77	22.080	1.948	20.132	2003-04	27.890	6.313	21.577

Source: (Basic Data): *Indian Public Finance Statistics*.

In the case of total expenditure, starting from a level of about 9 per cent of GDP, there was a steady expansion of the size of government reaching a peak level of about 29 per cent of GDP in 1986-87. This could not be sustained in the latter years. The total expenditure relative to GDP fell to a level of about 23.5 per cent in 1996-97. The fall in expenditure is due clearly to a fall in the ratio of revenue receipts to GDP. There was an attempt to make up for the erosion in the level of revenues relative to GDP by additional borrowing. However, as a result, interest payments started increasing and primary expenditure fell relative to GDP. Figures for primary expenditure to GDP show a steady rise from a level of 8.4 per cent of GDP in 1950-51 to a peak of 25.6 per cent in 1986-87. Thereafter, it started to fall. The lowest level was reached in 1996-97 at 18.4 per cent. Thereafter, it increased but has remained at about 21-22 per cent of GDP.

It becomes clear that an increase in primary expenditure cannot be sustained by borrowing alone unless there is growth. A reliable way of getting a sustained increase in the size of government as measured through the level of primary expenditure relative to GDP is through an increase in the level of revenue receipts relative to GDP. Once revenue receipts stabilize, the primary expenditure relative to GDP should also stabilize. Chart 1.1 shows the profile of growth of total and primary expenditures as also interest payments relative to GDP from 1950-51 to 2003-4.

1.11 Government: Role in the Macro Economy

Governments have a critical role to play in achieving macroeconomic objectives like growth and control of inflation. In traditional public finance theory, such as that discussed by Musgrave, 'stabilization' is an important function of the government. The impact of the size and composition of government expenditure on growth, inflation, interest rate and the external account requires consideration in a framework that takes into account relevant interrelationships and feedbacks. The structure of public finances relates, apart from other features, to the size and composition of expenditure. Government expenditure as a proportion of GDP is smaller in India in comparison to many other countries. Getting the right size of the government, and the right composition of government expenditure with a view to facilitating achievement of highest attainable growth rates, and meeting governments' social obligations including poverty reduction and provision of health and education should be considered integral to any plan for restructuring public finances. This requires increasing public spending in social and economic infrastructure for accelerating growth while reducing the overall fiscal imbalance.

Chart 1.1: Total and Primary Expenditure Relative to GDP

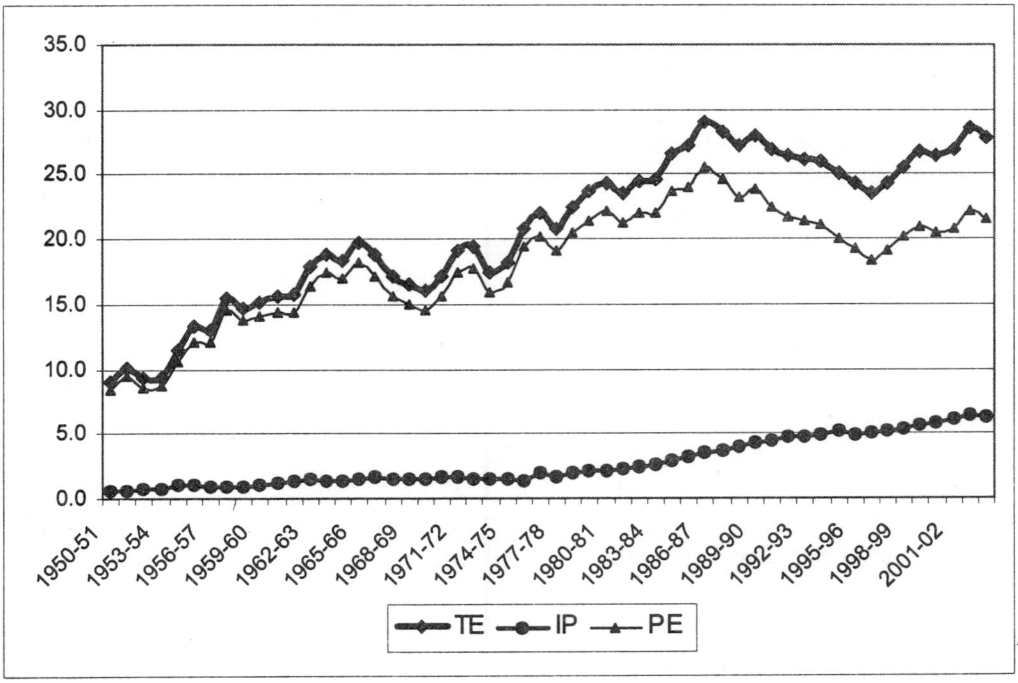

Macroeconomic stability refers to the capacity of the economy to keep close to levels of output consistent with full employment. At the same time, inflation should be contained within acceptable limits. In practice, there may be structural rigidities that keep the economy below full employment on a long term basis. Issues of stabilization are, therefore, considered with reference to growth of 'potential' or trend levels of output. Measurement of potential output requires that cyclical variations are removed to identify the level of output along its long term path. In a period of recession, real output may fall below potential output. In a period of expansion, inflation may exceed its long term levels. Both departures constitute departures from stability.

Achieving stability is facilitated if the economy has a built-in capacity to return to its long term path. In the context of fiscal policy, this capacity is provided by automatic stabilizers. Automatic stabilizers exist if the structure of public finances is such that the responsiveness of taxes is larger than that of expenditures following a change in nominal output. Thus, in an inflationary situation, taxes will withdraw more from the expenditure stream than what increased government expenditures inject, and there will be a net contraction in aggregate expenditures, thereby dampening the cycle. In a recessionary situation, government expenditures contribute more to the expenditures than taxation withdraws. This reduces the impact of recession. If automatic responses are not adequate, discretionary fiscal interventions are called for to bring about stabilization. The Reserve Bank of India in its Report on Currency and Finance for 2001-02, had estimated that the elasticity of receipts of the combined government sector is 1.07 whereas that for combined non-interest expenditure is 1.06. The Report of the Twelfth Finance Commission (TFC) also makes reference to this. It observes that since the difference in the two response coefficients is small, automatic stabilizers in India may be weak. Stabilisation therefore requires effective discretionary action.

In considering the issue of growth with stabilization, there is a need to examine (a) whether potential output along its growth path remains persistently below full employment levels and (b) whether actual output in any given year is above or below the growth path of potential output. In both cases, the structure of public finances and the management of fiscal policy have a role to play. We consider these issues in detail in Part V the book. When the long run growth path is below full employment levels, it is desirable to design public finances to remove the structural constraints such as supply bottlenecks and bring potential output closer to full employment levels. In this context, the structure of government expenditure, particularly government investment, is important. In regard to the second issue, in achieving stabilization, the management of aggregate government demand in response to the cyclical movements of potential output along its growth path is relevant.

The TFC observes that the manner of financing government expenditures also affects stabilization and growth. Governments have to resort to borrowing, i.e. fiscal deficit to the extent their expenditures are not covered by the revenue and non-debt capital receipts. Excessive dependence on domestic market borrowing can push the interest rates. Excessive dependence on borrowing from the central bank is likely to accelerate the inflation rate. The use of external borrowing can put pressure on the exchange rate. Fiscal deficit should also be viewed as consisting of two components: a structural or long term component and a cyclical component reflecting deviation from the long run average. The cyclical or the temporary component of fiscal deficit may be used to stabilize fluctuations around the trend growth of output.

Growth depends, among other factors, on the saving and investment rates. The saving rate depends, among other factors, on government's revenue deficit, which amounts to government's net dis-saving. The aggregate saving rate, consisting of the saving rate of the household sector, the private corporate sector, and the government sector, remains less than what is potentially achievable as long as government is using the saving of the private sector to finance consumption expenditure.

Chart 1.2, based on the TFC Report, depicts the growth rates derived from trend levels of output along with actual annual growth of GDP at factor cost at constant 1993-94 prices from 1950-51 to 2002-03. The analysis is with reference to GDP at factor cost with a view to focusing on the performance in respect of growth of output. The trend growth has been estimated by using the Hodrick-Prescott (H-P) filter. Chart 1.2 shows that a long term cyclical path has been followed by output where the trend growth fell from a little below 4.5 per cent to about 3.3 per cent in the early seventies, after which there was a rise bringing the trend growth to levels above 6 per cent in the mid-nineties. It is the fall in the trend growth rate to below 5 per cent since then that has been a cause of concern.

The TFC notes that the amplitude of variation from trend growth rate has come down in the late nineties. A corresponding analysis of actual and trend inflation rates indicates that the trend inflation rate during 1999-00 to 2002-03 has come down marginally below 5 per cent, although actual inflation rate was even lower remaining below 4 per cent. These may be seen as signs of recession that lasted until 2002-03. Table 1.2 gives the actual, trend, and the residual components of growth and inflation from 1990-91 to 2002-03. Following the strong recovery of agriculture in 2003-04 and the upturn in industry in both 2003-04 and 2004-05, the overall growth rate during 2003-04 and 2004-05 is estimated to be above 8 per cent and 6 per cent, respectively. To achieve a growth rate of above 7 per cent on a sustained basis, the investment and saving rates have to increase to levels equal to or above those achieved in the mid-nineties.

Table 1.3, also based on the TFC Report, gives the saving rate of the household, private corporate, and the public sector. Table 1.4 provides the rate of gross domestic investment for private and public sectors. The public sector saving rate became negative in 1998-99 and the magnitude of negative savings went on increasing until 2001-02. Within it, dis-saving of the government, consisting of administrative and departmental enterprises showed a sharp deterioration from 1.7 per cent of GDP in 1996-97 to 6.2 per cent in 2001-02. The aggregate saving rate had peaked in 1995-96 at 25.2 per cent. In 1998-99, it reached its lowest level in recent years at 21.5 per cent. Correspondingly, the investment rate had peaked in 1995-96 and reached its lowest level in recent years at 22.6 per cent in 1998-99. The three years in the mid-nineties provide some evidence for the kind of saving and investment rates required for a 7 plus growth.

Chart 1.2: Growth Rates of Actual and Trend GDP at Constant Prices

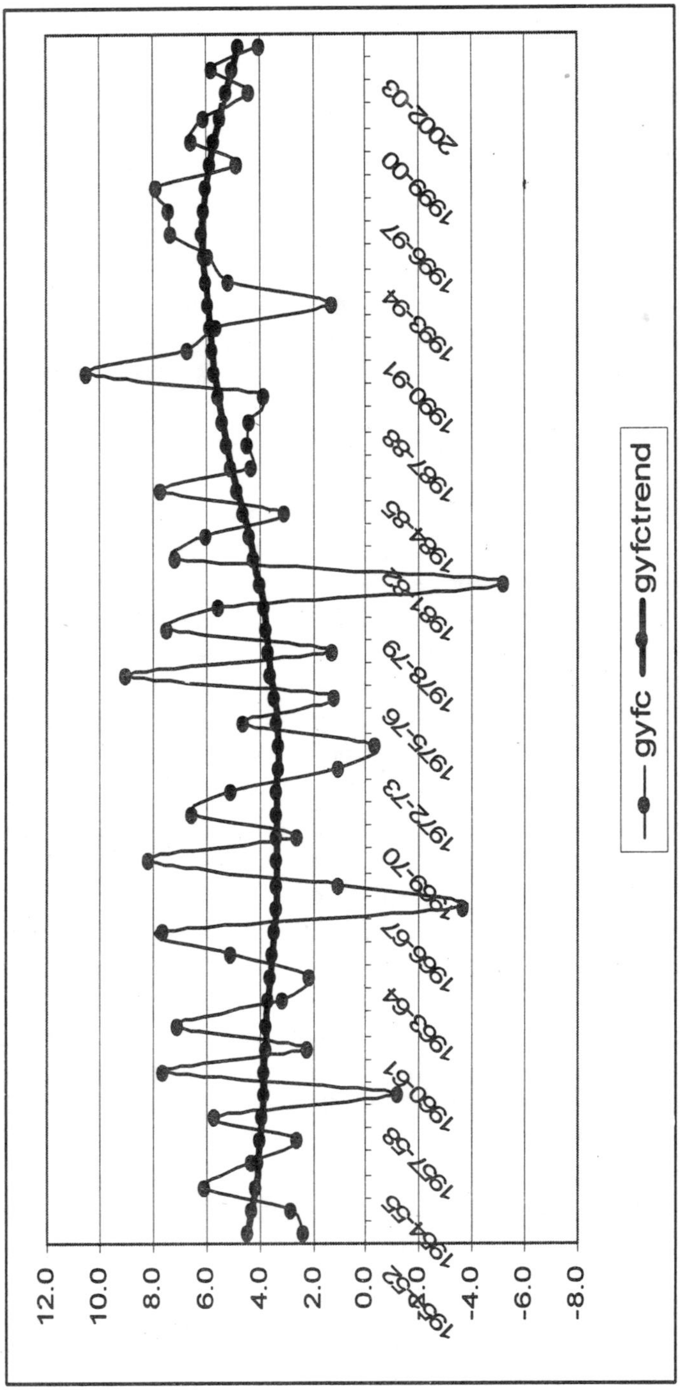

Table 1.2: Growth and Inflation Rates: Trends and Actuals (per cent)

	Actual growth in output*	Trend$ growth in output	Deviation from trend growth rate	Actual inflation rate**	Trend inflation rate	Deviation from trend inflation rate
1990-91	5.57	5.83	-0.27	10.50	9.65	0.85
1991-92	1.30	5.90	-4.60	13.81	9.46	4.35
1992-93	5.12	5.98	-0.86	8.72	9.15	-0.43
1993-94	5.90	6.06	-0.16	9.59	8.75	0.85
1994-95	7.25	6.10	1.15	9.43	8.27	1.16
1995-96	7.34	6.08	1.26	9.03	7.75	1.27
1996-97	7.84	6.00	1.84	7.44	7.21	0.23
1997-98	4.79	5.85	-1.05	6.67	6.68	0.00
1998-99	6.51	5.66	0.84	7.94	6.17	1.77
1999-00	6.06	5.45	0.61	3.94	5.70	-1.76
2000-01	4.37	5.21	-0.84	3.49	5.30	-1.82
2001-02	5.78	4.98	0.80	3.88	4.98	-1.10
2002-03	3.98	4.74	-0.76	3.46	4.72	-1.26

* Output refers to GDP at factor cost.
** Inflation refers to implicit price deflator of GDP at factor cost.
$Trend is calculated using Hodrick-Prescott filter covering 1950-51 to 2002-03 data.
Source: *Report of the Twelfth Finance Commission, 2004.*

The three years covering 1994-95 to 1996-97, as noted by the TFC, had an average investment rate of about 26 per cent and domestic saving rate of about 24.7 per cent. In contrast during 2000-01 to 2002-03, the investment rate on average was 23.6 per cent and the average saving rate was 23.8 per cent. There has been a persistent fall in public investment in the nineties. The rate of gross domestic capital formation in the public sector fell from an average of 10.1 per cent of GDP during 1985-1990 to 5.7 in 2002-03. Since private investment was increasing up to the mid-nineties, it made up for the fall in the public sector investment. However, after 1995-96, the private corporate sector investment also fell.

The TFC observes that for increasing and sustaining the growth rate at 7 per cent, an aggregate investment rate of 28 percent is required on the assumption that the incremental capital-output ratio (ICOR) is 4. The Tenth Plan had envisaged an average investment rate of 28.4 per cent to attain a growth of 8 per cent by assuming a lower ICOR. Such levels of total investment would require increasing levels of both public and private investment relative to GDP.

Table 1.3: Gross Domestic Saving at Current Prices as Per Cent of GDP

Year	Household Sector	Private corporate sector	Private sector	Public sector	Total (2+3+4)
Average (1985-86 to 1989-90)	16.03	1.96	17.99	2.39	20.37
1990-91	19.33	2.67	21.99	1.10	23.10
1991-92	16.96	3.11	20.06	1.97	22.03
1992-93	17.51	2.67	20.18	1.59	21.77
1993-94	18.42	3.48	21.90	0.63	22.53
1994-95	19.68	3.48	23.17	1.66	24.83
1995-96	18.19	4.93	23.12	2.03	25.15
1996-97	17.05	4.47	21.51	1.67	23.19
1997-98	17.63	4.17	21.80	1.33	23.13
1998-99	18.77	3.74	22.51	-0.99	21.52
1999-00	20.88	4.35	25.23	-1.04	24.20
2000-01	21.93	4.12	26.05	-2.31	23.74
2001-02	22.74	3.46	26.20	-2.75	23.45
2002-03	22.65	3.41	26.05	-1.85	24.20

Source: *Report of the Twelfth Finance Commission, 2004.*

As discussed in the TFC Report, there are four main features that can be highlighted in comparing the growth-saving-investment profile of the mid-nineties with that of the first three years of the new decade.

- In the mid-nineties, the average growth of GDP at factor cost was 7.5 per cent per annum, which fell to an average of 4.7 per cent during 2000-03;
- The public sector saving rate fell during this period from an average level of 1.8 per cent to -2.3 percent of GDP, amounting to a fall of 4.1 percentage points;
- The public sector investment fell by 1.9 percentage points from an average level of 7.8 percent of GDP to 5.9 per cent and the overall investment rate fell by 2.2 percentage points from an average level of 25.8 per cent to 23.6 per cent. The corporate investment fell from a high of 9.8 per cent of GDP in 1995-96 to 4.8 per cent in 2002-03;

- The excess of gross domestic investment over gross domestic saving between the two periods, showing the extent of reliance on current account deficit, fell from 1.4 percentage points to -0.2 percentage points.

Table 1.4: Gross Capital Formation at Current Market Prices as Per Cent to GDP

	Public sector	Private corporate	Household	Private sector	Total (12+13)	Errors& omissions	Adjusted total (14+15)
Average (1985-86 to 1989-90)	10.11	4.33	8.83	13.16	23.27	-0.56	22.70
1990-91	9.34	4.13	10.60	14.73	24.07	2.23	26.30
1991-92	8.82	5.66	7.45	13.11	21.93	0.62	22.55
1992-93	8.55	6.46	8.78	15.24	23.79	-0.17	23.61
1993-94	8.24	5.61	7.40	13.01	21.25	1.84	23.09
1994-95	8.71	6.91	7.76	14.67	23.38	2.62	26.00
1995-96	7.66	9.58	9.29	18.87	26.53	0.37	26.90
1996-97	7.03	8.05	6.69	14.74	21.77	2.71	24.48
1997-98	6.61	7.97	7.99	15.96	22.57	2.02	24.60
1998-99	6.58	6.39	8.41	14.80	21.38	1.20	22.57
1999-00	6.94	6.46	10.26	16.72	23.66	1.67	25.33
2000-01	6.29	5.06	11.27	16.33	22.62	1.73	24.35
2001-02	5.83	4.88	11.60	16.48	22.31	0.83	23.13
2002-03	5.68	4.80	12.34	17.15	22.83	0.45	23.28

Source: (Basic data): National Income Accounts, CSO.

1.12 Government Failures

It is well known that the market fails under certain circumstances. The rationale of a government often rests on these market failures. However, there are also various government failures. There are several sources of government failures.

1.13 Rigidities

Governments change slowly to changes in economic conditions as they are bound by rules and regulations and habit-persistence. A centralized decision–taking body responds slowly to changes in market conditions than decentralized decision takers. This makes governments a less efficient participant in the economic activities. If governments get excessively involved, particularly in the provision of private goods, they may fail to achieve efficient outcomes.

1.14 Adverse Incentives

In the functioning of governments, there are principal-agent problems leading problems of adverse incentives. The principal in the case of government is the public, and agents are the elected and appointed functionaries. Once in position, the motivations of the agents take over the objectives of the principals. Thus, a government, once in place may work according to the preferences not of the principal, that is people, but the by the motives of the bureaucracy and the politicians. There is a highly developed literature by Niskanen and others, which has argued that bureaucrats often act by the motive of maximizing the size of their bureaus rather than work for the welfare of the people.

1.15 Information Costs and Lags

Government also fails to deliver efficient outcomes, if it undertakes resource allocations in its hand and disturbs the market mechanisms that costlessly indicate relative scarcities in the system through price signals. When governments start to administer and regulate prices, information on relative scarcities must be exogenously compiled. This involves both costs and time lags. In addition, separate mechanisms are required to process the relevant information to make the resource allocation according to some objective function.

For an efficient functioning of the economic system, efficient outcomes can be generated when government and markets play a complementary role. The government, by suitable regulations, sets up rules for the market to operate, sets uniform weights and measures, ensures that contracts are adhered to, and provides currency to serve as the unit of exchange by regulating the central bank. The government also augments efficiency by doing what markets cannot do efficiently, namely, providing public and merit goods. But if the government exceeds its mandate and interfere too much in the functioning of the markets or enter itself in the production of various private goods, it is likely to dilute the overall efficiency of the economy.

1.16 Federal Government in India: Three-Tier Structure of Government

There have been some major changes in the structure of government in India over time. In particular, the number of states has increased over time because of continuing bifurcation of existing states and also because of salient changes in regard to the status of local bodies. We have a three-tier structure of government structure with the central government at the apex, state governments in the second tier, and rural and urban local bodies at the third tier. The rural local bodies themselves have a three-tier structure with district or *zila panchayat* at the first local tier, block or *anchal panchayat* in the middle, and *gram panchayat* at the root level of the village. The urban local bodies are of a single tier, but these are of three types, namely, municipal corporations, municipalities, and *nagar panchayats*.

Table 1.5 shows states arranged according to size of population. There are ten states with a population of less than 1 crore. This group includes all the special category states and Goa. The remaining two special category states, viz., Jammu and Kashmir and Assam are in the next group of states with population between 1 to 5 crore contains eight states. Six states have population between 5 to 8 crore. The remaining four states have population of more than 8 crore. Uttar Pradesh, even after the creation of Uttaranchal in 2000, is still the state with the largest population. Sikkim is the state with the smallest population size. In terms of population Uttar Pradesh is nearly 307 times as large as Sikkim, showing the tremendous heterogeneity that the organization of Indian states show.

Table 1.5: States Arranged According to Size of Population (2001)

Below 1 crore		(in lakh)	**1 to 5 crore**		(in lakh)
1.	Sikkim	5.4	11.	Jammu & Kashmir	101.4
2.	Mizoram	8.9	12.	Chhatisgarh	208.3
3.	Arunachal Pradesh	11.0	13.	Haryana	211.4
4.	Goa	13.5	14.	Punjab	243.6
5.	Nagaland	19.9	15.	Assam	266.6
6.	Manipur	21.7	16.	Jharkhand	269.5
7.	Meghalaya	23.2	17.	Kerala	318.4
8.	Tripura	32.0	18.	Orissa	368.0
9.	Himachal Pradesh	60.8			
10.	Uttaranchal	84.9			
5 to 8 crore			**Above 8 crore**		
19.	Gujarat	506.7	25.	West Bengal	801.8
20.	Karnataka	528.5	26.	Bihar	830.0
21.	Rajasthan	565.1	27.	Maharashtra	968.8
22.	Madhya Pradesh	603.5	28.	Uttar Pradesh	1662.0
23.	Tamil Nadu	624.1			
24.	Andhra Pradesh	762.1			

Source: *Census 2001*.

Table 1.6 gives two other indicators in respect of which the states can be compared: area and per capita comparable GSDP. The states are arranged in ascending order of per capita GSDP (pcGSDP). The least pcGSDP state is Bihar, and the highest pcGSDP is that for Goa, the ratio of the richest to the poorest being 8.6. States that may be listed as the five highest income states, considering pcGSDP as an indicator of per capita income are Goa, Punjab, Maharashtra, Haryana, and Himachal Pradesh. Kerala is the highest among the next five ahead of Tamil Nadu and Gujarat.

Table 1.6: Comparing States: Basic Size Indicators: Area and Per Capita GSDP

(Comparable GSDP in nominal terms: average over 1999-00 to 2001-02)

	Area	Per capita GSDP (Average 1999-00 to 2001-02)		Area	Per capita GSDP (Average 1999-00 to 2001-02)
	('000sq kms.)	Rs.		('000sq kms.)	Rs.
Bihar	94.16	6,539.3	Andhra Pradesh	275.05	18869.3
Uttar Pradesh	240.93	10,797.7	Tripura	10.49	18974.0
Orissa	155.71	11,234.3	Nagaland	16.58	20469.3
Jharkhand	79.71	11,717.0	Karnataka	191.79	20703.3
Assam	78.44	12,288.0	Sikkim	7.10	20928.7
Madhya Pradesh	308.25	13,340.3	Mizoram	21.08	21244.7
Chhatisgarh	135.19	13,710.3	Tamil Nadu	130.06	22587.3
Rajasthan	342.24	15,058.7	Gujarat	196.02	22708.3
Meghalaya	22.43	16,035.0	Kerala	38.86	22824.0
Arunchal Pradesh	83.74	16,579.0	Himachal Pradesh	55.67	24762.0
Uttaranchal	53.48	16,998.7	Haryana	44.21	26255.7
Manipur	22.33	17,263.7	Maharashtra	307.71	26994.3
West Bengal	88.75	17,376.7	Punjab	50.36	28030.0
Jammu & Kashmir	222.24	18,132.3	Goa	3.70	56589.3

Source (Basic Data): Census and CSO.

In terms of area, the largest state is Rajasthan followed by Madhya Pradesh, Maharashtra, and Uttar Pradesh. The smallest state in terms of area is Goa, followed by Sikkim and Tripura. Many of the special category states have small areas, but Jammu and Kashmir, and Uttaranchal have relatively larger areas and Himachal Pradesh and Uttaranchal are middle sized states in terms of area. The area of Rajasthan is nearly 92.5 times that of Goa.

1.17 Local Bodies

The local bodies in India are part of the state governments. Under constitutional arrangements, state governments by law assign to them responsibilities as well as resources from a list of items that are enumerated in the constitution. Different states need not assign the same functions to their respective local bodies, as long as they make it clear through a suitable legislation what functions and resources are being assigned to them. In India, there are both rural local bodies and urban local bodies. The rural local bodies have a three-tier structure: District *Panchayats* at the apex, Block *Panchayats* in the middle, and *Gram Panchayats* at the grass root level. In the case of urban bodies, there are three types, depending on the size of the locality. Municipal Corporations are the largest, Municipalities are for the intermediate size cities, and *Nagar Panchayats* are for smaller towns (Table 1.7).

Table 1.7: Number of Local Bodies in India

Rural		Urban	
Gram Panchayat	2,36,350	Municipal Corporation	109
Panchayat Samiti	6,795	Municipalities	1,432
Zila Parishad	531	Nagar Panchayats	2,182
Autonomous District Council	9		
	2,43,685		3,723

Source: Compiled from data in *Report of the Twelfth Finance Commission.*

1.18 Contemporary Issues in Indian Public Finance

Public finances must be managed in an efficient manner to augment people's welfare. Public finances also serve as a means to achieving equity in the distribution of incomes and resources. In the context of equity and efficiency, India's public finances require major restructuring. Some of the important issues that require to be discussed include the following:

1. Is the size of the government suitable given the large and diverse nature of the population? Should government size be increased, recognizing that in most western countries, the volume of government expenditure is tangibly higher?
2. The main instrument of increasing the size of the government is higher taxation. In what way can the tax-GDP ratio be raised so that efficiency of the system is not adversely affected? In fact, given the existing tax-GDP ratio, there are issues of getting the right balance between direct and indirect taxes, and minimizing the inefficiencies of the indirect tax system through the implementation of the value added tax system.
3. On the expenditure side, a major restructuring is required so that government can increase its focus on its core responsibilities like administration, health and education while shedding away its participation in producing many private goods, which can be entrusted to the private sector without much difficulty. A contemporary question is as to how speedily should this change be implemented?
4. Related to the previous issue is the relative role that central and state governments should play in providing public, merit, and private goods. In this context, whether centre's intervention in many fields that are the assigned responsibilities of state governments is excessive is worthy discussing.
5. Many services require to be provided at the local level. What are the appropriate ways of recovering their costs directly by the beneficiaries is an important question.
6. The option of spending based on borrowing does not seem to be a practical answer beyond a certain limit. Once that is crossed, additional borrowing proves to be counterproductive. The issue of containing debt without compromising the basic objectives of the government is a major challenge present before us.
7. Designing a suitable scheme of transfer of resources from the central to state and local governments is another important question.
8. Government must play an active role in alleviating poverty. So far, it has been possible to reduce the incidence of poverty as a result of government intervention as well as growth. Poverty is still rampant and ways need to be found to tackle it effectively.
9. Subsidies consume an inordinately large proportion of the resources in India. The issue is how to reduce the volume of subsidies without compromising the basic objectives of subsidization, which could be justified on grounds of equity or externalities.

10. What is the role of the government in maintaining macroeconomic stability in reference to both output and price stabilization? How far has the Indian government been successful in achieving the stabilization objectives?

2

Fiscal Trends in India

> Arguably, the six years from1997-98 to 2002-03, have had a debilitating impact on government finances. The first three years put finances under pressure because of salary revision and high interest rates, and the next three years, due to low growth and severe drought.
>
> Report of the Twelfth Finance Commission, 2004

In this Chapter, we have looked at the long term fiscal trends in India with particular emphasis on developments during the reform era since the nineties. In describing the status of government finances, we look at four aspects: fiscal imbalance, taxation, expenditure, and government debt. The analysis has been done separately for the centre, the aggregate of state finances, and the combined finances of the centre and the states. The period covered is 1950-51 to 2001-02. The period since the late eighties, and particularly the nineties are particularly emphasized.

2.1 Trends in Revenue Receipts

The combined revenue receipts of the centre and the states have evolved in a clear pattern since 1950-51 consisting of two phases. In particular, while non-tax revenues have remained more or less at comparable levels throughout the period since 1950-51, the tax revenues have shown an upward trend until the late eighties. After that year, there has been a decline. Since it is the tax revenues that constitute the core of total revenues, there has been a significant effect of the decline in the tax revenues on fiscal imbalance and expenditures relative to GDP since the late eighties.

Table 2.1 shows the trend in the combined revenue receipts as percentage of GDP since 1950-51. Tax and non-tax revenues are shown separately. It may be noted that that their total does not precisely add up to the total given because of various adjustments that are described in the note to the table. The total revenue receipts show a steady growth from a level of 7.7 per cent in 1950-51 to a peak of 18.9 per cent in 1986-87. It fell to 15.8 per cent in 1998-99 and remained at 16.7 per cent in 2001-02. It is apparent that the fall in the revenue receipts relative to GDP is due to a corresponding pattern in the tax-GDP ratio as the non-tax to GDP ratio has remained in the range of 2 to 3 per cent throughout the period since 1958-59. There is only one year in which the non-tax revenues were marginally higher than 3 per cent of GDP. Chart 2.1 exhibits the profile of growth in tax and non-tax revenues relative to GDP since 1950-51.

Table 2.1: Trends in Combined Revenue Receipts (per cent to GDP)

Year	Tax revenue	Non-tax revenue	Total revenue receipts*	Year	Tax revenue	Non-rax revenue	Total revenue receipts*
1950-51	6.307	1.511	7.863	1976-77	13.742	3.075	17.003
1951-52	6.991	1.463	8.549	1977-78	13.029	2.986	16.177
1952-53	6.502	1.519	8.021	1978-79	14.099	2.867	17.048
1953-54	5.967	1.560	7.527	1979-80	14.633	2.873	17.553
1954-55	6.749	1.801	8.549	1980-81	13.803	2.630	16.579
1955-56	7.059	1.949	9.064	1981-82	14.319	2.629	17.130
1956-57	6.875	1.753	8.665	1982-83	14.470	2.964	17.574
1957-58	7.829	1.896	9.733	1983-84	14.363	2.459	16.838
1958-59	7.324	1.985	9.325	1984-85	14.587	2.786	17.487
1959-60	7.760	2.427	10.197	1985-86	15.564	2.888	18.350
1960-61	7.866	2.104	10.250	1986-87	15.920	2.999	18.779
1961-62	8.480	2.138	10.918	1987-88	16.079	2.733	18.863
1962-63	9.532	2.257	12.393	1988-89	15.875	2.423	18.387
1963-64	10.340	2.359	13.190	1989-90	15.980	2.938	18.981
1964-65	9.912	2.118	12.614	1990-91	15.426	2.161	17.458
1965-66	10.559	2.485	13.386	1991-92	15.801	2.825	18.621
1966-67	10.417	2.391	12.883	1992-93	15.255	2.834	18.096
1967-68	9.429	2.437	11.908	1993-94	14.194	2.783	17.136
1968-69	9.682	2.684	12.400	1994-95	14.599	2.868	17.577
1969-70	9.825	2.627	12.470	1995-96	14.752	2.767	17.438
1970-71	10.404	2.421	12.835	1996-97	14.622	2.417	17.107
1971-72	11.394	2.678	14.102	1997-98	13.994	2.430	16.945
1972-73	11.930	2.511	14.452	1998-99	13.384	2.377	15.782
1973-74	11.261	2.128	13.395	1999-00	14.177	2.527	16.888
1974-75	11.904	2.298	14.259	2000-01	14.612	2.362	16.749
1975-76	13.428	2.820	16.437	2001-02	14.619	2.744	16.698

*Adjusted for self-balancing items, transfer from funds, differences in figures from centre and states, and other adjustments.

Source: (Basic Data): *Indian Public Finance Statistics.*

Chart 2.1: Growth of Combined Revenue Receipts

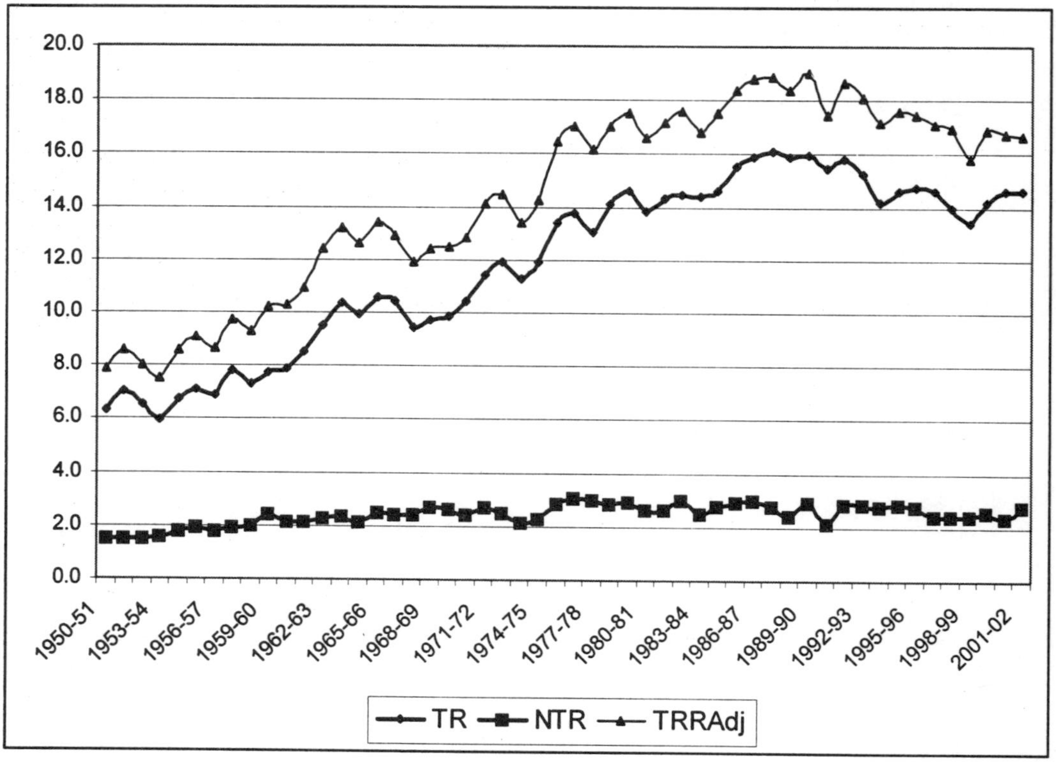

2.2 Tax Revenues of the Centre: Experience of the Nineties

The overall tax-GDP ratio fell during the nineties primarily because of the performance of the central taxes. The central government has four major taxes: personal income tax, corporate income tax, Union excise duties, and customs duties. In more recent times, the service tax is also emerging as an important source of revenue. The two income taxes are classified as direct taxes. The main indirect taxes are the Union excise duties, customs duties, and the service tax. We discuss below the performance of the central taxes in the nineties, which is the period where significant changes occurred with respect to the buoyancy of direct and indirect central taxes.

Table 2.2 gives, relative to GDP, revenues from the four major central taxes, namely, corporation tax, income tax, customs duty, and Union excise duties. Considering the gross receipts from the central taxes, the tax-GDP ratio of the centre declined from 10.1 per cent in 1990-91 to 8.8 per cent in 2002-03.

Table 2.2: Major Taxes of the Centre: Performance since 1990-91 (Per cent of GDP)

	Corporation tax	Income Tax	Customs duties	Union excise duties	Total Central tax revenues (gross)
1990-91	0.94	0.95	3.63	4.31	10.12
1991-92	1.20	1.03	3.41	4.30	10.31
1992-93	1.19	1.06	3.18	4.12	9.97
1993-94	1.17	1.06	2.58	3.69	8.82
1994-95	1.36	1.19	2.65	3.69	9.11
1995-96	1.39	1.31	3.01	3.38	9.36
1996-97	1.36	1.33	3.13	3.29	9.41
1997-98	1.31	1.12	2.64	3.15	9.14
1998-99	1.41	1.16	2.34	3.06	8.26
1999-00	1.58	1.32	2.50	3.20	8.87
2000-01	1.71	1.52	2.28	3.28	9.03
2001-02	1.60	1.40	1.76	3.18	8.20
2002-03	1.87	1.49	1.82	3.33	8.76
2003-04r	2.27	1.45	1.78	3.33	9.20
				%age of centre's gross tax revenues	
1990-91	9.27	9.34	35.85	42.58	
1991-92	11.66	9.99	33.04	41.73	
1992-93	11.92	10.58	31.86	41.31	
1993-94	13.28	12.04	29.30	41.85	
1994-95	14.98	13.03	29.02	40.46	
1995-96	14.82	14.02	32.15	36.13	
1996-97	14.42	14.16	33.28	34.95	
1997-98	14.38	12.28	28.87	34.45	
1998-99	17.06	14.08	28.28	37.03	
1999-00	17.87	14.94	28.19	36.04	
2000-01	18.93	16.84	25.21	36.33	
2001-02	19.57	17.11	21.53	38.79	
2002-03	21.35	17.04	20.74	38.06	
2003-04r	24.71	15.80	19.36	36.24	

Source: (Basic Data): *Report of the Twelfth Finance Commission, 2004.*

The major contributor to this decline was customs duty, which, relative to GDP, halved from 3.6 per cent in 1990-91 to 1.8 per cent in 2002-03. This was due to a phased reduction in import duty rates in the wake of commitments to the World Trade Organization. More important was the decline in the ratio of excise duty collections to GDP, which fell by 1 percentage point during the same period from 4.3 per cent of GDP to 3.3 per cent. The direct tax revenues grew from 1.9 per cent of GDP in 1990-91 to 3.4 per cent in 2002-03, but the loss in the revenue from customs and excise duties could not be made up, leading to a fall in the tax-GDP ratio. The main reason for the fall in the revenues from Union excise duties relative to GDP was the reduction in the average tax rates, which could not be accompanied by an adequate rise in the tax base.

The Twelfth Finance Commission has recently examined the composition of centre's gross tax revenues, which the Commission observes, has changed in a fundamental way, in favour of corporation tax and income tax. The share of corporation tax increased from 9.3 per cent of centre's gross revenue receipts in 1990-91 to 24.7 per cent in 2003-04 RE, amounting to an increase of 15.4 percentage points. During this period, the increase in income tax was 6.5 percentage points, which in 2003-04 RE accounted for 15.8 per cent of centre's gross revenue receipts. The fall during the period was 16.5 and 6.4 percentage points in customs duties and Union excise duties. This is shown in Table 2.2.

2.3 States' Revenue Receipts: Performance in Recent Years

States' revenue receipts consist of own taxes, own non-tax revenues, share in central taxes, and grants. Apart from the share in central taxes, the main tax that the states have is the sales tax. In addition, they have state excise duties, motor vehicle tax, and stamp and registration duties and the entertainment tax.

While the performance of individual state taxes will be reviewed in a later chapter, here we look at the aggregate category of states 'own tax revenue' relative to GDP. The overall availability of tax revenues to the states depends apart from the own tax revenues on the tax devolution from the centre. The fall in the centre's tax ratio therefore has affected the availability of tax resources to the states. As shown in Table 2.3, the ratio of own tax revenues to GDP for all states fell from 5.3 percent to 4.9 per cent in 1998-99 and was at 5.1 percent in1999-00. There was a substantial improvement in 2000-01 as most states agreed to the implementation of floor rates in sales tax and to reduce and rationalize various exemptions. In 2002-03, the states' own tax revenues as percentage of GDP had improved to 5.5 per cent.

Table 2.3: Aggregate State Finances: Main Fiscal Indicators

(per cent to GDP)

Year	Own tax revenues	Own non-tax revenues	Finance Commission Transfers	Non-Finance Commission Transfers	Total revenue receipts
1993-94	5.30	1.59	3.05	2.02	11.96
1994-95	5.31	1.55	2.86	1.55	11.27
1995-96	5.20	1.51	2.90	1.30	10.91
1996-97	5.01	1.47	2.94	1.29	10.71
1997-98	5.14	1.43	2.90	1.33	10.80
1998-99	4.93	1.26	2.44	1.17	9.81
1999-00	5.09	1.38	2.50	1.29	10.26
2000-01	5.46	1.37	3.02	1.20	11.04
2001-02	5.32	1.19	2.84	1.28	10.63
2002-03	5.52	1.23	2.80	1.22	10.77
Average					
1993-96 [A]	5.27	1.55	2.94	1.62	11.38
2000-03 [B]	5.44	1.26	2.88	1.23	10.81
[B]-[A]	0.17	-0.29	-0.05	-0.39	-0.57

Source: *Report of the Twelfth Finance Commission, 2004.*

While reviewing trends in state revenues, the Twelfth Finance Commission notes that during 1993-2003, the Finance Commission's transfers relative to GDP were the lowest in 1998-99 and 1999-2000 at 2.4 per cent and 2.5 per cent respectively. There has been an improvement since. In the case of transfers other than Finance Commission transfers, the fall was even more significant. In 1993-94, non-Finance Commission transfers accounted for about 2 per cent of GDP. These fell to below 1.3 per cent in the period sine 1998-99. Together, the Finance Commission and non-Finance Commission transfers from the centre fell by about 0.44 percentage points comparing the 2000-03 average with that of 1993-96. Thus, the aggregate revenue receipts of the states as percentage of GDP were the lowest in 1998-99 at 9.8 per cent. Comparing the two period averages of 1993-96 and 2000-03, there has been a fall of little less than 0.6 percentage points in the total revenue receipts of the states.

2.4 Trends in Combined Expenditures

Table 2.4 looks at the long-term profile of government expenditure on the combined account of the central and all state governments. It divides total expenditure into revenue and capital expenditure.

Table 2.4: Trends in Combined Expenditures of central and State Governments (per cent to GDP)

Year	Revenue expenditure	Capital expenditure	Total expenditure	Year	Revenue expenditure	Capital expenditure	Total expenditure
1950-51	7.302	1.702	9.004	1976-77	15.449	6.631	22.080
1951-52	7.254	2.685	9.940	1977-78	14.751	6.099	20.850
1952-53	7.709	1.583	9.292	1978-79	15.752	6.720	22.472
1953-54	7.421	1.521	8.942	1979-80	16.846	6.834	23.680
1954-55	8.362	3.175	11.537	1980-81	16.493	7.745	24.238
1955-56	9.047	3.746	12.794	1981-82	16.526	6.986	23.512
1956-57	8.103	4.647	12.749	1982-83	17.768	6.718	24.486
1957-58	9.238	5.883	15.121	1983-84	17.831	6.705	24.536
1558-59	9.036	5.344	14.379	1984-85	19.277	7.321	26.599
1959-60	9.672	5.760	15.432	1985-86	20.156	6.989	27.144
1960-61	9.813	5.684	15.496	1986-87	21.271	7.746	29.016
1961-62	10.482	5.280	15.763	1987-88	21.734	6.557	28.291
1962-63	11.696	6.193	17.889	1988-89	21.314	5.855	27.169
1963-64	11.984	6.832	18.816	1989-90	22.153	6.005	28.159
1964-65	11.353	6.968	18.321	1990-91	21.620	5.311	26.931
1965-66	12.354	7.396	19.750	1991-92	21.976	4.406	26.383
1966-67	12.321	7.438	19.759	1992-93	21.254	4.942	26.196
1967-68	11.628	5.457	17.084	1993-94	21.348	4.629	25.977
1968-69	12.140	4.419	16.558	1994-95	21.191	3.925	25.116
1969-70	12.332	3.733	16.064	1995-96	20.676	3.613	24.289
1970-71	12.516	4.658	17.175	1996-97	20.668	2.806	23.473
1971-72	14.288	4.847	19.135	1997-98	21.093	3.156	24.248
1972-73	14.548	4.795	19.344	1998-99	22.133	3.400	25.532
1973-74	13.214	4.273	17.486	1999-00	23.154	3.441	26.595
1974-75	12.754	5.387	18.141	2000-01	23.230	2.917	26.147
1975-76	14.227	6.555	20.782	2001-02	23.613	3.086	26.698

Source (Basic Data): *Indian Public Finance Statistics.*

The revenue expenditure has persistently increased from a level of 7.3 per cent of GDP in 1950-51 to 9.8 per cent in 1960-61, 12.5 per cent in 1970-71, 16.5 per cent in 1980-81, 21.6 per cent in 1990-91, and 23.62 per cent in 2001-02. Capital expenditure, on the other hand, shows a more cyclical pattern, reaching peaks above 7 per cent of GDP in 1965-66 and 1966-67, and again in 1980-81, 1984-85 and 1986-87. Since then, capital expenditure relative to GDP has been declining.

These trends are shown by Chart 2.2 highlighting the secular growth in revenue expenditure and the cyclical pattern of capital expenditure relative to GDP, which seems to have gone into a disturbing decline since the late eighties. The major causes of the growth in the revenue expenditure including revision in salaries are discussed below.

Chart 2.2: Profile of Combined Expenditure: Revenue and Capital

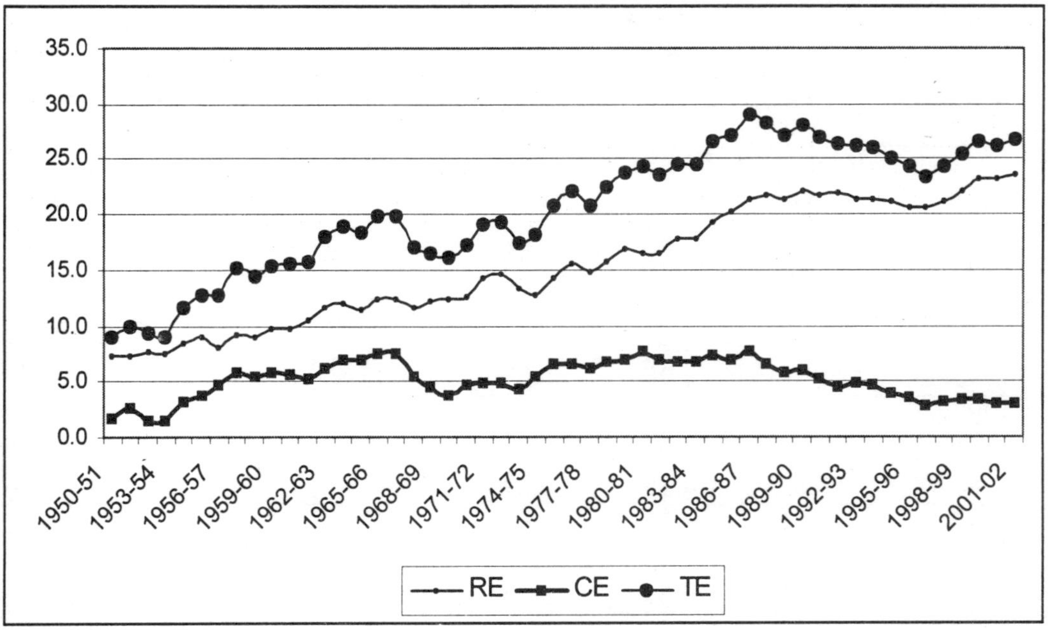

2.5 Central Expenditures: Trends in Recent Years

In order to understand the trends in expenditure in recent years, we look at central and state expenditures separately. In particular, we look at the trends in central expenditures focusing on the nineties. The total expenditure of the central government, comprising revenue and capital expenditure, after witnessing some fall relative to GDP in the first half of the nineties, started rising in 1997-98. It declined as a proportion of GDP from 18.52 per cent in 1990-91 to 14.69 per cent in 1996-97, rising thereafter to 16.77 per cent in 2002-03. As observed by the Twelfth Finance Commission, the quality of expenditure has also witnessed deterioration over the years as the share of capital expenditure declined from 5.6

per cent of GDP in 1990-91 to 3.02 percent in 2002-03. Interest payments, subsidies, pensions and defence revenue expenditure account for 60 to 65 per cent of revenue expenditure. The TFC noted that interest payments form the single largest component of centre's revenue expenditure, accounting for about 35 per cent of revenue expenditure. As a proportion of centre's revenue receipts, these accounted for about 51 per cent of centre's revenue receipts in 2002-03.

Table 2.5 provides details of some other major expenditures of the centre. Considering three year period averages over 1990-93 and 2000-03, Table 2.5 indicates that interest payments increased by about 0.6 percentage points of GDP, and pensions, by about 0.24 percentage points. Capital expenditure, on the other hand fell by a little less than 3 percentage points of GDP. Table 2.6 gives more details on centre's explicit subsidies.

Table 2.5: Trends in Central Government Expenditures (Per cent of GDP)

	Revenue expenditure	Interest payments	Pensions	Subsidies	Capital expenditure	Total expenditure
1990-91	12.93	3.78	0.38	2.14	5.59	18.52
1991-92	12.60	4.07	0.37	1.88	4.46	17.06
1992-93	13.76	4.61	0.45	1.78	4.44	18.20
1993-94	12.59	4.28	0.39	1.35	3.92	16.51
1994-95	12.06	4.35	0.36	1.17	3.81	15.87
1995-96	11.77	4.21	0.36	1.07	3.23	15.01
1996-97	11.62	4.35	0.37	1.13	3.08	14.69
1997-98	11.84	4.31	0.45	1.22	3.40	15.24
1998-99	12.43	4.47	0.58	1.36	3.61	16.04
1999-00	12.86	4.66	0.74	1.26	2.53	15.39
2000-01	13.30	4.75	0.69	1.28	2.29	15.58
2001-02	13.21	4.71	0.63	1.37	2.67	15.88
2002-03	13.75	4.77	0.59	1.76	3.02	16.77
2003-04 (RE)	13.09	4.49	0.55	1.61	4.02	17.11
Average (1990-93) A	13.09	4.15	0.40	1.93	4.83	17.92
Average (2000-03) B	13.42	4.74	0.64	1.47	2.66	16.08
B-A	0.32	0.59	0.24	-0.46	-2.17	-1.85

Source: (Basic Data): *Report of the Twelfth Finance Commission, 2004.*

The main subsidies provided by the centre are food and fertilizer subsidies and more recently, on some petroleum products like kerosene and cooking gas. Various studies, discussed in a subsequent chapter, have shown that budgetary subsidies are ill targeted and inefficiency promoting. Table 2.6 shows that the food subsidies have grown sharply in recent years rising from a level of 4.8 per cent of centre's gross revenue receipts in 1996-97 to 10.4 per cent in 2002-03. There has been a fall in the fertilizer subsidies relative to centre's gross revenue receipts. The fertilizer subsidies arose because of administered prices for purchase of fertilizers by the farmers and a retention price scheme in the case of indigenous urea fertilizer, which allowed a guaranteed return on net worth. The amount of subsidies depends on the difference between the consumer's and the retention price, and the level of production. There are subsidies also for imported urea fertilizers and sale of decontrolled fertilizers with concession to farmers.

Table 2.6: Explicit Subsidies Relative to Centre's Gross Revenue Receipts

(per cent)

	Food	Fertilizer	Others	Total
1990-91	4.45	7.98	9.67	22.11
1991-92	4.32	7.85	6.39	18.56
1992-93	3.78	7.82	3.01	14.60
1993-94	7.31	6.02	1.99	15.31
1994-95	5.58	6.32	1.08	12.98
1995-96	4.88	6.12	0.50	11.50
1996-97	4.80	6.00	1.47	12.27
1997-98	5.90	7.41	0.54	13.85
1998-99	6.09	7.76	1.94	15.78
1999-00	5.20	7.30	1.00	13.49
2000-01	6.26	7.16	0.51	13.93
2001-02	8.69	6.26	0.55	15.50
2002-03	10.43	4.75	3.59	18.78
2003-04 (RE)	9.58	4.48	2.93	17.00

Source (Basic Data): Centre's Budget Documents.

2.6 State Expenditures: Changes in Recent Years

Table 2.7 shows the main trends in the all-state revenue expenditures. A review of state expenditures was recently undertaken by the Twelfth Finance Commission. It shows the position of interest payments and pensions relative to GDP as well as the aggregates of plan and non-plan revenue expenditures. In comparison to the trends in revenue receipts, almost all expenditure categories show tangible increases in the nineties. These increases are particularly noticeable in the case of interest payments and pensions. Interest payments rose from about 1.8 per cent of GDP in 1993-94 to 2.8 per cent in 2002-03 showing a rise of 1 percentage point in a span of 10 years. Pensions also show a sharp rise, increasing from 0.6 per cent in 1993-94 to 1.24 per cent in 2002-03, showing a rise of more than 100 per cent. Both these heads of expenditure constitute transfer payments. Increased claims on their account led to a fall in plan revenue expenditure, which fell from the level of 2.2 per cent of GDP in 1993-94 to 1.8 per cent by 2002-03.

Table 2.7: Aggregate State Finances: Expenditure Indicators

(per cent to GDP)

Year	Total revenue expenditure	Interest payments	Pension	Plan revenue expenditure	Non-Plan revenue expenditure
1993-94	12.41	1.82	0.61	2.22	10.19
1994-95	11.96	1.92	0.63	2.06	9.91
1995-96	11.63	1.83	0.66	2.01	9.63
1996-97	12.02	1.87	0.72	2.10	9.93
1997-98	12.03	2.01	0.77	1.93	10.10
1998-99	12.41	2.07	0.93	1.99	10.43
1999-00	13.08	2.30	1.16	1.87	11.21
2000-01	13.65	2.48	1.24	1.91	11.74
2001-02	13.31	2.68	1.26	1.85	11.46
2002-03	13.06	2.80	1.24	1.81	11.24
Avg.					
1993-96 [A]	12.00	1.86	0.63	2.09	9.91
2000-03 [B]	13.34	2.65	1.25	1.86	11.48
[B]-[A]	1.34	0.79	0.62	-0.24	1.57

Source: (Basic Data): *Report of the Twelfth Finance Commission, 2004.*

Also, as the TFC observes, due to the increase in interest payments and pensions, total revenue expenditure increased from 12.4 per cent in 1993-94 to 13 per cent in 2002-03. Comparing the period averages of 1993-96 and 2000-03, there has been a rise of 1.34 percentage points of GDP. At the aggregate level, total revenue expenditure of all the states was at its lowest at 11.6 per cent of GDP in 1995-96. Thereafter, it increased steadily to reach a level of 13.7 per cent in 2000-01, after which it came come down to 13.1 per cent in 2002-03. The increase during 1998-2001 can be attributed to the large increases in salaries and pensions due to the revision of salaries and pensions following the recommendations of the Fifth Central Pay Commission. Within the overall revenue expenditure, the non-plan component increased steadily from 9.6 per cent in 1995-96 to 11.7 per cent in 2000-01, after which it started coming down.

Among several factors that have contributed to the deterioration of the state finances, the large volume of subsidies is also an important one. The subject of implicit subsidies is discussed in a later Chapter. The bulk of the subsidies provided by the states are implicit rather than explicit. These arise when services are provided at prices that do not recover costs. Low user charges that could recover only a fraction of the costs have characterized all states without exception. Budgetary support to the power sector in particular has been an important source of drain in states where explicit subsidy for this purpose has been provided for in the budgets.

2.7 State Finances: A Comparative Perspective

In this section, we look at the relative performance of individual states in regard to revenue and expenditure trends in a comparative perspective. The discussion is based on the recent review undertaken by the Twelfth Finance Commission. Comparisons are made for two three-year period averages, 1993-96 and 2000-03. All variables are taken as percentages to the respective GSDPs of the states. States other than the eleven special category states (SCS) are referred to as the general category states (GCS). States of Uttar Pradesh, Madhya Pradesh, and Bihar are taken as undivided states for purposes of comparison for the entire period.

2.8 Comparative Performance of States: Own Tax Revenues

Table 2.8 shows that the ratio of states' own tax revenue to GDP increased, considering the two period-averages over 1993-96 and 2000-03, for the groups of special category and general category states, and all the individual states except a few. The overall increase over the period-averages for the states as a whole was 0.67 percentage points for all states relative to the all-state GSDP, 0.66 for the SCS and 0.69 for the GCS group, relative to their respective group-GSDPs. The only exceptions in terms of individual states, where the tax-GDP ratio declined in terms of their 2000-03 averages were Goa, Karnataka, Kerala, and West Bengal. While the first three went from high to less high, West Bengal had a somewhat lower tax-GSDP ratio even in the 1993-96 period. Among the SCS group, only Manipur has shown a decline in tax-GSDP ratio.

Table 2.8: Own Tax Revenues: Comparative Performance of States

	Average OTR/GSDP (%)			Buoyancy
	1993-96 [A]	2000-03 [B]	B-A	1993-03
Arunachal Pradesh	0.55	1.47	0.91	2.543
Assam	3.69	4.58	0.90	1.326
Himachal Pradesh	4.87	5.08	0.21	1.043
Jammu & Kashmir	3.11	4.51	1.40	1.443
Manipur	1.44	1.21	-0.23	0.842
Meghalaya	3.02	3.26	0.23	1.089
Mizoram	0.59	0.97	0.38	1.608
Nagaland	1.18	1.19	0.01	0.980
Sikkim	3.44	4.58	1.15	1.303
Tripura	1.95	2.19	0.24	1.105
Total: SCS	3.30	3.96	0.66	1.226
Andhra Pradesh	5.90	7.30	1.40	1.271
Bihar	3.71	4.46	0.75	1.290
Goa	7.91	6.46	-1.45	0.806
Gujarat	7.51	7.71	0.20	1.010
Haryana	7.22	8.30	1.09	1.205
Karnataka	8.53	8.33	-0.19	0.969
Kerala	8.45	8.11	-0.34	0.946
Madhya Pradesh	4.91	6.45	1.53	1.452
Maharashtra	6.64	7.76	1.12	1.221
Orissa	3.93	5.81	1.87	1.639
Punjab	6.88	7.13	0.25	1.061
Rajasthan	5.50	6.48	0.98	1.231
Tamil Nadu	8.40	9.00	0.60	1.110
Uttar Pradesh	4.76	5.88	1.12	1.318
West Bengal	5.46	4.26	-1.20	0.690
Total: GCS	6.26	6.95	0.69	1.143
All States	6.12	6.79	0.67	1.141

Source: *Report of the Twelfth Finance Commission.*

During 2000-03, the highest tax-GSDP ratio was that for Tamil Nadu at 9.0 per cent of GSDP, and the lowest for West Bengal at 4.26 per cent, among the general category states.

2.9 Comparative Performance of States: Expenditures

Table 2.9 shows, as discussed in the TFC Report, a general upward trend in respect of revenue expenditures relative to GSDP levels, comparing averages over the two periods, viz., 1993-96 and 2000-03. The corresponding ratio for capital expenditure, however, shows a change in the reverse direction. For the special category states, there is an increase of 1.4 percentage points between the two period averages.

Table 2.9: States: Comparative Trends in Expenditure (Per cent of GSDP)

	Revenue Expenditure			Capital Expenditure		
	1993-96 (A)	2000-03 (B)	[B-A]	1993-96 [C]	2000-03 [D]	[D-A]
Andhra Pradesh	13.47	15.56	2.08	3.87	2.93	-0.94
Bihar	16.50	18.11	1.60	1.04	2.67	1.63
Goa	17.11	17.25	0.13	3.86	2.33	-1.54
Gujarat	12.52	18.37	5.85	2.37	2.43	0.06
Haryana	13.06	13.45	0.39	2.33	2.52	0.18
Karnataka	13.96	15.33	1.36	3.08	2.44	-0.64
Kerala	14.93	16.11	1.18	2.23	1.07	-1.16
Madhya Pradesh	13.29	16.74	3.45	1.90	2.37	0.47
Maharashtra	10.68	14.10	3.42	2.56	1.47	-1.09
Orissa	16.49	22.22	5.74	2.83	3.23	0.40
Punjab	12.75	15.33	2.59	2.65	2.11	-0.54
Rajasthan	15.43	18.06	2.63	3.89	2.30	-1.59
Tamil Nadu	13.95	15.60	1.66	1.85	1.51	-0.34
Uttar Pradesh	14.28	16.78	2.50	2.63	2.23	-0.40
West Bengal	11.80	15.02	3.23	1.78	1.94	0.16
General Category	13.33	16.05	2.72	2.51	2.12	-0.38
Special Category	26.27	27.66	1.40	5.71	4.69	-1.03
All States	13.94	16.67	2.72	2.66	2.26	-0.40

Source: *Report of the Twelfth Finance Commission, 2004.*

Among the general category states, the largest increase in ratio of revenue expenditure to GSDP is in respect of Gujarat (5.9 per cent) and Orissa (5.7 per cent). The states where this increase is least are Goa (0.1 per cent) and Haryana (0.4 per cent). These increases are due no doubt largely to the increases in salaries and pensions during the period as well as on account of increasing interest payments.

Considering the levels of revenue expenditures relative to GSDP, the average for 2000-03 indicates that for the special category states, the ratio is about 10 percentage points higher than that for the general category states. In this group, Orissa has an exceptionally high ratio at 22.2 per cent. At the lower end, Haryana was at 13.5 per cent and Maharashtra at 14.1 per cent, which are the only states below 15 per cent.

The increase in revenue expenditure was accompanied by a fall in capital expenditure. In this respect, the special category states showed the larger reduction in capital expenditure to GSDP ratio between 1993-96 and 2000-03, as compared to the general category states taken as a group. Among the general category states, Orissa has the highest level of capital expenditure at 3.2 per cent in 2000-03 while Kerala has the lowest at 1.1 per cent.

Table 2.10 shows comparisons for two other important ratios, namely, interest payments relative to total revenue receipts and pension expenditures relative to GSDP. These reflect transfer payments and discussed at length by the TFC. The ratio of interest payments to TRR has increased to unsustainable levels in many cases. Among special category states, this ratio is the highest for Himachal Pradesh at 28.78 per cent during 2000-03. This state has witnessed the largest increase in this ratio at 12.90 percentage points over 1993-96. The increase in debt servicing burden has affected the general category states more than the special category states. West Bengal has registered the largest increase in IP-TRR ratio in 2000-03 over 1993-96 at 23.98 percentage points. As a consequence, its IP-TRR ratio at 44.33 per cent during 2000-03 is the highest among all states. Punjab follows next at 38.51 per cent. A consistently high level of this ratio for this state during the nineties is reflected by the fact that its IP-TRR ratio was the highest at 32.13 per cent during 1993-96. Orissa and Rajasthan have also shown large increases in their IP-TRR ratios at 13.46 and 13.19 percentage points, respectively between the two periods. During 2000-03, Karnataka, undivided Madhya Pradesh, and Tamil Nadu have displayed lower levels of the IP-TRR ratios at about 18 per cent.

The sharp growth of pension liabilities consequent upon the revision of pay scales, shows, as indicated by Table 2.10, that during 2000-03, pension liabilities as a percentage of GSDP were higher than the corresponding average over 1993-

96 by 1.28 percentage point for the general category states and by 0.8 percentage points for the special category states. During 2000-03, pension expenditures relative to GSDP varied from 1 per cent to 3 per cent across all states. Among the general category states, the increase in terms of percentage points, in the ratio of pension expenditures to GSDP, was the highest for undivided Bihar (1.82), Orissa (1.53), Rajasthan (1.18) and Tamil Nadu (1.19).

Table 2.10: State Expenditure Trends: Comparative Profile

(Per cent of GSDP)

	Interest payment/TRR			Pension expenditure/GSDP		
	1993-96 (A)	2000-03 (B)	[B-A]	1993-96 [C]	2000-03 [D]	[D-A]
Andhra Pradesh	14.07	22.37	8.30	1.01	1.49	0.48
Bihar	21.78	24.92	3.14	1.01	2.82	1.82
Goa	14.21	19.50	5.29	0.55	1.28	0.74
Gujarat	15.18	24.59	9.41	0.60	1.25	0.65
Haryana	15.26	23.35	8.09	0.54	1.10	0.56
Karnataka	12.08	18.07	6.00	0.92	1.42	0.50
Kerala	17.61	27.34	9.73	1.72	2.57	0.85
Madhya Pradesh	13.34	18.36	5.02	0.67	1.17	0.50
Maharashtra	11.93	20.75	8.82	0.36	0.88	0.52
Orissa	22.39	35.85	13.46	0.68	2.21	1.53
Punjab	32.13	38.51	6.38	0.64	1.62	0.98
Rajasthan	17.38	30.57	13.19	0.73	1.91	1.18
Tamil Nadu	11.98	18.61	6.63	0.93	2.11	1.19
Uttar Pradesh	22.30	28.27	5.97	0.54	1.21	0.67
West Bengal	20.34	44.33	23.98	0.61	1.44	0.83
General Category	16.70	25.40	8.70	0.72	1.51	0.80
Special Category	13.41	16.98	3.57	1.11	2.39	1.28
All States	16.37	24.57	8.20	0.73	1.56	0.83

Source: *Report of the Twelfth Finance Commission, 2004.*

2.10 Profile of Fiscal Imbalance

Growth in fiscal imbalance is an unavoidable outcome of the fall in revenue receipts relative to GDP accompanied by the continued rise in revenue expenditures. Fiscal imbalance as indicated by revenue, fiscal, and primary deficits was at high levels at the end of the eighties, showed improvement in the mid-nineties, but deteriorated since then. As indicated by Chart 2.3, revenue and fiscal deficits as percentage of GDP were higher in 1999-2002 on average as compared to their levels in the late eighties. Revenue deficit shows the most persistent deterioration, increasing by more than double, from the 1987-1990 average of 3 per cent of GDP to 6.7 per cent in 1999-2002. It had declined to 3.2 per cent in 1995-96, after which it steadily climbed up.

Chart 2.3: Revenue, Fiscal, and Primary Deficits as % of GDP

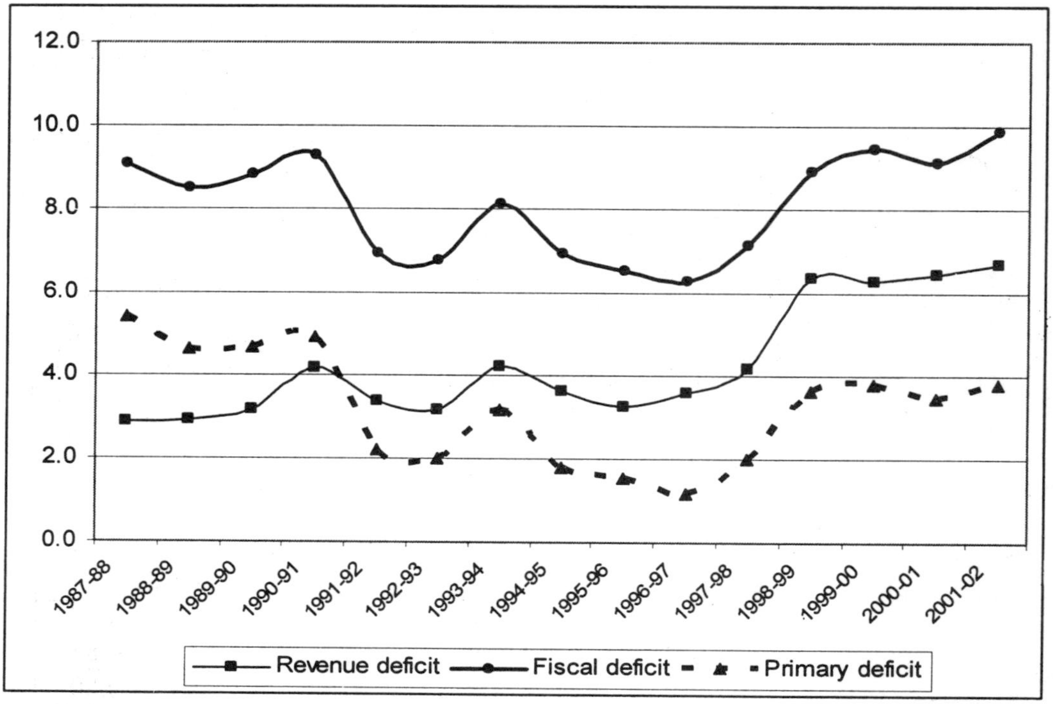

In the case of fiscal deficits, there is a deterioration of 0.7 percentage points. At the end of the eighties, the average level of fiscal deficit was 8.8 per cent of GDP, which increased to 9.5 percent in 1999-2002. However, there was an improvement in the mid-nineties. As the TFC notes, in 1996-97, fiscal deficit had fallen to 6.3 per cent of GDP. The primary deficit was 4.9 per cent of GDP on average at the end of the eighties. It fell to 1.1 per cent in 1996-97, after which it deteriorated but the average over 1999-2002 was lower than that in 1987-1990. Thus, the primary deficit as percentage of GDP was lower by 1.2 percentage points as compared to its average level in 1987-1990.

The ratio of revenue to fiscal deficits, as noted by the TFC, indicates the 'quality' of fiscal deficit by highlighting the proportion of government borrowing that does not lead to creation of assets, which can give returns in the future to service the borrowing. This ratio has increased from about 34 per cent at the end of the eighties to 68 per cent on average during 199-2002. This underlies a major weakness of the government finances, indicating that a progressively larger share of borrowing is being spent on consumption.

The nature, extent, and causes of growth of fiscal imbalance are discussed at length in the chapter on fiscal imbalance.

2.11 Growth in Debt: Centre and States

Fiscal deficits accumulate into debt. The debt-GDP ratio rises depending on primary deficit relative to GDP and the excess of interest rate over growth rate. This relationship is discussed later in Chapters 12 and 13. In India, the debt-GDP ratio relating to the combined account of the central and state governments as well as on their individual accounts has risen steadily over time. The increase has been particularly sharp after the mid-nineties.

As noted by the TFC, measurement of government debt is not a straightforward exercise. Debt consists of domestic and external debt. In some estimates liabilities of governments on account reserve funds and deposits are not included. Similarly, external debt requires to be measured in terms of the current exchange rates. However, conventionally, external debt has been taken into account in terms of the historical exchange rates, that is, the rates that prevailed in the year in which the debt was incurred.

The combined debt-GDP ratio of the central and state governments at the end of 1950-51 was 29.6 percent. During 1951-52 to 1959-60 a little less than 13 percentage points were added to the debt-GDP ratio. An additional accretion of about 4 percentage points took place in the sixties. In the seventies, there was hardly any change in the debt-GDP ratio. The TFC notes that it was in the eighties and nineties that there was a significant increase in the debt-GDP ratio. At the end of 2002-03, the combined debt-GDP ratio stood at 76 percent when external debt is evaluated at historical exchange rates and, for the states, reserve funds and deposits are not included. If these adjustments are made, the combined debt-GDP ratio at the end of 2002-23 is estimated to be about 85 percent of GDP.

High levels of debt-GDP ratio result in high interest payments relative to revenue receipts. Since interest payments are committed expenditure, revenue deficits are bound to increase when revenue receipts to GDP ratios remain sluggish. This has the effect of lowering the saving rate on the one hand and increasing the fiscal deficit on the other to maintain primary expenditures.

Eventually, these changes have the potential of developing into a spiral of rising fiscal deficits, debt, interest payments, revenue deficits, back to fiscal deficits. This gives rise to issue of sustainability of debt.

2.12 Structural Changes in India's Public Finances

Bringing together trends in revenues, expenditures, and fiscal imbalance, we can now summarize the major changes that took place in India's public finances covering both central and state governments since 1987-88. We have looked at selected fiscal aggregates relative to GDP during 1987-88 to 2001-02. This comprises a period when the public finances underwent major changes.

Table 2.11: Combined Account of Central and State Governments: Selected Variables Relative to GDP (per cent)

	TR	IP	CE	RR	RE	IP to RR (%)	RD	FD	PD	Ratio of RD to FD (%)
1987-88	16.1	3.7	6.6	18.9	21.7	19.4	2.9	9.1	5.4	31.6
1988-89	15.9	3.9	5.9	18.4	21.3	21.2	2.9	8.5	4.6	34.3
1989-90	16.0	4.2	6.0	19.0	22.2	22.2	3.2	8.9	4.6	35.8
1990-91	15.4	4.4	5.3	17.5	21.6	25.2	4.2	9.3	4.9	44.7
1991-92	15.8	4.7	4.4	18.6	22.0	25.5	3.4	6.9	2.2	48.3
1992-93	15.3	4.8	4.9	18.1	21.3	26.5	3.2	6.8	2.0	46.6
1993-94	14.2	5.0	4.6	17.1	21.3	28.9	4.2	8.1	3.2	51.9
1994-95	14.6	5.1	3.9	17.6	21.2	29.2	3.6	6.9	1.8	52.2
1995-96	14.8	5.0	3.6	17.4	20.7	28.5	3.2	6.5	1.6	49.7
1996-97	14.6	5.1	2.8	17.1	20.7	29.9	3.6	6.3	1.1	56.9
1997-98	14.0	5.2	3.2	16.9	21.1	30.4	4.1	7.2	2.0	57.9
1998-99	13.4	5.3	3.4	15.8	22.1	33.7	6.4	8.9	3.6	71.0
1999-00	14.2	5.7	3.4	16.9	23.2	33.6	6.3	9.5	3.8	66.2
2000-01	14.6	5.7	2.9	16.7	23.2	34.2	6.5	9.2	3.5	70.4
2001-02	14.5	6.1	3.6	17.8	24.5	34.2	6.7	9.9	3.8	67.5
Average (1987-88 to 1989-90) [I]	16.0	3.9	6.1	18.7	21.7	21.0	3.0	8.8	4.9	33.9
Average (1999-00 to 2001-02) [II]	14.4	5.8	3.3	17.2	23.6	34.0	6.5	9.5	3.7	68.0
(II-I)	-1.6	1.9	-2.8	-1.6	1.9	13.0	3.5	0.7	-1.2	34.1

TR=Tax Revenue; IP=Interest Payments; CE=Capital Expenditure; RR=Revenue Receipts; RE=Revenue Expenditure; RD=Revenue Deficit; FD=Fiscal Deficit; PD=Primary Deficit.
Source: *Report of the Twelfth Finance Commission.*

Table 2.11 shows the structural changes in some of the major heads of the combined revenues and expenditures of the central and state governments after netting out all intergovernmental flows. The combined tax-GDP ratio fell from a level of 16 per cent of GDP towards the end of the eighties to about 14.4 per cent, i.e. a fall of 1.6 percentage points. This translated into a corresponding fall in the ratio of total revenue receipts relative to GDP as that there was no perceptible change in the contribution of non-tax revenues relative to GDP.

On the other hand, the average revenue expenditure increased from 21.7 per cent of GDP to 23.6 percentage points showing a rise of 1.8 percentage points. This was mainly accounted for by the increase in interest payments relative to GDP, which increased from 3.9 to 5.8 per cent. The resulting pressure was shown up in two changes: fall in capital expenditure, which fell by 2.8 percentage points, from 6.1 to 3.3 per cent of GDP on average during 1999-2002 and a rise in fiscal imbalance as shown by the increases in revenue and fiscal deficits.

3

Fiscal Reforms in India

> Fiscal consolidation has been high among the reform priorities of the Government....Fiscal consolidation, after a promising start in the early 1990s, had started deteriorating since 1997-98....The fiscal health of State Governments has been equally worrisome.
>
> Economic Survey, 2004-05

In the pre-reform era, at the centre of the economic strategy that informed economic policy making in India, and determined its performance, was an auto-centric, inward looking, import substituting, plan-centered strategy that gave a preeminent position to the public sector. The objective was to establish a socialist pattern of society with equitable distribution of income and economic opportunities. This laudable objective, however, remained elusive. Three events are known to have triggered economic reforms in India at the beginning of the nineties. First, the collapse the erstwhile USSR, which signaled the need to recast economic policies that had hitherto been inward-looking, centered on five year plans, and had relied heavily on administrative mechanisms for controlling prices as well as outputs. Secondly, the transformation of the General Agreement on Tariff and Trade (GATT) into the World Trade Organization (WTO) increased the urgency to bring reforms that would foster globalization of the economy. Thirdly, in 1991, the foreign exchange reserves had dwindled to such low levels that reform of the exchange rate regime could brook no further delay. These events made reforms politically more acceptable than had hitherto been the case. In particular, comprehensive economic and fiscal reforms were initiated in the early nineties leading to a substantial rise in the overall growth rate by the mid-nineties.

The nineties witnessed momentous changes in the macroeconomic scenario of India in terms of economic growth, changes in the sectoral composition of output, public finances, and the overall policy environment that characterized and influenced the macroeconomic outcomes. Towards the close of the decade, reforms appeared to have slowed down even as industrial recession seriously beset the economy for three consecutive years toward the end of the decade. Several events in the latter part of the nineties clouded the gains from the fiscal reforms of the initial years, leading the public finances of the centre as well as the states to exhibit chronic imbalances showing themselves up in the form of large revenue and fiscal deficits. Important among these was the revision of salaries of central and state government employees in the wake of the recommendations of the fifth central pay commission. A second reason was a substantial rise in the nominal and real interest rates, with low inflation rate. A third reason was the onset of recession that led to a fall in government revenues relative to GDP and large fiscal imbalances, with government expenditures adjusting much less than revenues. The new crisis led to new responses. The central and many state governments emerged with fiscal responsibility legislations and medium term adjustment programmes.

In this Chapter, we look at the evolution and progress of reforms of fiscal reforms, based as it was on the recommendations of several committees and advisory groups.

3.1 Reforms: The Early Phase

Economic reforms were ushered with two massive doses of devaluation in 1991 within the span of two months. The exchange rate regime was formally changed in 1993, and imparted the necessary flexibility for the exchange rate to respond to market signals. Up to the mid-nineties, reforms proceeded at a fast pace with the lowering of tariff barriers, lifting of quantitative restrictions on imports, lowering of personal and corporate income taxes, reduction and rationalisation of import duties, and reforms of domestic commodity taxation. The central government entered into an agreement with the Reserve Bank of India (RBI) to certain nominal limits to borrowing by the government from RBI through ad hoc treasury bills. Bank interest rates were deregulated from October 1, 1998. Industries reserved for the public sector were limited to only six areas, viz., defense products, atomic energy, coal and lignite, mineral oils, railway transport, and minerals related to atomic energy. The number of items requiring industrial licensing was reduced to 15. These accounted for less than 15 percent of the value added in the manufacturing sector.

Fiscal reforms, particularly those relating to taxation constituted the core of economic reforms in the early stages. Fiscal reforms that have been carried out so far and those that are forthcoming can be studied under the following broad heads:

1. Revenue side reforms consisting of (a) taxation reforms at the central and state level and (b) reforms affecting non-tax revenues;
2. Expenditure reforms affecting (a) subsidies, (b) salaries of government employees, and (c) pensions;

3. Reforms relating to managing fiscal imbalance including fiscal responsibility legislations;
4. Public sector reforms including disinvestment and power sector reforms; and
5. Budgetary reforms.

3.2 Revenue Side Reforms

Central to revenue related reforms are tax reforms. Non-tax revenues are however also important.

3.3 Tax Reforms

Prior to reforms, the system of taxation was characterized by various deficiencies. In the case of direct taxes, there was a reliance on high marginal tax rates, large number of rate categories, many exemption categories, and complicated rules that left scope for discretion. In the case of commodity taxes also, there was a complex structure of taxation with both the centre and the states entitled to taxing the production and sale of commodities respectively. There was a limited taxation of some services. The tax structure fragmented the domestic market. The central government relied heavily on the central excise duties and customs duties for raising its taxes. The state governments had heterogeneous sales tax structures, and were engaged in revenue-depleting tax competition. The existence of a central sales tax provided a barrier to achieving a common market, and also provided an avenue for tax exportation as well as tax evasion. Since inputs as well as outputs were taxed by multiple jurisdictions, there was extensive cascading of taxes. The following provides a chronological listing of some of the major changes that occurred in central taxes during the reform era.

1990-91 Budget:

- Corporation tax rate for widely held companies was reduced from 50 to 40 per cent.
- Customs duty structure was rationalized.
- Most items were placed in a limited number of slots in the range of zero to 125 per cent taking together the basic and auxiliary duties.

1991-92 Budget

- MODVAT was extended to manmade fibres, filament yarns, and aerated water.
- Tax Reforms Committee (TRC) set up in August 1991 under the chairmanship of Dr R.J. Chelliah; interim report submitted in February 1992.

1992-93 Budget

- The distinction between registered and unregistered firms was eliminated for purposes of corporate taxation.

- Several changes were introduced in the case of personal income taxation, as highlighted below:
- Exemption limit was raised from Rs.22000 to Rs. 28000
- New income tax slabs were introduced
  Up to Rs.50000—20%
  Rs.50000 to Rs.1lakh30 %
  Above Rs.1 lakh 40 %
  Surcharge was continued on the last slab.
- Presumptive income tax of Rs.1400 was brought in for shopkeepers and retail traders with an annual turnover of Rs. 5lakh and below.
- Long term capital gains was to be taxed at flat rates of 20 % for individuals and HUFs, 30 per cent for firms, and 40 per cent for companies.
- Peak tariff duty was reduced to 110 per cent.

1993-94 Budget

- Customs peak duty rate was reduced from 110 to 85 per cent.
- Excise duty rates were reduced on major items: that on motor cars from 55 to 40 per cent; non-petrol driven commercial vehicles, from 23 to 15 per cent.
- Small-scale industry limit for exemption from registration was raised from Rs.7.5 lakh to Rs. 30 lakh.

1994-95 Budget

- The income tax slabs (in terms of Rs.) were revised as under:
  From 0-30000 to 0-35000
  From 30001 –50000 to 35001-60000
  From 50001-10000 to 60001-120000
  From above 100000 to above 120000
- In the area of corporate taxation, the distinction between widely and narrowly held companies was removed, which were previously taxed at 45 and 50 per cent respectively. In both cases, the tax rate for domestic companies was set at 40 per cent.
- Peak customs duty rate was reduced from 85 to 65 per cent.
- Service tax was introduced on telephones, non-life insurance, and stockbrokers.

1995-96 Budget

- Income tax slabs were revised to
  0-40000 at zero per cent
  40001-60000 at 20 per cent
  60001-12000 at 30 per cent
  Above 120000 at 40 per cent

- Peak Customs duty rate was reduced from 65 per cent to 50 per cent.

1996-97 Budget

- In the case of personal income taxation, the tax rate on the first slab was reduced from 20 to 15 per cent. The standard deduction was raised Rs.15000 to Rs.18000.
- In respect of corporation tax, the surcharge was reduced from 15 to 7.5 per cent.
- A Minimum Alternate Tax (MAT) was brought in to cover the so-called zero tax companies.

1997-98 Budget

This budget is often described as a Dream Budget for the rate reductions and incentives that it contained. Its highlights are summarized below.

- The maximum marginal rate of income tax was reduced to 30 per cent from 40 per cent, and the lowest rate was reduced to 10 per cent from 15 per cent. A new slab between Rs.60001 to Rs150000 at 20 per cent was instituted.
- The dividend taxation at individual level was abolished.
- The surcharge on corporation income was abolished.
- The corporate tax rates applicable to domestic and foreign companies reduced from 40 to 35 per cent.
- A Voluntary Disclosure Scheme (VDIS) was introduced for declaring hitherto undisclosed incomes for payment of taxes.
- The peak customs duty rates reduced from 50 to 40 per cent.
- In the case of excise duty, three new rates of 8,13 and 18 per cent introduced with the objective of moving towards fewer rates.

1998-99 Budget

- The income tax exemption limit was raised to Rs. 50000 from RS. 40,000 for non-corporate assessees.
- Introduction of a simple one page taxpayer-friendly return called SARAL

1999-2000 Budget

- A one-by-six scheme was introduced for identifying potential tax assessees.
- Customs peak duty rates were reduced from 45 to 40 per cent.
- In excise duty, a 3-rate structure consisting of a central rate of 16 per cent, a merit rate of 8 per cent, and a demerit rate of 24 per cent was introduced.

2000-01 Budget

- One-by-six scheme was extended to 79 more cities from the existing coverage of 54 cities having population of 2 lakh or more.

- Surcharge at the rate of 10 per cent and 15 per cent was levied for income of non-corporate assessees with an income of Rs.60,001 to Rs. 1,50,000 and with income above Rs.1,50,000 respectively.
- Peak customs duty rate reduced from 40 to 35 per cent ad valorem.
- MODVAT was converted into CENVAT with a uniform rate of 16 per cent with three special excise duty rates of 8,16, and 24 per cent.

2001-02 Budget

- Surcharges were abolished except a 2 per cent surcharge leviable on all corporate and non-corporate assessees except foreign companies.
- One-by-six scheme was extended to all urban areas.
- In customs duty surcharge of 10 per cent was discontinued.
- In the case of Excise duty, one CENVAT rate of 16 per cent and one single special excise duty of rate of 16 per cent was brought in.

While there was a determined progress made over the nineties to simplify the tax structure, generally reduce the rates, and improve administration, the tax system lost, over the nineties, some of the aggregate buoyancy and the tax-GDP ratio fell. This is discussed at length in a later Chapter. The reform process of the central taxes is far from over. The reforms that were brought about and those that are prospective could be considered to be largely based on the recommendations of committees, task forces, and advisory groups that the central government set up from time to time. This was the period in which the Eleventh and Twelfth Finance Commissions also gave their recommendations. We will briefly summarize here the recommendations of a select list of committees/groups.

3.4 Tax Reforms (Chelliah) Committee

In the early nineties, one of the first comprehensive analysis of the Indian tax system was undertaken by the Chelliah Committee, which suggested a basic overhaul of the tax system. In regard to income taxation, the Committee stressed the importance of lower tax rates, a narrower spread between the entry rate and the maximum marginal rate, and few exemptions and deductions. This, it recommended, should be combined with effective enforcement.

The Committee's main recommendations relating to corporation tax are summarized below.

1. The tax rate on corporate incomes for domestic companies be lowered to 45 per cent.
2. Agricultural income in excess Rs. 25000 accruing to the non-agriculturists be taxed by aggregating it with non-agricultural income.
3. Interest tax should be abolished.

4. Perquisites and fringe benefits should be taxed.

In regard to customs and central excise, the committee recommended:

- Tariffs on finished goods should be higher than on basic raw materials and those on components and machinery.
- Agricultural imports should be taxed.
- A three rate MODVAT at 10, 20 and 30 percent should be introduced with selective excises at 30,40, and 50 per cent.

3.5 Advisory Group on Tax Policy and Tax Administration for the Tenth Plan

In the context of finding resources for the Tenth Plan, the Planning Commission set up an Advisory Group headed by P. Shome to make recommendations on reforming the tax system. The Advisory Group made the following main recommendations in regard to direct taxes:

1. The maximum marginal rate of personal income tax rate be retained at 30 per cent. Also, correction should be made to remove bracket creep from the structure by broad-basing the various brackets/slabs even though it may lead to some revenue loss at existing levels of compliance.
2. Tax incentives under sections 80CCC, 88, 80L and 10(15) of the Income Tax Act be abolished, at least in phases. Tax concessions under Sections 80 D, 80DD, 80 DDB and 80 E be given in the form of tax credit rather than as deduction from income (to improve equity); and the rollover provision relating capital gains under sections 54, 54B, 54D, 54EA, and 54EB be removed. This reform would enable further reduction in the overall tax rate structure that should enable improved savings behaviour by all taxpayers.
3. Corporate tax rate should not exceed the maximum marginal personal income tax. Hence, the corporate tax rate should be reduced to 30 per cent to bring it in line with the existing level of maximum marginal personal income tax. Abolition of the distribution tax on dividends and consequent reduction of the tax rate for foreign companies to the level for domestic companies.
4. Minimum alternate tax (MAT) should be reconstituted as a tax equal to the aggregate of 0.75 per cent of adjusted net worth plus 10 percent of the dividend distributed. The MAT should be allowed to be carried forward for set-off against future tax liability in excess of the MAT as provided in Section 115JAA.

In regard to the indirect taxes, the Advisory Group recommended as follows:

1. For Union excise duties, introduction of two-rate structure of 16 per cent together with a higher rate.

2. Definition of manufacture be widened to include the chain of value addition by or on behalf of the manufacturer (undertaken before the marketing of the product) be charged to duty.
3. Both capital goods and other inputs used in the factory of the manufacturer should be allowed CENVAT credit. Thus, capital goods and other inputs should not be distinguished for purposes of input tax credit.
4. The median tariff rate in India is much higher. At 35 percent, it is still among the highest in the world. This should be brought down to 25 per cent in the 2002-03 budget. The objective should now be to bring down the median tariff rate to 20 per cent in 2003-04 and 15 per cent in 2004-05.
5. Remove as many exemptions as possible. The countervailing duty of 16 per cent be levied uniformly without exemptions.
6. No need for so many export promotion schemes in the nature of remission, exemption, entitlements, etc. They need to be rationalized by combining them and removing the overlapping.

In regard to the state level Value Added Tax, the Advisory Group made the following recommendations:

1. States should adopt a consumption type VAT i.e. there should be no distinction between raw materials and capital goods in allowing VAT credit. Only this VAT variant is equivalent to a retail sales tax. The consumption base must be as wide as possible and must comprehensively include manufacturers and dealers of all goods indicated in sales tax schedule.
2. A two floor VAT rate structure in addition to the zero rate; one for essential commodities and another for all other items would be best.
3. The States must draw up a common exemption list: unprocessed food articles, life-saving drugs and commodities with negative externalities whose consumption needs to be checked should be exempted from State VAT.
4. All concessions with regard to the sales tax should be eliminated under the State VAT and benefits if any should be given only in exceptional circumstances through budget based subsidies.
5. Small dealers whose annual turnover does not exceed Rs.15 lakh should be exempt from the liability of VAT but subjected to a sales tax of one per cent. All international exports should be zero-rated.
6. Commodities with negative externalities whose consumption needs to be checked should, however, be subject to the Special Additional Tax (SAT) against which no input tax credit should be granted. Luxuries should not be taxed under the SAT. Instead, it would be better to have a common, high, third VAT rate for luxuries.

7. The local VAT rates should be close to uniform across States. A destination based VAT is recommended for the Indian State level VAT.

3.6 Kelkar Committee on Direct and Indirect Taxes

There have been numerous attempts to reform the tax system from time to time. The latest in this series were two committees headed by Dr. Kelkar covering direct and indirect taxation. The committee estimated that as a result of their recommendations, there will be a reduction in the transaction costs almost by 50 per cent, which would translate into potential gain of about Rs. 4000-5000 crore per annum. The Kelkar Committee set out an ultimate goal and specified a road map in which stepwise changes were indicated so as to achieve the reform objective. For excise duties, they suggested four rates of categories of zero, 10 per cent, 20 per cent and 150 per cent dealing with respectively with life saving items, raw materials, inputs and intermediate goods, final goods and demerit goods. The committee also suggested the removal of most of the exemptions with limited exceptions. For the central excise duty, the committee recommended 16 per cent as the core rate and zero and 8 per cent for life saving drugs and food products respectively. A separate duty structure was suggested for the petroleum sector.

The Committee emphasized the need for building up capacitates to deal with the requirements of a modern transparent tax system. It observed that as a result of some of the initial reforms, there was a fall in the tax-GDP ratio of central commodity taxes has been only partially mitigated by the rise in the central direct taxes. This has adversely affected the finances of both central and state governments.

However, some of these changes might have been efficiency augmenting by reducing cascading of taxes. Large tax bases and low rates, limited rate categories, absence of tax cascading, minimum exemptions, and absence of tax barriers in inter-state trade would characterize a desirable system of taxation of goods and services. Such a system should also be harmonized across states so that competitive reduction of tax rates can be avoided. Where tax related decisions of the central government affect the tax bases of the state governments and vice versa, such as in the case of sales tax and Union excise duties, there is need for vertical coordination in using common tax fields. Implementation of state level VAT and removal of tax-related barriers to an integrated country-wide market like the central sales tax would therefore strengthen the efficiency effects of tax reforms.

3.7 Reforms Suggested by the Kelkar Task Force

The Ministry of Finance set up a Task Force headed by Vijay Kelkar to suggest ways and means of achieving the targets under the Fiscal responsibility and Budget Management Act (FRBMA) of the central government. The Task Force used four data sets for carrying out its analysis: (a) time-series of tax revenues, (b) previously unpublished data about the composition of excise revenues, (c) a data set of roughly 1 million records of filings for personal income tax, and (d) the CMIE database of 2,74,446 firms of India. The Task Force adopted four principles for the strategy for fiscal consolidation:

- Fiscal consolidation should be revenue-led.
- Fiscal consolidation should be front-loaded.
- Capital expenditure should be enhanced, to counter-balance the contractionary effects of the fiscal consolidation, but expenditures should be conditional on institutional reform to ensure that the expenditure is well utilized.
- The reform efforts on revenue expenditure should be further intensified.

The Task Force suggested the following eight-part strategy for tax reforms:

1. Widening the tax base. This involves removing exemptions and broadening the scope of the tax system to bring within its fold economic activities, which are presently exempted.
2. Few rates; Low rates. High tax rates distort economic decisions and fuel the deployment of resources into tax avoidance and tax evasion. The Task Force observed that a large number of rates of taxes generate problems of bracket creep, classification disputes, and political lobbying about rates. These arguments suggest that a rational tax system is one with very few rates and low rates.
3. Enhancing equity of the tax system. In its view, reform of the tax system should further both vertical and horizontal equity.
4. Shift to non-distortionary consumption taxes to increase efficiency in production and enhance international competitiveness of Indian goods and services: A key idea of sound public finance is to shift the incidence of taxation upon consumption. In the view of the Task Force, tariffs, excises and turnover taxes on domestic goods and services have cascading effects. The destination-based VAT on all goods and services would be the best alternative.
5. Enhancing the neutrality between present consumption and future consumption: The Task force observes that neutrality between consumption

and savings tends to depress savings rates and investment. Tax reform should impart inter- temporal neutrality in consumption.

6. Enhancing neutrality of the tax system to the form of organization: The choice of organizational structure adopted by decision-makers in the economy should be driven by efficiency considerations and not tax considerations.
7. Enhancing the neutrality of the tax system to sources of finance. The choice between debt and equity and between retention and distribution of profits should not be distorted by tax considerations.
8. Establishing an effective and efficient compliance system: A well-executed tax administration will enhance transparency and integrity, thereby inspiring public confidence.

The Task Force came out with a plan of restructuring central finances. This plan also has significant implications for state finances. The salient features of the Report of the Task Force may be summarized as below:

- Vide article 268A, the power to tax services has been vested in the central government.
- The value-added in the case of goods beyond manufacturing is in the nature of trade arising from wholesaling or retailing, which can be considered as a service. The centre is therefore entitled to tax this value added.
- States are not entitled to tax services as the subject is in the Union list. However, under article 268 A, the taxation of services can be assigned fully or partially to the states.
- A 'grand bargain' can then be proposed to the states whereby they may agree to participate in a national Goods and Services Tax (GST), which can be levied at the rate of 20 per cent, of which the centre will levy 12 per cent and states can levy 8 per cent.

The estimates provided by the Task Force indicate that these changes will have significant revenue implications. Their base scenario assumes a buoyancy of 1.87 for direct taxes and 0.74 for indirect taxes, which include taxation of services under the present laws. These result in considerable improvement in the ratio of centre's gross tax revenues to GDP, which rises from 9.2 per cent of GDP in 2003-04 to 10.7 in 2008-09, showing an improvement of 1.5 percentage points. Even after this margin of improvement, the FRBMA target is not met, with revenue deficit at 1.66 per cent of GDP in 2008-09. In the reform scenario also, the core adjustment comes from a substantial improvement in the ratio of gross tax revenues of the centre to GDP taking it above 13 percent in 2008-09. In relation to Task Force's recommendation of GST under a 'grand bargain', several issues have been raised in the related discussions. These are discussed in the Report of the Twelfth Finance Commission as summarized below:

- The legal status of centre's power to tax value added of goods interpreting as services has been questioned. It is a matter that can lead to legal issues, once the actual legislation is made and notified.
- The 12: 8 ratio of in favor of the centre can increase the vertical imbalance in the system, particularly because stamp fees, registration duties and sales tax on works contracts will be merged under the GST. The states will also lose the autonomy to fix rates, which is the essence having autonomy over tax bases.
- Aspects of inter-state taxation of services raise additional problems. Some have argued for the need for a negative list of taxes that have an inter-state character. The proposal of a clearing house mechanism to address issues of inter-state taxation and settlement of rebate claims and counter claims may run into a variety of practical problems.
- Inefficiencies will increase, if decisions to spend are totally divorced from decisions to tax.
- The status of divisibility of the tax on services will remain open-ended as these will not be subject to sharing under article 270, and therefore, under the recommendations of the Finance Commission.

3.8 Tax Reforms Suggested by the Twelfth Finance Commission

In the TFC's restructuring plan, the tax-GDP ratio goes up 2 by percentage points with both centre and states contributing to it. For the states, the adoption of the Value Added Tax is likely to be revenue-augmenting in the medium to long term. These changes, according to the TFC, will have both vertical and horizontal benefits. The vertical benefit would be due to augmentation of the tax base as distortion related inefficiencies are reduced. The horizontal benefit will accrue from the fact that consuming states will gain more in relative terms. The TFC has urged that the issue of taxation of services following the 88th amendment to the constitution should be resolved. Since the service tax has been put under article 268A, the sharing of its revenues with the states has been taken out of the purview of the Finance commission. The centre can assign certain services to the states for collecting and retaining the revenues, but the tax will be levied by the centre. The TFC has suggested that it is necessary to ensure that the revenue accruing to the states, under the new arrangement should not be less than the share that would accrue to the states, had the entire service tax proceeds been part of the shareable pool.

While commenting on the reforms suggested by the Task force, particularly the idea of the GST, the TFC observes that the proposal of a comprehensive GST is an attractive one and should be pursued as a long-term objective. The relevant legal and administrative aspects should be extensively discussed, particularly with the states. The implementation of a state-level VAT would facilitate its introduction in due course. However, even without this radical change, it should be possible to raise the tax-GDP ratio adequately.

3.9 Non-tax Revenues

Non tax revenues in India have stagnated between 2 to 3 per cent of GDP over the years on the combined account of the centre and states. Non tax revenues consist of a heterogeneous mix of sources encompassing interest receipts on loans given by the governments, dividends on equity investment, and user charges and tariffs for services provided by the governments. The TFC observes in this context that in the case of goods and services that are private in nature, the principle of cost recovery should apply, and where costs are not meant to be recovered fully, explicit subsidies should be provided. The management of government finances in such a way would impart the necessary transparency and improve the efficacy of fiscal intervention. In the context of interest receipts and dividends, the issue is linked to the reform of public enterprises, and the question of user charges is linked to subsidies. Where royalties are payable, these should be on ad valorem basis. Our restructuring plan proposes a tangible increase in the non-tax revenues relative to GDP.

3.10 Reforms in State Level Finances

States initiated tax reforms somewhat later than the centre. In particular, they reduced the rate categories in the case of sales taxes, reduced exemptions, and introduced floor rates. There were tangible revenue benefits after these changes. Efforts have been underway for some time now under the guidance of the empowered committee of the state finance ministers to facilitate the implementation of state level VAT. In his speech introducing the 2004-05 budget, the Union Finance Minister made reference to 'broad consensus among the states to implement VAT' and that 'April 1, 2005 has been set as the date for implementation'. With the State level VAT, there would be further reduction in distortions due to cascading. The TFC has recommended that the tax rental arrangement regarding the additional excise duty items, viz., textiles, tobacco and sugar should be formally revoked and these items should be integrated into the overall design of State VAT. Any ceiling of 4 per cent should not be there, and in fact the relevance of the entire mechanism of declared goods should be reexamined. The TFC observes that the taxation of services has remained fragmented and piecemeal.

3.11 Expenditure Reforms

Five items are important under expenditure reforms: reforms of subsidies, reforms relating to growth of government salaries, pension reforms, restructuring of expenditure towards capital expenditure, and strategies for the reduction of interest payments. Various bodies including the Expenditure Reforms Commission and the Eleventh and Twelfth Finance Commissions have examined the question of expenditure reforms. Some of their recommendations are highlighted below.

3.12 Expenditure Reforms Commission

The recommendations of the Expenditure Reforms Commission (ERC) covered the following main areas: food subsidy, fertilizer subsidy, and government employment policies.

Food Subsidy: In respect of those States where the total distribution under the PDS is in excess of the quantities earmarked for BPL population and at prices at or below the price at which the sales are to be made to the BPL population, the ERC suggested that the Government of India could provide the subsidy amounts directly to the State Governments, leaving it to them to procure the food-grains required for the BPL population. The ERC recommended a National Food Security buffer stock of 10 million tonnes – 4 million tonnes of wheat and 6 million tonnes of rice – should be maintained at all times. It observed that the cost of buffer stocks held in excess of the above requirements should be treated as "producer's subsidy" and action taken to phase it out through.

- Moderating the increase in minimum support prices and;
- Moving towards procurement of single (common) variety of paddy/rice, as in the case of wheat. Besides, through a suitable adjustment in the pricing mechanism, reduce procurement of paddy and increase procurement of rice through a levy system.
- Encouraging State Governments and private sector to enter procurement, trade and export of food-grains through an assurance of continuity of policy over the next 15 years.

Fertilizer Subsidies: The Retention Price Scheme (RPS) in ERC's view had led to the development of a large domestic industry and near self-sufficiency. However, the unit wise RPS is a cost plus scheme. It results in high cost fertilizers, excess payments to industry and provides no incentives to be cost efficient. Besides, fertilizer subsidies have grown over the years. The package suggested to rationalize fertilizer subsidies takes care of the needs of small farmers and proposes to bring fertilizer prices to the level of import parity price in a gradual and phased manner over a period of time as follows:

To protect small farmers and marginal farmers who consume a large part of their output from a loss in their real incomes arising out of increase in farm gate prices of fertilizers two options are suggested:

- introduction of a dual price scheme under which all cultivator households are given 120 Kgs. of fertilizers at subsidized prices and;
- Expansion of Employment Guarantee Scheme and Rural Works Programmes to provide additional incomes to small farmers.

Dismantling of the control system in a phased manner, leading to a decontrolled fertilizer industry which can compete with import albeit with a small level of protection and a feedstock cost differential compensation to naphtha/liquefied natural gas (LNG) based units to ensure self-sufficiency.

3.13 Optimizing Government Staff Strength

The ERC suggested a cut of 10 per cent on the staff strength as on 1.1.2000 to be carried out by the year 2004-2005. Besides, an annual direct recruitment plan for all cadres should be prepared by a Screening Committee. It said that there should be a total ban on creation of new posts for two years. Staff declared surplus should be transferred to the Surplus Cell to be redesignated as the Division of Retraining and Deployment, which will pay their salary, requirement benefits etc. Further, surplus staff should be made eligible for a liberal Voluntary Retirement Scheme recommended by the Fifth Central Pay Commission with the exception that commutation entitlements will be as at present and the ex-gratia amount will be paid in monthly installments covering a five year period. Those who do not opt for Voluntary Retirement Scheme and are not re-deployed within one year will be discharged from service.

3.14 Expenditure Restructuring Suggested by TFC

In restructuring expenditures, the TFC noted that there is need to make reference to the basic objectives of government intervention in economic activities, as also to the basic objectives for assignment of responsibilities as between central and sub-national governments. It is also important to relate government expenditures to outcomes in terms of the quality, reach, and impact of government services. This would be facilitated if governments focus more on their primary responsibilities rather than spreading resources thinly in many areas where the private sector can provide the necessary services. The primary role of government is to provide public goods like defence, law and order, and general administration as public goods. This represents one kind of market failure. The role of governments extends to merit goods and services with large positive externalities like education and health. The services should be assigned to the central government if the scope of public goods is nation wide like defence. The services get assigned to state governments if the scope of the public good is limited to regions or if externalities are more local in character like the health services. Admittedly there may be many examples of benefit spillovers, some of which can be internalized to the state level decision makers by a suitable scheme of grants. There is a felt need to examine whether the central government is not partaking in many responsibilities that legitimately belong to the domain of the states. Governments at both levels have also stepped into the provision of many private goods, which adversely affects the quantum and quality of service in regard to public and merit goods. Two key elements of restructuring government expenditures relate to augmentation of capital expenditure relative to GDP, focused on infrastructure and a reduction of central government's expenditures on subjects listed as state responsibilities.

The TFC observes that the conventional budget exercises have focused on allocation of resources to different heads, without taking into account how these government expenditures get translated into outputs and outcomes. Outputs are the direct result of government expenditure and outcomes are the final results. Thus, in the context of education, opening a new school or appointing a new teacher is an output and reduction in the rate of illiteracy is an outcome. Issues of efficiency require consideration whether the same outcome can be achieved at lower costs and whether then same costs can produce better outcomes. A critical part of budgetary reforms must include information on the relationship between expenditures and the corresponding performance in producing real results as in determining the size of the budget and its allocation among different heads. Although in the past there have been attempts at introducing performance budgeting, such endeavors have receded in importance. There is need to bring back performance budgeting as an integral part of the preparation and evaluation of budgets, both for the centre and the states. Thus, the management of public expenditures should be guided by economy, efficiency, and effectiveness.

3.15 Subsidies: The 1997 Discussion Paper and Beyond

The subject of subsidies was extensively examined by the Discussion Paper brought out by the Ministry of Finance in 1997. It had argued that government subsidies in India are largely of the non-merit type, poorly targeted, and mainly administered through inputs. It argued for an extensive reform of the subsidy regime. Budgetary subsidies can be explicit or implicit. When subsidies are explicitly stated in the budget it adds to transparency in expenditure management. According to the Discussion Paper brought out by the Ministry of Finance in 1997, there are many hidden subsidies in the budget. These arise because the costs of providing these are not recovered from the users or beneficiaries. In the case of merit goods like education and health, subsidization may be desirable. But the desired extent of subsidization should be clearly worked out. Various studies have highlighted that government subsidies, measured as un-recovered costs in the public provision of private goods, are large in volume, amounting to 13 to 14 per cent of GDP. In many instances, subsidies promote or subsidize inefficiencies. Subsidies are often wasted, as these do not reach the intended beneficiary. The 1997 Discussion Paper did highlight many of these problems and suggested a course for subsidy reforms that included reducing their volume, eliminating input-based subsidies, making these subsidies explicit, and improving their targeting. Following the recommendations of the Expenditure Reforms Commission, some changes were introduced in the regime of subsidization of fertilizers. In spite of these efforts, the volume of subsidies in the central budget has remained large. Some of the earlier commitments for reducing subsidies, particularly in areas of fertilizers and petroleum, must be implemented. In the case of states, subsidies largely remain hidden as cost of services keeps increasing, while recoveries as proportion of costs become less and less. There is a clear need to link user charges with costs. The TFC has also recommended that the determination of user charges for a variety of private services provided by the governments should be supervised by an autonomous regulatory commission, which can protect both the interests of the consumer and the revenues of the government.

3.16 Government Salaries

The TFC observed that salaries and allowances in many states have tended to converge with those of the central government and that they find it difficult to implement a salary structure that is different from that of the centre. The problems have become acute for some states, as the share of salaries in their total expenditure is very large. The initial conditions for the states differ because in the past their salary scales were different from the centre and they also followed different recruitment policies. If salary structures across the states are allowed to converge, the number of employees in a state also needs to follow some comparable norms in relation to the size of population, fiscal capacity, and other relevant considerations. The per employee salary expenditure may still differ because of the composition of the workforce. Normalization can be done in respect of the total salary bill relative to their fiscal capacities. The salary burden is already heavy and at the minimum, the ratio of salaries to revenue expenditure net of interest payments and pensions must not be allowed to increase. It should be progressively brought down to levels prevalent in 1996-97. The EFC had recommended that there is no need to appoint Pay Commissions as a routine at the interval of 10 years. It also recommended that states should be consulted while appointing a new Pay Commission, which is endorsed by the TFC.

3.17 Pension Reforms

Pension payments constitute an important component of committed expenditures in the central and state budgets. The TFC favoured the initiative taken by the central government in this context. The central government has taken steps for pension reforms, particularly in respect of new appointments. A defined contribution pension scheme was introduced by the central government with effect from January 1, 2004 for Central Government employees recruited on or after that date, (except Armed Forces, in the first stage) replacing the existing defined benefit pension system. The central government has also initiated the process for bringing out legislation for the appointment of an independent pension regulatory authority, which can ensure proper investment of pension funds. The Pension Fund regulator will have the responsibility of regulating, promoting and ensuring the orderly growth of the pension funds. The pension liabilities in the case of the states account for a larger share of its revenue receipts. This share may increase further in view of the increasing longevity and the number of appointments in the late sixties and early seventies, when the size of state governments was expanding. The TFC has recommended that the state governments need to take up initiatives similar to those of the central government for pension reforms.

3.18 Towards Productive Capital Expenditure

While much emphasis is placed on the quantum of capital expenditure, the TFC observes that the quality of such expenditure is equally important. In the proposed restructuring plan suggested by the TFC, the level of capital expenditure, on the combined account of the centre and the states relative to GDP, is set to rise to about 7 per cent of GDP by 2009-10. It is indicated that this capital expenditure is meant for administrative departments and departmental enterprises. Separate borrowing limits have been prescribed by the TFC for non-departmental enterprises. The increase in capital expenditure is for augmenting investment and building physical assets for the various publicly provided services aimed at promoting growth and improving the quality of services provided by the central and state governments. It is not meant for covering losses of non-departmental public enterprises, by contributing to their share capital, or for servicing debt arising from off-budget borrowing.

3.19 Reforms for Managing Fiscal Imbalance

Chronic and ever growing revenue deficits became what was described by the Eleventh Finance Commission (EFC), as "malefic fixtures" in the central, combined, and all state fiscal profiles since 1979-80, 1982-83, and 1987-88, respectively. Individual states, first the fiscally weaker ones, and then, even the higher per capita income states have successively slid into revenue deficit. These revenue deficits, embedded as they are in unsustainable fiscal deficits, are only visible manifestations of multiple and deeper deficiencies in government finances.

For the accentuation of the crisis in government finances in the late nineties, three proximate reasons can be stated. First, an industrial recession, that had an unmitigated run for nearly three years, depressed tax revenues; secondly, the revision of salaries and pensions of central government employees subsequent to the recommendations of the Fifth Central Pay Commission, and the consequent in-tandem revisions of salaries and pensions of state government employees pushed state budgets deep into the red; and thirdly, the high level of nominal interest rates, itself being caused by ballooning government borrowing requirements, further deepened the crisis.

The causalities however, run deeper into the system. Important among these is the long-term erosion of the tax-GDP ratio, which reflects an amalgam of causes like under - taxation of services and of agriculture, and inefficiencies of tax administration. As shown by Table 2.1, the long-term history of tax revenues indicates a steady upward trend up to 1987-88. Between 1960-61 and 1987-88, tax revenues as a percentage of GDP (new series) increased by about 8 percentage points from 7.86 to 16.68. This ratio was still about 16 percent in 1989-90. Since then, it declined to 13.25 percent in 1998-99. It recovered marginally next year and was around 14 percent in 1999-00. The break-up of the aggregate tax-GDP ratio between direct and indirect taxes indicates that while the direct taxes have picked up by about 1 percentage point in the nineties, the indirect taxes have lost ground by more than 2 percentage points. States' own tax revenues, as percentage of GDP, had reached a level of 5.49 percent in 1991-92 and 1994-95, but declined from this peak in later years. States tax revenues have remained stagnant relative to GDP during the nineties, and show a marginal decline (0.38 percentage points) between 1987-88 and 1997-98. There was some improvement subsequently following the introduction of uniform floor rates in sales taxes. States own tax revenues in 1999-2000 amounted to 5.41 percent of GDP. On the other hand, centre's gross tax collections show a larger decline, the fall being close to 1.6 percentage points from the peak of 10.31 percent achieved in 1987-88 to 8.69 percent of GDP in 1999-00. Tax revenue buoyancies, as discussed in a later chapter, had peaked in the seventies for both the central and state governments.

3.20 Fiscal Frameworks for Reforms

In the nineties many countries around the world were able to achieve fiscal consolidation, attaining primary surpluses. The TFC has provided a brief review of it in its Report. Widespread reforms including debt ceilings and deficit targets have strengthened fiscal frameworks. Expenditure rules and transparency in the fiscal management has also been emphasized in these fiscal frameworks.

Evaluations of these fiscal consolidation efforts have identified certain factors that account for reliable and durable adjustments. In particular, fiscal consolidation is more likely to be successful when based on cuts in expenditure, especially when undertaken by countries with high levels of debt. Widespread reforms in fiscal frameworks require institutional reforms aimed at achieving and maintaining fiscal consolidation, while leaving room for fiscal policy to respond to business cycles through automatic stabilizers and policy actions.

Recent institutional reforms can be classified into three broad groups: formal deficit and debt rules, expenditure limits, and transparency. The main examples of this approach are European countries bound by the Maastricht Treaty as supplemented by the Stability and Growth Pact. The UK since 1997 has operated a Golden Rule whereby borrowing is done only to finance capital spending and the limit on net debt is 40 per cent of GDP over a cycle. Several countries have deficit and debt rules at the sub national level. In the US, all but two states have laws requiring balanced budgets and limiting the states to raise debt. Nine provinces and territories of Canada have fiscal rules with balanced budgets requiring them to take on debt only for the purpose of financing investment projects. Canada has also focused on instituting a rigorous expenditure review process. Debt ceiling should be prescribed along with the deficit rules. In practice debt ceilings have not been based on theory, but governed by the concern about reducing high debt levels and are thus generally been chosen on the basis of the experience individual countries. The main criticism of the deficit rules in general and balanced budget rules in particular is that they are invariant and therefore tend to be pro-cyclical. This is a more important consideration for national governments as compared to sub national governments. For this reason the deficit rules for the national government have increasingly been defined in terms of a cyclically adjusted deficit measures or as an average over the economic cycle. Thus these rules allow the operation of domestic stabilizers and to some extent also provide room for discretionary policy within the cycle.

Transparency in fiscal management has been emphasized by countries like New Zealand, Australia and the UK. The key element in this approach requires an explicit legal basis, elaboration of guiding principles of fiscal policy, requirement that objectives are clearly stated and emphasis on the need for a long-term focus to fiscal policy, and requirements for fiscal reporting to the public. The UK, New Zealand, and US have enacted legislations for transparency, which require statements providing the objectives for deficits and debt. The US places relatively greater emphasis on expenditure and deficit rules. Expenditure rules typically emphasize ceilings on specific areas of expenditure like discretionary expenditure as opposed to non-discretionary expenditure and in some cases with respect to particular programmes. Thus, three structural changes can help restore the fiscal health in India, namely, (1) legislative enactments that can restrict fiscal imprudence and set targets such as those relating to fiscal and revenue deficits, debt, and rules for expenditure cuts contingent on specified conditions, (2) transparency requirements in fiscal management, which help a better understanding of the fiscal health of a government by its citizens and their representatives, and (3) exposure to market discipline, particularly in raising debt.

As noted by the TFC, there has been some notable improvement in the institutional environment that can support fiscal reforms. The central government has enacted a Fiscal Responsibility and Management Act (FRBMA) in 2003, which had set the target for eliminating revenue deficit by 2007-08, and reducing fiscal deficit to 3 per cent of GDP. The July 2004 budget has shifted the target year to 2008-09. The states of Karnataka, Kerala, Tamil Nadu, Punjab, and Uttar Pradesh have enacted fiscal responsibility legislations. Many states have drawn up their medium term reform programs with specific monitorable targets in the context of the Medium Term Fiscal Reform Facility instituted on the basis of EFC's recommendations.

Clause 3 of the FRBMA provides that the Central Government shall lay in each financial year before both the Houses of Parliament, three statements relating to (i) Mid Term Financial Policy Statement (ii) Fiscal Policy Strategy Statement, and a (iii) Macroeconomic Framework Statement, which shall contain an assessment regarding (a) growth in GDP (b) fiscal balance of the Union Government as reflected in the revenue balance and gross fiscal balance, and (c) external sector balance of the economy as reflected in the current account balance in the balance of payments.

The TFC observes that the targets for revenue and fiscal deficits are essential ingredients of a restructuring program. Like the central government, similar targets are indicated for the states. These targets take into account an underlying growth scenario along with levels of interest rates and other macroeconomic parameters. In fixing such targets, account is taken of the determinants of debt dynamics. Growth in the debt-GDP ratio depends on two factors: (a) primary deficit to GDP ratio and (b) the excess of growth over interest rate. If growth rate is equal to interest rate, debt relative to GDP would be the outcome of accumulated primary deficits only. However, as long as growth rate is higher than interest rate, it absorbs some of primary deficits being translated into higher debt relative to GDP. On the other hand, if interest rate exceeds growth rate, the debt-GDP ratio would increase as a result of both factors. Fiscal deficit can have an impact on the growth rate as well as on interest rates, particularly when the household savings in the financial form are not adequate to cover the demand for those savings from the government leaving enough for the private corporate sector. Using the equation of debt dynamics, the TFC derives conditions that would stabilize debt and fiscal deficit relative to GDP. Nominal growth rate (g) and the nominal effective interest rate are taken as exogenous. The relevant conditions state that:

- The debt-GDP ratio will be stabilized at a level b* where b*= p (1+g)/ (g-i).
- The fiscal deficit to GDP ratio will be stabilized at f* where f*= p.g/ (g-i).

Indicating the ratio of revenue receipts to GDP indicated by (r), these conditions are written equivalently, in terms of the ratio of interest payments to revenue receipts (ip)* instead of primary deficit, as follows [12]:

- The debt-GDP ratio will be stabilized at a level b* where b*= (ip)*r (1+g)/ i.
- The fiscal deficit to GDP ratio will be stabilized at f* where f*= (ip)*r.g/ i.

In the case of states, the ratio of revenue receipts to GSDP and that of interest payment to revenue receipts differ widely across states. The TFC observes that it is more useful to cast the debt-sustainability conditions in terms of the ratio of interest payments to revenue receipts although the two sets of conditions are equivalent.

In the present Indian context, the FRBMA has fixed a fiscal deficit target for the central government at 3 per cent of GDP. Using relations given above, which imply [b*=f*(1+g)/g], it is seen that for this level of fiscal deficit and a nominal growth rate of 12 per cent, the debt-GDP ratio will eventually be stabilized at 28 per cent. At the end of 2004-05, the centre's debt-GDP ratio is estimated at 53 per cent, with external debt measured at historical exchange rates, and not taking into account that part of the NSSF liabilities against which there are assets in the form of state securities and also excluding the Market Stabilization Scheme (MSS) liabilities against which an equal amount of cash balance is held. Since the fiscal deficit target is given by the FRBMA, as long there is an excess of growth over interest rate, a primary deficit can be maintained in the stabilization phase. The TFC observes that for a combination of 12 per cent nominal growth rate and 7 per cent interest rate, this would be equal to 1.25 per cent of GDP. They prescribe a combined fiscal deficit target, relative to GDP, of 6 per cent as consistent with the availability of savings of the household sector in financial assets, which is of the order of 10 per cent, the desirable level of current account deficit, and the requirements of the corporate sector and the non-departmental public sector undertakings. The transferable savings of the household sector of 10 per cent of GDP combined with an acceptable level of current account deficit of 1.5 per cent would be adequate to provide for a government fiscal deficit of 6 per cent, an absorption by the private corporate sector of 4 per cent, and by non-departmental public enterprises of 1.5 per cent of GDP. The argument is that when the revenue deficit becomes zero, the entire fiscal deficit would lead to an augmentation of investment with the total investment as percentage of GDP touching a level in the range of 28 to 30 per cent. Of this total, the household sector could invest about 12 per cent of GDP, the private corporate sector, about 8 per cent of GDP, and the public sector, about 8 to 10 per cent of GDP.

Limiting the combined fiscal deficit at 6 per cent of GDP is also necessary in TFC's view to bring down the ratio of interest payments to revenue receipts from the very high levels of almost 50 per cent in 2002-03 for the centre, 26 per cent for the states, and 37 per cent on their combined account. In TFC's plan for restructuring government finances, these are to be brought down by 2009-10, respectively, to 28 per cent for the centre, 15 per cent for the states, and 22 per cent, on their combined accounts.

The TFC particularly emphasises two phases of fiscal consolidation: adjustment phase and stabilization phase. In the adjustment phase, the debt-GDP ratio will steadily fall as primary deficit follows a path of adjustment so that the fiscal deficit target of 6 per cent is achieved. After the debt-GDP ratio has fallen to the desirable levels, primary deficit and fiscal deficit will be stabilized.

In summary, the TFC recommended as follows:

1. The overall debt-GDP ratio on the combined account (with external debt measured at historical exchange rates) may be targeted to be brought down to 56 percent of GDP over a period of time. Since the level is estimated to be as high as 81 percent of GDP at the end of 2004-05, it should be brought down to at least 75 per cent by the end of 2009-10.

2. The level of combined interest payments relative to revenue receipts should be brought down from 34 per cent in 2004-05 to 22 per cent in 2009-10, and eventually to about 17 per cent.
3. The system of on-lending by the centre to the states should be phased out. The long-term goal for the centre and state for the debt-GDP ratio should be 28 per cent each. Their fiscal deficit to GDP ratio targets should be 3 per cent each.

3.21 Public Sector Reforms

As pointed out by the Eleventh and Twelfth Finance Commissions, large amounts of capital is locked up in the public sector showing extremely low returns in relation to the average cost of funds to the government. The TFC notes that 109 central public sector companies were running in losses. The problem is particularly acute in the case of the states. Out of 1003 state level public enterprises (SLPEs), 599 SLPEs are reported to be either non-functioning or running into losses. Not only the returns on government investment are non-existent or low, but also a large number of SLPEs fail to finalize their accounts. The total amount of investment in respect of the SLPEs where accounts were finalized, was estimated to be Rs. 2,38,220 crore at the end of 2000-01. Many states have, however, taken steps for closing down many of the SLPEs and for disinvestment in others. The TFC recommended that this process should be further strengthened. In particular, in the period of restructuring, that is 2005-10, state governments should draw up a programme that includes closure of almost all loss making SLPEs. The TFC also favoured that reforms of state electricity boards and transport enterprises should be taken up separately. By the end of 2009-10, states should have a small but viable set of SLPEs.

3.22 Restructuring: Recommendations of the Twelfth Finance Commission

A summary of the multi-dimensional restructuring of government finances aimed at both the qualitative and quantitative aspects of managing government finances recommended by the TFC is given below.

1. Taxation reforms aimed at building up non-distortionary and revenue-elastic system of taxation with tax rates that are low, limited in number of rate categories, and stable;
2. Non-tax revenues where user charges, as a short term objective, ensure recoveries of current costs, and aim at full recovery of costs measured at acceptable efficiency levels in the longer run, in the case of services where there is no clear cut case for subsidization and ensure rates of return on investment that covers the average cost of borrowing;

3. Expenditure restructuring relating to both its size and sectoral allocations aimed at removing inefficiencies arising from misallocations, design and implementation of schemes, and delivery of services;
4. Rationalizing subsidies by reducing their overall volume, increasing their transparency by making them explicit, and improving their targeting;
5. Public sector restructuring where, apart from natural monopolies and strategic reasons, there is a strong case for reducing government's involvement;
6. Fiscal transfer system where equalizing transfers are given much greater weight and extended to local bodies;
7. Suggesting a reformed role for the plan process;
8. Strengthening the role of local bodies to become a more effective instrument in the delivery of local public goods;
9. Role of the central government in intermediating loans for the states including the need to specify annual ceiling of borrowing for each state and implementing a hard-budget constraint; and,
10. Suggesting institutional frameworks including ceiling on debt and deficits and mechanisms for their monitoring through state level fiscal responsibility legislation.

Part II: Issues in Taxation

4

Issues in Taxation: Performance of Central Taxes

"Tax Policy…is an art no less than a science; and equity is to be sought as a matter of degree rather than an absolute norm"

Musgrave and Musgrave

Taxes are levied with a view to financing the provision of public goods and goods of high merit even if they are private. The Government is able to finance the provision of these goods and undertake investment that can serve as a catalyst in the development process. Tax revenues as supplemented by a limited amount of non-tax revenues largely finance the required expenditures. The design of a good tax system is a central problem in managing a country's public finances. It has an impact not only on the government but also the private economic activities. Fairness and neutrality in the allocation of resources characterize a robust tax system. A tax system with multiple rate categories, numerous exemptions and provisions for discretion in the hands of revenue administrators not only adds to distortions but also involves considerable transaction costs.

In theory, a good tax system is characterized by fairness and neutrality in the allocation of resources. A tax system with multiple rate categories, numerous exemptions and provisions for discretion in the hands of revenue administrators not only adds to distortions but also involves considerable transaction costs. Musgrave and Musgrave (1989) describe the following as characteristics of a good tax system:

1. **Adequacy of Revenue:** The tax system should be revenue productive in a manner that the government is able to finance the provision of public and merit goods to the desired extent.
2. **Equitable Distribution:** The tax system should be such that every body pays his fair share of taxes according to his ability to pay. This issue should be considered in terms of final incidence of tax.
3. **Minimum Distortions:** Taxes should be chosen so as to minimize interference with economic decisions relating to allocation of resources in markets that may otherwise be efficient. In fact, taxes impose excess burdens, and the design of the tax system should be such that these are minimized.
4. **Facilitation of Stabilization and Growth Objectives of Fiscal Policy:** The tax structure should facilitate the use of fiscal policy for stabilization and

growth by suitably providing for automatic stabilizers as well supporting the saving performance of the economic agents.

5. **Fair Administration:** The tax system should permit a fair, transparent, non-arbitrary, and easily understandable administration for the taxpayers.
6. **Minimum Administration and Compliance Costs:** The tax system should involve minimum costs of administration for the government and compliance costs for the taxpayer.

4.1 Assigning Taxes in a Federal System

In designing a tax system in a federal system, there is the additional dimension of assigning taxes between the central and sub-national governments. The general principle is that nationwide services should be financed through federation level taxes, and services whose benefits are likely to be limited to the regional or local jurisdictions should be financed through sub-national taxes. One key issue in assigning taxes to different jurisdictions relates to efficiency. By definition, the federation is a common market in which goods and factors of production should be able to move across jurisdictions without intervention. This requires that attention be paid to the effects of differential taxation in different sub-national jurisdictions on the efficiency of the economy. Efficiency may be adversely affected in terms of movement of goods as well as factors due to tax competition among jurisdictions. Such inefficiencies may be reduced by coordination. Musgrave and Musgrave suggest the following broad classification of taxes for addressing the assignment issue (Table 4.1).

Table 4.1: Assignment of Taxes by Levels

Central Level	Middle Level	Local Level
1. Income tax 2. Death duties 3. Natural resource taxes	1. Income tax on residents 2. Income tax on income to factors owned by residents and on income accruing to non-residents but originating within jurisdiction 3. Retail sales tax 4. Origin-type product tax as benefit Charge	1. Real estate 2. Payroll tax 3. Benefit charges

Source: *Musgrave and Musgrave* (1989).

4.2 Assignment of Taxes in India

In India, taxes have been assigned between the central and state governments as specified in the Union List and State List in Seventh Schedule to the Constitution. From among the resources assigned to the states, they can assign resources to the local bodies as per the provisions of the 73rd and 74th amendments to the constitution. Any unlisted sources of taxation are taxable by the Union government, which has been vested with residuary powers of taxation. Table 4.2 summarizes the constitutional assignment of taxes between the Union and state governments.

Table 4.2: Assignment of Taxes: Union and State Governments

Union Taxes	State Taxes
1. Taxes on income other than agricultural income 2. Duties of customs including export duties 3. Duties of excise on tobacco and other goods manufactured and produced in India except – a. Alcoholic liquors for human consumption b. Opium, Indian hemp and other narcotic drugs and narcotics but including medicinal and toilet preparations containing alcohol or any substance included in sub-paragraph (b) of this entry 4. Corporation tax 5. Taxes on the capital value of the assets, exclusive of agricultural land 6. Duties in respect of succession to property other than agricultural land 7. Terminal taxes on goods and passengers, carried by railway, sea or air, taxes on railway fares and	1. Land revenue, including the assessment and collection of revenue, the maintenance of land records, survey for revenue purposes and records of rights, and alienation of revenues 2. Taxes on agricultural income 3. Duties in respect of succession to agricultural land 4. Estate duty in respect of agricultural land 5. Taxes on land and buildings 6. Taxes on mineral rights subject to any limitations imposed by Parliament by law relating to mineral development 7. Duties of excise on the following goods manufactured or produced in the State and countervailing duties at the same or lower rates on similar goods manufactured or produced elsewhere in India 8. alcoholic liquors for human consumption 9. opium, Indian hemp and other narcotic drugs and narcotics, but not including medicinal and toilet preparations

freights 8. Taxes other than stamp duties on transactions in stock exchanges and futures markets 9. Rates of stamp duty in respect of bills of exchange, cheques, promissory notes, bills of lading, letters of credit, policies of insurance, transfer of shares, debentures, proxies and receipts 10. Taxes on the sale and purchase of newspapers and on advertisement published therein 11. Taxes on the sale and purchase of goods other than newspapers, where such sale or purchase takes place in the course of inter-state trade or commerce 12. Taxes on the consignment of goods (whether the consignment is to the person making it or to any other person), where such consignment takes place in the course of the inter-state trade or commerce	containing alcohol or any substance included in sub-paragraph (b) of this entry 10. Taxes on entry of goods into a local area for consumption, use or sale therein 11. Taxes on the consumption or sale of electricity 12. Taxes on the sale or purchase of goods other than newspapers, subject to the provisions of entry 92 A of List 1 13. Taxes on advertisements other than advertisements published in newspapers and advertisements broadcast by radio or television 14. Taxes on goods and passengers carried by road or inland waterways 15. Taxes on vehicles, whether mechanically propelled or not, suitable for use on roads, including tramcars subject to the provisions of entry 35 of List III 16. Taxes on animals and boats 17. Tolls 18. Taxes on professions, trades, callings and employments 19. Capitation taxes 20. Taxes on luxuries, including taxes on entertainments, amusements, betting and gambling 21. Rates of stamp duty in respect of documents other than those specified in the provisions of List I with regard to rates of stamp duty

The constitution, under articles 268 and 269 makes provision for the assignment of some of the Union taxes to the states for collection and sharing or retaining the amount of revenues raised. The specific provisions are described below.

4.3 Article 268: Taxes Levied by the Union but Collected and Appropriated by the States

(1) Such stamp duties and such duties of excise on medicinal and toilet preparations as are mentioned in the Union List shall be levied by the Government of India but shall be collected—

(a) in case where such duties are leviable within any [Union territory], by the Government of India, and

(b) in other cases, by the States within which such duties are respectively leviable.

(2) The proceeds in any financial year of any such duty leviable within any State shall not form part of the Consolidated Fund of India, but shall be assigned to that State.

4.4 Article 269: Taxes Levied and Collected by the Union but Assigned to the States

(1) Taxes on the sales or purchase of goods and taxes on the consignment of goods shall be levied and collected by the Government of India but shall be assigned and shall be deemed to have been assigned to the States on or after the 1st day of April, 1996 in the matter provided in clause (2).

Explanation—for the purposes of this clause,

(a) the expression "taxes on the sale or purchase of goods" shall mean taxes on sale or purchase of goods other than newspapers, where such sale or purchase takes place in the course of inter-State trade or commerce;

(b) the expression "taxes on the consignment of goods" shall mean taxes on the consignment of goods (whether the consignment is to the person making it or to any other person), where such consignment takes place in the course of inter-State trade or commerce.

(2) The net proceeds in any financial year of any such tax, except in so far as those proceeds represent proceeds attributable to Union territories, shall not form part of the Consolidated Fund of India, but shall be assigned to the States within which that tax is leviable in that year, and shall be distributed among those States in accordance with such principles of distribution as may be formulated by Parliament by law.

(3) Parliament may by law formulate principles for determining when a sale or purchase of, or consignment of, goods takes place in the course of inter-State or commerce.

In a recent amendment (88th amendment), the service tax has been brought in as Article 268 A. This article provides that taxes on services shall be levied by the Government of India and such tax may be collected and appropriated by the

Government of India and the States. The principles of collection and appropriation may be formulated by Parliament by law.

4.5 Major Central Taxes: Basic Features

The central government has four major taxes: personal income tax, corporation tax, central excise duties, and customs duties. More recently, the taxation of services has also assumed growing importance.

Customs Duties: The customs duty in India consists of 'basic' tariff, the additional duty of customs (AD), and special excise duty (SAD). The additional duty is the counterpart of excise duties paid by domestic manufacturers i.e. countervailing duty (CVD). The special additional duty has been introduced to serve as the counterpart of state sales taxes on domestically produced goods. Since the customs duty is collected under the three sub-heads (basic, AD & SAD), its customs duty collection rate should be obtained by dividing total collections under the three heads by the total value of imports during the year. The "peak" tariff rate refers to the 'basic' customs tariffs. It is the highest general rate applicable to a large majority of imports. At present, there are certain additional surcharges or cesses also being levied on, like the national calamity contingency duty and education cess. There are also some export duties and cesses on exports.

Some commodities like alcohol have a 'basic' rate higher than the 'peak' rate. During the reform years, the "peak" rate has progressively come down from 150 per cent in 1991-92 to 40 per cent in 1997-98. The "peak" rate was reduced to 35 per cent in 2001-02 and 30 per cent in 2002-03. The reduction in the peak duty rates has continued. The 2005-06 Budget has reduced the peak duty rate to 15 per cent for non-agricultural products. The average tariff rate has therefore declined over the 1990s. As a result the customs duty collection rate has declined from about 47 per cent in 1990-91 to 29 per cent in 1995-96, and further to 23 per cent in 1998-99, and to 21 per cent in 2000-01 (See, Virmani, 2002). The average customs tariffs rates still remain among the highest in the world.

India is known to have had one of the highest customs tariff rates, which was one the instruments in the earlier policy of protection of domestic industry. Virmani (2001) reports that out of a set of 122 countries for which data on (simple i.e. unweighted) average customs tariffs were available for 1999 or one of the three preceding years, India had the third highest average tariff rate (32.2 per cent; rank 120th). Only Cambodia and Pakistan had higher average tariffs than India. Emerging market economies like Czech republic (6.8 per cent), Turkey (8.2 per cent), S. Africa (8.5 per cent), Chile (10 per cent), Mexico (10.1 per cent), Argentina (11per cent), Venezuela (12.6 per cent), Russia (13.9 per cent), Poland (15.9 per cent) and Egypt (20.5 per cent) had average rates ranging from 1/5th to 2/3rd of India's 32.2 per cent. After Cambodia, Thailand had the highest average tariff of 17.1 per cent, followed by Vietnam (15.1 per cent), Indonesia (10.9 per cent), Philippines (10.1 per cent), Taiwan (8.8 per cent), S. Korea (8.7 per cent), Malaysia (7.1 per cent) and Singapore & Hong Kong (0 per cent). All the South Asian neighbours of India like Sri Lanka (20 per cent), Bangladesh (22.2 per cent) and Nepal (17.7 per cent) and China (16.8 per cent) had lower average tariffs.

Central Excise Duties: Union excise duties and cesses are levied on commodities covered by the Central Excise Act, 1944 and other Acts. The central excise duties have historically been an important tax on the manufacture or production of domestic goods. Since the late eighties, these excise duties have been transformed as taxes levied under the value-added principle going up to the manufacturing or production stage. It was first transformed into what was called a modified value added tax (MODVAT) and later as central value added tax (CENVAT) in the latter part of the nineties.

The MODVAT was introduced in the 1986-87 budget. With effect from March 1,1986, the proforma credit scheme was extended to products with reference to specified Chapters of the Central Excise Tariff Act, 1985. A major objective of the MODVAT scheme was to initiate a system of taxation, which can reduce cascading of taxes, and thereby also reduce costs and prices. At first, the coverage was limited to 37 out of 91 Chapters. With effect from March 1, 1987, all commodities except petroleum products, textiles, tobacco, cinematographic films and matches were covered. In the MODVAT system, early in the nineties, full rebate on the excise tax paid on capital goods was allowed instead of setting up a system of annual depreciation related deductions. With effect from 1995-96, the entire manufacturing chain was brought under MODVAT. In the 2000-01 Budget, the excise deduction on capital goods was permitted to be spread over two years. In the case of CENVAT, an attempt was made to reduce the rate to a limited number of core rates. The favoured core rate has been 16 per cent, accompanied by a concessional merit rate of 8 per cent and demerit rate of 24 per cent.

In view of revenue and equity considerations, a few higher rates for demerit goods like tobacco products (cigarettes, cigars, chewing tobacco or mixed in pan masala) and for final, finished, luxury consumer durable goods like cars appear to be justifiable. If these are levied as special excises, the eligibility for VAT credit is not there. Special excises can also be imposed on grounds of environmental pollution. Thus, polluting fuels like motor spirit and diesel as well as selected dyes & chemicals that damage water sources could have special excise taxes on top of the general rate. The taxation of petroleum products has been handled separately both in the case of custom and central excises, considering the large contribution they make in government's tax revenues. The 2005-06 Budget has reduced the customs duty rate on petroleum products from 10 per cent to 5 per cent. On other petroleum products including motor spirit and diesel, customs duty rate in the 2005-06 Budget have been brought down from 20 to 15 per cent. There is also a change in the excise duties on petroleum products. While these used to be ad valorem, the 2005-06 Budget has introduced a system, which provides a combination of specific and ad valorem duties.

Services Tax: A service tax has been levied by the central government under its residuary powers, as the subject has not been mentioned in any of the Lists of the seventh schedule to the constitution. The main services that are have proved to revenue productive in the case of service are telephones, insurance, brokerage, advertising, courier services, air travel agent services, clearing and forwarding agent services, banking and other financial services, and port services. Central Service tax reform and extension must be designed to integrate it with the CENVAT by the end of the 10th Plan, keeping in mind the ultimate objective of a National VAT. All services, particularly modern production services such as transport, communication and financial services, under the tax authority of the centre should be subject to the same basic CENVAT rate. Similarly the tax paid on any services used as input into the production of excisable services or goods should be given set-off. Any comprehensive Service Tax law must keep these objectives in view. The general service tax rate is presently 10 per cent.

Income Tax: The income tax levied is under the Income-tax Act of 1961 as amended from time to time. This Act provides that income tax would be charged for any assessment year at the relevant rate on the total income of any previous year of a person who is a resident. The total income would include all income derived from different sources, which

(*a*) is received or is deemed to be received in India in such year by or on behalf of such person; or

(*b*) accrues or arises or is deemed to accrue or arise to him in India during such year; or

(*c*) accrues or arises to him outside India during such year.

It is provided that, in the case of a person not ordinarily resident in India the income which accrues or arises to him outside India shall not be so included unless it is derived from a business controlled in or a profession set up in India.

The present income tax rate structure, as specified by the 2005-06 Budget is as follows:

Up to Rs. 1 lakh	: Nil
Rs. 1 lakh to Rs. 1.5 lakh	: 10 per cent
Rs. 1.5 lakh to Rs. 2.5 lakh	: 20 per cent
Above Rs. 2.5 lakh	: 30 per cent

A surcharge of 10 per cent applies on a taxable income above Rs. 10 lakh.

Corporation Tax: In the earlier years, the tax rate on corporate income was higher than the highest marginal rate on personal income. The 2005-06 Budget has provided that for domestic companies, the corporate income tax rate is 30 per cent along with a surcharge of 10 per cent. This has brought the corporation tax rate for domestic companies equal to the highest marginal personal income tax rate.

In the case of corporation tax, there is also a Minimum Alternate Tax (MAT) for companies who otherwise do not pay corporation tax claiming benefits from various exemptions and provisions.

4.6 Revenue Performance of Central Taxes

From the viewpoint of revenue, four central taxes have contributed the most, although their relative shares in the total gross central revenues show considerable changes particularly in the reform years. Two of these are direct taxes: income tax and corporation tax. The other two are commodity taxes: Union excise duties and customs duties.

We look at the revenue performance of these taxes in terms of -

1. Their share in GDP;
2. Their relative share in total gross central taxes; and
3. Their annual and decade wise buoyancy.

Tax buoyancy is measured as percentage change in tax revenue over a given period divided by percentage change in tax base, which is generally taken to be GDP, over the same period. Where a longer period is involved, the estimate of the response coefficient is obtained by fitting a regression using a double log specification.

4.7 Major Central Taxes Relative to GDP

Table 4.3 gives the share of the four major taxes along with that of the gross amount of central taxes prior to sharing with the state governments as percentage of GDP at market prices. Different taxes show quite distinct time profiles. Thus, the income tax between 1950-51 to 1999-2000 has been varying within a limited range from 0.9 at the lower end and 0.135 at the upper end with some exceptions. One important period of exception was in the early part of the eighties, when the share of income tax in GDP fell to as low as 0.77 in 1983-84. After 1999-2000, there has been a noticeable improvement in the performance of the income tax.

Table 4.3: Share of Central Taxes in GDP: 1950-51 to 2002-03

(per cent)

Year	Income tax	Corporation tax	Union excise duties	Customs duties	Gross central tax revenues
1950-51	1.346	0.396	0.680	1.582	4.077
1951-52	1.388	0.386	0.811	2.205	4.846
1952-53	1.185	0.401	0.801	1.676	4.293
1953-54	1.084	0.331	0.842	1.407	3.723
1954-55	1.230	0.347	1.014	1.731	4.261
1955-56	1.214	0.336	1.336	1.533	4.461
1956-57	1.167	0.389	1.470	1.338	4.401
1957-58	1.233	0.417	2.051	1.348	5.184
1958-59	1.156	0.365	2.104	0.930	4.713
1959-60	0.950	0.680	2.301	0.996	5.065
1960-61	0.983	0.639	2.425	0.990	5.213
1961-62	0.909	0.860	2.689	1.166	5.792
1962-63	0.950	1.132	3.058	1.257	6.568
1963-64	1.128	1.221	3.245	1.489	7.268
1964-65	1.017	1.198	3.057	1.516	6.945
1965-66	0.982	1.102	3.245	1.948	7.449
1966-67	0.986	1.051	3.302	1.870	7.369
1967-68	0.889	0.847	3.133	1.401	6.420
1968-69	0.975	0.772	3.402	1.150	6.465
1969-70	1.049	0.827	3.566	0.990	6.601
1970-71	1.036	0.811	3.850	1.147	7.019
1971-72	1.097	0.965	4.212	1.422	7.915
1972-73	1.159	1.034	4.308	1.588	8.351
1973-74	1.130	0.888	3.966	1.519	7.727
1974-75	1.129	0.916	4.170	1.720	8.160
1975-76	1.458	1.035	4.017	1.705	9.138
1976-77	1.331	1.097	4.704	1.731	9.208

Contd...

1977-78	0.986	1.202	4.378	1.795	8.719
1978-79	1.069	1.136	4.873	2.201	9.557
1979-80	1.109	1.152	4.974	2.420	9.909
1980-81	1.048	0.912	4.521	2.371	9.167
1981-82	0.875	1.168	4.401	2.551	9.399
1982-83	0.834	1.160	4.280	2.719	9.400
1983-84	0.774	1.136	4.657	2.544	9.440
1984-85	0.785	1.041	4.542	2.868	9.560
1985-86	0.903	1.031	4.660	3.427	10.314
1986-87	0.925	1.015	4.650	3.688	10.553
1987-88	0.901	0.969	4.636	3.867	10.630
1988-89	1.016	1.045	4.469	3.749	10.550
1989-90	1.045	0.973	4.609	3.710	10.621
1990-91	0.946	0.938	4.311	3.630	10.125
1991-92	1.031	1.202	4.304	3.408	10.314
1992-93	1.055	1.189	4.120	3.177	9.973
1993-94	1.062	1.171	3.689	2.583	8.815
1994-95	1.188	1.365	3.688	2.645	9.113
1995-96	1.312	1.388	3.383	3.010	9.362
1996-97	1.333	1.357	3.290	3.132	9.484
1997-98	1.123	1.315	3.150	2.640	8.645
1998-99	1.163	1.409	3.058	2.336	8.260
1999-00	1.325	1.585	3.196	2.500	8.868
2000-01	1.520	1.708	3.280	2.275	9.026
2001-02	1.409	1.611	3.193	1.772	8.233
2002-03	1.496	1.874	3.341	1.821	9.009

Source (Basic Data): *Indian Public Finance Statistics.*

The corporation tax shows a more regular upward trend. It started at a level much below that of the income tax in 1950-51 at just 0.4 per cent of GDP. By the end of the fifties, it was at 0.7 per cent of GDP. By the end of the sixties, it reached a level of 0.83 per cent of GDP. Its rise was steady through the seventies, ending the decade at a level of 1.15 per cent of GDP. After some fall in some of the years of the eighties, it grew again at a steady rate during the nineties, progressively overtaking the contribution by the income tax in recent years.

The profile of the share of the Union excise duties shows more of an inverted U-shape, particularly after 1962-63. Up to this year, the Union excise duties were rising steadily starting from a level of 0.68 per cent of GDP and reaching a level of more than 3 per cent in 1962-63. After this, it continued to rise and reached a peak of nearly 5 per cent of GDP in 1979-80, after which, it started falling steadily. It fell to a level close to 3.2 per cent of GDP in 2001-02, which was only slightly above that attained in the early sixties.

The customs duties follow a similar pattern although these started at a level much higher than that of the Union excise duties. In 1950-51, the customs duties accounted for nearly 1.6 per cent of the GDP, which was the highest among all major central taxes. These were overtaken by the Union excise duties in 1957-58. Following a slightly volatile pattern, these reached a peak of 3.9 per cent in 1986-87, after which they started declining. By 2001-02, these had reached a level, relative to GDP, of 1.8 per cent, which is compared to its level in the mid sixties.

Thus, while income tax was the second highest contributor relative to the GDP in the early fifties, it was in 2001-02, even after improvement, the lowest contributor. The customs duty, which was the highest contributor, is fast becoming the lowest contributor now. These were overtaken first by the Union excise duties, which although it started falling in more recent years is still the highest contributor to the gross tax revenues of the central government. These trends become clearer, when we look at the share of these taxes as percentage of the gross central tax revenues.

4.8 Structure of Central Taxes

The structure of central taxes is captured by examining the changing profile of the share of the major direct and indirect taxes of the centre. Chart 4.1 and Table 4.4 show the share of four major taxes in the gross tax revenues of the centre since 1950-51. At the top end, in 1950-51, were the customs duties contributing nearly 39 per cent of the total central tax revenues while income tax was a close second, contributing nearly 33 per cent. The share of both the customs duties and the income tax in total central tax revenues had, by the end of the fifties, fallen to about 20 per cent. In the seventies, the Union excise duties had become the star performer, contributing more than fifty per cent. It was the corporation tax, which had remained in the range of 10 to 12 per cent, except for the decade of the sixties, when its share was higher, started rising in the nineties crossing 20 per cent of centre's total tax revenues by 2002-03.

Chart 4.1 highlights the inverted U-shape of the curve representing the share of the Union excise duties, which can be contrasted with the more U-shaped type of curve of the customs excise duties until the beginning of the nineties. What is also clearly observable is that the four taxes are tending to come close to each other in terms of their shares in the centre's gross revenue receipts. Table 4.4 gives the profile of shares of these four taxes.

Table 4.4: Relative Share of Central Taxes in Gross Central Taxes

(per cent)

Year	Income tax	Corporation tax	Union excise duties	Customs duties
1950-51	33.025	9.711	16.677	38.805
1951-52	28.646	7.959	16.738	45.498
1952-53	27.602	9.335	18.658	39.045
1953-54	29.110	8.888	22.614	37.788
1954-55	28.870	8.141	23.787	40.629
1955-56	27.221	7.530	29.951	34.371
1956-57	26.525	8.842	33.409	30.391
1957-58	23.788	8.043	39.564	26.010
1958-59	24.538	7.750	44.642	19.728
1959-60	18.747	13.421	45.422	19.661
1960-61	18.853	12.257	46.520	18.998
1961-62	15.692	14.844	46.424	20.138
1962-63	14.472	17.237	46.563	19.141
1963-64	15.526	16.805	44.647	20.487
1964-65	14.638	17.246	44.015	21.829
1965-66	13.188	14.791	43.567	26.151
1966-67	13.381	14.257	44.811	25.374
1967-68	13.850	13.196	48.799	21.817
1968-69	15.078	11.943	52.616	17.789
1969-70	15.891	12.523	54.015	15.000
1970-71	14.759	11.557	54.852	16.345
1971-72	13.859	12.189	53.217	17.962
1972-73	13.884	12.383	51.593	19.015
1973-74	14.623	11.491	51.324	19.653
1974-75	13.831	11.222	51.099	21.084
1975-76	15.960	11.325	43.958	18.654
1976-77	14.455	11.911	51.089	18.803
1977-78	11.312	13.782	50.209	20.593
1978-79	11.187	11.890	50.994	23.026

Contd...

1979-80	11.194	11.624	50.201	24.421
1980-81	11.430	9.946	49.321	25.869
1981-82	9.311	12.431	46.827	27.137
1982-83	8.870	12.345	45.539	28.930
1983-84	8.200	12.030	49.330	26.946
1984-85	8.213	10.890	47.509	29.997
1985-86	8.753	9.993	45.188	33.224
1986-87	8.767	9.623	44.067	34.945
1987-88	8.476	9.114	43.609	36.379
1988-89	9.631	9.910	42.365	35.538
1989-90	9.836	9.158	43.393	34.929
1990-91	9.339	9.266	42.577	35.854
1991-92	9.993	11.658	41.730	33.041
1992-93	10.579	11.923	41.309	31.856
1993-94	12.044	13.282	41.848	29.300
1994-95	13.033	14.975	40.464	29.025
1995-96	14.018	14.823	36.132	32.148
1996-97	14.052	14.308	34.685	33.023
1997-98	12.992	15.207	36.438	30.536
1998-99	14.076	17.058	37.029	28.282
1999-00	14.937	17.870	36.041	28.192
2000-01	16.842	18.927	36.334	25.208
2001-02	17.109	19.571	38.787	21.527
2002-03	16.609	20.806	37.090	20.211

Source (Basic Data): *Indian Public Finance Statistics*

4.9 Central Taxes: Analysis of Growth Rates and Yearly Buoyancy

While the contribution that a tax makes to overall collection of tax revenues is an important consideration, another important feature of the tax sources is their volatility. To examine their comparable volatility we look at their yearly growth rates, which can show both the direction of the change and amplitude of variation.

Table 4.5 gives the relevant growth rates. Some of the highest growth rates attained, for example, in the case of income tax are in the years 1975-76 at 38.9 per cent, 1985-86 at 30.2 per cent, 1988-89 at 34 per cent, and 1995-96 at 30.0 per cent. There were eight years when there was a negative growth, which means that the tax revenue fell in absolute terms.

Chart 4.1: Relative Shares of Major Central Taxes in Centre's Gross Tax Revenues

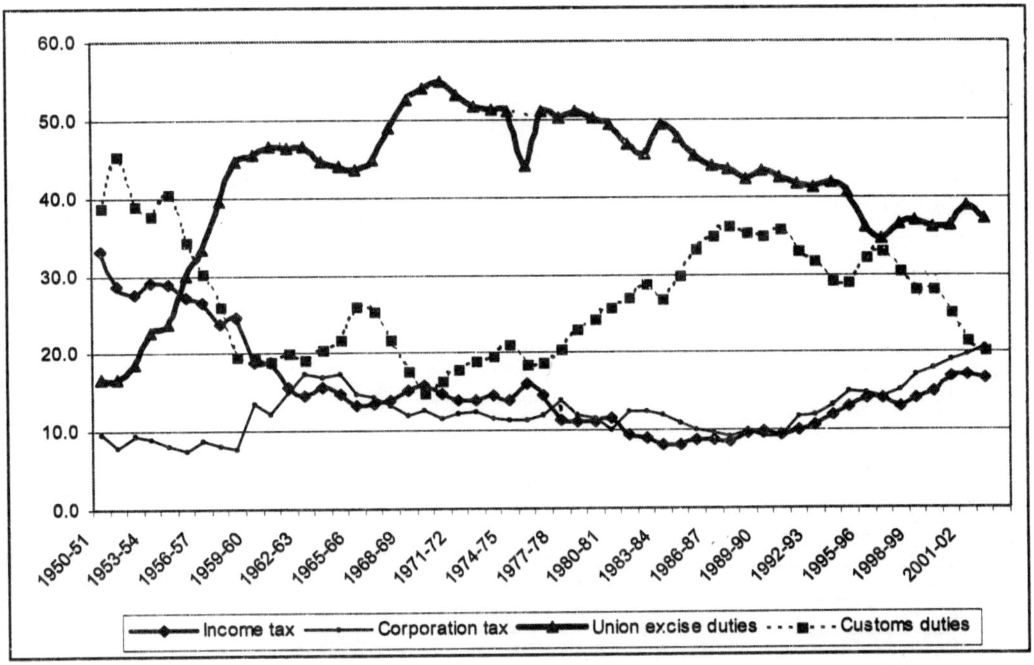

Table 4.5: Major Central Taxes: Yearly Growth Rates

(per cent)

Year	Income tax	Corporation tax	Union excise duties	Customs duties	Gross central tax revenues
1951-52	9.66	3.61	26.89	48.22	26.42
1952-53	-16.25	1.94	-3.12	-25.41	-13.09
1953-54	-0.46	-10.13	14.39	-8.66	-5.62
1954-55	7.44	-0.78	13.95	16.48	8.33
1955-56	0.50	-1.40	34.21	-9.82	6.59
1956-57	14.52	38.01	31.10	3.92	17.53
1957-58	8.88	10.44	43.77	3.90	21.40
1958-59	4.50	-2.39	14.30	-23.17	1.30
1959-60	-13.46	96.13	15.25	12.89	13.27
1960-61	13.36	2.95	15.44	8.92	12.72
1961-62	-1.98	42.63	17.52	24.83	17.77
1962-63	12.44	41.57	22.28	15.88	21.92

Contd...

1963-64	36.42	23.97	21.93	36.10	27.16
1964-65	5.07	14.37	9.87	18.75	11.44
1965-66	1.97	-2.93	12.03	35.59	13.18
1966-67	13.57	7.89	15.13	8.61	11.94
1967-68	5.57	-5.59	11.07	-12.30	1.99
1968-69	16.13	-3.46	15.02	-13.02	6.67
1969-70	18.49	17.89	15.42	-5.19	12.43
1970-71	5.51	4.84	15.37	23.79	13.61
1971-72	13.43	27.41	17.20	32.76	20.80
1972-73	16.53	18.17	12.77	23.14	16.32
1973-74	18.53	4.43	11.96	16.32	12.54
1974-75	17.95	21.78	24.15	33.77	24.69
1975-76	38.88	21.46	3.54	6.49	20.36
1976-77	-1.65	14.22	26.21	9.46	8.60
1977-78	-16.11	24.03	5.36	17.40	7.20
1978-79	17.50	2.51	20.68	32.86	18.82
1979-80	13.84	11.22	12.00	20.66	13.77
1980-81	12.39	-5.83	8.13	16.59	10.06
1981-82	-2.05	50.29	14.16	26.14	20.24
1982-83	6.39	10.89	8.59	19.05	11.67
1983-84	8.24	14.11	26.84	9.06	17.09
1984-85	13.46	2.53	9.09	26.10	13.27
1985-86	30.18	12.10	16.19	35.30	22.15
1986-87	14.72	10.29	11.69	20.46	14.53
1987-88	10.90	8.64	13.51	19.41	14.71
1988-89	34.16	28.38	14.71	15.35	18.07
1989-90	18.58	7.30	18.92	14.12	16.10
1990-91	5.87	12.82	9.41	14.46	11.51
1991-92	25.18	47.19	14.67	7.81	16.99
1992-93	17.30	13.31	9.68	6.83	10.80
1993-94	15.54	13.05	2.81	-6.66	1.48
1994-95	31.86	37.39	17.83	20.71	21.86
1995-96	29.62	19.28	7.60	33.48	20.51
1996-97	16.95	12.61	12.00	19.84	16.67
1997-98	-6.22	7.81	6.56	-6.20	1.44
1998-99	18.36	22.55	11.02	1.18	9.25
1999-00	26.75	25.13	16.26	19.06	19.44
2000-01	23.81	16.30	10.70	-1.81	9.81
2001-02	0.76	2.56	5.88	-15.30	-0.82
2002-03	15.17	26.12	13.44	11.38	18.63

Source (Basic Data): *Indian Public Finance Statistics.*

In the case of the corporation tax, there are some years of negative growth, but these occur largely in the first two decades. Customs duties are more noticeable for their negative growth in more recent years. For gross tax revenues, except for two years in the fifties there was never a negative growth except in 2001-02.

4.10 Buoyancy of Central Taxes

It is one thing, if tax revenues fall because of a fall in GDP. But it is more serious when tax revenues fall while the GDP is increasing. This feature is captured by looking at the profile of buoyancies estimated on a yearly basis. The benchmark figure of 1 is notable for it indicates that tax revenues rise in proportion to the rise in GDP. Table 4.6 gives year-wise buoyancies for the period from 1951-52 to 2002-03. Noticeable patches where the tax buoyancy is less than one are: for corporation tax in the sixties and mid eighties, for the Union excise duties in the late eighties, for the customs duties, in the early nineties and the first two years of the new decade. In the gross tax revenue of the centre, there are several years in since 1990-91, when the buoyancy is less than 1, which explains why the tax-GDP ratio fell in the nineties. Much of this fall in the aggregate tax-GDP ratio was due to the less than 1 buoyancy during these years of the Union excise duties and the Customs duties.

Table 4.6: Estimated Annual Buoyancy of Central Taxes

Year	Income tax	Corporation tax	Union excise duties	Customs duties	Gross central tax revenues
1951-52	1.518	0.568	4.226	7.580	4.153
1952-53	8.587	-1.024	1.646	13.426	6.913
1953-54	-0.053	-1.147	1.629	-0.980	-0.636
1954-55	-1.390	0.145	-2.606	-3.078	-1.557
1955-56	0.275	-0.769	18.735	-5.379	3.610
1956-57	0.760	1.989	1.627	0.205	0.917
1957-58	2.888	3.396	14.243	1.270	6.965
1958-59	0.394	-0.209	1.252	-2.028	0.114
1959-60	-2.500	17.852	2.831	2.393	2.464
1960-61	1.403	0.310	1.623	0.937	1.336
1961-62	-0.330	7.111	2.924	4.143	2.964
1962-63	1.652	5.521	2.959	2.109	2.911
1963-64	2.444	1.608	1.471	2.422	1.822

Contd...

1964-65	0.305	0.864	0.593	1.127	0.688
1965-66	0.357	-0.531	2.178	6.445	2.387
1966-67	1.033	0.600	1.151	0.655	0.908
1967-68	0.326	-0.328	0.649	-0.721	0.117
1968-69	2.720	-0.583	2.531	-2.195	1.125
1969-70	1.828	1.769	1.524	-0.513	1.229
1970-71	0.805	0.708	2.244	3.475	1.987
1971-72	1.885	3.846	2.414	4.597	2.920
1972-73	1.613	1.773	1.246	2.258	1.592
1973-74	0.857	0.205	0.553	0.755	0.580
1974-75	0.992	1.204	1.335	1.867	1.365
1975-76	5.202	2.871	0.473	0.868	2.724
1976-77	-0.212	1.830	3.373	1.218	1.106
1977-78	-1.219	1.819	0.405	1.317	0.545
1978-79	2.083	0.299	2.461	3.911	2.240
1979-80	1.423	1.154	1.234	2.125	1.416
1980-81	0.653	-0.307	0.429	0.875	0.531
1981-82	-0.119	2.911	0.820	1.513	1.172
1982-83	0.548	0.934	0.737	1.633	1.001
1983-84	0.497	0.850	1.618	0.546	1.030
1984-85	1.135	0.214	0.767	2.201	1.120
1985-86	2.282	0.914	1.224	2.669	1.675
1986-87	1.233	0.862	0.979	1.714	1.217
1987-88	0.786	0.623	0.974	1.399	1.060
1988-89	1.801	1.496	0.775	0.809	0.953
1989-90	1.212	0.476	1.235	0.921	1.051
1990-91	0.346	0.756	0.554	0.852	0.678
1991-92	1.696	3.178	0.988	0.526	1.144
1992-93	1.186	0.913	0.664	0.468	0.741
1993-94	1.049	0.881	0.189	-0.450	0.100
1994-95	1.783	2.092	0.998	1.159	1.223
1995-96	1.712	1.114	0.439	1.935	1.185
1996-97	1.117	0.832	0.791	1.308	1.099
1997-98	-0.551	0.692	0.582	-0.550	0.127
1998-99	1.280	1.572	0.768	0.082	0.645
1999-00	2.378	2.234	1.445	1.694	1.728
2000-01	3.021	2.068	1.358	-0.230	1.245
2001-02	0.087	0.293	0.673	-1.752	-0.094
2002-03	1.801	3.102	1.596	1.352	2.213

Source (Basic Data): *Indian Public Finance Statistics.*

Chart 4.2 shows the annual buoyancy for the two direct central taxes: income tax and corporation tax. It is apparent that both income tax and corporation tax show a regular cyclical pattern over the years. The volatility was however higher in the fifties and the sixties, the amplitude of variation as measured by yearly growth rates has come down. The pattern is relatively steady since the seventies.

Chart 4.2: Buoyancy Pattern of Income and Corporation Tax

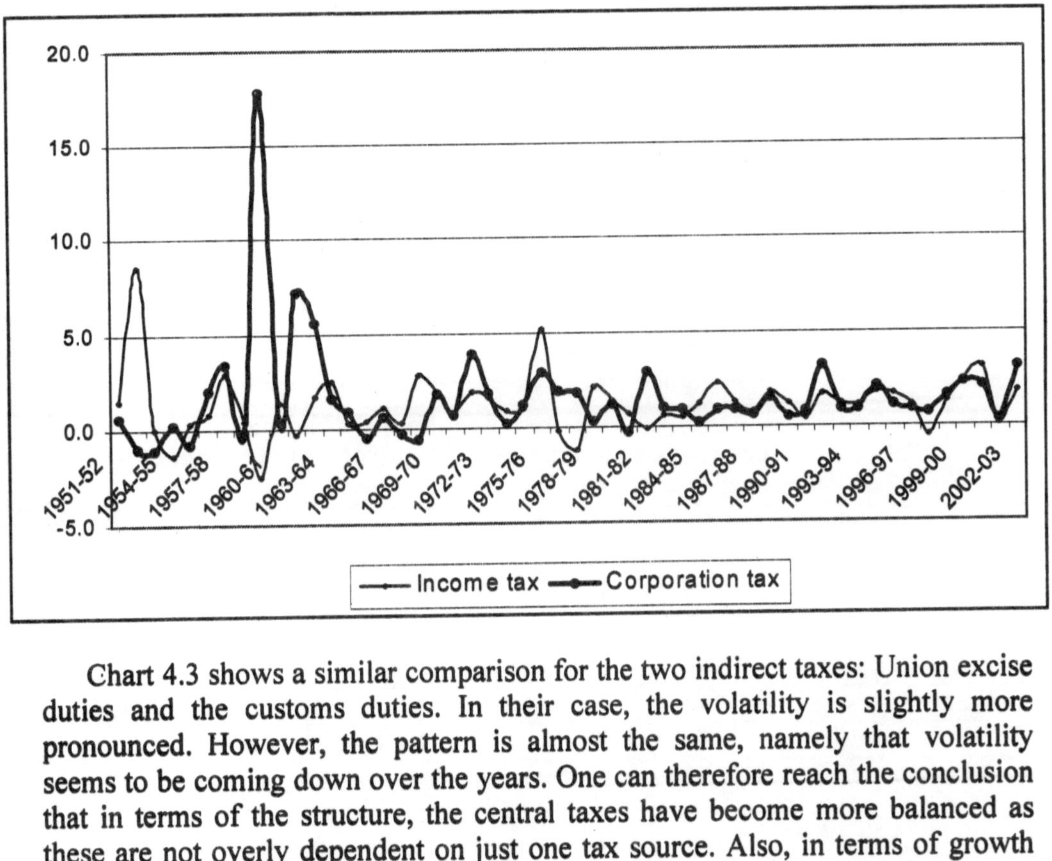

Chart 4.3 shows a similar comparison for the two indirect taxes: Union excise duties and the customs duties. In their case, the volatility is slightly more pronounced. However, the pattern is almost the same, namely that volatility seems to be coming down over the years. One can therefore reach the conclusion that in terms of the structure, the central taxes have become more balanced as these are not overly dependent on just one tax source. Also, in terms of growth rates, there is volatility, but the amplitude of variation has come down over the years. As such, there is greater stability in the tax revenues.

It is also useful to look at the decade wise buoyancies of the central taxes. Table 4.7 provides estimates given in the report of the Twelfth Finance Commission. This is done terms of the direct and indirect central taxes. It is the erosion of the buoyancy of the central indirect taxes, which is particularly noticeable.

Chart 4.3: Buoyancy Pattern of Union Excise Duties and Customs Duties

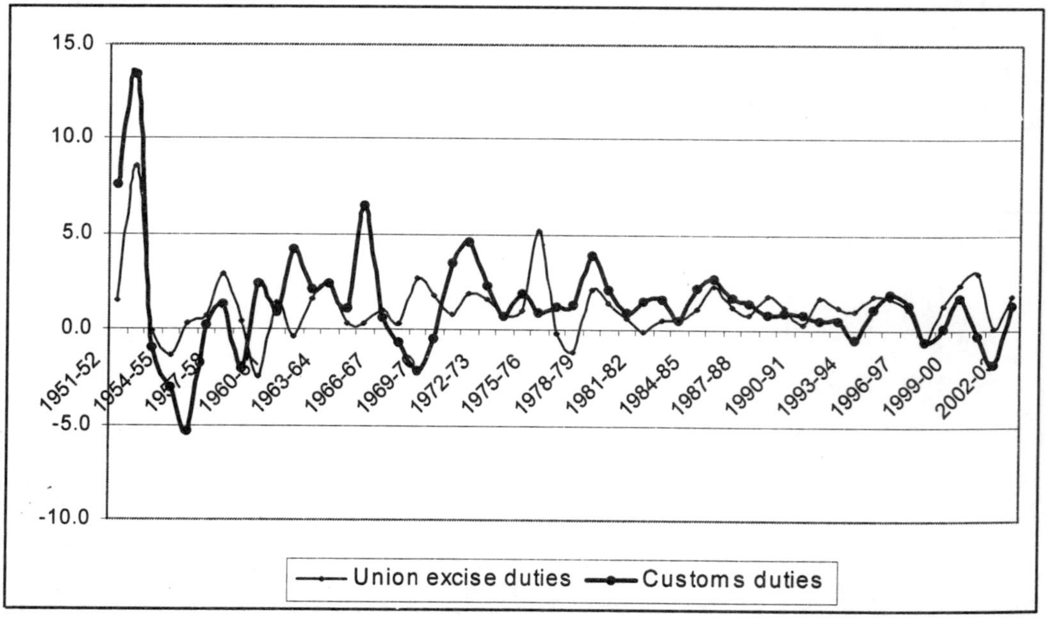

Table 4.7: Decade-wise Buoyancies of Central Tax Revenues

	1950-51 to 1959-60	1960-61 to 1969-70	1970-71 to 1979-80	1980-81 to 1989-90	1991-92 to 2001-02	1950-51 to 2001-02
Central Taxes: Gross Revenues						
Direct	0.94	0.96	1.18	0.94	1.30	1.09
Indirect	1.65	1.24	1.30	1.20	0.72	1.16
Total	1.38	1.15	1.27	1.14	0.89	1.14

Source: *Report of the Twelfth Finance Commission, 2004.*

5

Structure of Taxes and Comparative Performance

> The decline in the tax-GDP ratio in the 1990's is due partly to the "costs of reforms", reflecting the reduction in customs and excise duties to increase competition and enhance efficiency. But it also reflects the costs of incomplete reforms.
>
> India: Sustaining Reform, Reducing Poverty: World Bank, 2003

In this Chapter, we look at the structural changes in the aggregate tax revenues of the central and state governments, examining changes in the structure in terms of direct and indirect taxes. The aggregate tax revenues may be obtained by the adding together the gross tax revenues of the centre, prior to transfers, and own tax revenues of the states. This is equivalent to states' tax revenues, post transfers, and centre's net tax revenues. The classification of direct and indirect taxes is based on the one used in the Indian Public Finance Statistics published by the Ministry of Finance, Government of India. In view of the loss of buoyancy in the central indirect taxes in the nineties discussed in Chapter 4, the comparison between the performance of central and state taxes is particularly interesting in the period since the early nineties.

5.1 Combined Tax Revenues of the Central and State Governments

We first examine the profile of the aggregate tax revenues of the central and state governments. Appendix Table A5.1 and Chart 5.1 give the long term profile of the structure of aggregate taxes as divided between direct and indirect taxes. Chart 5.1 shows the shares of direct and indirect taxes in total taxes over time. It is clear that, to begin with, in the early fifties, the indirect taxes accounted for a larger share of the aggregate taxes. This difference went on widening, with the share of direct taxes falling over time. This trend was arrested to some extent in the late eighties after which, the share of direct taxes started picking up. As already discussed in the preceding chapter, this was due mainly to asymmetric performance of the major central taxes. The Union excise duties and customs duties slowed down in terms of growth relative to GDP growth while the direct taxes like income tax and corporation tax accelerated in terms of growth relative to GDP growth during the same period. However, even after this shift in relative performance, the contribution of the indirect taxes in total taxes remains larger than what it was in the early fifties.

Chart 5.1: Share of Direct and Indirect Taxes in Total Taxes of the Centre and States

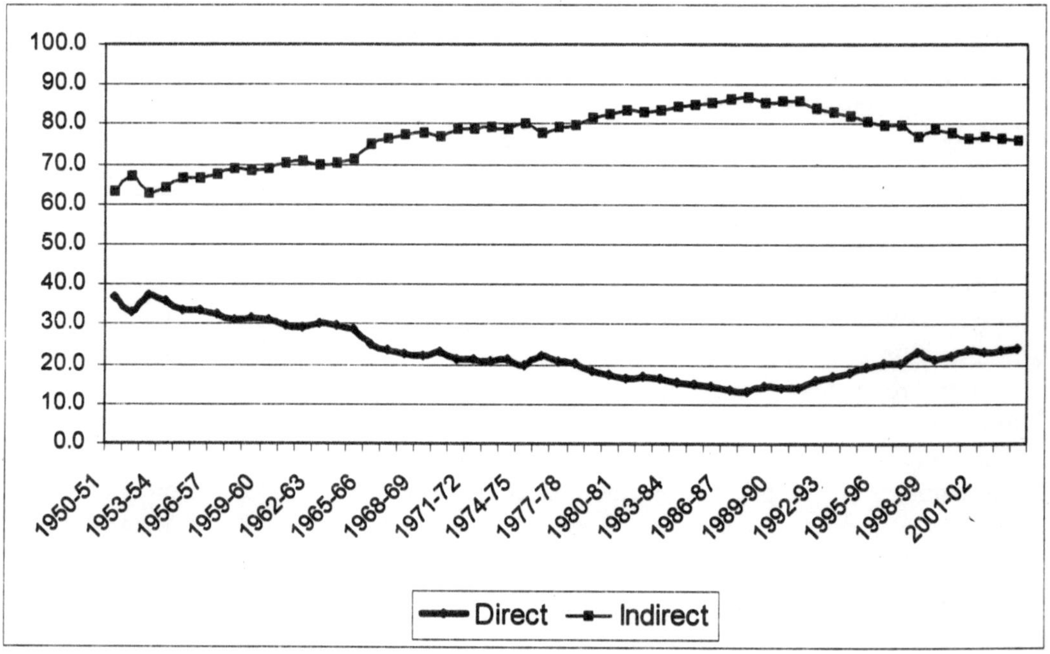

As is well known, controlling the incidence of taxation is easier in the case of direct taxes. The heavy dependence of India's tax system on the indirect taxes does not support the case for rating the design of India's tax structure as of high quality. Furthermore, as the indirect taxes have started showing falling buoyancy since the nineties, growth in the over all tax-GDP ratio has been stalled. Chart 5.2 shows the profile of the tax-GDP ratio since 1950-51. It will be observed that starting from a little above 7 per cent of GDP, the tax-GDP ratio continued to increase until in 1987-88, it reached a level slightly more than 16 per cent of GDP. After that, there has been erosion in the tax-GDP ratio. Only very recently, there has been some recovery, mainly due to the direct taxes with marginal supplementation by the service tax. Since the previous peak has not yet been crossed, there are signs of stagnation as far as the growth of the tax-GDP ratio is concerned.

Chart 5.2: Profile of Tax-GDP Ratio: Aggregate, Centre, and States

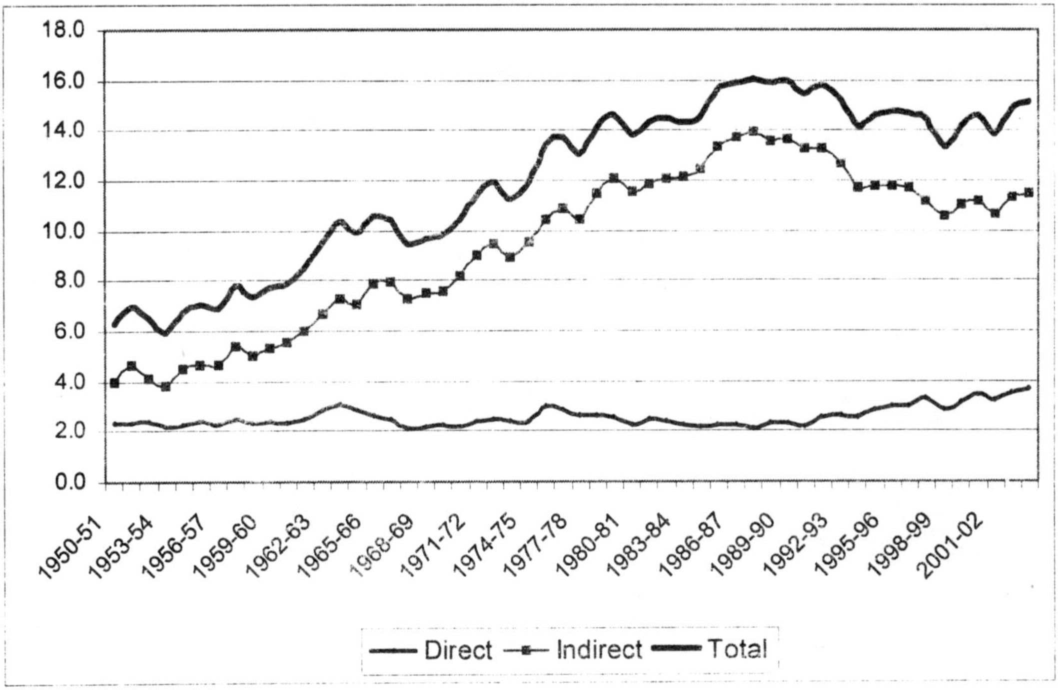

There are several reasons given as to why there has been a decline in the performance of the central indirect taxes, as listed below:

1. The customs duty rates were reduced as part of the WTO commitments and also to facilitate the opening up of the Indian economy.
2. The rates in the case of the Union excise duties were also reduced by and large as part of the overall rationalization of the tax regime.
3. The structure of GDP has progressively changed in favour of the services, whose tax potential has not been fully utilized.
4. There has been an increase in evasion due to lack of inadequate computerization and other information coordination activities that are needed for a successful implementation of the VAT system of taxation.
5. VAT that extends only up to the manufacturing stage often has to deal with large amounts of tax rebates on taxes paid on inputs. The revenue buoyancy of VAT comes from a comprehensive approach to VAT, which can extend its coverage to the retail stage.

While it is difficult to say, which of these reasons may the most important, but clearly, they may all have contributed to the erosion in the buoyancy of central indirect taxes. It is notable that even though tax rates were reduced in the case of direct taxes, their buoyancy improved as the augmentation in the tax base overtook any negative effect of the reduction in the tax rate. Table 5.1 summarizes the structure of aggregate taxes, as it evolved since 1985-86.

Table 5.1: Aggregate Tax Revenues of Centre and States: Structure and as % of GDP

Year		(% to Total Taxes)			(As % of GDP)
	Direct	Indirect	Direct	Indirect	Total
1985-86	14.45	85.55	2.25	13.32	15.56
1986-87	13.91	86.09	2.21	13.71	15.92
1987-88	13.13	86.87	2.11	13.97	16.08
1988-89	14.58	85.42	2.31	13.56	15.88
1989-90	14.37	85.63	2.30	13.68	15.98
1990-91	13.98	86.02	2.16	13.27	15.43
1991-92	16.14	83.86	2.55	13.25	15.80
1992-93	16.98	83.02	2.59	12.66	15.26
1993-94	17.80	82.20	2.53	11.67	14.19
1994-95	19.53	80.47	2.85	11.75	14.60
1995-96	20.41	79.59	3.01	11.74	14.75
1996-97	20.42	79.58	3.00	11.69	14.69
1997-98	22.90	77.10	3.32	11.17	14.49
1998-99	21.08	78.92	2.82	10.56	13.38
1999-00	22.17	77.83	3.14	11.03	14.18
2000-01	23.50	76.50	3.43	11.18	14.61
2001-02	23.24	76.76	3.22	10.63	13.84
2002-03 b	23.63	76.37	3.52	11.36	14.87
2003-04 r	24.15	75.85	3.65	11.47	15.12

Source (Basic data): *Indian Public Finance Statistics and NAS.*

One important consideration in analyzing the growth of tax revenues relative to GDP relates to the impact that the changing structure of GDP has on it. Table 5.2 gives the result of a regression exercise where the dependent variable is the log of total tax revenues. The independent variables, apart from log of real income, are log of the implicit price deflator, share of manufacturing in GDP and the share of one component of the service sector relating to financial and business services (S2). Other components of GDP including agriculture and other service sectors were not found to be significant. There is dummy variable reflecting the impact of the reform years. It is seen that the elasticity of tax revenues with respect to real income and the implicit price deflator are both marginally above 1. As the share of manufacturing increases, it increases the buoyancy in a small way. However the service sector growth has had a negative impact on the tax buoyancy because it has historically not been captured in the tax net. The reform dummy also shows a negative sign which is statistically significant showing that reforms have had a negative impact on the growth of tax revenues.

Table 5.2: Determinants of Total Tax Revenues

Dependent Variable: LTTR				
Method: Least Squares				
Sample: 1950-51 to2001-02				
Included observations: 52				
Variable	Coefficient	Std. Error	t-Statistic	Prob.
C	-8.635316	1.354601	-6.374803	0
LYR	1.055957	0.133508	7.909295	0
SHM	0.071856	0.007924	9.067953	0
LIPD	1.020184	0.074297	13.7311	0
SHS2	-0.03699	0.01209	-3.059439	0.0037
DREFORMS	-0.09223	0.047905	-1.925279	0.0604
R-squared	0.999269	Mean dependent var		9.384452
Adjusted R-squared	0.99919	S.D. dependent var		2.00324
S.E. of regression	0.057027	Akaike info criterion		-2.782401
Sum squared resid	0.149598	Schwarz criterion		-2.557258
Log likelihood	78.34243	F-statistic		12577.11
Durbin-Watson stat	1.341114	Prob (F-statistic)		0

A similar exercise was done in respect of examining the determinants of the variability of the tax revenues relative to the variability of the GDP growth rate. In this case, the dependent variable was taken to be the annual buoyancy of total tax revenues. Once again, we include variables reflecting the structure of the GDP. We have taken the share of agricultural along with a lagged term, the share of manufacturing, and the share of service sector as represented by S1, which represents trade, transport, and communications. There is a first difference term of log of real income and also first difference terms of the implicit price deflator along with lags. The sample for this exercise was taken to be 1961-62 to 2001-02. While the share of manufacturing has a positive impact on the yearly buoyancy of tax revenues, current share of agriculture has a negative impact on the buoyancy. Lagged price term has also a positive impact. These results are summarized in Table 5.3.

Table 5.3: Determinants of Annual Variability of Tax Revenues

Dependent Variable: Annual Buoyancy of Total Tax Revenues				
Method: Least Squares				
Sample: 1961 2002				
Included observations: 42				
Variable	Coefficient	Std. Error	t-Statistic	Prob.
C	8.431	4.904	1.719	0.095
SHA	-0.295	0.073	-4.028	0.000
SHA(-1)	0.201	0.050	3.999	0.000
SHM(-1)	0.133	0.076	1.752	0.089
SHS1	-0.348	0.138	-2.525	0.017
DLYR	-4.033	2.832	-1.424	0.164
DLIPD	-8.520	2.373	-3.591	0.001
DLIPD(-1)	3.103	1.987	1.562	0.128
DLIPD(-3)	-3.242	1.596	-2.032	0.050
R-squared	0.7685	Mean dependent var		1.268
Adjusted R-squared	0.7124	S.D. dependent var		0.606
S.E. of regression	0.3249	Akaike info criterion		0.777
Sum squared resid	3.4842	Schwarz criterion		1.149
Log likelihood	-7.3175	F-statistic		13.693
Durbin-Watson stat	2.1136	Prob(F-statistic)		0.000

5.2 Structure of Central Taxes: Direct and Indirect

A corresponding analysis of the structure of taxation can be undertaken separately for the centre and the states. Table 5.4 describes the changes in the structure of centre's taxes since 1985-86. The share of indirect taxes has come down from a peak of about 82 per cent in 1987-88 to about 62 per cent in 2003-04, implying a fall of about 20 percentage points. As percentage of GDP, the direct taxes have increased from 2 per cent in 1985-86 to 3.5 per cent in 2002-03, a gain of 1.5 percentage points. This has not yet been enough to make up for the shortfall in the indirect tax revenues. As a result, the total tax revenues fell, as percentage of GDP, from 10.3 per cent in 1985-86 to 9.1 per cent in 2003-04.

Table 5.4: Aggregate Tax Revenues of Centre: Structure and as % of GDP

Year	As % of total tax revenues		(As % of GDP)		
	Direct	Indirect	Direct	Indirect	Total
1985-86	19.60	80.40	2.02	8.29	10.31
1986-87	18.99	81.01	2.00	8.55	10.55
1987-88	17.93	82.07	1.91	8.72	10.63
1988-89	19.85	80.15	2.09	8.46	10.55
1989-90	19.37	80.63	2.06	8.56	10.62
1990-91	19.16	80.84	1.94	8.19	10.12
1991-92	22.79	77.21	2.35	7.96	10.31
1992-93	24.30	75.70	2.42	7.55	9.97
1993-94	26.80	73.20	2.36	6.45	8.82
1994-95	29.22	70.78	2.66	6.45	9.11
1995-96	30.18	69.82	2.83	6.54	9.36
1996-97	29.98	70.02	2.84	6.64	9.48
1997-98	34.68	65.32	3.17	5.97	9.14
1998-99	32.41	67.59	2.68	5.58	8.26
1999-00	33.75	66.25	2.99	5.88	8.87
2000-01	36.22	63.78	3.27	5.76	9.03
2001-02	36.99	63.01	3.05	5.19	8.23
2002-03 b	37.15	62.85	3.35	5.66	9.01
2003-04 r	38.05	61.95	3.47	5.65	9.11

Source (Basic data): *Indian Public Finance Statistics and NAS*

The longer-term picture is given in Chart 5.3 and Appendix Table A5.2. Considering the centre's tax-GDP ratio, a steady upward trend was maintained from 1950-51 to 1986-87, after that a decline set in (Chart 5.4). This is the cause of the corresponding pattern already noted in the case of the combined tax revenues of the centre and the states.

5.3 State Taxes: Structure and Growth

In this section, we undertake an analysis of the state taxes. As compared to the centre, state taxes are predominated by the indirect taxes since all the major tax sources available to the states like the sales tax, motor vehicle tax, stamp duty and registration fees, state excise duties, and the entertainment tax are in the nature of indirect taxes.

Chart 5.3: Share of Direct and Indirect Taxes in Centre's Tax Revenues

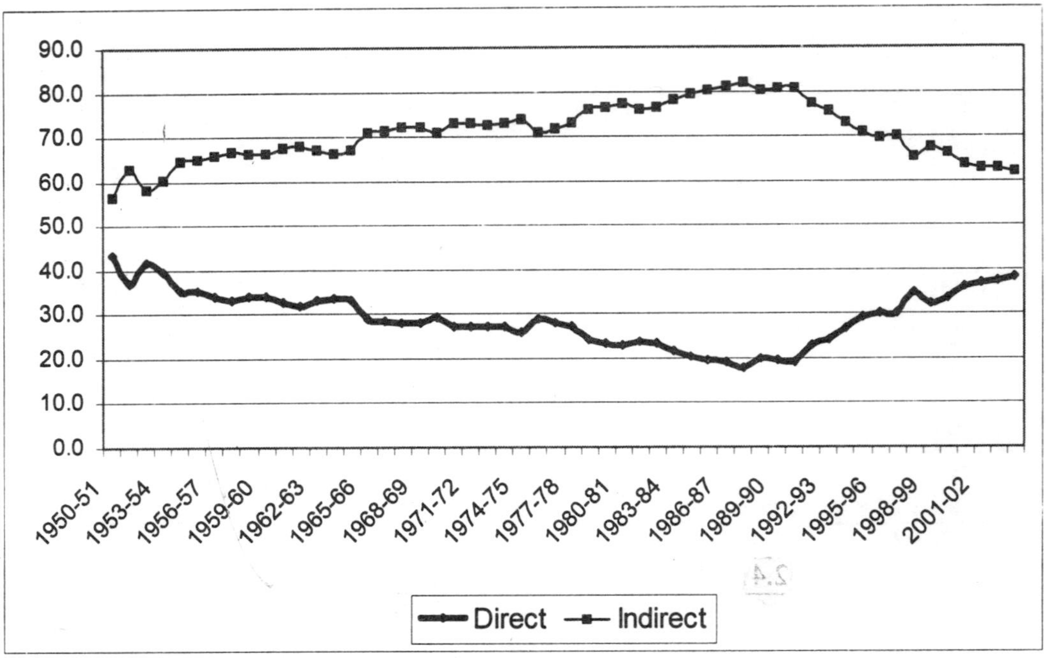

Chart 5.4: Central Taxes as percentage of GDP: Direct, Indirect and Total

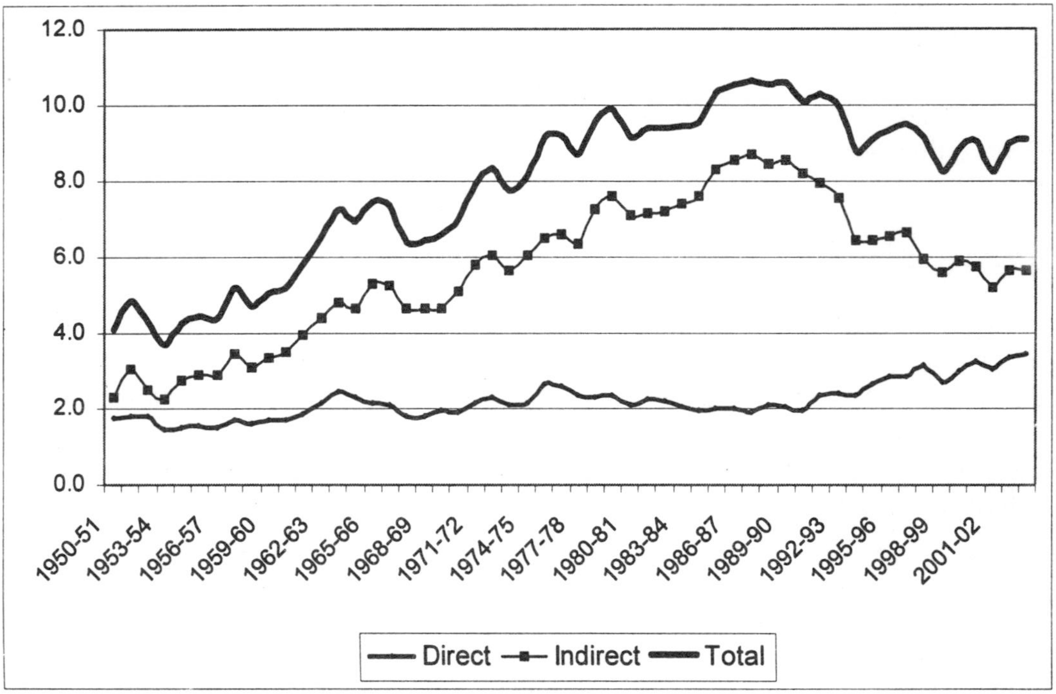

The direct taxes in the case of the states have contributed less than one quarter of a percentage point. It has come down below .20 per cent of GDP since 1992-93. On the other hand, the contribution of indirect taxes has been in excess 5 per cent of GDP. In the late 90's and the early part of the new decade even while the central indirect taxes relative to GDP went down, those of the states actually improved (Table 5.5).

Table 5.5: Own Tax Revenues of States: Structure and as % of GDP

Year		(% to Total Taxes)			(As % of GDP)
	Direct	Indirect	Direct	Indirect	Total
1985-86	4.33	95.67	0.23	5.02	5.25
1986-87	3.91	96.09	0.21	5.16	5.37
1987-88	3.79	96.21	0.21	5.24	5.45
1988-89	4.13	95.87	0.22	5.11	5.33
1989-90	4.46	95.54	0.24	5.12	5.36
1990-91	4.08	95.92	0.22	5.08	5.30
1991-92	3.64	96.36	0.20	5.29	5.49
1992-93	3.15	96.85	0.17	5.12	5.28
1993-94	3.06	96.94	0.16	5.21	5.38
1994-95	3.43	96.57	0.19	5.30	5.49
1995-96	3.46	96.54	0.19	5.20	5.39
1996-97	3.03	96.97	0.16	5.05	5.21
1997-98	2.77	97.23	0.15	5.20	5.35
1998-99	2.82	97.18	0.14	4.98	5.12
1999-00	2.82	97.18	0.15	5.16	5.31
2000-01	2.96	97.04	0.17	5.42	5.59
2001-02	3.07	96.93	0.17	5.44	5.61
2002-03 b	2.87	97.13	0.17	5.70	5.87
2003-04 r	3.06	96.94	0.18	5.83	6.01

Source (Basic data): *Indian Public Finance Statistics and NAS.*

Charts 5.5 and 5.6 describe, respectively, the relative shares of states' direct and indirect taxes in total own taxes of the states and as percentage of GDP. Clearly, direct taxes have had a very small share in the states' own tax revenues limited to about 4 per cent until the nineties. Since then, even this share could not been maintained. Chart 5.5 indicates that the gap between the relative shares of direct and indirect taxes in the case of the states has widened.

Chart 5.5: State Taxes: relative Share of Direct and Indirect Taxes

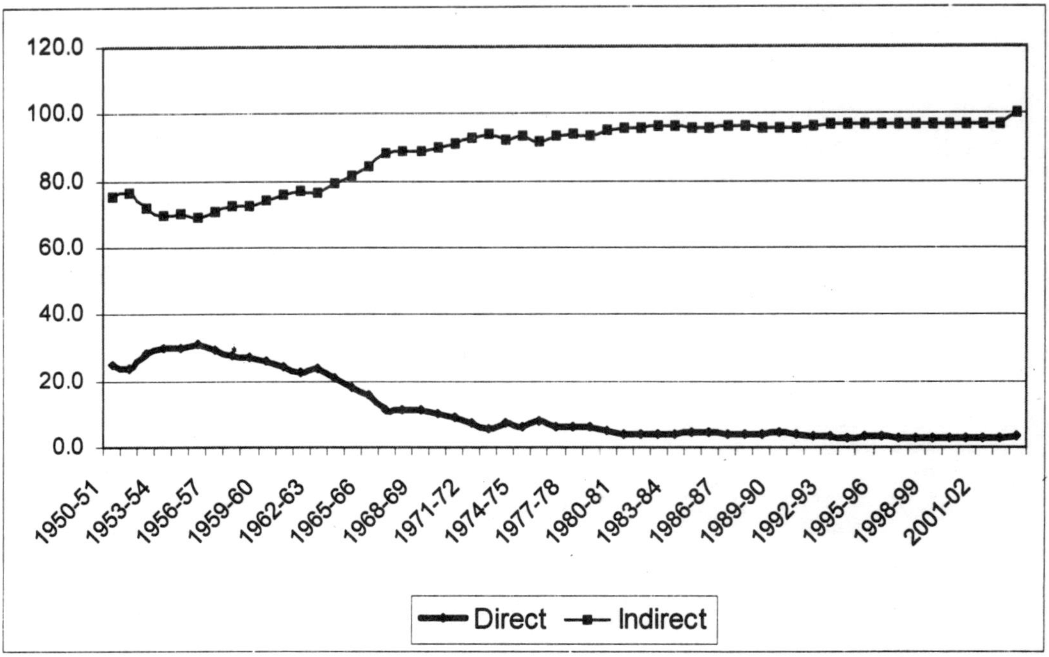

Chart 5.6: State Taxes: Direct and Indirect Taxes Relative to GDP

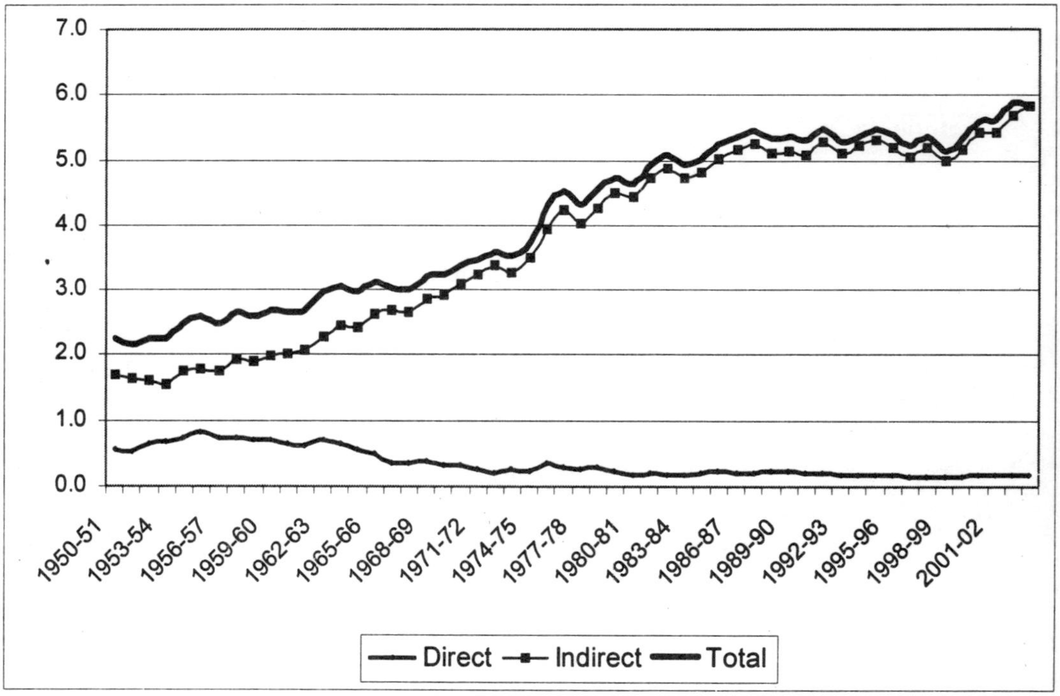

This also implies as reflected by Chart 5.6 that the curve reflecting total own tax revenues of the states is almost parallel to the curve reflecting the share of the indirect taxes relative to GDP.

5.4 Comparative Performance of Central and State Taxes

In this section, we look at the comparative performance of the central and state taxes, direct and indirect, over the five decades from 1950-51, in terms of decade wise buoyancies. Table 5.6 gives the decade wise buoyancies as given in the report of the Twelfth Finance Commission. In the case of central indirect taxes there is a clear pattern of declining buoyancies since the seventies. The buoyancy in the seventies is in fact also lower than its value in the fifties. However, in all the four decades before the nineties, the indirect tax buoyancy of the centre was more than one. Almost a reverse pattern is seen in the case of central direct taxes where the buoyancy was less than one in three of the five decades and increased tangibly only in the last decade. The aggregate buoyancy was highest in the fifties and next highest in the seventies. It was the lowest in the nineties.

Table 5.6: Decade wise Buoyancies of Central and State Tax Revenues

	1950-51 to 1959-60	1960-61 to 1969-70	1970-71 to 1979-80	1980-81 to 1989-90	1991-92 to 2001-02	1950-51 to 2001-02
Central Taxes: Gross Revenues						
Direct	0.94	0.96	1.18	0.94	1.30	1.09
Indirect	1.65	1.24	1.30	1.20	0.72	1.16
Total	1.38	1.15	1.27	1.14	0.89	1.14
States Own Tax Revenues						
Direct	-8.43	3.61	-6.32	-8.20	-4.34	-2.46
Indirect	1.41	1.37	1.37	1.11	1.02	1.23
Total	1.39	1.17	1.35	1.11	1.02	1.17
Total Tax Revenues						
Direct	1.05	0.79	1.16	0.96	1.26	1.03
Indirect	1.55	1.29	1.33	1.16	0.86	1.19
Total	1.38	1.16	1.30	1.13	0.93	1.15

Source: *Report of the Twelfth Finance Commission, 2004.*

In the case of the states, the direct tax buoyancies are generally negative reflecting a fall in the tax-GDP ratio. In the case of states' own indirect tax revenues, the pattern of buoyancy shows a clear downward fall decade after decade although it has remained above one in all the decades. For the first thirty years, this buoyancy was close to 1.4, which explains the sharp rise in the states own tax revenues to GDP ratio. The net outcome of the differential behaviour of centre's and states' taxes has been the less than one buoyancy of the aggregate taxes in the nineties. It broadly follows the pattern of centre's indirect taxes reflecting their larger weight

5.5 States' Relative Share in Raising Taxes.

In raising tax revenues, states' own tax revenues have contributed about 33 per cent of the combined tax revenues of the centre and the states. Chart 5.7 traces the share accounted by the states' own tax revenues in total tax revenues since 1950-51. Starting with a share of about 35 per cent, the share of the states in total tax revenues fell to a little above 30 per cent during the seventies. It started rising again in the nineties. In the latter part of the nineties, states' share of tax revenues increased to a level close to 40 per cent.

Chart 5.7: Share of States' Own Tax Revenues in Total Tax Revenues

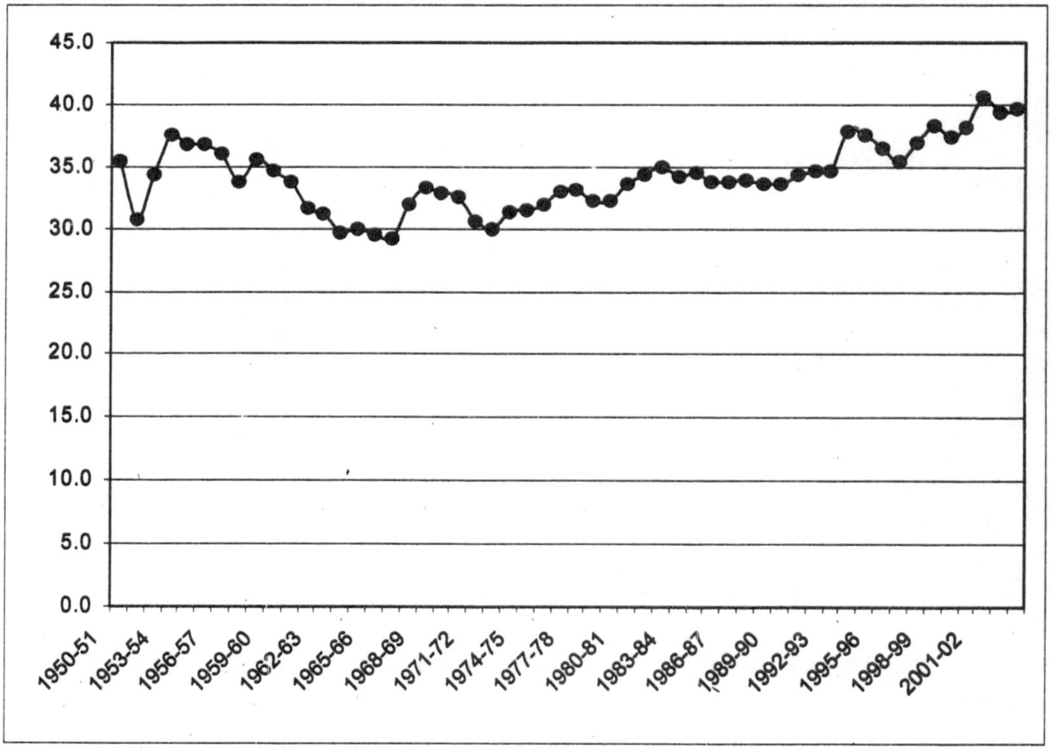

Appendix Table A5.1: Combined Tax Revenues of Centre and States: Structure and as % of GDP

Year		(% to Total Taxes)			(As % of GDP)
	Direct	Indirect	Direct	Indirect	Total
1950-51	36.84	63.16	2.325	3.986	6.312
1951-52	33.02	66.98	2.309	4.685	6.994
1952-53	37.17	62.83	2.431	4.110	6.541
1953-54	36.01	63.99	2.145	3.811	5.956
1954-55	33.33	66.67	2.248	4.495	6.743
1955-56	33.72	66.28	2.382	4.681	7.063
1956-57	32.36	67.64	2.224	4.648	6.872
1957-58	31.29	68.71	2.450	5.379	7.828
1958-59	31.59	68.41	2.313	5.009	7.322
1959-60	31.09	68.91	2.411	5.346	7.758
1960-61	29.78	70.22	2.342	5.522	7.864
1961-62	29.10	70.90	2.468	6.012	8.480
1962-63	30.03	69.97	2.862	6.670	9.532
1963-64	29.81	70.19	3.082	7.259	10.342
1964-65	28.59	71.41	2.834	7.079	9.912
1965-66	25.12	74.88	2.653	7.908	10.561
1966-67	23.52	76.48	2.450	7.967	10.417
1967-68	22.57	77.43	2.128	7.302	9.430
1968-69	22.35	77.65	2.164	7.519	9.682
1969-70	22.93	77.07	2.253	7.572	9.825
1970-71	21.23	78.77	2.209	8.194	10.403
1971-72	21.00	79.00	2.393	9.000	11.393
1972-73	20.91	79.09	2.495	9.435	11.930
1973-74	21.00	79.00	2.365	8.896	11.261
1974-75	19.89	80.11	2.367	9.537	11.904
1975-76	22.29	77.71	2.994	10.435	13.429
1976-77	20.96	79.04	2.881	10.861	13.742
1977-78	20.25	79.75	2.638	10.391	13.029
1978-79	18.36	81.64	2.589	11.511	14.099
1979-80	17.51	82.49	2.562	12.071	14.633
1980-81	16.47	83.53	2.273	11.530	13.803
1981-82	17.12	82.88	2.451	11.868	14.319

Contd...

1982-83	16.49	83.51	2.386	12.084	14.470
1983-84	15.57	84.43	2.236	12.127	14.362
1984-85	14.88	85.12	2.171	12.416	14.587
1985-86	14.45	85.55	2.249	13.315	15.564
1986-87	13.91	86.09	2.214	13.706	15.920
1987-88	13.13	86.87	2.112	13.968	16.080
1988-89	14.58	85.42	2.314	13.561	15.875
1989-90	14.37	85.63	2.296	13.684	15.980
1990-91	13.98	86.02	2.156	13.270	15.426
1991-92	16.14	83.86	2.550	13.250	15.801
1992-93	16.98	83.02	2.591	12.665	15.255
1993-94	17.80	82.20	2.527	11.667	14.194
1994-95	19.53	80.47	2.851	11.747	14.598
1995-96	20.41	79.59	3.012	11.741	14.752
1996-97	20.42	79.58	3.001	11.694	14.695
1997-98	22.90	77.10	3.319	11.173	14.493
1998-99	21.08	78.92	2.821	10.563	13.384
1999-00	22.17	77.83	3.142	11.034	14.177
2000-01	23.50	76.50	3.434	11.178	14.612
2001-02	23.24	76.76	3.218	10.626	13.844
2002-03 re	23.63	76.37	3.515	11.359	14.874
2003-04be	24.15	75.85	3.652	11.470	15.122

Source (Basic data): *Indian Public Finance Statistics and NAS.*

Appendix Table A5.2: Tax Revenues of Centre: Structure and as % of GDP

Year		(% to Total Taxes)			(As % of GDP)
	Direct	Indirect	Direct	Indirect	Total
1950-51	43.46	56.54	1.772	2.305	4.077
1951-52	37.11	62.89	1.798	3.048	4.846
1952-53	41.80	58.20	1.794	2.499	4.293
1953-54	39.52	60.48	1.471	2.251	3.723
1954-55	35.38	64.62	1.508	2.753	4.261
1955-56	35.26	64.74	1.573	2.888	4.461
1956-57	34.04	65.96	1.498	2.903	4.401
1957-58	33.24	66.76	1.723	3.461	5.184
1958-59	33.95	66.05	1.600	3.113	4.713
1959-60	33.88	66.12	1.716	3.349	5.065
1960-61	32.63	67.37	1.701	3.513	5.213
1961-62	31.97	68.03	1.852	3.940	5.792
1962-63	32.92	67.08	2.162	4.406	6.568
1963-64	33.66	66.34	2.446	4.822	7.268
1964-65	32.95	67.05	2.288	4.657	6.945
1965-66	29.02	70.98	2.161	5.288	7.449
1966-67	28.48	71.52	2.099	5.271	7.369
1967-68	27.84	72.16	1.787	4.633	6.420
1968-69	27.81	72.19	1.798	4.667	6.465
1969-70	29.27	70.73	1.932	4.669	6.601
1970-71	27.11	72.89	1.902	5.116	7.019
1971-72	27.03	72.97	2.140	5.775	7.915
1972-73	27.37	72.63	2.286	6.065	8.351
1973-74	27.12	72.88	2.096	5.632	7.727
1974-75	26.10	73.90	2.130	6.030	8.160
1975-76	28.98	71.02	2.648	6.490	9.138
1976-77	28.08	71.92	2.585	6.623	9.208
1977-78	27.15	72.85	2.367	6.352	8.719
1978-79	24.02	75.98	2.295	7.261	9.557
1979-80	23.53	76.47	2.332	7.577	9.909
1980-81	22.74	77.26	2.085	7.083	9.167
1981-82	23.89	76.11	2.246	7.154	9.399
1982-83	23.39	76.61	2.199	7.201	9.400

Contd...

1983-84	21.71	78.29	2.049	7.391	9.440
1984-85	20.44	79.56	1.954	7.606	9.560
1985-86	19.60	80.40	2.022	8.292	10.314
1986-87	18.99	81.01	2.004	8.549	10.553
1987-88	17.93	82.07	1.905	8.724	10.630
1988-89	19.85	80.15	2.095	8.455	10.550
1989-90	19.37	80.63	2.057	8.563	10.621
1990-91	19.16	80.84	1.940	8.185	10.125
1991-92	22.79	77.21	2.351	7.963	10.314
1992-93	24.30	75.70	2.424	7.549	9.973
1993-94	26.80	73.20	2.362	6.453	8.815
1994-95	29.22	70.78	2.663	6.450	9.113
1995-96	30.18	69.82	2.825	6.537	9.362
1996-97	29.98	70.02	2.843	6.641	9.484
1997-98	34.68	65.32	3.171	5.973	9.144
1998-99	32.41	67.59	2.677	5.583	8.260
1999-00	33.75	66.25	2.993	5.875	8.868
2000-01	36.22	63.78	3.269	5.757	9.026
2001-02	36.99	63.01	3.046	5.188	8.233
2002-03 re	37.15	62.85	3.347	5.662	9.009
2003-04be	38.05	61.95	3.468	5.645	9.113

Source (Basic data): *Indian Public Finance Statistics and NAS.*

Appendix Table A5.3: Own Tax Revenues of States: Structure and as % of GDP

year		(% to Total Taxes)			(As % of GDP)
	Direct	Indirect	Direct	Indirect	Total
1950-51	24.77	75.23	0.554	1.681	2.235
1951-52	23.79	76.21	0.511	1.637	2.148
1952-53	28.33	71.67	0.637	1.611	2.248
1953-54	30.16	69.84	0.674	1.560	2.234
1954-55	29.81	70.19	0.740	1.742	2.482
1955-56	31.10	68.90	0.809	1.793	2.603
1956-57	29.38	70.63	0.726	1.745	2.471
1957-58	27.48	72.52	0.727	1.918	2.644
1958-59	27.32	72.68	0.713	1.896	2.609
1959-60	25.83	74.17	0.695	1.997	2.692
1960-61	24.18	75.82	0.641	2.010	2.650
1961-62	22.90	77.10	0.616	2.072	2.687
1962-63	23.62	76.38	0.700	2.264	2.964
1963-64	20.69	79.31	0.636	2.438	3.074
1964-65	18.38	81.62	0.545	2.422	2.967
1965-66	15.80	84.20	0.492	2.620	3.112
1966-67	11.53	88.47	0.351	2.696	3.047
1967-68	11.33	88.67	0.341	2.669	3.010
1968-69	11.37	88.63	0.366	2.851	3.217
1969-70	9.94	90.06	0.320	2.903	3.223
1970-71	9.06	90.94	0.306	3.078	3.385
1971-72	7.29	92.71	0.253	3.225	3.478
1972-73	5.85	94.15	0.209	3.370	3.579
1973-74	7.63	92.37	0.270	3.265	3.534
1974-75	6.34	93.66	0.237	3.507	3.744
1975-76	8.06	91.94	0.346	3.945	4.291
1976-77	6.33	93.67	0.286	4.239	4.525
1977-78	6.28	93.72	0.271	4.039	4.310
1978-79	6.46	93.54	0.293	4.249	4.543
1979-80	4.87	95.13	0.230	4.494	4.724
1980-81	4.07	95.93	0.189	4.448	4.636
1981-82	4.18	95.82	0.206	4.714	4.920

Contd...

1982-83	3.70	96.30	0.188	4.883	5.071
1983-84	3.79	96.21	0.186	4.736	4.922
1984-85	4.31	95.69	0.217	4.811	5.027
1985-86	4.33	95.67	0.227	5.024	5.251
1986-87	3.91	96.09	0.210	5.157	5.367
1987-88	3.79	96.21	0.206	5.244	5.450
1988-89	4.13	95.87	0.220	5.106	5.326
1989-90	4.46	95.54	0.239	5.121	5.360
1990-91	4.08	95.92	0.216	5.085	5.301
1991-92	3.64	96.36	0.200	5.287	5.487
1992-93	3.15	96.85	0.167	5.116	5.282
1993-94	3.06	96.94	0.165	5.215	5.379
1994-95	3.43	96.57	0.188	5.297	5.485
1995-96	3.46	96.54	0.186	5.204	5.390
1996-97	3.03	96.97	0.158	5.053	5.211
1997-98	2.77	97.23	0.148	5.201	5.349
1998-99	2.82	97.18	0.145	4.980	5.125
1999-00	2.82	97.18	0.150	5.159	5.309
2000-01	2.96	97.04	0.165	5.420	5.586
2001-02	3.07	96.93	0.172	5.439	5.611
2002-03 re	2.87	97.13	0.168	5.697	5.865
2003-04be	3.06	96.94	0.184	5.825	6.009

Source (Basic data): *Indian Public Finance Statistics and NAS.*

6

State Taxes: Inter-State Comparisons

> The single positive feature in this otherwise depressing narrative of state finances was the performance of states in regard to their own tax effort.
>
> Report of the Twelfth Finance Commission

The sales taxes constitute the core of state taxes. As part of the nation wide efforts to redesign the sphere of commodity taxation, after the implementation of CENVAT at the level of the centre, many states have modified their sales tax regimes to launch a state level VAT under the scheme prepared by the Empowered Committee for this purpose. Apart from sales taxes, other important state level taxes are state excise duties, motor vehicle tax, stamp duties and registration fees, entertainment tax, and electricity duties. This chapter looks at comparative performance of the state governments in raising taxes and the need for reforms in state level taxation both with a view to augmenting revenues and supporting economic growth.

6.1 State Level Taxes: Basic Features

In this section, we look at the basic features of some of the main state level taxes.

Sales Taxes: The constitution empowers the states to levy 'taxes on sale or purchase of goods other than newspapers, subject to provisions of entry 92 A of List I'. This entry provides that the central government is empowered to levy a tax on the sale and purchase of goods other than newspapers where such sale or purchase takes place in the course of inter-state trade or commerce. Thus, states are entitled to levy a sales tax on transactions within a state. However, the central government has levied a central sales tax on inter-state sales, which under article 269, are collected and retained by the states.

The structure of sales tax, prior to reforms undertaken in late nineties was characterized by a multiplicity of tax rate and exemptions, lack of uniformity across states, large number of incentives, and cascading of taxes. During reforms of sales taxes prior to the introduction of state VAT, most states had agreed to phase out the incentive related exemptions and implement floor rates. The implementation of state level VAT is discussed in the next chapter.

Motor Vehicle Tax: In most states a compounded system of motor vehicle tax exists, where a one time levy is paid for the life of the vehicle. This may be useful, particularly if the tax payers are to be saved from the hassle of interacting with the tax department every year. However, compounded levies are not very revenue productive. These levies need to be revised from time to time to reflect the increasing costs of maintaining roads. It is also difficult to bring in considerations of congestion and pollution, which change over time.

Stamp Duty and Registration Fees: The stamp duty on the registration of property or other conveyances has the main difficulty of getting the correct method of evaluation. Until recently, the stamp duty rates were excessively high in most states and the procedures for evaluating the conveyances were also complicated. The linkage between stamp duty and registration fees was also not very efficient. In recent years, states have undertaken reforms by reducing the duty rates and streamlining procedures for evaluation of property. Even after the reduction of rates, the general experience has been revenue-augmenting as the effect of rate reduction has been overcome by the higher values of the conveyances.

State Excise Duties: The power of states to levy excise duties is limited to alcoholic liquors for human consumption, and opium, Indian hemp and other narcotic drugs excluding those used for medicinal purposes or for toilet preparations. The revenues accrue to the states in the form of licence duties from the vendors as well as the tax, which can be specific or ad valorem.

Excise duties in the states have a special position in the armory of taxes since they are applied on consumption that is known to be harmful. Consumption of alcohol and other beverages containing spirit are known to be hazardous and injurious to health. The constitution has provided the state governments with a monopoly to tax the production and sale of alcoholic beverages that are not meant to be used for medicinal purposes. The state governments also control the production of these by giving licenses and often specifying the quantity to which the production should be limited. Since demand for alcoholic beverages is generally assessed to be price-inelastic, this tax provides a case for keeping high tax rates for controlling the level of consumption. In fact high tax rates yield both high revenues and greater control on consumption. Some states have from time to time embarked upon the path of total prohibition. However, it is difficult to totally prohibit the consumption of alcohol in the states. Attempts at full prohibition lead to illegal production and export of the tax base to the neighboring states.

Electricity Duty: The electricity duty is charged to consumers along with the electricity tariffs or rates. The rates are meant for electricity boards or the providers of electricity, while the electricity duty is meant for the state coffers. In this sector there is considerable non-transparency. The state government administers the electricity prices, and often owes to the electricity boards payments on account of unpaid but committed subsidies. In actual practice, as state governments are unable to pay the requisite amounts due to the electricity boards, the boards in turn collect the electricity duty but do not pass these on to the state government.

Entertainment Tax: The entertainment tax is a levy on admission to places of amusement or entertainment including cinema, circus, theatrical performances, exhibitions, etc. The entertainment tax used to be an important source of revenue for the states, but has lost its importance in recent times due to proliferation of means of home-based entertainment, which has also made it difficult to revise tax rates upwards. The levy of this tax also suffers from inefficient administration.

Profession Tax: The levy of profession tax is subject to a ceiling prescribed in the constitution. Most states either do not tap this source or use it only to a limited extent. At the same time, since the levy eventually falls on the income of the tax payer, it can not be tapped excessively. The Eleventh Finance Commission had recommended that the ceiling prescribed should be raised and that the states should tap this source up to the ceiling amount. The ceiling amount has been raised to Rs. 2500.

6.2 Own Tax Revenues: Analysis of Inter-State Performance

We examine the tax performance of the states in terms of

1. their aggregate all-state level performance;
2. comparative inter-state performance; and
3. performance of selected individual states.

6.3 Aggregate All-State Tax Performance

As noted by the TFC, the ratio of own tax revenues to GDP for all states fell from 5.3 per cent to 4.9 per cent in 1998-99 and was at 5.1 percent in1999-00. As a result of introducing the floor rates, there was a substantial improvement in 2000-01. This followed the agreement among states to implement the floor rates in sales tax and to reduce and rationalize various exemptions. In 2002-03, the states' own tax revenues as percentage of GDP had increased to 5.5 per cent. Comparing the 2000-01 to 2002-03 average with that of 1993-94 to 1995-96, there was an improvement of 0.17 percentage points. The tax performance compares well the performance in the case of the non-tax revenues, where there was a downward slide. It fell from 1.6 per cent of GDP in 1993-94 to 1.2 per cent in 2001-02. Comparing the average over 2000-01 to 2002-03 average to the average over the period from 1993-94 to 1995-96, there is a fall of 0.3 percentage points in the own non tax revenues of the states (Table 6.1).

Table 6.1: Aggregate State Finances: Main Fiscal Indicators

(per cent to GDP)

Year	Own tax revenues	Own non-tax revenues	Finance Commission Transfers	Non-Finance Commission Transfers	Total Revenue Receipts
1993-94	5.30	1.59	3.05	2.02	11.96
1994-95	5.31	1.55	2.86	1.55	11.27
1995-96	5.20	1.51	2.90	1.30	10.91
1996-97	5.01	1.47	2.94	1.29	10.71
1997-98	5.14	1.43	2.90	1.33	10.80
1998-99	4.93	1.26	2.44	1.17	9.81
1999-00	5.09	1.38	2.50	1.29	10.26
2000-01	5.46	1.37	3.02	1.20	11.04
2001-02	5.32	1.19	2.84	1.28	10.63
2002-03	5.52	1.23	2.80	1.22	10.77
Average					
1993-94 to 1995-96 [A]	5.27	1.55	2.94	1.62	11.38
2000-01 to 2002-03 [B]	5.44	1.26	2.88	1.23	10.81
[B]-[A]	0.17	-0.29	-0.05	-0.39	-0.57

Source (Basic Data): *Report of the Twelfth Finance Commission, 2004.*

In the period under review, the Finance Commission's transfers relative to GDP were the lowest in 1998-99 and 1999-2000 at 2.4 per cent and 2.5 per cent respectively. There has been an improvement since. In the case of non-Finance Commissions' transfers, the fall was even more significant. In 1993-94, non-Finance Commission transfers accounted for about 2 per cent of GDP. These fell to below 1.3 per cent in the period sine 1998-99. Together, the Finance Commission and non-Finance Commission transfers from the centre fell by about 0.44 percentage points comparing the 2000-01 to 2002-03 average with that of 1993-94 to 1995-96. Taking these revenue flows together, the aggregate revenue receipts of the states as percentage of GDP were the lowest in 1998-99 at 9.8 per cent. Comparing the two period averages of 1993-94 to 1995-96 and 2000-01 to

2002-03, there has been a fall of little less than 0.6 percentage points in the total revenue receipts of the states.

6.4 Comparative Performance of States: Own Tax Revenues

In this section, we look at the comparative position of the states in the interstate ladder of tax-GSDP ratios. The Twelfth Finance Commission in its review of state finances had observed: "The single positive feature in this otherwise depressing narrative of state finances was the performance of states in regard to their own tax effort." Table 6.2 shows that the tax-GDP ratio increased considering the period-averages over 1993-94 to 1995-96 and 2000-01 to 2002-03. This applies for both the group of special category and general category states. It applies to all the individual states except for five states. These states are: West Bengal, Kerala, Karnataka, Goa and Manipur. The overall increase comparing the 2000-03 average with the 1993-96 average for the states as a whole was 0.67 percentage points for all states relative to the all-state GSDP and, 0.66 for the group of special category states. The increase was 0.69 percentage points for the group of the general category states, relative to their respective group-GSDPs.

As noted, the only exceptions in terms of individual states, where the tax-GDP ratio declined in terms of their 2000-01 to 2002-03 averages are Goa, Karnataka, Kerala, and West Bengal, although while the first three went from high to less high, West Bengal had a somewhat lower tax-GSDP ratio even in the 1993-94 to 1995-96 period. Among the special category states only Manipur has shown a decline in tax-GSDP ratio.

During 2000-01 to 2002-03, the highest tax-GSDP ratio was that for Tamil Nadu at 9.0 per cent of GSDP, and the lowest for West Bengal at 4.26 per cent, among the general category states.

Chart 6.1 shows the tax-GSDP ratios of the general category states along with Assam. States are arranged in ascending order of per capita comparable GSDP (average over 1999-00 to 2001-02). This is on the basis of the TFC report in which a logarithmic trend line was drawn. It is clear that there is a positive relationship between tax effort and per capita GSDP. The relationship would have been clearer if only Punjab and Goa at the higher income end, West Bengal, in the middle range, and Assam and Bihar, at the lower per capita GSDP end would have been closer to the fitted line. These states, the TFC observes have, in terms of the tax-GSDP ratio, performed below the par set by other states in their neighborhood in terms of the level of per capita GSDP.

Table 6.2: Own Tax Revenues: Comparative Performance of States

	Average OTR/GSDP (%)			Buoyancy
	1993-94 to 1995-96 [A]	2000-01 to 2002-03 [B]	B-A	1993-03
Arunachal Pradesh	0.55	1.47	0.91	2.543
Assam	3.69	4.58	0.90	1.326
Himachal Pradesh	4.87	5.08	0.21	1.043
Jammu & Kashmir	3.11	4.51	1.40	1.443
Manipur	1.44	1.21	-0.23	0.842
Meghalaya	3.02	3.26	0.23	1.089
Mizoram	0.59	0.97	0.38	1.608
Nagaland	1.18	1.19	0.01	0.980
Sikkim	3.44	4.58	1.15	1.303
Tripura	1.95	2.19	0.24	1.105
Total: Special Category States	3.30	3.96	0.66	1.226
Andhra Pradesh	5.90	7.30	1.40	1.271
Bihar	3.71	4.46	0.75	1.290
Goa	7.91	6.46	-1.45	0.806
Gujarat	7.51	7.71	0.20	1.010
Haryana	7.22	8.30	1.09	1.205
Karnataka	8.53	8.33	-0.19	0.969
Kerala	8.45	8.11	-0.34	0.946
Madhya Pradesh	4.91	6.45	1.53	1.452
Maharashtra	6.64	7.76	1.12	1.221
Orissa	3.93	5.81	1.87	1.639
Punjab	6.88	7.13	0.25	1.061
Rajasthan	5.50	6.48	0.98	1.231
Tamil Nadu	8.40	9.00	0.60	1.110
Uttar Pradesh	4.76	5.88	1.12	1.318
West Bengal	5.46	4.26	-1.20	0.690
Total: General Category States	6.26	6.95	0.69	1.143
All States	6.12	6.79	0.67	1.141

Source: *Report of the Twelfth Finance Commission, 2004.*

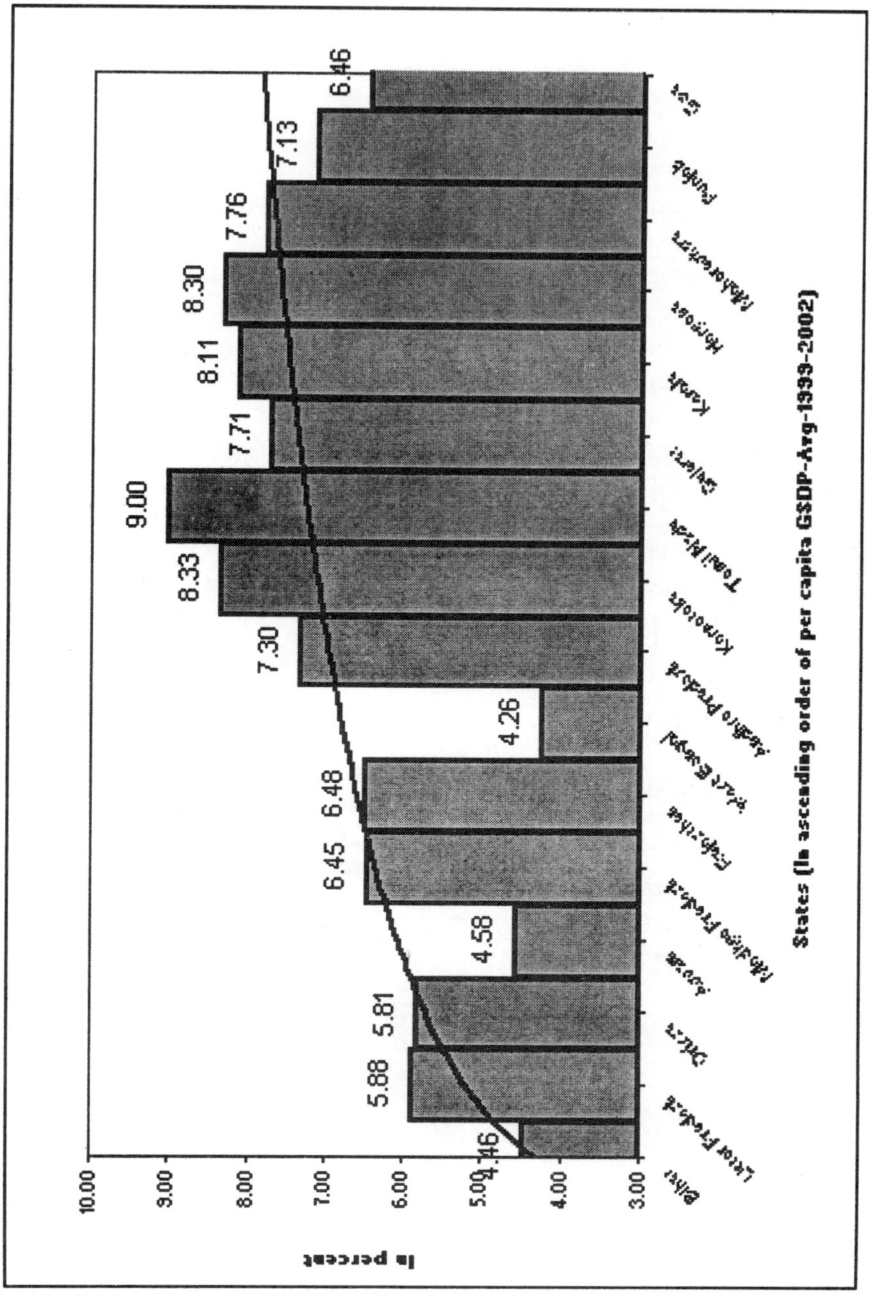

Chart 6.1: State's Own Tax Revenues Relative to GSDP (2000-01 to 2002-03)

6.5 Buoyancy of Own Tax Revenues: Inter-state Comparison

In this section, we look at the buoyancy of own tax revenues of the states. As noted earlier, buoyancy reflects the percentage increase in tax revenues following a one percent increase in the GSDP. This means that states with a buoyancy which is more than one will experience over time an increase in the own tax-GSDP ratio as tax revenues grow at a rate faster than the GSDP growth. Table 6.3 gives the buoyancy estimated over the period 1993-94 to 2001-02 for sixteen states.

Table 6.3 shows the buoyancy of own tax revenues of the states with respect to their respective per capita GSDPs, which indicates the extent of increase in own tax revenues following a one per cent change in per capita comparable GSDP, taking the latter as a macro indicator of the tax base. The tax-buoyancy has been estimated over the period 1993-2002. If the states with a low tax-GSDP ratio have high buoyancy, they would find improvement in their tax-GSDP ratios over time. If the tax-buoyancy is less than 1, the tax-GSDP ratio would fall over time. Subject to adjustment for levels of per capita GSDPs, it would be desirable if states at the lower end of the chart show higher buoyancy. In this sense, the states at the lower to middle income ranges, with the exception of West Bengal, do show an improving picture.

Table 6.3: Buoyancy of Own Tax Revenues: 1993-2002

(General Category States and Assam)			
Andhra Pradesh	1.27	Madhya Pradesh	1.45
Assam	1.33	Maharashtra	1.22
Bihar	1.29	Orissa	1.64
Goa	0.81	Punjab	1.06
Gujarat	1.01	Rajasthan	1.23
Haryana	1.21	Tamil Nadu	1.11
Karnataka	0.97	Uttar Pradesh	1.32
Kerala	0.95	West Bengal	0.69

Source: (Basic Data): *State Finance Accounts and CSO.*

Chart 6.2 provides a comparison of the states in terms of own tax buoyancy. Clearly West Bengal has the lowest buoyancy. Goa, Kerala, and Karnataka, also have buoyancy which is less than one. It is expected that the states that are starting with a low tax-GSDP ratio may find it easier to show buoyancy which is substantially larger than one. Assam and Orissa show a high buoyancy due to better performance in recent years but starting with a low tax-GSDP ratio. High income states like Gujarat, Tamil Nadu and Punjab show buoyancy close to one. Haryana in recent years has shown substantial growth in the own tax revenues following the imposition of floor rate in the case of sales tax. That is why it has a buoyancy exceeding 1.2.

Chart 6.2: Own Tax Buoyancy: Comparison of States

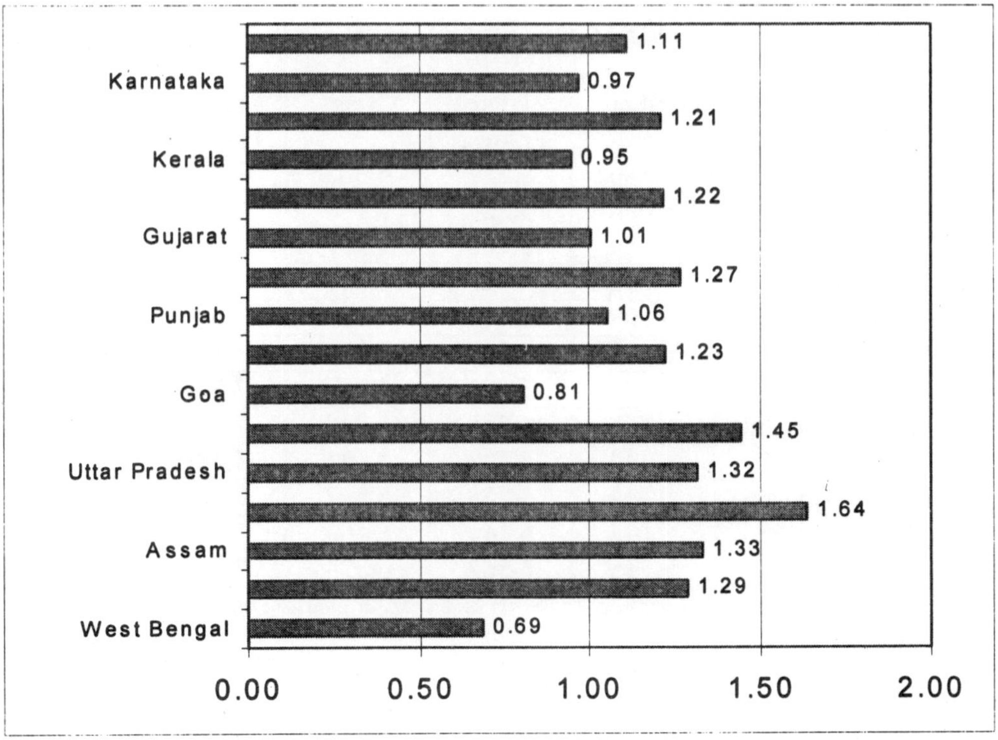

6.6 Tax-GSDP Ratio: Group-wise Comparisons

In this section, we look at the tax-GSDP ratios of different states over the period from 1993-94 to 2004-05 (BE) and look at their performance within respective groups of low income, middle income, and high income groups. For this purpose, 16 states are chosen, which include all the general category states except the newly created ones, and one special category state, namely, Assam.

6.7 Low Income States: Tax Performance

In the group of low income states, we have included Bihar, Uttar Pradesh, Orissa, Rajasthan, Madhya Pradesh, and Assam. The tax-GSDP ratio in the case of Assam has increased from a level just above 3.5 per cent in 1994-95 to an estimated 5.8 per cent in 2004-05. Orissa and Rajasthan also show sharp increases in their own tax to GSDP ratio. In the case of Orissa, it went from 4.065 in 1993-94 to 6.384 in 2004-05 while in the case of Rajasthan it increased from 5.683 in 1993-94 to 7.428 in 2004-05 (Table 6.4).

Table 6.4: Tax-GSDP Ratios: Low Income Group (per cent)

Year	Assam	Bihar	Uttar Pradesh	Orissa	Madhya Pradesh	Rajasthan
1993-94	3.971	6.380	5.257	4.065	7.248	5.683
1994-95	3.525	6.096	5.224	3.738	6.587	5.306
1995-96	3.562	7.289	5.206	3.997	6.905	5.510
1996-97	3.663	6.588	4.959	4.621	7.009	5.014
1997-98	3.904	6.808	5.043	4.384	7.095	5.513
1998-99	3.807	6.063	5.059	3.924	7.134	5.330
1999-00	4.169	6.400	5.593	4.390	7.320	5.692
2000-01	4.168	4.851	6.258	5.440	7.489	6.465
2001-02	4.509	4.240	5.449	5.581	5.486	6.230
2002-03	5.066	4.774	6.275	6.397	7.321	6.734
2003-04 RE	5.556	5.194	6.141	6.400	7.201	7.491
2004-05 BE	5.774	5.535	6.562	6.384	7.757	7.428

Source: (Basic Data): *State Finance Accounts and Budget Documents.*

There is an increase the tax-GSDP ratio for Uttar Pradesh and Madhya Pradesh. However the improvement is marginal. The only case where there is a fall in the ratio of own-tax to GSDP is that of the Bihar. The other notable feature is the rise in this ratio in the case of most states during the early years of this decade. For example, in Assam there was a rise of more than 1.5 percentage points from the level of 2000-01 by 2003-04. There were similar tangible increases in the case most other states.

Next we look at the trends in the case of the middle income group states, which comprise West Bengal, Andhra Pradesh, Kerala, Karnataka and Tamil Nadu (Table 6.5). As already noted, West Bengal has shown the lowest tax own tax-GSDP ratio in this group of states. Not only has it been low, but it has also fallen over time. In terms of the magnitude of this ratio, Andhra Pradesh has been the next highest. It has shown a reasonable rise in the ratio over the nineties but its ratio is still lower than the other three states. In terms of the tax GSDP ratio, Kerala, Karnataka and Tamil Nadu all show currently a ratio of more than nine per cent of GSDP. This takes them to the category of the highest tax-GSDP ratio states. The middle income states also show a rise in the early years of the new decade but the increase is not so sharp. This is because they have been able to exploit their tax bases more fully in the earlier years also.

Table 6.5: Tax-GSDP Ratios: Middle Income Group (per cent)

Year	West Bengal	Andhra Pradesh	Kerala	Karnataka	Tamil Nadu
1993-94	5.190	6.610	8.573	8.587	8.146
1994-95	5.752	6.001	8.461	8.195	8.206
1995-96	5.435	5.081	8.317	8.797	8.839
1996-97	5.064	5.261	8.241	8.017	8.490
1997-98	4.588	7.353	7.981	8.249	8.043
1998-99	4.059	6.867	7.775	7.482	7.872
1999-00	4.018	7.163	7.645	7.807	8.422
2000-01	4.364	7.332	7.842	8.164	8.479
2001-02	4.260	7.300	7.935	8.509	8.968
2002-03	4.149	7.268	8.543	8.325	9.555
2003-04 RE	4.546	7.220	9.034	9.272	9.606
2004-05 BE	4.721	7.835	9.240	9.619	9.526

Source: (Basic Data): *State Finance Accounts and Budget Documents.*

In summary, among the middle income states, there is deterioration seen in the case of West Bengal. All the other four states show improvement from their already attained high levels of Tax-GSDP ratios. As shown in the next section, it is the middle income states which have performed better even as compared to the high income states.

6.8 High Income Group

In the case of the high income states, which include Punjab, Haryana, Goa, Gujarat, and Maharashtra, the tax-GSDP ratio could not exceed the level of nine per cent which has been achieved by some of the middle income states. Table 6.6 shows the relative variation in the tax-GSDP ratios of this group of states.

Haryana shows the highest tax-GSDP ratio in this group of states followed by Maharashtra, Punjab, Gujarat and Goa. Among these states Gujarat and Goa do not show any increase in recent years as compared to the mid nineties. In fact, there is a fall in the case of Goa.

Table 6.6: Tax-GSDP Ratios: High Income Group (per cent)

Year	Gujarat	Punjab	Haryana	Maharashtra	Goa
1993-94	7.848	6.878	7.281	6.485	7.634
1994-95	7.353	7.190	7.147	6.958	8.060
1995-96	7.316	6.576	7.223	6.478	8.041
1996-97	7.357	5.791	5.853	6.386	6.560
1997-98	7.114	5.890	5.815	7.288	7.344
1998-99	7.106	5.728	6.868	6.531	5.843
1999-00	7.495	6.303	6.890	6.903	6.634
2000-01	8.410	7.228	7.963	7.818	6.687
2001-02	7.382	6.646	8.387	7.721	7.052
2002-03	7.323	7.517	8.561	7.736	5.647
2003-04 RE	7.905	7.822	8.607	8.037	6.191
2004-05 BE	7.537	7.706	8.597	7.996	6.111

Source: (Basic Data): *State Finance Accounts and Budget Documents.*

6.9 Own Tax Revenues: Growth Pattern

In this section, we look at the growth pattern of own tax revenues, with a view to comparing relative performance of different states during the nineties and in more recent years. Table 6.7 shows the growth pattern in the case of the low income states. The years marked with negative growth are 2000-01 and 2001-02 for Bihar and Madhya Pradesh, and 2001-02 for Uttar Pradesh. The high growth years are 1999-00 for Assam 2002-03 for Bihar and Uttar Pradesh, 2000-01 for Orissa and Rajasthan.

In contrast to the low income states, the middle and high income states show a more uniform performance. Table 6.8 gives the growth rates for both middle and high income states. The high growth years for this group of states may be noted as follows: 2000-01 and 2003-04 for West Bengal, 2000-01 for Andhra Pradesh, 2002-03 for Kerala, and 2000-01 for Karnataka. A negative growth is seen only for one year (1995-96) in the case of Andhra Pradesh.

Among the high income states, there are relatively more negative tax-growth years but these are also few. It may be noted that it is quite rare to get a negative growth in own tax revenues, since the tax base, that is, GSDP is growing. In the case of the high income states, 2000-01 is a notable year where almost all states had a reasonably high growth in the own tax revenues.

Table 6.7: Growth in Tax Revenues: 1994-95 to 2004-05

Year	Assam	Bihar	Uttar Pradesh	Orissa	Madhya Pradesh	Rajasthan
1994-95	3.17	15.94	18.06	7.29	7.23	18.30
1995-96	11.11	18.22	12.11	22.17	22.56	18.35
1996-97	9.17	14.43	15.31	19.06	16.64	14.40
1997-98	15.00	6.61	10.97	5.94	11.23	15.58
1998-99	11.41	11.73	13.03	4.60	11.92	9.11
1999-00	24.65	15.05	18.85	14.59	13.44	15.02
2000-01	15.10	-8.93	16.80	28.16	-2.69	16.97
2001-02	10.45	-17.45	-5.92	12.95	-17.03	7.00
2002-03	24.25	19.12	23.59	16.42	31.75	10.27
2003-04 RE	22.86	21.67	7.37	10.31	7.60	21.58
2004-05 BE	16.16	18.90	16.95	9.74	17.55	8.12

Source: (Basic Data): *State Finance Accounts and Budget Documents.*

6.10 Relative Share of State Level Taxes in Total Own Tax Revenues

In this section, we look at the relative share of different sources of tax revenues in states' total own tax revenues. This analysis has been done at an aggregate level of all states. The trends are given for the period of the nineties, as shown in Table 6.9. The overwhelming contribution of the state sales taxes is clearly visible. In fact, it has gone up during the nineties from a level of 58 per cent in 1990-91 to more than 62 per cent in 2000-01. There is however also some volatility in the share of the sales taxes.

The other most important tax for the states in terms of its revenue contribution is state excise duties followed by stamp duty and registration fees. The stamp duties and registration duties exhibited their highest share in the mid-nineties, but has come down since. What is more of a concern is that the contribution of state excise duties has also come down. This would be welcome if it reflects any lowering of alcohol consumption, but is more likely due to lack of revision of the excise duty rates.

Table 6.8: Growth in Tax Revenues: 1994-95 to 2004-05

Year	West Bengal	Andhra Pradesh	Kerala	Karnataka	Tamil Nadu
1994-95	28.06	10.29	19.37	12.51	21.50
1995-96	10.79	-2.53	20.85	22.96	22.58
1996-97	3.05	18.48	15.25	9.37	11.64
1997-98	6.06	45.71	15.46	11.17	8.80
1998-99	5.70	11.92	3.30	8.28	10.82
1999-00	6.84	13.15	11.70	11.54	13.44
2000-01	16.54	17.13	13.03	16.76	12.49
2001-02	9.92	9.46	0.91	8.96	5.92
2002-03	7.83	9.24	23.28	5.95	10.24
2003-04 RE	25.24	12.05	17.52	24.17	11.16
2004-05 BE	18.40	22.10	13.41	15.39	9.39
	Gujarat	Punjab	Haryana	Maharashtra	Goa
1994-95	20.32	20.91	18.81	22.85	20.40
1995-96	12.23	2.00	14.89	15.65	20.22
1996-97	13.96	3.16	-1.19	7.14	11.42
1997-98	8.66	11.34	10.52	17.11	20.67
1998-99	15.55	7.15	31.71	3.52	-2.21
1999-00	7.17	21.00	12.76	21.56	28.35
2000-01	10.84	24.01	22.57	14.23	12.28
2001-02	2.21	-1.53	15.33	7.94	10.59
2002-03	3.05	18.47	11.61	7.10	5.77
2003-04 RE	19.11	14.81	12.12	14.31	24.33
2004-05 BE	4.97	8.46	11.14	9.21	11.68

Source: (Basic Data): *State Finance Accounts and Budget Documents.*

6.11 Fiscal Adjustment and the Role of Own Tax Revenues

The TFC envisages a small increase in the states' own tax revenue which should rise from a level of 5.9 per cent of GDP to 6.8 per cent by 2009-10. As indicated in Table 6.10, This involves a per year increase of 0.17 percentage points of GDP. This combined with a small rise in the non tax revenues accompanied by a rise in transfers enable adjustment to take place in the state finances, in which an increase in the revenue receipts has to play an important role.

Table 6.9: States: Structure of Own Tax Revenues (Rs. crore)

Year	States' own tax revenue	Sales tax	State excise	Tax on vehicles	Stamp duties & registration fees	Others
1990-91	30344.83	17667.03	4795.15	1566.27	2112.31	4204.07
1991-92	35756.05	16810.68	5438.77	1837.1	2653.93	9015.57
1992-93	39868.28	23348.99	6264.76	2194.42	2978.1	5082.01
1993-94	45873.87	21246.53	7008.74	2569.44	3535.05	11514.11
1994-95	53947.07	31883.05	7438.44	3014.95	4978.61	6632.02
1995-96	61754.14	33938.12	8180.69	3655.82	5770.08	10209.43
1996-97	68566.65	42112.09	8358.78	4039.22	6152.59	7903.97
1997-98	78287.85	46812.78	10755.68	4748.76	7025.58	8945.05
1998-99	85906.47	51003.04	12811.9	4898.61	7281.08	9911.84
1999-00	99151.48	59954.72	14465.54	5992.25	8368.19	10370.78
2000-01	113580.38	69976.05	15478.31	6523.21	9483.02	12119.79
						(Per cent to Total)
	States' own tax Revenue	Sales tax	State excise	Tax on vehicles	Stamp duties & registration fees	Others
1990-91	100.0	58.2	15.8	5.2	7.0	13.9
1991-92	100.0	47.0	15.2	5.1	7.4	25.2
1992-93	100.0	58.6	15.7	5.5	7.5	12.7
1993-94	100.0	46.3	15.3	5.6	7.7	25.1
1994-95	100.0	59.1	13.8	5.6	9.2	12.3
1995-96	100.0	55.0	13.2	5.9	9.3	16.5
1996-97	100.0	61.4	12.2	5.9	9.0	11.5
1997-98	100.0	59.8	13.7	6.1	9.0	11.4
1998-99	100.0	59.4	14.9	5.7	8.5	11.5
1999-00	100.0	60.5	14.6	6.0	8.4	10.5
2000-01	100.0	61.6	13.6	5.7	8.3	10.7

Source: (Basic Data): *RBI Bulletin on State Finances.*

Table 6.10: TFC Restructuring Plan: Role of Own Tax Revenues

State Finances				
States' Own Tax Revenues	5.9	6.8	0.8	0.17
Tax Revenues	8.4	9.7	1.3	0.25
Own Non-tax Revenues	1.2	1.4	0.2	0.03
Non Tax Revenues	3.2	3.5	0.3	0.07
Total Revenue Receipts	11.6	13.2	1.6	0.32

In summary, it is apparent that own tax revenues constitute the core of state taxation. Contrary to the trend for the central indirect taxes, they have not fallen relative to GDP during the nineties but have shown a marginal improvement. Many states have shown a higher than one buoyancy in the nineties. The middle income states are particularly praiseworthy as they have maintained an average close to 9 per cent of GSDP. There is some scope for improving the revenues from state level excise duties. There is a great need to convert the sales taxes into state level value added tax system, eliminate the central sales tax while ensuring that state level VAT proves eventually revenue augmenting. The options and issues in regard to State level VAT are discussed in the next Chapter.

6.12 State Taxes: Relative Importance of the Central Sales Taxes

In any design of commodity taxes, it is best to minimise taxes that fragment the common market that extends over the entire country. The central taxes were initially introduced under article 269 more for keeping track of the inter-state flow of goods. Over time the tax rate was increased to 4 per cent. The central sales tax is levied by the central governments but administered and collected by the producing state, whereas it is paid by the purchasers of the consuming state. In this sense, tax exportation becomes possible. For a tax design that is consistent with a destination based principle, this arrangement constitutes a distortion. In a robust state level VAT system, the central sales tax would require to be phased out as quickly as possible.

Table 6.11: Central Sales Tax: Relative Importance for States (Rs. crore)

State	1998-99	1999-2000	2000-01	2001-02	2002-03
Andhra Pradesh	448.77	562.01	981.63	646.07	879.10
Bihar	335.21	444.95	253.29	578.70	124.68
Chhattisgarh	0.00	0.00	24.77	376.19	334.35
Goa	19.01	28.19	41.09	36.10	27.55
Gujarat	749.87	956.81	1,051.66	1,015.71	1,157.13
Haryana	483.68	613.45	927.77	838.14	867.27
Himachal Pradesh	24.06	31.14	32.07	43.14	44.41
Jharkhand	0.00	0.00	197.39	450.15	266.54
Karnataka	448.49	550.75	772.13	679.35	814.80
Kerala	273.65	287.31	356.95	260.98	355.88
Madhya Pradesh	453.06	474.00	439.29	332.55	350.46
Maharashtra	1.334.88	1,655.18	1,865.31	2,059.50	1,718.47
Meghalaya	28.57	19.33	31.76	21.11	23.60

Contd...

Orissa	0.00	45.81	48.13	51.82	72.53
Punjab	259.72	387.35	377.21	620.47	349.57
Rajasthan	134.25	144.69	176.70	199.80	208.11
Tamil Nadu	714.45	830.09	2,183.86	1,546.71	928.67
Uttar Pradesh	182.25	424.07	599.20	498.37	707.48
Uttaranchal	0.00	0.00	13.58	34.37	52.15
West Bengal	400.04	442.85	461.61	512.43	566.85
Total	**6.291.02**	**7,899.09**	**10,842.45**	**10,811.53**	**10,097.45**
					(Per cent to Total)
Andhra Pradesh	7.13	7.11	9.05	5.98	8.71
Bihar	5.33	5.63	2.34	5.35	1.23
Chhattisgarh	0.00	0.00	0.23	3.48	3.31
Goa	0.30	0.36	0.38	0.33	0.27
Gujarat	11.92	12.11	9.70	9.39	11.46
Haryana	7.69	7.77	8.56	7.75	8.59
Himachal Pradesh	0.38	0.39	0.30	0.40	0.44
Jharkhand	0.00	0.00	1.82	4.16	2.64
Karnataka	7.13	6.97	7.12	6.28	8.07
Kerala	4.35	3.64	3.29	2.41	3.52
Madhya Pradesh	7.20	6.00	4.05	3.08	3.47
Maharashtra	21.22	20.95	17.20	19.05	17.02
Meghalaya	0.45	0.24	0.29	0.20	0.23
Orissa	0.00	0.58	0.44	0.48	0.72
Punjab	4.13	4.90	3.48	5.74	3.46
Rajasthan	2.13	1.83	1.63	1.85	2.06
Tamil Nadu	11.36	10.51	20.14	14.31	9.20
Uttar Pradesh	2.90	5.37	5.53	4.61	7.01
Uttaranchal	0.00	0.00	0.13	0.32	0.52
West Bengal	6.36	5.61	4.26	4.74	5.61
Total	100.00	100.00	100.00	100.00	100.00

Source: *State Finance Accounts and Budget Documents.*

Table 6.11 gives the amounts that are raised under the central sales tax by the different states. This also gives an idea as to states which will have to make up for the loss under the destination based VAT. While in all more than Rs. 10,000 crore are being raised, states which account for a high share of this total are Andhra Pradesh, Gujarat, Haryana, Karnataka, Maharashtra, Tamil Nadu, and Uttar Pradesh. Although the share of Maharashtra was the highest in 2002-03, at more than 17 per cent, it fell over time. The share of Tamil Nadu has also fallen.

The shares of Karnataka, Andhra Pradesh, and Uttar Pradesh have increased marginally.

7

Value Added Tax in India: Principles and Practice

From an economist's point of view, a properly implemented value-added tax is equivalent to a corresponding single-stage tax. Unlike the expenditure tax, the value-added tax is not a genuinely new form of taxation but merely a sales tax administered in a different form.

Musgrave and Musgrave

Among taxation systems relating to goods and services, the Value Added Tax has come to enjoy an overwhelming popularity in the world. Over 130 countries across the world have a Value Added Tax system of indirect taxes. VAT is a multi-stage levy imposed on business at all levels of the manufacture and production of a good or service and based on the increase in price, or value, provided by each level. The tax paid at the earlier input stages is rebated at each successive stage. The consumer ultimately pays the tax on his purchases. As such, the VAT is essentially a sales tax. Originally introduced in France (1954), it is now a major part of the tax structure of most Western European nations. In the early 1990s the U.S. government considered instituting a VAT to fund national health care programs. In Brazil, which is a federal country, a full-fledged VAT was brought in the mid-1960s. In the European countries, VAT has operated since the 1970's. In Asia, it has been introduced by a large number of countries from China to Sri Lanka. In India, there has been a VAT system introduced by the Government of India in the form of CENVAT.

The popularity of VAT arises from some its well known advantages. First, because of its broad base, it has a high revenue buoyancy. Its buoyancy can easily exceed 1. Secondly, VAT is also known to be neutral in its impact on foreign trade flows. Exports are generally not taxed under VAT and imports are taxed at the same rate as domestically produced goods. Since the developing countries rely more on taxes on foreign trade, the raising of additional revenue from a VAT will have beneficial effect in terms of reducing the responsiveness of total tax revenue to trade fluctuations. Thirdly, emphasis on domestic consumption taxes in the form of VAT also reduces the fiscal cost of trade liberalization. Fourthly, since the tax is paid by customers in small amounts, it has low visibility, once it is established.

There may be however some disadvantages associated with VAT. If it is levied as a comprehensive, single rate VAT, it would turn out to be proportional rather than a progressive tax. It is therefore likely to be less equitable than an income tax with a threshold and rising marginal rates, and no exemptions. However, it is possible to impart some progressivity to VAT by having two or more rates including zero rates, which may be applied on basic needs goods such as food and clothing. It requires a comprehensive information base where transactions can be recorded and tracked. It has been argued that VAT has a detrimental effect on the informal sector. As this sector is brought into the tax net, its attractiveness for drawing investment and its role as employment generator will be depleted. In a federal country like India, there are additional difficulties because the division of tax powers between the federal and the state governments is constitutionally entrenched, and making provision for a comprehensive VAT requires new arrangements. If states are unwilling to support the constitutional amendment that would give the center the power to levy the VAT on common principles across the country, various working principles have to be evolved for sharing of the tax base linked to value added in the production and sale of goods and services.

The United States, which is also a federal country, represents an interesting example of a developed country where VAT has not been implemented despite several attempts in the last thirty years. One of the reasons, often cited, is the concern that with VAT the Federal Government may usurp a large part of the states' power of sales taxation.

7.1 Essential Characteristics of VAT

The idea in VAT is to tax the value added at each stage of manufacturing or sale so that eventually the total value of the product is taxed. In this sense it amounts to a retail sales tax. However, the difference is that in following the principle of taxing at every stage and rebating at every stage, it creates a paper chain of transactions and thereby minimizes any sales that may be done outside the tax net.

In the literature three variants of VAT are discussed: Gross Product, Income, and Consumption. The economic base of the gross product variant is the gross national product. In this deduction is allowed for all purchases of raw materials and components but deduction is not allowed for business inputs like capital goods such as plant and machinery. In the income tax variant, the tax is levied at all stages and set off is given for depreciation of capital goods. In the consumption variant, tax is levied on all sales and deduction is allowed for business inputs.

7.2 VAT in a Federal Country

In a federal country, introducing VAT requires to take into account the assignment of powers between the central and state governments in relation to the taxation of commodities and services. It also requires addressing the issues of co-ordination and harmonization so that the objective of having a unified country wide market may be achieved. In India, the powers to tap the value added in the case of goods are up to the extent of manufacturing or production. Beyond this are the stages of stages of wholesale and retail. The states, in the form of sales taxes, can tap the entire value added up to the retail level. In the case of services, the power of taxation is vested only with the central government.

A federal country can select from several alternatives in designing a suitable VAT system. A suitable design of VAT should ensure that it guided by the destination principle, that the incidence of tax should be on consumers and accrue to states where they reside. The main alternatives, considered in the literature are briefly mentioned below:

Federal VAT: The federal VAT (FVAT), which may also be called the Union or Federal VAT is levied and administered by the central government comprehensively. In the Indian case, this would imply replacing both the existing central excise duties/CENVAT and state sale taxes. The central sales tax would also be eliminated automatically. In FVAT, the tax rates would be automatically harmonized across the states. It will be able to cover the entire value added from the manufacturing to retail. In this sense, there is much to recommend for a federal VAT except for its main drawback that it would entirely disturb the nature of the federal structure in terms of powers to levy taxes and ownership of tax revenues. States will be required to surrender their autonomy to levy and collect taxes. This may lead to greater centralization of powers.

State VAT: The other alternative is to go the other extreme and vest states with the power to levy a state level VAT (SVAT). Even the state level VAT can be nationally regulated. In one version, the state level VAT can be levied by the central government but administered and collected by the state governments. In this case the central government will also determine the exemptions and the procedures. This would mean that the centre will have to vacate the field of central excise taxation and the taxes will be collected and retained by the states. The loss of revenue to the centre could be made up by a limited number of sumptuary excises that are neither rebatable nor sharable. Although the states will gain in revenue, they will lose the autonomy to vary tax rates. One important implication of this version of state VAT is in relation to centre-state transfers. With vertical imbalance being almost eliminated, the centre will not be able to play a redistributive role through progressive transfers. One benefit however is that, apart from automatic harmonization, the central sales tax can also be eliminated. If the destination principle is adopted, problems of coordination will be eased because of common rates.

An alternative version of state level VAT (SVAT2) argues for a system of state VAT's, which is regulated by the states themselves. In this case, the tax is levied, administered, collected and retained by the states. The states will also have the autonomy to fix tax rates and exercise discretionary choices relating to exemptions and administration. In this case also the centre will have to forgo its power to levy central excises except for a few sumptuary duties. Such an arrangement will work when states agree voluntarily to harmonize or at least agree to floor rates. This will also imply revenue depletion for the centre and its capacity to make redistributive transfers will be compromised because of loss of vertical imbalance in resources in favor of the states. Neither of the two versions of state VAT has found favor with the policy makers mainly for this reason.

7.3 Systems of Dual VAT

In the literature three alternative versions of a system of dual VAT, which is a combination of central VAT and state level VAT. The three main versions maybe referred to as follows:

1. Concurrent VAT
2. Dual VAT with centre's power extended up to the wholesale stage
3. Dual VAT with independent tiers

Concurrent VAT: In concurrent VAT, both centre and states levy the tax on a common base but collect it according to their own rates. For both tiers of government, the tax base will extend up to the retail stage. The states may be allowed to vary their rates within agreed bands. In this case, the inter state sales will be subject to the central VAT, but zero rated for state VATs. There can be common registration by the dealers and the VAT return form will also be common for both tiers. The taxes may be remitted directly to centre and states. In the present Indian setup, such a concurrent VAT will require a constitutional change which will confer concurrent powers. In particular the centre would need to be given powers to enter into state's field of taxation, which extend beyond manufacturing to wholesale and retail level. The centre will also require additional administrative staff if a dual administrative structure is built up. However the centre may ask the state governments to collect central VAT on its behalf. While this option is appealing, the main hurdle is the need for a constitutional amendment. An arrangement like this will also create issues of vertical externality in taxes because tax rate decisions by one tier will affect the tax base of the other tier.

Dual VAT with centre's Power Extended up to Wholesale Stage: The version of dual VAT where centre's jurisdiction is extended up to the whole sale stage was suggested by the Tax Reform Committee headed by Dr. Chelliah. In the version that was suggested, the state system of VAT was to operate beyond the whole sale stage. While the tax beyond manufacture up to the whole sale stage was to be levied by the centre at a common rate it was to be collected and retained by the states. As such, states were not to lose any revenue from the value added from manufacturing to whole sale, but the advantage is that uniformity of the tax rates is ensured up to the whole sale stage. One argument in favor of this system was that this will discourage shifting of marketing or other ancillary activities by the firms beyond manufacturing to avoid the CENVAT. It will also solve valuation problems, which are a major irritant in administering the central excise duties. The implementability of this option depends entirely on the agreement of the state to allow the centre to levy the tax up to the whole sale stage. It may require a constitutional change.

Dual VAT with Independent Jurisdictions: The third version of dual VAT consists of two independent systems of CENVAT and state VAT. In this case, both the centre and the states are supposed to exercise their existing taxation powers but convert their commodity taxes into VAT. The CENVAT extends up to manufacturing and the states opt for state level VATs. Both tiers retain the autonomy in fixing tax rates, exemptions and other discretionary decisions. No constitutional change is required. However arrangements for harmonization across states need to be worked out. There is also the problem of dealing with the central sales tax, which should be eliminated and exports from states should be zero rated. The federal fiscal equations do not undergo any change as long as the conversion of central excise into CENVAT and state sales taxes into state VAT is revenue neutral. The main problem in this system is that cascading of taxes may not be fully eliminated. Sales taxes may cascade into central excises and vice versa.

7.4 Services in a VAT System

In all the systems of VAT discussed above, taxation is limited to the value added in the production and sale of goods. In modern day economies, services constitute not only a large part, but the service sector also grows relatively fast. Services become an input in the production of goods while goods may be required in the production of services. Ideally taxation of gods and services should be considered together. Under the existing constitutional arrangements, the power to levy the service tax is with the centre under its residuary powers. As long as goods and services are subjected to different regimes of taxation, neither harmonization can be achieved nor cascading of taxes can be fully avoided. In most countries of the world, an integrated system capturing the value added in production and sale both of goods and services is in vogue.

In evaluating the available options in the Indian context, one should realize that the basic objective in imposing a harmonized VAT is to support economic efficiency, which can eliminate tax related distortions in the allocation of resources and the productive activities of the economy. Other important objectives relate to issues of harmonization and administrative efficiency. In a federal system like that in India, both tiers of governments require to retain their autonomy but still agree to harmonization in terms of floor rates. Issues of cross cascading between taxation of goods and that of services raise additional problems. It may be best for the medium term to settle for options that do not require constitutional changes as it is neither easy for the central government nor the state governments to vacate existing powers of taxation. The system must develop mechanisms whereby problems of interstate sales and excessive rate variation across states may be tackled. The present trends indicate that the system is evolving towards a dual VAT with independent jurisdictions with some degree of harmonization.

7.5 Need for Reforming State Sales Taxes

While the centre has already taken the initiative in introducing the VAT principle in central excises, there is clear need to reform the state level sales taxes. In the existing sales tax structure, there are problems of double taxation of commodities and multiplicity of taxes, resulting in a cascading tax burden. There is a multiplicity of tax rates, proliferation of exemptions where the tax incidence is opaque and difficult to control. In the existing structure, before a commodity is produced, inputs are first taxed, and then after the commodity is produced with the input tax load, output is taxed again. This leads to cascading effects.

7.6 Scheme of VAT as Proposed by the Empowered Committee

Within the context of a dual VAT system with independent jurisdictions, the Empowered Committee of State Finance Ministers has recommended a scheme of implementing State-level VAT. This is elaborated in the White Paper that has been brought out by the Government of India. The empowered committee was constituted in July 2000 to monitor the process of introduction of VAT at the state level. After missing several deadlines, many states have gone ahead with the introduction of VAT with effect from 1.4.2005 on the basis of the scheme developed by the committee. The Empowered Committee commends this scheme having some distinct advantages over the existing sales tax structure.

Accordingly, the VAT will not only provide full set-off for input tax as well as tax on previous purchases, but it will also abolish the burden of several of the existing taxes, such as turnover tax, surcharge on sales tax, additional surcharge, special additional tax, etc. In addition, it recommends phasing out of the Central Sales Tax. This will entail that the overall tax burden will be rationalized. VAT will replace the existing system of inspection by a system of built-in self-assessment by traders and manufacturers. The tax structure will become simple and more transparent, facilitating tax compliance and supporting revenue growth.

The state-level VAT is a State subject derived from Entry 54 of the State List, for which the States are sovereign in taking decisions. The Empowered Committee notes that the states have found it in their interest, to avoid unhealthy competition and have certain features of VAT to be common for all the States. These features will constitute the basic design of VAT. The States will have freedom for appropriate variations consistent with this basic design. The main features of the scheme may be described as follows:

- uniform schedule of rates of VAT for all states, making the system simple and uniform and prevent unhealthy tax competition among states;
- the provision of input tax credit meant for preventing cascading effect of tax;
- the provision self assessment by dealers aimed at reducing harassment; and
- the zero rating of exports aimed at increasing the competitiveness of Indian exports

Concept of VAT and Set-off/Input Tax Credit: The essence of VAT, as noted by the Empowered Committee is in providing set-off for the tax paid earlier, and this is given effect through the concept of input tax credit/rebate. This input tax credit in relation to any period means setting off the amount of input tax by a registered dealer against the amount of his output tax. The Value Added Tax (VAT) is based on the value addition to the goods, and the related VAT liability of the dealer is calculated by deducting input tax credit from tax collected on sales during the payment period (say, a month). If, for example, input worth Rs. 1,00,000/- is purchased and sales are worth Rs. 2,00,000/- in a month, and input tax rate and output tax rate are 4 per cent and 10 per cent respectively, then input tax credit/set-off and calculation of VAT will be as shown below:

(a) Input purchased within the month: Rs. 1,00,000/-
(b) Output sold in the month: Rs. 2,00,000/-
(c) Input tax paid: Rs. 4,000/-
(d) Output tax payable: Rs. 20,000/-
(e) VAT payable during the month: Rs. 16,000/-
after set-off/input tax credit [(d) – (c)]

Coverage of Set-Off/Input Tax Credit: The Empowered Committee stipulates that this input tax credit will be given for both manufacturers and traders for purchase of inputs/supplies meant for both sales within the State as well as to other States, irrespective of when these will be utilized/sold. This will also reduce the immediate tax liability. Even for stock transfer/consignment sale of goods out of the State, input tax paid in excess of 4 per cent will be eligible for tax credit.

Carrying Over of Tax Credit: In relation to tax credit, the Empowered Committee stipulates that if the tax credit exceeds the tax payable on sales in a month, the excess credit will be carried over to the end of next financial year. If there is any excess unadjusted input tax credit at the end of second year, then the same will be eligible for refund. Input tax credit on capital goods will also be available for traders and manufacturers. Tax credit on capital goods may be adjusted over a maximum of 36 equal monthly installments. The States may at their option reduce this number of installments. There will be a negative list for capital goods (on the basis of principles already decided by the Empowered Committee) not eligible for input tax credit.

Treatment of Exports etc.: As per the basic principles of VAT, the state VAT also provides that for all exports made out of the country, tax paid within the State will be refunded in full, and this refund will be made within three months. Units located in SEZ and EOU will be granted either exemption from payment of input tax or refund of the input tax paid within three months.

Inputs Procured from Other States: It is provided that, tax paid on inputs procured from other States through inter-State sale and stock transfer, will not be eligible for credit. However, a decision has been taken for duly phasing out of inter-State sales tax or Central sales tax. The Empowered Committee recommends setting up of a comprehensive inter-State tax information exchange system.

Treatment of Opening Stock: In State VAT scheme designed by the Empowered Committee, all tax-paid goods purchased on or after April 1, 2004 and still in stock as on April 1, 2005 will be eligible to receive input tax credit, subject to submission of requisite documents. Resellers holding tax-paid goods on April 1, 2005 will also be eligible. VAT will be levied on the goods when sold on and after April 1, 2005 and input tax credit will be given for the sales tax already paid in the previous year. This tax credit will be available over a period of 6 months after an interval of 3 months needed for verification.

Compulsory Issue of Tax Invoice, Cash Memo or Bill: Since the entire design of state-VAT with input tax credit is crucially based on documentation of tax invoice, cash memo or bill, it is provided that every registered dealer, having turnover of sales above an amount specified, shall issue to the purchaser serially numbered tax invoice with the prescribed particulars. This tax invoice will be signed and dated by the dealer or his regular employee, showing the required particulars. The dealer shall keep a counterfoil or duplicate of such tax invoice duly signed and dated. Failure to comply with the above will attract penalty.

Registration, Small Dealers and Composition Scheme: In the original proposal, registration of dealers with gross annual turnover above Rs. 5 lakh was made compulsory. There is a provision for voluntary registration. All existing dealers are supposed to be automatically registered under the VAT Act. A new dealer will be allowed some time from the date of liability to get registered. Small dealers with gross annual turnover not exceeding Rs. 5 lakh will not be liable to pay VAT.

The Empowered Committee has given the States flexibility to fix threshold limit. Small dealers with annual gross turnover not exceeding Rs. 50 lakh who are otherwise liable to pay VAT, may be given the option for a composition scheme with payment of tax at a small percentage of gross turnover. The dealers opting for this composition scheme will not be entitled to input tax credit.

Tax Payer's Identification Number (TIN): For better inter-state coordination, the Empowered Committee has suggested that there should be a Tax Payer's Identification Number, which will consist of 11 digit numerals throughout the country. The first two characters will represent the State Code as used by the Union Ministry of Home Affairs. The set-up of the next nine characters may, however, be different in different States.

Filing of Return: Under VAT, simplified form of returns will be notified. Returns are to be filed monthly/quarterly as specified in the State Acts/Rules, and will be accompanied with payment challans. Every return furnished by dealers will be scrutinized expeditiously within prescribed time limit from the date of filing the return. If any technical mistake is detected on scrutiny, the dealer will be required to pay the deficit appropriately.

Procedure of Self-Assessment of VAT Liability: The basic simplification in VAT, as the White Paper observes, is that VAT liability will be self-assessed by the dealers themselves in terms of submission of returns upon setting off the tax credit. Return forms as well as other procedures will be simple in all States. There will no longer be compulsory assessment at the end of each year as exists now. If no specific notice is issued proposing departmental audit of the books of accounts of the dealer within the time limit specified in the Act, the dealer will be deemed to have been self-assessed on the basis of returns submitted by him. Because of the importance of the concept of self-assessment in VAT, provision for "self-assessment" will be stated in the VAT Bills of the States.

Audit: In a system of self-assessment, provision for audit is important. The Empowered Committee provides that correctness of self-assessment will be checked through a system of Departmental Audit. A certain percentage of the dealers will be taken up for audit every year on a scientific basis. If, however, evasion is detected on audit, the concerned dealer may be taken up for audit for previous periods. This Audit Wing will remain delinked from tax collection wing to remove any bias. The audit team will conduct its work in a time bound manner and audit will be completed within six months. The audit report will be transparently sent to the dealer also.

This should be accompanied by a cross-checking. A computerized system is being worked out on the basis of coordination between the tax authorities of the State Governments and the authorities of Central Excise and Income Tax to compare constantly the tax returns and set-off documents of VAT system of the States and those of Central Excise and Income Tax. This comprehensive cross-checking system will help reduce tax evasion and also lead to significant growth of tax revenue. At the same time, by protecting transparently the interests of tax-complying dealers against the unfair practices of tax-evaders, the system will also bring in more equal competition in the sphere of trade and industry.

The Empowered Committee provides that the existing incentive schemes may be continued in the manner deemed appropriate by the States after ensuring that VAT chain is not affected. However, all other existing taxes such as turnover tax, surcharge, additional surcharge and Special Additional Tax (SAT) should be abolished. The Empowered Committee has left out Octroi from this stipulation.

Coverage of Goods under VAT: In the state-VAT scheme, all the goods, including declared goods will be covered and get the benefit of input tax credit. The only few goods which will be outside VAT will be liquor, lottery tickets, petrol, diesel, aviation turbine fuel and other motor spirit since their prices are not fully market determined. These will continue to be taxed under the Sales Tax Act or any other State Act or even by making special provisions in the VAT Act itself, and with uniform floor rates decided by the Empowered Committee.

VAT Rates and Classification of Commodities: The most important part of the VAT scheme relates to the tax rates. Under the VAT system covering about 550 goods, there will be only two basic VAT rates of 4 per cent and 12.5 per cent, plus a specific category of tax-exempted goods and a special VAT rate of 1 per cent only for gold and silver ornaments.

Under exempted category, there will be 46 commodities comprising natural and unprocessed products in the un-organized sector, items that are legally barred from taxation and items which have social implications. Under the state-VAT, there is the proposal to give flexibility to the states to select a set of maximum of

10 commodities for exemption from a list of goods specified by the Empowered Committee, which are of local social importance for the individual States without having any inter-state implications.

The rest of the commodities in the list are common for all the States. Under 4 per cent VAT rate category, there will be the largest number of goods (about 270), common for all the States, comprising items of basic necessities such as medicines and drugs, all agricultural and industrial inputs, capital goods and declared goods. The remaining commodities, common for all the States, will fall under the general VAT rate of 12.5 per cent.

It is proposed that VAT on AED items relating to sugar, textile and tobacco, because of initial organizational difficulties, will not be imposed for one year after the introduction of VAT and till then the existing arrangement will continue.

The Empowered Committee Empowered Committee is of the opinion that this proposed VAT system will be able to rationalize the tax burden and stop unhealthy tax-rate "war" and trade diversion among the States, which had adversely affected interests of all the States in the past. It will also bring in simplicity and transparency in the tax structure, thereby improving tax-compliance and eventually also the revenue growth, as mentioned in the beginning.

The highlights of the scheme proposed in the White Paper are captured in Box 7.1.

7.7 Progress by States

According to available information, 21 states have launched VAT broadly consistent with the design recommended by the Empowered Committee. The states have initiated, and in many cases also completed, steps for computerization up to the levels of assessing officers and also at the check posts. This process will continue since this is extremely important for document-based verification and integration with Taxation Information Exchange System as well as with information of the Central excise and income tax systems as indicated earlier. In order to support the states, and protect them against revenue loss, in the initial years of transition, the central government has agreed to compensate for 100 per cent of the loss in the first year, 75 per cent of the loss in the second year and 50 per cent of the loss in the third year of introduction of VAT, and the loss would be computed on the basis of an agreed formula.

The Empowered Committee emphasizes that after introduction of VAT, there is need for phasing out of Central Sales Tax (CST). However, the states are now collecting a large sum every year from CST. There is accordingly a need of compensation from the Government of India for this loss of revenue as CST is phased out. Moreover, while CST is phased out, there is also a critical need for putting in place a regulatory frame-work in terms of Taxation Information Exchange System to give a comprehensive picture of inter-State trade of all commodities. As already mentioned, this process of setting up of Taxation Information Exchange System has already been started by the Empowered Committee, and is expected to be completed within one year. The position regarding CST will be reviewed by the Empowered Committee during 2005-06, and suitable decision on the phasing out of CST will be taken.

Box 7.1 Highlights of White Paper on State Level VAT

- Introduction of VAT would help avoid cascading nature of sales tax.
- Present multiple rates and taxes can converge into a few rates and a single VAT
- Transparency in the system of tax administration through simple self-assessments and departmental audit.
- Nationalization of taxes to result in lower tax burden and higher tax revenues.
- To avoid tax competition, the design of state VAT needs to be harmonized even as the distinctive needs of individual states are recognized.
- State VAT to have two basic rates of 4 per cent and 12.5 per cent and to over 550 commodities.
- About 270 commodities will be under 4 per cent rate.
- 46 items, comprising natural and unprocessed products in the unorganized sector, items legally barred and items having social implications, are exempt from VAT.
- Gold and silver ornaments subject to a special VAT rate of 1 percent

Source: *Economic Survey*, 2004-05

It is also essential to bring imports into the VAT chain. Because of the set-off, this will not result in any tax cascading effect, but will only improve tax compliance. A proposal for VAT on imports, including the collection mechanism with adequate safeguards for the protection of interest of land-locked States, is being discussed with the Government of India. Similarly, discussion between the Empowered Committee and the Government of India is going on for an early decision on the question of collection and appropriation of service tax by the Centre and the States. If decisions on VAT on imports and service tax are taken expeditiously at the national level, then these two important spheres of taxation can be integrated, along with the items subject to the additional excise duty, into the VAT system of the States from the second year of introduction of VAT.

It may be noted that this VAT design has been worked out by the Empowered Committee to strike a balance not only between the common points of convergence and federal flexibility, but also a balance between short term and medium term objectives in the context of the VAT system. For successful implementation of State-level VAT, close interaction with trade and industry is especially important. The Empowered Committee has therefore also set up a Consultative Committee with one representative from each of the national level trade organizations and national level chambers of commerce and industry. This process of interaction will continue regularly to discuss issues and sort out problems of implementation of VAT. Such Consultative Committees will also be set up at the level of each State, and interaction with the State Government will take place in a similarly regular manner.

There are some important points on the ground-level implementation of VAT which have been raised by the representatives of trade and industry. A comprehensive campaign based on written materials as well as publicity through all media is necessary to educate the dealers as well as the tax administrators.

7.8 Goods and Services Tax

A long-term solution is needed in respect of the problem of fragmentation of the taxation space between goods and services and the fact that cross cascading cannot be fully avoided as long as these are subject to separate taxation regimes. The Task Force recently appointed by the central government to examine the medium term fiscal restructuring came out with a plan of restructuring central finances that also involved the levy a comprehensive Goods and Services Tax (GST).

The Task Force argues that vide article 268A, the power to tax services has been vested in the central government. Further, the value-added in the case of goods beyond manufacturing is in the nature of trade arising from wholesaling or retailing, which can be considered as a service. The centre, according to the Task Forces is therefore entitled to tax this value added. At the same time, states are not entitled to tax services as the subject is in the Union list. However, under article 268 A the taxation of services can be assigned fully or partially to the states. The Task Force then suggests that a 'grand bargain' can then be proposed to the states whereby they may agree to participate in a national Goods and Services Tax (GST), which can be levied at the rate of 20 per cent, of which the centre will levy 12 per cent and states can levy 8 per cent. As per the estimates provided by the Task Force, these changes will have significant revenue implications.

However, there are several problems with the Task Force's recommendation of GST under a 'grand bargain'. First, the legal status of centre's power to tax value added of goods interpreted as services has been questioned. It is a matter that can lead to legal issues, once the actual legislation is made and notified. Secondly, the 12: 8 ratio in favor of the centre, as suggested by the Task Force, can increase the vertical imbalance in the system, particularly because stamp fees, registration duties and sales tax on works contracts will be merged under the GST. The states are also likely to lose the autonomy to fix rates, which is the essence having autonomy over tax bases. Thirdly, aspects of inter-state taxation of services raise additional problems. It has been argued that there is the need for a negative list of taxes that have an inter-state character. The proposal of a clearing house mechanism to address issues of inter-state taxation and settlement of rebate claims and counter claims may run into a variety of practical problems. Fourthly, inefficiencies may well increase, if decisions to spend are totally divorced from decisions to tax. Finally, the status of divisibility of the tax on services will remain open-ended as these will not be subject to sharing under article 270, and therefore, not under the recommendations of the Finance Commission.

Commenting on the proposal for GST, the TFC observes, "In our view, the proposal of a comprehensive GST is an attractive one, and should be pursued. However, the relevant legal and administrative aspects should be extensively discussed, particularly with the states. The implementation of a state-level VAT would facilitate its introduction in due course. However, even without this radical change, it should be possible to raise the tax-GDP ratio adequately."

7.9 Recent Developments in Implementing State Level VAT in Federal Systems

In recent years, particularly while dealing with problems of cross-border trade in the European countries, some new concepts have been proposed. The first effort was that by Versano in 1995. It was in the context of the attempts to convert the origin based VATs of Brazil into the destination system. The original Versano proposal came to be known as compensating VAT (CVAT). An alternative formulation to attend to the same problems was proposed by Keen and Smith in 1996, which came to be known as the Viable Integrated VAT (VIVAT). Yet another alternative was proposed by Bird and Gendron in 1998, which is referred to as the Dual VAT (DVAT).

The main characteristics of the Versano proposal as modified by Mclure Jr. (2000) may be described s follows:

1. There is uniform definition of the state and federal tax base.

2. There is uniform administration including all the relevant laws.
3. The VAT rates are set by the individual states (in the original proposal, there was to be the same VAT rate in all states).
4. There is zero rating of all inter state exports in respect of the state VAT.
5. There is application of the compensating VAT to all inter-state exports.
6. There is a system of deferred payment of state VAT on inter state imports by registered dealers in respect of state VAT.
7. A system of credit for the compensating VAT on inter-state imports by the registered dealers is provided

In this case, the federal government levies both the federal VAT and the Compensating VAT.

The VIVAT proposal was formulated particularly in the context of the inter-country trade of EU member countries. In this, there is no federal VAT. The objective is to maintain the destination principle. VAT is entirely assigned to the member countries/states. There is compliance cost symmetry, in the sense that VAT compliance costs on intra-EU trade are similar to VAT compliance costs on corresponding domestic supply. There is no requirement of a central administration. The VIVAT scheme proposes to establish a uniform Union wide rate of VAT for all intermediate purchases, that is, for sales between registered dealers. This would be applied to transactions within a member state to sales between member states, thus continuing the VAT chain across intra-EU borders.

	Dual VAT	CVAT	VIVAT
Rate autonomy	Yes	Some	Some
Central rate setting	No	Some	Some
Collection incentive	Some	Unknown	Unknown
Compliance symmetry	No	No	Yes
Identify destination state	No	No	Yes
Administrative cost	Low	Higher	Highest?
Distinguish type of purchases	No	Yes	Yes
Credit tracking	No	No	Yes
Excess credits	Few	Some	Yes
Needed administrative capacity	High	Low	High
Central agency	Yes	Yes	No

Source: Bird and Gendron (2000).

In the dual VAT system, the existence of a federal VAT is required. But the member-states are free to set their VAT rates. The central VAT is included in the tax base of the sub-national VAT, which provides a direct financial incentive to apply correctly the central VAT, if they are collecting it. Bird and Gendron (2000) provide a summary of the main differences between the three alternative systems proposed to take care of the problems of inter-state in a federal kind of set-up.

In India, VAT has to evolve over time. In the medium term, the movement is towards a dual VAT with both tiers free to fix their rates. As yet, a viable solution to the taxation of inter-state sales has not been found. The problem of integrating taxation of goods and services in an integral framework also remains.

Part III: Issues in Government Expenditure

8

Trends in Expenditure: Combined and Central Government

> Getting the right size of the government, and the right composition of government expenditure with a view to facilitating achievement of highest attainable growth rates, and meeting governments' social obligations including poverty reduction and provision of health and education should be considered integral to any plan for restructuring public finances.
>
> Report of the Twelfth Finance Commission

In this chapter, we look at the trends in expenditures. The first part deals with trends in the combined expenditures of central and state governments. In the second part, we focus only on the expenditures of the central government. Expenditures in the Indian budgets are classified in several ways. First, there is the distinction between revenue and capital expenditures, which broadly correspond to expenditure that may classified as consumption expenditure as against that, which may be judged to be investment expenditure leading to creation of assets, physical and financial.

A typical budget in India generally will have three broad categories of expenditures: general, social, and economic. The general category consists of heads including general administration, interest payments and pensions. The social services include expenditures on education, health, water supply and sanitation, and the social security programmes. The economic services include agriculture, industry, roads, energy, transport, etc. There is also the distinction between developmental and non-development expenditures. By convention, all expenditures on social and economic heads are considered developmental while that on general services are considered non-developmental. There is also the important distinction between plan and non-plan expenditure. Plan expenditure is taken to be incremental development expenditure while non-plan expenditures are committed expenditures. While these categories were designed to keep an eye on the productive expenditures, excessive categorisation in practice has also led to many inefficiencies. Conventionally, capital expenditure, development expenditure, and plan expenditure were considered to be in some sense the more desirable expenditures. In this chapter, we look at some of the trends in expenditures, including changes in the structure to consider whether changes have been efficiency augmenting and whether governments have been enabled to fulfil their responsibilities by the kind of level and structure of expenditures, they have maintained.

8.1 Trends in Combined Expenditures

We begin by examining the trends in the combined expenditures of central and state governments net of intergovernmental flows. The main flows are transfers made by the central to the state governments and interest payments made by the states to the central government. We first look at the combined total expenditures and trends relating to the broad aggregates of revenue and capital expenditures in relation to GDP as also their relative shares in total expenditure. We then look at the revenue expenditure in greater detail. The relevant data are given in Appendix Table A8.1. Chart 8.1 describes the growing chasm between the shares of revenue and capital expenditures in total expenditures.

Although in the early years beginning from 1950-51, the share of revenue expenditure was large, it began to come down, and the share capital expenditure started to increase. This process continued until the late fifties, and again during the late seventies. At their highest, capital expenditure accounted for 38.9 per cent in 1957-58, 38 per cent in 1964-65, and 32 per cent in 1980-81. Since then, the share of capital expenditure has been on a continuous decline. It became as low as 12 per cent in 2000-01 and the years immediately after. There is thus a clear trend of declining capital expenditures, mirrored in the rise of the share of revenue expenditures. There is a degree of compulsion in the revenue expenditures as salary payments, pensions, and interest payments are all in the nature of committed expenditures. It is possible to say that revenue expenditures have crowded out capital expenditures in a context, as noted in the chapter on fiscal trends, where total expenditures stagnated due to stagnation or decline in the revenue receipts relative to GDP.

Looking at revenue expenditures as percentage of GDP, one notices a secular rise. Revenue expenditure rose from 7.3 per cent of GDP in 1950-51 to 9.81 per cent in 1960-61, 12.52 per cent in 1970-71, 16.5 per cent in 1980-81, 21.62 per cent in 1990-91, and 23.23 per cent of GDP in 2000-01. The rise has been particularly sharp in the seventies and nineties. Chart 8.2 shows the time profile of revenue, capital, and total expenditure as percentage of GDP.

It has been noted in an earlier chapter, that the size of the government as measured by total expenditure had peaked in the late eighties. It fell to a level of 23.5 per cent in 1996-97, but has started increasing again. A similar trend was followed by the revenue expenditures but to a lesser degree. In their case, a local peak occurred in 1987-88 at 21.8 per cent. After that there is an imperceptible fall. These have remained marginally above 21 per cent until 1997-98.

Chart 8.1: Share of Revenue and Capital Expenditures in Combined Expenditure

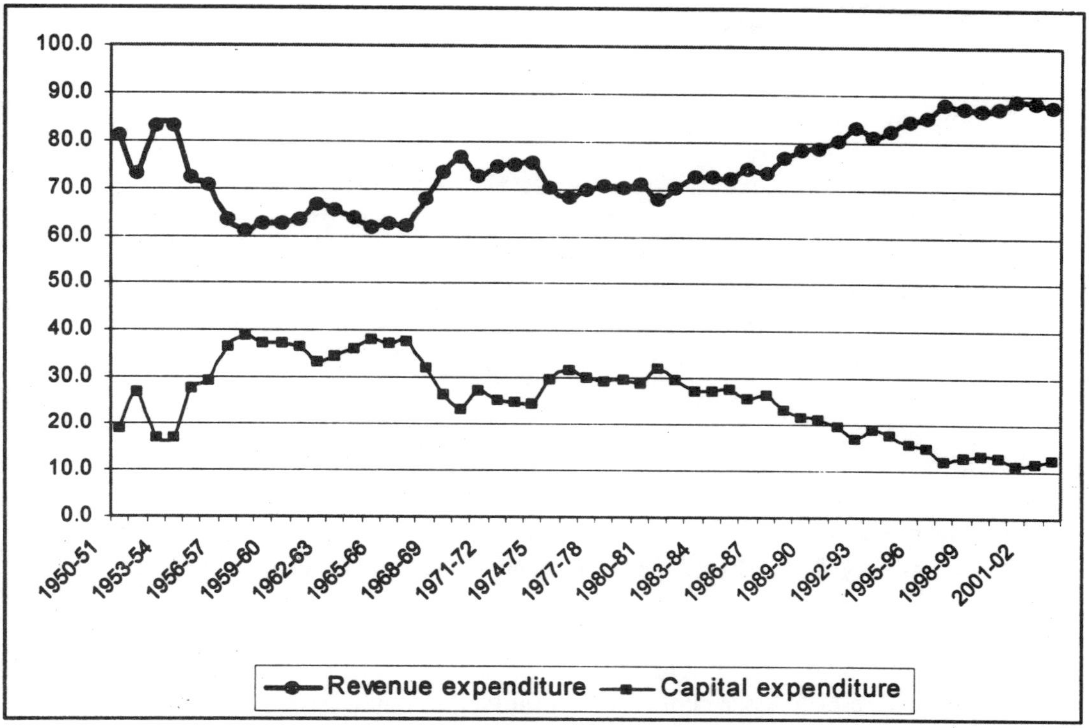

Chart 8.2: Combined Revenue, Capital and Total Expenditure as % of GDP

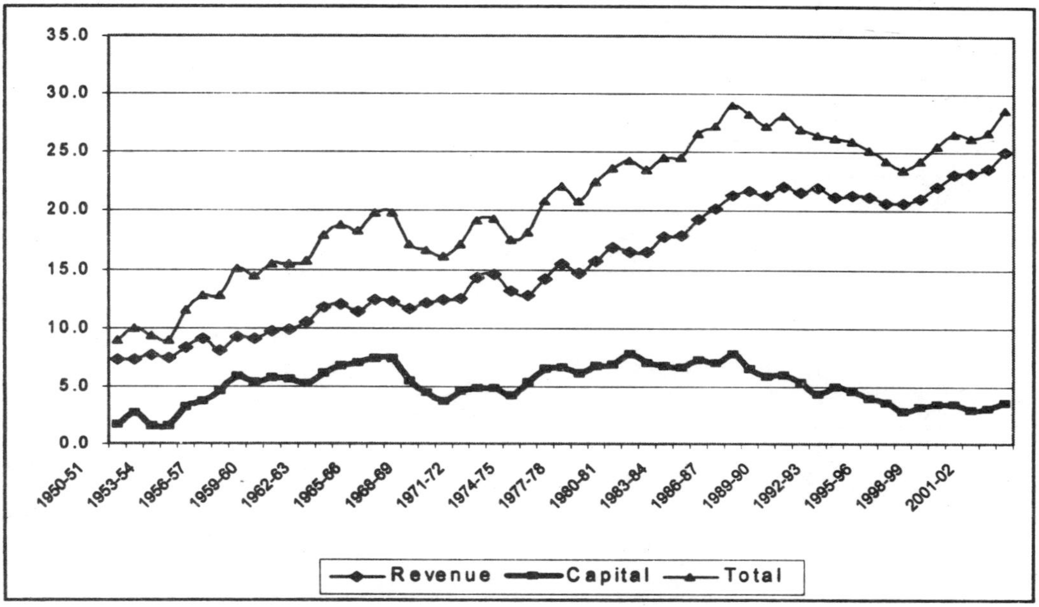

After that year, there is a sharp increase. This is often attributed to the impact on salary payments following the recommendations of the Fifth Central Pay Commission. It is also due to the mounting debt of the central and state governments and high cost of borrowing. Capital expenditure as percentage of GDP fell to levels close to those obtained in the fifties.

8.2 Trends and Structure of Combined Revenue Expenditure

Given the overwhelming importance of the revenue expenditures, we now consider a decomposition of revenue expenditures in terms of selected broad heads. Table 8.1 shows the relative share of major aggregates of expenditure as percentage of total revenue expenditure on the combined account of the central and state governments. The period covered is from 1974-75 to 2002-03. Interest payments rise from about 10 per cent in 1975-76 to 26 percent by 2001-02. In contrast, the share of defence expenditure has come down in terms of the relative share in total revenue expenditure, falling from 19.4 per cent in 1974-75 to 7.4 per cent in 2002-03. This implies a fall of nearly 12 percentage points of total expenditure. Pensions also show a secular rise, increasing from 1.2 per cent in 1974-75 to 7.2 percent in 2002-03. Among the social services, education has commanded a small share as also medical and public health. The share of education in the combined revenue expenditure was 15.8 per cent in 1974-75. It has come down to 11.9 per cent by 2004-05. In the case of medical and public health, the share at 5.6 per cent of the combined revenue expenditure was small to begin with. It has come down further to 4 per cent in 2002-03.

Table 8.1: Structure of Combined Revenue Expenditure of Central and State Governments: Profile over Time (Per cent to Total)

Year	Interest payments	Defence	Pensions	Education	Medical and public health
1974-75	11.825	19.432	1.174	15.770	5.624
1975-76	9.799	19.002	1.357	15.246	5.260
1976-77	12.612	13.851	1.418	14.363	5.163
1977-78	11.620	15.021	1.456	15.077	5.546
1978-79	12.623	15.068	1.501	14.709	5.609
1979-80	13.091	15.197	1.507	13.901	5.672
1980-81	12.469	14.931	1.667	14.375	5.862
1981-82	13.441	14.956	1.826	14.149	5.930

Contd...

1982-83	13.861	14.594	1.898	14.292	5.757
1983-84	14.113	14.479	1.955	13.933	5.892
1984-85	14.500	13.521	2.054	0.203	5.546
1985-86	15.360	13.478	2.102	13.397	5.432
1986-87	16.001	14.909	2.179	12.943	5.409
1987-88	16.868	11.022	4.575	13.671	5.387
1988-89	18.304	10.638	4.593	13.508	5.203
1989-90	19.035	9.465	4.491	24.062	4.882
1990-91	20.338	8.844	4.216	13.674	4.871
1991-92	21.594	7.971	4.277	12.985	4.577
1992-93	22.548	7.613	4.650	13.114	4.682
1993-94	23.199	8.165	4.663	12.899	4.703
1994-95	24.198	7.654	5.704	12.525	4.581
1995-96	23.997	7.670	4.954	12.801	4.538
1996-97	24.730	7.425	5.282	12.793	4.527
1997-98	24.460	8.150	5.775	12.834	4.723
1998-99	24.030	7.750	6.815	13.336	4.733
1999-00	24.541	7.853	8.255	13.826	4.462
2000-01	25.298	7.672	7.997	12.883	4.253
2001-02	26.262	7.094	7.516	12.384	4.079
2002-03	25.860	6.652	7.116	11.861	3.996

Source: (Basic Data): *Indian Public Finance Statistics*.

Table 8.2 describes the relative share of major items under the economic services in aggregate revenue expenditure of the centre and states. Agriculture had a share of 7.6 per cent in 1974-75, witnessed a small rise until the mid nineties, and has then experienced a fall. Industry has a share of les than two percent in 1974-75, which increases only marginally. The share of transport has remained almost stagnant. The power and irrigation sectors, considered together, show a rise in their share in the combined revenue expenditure, rising from less than one per cent in 1974-75 to close to 4 per cent in recent years.

In summary, the following may be highlighted as the main trends characterizing the changes in the structure of the combined expenditures of the central and state governments.

1. The share of revenue expenditure in total expenditure has risen steadily over time. This increase has been particularly sharp in the nineties. There has been a corresponding fall in the share of capital expenditure.

Table 8.2: Share of Economic Services in Combined Revenue Expenditure of Central and State Governments: Profile over Time (Per cent to Total)

Year	Agriculture	Industry and Minerals	Power and irrigation	Transport	Public Works
1974-75	7.570	1.867	0.806	3.150	0.982
1975-76	7.466	2.482	0.833	2.984	0.719
1976-77	7.723	2.278	0.884	3.292	0.552
1977-78	8.435	2.844	0.974	3.152	0.466
1978-79	9.335	2.177	1.238	3.590	0.556
1979-80	9.653	2.646	1.074	3.718	0.758
1980-81	9.787	2.502	1.668	3.680	0.748
1981-82	9.677	2.886	1.214	3.533	0.713
1982-83	9.681	2.657	1.284	3.138	0.728
1983-84	9.875	2.326	0.956	2.972	0.645
1984-85	10.546	3.286	1.604	2.915	0.729
1985-86	8.100	2.613	2.836	2.744	0.722
1986-87	8.258	2.730	2.335	2.459	0.741
1987-88	8.708	2.831	2.567	2.497	0.793
1988-89	8.592	2.485	2.389	2.339	0.732
1989-90	8.491	2.785	2.262	2.811	0.733
1990-91	8.985	2.010	2.195	2.142	0.735
1991-92	8.563	1.710	5.500	2.353	0.661
1992-93	9.097	1.908	3.548	2.401	0.710
1993-94	8.945	1.857	3.849	2.410	0.681
1994-95	8.891	1.418	3.517	2.325	0.601
1995-96	8.396	1.525	3.506	1.952	0.630
1996-97	7.808	1.842	4.770	2.111	0.652
1997-98	7.657	1.302	3.710	2.146	0.667
1998-99	8.004	1.221	3.475	2.068	0.572
1999-00	7.522	1.305	3.171	2.354	0.616
2000-01	6.475	1.146	3.950	3.293	0.635
2001-02	6.517	1.175	4.309	3.455	0.603
2002-03	6.945	2.511	3.854	3.135	0.480

Source: (Basic Data): *Indian Public Finance Statistics.*

2. This increase in revenue expenditure has been due primarily to a rise in interest payments relative to GDP.

3. Among general services, defense expenditure has gone down in terms of relative importance in the revenue expenditures, while the share of pensions has gone up.
4. Among social services, there has been a fall in the share of education and health since 1974-75.
5. Among economic services, agriculture and transport have had the larger share. Particularly, the share of power and irrigation sectors has increased.

8.3 Analysis of Central Expenditure

We now look at the salient changes in the profile of central expenditures. It is important to trace the evolution of centre's revenue and capital expenditures that are shown in Appendix Table A8.2. The long term profile is also depicted in Chart 8.3. It is indicated that the pattern of rise of revenue expenditure at the cost of capital expenditure has been even sharper than that in the case the combined expenditures. In fact there was a period in which capital expenditures were almost as important as the revenue expenditures and the two curves met in the late sixties. However, the period beyond these years indicates first a patch in which the two shares remain stable. After that there is a secular fall in the share of capital expenditures, which is mirrored in the rise of the share of revenue expenditure that is clearly very sharp towards the end of the nineties.

Chart 8.3: Central Expenditures: Relative Shares of Revenue and Capital Expenditures in Total Central Expenditure

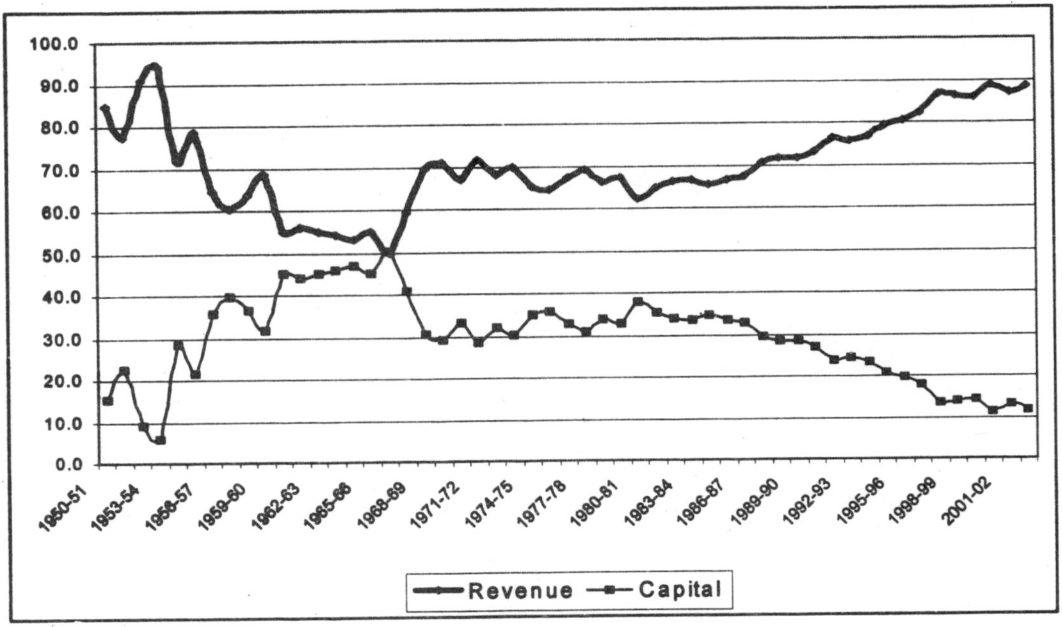

As mentioned earlier, expenditures are also classified into the broad categories of developmental and non developmental expenditures. This is taken to indicate quality expenditures as compared to compulsory expenditures which may not be critical for development. However this perception is not entirely correct because general services including law and order and general administration are quite important for development. Bearing this qualification in mind, we also look at the profile of developmental and non-developmental expenditures, on the revenue account, in terms of their share in central revenue expenditures. Except for the first few years in the period after 1974-75, these expenditure categories indicate roughly stable shares with that of developmental expenditure being in the range of 34-35 percent and that of non developmental expenditure in the range of 65-66 per cent for most years. There has been however some increase in the share of non developmental expenditures in more recent years (Table 8.3).

Table 8.3: Structure of Central Revenue Expenditure: Developmental and Non-developmental (As percent of Total Central Revenue Expenditure)

Year	Developmental	Non-developmental	Total (Rs. crore)
1974-75	23.467	68.869	5,713.76
1975-76	26.701	66.283	7,071.14
1976-77	28.021	64.930	8,319.98
1977-78	32.199	60.361	9,161.79
1978-79	34.790	58.699	10,711.07
1979-80	35.464	62.045	11,755.40
1980-81	33.927	63.525	13,260.75
1981-82	33.885	63.806	15,433.12
1982-83	34.906	62.718	18,761.12
1983-84	35.074	62.831	22,114.69
1984-85	36.339	61.653	27,046.98
1985-86	34.906	61.897	33,608.39
1986-87	34.542	63.072	40,725.85
1987-88	36.398	60.797	46,167.02
1988-89	36.910	60.567	54,106.70
1989-90	38.525	58.977	64,010.78
1990-91	36.084	59.294	73,556.78
1991-92	35.350	60.462	82,290.80

Contd...

1992-93	34.517	61.324	92,691.85
1993-94	32.529	63.752	1,08,499.83
1994-95	33.275	65.334	1,22,346.70
1995-96	30.355	65.861	1,39,714.95
1996-97	30.198	66.441	1,58,810.74
1997-98	30.473	67.807	1,79,996.53
1998-99	29.655	68.779	2,16,417.41
1999-00	29.482	68.996	2,48,869.34
2000-01	29.042	66.793	2,77,975.49
2001-02	29.563	66.165	3,01,774.76
2002-03 RE	31.921	64.434	3,42,261.26

Source: (Basic Data): *Indian Public Finance Statistics.*

8.4 Profile of Relative Shares in Revenue Expenditures: General Services

We now review the changing structure of the revenue expenditures of the central government. Important among the general services are interest payments, defence services, administrative services and pensions and other retirement benefits. As expected, the share of interest payments in total central expenditure has gone up from 17.5 percent in 1974-75 to a peak of more than 37 percent in 1996-97. It has come down marginally after that period primarily due to a fall in the nominal interest rates. As noted earlier, defence expenditures show a secular fall in their share of total central revenue expenditure. However, defence also gets a tangible share in the capital expenditures. The share of pensions has increased but it is less than the share of pensions noted in the case of combined expenditures indicating that it is the states that are bearing the larger burden of the increase in the pension payments (Table 8.4).

Table 8.4: Structure of Central Revenue Expenditure: Selected General Service Heads (As percent of Total Central Revenue Expenditure)

Year	Interest payments	Defence services	Administ-rative. services	Pension and others retire-ment. benefits	Other non-developmental expenditures
1974-75	17.515	33.607	5.712	0.342	11.693
1975-76	17.369	31.836	5.505	0.380	11.194
1976-77	16.520	28.212	4.806	0.384	15.008
1977-78	16.605	26.042	4.600	0.389	12.724

Contd...

1978-79	17.076	24.404	4.233	0.432	12.554
1979-80	18.799	26.317	4.115	0.467	12.348
1980-81	19.639	26.698	4.351	0.561	12.276
1981-82	20.700	27.002	4.334	0.553	11.217
1982-83	20.988	26.020	4.068	0.518	11.123
1983-84	21.685	25.624	3.722	0.539	11.261
1984-85	22.089	23.660	3.684	0.566	11.653
1985-86	22.326	22.471	3.525	0.582	12.993
1986-87	22.703	24.230	3.688	0.566	11.884
1987-88	24.371	18.386	3.765	4.241	10.035
1988-89	26.389	17.665	3.707	3.723	9.082
1989-90	27.741	15.926	3.654	3.635	8.021
1990-91	29.227	14.783	3.899	2.907	8.478
1991-92	32.319	13.904	3.846	2.936	7.456
1992-93	33.526	13.063	4.689	3.242	6.805
1993-94	33.862	13.804	4.001	3.077	9.008
1994-95	36.012	13.426	4.335	2.986	8.575
1995-96	35.819	13.485	4.326	3.069	9.161
1996-97	37.452	13.221	4.458	3.208	8.102
1997-98	36.466	14.542	4.614	3.823	8.362
1998-99	35.987	13.798	4.594	4.647	9.753
1999-00	36.264	14.150	4.614	5.740	8.227
2000-01	35.728	13.396	4.821	5.116	7.732
2001-02	35.609	12.612	4.641	3.829	9.473
2002-03 RE	33.891	12.005	4.439	3.486	10.614

Source: (Basic Data): *Indian Public Finance Statistics.*

8.5 Profile of Central Expenditures: Share of Social Service Heads

Social services, in terms of their relative importance, do not carry a large weight in the revenue expenditures of the centre. The largest social sector for the central government is education. The share of education in total central expenditure has gone up only marginally. Other social sectors claim a smaller share, which have remained stable (Table 8.5).

Table 8.5: Structure of Central Revenue Expenditure: Selected Social Service Heads (As percent of Total Central Revenue Expenditure)

Year	Education	Scientific & research	Medical and public health	Family welfare
1974-75	2.614	1.961	1.204	1.025
1975-76	2.700	1.896	1.638	1.702
1976-77	2.568	1.874	1.317	1.786
1977-78	2.563	1.863	1.541	0.956
1978-79	2.515	1.759	1.462	0.960
1979-80	2.237	1.741	1.332	0.922
1980-81	2.210	1.671	1.189	0.957
1981-82	2.217	1.884	1.313	1.093
1982-83	2.296	1.927	1.140	1.571
1983-84	2.160	1.851	1.109	1.701
1984-85	2.202	1.887	1.087	1.565
1985-86	2.188	1.972	1.039	1.442
1986-87	2.132	1.825	1.061	1.285
1987-88	3.563	1.710	0.935	1.245
1988-89	3.552	1.794	0.979	1.169
1989-90	2.962	1.686	0.988	1.017
1990-91	2.781	1.589	0.961	1.068
1991-92	2.632	1.621	0.865	1.044
1992-93	2.478	1.533	0.960	1.115
1993-94	2.344	1.514	0.881	1.298
1994-95	2.246	1.456	0.916	1.252
1995-96	2.529	1.392	1.030	1.098
1996-97	2.464	1.427	0.970	0.992
1997-98	2.731	1.513	1.063	1.012
1998-99	3.090	1.404	1.081	1.077
1999-00	3.097	1.315	1.066	1.244
2000-01	2.996	1.312	1.113	1.117
2001-02	2.822	1.415	1.105	1.178
2002-03 RE	2.648	1.420	0.995	1.089

Source: (Basic Data): *Indian Public Finance Statistics.*

8.6 Share of Economic Services in Central Expenditures

It is the economic services, which have a larger share in the case of central revenue expenditures. The industrial sector has the largest share followed by the agricultural sector, transport and communications, fertilizer subsidies, and power, irrigation and flood control. In 2002-03, the share of industry was 3.6 per cent and that of transport and communications also at this level. The fertiliser subsidies had a share 2.2 per cent in centre's revenue expenditure in 2002-03. The share of agriculture was 5.6 per cent in centre's revenue expenditures, having risen from 2.5 per cent in 1974-75 (Table 8.6).

Table 8.6: Structure of Central Expenditure: Selected Economic Service Heads (As percent of Central Revenue Expenditure)

Year	Agriculture and allied services	Industry & minerals	Fertiliser subsidies	Power, irrig. and flood control	Transport & communica-tions
1974-75	2.249	2.357		0.312	1.746
1975-76	2.270	3.366		0.306	1.826
1976-77	2.059	2.909	0.719	0.430	1.565
1977-78	2.788	3.742	1.171	0.504	1.528
1978-79	3.246	2.503	1.617	0.426	1.766
1979-80	2.743	3.273	2.729	0.220	2.133
1980-81	2.463	2.987	1.282	0.358	2.160
1981-82	2.656	3.616	1.782	0.396	2.106
1982-83	2.786	3.290	2.932	0.549	2.035
1983-84	2.781	2.481	4.070	0.763	1.876
1984-85	2.769	4.212	4.437	0.499	1.771
1985-86	2.282	2.793	4.761	0.214	1.789
1986-87	2.578	2.891	4.658	0.261	1.424
1987-88	2.273	3.224	4.687	0.264	1.355
1988-89	2.795	2.594	5.916	0.567	1.374
1989-90	5.741	3.100	7.096	0.381	2.474
1990-91	4.313	2.023	5.982	0.511	1.267
1991-92	4.511	1.538	5.833	0.658	1.278
1992-93	4.449	1.866	6.253	0.314	1.346
1993-94	4.542	1.853	4.205	0.397	1.461
1994-95	5.997	1.126	4.284	0.450	1.481

Contd...

1995-96	6.205	1.302	4.463	0.418	1.295
1996-97	5.630	1.942	3.719	0.433	1.254
1997-98	5.692	1.233	4.068	0.546	1.352
1998-99	5.518	1.185	3.607	0.622	1.383
1999-00	5.276	1.522	3.601	0.644	2.036
2000-01	4.592	1.194	3.415	0.668	3.746
2001-02	4.976	1.274	2.681	0.799	4.226
2002-03 RE	5.614	3.614	2.194	0.702	3.559

Source: (Basic Data): *Indian Public Finance Statistics.*

In summary, the main trends characterizing the expenditure profile may be summarised as below:

1. Revenue expenditures, having a large share to begin with in 1974-75, the centre's total expenditures have increased in relative importance.
2. This has been driven largely by the rise in interest payments, which claimed in 2002-03 nearly 37 per cent of centre's revenues expenditures.
3. Social services do not have a large share in centre's revenue expenditure profile. The largest sector within the social sector is education.
4. Among the economic sectors, agriculture has the largest share, but industry and minerals, transport and communications are also quite important.
5. The transport and communications head has witnessed a sharp rise since the early nineties.

8.7 Expenditure Reforms

The structure of expenditures requires restructuring at the level both of the centre and the states. In particular, larger government expenditure in the form of capital expenditures, focus on the primary services that the government should provide including public goods like general administration and merit goods like education and health would require restructuring of the government expenditures. Such restructuring would be possible only if the debt-burden and consequently the claim of interest payments in revenue expenditures is brought down. The Twelfth Finance Commission has recently reviewed these trends and suggested a programme of restructuring. The TFC has suggested a broad restructuring of public finances aimed at macroeconomic stabilization and achieving revenue account balance. The impact of the size and composition of government expenditure on growth, inflation, interest rate and the external account has to be considered in a framework that takes into account relevant interrelationships and feedbacks. We summarise below some of the main suggestions made by the TFC.

In restructuring expenditures, the TFC observes that there is need to make reference to the basic objectives of government intervention in economic activities, as also to the basic objectives for the assignment of responsibilities as between central and sub-national governments. It is also important to relate government expenditures to outcomes in terms of the quality, reach, and impact of government services. This would be facilitated, according to the TFC, if governments focus more on their primary responsibilities rather than spreading resources thinly in many areas where the private sector can provide the necessary services.

The primary role of government, it should be realized, is to provide public goods like defence, law and order, and general administration as public goods. This represents one kind of market failure. The role of governments extends to merit goods and services with large positive externalities like education and health. The services should be assigned to the central government if the scope of public goods is nation wide like defence. The services get assigned to state governments if the scope of the public good is limited to regions or if externalities are more local in character like the health services. The TFC has suggested some guiding principles of expenditure reforms, as indicated in the following discussion.

8.8 From Expenditures to Outcomes

The conventional budget exercises have focused on allocation of resources to different heads, without taking into account how these government expenditures get translated into outputs and outcomes. This should change. Outputs are the direct result of government expenditure and outcomes are the final results. In the case of education, opening a new school or appointing a new teacher is an output and reduction in the rate of illiteracy is an outcome. Issues of efficiency require consideration whether the same outcome can be achieved at lower costs and whether then same costs can produce better outcomes.

A critical part of budgetary reforms, according to the TFC, must include information on the relationship between expenditures and the corresponding performance in producing real results as in determining the size of the budget and its allocation among different heads. Although in the past there have been attempts at introducing performance budgeting, such endeavors have receded in importance. There is need to emphasise performance budgeting, both for the centre and the states. In summary, the management of public expenditures should be guided by economy, efficiency, and effectiveness.

8.9 Shift towards Productive Capital Expenditure

In the proposed restructuring plan of the TFC, the level of capital expenditure, on the combined account of the centre and the states relative to GDP, is set to rise to about 7 per cent of GDP by 2009-10. The TFC has indicated that this capital expenditure is meant for administrative departments and departmental enterprises. The increase in capital expenditure is for augmenting investment and building physical assets for the various publicly provided services and should be aimed at promoting growth and improving the quality of services provided by the central and state governments. The increase in capital should not be wasted for covering losses of non-departmental public enterprises, by contributing to their share capital, or for servicing debt arising from off-budget borrowing.

8.10 Government Salaries

The biggest cause of increase in revenue expenditures, apart from interest payments has been the rise in the share of salary expenditures. The problem is quite acute for the states. There is need to control growth of salary expenditures by linking it to the growth of state economy and the growth of state government's revenue receipts. We have discussed this issue further in the next Chapter.

8.11 Pension Reforms

Equally important are pension reforms. The TFC observes that the pension payments constitute an important component of committed expenditures in the central and state budgets. The central government has taken steps for pension reforms, particularly in respect of new appointments by providing for a defined contribution pension scheme. This has taken effect from January 1, 2004 for Central Government employees recruited on or after that date, (except Armed Forces, in the first stage). It has replaced the existing defined benefit pension system. The central government has also initiated the process for bringing out legislation for the appointment of an independent pension regulatory authority, which can ensure proper investment of pension funds. The Pension Fund regulator will have the responsibility of regulating, promoting and ensuring the orderly growth of the pension funds. The pension liabilities in the case of the states account for a larger share of its revenue receipts, and this share may increase further in view of the increasing longevity and the number of appointments in the late sixties and early seventies, when the size of state governments was expanding. The TFC has recommended that the state governments also need to take up initiatives similar to those of the central government for pension reforms.

Appendix Table A8.1: Combined Revenue and Capital Expenditure: Relative Shares and as Percentage of GDP

Year	As percentage of Total Expenditure		As percentage of GDP		
	Revenue	Capital	Revenue	Capital	Total
1950-51	81.09	18.91	7.302	1.702	9.004
1951-52	72.98	27.02	7.254	2.685	9.940
1952-53	82.96	17.04	7.709	1.583	9.292
1953-54	82.99	17.01	7.421	1.521	8.942
1954-55	72.48	27.52	8.362	3.175	11.537
1955-56	70.72	29.28	9.047	3.746	12.794
1956-57	63.55	36.45	8.103	4.647	12.749
1957-58	61.10	38.90	9.238	5.883	15.121
1558-59	62.84	37.16	9.036	5.344	14.379
1959-60	62.67	37.33	9.672	5.760	15.432
1960-61	63.32	36.68	9.813	5.684	15.496
1961-62	66.50	33.50	10.482	5.280	15.763
1962-63	65.38	34.62	11.696	6.193	17.889
1963-64	63.69	36.31	11.984	6.832	18.816
1964-65	61.97	38.03	11.353	6.968	18.321
1965-66	62.55	37.45	12.354	7.396	19.750
1966-67	62.36	37.64	12.321	7.438	19.759
1967-68	68.06	31.94	11.628	5.457	17.084
1968-69	73.31	26.69	12.140	4.419	16.558
1969-70	76.76	23.24	12.332	3.733	16.064
1970-71	72.88	27.12	12.516	4.658	17.175
1971-72	74.67	25.33	14.288	4.847	19.135
1972-73	75.21	24.79	14.548	4.795	19.344
1973-74	75.57	24.43	13.214	4.273	17.486
1974-75	70.30	29.70	12.754	5.387	18.141
1975-76	68.46	31.54	14.227	6.555	20.782
1976-77	69.97	30.03	15.449	6.631	22.080
1977-78	70.75	29.25	14.751	6.099	20.850
1978-79	70.09	29.91	15.752	6.720	22.472
1979-80	71.14	28.86	16.846	6.834	23.680
1980-81	68.05	31.95	16.493	7.745	24.238

Contd...

1981-82	70.29	29.71	16.526	6.986	23.512
1982-83	72.56	27.44	17.768	6.718	24.486
1983-84	72.67	27.33	17.831	6.705	24.536
1984-85	72.48	27.52	19.277	7.321	26.599
1985-86	74.25	25.75	20.156	6.989	27.144
1986-87	73.31	26.69	21.271	7.746	29.016
1987-88	76.82	23.18	21.734	6.557	28.291
1988-89	78.45	21.55	21.314	5.855	27.169
1989-90	78.67	21.33	22.153	6.005	28.159
1990-91	80.28	19.72	21.620	5.311	26.931
1991-92	83.30	16.70	21.976	4.406	26.383
1992-93	81.13	18.87	21.254	4.942	26.196
1993-94	82.18	17.82	21.348	4.629	25.977
1994-95	84.37	15.63	21.191	3.925	25.116
1995-96	85.12	14.88	20.676	3.613	24.289
1996-97	88.05	11.95	20.668	2.806	23.473
1997-98	86.99	13.01	21.093	3.156	24.248
1998-99	86.69	13.31	22.133	3.400	25.532
1999-00	87.06	12.94	23.154	3.441	26.595
2000-01	88.84	11.16	23.230	2.917	26.147
2001-02	88.44	11.56	23.613	3.086	26.698
2002-03 (RE)	87.61	12.39	25.074	3.545	28.619

Source: (Basic Data): *Indian Public Finance Statistics.*

Appendix Table A8.2: Centre: Revenue and Capital Expenditure: Share in Total and as Percentage of GDP

Year	As percentage of Total Expenditure		As percentage of GDP		
	Revenue	Capital	Revenue	Capital	Total
1950-51	84.868	15.132	3.7742	0.6729	4.4472
1951-52	77.397	22.603	3.8002	1.1098	4.9100
1952-53	90.896	9.104	3.7678	0.3774	4.1452
1953-54	94.317	5.683	3.5557	0.2142	3.7699
1954-55	71.520	28.480	3.9371	1.5678	5.5049
1955-56	78.417	21.583	4.2371	1.1662	5.4033
1956-57	64.345	35.655	3.8441	2.1301	5.9742
1957-58	60.497	39.503	4.9461	3.2296	8.1757
1558-59	63.740	36.260	4.7493	2.7018	7.4511
1959-60	68.338	31.662	4.9227	2.2808	7.2034
1960-61	55.087	44.913	5.5555	4.5295	10.0850
1961-62	55.902	44.098	5.8364	4.6041	10.4405
1962-63	54.794	45.206	6.8568	5.6571	12.5139
1963-64	54.322	45.678	7.4409	6.2568	13.6977
1964-65	53.155	46.845	7.0052	6.1736	13.1789
1965-66	54.852	45.148	7.2967	6.0057	13.3024
1966-67	49.751	50.249	7.2398	7.3123	14.5521
1967-68	59.369	40.631	6.7650	4.6299	11.3949
1968-69	69.525	30.475	6.9544	3.0483	10.0027
1969-70	70.885	29.115	6.8422	2.8104	9.6526
1970-71	66.736	33.264	6.9033	3.4408	10.3441
1971-72	71.577	28.423	8.3715	3.3243	11.6958
1972-73	68.087	31.913	8.3928	3.9338	12.3266
1973-74	69.978	30.022	7.3088	3.1356	10.4443
1974-75	65.065	34.935	7.3746	3.9596	11.3342
1975-76	64.357	35.643	8.4919	4.7032	13.1951
1976-77	67.095	32.905	9.2713	4.5469	13.8182
1977-78	69.036	30.964	9.0178	4.0447	13.0625
1978-79	66.293	33.707	9.7256	4.9451	14.6707
1979-80	67.352	32.648	9.7280	4.7155	14.4435
1980-81	62.051	37.949	9.2241	5.6413	14.8654
1981-82	64.826	35.174	9.1537	4.9667	14.1204

1982-83	66.357	33.643	9.9654	5.0524	15.0178
1983-84	66.510	33.490	10.0752	5.0732	15.1484
1984-85	65.433	34.567	11.0164	5.8199	16.8363
1985-86	66.657	33.343	12.0897	6.0475	18.1372
1986-87	67.398	32.602	13.0877	6.3307	19.4184
1987-88	70.696	29.304	13.0289	5.4005	18.4294
1988-89	71.570	28.430	12.8347	5.0983	17.9329
1989-90	71.664	28.336	13.1661	5.2058	18.3719
1990-91	72.912	27.088	12.9348	4.8054	17.7402
1991-92	76.264	23.736	12.5997	3.9215	16.5212
1992-93	75.656	24.344	12.3859	3.9854	16.3713
1993-94	76.576	23.424	12.6277	3.8628	16.4905
1994-95	79.117	20.883	12.0804	3.1887	15.2691
1995-96	80.195	19.805	11.7604	2.9044	14.6648
1996-97	82.139	17.861	11.6072	2.5240	14.1312
1997-98	86.677	13.323	11.8221	1.8172	13.6393
1998-99	86.279	13.721	12.4307	1.9768	14.4075
1999-00	85.995	14.005	12.8493	2.0926	14.9419
2000-01	88.807	11.193	13.3034	1.6768	14.9802
2001-02	87.064	12.936	13.2824	1.9735	15.2560
2002-03 RE	88.346	11.654	13.8943	1.8328	15.7271

Source: (Basic Data): *Indian Public Finance Statistics.*

9

State Expenditures: Structure and Comparative Trends

Though the fiscal deterioration of states began much later than that of the centre, the fiscal stress of some of the State Governments is more acute...

Economic Survey, 2004-05

State level expenditures have grown over time. The size of the state governments grew in terms of total expenditures and primary expenditures relative to GDP. But the structure of state of governments has tilted heavily towards committed expenditures like interest payments, salaries, and pensions. In this Chapter, we look at the trend and evolution of state expenditures since 1950-51. The analysis is done, first at the aggregate level of all states. Then a comparative picture is drawn across states.

Chart 9.1 depicts the long term profile of the relative shares of revenue and capital expenditures in total expenditure. The two curves are almost similar in their shape as was the case for central expenditures. However, whereas in that case there were some years in which the share of capital expenditure had become almost as much as that of the revenue expenditures. In the case of states, the share of the revenue expenditures was always relatively much larger.

Chart 9.1: Relative Share of Revenue and Capital Expenditure in Total Expenditure

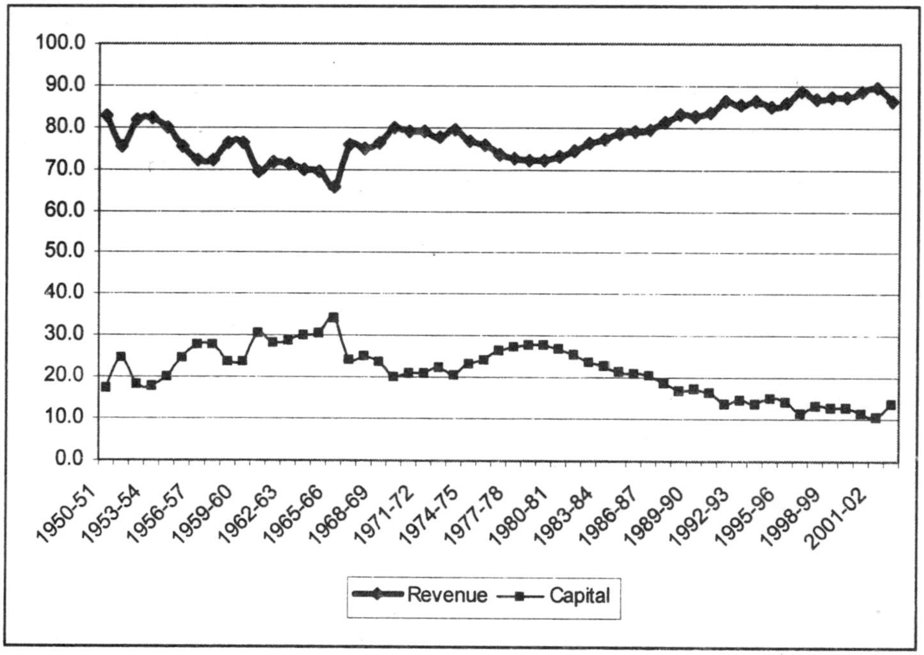

After the mid-sixties, when the share of revenue expenditure was about sixty five per cent, this share started rising reaching a level of nearly 89 percent in 2000-01. The states have the larger share of expenditure as compared to the centre when spending for current purchases is taken in to account and intergovernmental transfers are netted out. As percentage of GDP, the total state expenditure, as given in appendix Table A9.1, started at about 4 per cent of GDP in 1950-51 and rose to as much 16 per cent in recent years.

Considering the large share of revenue expenditures in the total expenditures, it is useful to examine the broad structure of the state level revenue expenditure. Table 9.1 gives the share of different components of non-development revenue expenditure at the aggregate level for the states from 1974-75. Accounting for a little more than 38 per cent of total revenue expenditure, the non-developmental expenditures started rising since the early 90's reaching a level of nearly 50 per cent by 2002-03. The largest expenditure head within the category of non-developmental expenditure is interest payment. Interest payments alone accounted for nearly 40 per cent of the revenue expenditures of the state government in 2002-03. This share was only 10 per cent in 1974-75.

Table 9.1: States: Share of Selected Non-developmental Services in Total Revenue Expenditure

Year	Non-Dev. expenditure	Interest payments	Pension & oth. Ret. benefits	Compensation to local bodies	other non-dev. expenditure
1974-75	38.48	9.67	1.72	1.29	25.80
1975-76	38.62	10.57	2.05	1.13	24.86
1976-77	36.25	10.11	2.18	1.63	22.33
1977-78	35.15	9.74	2.18	1.55	21.68
1978-79	33.46	9.75	2.17	1.45	20.10
1979-80	33.03	8.29	2.19	1.45	21.10
1980-81	33.24	8.78	2.27	1.38	20.81
1981-82	33.74	9.01	2.61	1.41	20.71
1982-83	35.17	8.93	2.78	1.37	22.10
1983-84	34.89	8.78	2.85	1.40	21.86
1984-85	34.37	9.23	3.02	1.38	20.74
1985-86	35.88	9.49	3.13	1.33	21.94
1986-87	35.65	11.40	3.37	0.98	19.89
1987-88	35.93	11.31	3.62	1.08	19.91

Contd...

1988-89	36.67	11.98	4.26	1.07	19.37
1989-90	37.99	12.61	4.42	0.97	19.99
1990-91	38.93	12.79	4.49	1.16	20.50
1991-92	38.04	13.11	4.45	1.18	19.29
1992-93	39.59	13.71	4.76	1.33	19.79
1993-94	40.26	14.58	4.95	1.11	19.63
1994-95	43.94	15.40	6.94	0.90	20.70
1995-96	45.83	15.59	5.61	0.96	23.67
1996-97	42.78	15.75	6.05	1.07	19.92
1997-98	44.77	16.74	6.43	1.63	19.97
1998-99	44.03	16.64	7.50	1.57	18.31
1999-00	46.43	17.75	8.92	1.78	17.91
2000-01	47.44	18.51	9.04	1.73	18.17
2001-02	49.39	20.19	9.42	1.52	17.72
2002-03	49.63	21.13	9.16	1.80	19.34

Source: (Basic Data): *Indian Public Finance Statistics.*

Table 9.2 shows the shares of different components of social services in the aggregate revenue expenditures of state governments. The share of total development expenditure in total revenue expenditure is also given over the period from 1974-75 to 2002-03. The share of development expenditure of the states in revenue expenditure shows a secular decline falling from a level of sixty per cent in the seventies to close to 48 per cent in the first few years of the new decade. Development expenditure consists of social and economic services. The share of social services has also fallen over this period from a level of 39 per cent in 1974-75 to 31 per cent. Clearly, it is the economic services which have fallen even more in terms of their relative share in the revenue expenditures of the state governments. Among the social services, education commands the largest weight. The share of education in total revenue expenditure was about 25 per cent in 1974-75. This share has fallen to about 16 per cent, which can be considered to be a highly undesirable trend. The medical and public health services accounted for a little less than 10 per cent of the state governments' revenue expenditure in the mid-seventies. This share has fallen to just a little above 6 per cent.

Table 9.3 shows the share of selected economic services in total revenue expenditures. Some of the important economic services are agriculture, road and transport, industry and minerals, and power and irrigation. The agricultural sector is the relatively more important sector in the case the states.

Table 9.2: States: Share of Selected Social Services in Total Revenue Expenditure

Year	Development expenditure	Social and community services	Education	Medical and public health	Family welfare	Social security and welfare
1974-75	60.13	39.28	25.29	9.21	1.06	1.14
1975-76	60.09	39.47	25.00	8.89	1.24	1.24
1976-77	61.32	38.55	23.77	8.73	2.14	1.17
1977-78	62.25	39.24	24.43	9.14	1.04	1.60
1978-79	64.40	38.92	23.47	9.15	1.00	1.62
1979-80	64.29	37.99	22.57	9.38	0.96	1.44
1980-81	64.29	37.94	22.24	9.16	0.92	1.92
1981-82	63.90	38.58	22.42	9.51	1.05	2.04
1982-83	62.54	38.32	22.69	9.24	1.32	2.07
1983-84	63.13	38.36	22.13	9.49	1.49	2.43
1984-85	63.87	37.74	21.63	9.03	1.36	2.36
1985-86	62.40	35.52	20.29	8.98	1.44	2.10
1986-87	62.71	37.89	21.61	9.06	1.35	2.63
1987-88	62.26	36.64	21.33	8.88	1.28	2.48
1988-89	61.21	36.87	21.90	8.60	1.25	24.87
1989-90	60.03	38.37	23.74	8.36	1.24	2.43
1990-91	59.48	36.18	22.51	7.97	1.19	1.98
1991-92	60.39	32.99	20.32	7.17	1.11	2.01
1992-93	58.39	33.07	20.67	7.32	1.01	1.81
1993-94	58.36	33.18	20.52	7.45	1.14	1.89
1994-95	54.62	32.67	19.96	7.27	1.09	2.02
1995-96	54.11	33.33	20.31	7.12	1.18	2.14
1996-97	55.85	33.17	20.23	7.12	0.96	2.15
1997-98	53.72	33.47	20.30	7.49	0.96	2.03
1998-99	54.18	34.01	21.03	7.48	0.86	1.92
1999-00	52.38	33.95	21.85	6.93	0.83	1.85
2000-01	50.89	32.33	20.55	6.58	0.78	1.99
2001-02	48.76	30.70	19.43	6.18	0.78	2.03
2002-03	48.24	30.64	18.47	6.16	0.89	2.51

Source: (Basic Data): *Indian Public Finance Statistics.*

Agriculture had a share of about 12 per cent in 1974-75 in the revenue expenditures of the states. Initially this share increased in the late seventies and early eighties reaching a peak of 16.6 per cent in 1984-85. After that its share started to fall steeply, becoming only 7 percent in 2002-03. The transport and communications sector is next in order of importance. Its share however was only about 4.4 per cent in 1974-75, which fell over time to a level of 2.2 per cent only by 2002-03.

Table 9.3: States: Share of Selected Economic Services in Total Revenue Expenditure

Year	Agriculture	Industry and minerals	Power and irrigation	Transport and communication
1974-75	11.86	1.03	1.25	4.38
1975-76	12.23	0.98	1.24	4.11
1976-77	12.61	1.15	1.20	4.88
1977-78	13.19	1.26	1.23	4.45
1978-79	14.18	1.47	1.77	4.96
1979-80	15.03	1.41	1.71	4.85
1980-81	14.75	1.42	2.62	4.47
1981-82	14.62	1.57	1.87	4.43
1982-83	14.53	1.45	1.90	3.78
1983-84	15.19	1.64	1.71	3.60
1984-85	16.60	1.58	1.64	3.65
1985-86	14.45	1.72	4.80	3.34
1986-87	13.35	1.80	3.91	3.19
1987-88	13.98	1.64	4.22	3.25
1988-89	13.48	1.71	3.72	2.74
1989-90	10.62	1.83	3.86	2.78
1990-91	12.66	1.48	3.43	2.73
1991-92	11.68	1.45	8.80	2.97
1992-93	12.71	1.44	5.81	2.99
1993-94	12.50	1.32	6.29	2.87
1994-95	10.40	1.35	5.66	2.74
1995-96	9.40	1.38	5.71	2.29
1996-97	9.04	1.31	7.87	2.59
1997-98	8.64	1.08	6.03	2.64

Contd...

1998-99	9.35	0.99	5.58	2.46
1999-00	8.62	0.81	4.95	2.31
2000-01	7.39	0.83	6.37	2.22
2001-02	6.91	0.81	6.78	2.05
2002-03	7.05	0.91	6.12	2.20

Source: (Basic Data): *Indian Public Finance Statistics.*

9.1 Comparative Performance of States: Expenditures

Having looked at the aggregate trends in state level expenditures, it is also useful to consider some broad comparisons in expenditure patterns across states. In appendix Tables A9.4 to A9.9, we have looked at the prevailing trends in the case of social and economic services in selected states. Among these services, attention is focused on education, and medical and public health. The period covered is from 1993-94 to 2002-03. Expenditure are given in absolute terms as also relative to the respective GSDP of different states. Data for five states are given, namely, West Bengal, Uttar Pradesh, Tamil Nadu, Maharashtra and Rajasthan. These states are drawn from different income groups reflecting the situation in low, middle, and high income groups. In general the share of social services relative to GSDP is higher than that of economic services. Further the share of economic services has gone down over time in most cases. Among the social services, the highest level relative to GSDP is shown by Rajasthan among the selected states. In all cases, the share of education is the largest among the social services.

The TFC has provided a review in a comparative perspective of some important dimensions of expenditures. They have made comparisons over two periods to draw attention to the structural changes: average of 1993-94 to 1995-96 and 2000-01 to 2002-03. In respect of revenue expenditures relative to GSDP levels, comparing averages over the two periods, viz., 1993-96 and 2000-03, Table 9.4 shows a general upward trend. The corresponding ratio for capital expenditure, however, shows a change in the reverse direction. For the group of special category states, there is an increase of 1.4 percentage points between the two period averages. Among the general category states, the TFC finds that the largest increase in RE/GSDP ratio is in respect of Gujarat (5.9 per cent) and Orissa (5.7 per cent). The states where this increase is least are Goa (0.1 per cent) and Haryana (0.4 per cent). The main reason for the increase in revenue expenditure in relation to GSDP can be attributed to the increases in salaries and pensions during the period as well as on account of an increasing debt servicing burden.

Looking at the levels of revenue expenditures relative to GSDP, the average for 2000-03 indicates that for the group of special category states, the ratio is about 10 percentage points higher than that for the general category states. In this group, Orissa has an exceptionally high ratio at 22.2 per cent. At the lower end, we have Haryana at 13.5 per cent and Maharashtra at 14.1 per cent, which are the only states below 15 per cent.

Table 9.4: States: Comparative Trends in Expenditure

(Per cent of GSDP)

State	Revenue Expenditure			Capital Expenditure		
	1993-96 (A)	2000-03 (B)	[B-A]	1993-96 [C]	2000-03 [D]	[D-A]
Andhra Pradesh	13.47	15.56	2.08	3.87	2.93	-0.94
Bihar	16.50	18.11	1.60	1.04	2.67	1.63
Goa	17.11	17.25	0.13	3.86	2.33	-1.54
Gujarat	12.52	18.37	5.85	2.37	2.43	0.06
Haryana	13.06	13.45	0.39	2.33	2.52	0.18
Karnataka	13.96	15.33	1.36	3.08	2.44	-0.64
Kerala	14.93	16.11	1.18	2.23	1.07	-1.16
Madhya Pradesh	13.29	16.74	3.45	1.90	2.37	0.47
Maharashtra	10.68	14.10	3.42	2.56	1.47	-1.09
Orissa	16.49	22.22	5.74	2.83	3.23	0.40
Punjab	12.75	15.33	2.59	2.65	2.11	-0.54
Rajasthan	15.43	18.06	2.63	3.89	2.30	-1.59
Tamil Nadu	13.95	15.60	1.66	1.85	1.51	-0.34
Uttar Pradesh	14.28	16.78	2.50	2.63	2.23	-0.40
West Bengal	11.80	15.02	3.23	1.78	1.94	0.16
General Category	13.33	16.05	2.72	2.51	2.12	-0.38
Special Category	26.27	27.66	1.40	5.71	4.69	-1.03
All States	13.94	16.67	2.72	2.66	2.26	-0.40

Source: *Report of the Twelfth Finance Commission, 2004.*

As evident, the increase in revenue expenditure implies a fall in capital expenditure if revenue receipts are stagnant. In this case, the special category states display the larger reduction in capital expenditure to GSDP ratio between 1993-96 and 2000-03, comparing group to group. In the group of general category states, Orissa has the highest level of capital expenditure at 3.2 per cent in 2000-03 while Kerala has the lowest at 1.1 per cent.

Table 9.5 shows comparisons over the two period-averages for two other important ratios, namely, interest payments relative to total revenue receipts and pension payments relative to GSDP. The TFC observes that in the absence of adequate availability of non-debt resources, many states relied on increased borrowing to finance the upward revision of salary scales and pensions during 1997-2000. Consequently, the debt servicing burden of states in the form of the interest payments to TRR ratio has increased to unsustainable levels. Among special category states, the ratio of interest payments to total revenue receipts is the highest for Himachal Pradesh at 28.78 per cent during 2000-03, which amounts to the largest increase in this ratio at 12.90 percentage points over 1993-96. The increase in debt servicing burden has affected the general category states more than the special category states. West Bengal has registered the largest increase in ratio of interest payments to total revenue receipts in 2000-03 over 1993-96 at 23.98 percentage points.

Table 9.5: State Expenditure Trends: Comparative Profile

(Per cent of GSDP)

State	Int. Payment/TRR			Pension Exp./GSDP		
	1993-96 (A)	2000-03 (B)	[B-A]	1993-96 [C]	2000-03 [D]	[D-A]
Andhra Pradesh	14.07	22.37	8.30	1.01	1.49	0.48
Bihar	21.78	24.92	3.14	1.01	2.82	1.82
Goa	14.21	19.50	5.29	0.55	1.28	0.74
Gujarat	15.18	24.59	9.41	0.60	1.25	0.65
Haryana	15.26	23.35	8.09	0.54	1.10	0.56
Karnataka	12.08	18.07	6.00	0.92	1.42	0.50
Kerala	17.61	27.34	9.73	1.72	2.57	0.85
Madhya Pradesh	13.34	18.36	5.02	0.67	1.17	0.50
Maharashtra	11.93	20.75	8.82	0.36	0.88	0.52
Orissa	22.39	35.85	13.46	0.68	2.21	1.53
Punjab	32.13	38.51	6.38	0.64	1.62	0.98
Rajasthan	17.38	30.57	13.19	0.73	1.91	1.18
Tamil Nadu	11.98	18.61	6.63	0.93	2.11	1.19
Uttar Pradesh	22.30	28.27	5.97	0.54	1.21	0.67
West Bengal	20.34	44.33	23.98	0.61	1.44	0.83
General Category	16.70	25.40	8.70	0.72	1.51	0.80
Special Category	13.41	16.98	3.57	1.11	2.39	1.28
All States	16.37	24.57	8.20	0.73	1.56	0.83

Source: *Report of the Twelfth Finance Commission.*

As a result, its ratio of interest payments to total revenue receipts at 44.33 per cent during 2000-03 is the highest among all states. Punjab follows next at 38.51 per cent. A consistently high level of this ratio for this state during the nineties is reflected by the fact that its ratio of interest payments to total revenue receipts was the highest at 32.13 per cent during 1993-96. Orissa and Rajasthan have also shown large increases in their ratio of interest payments to total revenue receipts at 13.46 and 13.19 percentage points, respectively between the two periods. During 2000-03, Karnataka, undivided Madhya Pradesh, and Tamil Nadu have displayed lower levels of the ratio of interest payments to total revenue receipts at about 18 per cent.

One serious concern in the context of state finances is the phenomenal growth of pension liabilities consequent upon the revision of pay scales. As indicated by Table 9.5, during 2000-03, pension liabilities as a percentage of GSDP were higher than the corresponding average over 1993-96 by 1.28 percentage point for the general category states and by 0.8 percentage points for the special category states. During 2000-03, pension payments relative to GSDP varied from 1 per cent to 3 per cent across all states. Among the general category states, the increase in terms of percentage points, in the ratio of pension payments to GSDP, was the highest for undivided Bihar (1.82), Orissa (1.53), Rajasthan (1.18) and Tamil Nadu (1.19).

9.2 Disparities across States in Outcomes

The state has to play an important role in providing merit services like health and education. Although the private sector can play a role, disparities in state level expenditures translate into disparities in outcomes. The inter-state pattern of per capita government expenditures, particularly in social and economic services shows the prevailing disparities in respect of publicly provided services. Table 9.6, as given by the TFC Report, shows per capita average state government expenditures over the period 1998-99 to 2000-01 in general, social, and economic services. In the general services, interest payments, pensions, and lotteries are excluded.

Within the social sector expenditures, per capita expenditures on education, health, and water supply and sanitation are also shown. States are arranged in ascending order of per capita GSDP. The general pattern with some exceptions is that states with low per capita GSDPs also have low per capita expenditures. The ratio of minimum to maximum expenditure and that of minimum to mean expenditure indicates that in the case of general category states, the minimum expenditure is only 28 per cent of maximum expenditure, excluding Goa, and it is 59 per cent of average expenditure. In the case of social services the minimum per capita expenditure is 35 per cent of the maximum and 46 per cent of the mean. The corresponding ratios for economic services, covering plan and non-plan expenditures, are 15 per cent and 34 per cent. In the case of education, the minimum to mean ratio is 57 per cent. The corresponding figures are 45 per cent and 34 per cent for health and water supply and sanitation.

Table 9.6: Per capita Expenditure on General, Social and Economic Services

(Rs.)

State	1998-99 to 2000-01			1998-99 to 2000-01		
	GEN	SOC	ECO	EDN	HTH	WSS
Bihar	182.20	460.22	198.29	311.14	38.89	19.13
Orissa	224.20	931.18	406.54	463.08	68.31	56.18
Uttar Pradesh	208.88	549.54	318.14	340.41	52.74	19.96
Assam	334.39	929.88	369.27	615.21	64.58	59.23
Madhya Pradesh	228.19	697.03	411.75	344.49	70.08	63.38
Rajasthan	265.36	1,020.65	405.00	545.30	101.98	111.46
West Bengal	262.41	958.23	392.62	512.29	107.77	42.51
Andhra Pradesh	264.50	905.72	623.67	411.70	83.61	57.72
Kerala	328.99	1,254.80	716.48	713.26	131.37	52.35
Karnataka	279.17	1,083.89	755.77	558.33	59.28	60.27
Tamil Nadu	321.50	1,240.90	685.30	651.46	110.81	38.34
Gujarat	276.34	1,331.35	1,285.75	664.44	109.55	39.03
Haryana	320.94	1,145.38	902.40	587.60	73.14	102.14
Maharashtra	639.84	1,276.05	647.73	730.93	59.69	79.69
Punjab	533.63	1,220.48	733.94	716.27	178.32	55.04
Coeff of variation	39.24	26.62	46.93	26.30	41.49	45.11
Min/Max	0.28	0.35	0.15	0.43	0.22	0.17
Min/Mean	0.59	0.46	0.34	0.57	0.45	0.34

Note: Per capita Revenue Expenditure on General Services is net of Interest Payments and Pension & Lottery.
Source: *Report of the Twelfth Finance Commission.*

These differences are reflected in the index of human development. In the ranking given by the Table on HDI given in the TFC Report, the lowest ranked state is Bihar, followed by Uttar Pradesh, Orissa, and Madhya Pradesh. There is a clear positive relationship, as expected, between per capita GSDP and the HDI. At the same time, states, which have provided more in terms of per capita budgetary expenditures on health and education, have ranks that are higher than their relative position in the ranking of per capita GSDP. This is so also for the special category states. In the TFC report, the ranking in terms of infrastructure index is also given. Based on the relative ranking of an index of infrastructure, the states have also been grouped into five categories. While the HDI reflects access to social services, the infrastructure index reflects access to physical infrastructure. Together, these capture two different dimensions of disparities. While the special category states do better in the HDI, there position in terms of access to infrastructure is a major handicap. For the low income states like Bihar and Rajasthan, both HDI and the Infrastructure index show a handicap (Table 9.7).

Table 9.7: States Grouped According to Selected Indicators

Human Development Index	Infrastructure Index
High	**High**
Goa, Kerala, Maharashtra, Mizoram	Goa, Maharashtra, Punjab
High Middle	**High Middle**
Gujarat, Manipur, Nagaland, Punjab, Sikkim, Tamil Nadu	Gujarat, Haryana, Kerala, Tamil Nadu
Middle	**Middle**
Andhra Pradesh, Arunachal Pradesh, Haryana, Himachal Pradesh, Meghalaya, Karnataka, Tripura, West Bengal, Uttaranchal	Andhra Pradesh, Karnataka
Lower Middle	**Lower Middle**
Assam, Chattisgarh, J &K, Jharkhand, Rajasthan	Himachal Pradesh, Madhya Pradesh Orissa, U.P., Uttaranchal, West Bengal
Low	**Low**
Bihar, Madhya Pradesh, Orissa, Uttar Pradesh	Arunachal Pradesh., Manipur, Meghalaya, Jharkhand, Mizoram, Nagaland, Assam, Chattisgarh, Sikkim, Tripura, J&K, Bihar, Rajasthan

Source: *Report of the Twelfth Finance Commission, 2004.*

Levels of income and its growth depend on many factors that include states' own efforts and policies, the inter-state distribution of private capital, domestic and foreign, and the inter-state pattern of the benefit of central investment and current expenditures. Much of the required correction has to come from the distribution and allocation of plan funds.

9.3 Growth of State Level Salaries since the Mid-nineties

Salary payments account for a major share of the committed expenditures in the state budgets. In the discussion below, we look at the state-wise pattern of government employment, average salaries, and the share of salaries in the revenue expenditures of the states have been examined over the period 1994-95 to 2002-03. This discussion is based on the data and review of this subject, given by the Twelfth Finance Commission in an appendix to the Report. The inordinate rise in the burden of salary payments in the latter part of the nineties has been one of main reasons for the sharp deterioration of state finances. Almost all states had decided to follow the recommendations of the Fifth central pay commission without taking into account the differences in their initial conditions. These initial conditions differed for the states because in the past their salary scales were different from the centre and they also followed different recruitment policies. The TFC for the first time has provided some comparable data for making inter-state comparisons of the impact of the salary revisions. It can be seen that expenditure on salaries relative to revenue expenditure excluding interest payments and pensions has gone up from 35 per cent in 1996-97 to 42 per cent in 1999-00. The EFC as also the TFC have recommended that there is no need to appoint Pay Commissions as a routine at the interval of 10 years.

In spite of the increasing convergence in the salary structures, there are considerable differences in the average salaries per employee, which may be due to the differences in the composition of government employees and their age-profile, as well as differences in some allowances, among other factors.

The Eleventh Finance Commission had recommended that states should attempt to limit their salary expenditures relative to revenue receipts or revenue expenditures. Decisions relating to salary levels and levels of government employment should be taken keeping in view the fiscal capacity of the state and the size of population that needs to be served by the government. If the number of employees is relatively large, average salaries should be relatively less. Table A9.2 gives the number of employees in the states. A state that has a large work force, a high level of per employee salary, and low fiscal capacity, will find a large part of its revenue receipts being claimed by the overall salary bill. The work force, even if large, would not prove to be productively employed unless the state is able to provide complementary expenditures, that is, non-salary revenue expenditure and capital expenditure. Different states implemented the salary revisions with effect from 1st January 1996, or some other specified date around this period, but were given effect to much later. Employees were given arrears, payments of which were also spread out in different ways across states. In order to consider the impact of salary revisions, the TFC provides a comparison of the pre-revised salary, i.e. of 1995-96 with the average of per employee salary in the later years.

Table 9.8: Per Employee Salary Expenditure: Per cent Increase after Salary Revisions (Rs. Per employee)

State	1995-96 (A)	Average (1997-98 to 1999-00) [B]	Percentage increase (B over A)
Andhra Pradesh	38,033	50,278	32.20
Arunachal Pradesh	51,369	79,101	53.99
Assam	41,616	60,709	45.88
Bihar	62,482	1,00,948	61.56
Goa	51,333	83,268	62.21
Gujarat	58,745	83,302	41.80
Haryana	44,201	66,869	51.28
Himachal Pradesh	50,975	78,364	53.73
Karnataka	38,344	63,997	66.90
Kerala	42,762	63,130	47.63
Madhya Pradesh	52,963	82,372	55.53
Maharashtra	49,083	73,934	50.63
Meghalaya	62,001	83,172	34.15
Orissa	36,040	66,285	83.92
Punjab	51,659	92,325	78.72
Rajasthan	47,682	72,327	51.69
Sikkim	49,012	1,00,815	105.70
Tamil Nadu	52,731	88,570	67.97
Tripura	50,654	59,654	17.77
Uttar Pradesh	45,998	84,675	84.09
West Bengal	45,838	78,723	71.74
Weighted Average (21 states)	47,398	75,364	**59.00**

Source: *Report of the Twelfth Finance Commission, 2004.*

The TFC has observed that the maximum impact of salary revision in different states was felt in 1997-98 to 1999-00. The average of these is centered in 1998-99. Table 9.8 shows that as compared to 1995-96, the average per employee salary over 1997-98 to 2000-01, centered in 1998-99, shows an increase of 59 per cent.

Table 9.9: Expenditure on Salaries Relative to Revenue Expenditures (Net of Interest Payments and Pensions) (per cent)

State	1994 -95	1995 -96	1996 -97	1997 -98	1998 -99	1999 -00	2000 -01	2001 -02	2002 -03
Andhra Pradesh	26.5	26.5	20.3	23.8	24.5	29.6	26.1	23.6	25.5
Arunachal Pradesh	40.5	41.1	39.7	45.2	50.1	48.6	46.7	43.6	47.8
Assam	60.7	60.7	70.4	71.7	74.3	75.9	71.1	71.5	71.7
Bihar	62.7	64.1	63.4	59.3	65.5	65.5	77.3	73.5	67.6
Goa	27.6	19.3	19.3	21.5	20.1	22.2	49.1	22.0	19.5
Gujarat	16.4	17.7	16.0	15.7	15.1	14.2	11.1	12.0	14.8
Haryana	20.8	29.6	27.5	28.3	39.6	52.5	52.6	47.0	49.6
Himachal Pradesh	45.9	46.7	47.6	45.9	51.4	51.7	51.5	58.9	58.3
Karnataka	37.3	35.9	34.6	39.3	39.3	40.0	37.6	36.3	38.3
Kerala	40.1	37.7	36.5	31.5	34.1	39.9	40.1	38.4	32.0
Madhya Pradesh	45.7	44.5	39.5	43.4	45.9	44.1	45.9	43.4	50.0
Maharashtra	25.3	25.4	22.3	22.5	22.7	31.2	21.2	21.8	19.8
Meghalaya	48.6	45.8	51.7	55.0	52.3	52.7	50.1	54.3	57.5
Orissa	44.0	43.2	54.0	61.5	65.4	57.2	64.6	57.0	65.5
Punjab	36.7	50.0	47.9	52.3	69.8	60.1	52.5	49.6	45.5
Rajasthan	39.6	37.8	45.9	50.4	54.4	52.6	49.2	49.3	48.0
Sikkim	16.8	11.6	10.6	11.1	17.9	18.3	37.6	17.1	16.5
Tamil Nadu	40.6	42.9	42.5	45.0	50.6	51.2	49.2	51.6	40.8
Tripura	53.1	68.8	54.5	55.8	59.9	64.4	60.2	67.0	69.9
Uttar Pradesh	33.8	34.1	34.7	39.7	37.3	38.5	38.8	35.4	37.5
West Bengal	31.8	31.2	29.8	31.5	36.6	30.4	30.1	30.1	35.4
Total (21states)	**35.2**	**36.2**	**34.8**	**37.0**	**39.7**	**41.3**	**38.3**	**36.8**	**37.3**

* excludes interest payments and pensions

Source: *Report of the Twelfth Finance commission, 2004.*

Table 9.9 shows the ratio of salary expenditure to revenue expenditure excluding interest payments and pensions. This ratio increased from a level of about 35 per cent prior to revisions to more than 40 per cent in 2000-01, after which it has started coming down, but it is still higher than the average pre-revision levels.

If salary structures across the states are allowed to converge, the number of employees in a state also needs to follow some comparable norms in relation to the size of population, fiscal capacity, and other relevant considerations. The per employee salary expenditure may still differ because of the composition of the workforce. Normalization can be done in respect of the total salary bill relative to their fiscal capacities. The salary burden is already heavy and at the minimum, the ratio of salaries to revenue expenditure net of interest payments and pensions must not be allowed to increase. The TFC has recommended that states should achieve a ratio of salary expenditure to revenue expenditure net of interest payments and pensions of 35 per cent, which is consistent with its average level in 1996-97.

The TFC also suggests that for reaching this target, for the states that are above it, there are three possible routes, viz.

- reducing the number of employees,
- reducing the average per employee salary, and
- increasing the level of revenue receipts without increasing the revenue deficit.

If the number of employees is relatively large, average salaries should be relatively less. In contrast, if the state has kept the growth in the number of government employees within prudent limits, it will be easier for it to attain prudent levels of salary expenditures relative to revenue receipts. Adjustments would be largest for a state that has both a large work force, a high level of per employee salary, and low fiscal capacity.

Table A9.1: Revenue and Capital Expenditure of States: Share and Relative to GDP

Year	As % of Total Expenditure		As % of GDP		
	Revenue	Capital	Revenue	Capital	Total
1950-51	82.79	17.21	3.795	0.789	4.584
1951-52	75.21	24.79	3.714	1.224	4.938
1952-53	81.72	18.28	4.289	0.960	5.249
1953-54	82.36	17.64	4.317	0.925	5.242
1954-55	80.04	19.96	5.011	1.250	6.261
1955-56	75.14	24.86	5.525	1.828	7.353
1956-57	72.20	27.80	4.972	1.914	6.886
1957-58	71.99	28.01	5.136	1.999	7.135
1558-59	76.26	23.74	5.166	1.608	6.774
1959-60	76.28	23.72	5.609	1.745	7.354
1960-61	69.21	30.79	5.919	2.633	8.552
1961-62	71.59	28.41	6.265	2.487	8.752
1962-63	71.40	28.60	6.368	2.551	8.919
1963-64	69.86	30.14	6.212	2.680	8.892
1964-65	69.24	30.76	6.098	2.710	8.808
1965-66	65.93	34.07	6.872	3.551	10.423
1966-67	75.65	24.35	7.086	2.281	9.367
1967-68	74.81	25.19	6.736	2.268	9.004
1968-69	76.46	23.54	7.194	2.215	9.408
1969-70	80.09	19.91	7.532	1.872	9.404
1970-71	79.16	20.84	7.530	1.983	9.513
1971-72	79.15	20.85	8.358	2.202	10.560
1972-73	77.83	22.17	8.640	2.461	11.100
1973-74	79.59	20.41	8.042	2.062	10.105
1974-75	76.81	23.19	7.230	2.183	9.414
1975-76	75.72	24.28	7.832	2.511	10.343
1976-77	73.70	26.30	8.419	3.004	11.423
1977-78	72.61	27.39	8.250	3.112	11.362
1978-79	72.03	27.97	8.964	3.480	12.444
1979-80	72.00	28.00	9.526	3.705	13.232
1980-81	72.91	27.09	9.833	3.654	13.487

Contd…

1981-82	74.31	25.69	9.605	3.321	12.926
1982-83	76.37	23.63	10.280	3.181	13.462
1983-84	77.20	22.80	10.338	3.052	13.390
1984-85	78.54	21.46	11.045	3.018	14.063
1985-86	78.97	21.03	11.282	3.004	14.285
1986-87	79.29	20.71	11.556	3.018	14.574
1987-88	81.28	18.72	12.193	2.808	15.001
1988-89	83.33	16.67	11.764	2.353	14.117
1989-90	82.76	17.24	11.689	2.436	14.125
1990-91	83.46	16.54	11.933	2.365	14.298
1991-92	86.28	13.72	12.802	2.035	14.837
1992-93	85.32	14.68	12.313	2.119	14.432
1993-94	86.36	13.64	12.272	1.938	14.210
1994-95	85.04	14.96	12.219	2.150	14.369
1995-96	85.80	14.20	11.826	1.958	13.784
1996-97	88.36	11.64	11.890	1.566	13.456
1997-98	86.64	13.36	11.919	1.838	13.757
1998-99	87.37	12.63	12.406	1.794	14.200
1999-00	87.09	12.91	13.159	1.951	15.110
2000-01	88.68	11.32	13.016	1.662	14.678
2001-02	89.51	10.49	13.444	1.575	15.019
2002-03RE	86.26	13.74	14.189	2.260	16.449

Source: (Basic Data): *Indian Public Finance Statistics.*

Table A9.2: State-wise Number of Government Employees (Number)

State	1994-95	1995-96	1996-97	1997-98	1998-99
Andhra Pradesh	5,60,138	5,64,583	5,68,907	6,97,619	5,89,998
Arunachal Pradesh	33,222	36,325	37,420	39,222	39,606
Assam	4,13,464	4,22,690	4,30,357	4,41,590	4,59,701
Bihar	6,27,990	6,13,440	5,95,612	5,70,241	5,48,075
Goa	31,241	31,880	33,807	34,056	34,230
Gujarat	2,09,873	2,08,680	2,04,355	1,97,768	2,15,874
Haryana	3,00,963	3,09,795	3,15,120	3,13,790	3,16,472
Himachal Pradesh	1,31,497	1,38,307	1,42,934	1,48,163	1,59,542
Karnataka	5,93,878	6,32,117	6,54,002	5,65,072	6,06,478
Kerala	3,57,203	3,62,540	3,61,115	3,67,572	3,77,037
Madhya Pradesh	5,23,583	5,26,378	5,14,677	5,13,475	5,18,381
Maharashtra	7,36,607	7,47,392	7,36,591	7,36,969	7,29,546
Meghalaya	36,194	38,014	39,613	42,830	44,928
Orissa	4,07,290	4,26,786	4,58,295	4,68,941	4,75,791
Punjab	3,65,703	3,67,935	3,73,468	3,71,462	3,73,270
Rajasthan	5,12,224	5,31,235	5,51,054	5,69,575	5,86,452
Sikkim	19,522	20,158	21,038	21,701	20,395
Tamil Nadu	6,90,546	6,91,515	6,91,644	6,91,644	7,08,201
Tripura	90,300	89,242	96,310	96,725	96,673
Uttar Pradesh	8,73,351	8,65,254	8,15,213	8,09,507	8,03,801
West Bengal	4,32,503	4,32,403	4,33,705	4,31,599	4,36,285
Total (21 states)	7,94,7292	80,56,669	80,75,237	81,29,521	81,40,736

State	1999-00	2000-01	2001-02	2002-03
Andhra Pradesh	5,81,456	5,43,147	5,14,163	545859
Arunachal Pradesh	39,445	40,231	40,322	41,165
Assam	4,53,245	4,47,424	4,41,634	4,35,534
Bihar	5,31,633	5,15,684	4,70,825	4,62,137

Contd...

Goa	35,341	35,379	34,276	34,499
Gujarat	2,06,036	2,05,935	2,11,008	2,03,286
Haryana	3,20,515	3,19,027	3,22,217	3,25,439
Himachal Pradesh	1,68,551	1,75,324	1,77,000	1,80,540
Karnataka	6,27,973	6,19,518	6,18,062	6,22,547
Kerala	3,89,563	3,85,234	3,85,881	3,52,730
Madhya Pradesh	5,16,230	5,10,115	5,05,682	4,97,985
Maharashtra	7,07,326	7,10,802	6,95,870	6,92,265
Meghalaya	46,644	47,427	48,776	49,813
Orissa	4,58,458	4,33,452	4,26,885	4,19,468
Punjab	3,78,147	3,73,702	3,76,222	NA
Rajasthan	5,96,143	6,00,835	6,11,583	6,07,469
Sikkim	22,728	22,859	23,426	23,973
Tamil Nadu	7,08,699	7,08,986	7,09,599	NA
Tripura	1,05,038	1,03,736	1,01,604	98,379
Uttar Pradesh	7,05,368	7,02,666	7,05,803	7,05,803
West Bengal	4,37,018	4,41,160	4,42,544	4,39,300
Total (21 states)	80,35,557	79,42,643	78,63,382	67,38,191

Source: *Report of the Twelfth Finance Commission, 2004.*

Table A9.3: Per Employee Salary Expenditure (in Rupees)

State	1994-95	1995-96	1996-97	1997-98	1998-99
Andhra Pradesh	35,138	38,033	40,899	37,991	49,282
Arunachal Pradesh	48,040	51,369	57,119	67,613	81,229
Assam	36,895	41,616	45,720	51,198	57,860
Bihar*	54,900	62,482	67,950	79,987	97,094
Goa	43,989	51,333	61,566	76,501	83,729
Gujarat	46,501	58,745	62,631	74,892	84,218
Haryana	38,922	44,201	50,667	50,027	68,620
Himachal Pradesh	45,542	50,975	56,717	66,669	83,728
Karnataka	36,314	38,344	42,800	58,445	61,759
Kerala	40,554	42,762	48,599	50,699	59,504
Madhya Pradesh*	46,205	52,963	60,517	67,392	85,515
Maharashtra	43,053	49,083	53,015	57,885	64,797
Meghalaya	53,434	62,001	70,568	77,378	82,668
Orissa	33,262	36,040	44,441	51,104	66,479
Punjab	45,432	51,659	62,492	77,198	98,641
Rajasthan	41,745	47,682	53,057	57,281	78,153
Sikkim	42,665	49,012	54,430	62,041	1,25,552
Tamil Nadu	45,173	52,731	61,775	71,807	91,394
Tripura	34,891	50,654	42,277	49,915	58,755
Uttar Pradesh*	40,045	45,998	56,940	74,531	79,486
West Bengal	41,846	45,838	52,430	57,728	84,631
Weighted Average(21 states)	**41,968**	**47,398**	**53,631**	**61,377**	**75,116**
Growth Rate(Average Salary)		12.94	13.15	14.44	22.38

State	1999-00	2000-01	2001-02	2002-03
Andhra Pradesh	63,562	75,365	75,897	80,909

Contd..

Arunachal Pradesh	88,462	94,136	93,558	98,221
Assam	73,070	77,432	81,745	83,720
Bihar*	1,25,763	1,25,198	97,677	1,05,125
Goa	89,573	92,510	1,00,053	1,02,491
Gujarat	90,795	94,320	96,782	1,08,095
Haryana	81,960	84,196	92,624	1,01,355
Himachal Pradesh	84,695	91,691	1,01,907	1,10,582
Karnataka	71,788	73,864	80,491	81,000
Kerala	79,187	79,443	72,359	85,961
Madhya Pradesh*	94,208	99,718	92,114	1,06,000
Maharashtra	99,119	87,452	90,126	86,281
Meghalaya	89,471	96,181	1,08,088	1,13,808
Orissa	81,272	82,980	78,748	92,876
Punjab	1,01,137	1,14,726	1,09,846	NA
Rajasthan	81,548	81,777	83,651	87,115
Sikkim	1,14,852	1,09,617	1,13,651	1,21,684
Tamil Nadu	1,02,509	1,01,463	1,02,998	NA
Tripura	70,292	77,736	89,609	99,631
Uttar Pradesh*	1,00,010	1,05,592	94,971	1,08,602
West Bengal	93,809	1,00,265	98,601	1,03,714
Weighted Average (21 states)	**89,600**	**92,214**	**90,353**	**94,603**
Growth Rate (Average Salary)19.28		2.92	-2.02	4.70

* These states were bifurcated in 2000. Data in 2000-01 and 2001-02 relate to the position after bifurcation.

Source: *Report of the Twelfth Finance Commission, 2004.*

Table A9.4: West Bengal: Selected Expenditures (Rs. crore)

Year	Social Services (a to d)	Education (2202 to 2205)	Health (2210 & 2211)	Buildings (2216 & 2059)	Other Social Services	Economic Services
1993-94	2401.8	1567.8	419.9	94.5	319.6	1018.5
1994-95	2738.0	1712.4	438.7	109.6	477.3	1000.2
1995-96	2980.6	1911.7	501.2	118.9	448.7	1071.2
1996-97	3552.3	2343.1	569.0	128.1	512.1	1244.7
1997-98	3801.1	2424.7	640.5	158.4	577.5	1408.8
1998-99	4723.8	2918.9	925.3	162.4	717.2	1818.0
1999-00	7170.0	4823.6	992.8	184.5	1169.0	1983.1
2000-01	7124.7	4396.6	1071.4	249.5	1407.3	2179.9
2001-02	6937.3	4321.5	1049.8	247.7	1318.3	2299.2
2002-03	6639.6	4276.6	1085.6	209.9	1067.4	2151.4
2003-04 RE	7538.2	4514.7	1134.8	281.2	1607.6	2428.6
2004-05 BE	7540.6	4696.0	1193.9	289.3	1361.3	2556.9
						As % of GSDP
1993-94	4.279	2.793	0.748	0.168	0.569	1.815
1994-95	4.222	2.640	0.676	0.169	0.736	1.542
1995-96	3.920	2.514	0.659	0.156	0.590	1.409
1996-97	4.224	2.786	0.677	0.152	0.609	1.480
1997-98	3.861	2.463	0.651	0.161	0.587	1.431
1998-99	4.016	2.481	0.787	0.138	0.610	1.545
1999-00	5.648	3.800	0.782	0.145	0.921	1.562
2000-01	5.231	3.228	0.787	0.183	1.033	1.600
2001-02	4.523	2.817	0.684	0.162	0.859	1.499
2002-03	3.909	2.518	0.639	0.124	0.629	1.267
2003-04 RE	3.883	2.326	0.585	0.145	0.828	1.251
2004-05 BE	3.407	2.122	0.539	0.131	0.615	1.155

Source: *State Finance Accounts.*

Table A9.5: Uttar Pradesh: Selected Expenditures (Rs. crore)

Year	Social Services (a to d)	Education (2202 to 2205)	Health (2210 & 2211)	Buildings (2216 & 2059)	Other Social Services	Economic Services
		a	b	C	d	
1993-94	3448.4	2232.6	633.7	163.2	419.0	2060.9
1994-95	3815.8	2591.6	600.8	157.7	465.6	2149.0
1995-96	4481.9	3023.1	733.8	194.8	530.3	2380.9
1996-97	5031.6	3447.3	809.2	216.9	558.2	2578.8
1997-98	5974.3	3780.6	1057.7	274.1	861.9	2888.4
1998-99	7476.8	5334.6	999.3	227.3	915.6	2947.7
1999-00	7383.6	5156.9	1010.9	404.5	811.3	3441.1
2000-01	7932.7	5583.1	1060.9	509.1	779.6	3755.7
2001-02	7910.8	5526.1	1062.5	494.2	828.0	3781.4
2002-03	8983.9	5751.9	1218.0	385.1	1629.0	4045.3
2003-04 RE	9013.6	6173.1	1389.3	131.0	1320.2	17354.5
2004-05 BE	9071.2	6065.1	1470.6	182.8	1352.7	4928.6
						As % of GSDP
1993-94	4.387	2.841	0.806	0.208	0.533	2.622
1994-95	4.086	2.775	0.643	0.169	0.499	2.301
1995-96	4.266	2.878	0.698	0.185	0.505	2.266
1996-97	3.957	2.711	0.636	0.171	0.439	2.028
1997-98	4.306	2.725	0.762	0.198	0.621	2.082
1998-99	4.782	3.412	0.639	0.145	0.586	1.885
1999-00	4.393	3.068	0.601	0.241	0.483	2.047
2000-01	4.521	3.182	0.605	0.290	0.444	2.140
2001-02	4.173	2.915	0.560	0.261	0.437	1.995
2002-03	4.416	2.827	0.599	0.189	0.801	1.988
2003-04 RE	4.038	2.766	0.622	0.059	0.591	7.775
2004-05 BE	3.713	2.483	0.602	0.075	0.554	2.017

Source: *State Finance Accounts.*

Table A9.6: Tamil Nadu: Selected Expenditures (Rs. crore)

Year	Social Services (a to d)	Education (2202 to 2205)	Health (2210 & 2211)	Buildings (2216 & 2059)	Other Social Services	Economic Services
		a	b	c	d	
1993-94	2860.1	1657.5	379.5	89.8	733.3	1675.4
1994-95	2975.3	1799.6	405.1	98.5	672.1	1957.4
1995-96	3352.6	2037.6	479.2	111.6	724.1	2124.3
1996-97	4003.0	2357.2	513.5	110.9	1021.5	2519.3
1997-98	4625.3	2727.0	629.6	103.9	1164.8	2882.2
1998-99	5899.2	3665.5	799.1	96.3	1338.3	2635.1
1999-00	6527.4	4137.9	858.3	127.6	1403.6	3308.5
2000-01	6766.8	4190.6	858.6	141.5	1576.1	3480.6
2001-02	6614.9	4058.7	858.6	93.9	1603.6	3239.4
2002-03	6485.3	3970.2	865.0	124.2	1525.8	5042.0
2003-04 RE	7081.7	4402.6	944.3	154.8	1580.0	2661.3
2004-05 BE	7206.2	4684.3	1022.5	167.0	1332.5	2735.6
						As % of GSDP
1993-94	4.853	2.812	0.644	0.152	1.244	2.843
1994-95	4.185	2.531	0.570	0.139	0.945	2.753
1995-96	4.144	2.519	0.592	0.138	0.895	2.626
1996-97	4.257	2.507	0.546	0.118	1.086	2.679
1997-98	4.283	2.525	0.583	0.096	1.079	2.669
1998-99	4.825	2.998	0.654	0.079	1.095	2.155
1999-00	5.035	3.192	0.662	0.098	1.083	2.552
2000-01	4.671	2.893	0.593	0.098	1.088	2.403
2001-02	4.560	2.798	0.592	0.065	1.105	2.233
2002-03	4.321	2.645	0.576	0.083	1.017	3.359
2003-04 RE	4.267	2.653	0.569	0.093	0.952	1.604
2004-05 BE	3.936	2.559	0.559	0.091	0.728	1.494

Source: *State Finance Accounts.*

Table A9.7: Rajasthan: Selected Expenditures (Rs. crore)

Year	Social Services (a to d)	Education (2202 to 2205)	Health (2210 & 2211)	Buildings (2216 & 2059)	Other Social Services	Economic Services
		a	b	c	D	
1993-94	1815.6	1043.9	261.1	45.2	465.4	1099.2
1994-95	1984.6	1171.2	289.4	33.7	490.3	948.8
1995-96	2308.1	1341.7	322.2	41.0	603.2	1048.1
1996-97	2702.7	1558.9	365.4	95.4	683.0	1353.3
1997-98	3146.8	1921.5	434.3	17.7	773.3	1229.0
1998-99	4062.9	2489.4	587.6	67.1	918.8	1535.8
1999-00	4408.8	2725.1	604.4	60.5	1018.8	1737.9
2000-01	4917.4	2782.4	632.9	78.3	1423.8	1710.6
2001-02	4928.0	2943.7	658.9	73.5	1251.8	1729.1
2002-03	5407.8	3155.3	699.4	67.4	1485.7	1790.1
2003-04 RE	6312.1	3455.3	752.5	77.7	2026.7	2130.3
2004-05 BE	5948.1	3679.8	831.5	88.6	1348.3	2399.1
						As % of GSDP
1993-94	5.291	3.042	0.761	0.132	1.356	3.203
1994-95	4.564	2.693	0.666	0.078	1.127	2.182
1995-96	4.658	2.707	0.650	0.083	1.217	2.115
1996-97	4.338	2.502	0.586	0.153	1.096	2.172
1997-98	4.805	2.934	0.663	0.027	1.181	1.876
1998-99	5.497	3.368	0.795	0.091	1.243	2.078
1999-00	5.539	3.424	0.759	0.076	1.280	2.183
2000-01	5.999	3.394	0.772	0.096	1.737	2.087
2001-02	5.414	3.234	0.724	0.081	1.375	1.899
2002-03	5.824	3.398	0.753	0.073	1.600	1.928
2003-04 RE	6.219	3.405	0.741	0.077	1.997	2.099
2004-05 BE	5.375	3.325	0.751	0.080	1.218	2.168

Source: *State Finance Accounts.*

Table A9.8: Maharashtra: Selected Expenditures (Rs. crore)

Year	Social Services (a to d)	Education (2202 to 2205)	Health (2210 & 2211)	Buildings (2216 & 2059)	Other Social Services	Economic Services
		a	B	c	d	
1993-94	3851.3	2450.2	503.4	247.0	650.7	2561.9
1994-95	4249.9	2744.4	559.4	165.9	780.2	2758.9
1995-96	4970.3	3206.5	617.8	241.0	905.0	2799.4
1996-97	5571.2	3656.5	654.3	340.0	920.4	3550.7
1997-98	6892.9	4471.7	808.1	472.4	1140.7	3785.7
1998-99	7774.5	4956.6	857.5	450.4	1510.1	4038.3
1999-00	10065.7	7004.3	1087.9	613.0	1360.6	4021.6
2000-01	13064.7	9086.7	1232.9	675.3	2069.8	6540.5
2001-02	12867.9	9076.1	1302.2	506.0	1983.6	4686.9
2002-03	12841.3	8695.2	1286.2	531.4	2328.4	6145.5
2003-04 RE	13912.6	9078.0	1379.5	462.5	2992.5	5335.0
2004-05 BE	14316.0	9133.2	1386.5	560.9	3235.5	5333.2
						As % of GSDP
1993-94	3.245	2.065	0.424	0.208	0.548	2.159
1994-95	3.128	2.020	0.412	0.122	0.574	2.030
1995-96	2.945	1.900	0.366	0.143	0.536	1.659
1996-97	3.037	1.993	0.357	0.185	0.502	1.936
1997-98	3.662	2.376	0.429	0.251	0.606	2.011
1998-99	3.575	2.279	0.394	0.207	0.694	1.857
1999-00	4.024	2.800	0.435	0.245	0.544	1.608
2000-01	5.179	3.602	0.489	0.268	0.820	2.593
2001-02	4.667	3.292	0.472	0.184	0.719	1.700
2002-03	4.357	2.950	0.436	0.180	0.790	2.085
2003-04 RE	4.290	2.799	0.425	0.143	0.923	1.645
2004-05 BE	4.022	2.566	0.390	0.158	0.909	1.498

Source: *State Finance Accounts.*

10

Budgetary Subsidies in India: Magnitudes and Issues

The definition of a subsidy, like that of beauty, varies with the beholder.
House Committee of Agriculture of the U.S. Congress

In this chapter, we look at the concept of subsidies and examine their role and rationale. We review at alternative ways of measuring subsidies, distinguishing between explicit and implicit subsidies. We examine the national income accounting approach to subsidies as also a more comprehensive method of measuring subsidies as un-recovered costs of providing goods and services that are essentially private in nature by the public authorities. Available estimates of the volume of central and state subsidies as well as their combined magnitude are surveyed. We also look at the composition of subsidies and the relevance of distinguishing merit from non-merit subsidies. Considering the large volume of budgetary subsidies in India that are largely input based, poorly targeted, and of the non-merit kind, we also look at the method and scope of reforming budgetary subsidies in India.

10.1 Subsidy: Meaning, Forms and Rationale

Subsidies and taxes on goods and services are both examples of indirect fiscal intervention in the working of the economy and are best understood as the converse of each other. Taxes appear on the revenue side of government budgets. Subsidies are part of government expenditures. While taxes withdraw money from the expenditure stream and reduce disposable income, subsidies inject money into the expenditure stream. Subsidies generally affect prices and alter the demand and supply conditions in the commodity markets. By lowering the relative price of the subsidized goods or services, subsidies generate an increase in its demand. On the other hand, other things remaining the same, an indirect tax will result in an increase of the price of the taxed commodity and a fall in the quantity at which the market for that commodity is cleared. Subsidies can have a major impact in augmenting welfare of the society provided. At the same time, subsidies can also be very costly if they are poorly designed and inefficiently administered.

Subsidies have been defined in a number of ways. The dictionary [Concise Oxford] defines it as "money granted by state, public body, etc., to keep down the prices of commodities, etc." Environmental economists define subsidies as uncompensated environmental damage arising from any flow of goods and services. Economists have used the term subsidy with different meanings and connotations in different contexts. It is no wonder that the House Committee on Agriculture of the U.S. Congress (1972) acknowledged that "the definition of a subsidy, like that of beauty, varies with the beholder". Houthakker (1972) had observed that "the concept of a subsidy is just too elusive to even attempt to define". Prest [1974] had observed that economists have not settled upon a commonly acceptable definition of subsidy. In a budgetary context, it may be defined as "unrecovered costs in the public provision of private goods". This was the definition used in Government of India's Discussion Paper on subsidies, which was presented to Parliament in May 1997.

10.2 Forms of Subsidies

Subsidies take many forms and ways in which these may be administered. Some of the important forms of subsidies are indicated below. These alternative forms are discussed in Srivastava and Sen (1997).

1. **Cash Subsides**: Given to producers or consumers in the form of cash like food subsidies are given as payment to the Food Corporation of India; fertilizer subsidy is given to the various fertilizer producing industrial units, export subsidies used to be given as cash to the exporters.
2. **Interest or Credit Subsidies**: When loans are given at less than market rates, an implicit subsidy emanates.
3. **Tax Subsidies**: Various tax exemptions, e.g. deductions of medical expenses, deducting interest payments on housing loans for purposes of exemption, postponing collection of arrears: these are also examples of implicit subsidies.
4. **Subsidies in the form of goods or services** (also known as **in-kind** subsidies) like provision of free medicines and medical consultation, free mid-day meal for children: these are explicit subsidies but given in kind and not in cash.
5. **Equity Subsidies:** These are subsidies implicit, when returns on equity investment of government, gives low dividends primarily as a result of administered prices.
6. **Procurement subsidies**: These arise when certain goods are procured from the producers at more than market prices like procurement of food grains in India at assured minimum support prices
7. **Regulatory Subsidies**: These arise when prices of some goods are fixed lower than average for certain category of consumers like electricity tariff for

agriculture and domestic consumer, while other categories of consumers are charged a lighter than average price. These give rise to cross- subsidies.

10.3 Rationale for Subsidies

Subsidies in areas such as education, health and environment are advocated on grounds that their benefits are spread well beyond the immediate recipients, and are shared by the population at large, present and future. Subsidies are also used with redistributive objectives, particularly for ensuring minimum consumption levels of food and other basic needs. Subsidies are justified mainly in the presence of positive externalities.

The presence of externalities implies that the social demand curve (Ds) lies above the private demand curve (Dp) as indicated in Figure 10.1. Given the supply curve Sp, market equilibrium is at a price-quantity combination of (p_0, q_0). However, this is sub-optimal with reference to the social demand curve (Ds), which requires that the quantity should be increased to q*. In order to induce the consumers to demand q*, price will need to be lowered to p_1. However, in order also to induce the suppliers to provide q*, they will need to be given a price p_2. This implies that per unit subsidy p_1p_2 will need to be injected into the system so that the suppliers obtain op_2, consumer pay op_1 and the government pays p_1p_2. The total subsidy bill then would be $p_1p_2oq^*$.

Figure 10.1: Rationale of A Price Subsidy in Partial Equilibrium

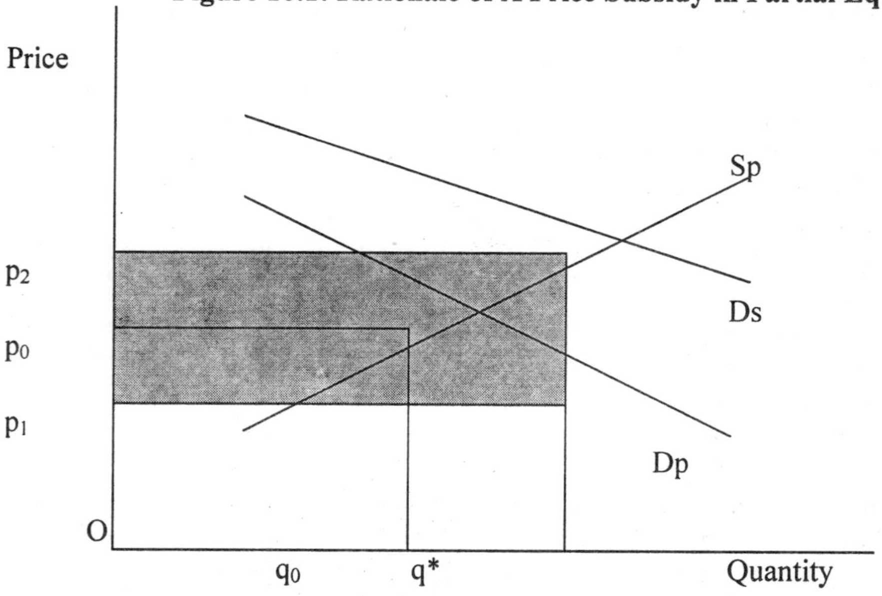

10.4 Measurement of Subsidies

It is commonly recognised that entries in the budget under the head 'subsidies' would give a very incomplete picture of subsidies. The national income accounting framework provides an alternative approach as discussed below. However, even that approach is not comprehensive enough.

A comprehensive approach is to define subsidies as un-recovered budgetary costs. While some subsidies are explicitly stated in the budget, there may be many others that are not shown explicitly. Therefore, explicit subsidies provide only a limited idea of the overall volume of budgetary subsidies in the system. Since observed or explicit subsidies cover only a fraction of total subsidies, methodologies have been developed to also estimate the implicit subsidies in the system as un-recovered costs of public provision of private goods/services. In these cases, in principle, it should be possible to recover the cost of providing services by charging the beneficiaries of the service a suitable price according to the extent of their consumption. In this exercise, it is customary to exclude pure public goods such as defence, general administration, etc., as these are meant to be financed by tax revenues, although, sometimes, subsidies are implicit in these cases also. For example, in the case of defence expenditure, a procurement subsidy may be provided in the purchase of defence goods.

10.5 National Income Accounting Approach

In national income accounts (NIA), indirect taxes are deducted and subsidies are added in order to arrive at estimates of gross domestic product (GDP) at factor cost from the estimates of GDP at current market prices. Indirect taxes that are part of the sale price of commodities do not create incomes for factors of production. These are, therefore, deducted from GDP at market prices to get at GDP at factor cost. On the other hand, subsidies have the opposite effect. A subsidy received by a firm is paid out as wages, rents or profits, and would therefore, become an income of the factors of production. This element of their income, however, is not generated by the sale of output. Hence, subsidies should be added to expenditure, i.e., GDP at market prices.

In the methodology adopted by the Central Statistical Organization, subsidies include grants on current account which private industries, public corporations and government enterprises receive from the government. These may be in the form of direct payments or those estimated on the basis of differentials between buying and selling prices of government trading organizations. The NIA approach focuses only on firms/producers or government departments. It does not fully cover all the budgetary costs in the public provision of non-public goods.

10.6 Comprehensive Estimates: Subsidies as Un-recovered Costs

Estimation of budgetary subsidies involves estimation of the "unrecovered" costs of governmental provision of goods/services that are not classified as public goods. Some of the important studies using this methodology are Rao and Mundle (1994) Tiwari (1996), Srivastava and Sen et al (1997), Srivastava and Amarnath (2001), and Srivastava and Bhujanga Rao and others (2002) The unrecovered costs are measured as the excess of aggregate costs over receipts from the concerned budgetary head. The aggregate costs comprise two elements: (i) current costs, and (ii) annualised capital costs. Current costs consist of revenue (current) expenditures directly related to the provision of services classified under different heads. Transfers to funds are not included as these do not contribute to the provision of service in the current cost. Transfers from funds are included. Transfers to individuals are also separated out, as these add to incomes of individuals and do not constitute provision of goods/services. For capital costs, we distinguish between three forms of government investment resulting in accumulated capital stock. If services are departmentally provided, there is investment in physical capital. In addition, there is investment in the form of equity and loans including those given to public enterprises. The annualised cost of capital is obtained by applying the interest rate at which funds have been borrowed by the government to capital stock. This represents the opportunity cost of capital. In the case of physical capital, a depreciation cost is calculated, in addition. The receipts come in three forms: revenue receipts from the user charges, interest receipts on loans, and dividends on equity investment.

In terms of symbols, these costs, following Srivastava and Sen (1997), may be written as:

$$C = RX + (i + d^*) K_0 + iZ_0$$

where

RX = revenue expenditure on the service head net of adjustments

i = effective interest rate

d^* = depreciation rate

K_0 = aggregate capital expenditure at the beginning of the period

Z_0 = sum of loans and equity investment at the beginning of the period

Adjustments in deriving RX relate to transfer to funds which are deducted and transfer from funds which are added. Transfers to individuals are also not counted, although these are separately compiled. Expenditure on running secretariat social and economic services are also not counted as these relate to general administration, and are also not decomposable among different heads of services.

Receipts are:

$R = RR + (I + D)$
where
RR = revenue receipts
I = interest receipts
D = dividends
Subsidy is defined as: $S = C - R$

Other parameters are effective interest rate and depreciation rate. These are estimated separately for the central government and each state government. The effective interest rate is obtained by dividing the interest payment by outstanding debt at the beginning of the concerned year.

10.7 Estimating Depreciation Costs

The depreciation rate is to be calculated with reference to the stock of capital at the beginning of the year. This stock of capital is the sum of nominal investments in previous years. Since these are additions of nominal figures, all at different prices, the calculation of depreciation rate has to take this into account. The methodology used for this purpose is explained below. This methodology is discussed in Srivastava and Amarnath (2001), and Srivastava and Bhujanga Rao and others (2002)

Let the life of a capital asset be T years. The rate of depreciation would be (1/T) per year for the asset to be written off. For example, if T = 50 (years), 1/T = .02. Let the current year be T + 1. The past years under consideration are from 1 to T. Let nominal investments in these years be written as

$I_1, I_2, \ldots, I_T$

Assuming an investment growth rate of z, we have

$I_2 = (1 + z) I_1$

$I_T = (1 + z)^{T-1} I_1$

Thus,

$I_1 = I_T/(1 + z)^{T-1}$

Correspondingly,

$I_1 = I_T/(1 + z)^{T-1}$

$I_2 = I_T/(1 + z)^{T-2}$

$I_{T-1} = I_T/(1 + z)$

$I_T = I_T$

If the long-term rate of inflation is `i', a nominal amount of 1 in year 1, is $(1 + i)^{T-1}$ in terms of the prices of the T_{th} year.

Then, the sum of I_1, etc. in terms of the prices of the T_{th} year can be written as

$$I_T\left(\frac{1+i}{1+z}\right)^{T-1} + I_T\left(\frac{1+i}{1+z}\right)^{T-2} + \ldots I_T$$

$= I_T\,[w^{T-1} + w^{T-2} + \ldots.. + 1]$

where

$$w = \left(\frac{1+i}{1+z}\right)$$

Let, $K_T = (I_T + I_{T-1} + \ldots.. + I_1)$ indicate aggregate capital expenditure obtained by summing investments measured in the prices of the respective years in which they were made. We can write:

$$K_T = I_T + \frac{I_T}{(1+z)} + \ldots + \frac{I_T}{(1+z)^{T-1}}$$

$$= I_T\left[1+\left(\frac{1}{1+z}\right)+\ldots+\left(\frac{1}{1+z}\right)^{T-1}\right]$$

$= I_T\,[1 + x + \ldots + (x)^{T-1}]$

where

$x = 1/(1 + z)$

or

$I_T = K_T/(1 + x + \ldots + x^{T-1})$

Depreciation for one year in terms of the prices of year T is given by

$$= \left(\frac{1}{T}\right) I_T\,(1 + w + w^2 + \ldots + w^{T-1})$$

$$= \left(\frac{1}{T}\right) K_T\,\frac{(1 + w + w^2 + \ldots + w^{T-1})}{(1 + x + \ldots + x^{T-1})}$$

Depreciation in terms of prices of year (T + 1), i.e., the current year, can be obtained by multiplying the above expression further by (1 + i). Thus, if K_T (i.e., outstanding accumulated capital stock in nominal terms) is to be used as the base, the depreciation rate on this should be

$$\left(\frac{1}{T}\right)\left(\frac{1 + w + w^2 + \ldots + w^{T-1}}{1 + x + x^2 + \ldots + x^{T-1}}\right)(1 + i)$$

We will refer to this expression as the adjusted depreciation rate (ADR). By simulating with alternative values of parameters (i, z) the following features regarding the impact of changes in the parameters on the depreciation rate can be derived.

- The higher the inflation rate, the higher is the depreciation rate, for any given rate of growth of investment.
- The higher the investment growth rate, the lower is the depreciation rate for any given inflation rate.

One more adjustment has been made. After investments are made, the stock of capital does not always start yielding service immediately. As an approximation, roughly 1/3rd of capital stock for three years immediately preceding the reference year is not counted and depreciation rate accordingly is adjusted.

10.8 Some Important Limitations

Although the methodology described above has been used in a number of studies, it is important to recognize that there are several qualifications and limitations, which arise primarily from the practical difficulties and lack of availability of relevant data. In particular, it may be noted that in the available studies, tax expenditures are not included in the estimates. The average life of an asset is assumed to be fifty years. Estimates are based on actual prices even if these are administered and not on the basis of market prices which would prevail in the absence of regulations. Subsidies arising from administered price regimes, or off-budget subsidies, are also not captured in the group of studies dealing with estimation of un-recovered costs of public provision of private goods.

10.9 Classifying Goods: Private, Public, Merit, and Non-Merit

A public good is distinguished from a private good by two characteristics: non-excludability and non-rivalry. Non-rivalry implies that the consumption of the good by one user does not reduce the quantity available for another. Non-excludability means that consumption of the good by one consumer cannot be distinguished from the consumption of the same good by another. Defence and law and order are examples of public goods. In the case of private goods, the consumer is identifiable, and the extent of his consumption is measurable. In modern economies, there are many goods/services that do not clearly fall into the exclusive categories of purely public or purely private goods. Both the characteristics of rivalry and excludability are matters of degree, and often there are some goods which can be seen as characterised by different degrees of publicness' and, therefore, fall in an intermediate category. An intermediate category is that of `club' goods or congestible goods like roads or swimming pools, which relate to goods that are non-rival for small groups but become rival when the group of users becomes large. In the case of congestible goods, user charges are leviable, although these may be varied only according to groups of consumers rather than individual consumers.

Government expenditures in India are classified into three broad service categories: general, social, and economic. In the general services, expenditure heads like organs of state, fiscal and administrative services are included. These services are in the nature of public goods. These are not supplied by the market although sometimes services can be individualised. In most cases, services cannot be charged to individuals according to the extent of their consumption. In such cases, these are appropriately paid for by taxation.

Governments in India, both central and the states, actively participate in the provision of a range of private goods or club goods under the head of social and economic services where users or groups of users are identifiable and user charges can be levied. The degree of 'externality' is a useful criterion to determine whether and to what extent the concerned service should be subsidised. In recent studies of subsidies in India, services were classified into merit and non-merit categories. The merit category has been further divided into Merit I, deserving of a high degree of subsidisation and Merit II, which deserve subsidisation to a lesser extent. There is no case for subsidising non-merit goods. In Srivastava, Bhujanga, C. Rao et al (2003) these categories included the services as specified below:

Merit I: Elementary education, primary health centres, prevention and control of diseases, social welfare and nutrition, soil and water conservation, and ecology and environment.

Merit II: Education (other than elementary), sports and youth services, family welfare, urban development, forestry, agricultural research and education, other agricultural programmes, special programmes for rural development, land reforms, other rural development programmes, special programmes for north-eastern areas, flood control and drainage, non-conventional energy, village and small industries, ports and light houses, roads and bridges, inland water transport, atomic energy research, space research, oceanographic research, other scientific research, census surveys and statistics, meteorology.

Non-Merit: All others.

10.10 Trends in Central Budgetary Subsidies

Most well known of the budgetary subsidies are the explicit subsidies of the central budget, mainly the food and fertilizer subsidies. We discuss first the volume of these subsidies and their trends in recent years. This is followed by an estimation of central budgetary subsidies in a comprehensive sense as per the methodology discussed above.

10.11 Explicit Subsidies

Some of the explicit subsidies of the central budget are the ones that are most frequently discussed in the Indian context. These include the well known food and fertilizer subsidies. More recently, the petroleum subsidies have also assumed importance. Table 10.1 gives the nominal amounts of the major central explicit subsidies. It is important to note the sharp rise in the volume of food subsidies in the latter part of the nineties.

Table 10.1: Volume of Explicit Central Subsidies (Rs. crore)

Year	Food	Fertilizer	Others	Total
1990-91	2,450	4,389	5,319	12,158
1991-92	2,850	5,185	4,218	12,253
1992-93	2,800	5,796	2,228	10,824
1993-94	5,537	4,562	1,506	11,605
1994-95	5,100	5,769	985	11,854
1995-96	5,377	6,735	554	12,666
1996-97	6,066	7,578	1,855	15,499
1997-98	7,900	9,918	722	18,540
1998-99	9,100	11,596	2,897	23,593
1999-00	9,434	13,244	1,809	24,487
2000-01	12,060	13,800	978	26,838
2001-02	17,499	12,595	1,116	31,210
2002-03	24,176	11,015	8,342	43,533
2003-04	25,160	11,847	7,249	44,256
2004-05RE	25,800	15,662	5,052	46,514
2005-06 BE	26,200	16,254	4,978	47,432

Source: *Central Budget Documents*.

The relative importance of the two major explicit subsidies is more clearly understood when these are looked relative to centre's revenue receipts. Table 10.2 shows the amount of central budgetary subsidies as percentage centre's revenue receipts. The main trend that is noticeable is the explosive growth in the food subsidies.

Chart 10.1 shows how the growth rate of food subsidies was far sharper than that of the fertilizer subsidies in recent years. The darker line, showing the ratio of food subsidies to centre's revenue receipts indicate sudden upsurge in their volume towards the end of the nineties.

Table 10.2: Central Explicit Subsidies as Percentage of Centre's Revenue Receipts

Year	Food	Fertilizer	Others	Total	Year	Food	Fertilizer	Others	Total
1980-81	5.21	4.05	6.99	16.24	1993-94	7.31	6.02	1.99	15.31
1981-82	4.62	2.52	5.68	12.82	1994-95	5.58	6.32	1.08	12.98
1982-83	4.06	3.44	5.42	12.92	1995-96	4.88	6.12	0.50	11.50
1983-84	4.23	5.28	4.42	13.94	1996-97	4.80	6.00	1.47	12.27
1984-85	4.68	8.19	4.28	17.15	1997-98	5.90	7.41	0.54	13.85
1985-86	5.88	6.86	4.36	17.10	1998-99	6.09	7.76	1.94	15.78
1986-87	6.07	5.76	4.71	16.54	1999-00	5.20	7.30	1.00	13.49
1987-88	5.40	5.84	4.90	16.15	2000-01	6.26	7.16	0.51	13.93
1988-89	5.05	7.34	5.35	17.74	2001-02	8.69	6.26	0.55	15.50
1989-90	4.75	8.72	6.63	20.10	2002-03	10.47	4.77	3.61	18.86
1990-91	4.45	7.98	9.67	22.11	2003-04	9.53	4.49	2.75	16.77
1991-92	4.32	7.85	6.39	18.56	2004-05 RE	8.57	5.20	1.68	15.46
1992-93	3.78	7.82	3.01	14.60	2005-06 BE	7.46	4.63	1.42	13.51

Source: *Central Budget Documents.*

Chart 10.1: Food and Fertilizer Subsidies as % of Centre's Revenue Receipts

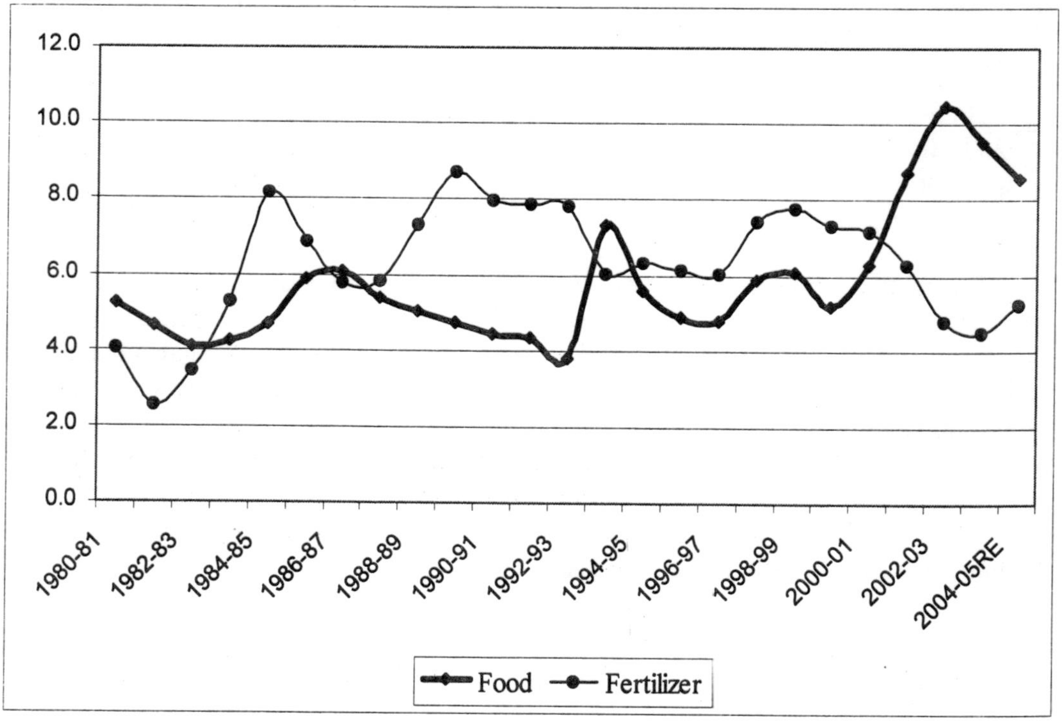

For a long period since the early eighties, the fertilizer subsidies have been larger than the food subsidies in terms of volume with the exception of a few years. It was in 2001-02 that the food subsidies rose sharply.

10.12 Central Subsidies: Comprehensive Estimates

Comprehensive estimates of central budgetary subsidies using a broadly similar methodology relating to the measurement of unrecovered costs in the public provision of private goods are now available for six years in the time span of 1987-88 to 1998-99. For the centre, four previous studies provide estimates for five years. The first in the series was that by Mundle and Rao (1992). Subsequent studies are by Tiwari (1996), Srivastava and Sen, *et. al.* (1997), Srivastava and Amar Nath (2001) and Srivastava and Bhujanga, C. Rao *et. al.* (2003). In all, estimates for six years have become available. These years are 1987-88, 1992-93, 1994-95, 1995-96, 1996-97 and 1998-99.

Table 10.3 shows a time profile of estimated central budgetary subsidies for six years over the eleven-year period from 1987-88 to 1998-99, as estimated in different studies from time to time. Because of differences in the methodology of estimation, the estimates are not directly comparable. However, in broad terms, a similar approach of measuring budgetary subsidies in a comprehensive way was used in these studies. There is a greater comparability in the last three estimates. In 1987-88, central budgetary subsidies were estimated to be 4.53 percent of GDP. In 1992-93, these increased to 4.92 percent of GDP. One major factor for this increase may have been the salary revisions following the recommendations of the Fourth Central Pay Commission. It would be evident that since 1994-95, subsidies in the central budget fell to 3.49 percent of GDP in 1996-97. After this, these show a sudden upward movement, rising from a level of 3.49 percent of GDP in 1996-97 to 4.59 percent in 1998-99. This takes it back beyond the level of 1987-88, indicating that attempts to contain subsidy amounts appear to have yielded little or no result over the eleven-year period under consideration.

A closer comparison of subsidy magnitudes between 1996-97 and 1998-99 further establishes the importance of salary revisions as a major factor that accounts for the upward surge in the volume of subsidies. Central budgetary subsidies were estimated at Rs. 47781 crore for 1996-97 which increased to Rs. 79828 crore in 1998-99. Thus, in a span of two years, subsidies of the central budget appear to have increased by Rs. 32047 crore. There are three possible reasons. First, the explicit subsidies (food, fertiliser, etc.) increased by a margin of Rs. 8094 crore from a figure of Rs. 15499 crore in 1996-97 to Rs. 23593 crore in 1998-99. Secondly, railways, which was a surplus sector in 1996-97 became a subsidy sector in 1998-99 with subsidies in this sector amounting to a little more than Rs. 4000 crore. Thirdly, salary revisions in the wake of the recommendations of the Fifth Central Pay Commission hiked up all current expenditures. The residual must be explained by increased cost of other inputs including petroleum products.

Table 10.3: A Comparison of Central Budgetary Subsidies: Selected Years

(Rs. crore)

Year	Subsidies	Revenue receipts	Fiscal deficit	GDP at market prices	Subsidies as percentage of		
					Revenue receipts	GDP	Fiscal deficit
1987-88 (M-R)	16,065	37,037	27,044	3,54,343	43.38	4.53	59.40
1992-93 (Tiwari)	36,829	74,128	40,173	7,48,367	49.68	4.92	91.68
1994-95 (NIPFP)	43,089	91,083	57,703	10,12,770	47.31	4.25	74.67
1995-96 (NIPFP)	42,941	1,10,130	60,243	11,88,012	38.99	3.61	71.28
1996-97 (NIPFP)	47,781	1,26,279	66,733	13,68,208	37.84	3.49	71.60
1998-99 (NIPFP)	79,828	1,49,485	1,13,348	17,40,935	53.40	4.59	70.43

Sources: Mundle and Rao (1992), Tiwari. A.C. (1996), Srivastava, D.K., *et.al.* (1997), Srivastava and Amar Nath (2001). Revenue Receipts and Fiscal Deficit: Receipts Budget of the Central Government.

In 1996-97, railways was surplus sector (Srivastava and Amar Nath, 2001). The estimated surplus was Rs. 4,624 crore. In 1998-99, railways became a subsidy sector, the estimated subsidy being Rs. 4,021 crore. This indicates a down-turn of Rs. 8,645 crore. The aggregate recovery rate in the case of the centre was shown to be 13.98 percent if railways is not included. The recovery rate in social services is 4.83 per cent of total cost. A comparison of recovery rates between 1996-97 and 1998-99 should be done by excluding railways in 1998-99 while calculating the aggregate recovery rate.

10.13 Central Merit and Non-Merit Subsidies

Subsidies have been divided into two main categories, merit and non-merit. The merit subsidies have been further divided into Merit I and Merit II groups. Table 10.4 provides group-wise totals of the subsidies. The share of non-merit subsidy is Rs. 60,100 crore in a total of 79,828 crore. This amounts to approximately 75 per cent of the total subsidies. Merit I subsidies are estimated at Rs. 4,006 crore which is only about 5 percent of the total subsidies. Merit II subsidies account for Rs. 15,722 crore, which is about 20 per cent of the total subsidies. The pattern shown by the recovery rate indicates that Merit I group has an average recovery rate of 1.63 percent whereas the Merit II group has an average recovery rate of 4.30 percent. The non-merit group shows an average recovery rate of 41.01 percent if railways is included. This provides the basis for working out the scope of additional recoveries by looking at the difference between category-wise defined subsidy rates and the actual subsidy rates.

Among the social services, the Merit I group comprises elementary education, primary health centres, prevention and control of diseases, welfare of SC, ST and other backward classes, and social welfare and nutrition. Except for social welfare and nutrition, in all the other categories, receipts are virtually zero.

Table 10.4: Classification of Central Subsidies: Merit and Non-Merit Categories: 1998-99 (Rs. crore)

Service	Cost			Receipts	Subsidy	Recovery Rate (%)
	Current	Capital	Total			
Social Services						
Merit I	3,567	285	3,852	66	3,786	1.72
Merit II	4,324	201	4,525	27	4,498	0.61
Total Merit	7,891	486	8,377	94	8,283	2.33
Non-Merit	6,434	854	7,288	663	6,625	9.10
Total Social Services	**14,325**	**1,340**	**15,665**	**757**	**14,908**	**4.83**
Economic Services						
Merit I	219	2	220	0	220	0.00
Merit II	8,717	3,186	11,903	678	11,225	5.70
Total Merit	8,936	3,188	12,123	678	11,445	5.70
Non-Merit	67,907	26,686	94,593	41,118	53,475	43.47
Total Economic Services	**76,842**	**29,874**	**1,06,716**	**41,797**	**64,920**	**39.17**
Social and Economic Services						
Merit I	3,785	287	4,072	66	4,006	1.63
Merit II	13,041	3,387	16,428	706	15,722	4.30
Total Merit	16,827	3,674	20,500	772	19,728	5.92
Non-Merit	74,340	27,541	1,01,881	41,781	60,100	41.01
Total Subsidy	**91,167**	**31,214**	**1,22,381**	**42,553**	**79,828**	**34.77**

Source: *Srivastava, Bhujanga Rao, et al (2003).*

In the Merit II group of social services, secondary and higher education, technical education, family welfare and urban development are included. In these cases also, the receipts are fairly small. The recovery rate for the Merit I group as a whole is higher than for the Merit II group under social services. In the non-merit social services, the recovery rate is above 9 percent and the volume of subsidy is Rs. 6625 crore. The aggregate volume of subsidies under the non-merit services in the social category, however, is less than the sum of the Merit I and Merit II group subsidies.

Among the economic services, the Merit I group consists of soil and water conservation and ecology and environment. In both cases, recoveries are nil and the total cost translates into subsidies. Merit II group of economic services accounts for a much larger share. The total volume of subsidies in this group is Rs. 11225 crore. However, the non-merit group subsidies in the economic services account for a much larger volume of subsidies. It is nearly 5 times as large as the subsidies in the Merit II group. The total volume of non-merit subsidies in the economic services is Rs. 53475 crore. However, in this group, the average recovery rate is 43.47 percent of the total costs excluding the surplus sectors, but including railways.

10.14 Budgetary Subsidies of the State Governments

Compared to the 1994-95 results used in Srivastava and Sen [NIPFP (1997)], there was a fall in the aggregate amount of subsidies relative to GDP in 1998-99, which amounted to 9.26 percent of the GDP at market prices when the same 1993-94 base series of GDP is used for comparison. However, the aggregate recovery rate had also fallen from 5.58 to 4.88. The fall in the volume of subsidies accompanied by a fall also in the recovery rate can only be explained by the fall in the total costs. These amounted to 9.83 percent of GDP in 1994-95 and to 9.32 percent in 1998-99. The lower expenditure in the provision of services is in spite of the higher salary expenditures. It was due to a fall both in capital expenditure and the non-salary revenue expenditure associated with these services. It, therefore, implies a fall in the quality and coverage of services rather than improvement through better recovery rates. It is indicative of subsidy reduction through the expenditure side rather than through the higher mobilization of non-tax revenues.

An idea about the overall trends in the movement of the subsidy bill relative to key fiscal and economic parameters may be obtained by a comparison with selected earlier studies for which estimates are available. However, it should be noted that because of differences in the methodology these comparisons are broadly indicative of the general trends. Table 10.5 provides information with respect to four years for which such information is available, namely, 1987-88, 1992-93, 1994-95 and 1998-99. Looking at the ratio of total estimated subsidies with respect to GDP at current market prices, it would appear that the subsidy bill had continued to rise until 1994-95 from 7.41 percent in 1987-88 to 7.82 percent in 1992-93 rising to a maximum of 9.26 percent in 1994-95. Since then it had declined to 8.96 percent. As percentage of fiscal deficit and revenue receipts, the profile of changes is also indicated in Table 10.5. As percentage of fiscal deficit, the same trend is visible but as percentage of revenue receipts subsidies had the highest share in 1998-99. This is because of the lower growth of revenue receipts, which have fallen relative to GDP.

Table 10.5: A Comparison of Budgetary Subsidies of the States: Selected Years (Rs. crore)

Year	Estimated subsidies	Fiscal deficit	GDP (at market prices)	Revenue receipts	Subsidies as percentage of		
					GDPmp	Fiscal deficit	Revenue receipts
1987-88 (M-R)	26,259	10,988	3,54,343	42,167	7.41	238.98	62.27
1992-93 (Tiwari)	58,544	20,000	7,48,367	87,091	7.82	292.72	67.22
1994-95 (NIPFP)	93,754	26,673	10,12,770	1,18,174	9.26	351.49	79.34
1998-99 (NIPFP)	1,55,923	72,660	17,40,935	1,72,414	8.96*	214.59	90.44

Notes: * 8.47 per cent with adjustment for salary arrears.
Sources: Mundle and Rao (1992), Tiwari. A.C. (1996), Srivastava, D. K., *et. al.* (1997), Srivastava and Amar Nath (2001), Fiscal Deficit and Revenue Receipts, Indian Public Finance Statistics, GDP (at market prices), Central Statistical Organisation and Economic Survey, 2001-02.

10.15 Composition of State Subsidies

Table 10.6 indicates that the maximum share of state budgetary subsidies goes to agriculture, rural development and allied activities (16.28), followed by irrigation and flood control (15.09) leaving out the residual category of other subsidies. The next few heads in order of importance are elementary education (10.54), energy (9.69), secondary education (9.07), medical and public health (7.86) and transport (5.89). Important among other sectors claiming budgetary subsidies are other education including technical education (4.69), water supply and sanitation (4.54), industry & minerals (3.21) and housing (1.25). Together these eleven broad heads account for 88 percent of the state budgetary subsidies. It is clear, therefore, that for rationalization and reduction of subsidies maximum effort should be made in the context of agriculture and irrigation and energy and transport. The education sector considered together accounts for a little less than 25 percent of the total state budgetary subsidies. In their case, while an attempt should be made to increase the service level, subsidies need to be rationalized by better targeting to support better quality and spread of education.

Table 10.6: Sectoral Shares of All State Subsidies: Arranged in Descending Order

Sector/Head	Amount (Rs. crore)	Share (per cent)
Agriculture, Rural Development & Allied Activities	25,380	16.28
Irrigation & Flood Control	23,525	15.09
Other Subsidies	18,661	11.97
Elementary Education	16,291	10.45
Energy	15,115	9.69
Secondary Education	14,147	9.07
Medical & Public Health	12,259	7.86
Transport	9,191	5.89
Other Education incl. Technical Education	7,319	4.69
Water Supply & Sanitation	7,082	4.54
Industry & Minerals	4,999	3.21
Housing	1,954	1.25
Total	**1,55,923**	**100.00**

Source: As in Table 10.1.

10.16 Per Capita Subsidies: Inter-State Pattern

Table 10.7 shows state-wise per capita subsidies in social and economic services arranged according to groups of states: three groups among the general category states (A, B, C) and two among the special category states (D and E). These results are on the basis of study by Srivastava, Bhujanga Rao and others (2003). Within each group, states are arranged in descending order of their per capita GSDP. Looking at the general category states, it would appear that the highest per capita subsidies are in Group A, followed by Group B. Group C, consisting of the low income states, has also the lowest per-capita subsidies. This pattern is common for both social and economic services. Among the special category states, again a pattern is visible where higher income states have higher per capita subsidies. Leaving Assam, all special category states have per capita subsidies higher than the general category states with the exception of Goa.

Table 10.7: State-Wise Per Capita Social and Economic Services Subsidies: 1998-99

State	Total (Rs. crore)		Per capita (Rupees)	
	Social	Economic	Social	Economic
Goa	407	218	2,718	1,453
Maharashtra	9,218	8,773	1,028	978
Punjab	2,207	2,965	953	1,280
Haryana	1,666	2,899	857	1,491
Gujarat	5,653	8,280	1,196	1,752
Tamil Nadu	6,423	4,607	1,053	755
Kerala	3,115	3,177	978	997
Karnataka	4,485	5,346	877	1,045
Andhra Pradesh	7,709	5,942	1,038	800
West Bengal	5,675	4,605	732	594
Rajasthan	4,543	4,108	870	786
Madhya Pradesh	4,382	4,899	563	630
Orissa	2,071	2,640	585	746
Uttar Pradesh	8,804	9,306	534	564
Bihar	2,579	3,887	265	399
Himachal Pradesh	1,362	726	2,106	1,122
Jammu & Kashmir	1,548	2,435	1,612	2,537
Assam	1,908	1,608	741	625
Nagaland	361	180	2,122	1,057
Mizoram	284	328	3,129	3,605
Sikkim	219	164	4,063	3,038
Arunachal Pradesh	300	531	2,875	5,095
Meghalaya	332	147	1,427	633
Manipur	371	392	1,688	1,782
Tripura	511	495	1,415	1,370

Source: Srivastava, D.K., Bhujanga, C. Rao et al (2003).

10.17 Merit and Non-Merit Subsidies

Table 10.8 per capita subsidies divided into the merit and non-merit groups. Again certain clear patterns emerge in the comparison across states. In the non-merit category, among the general category states, the highest per capita subsidies are given by the highest per capita income group and the lowest per capita non-merit subsidies are given by the lowest per capita income group. The smaller special category states gave high per capita subsidies both of the merit and non-merit kind. Within the special category states, a general regressive pattern is also visible.

Table 10.8: State-Wise Per Capita Merit and Non-Merit Subsidies: 1998-99

(Rupees)

State	Merit I	Merit II	Total	Non-Merit	Total
Goa	560	1,636	2,196	1,902	4,098
Maharashtra	436	524	961	1,046	2,006
Punjab	143	840	983	1,249	2,233
Haryana	216	626	842	1,506	2,348
Gujarat	544	772	1,315	1,632	2,948
Tamil Nadu	405	659	1,064	744	1,808
Kerala	304	921	1,224	751	1,975
Karnataka	412	503	916	1,006	1,922
Andhra Pradesh	598	511	1,109	729	1,838
West Bengal	217	573	789	537	1,326
Rajasthan	224	560	783	873	1,656
Madhya Pradesh	260	389	648	545	1,193
Orissa	203	456	658	673	1,331
Uttar Pradesh	281	376	657	441	1,098
Bihar	73	300	373	291	664
Himachal Pradesh	857	1,574	2,430	1,825	4,255
Jammu & Kashmir	469	1,043	1,512	2,636	4,148
Assam	386	547	934	433	1,366
Nagaland	814	1,415	2,229	1,872	4,101
Mizoram	1,444	2,391	3,835	2,899	6,734
Sikkim	1,754	2,301	4,055	4,926	8,981
Arunachal Pradesh	948	3,360	4,308	3,662	7,970
Meghalaya	565	1,282	1,847	1,117	2,964
Manipur	685	1,362	2,048	1,422	3,470
Tripura	673	1,146	1,819	966	2,785

Source: Srivastava, D.K. and Bhujanga, C. Rao, et al (2003).

10.18 Some Important Sectoral Subsidies

In this section, we discuss some of the important sectoral subsidies in India, like food, fertilizer, petroleum products, focusing on their particular problems, inefficiencies, and reforms.

Food Subsidy

The subsidy to food, administered through the central budget, subsidises not only the consumption of food, but also the farmers (producers) of wheat and rice, and the operational inefficiencies of the Food Corporation of India (FCI). The inefficiencies include costs of carrying excess food stocks and inefficiencies in procurement, transportation, processing, and storage operations of the FCI. Procurement and inefficiency costs have risen sharply in recent years, and the element of consumer subsidy has shrunk resulting in poor off-takes, leaving larger stocks with the FCI to carry forward, which entails additional cost as well as wastage of increasing stock of foodgrains. A reform of food subsidy would require both short-term and long-run measures.

Poor targeting of the food subsidy has often been highlighted as a major problem in administering this subsidy. For example, in Jha (1994), in respect of targeting through the Public Distribution System (PDS), a distinction was made between exclusion and inclusion errors, this has been discussed further in chapter 7. Jha found that the exclusion error for different commodities in the PDS ranged between 30 to 90 percent and was higher than the inclusion error which ranged from 30 to 60 percent. Targeting is bad also because of a clear urban bias in the PDS and because of the remoteness of many backward areas. Further, it is not only the number of poor covered by the PDS but also the lower magnitude of the benefit derived by the poor which indicates inadequate targeting. Jha had observed: "per capita subsidy to the poorest consumers is much below the average. The aggregate subsidy is only about Rs. 2.50 per capita per month – a meagre five percent of the mean expenditure of a person in the poorest decile".

Attempts have been made in recent years to improve PDS targeting through a Targeted Public Distribution System (TPDS). States have also now made a distinction between consumers above and below poverty line (APL/BPL) by using distinctly coloured cards. The central government has introduced a differentiation between the extent of subsidy for APL and BPL beneficiaries which is reflected in the PDS retail prices of the commodity. However, most of the APL quota is not being lifted. It is the BPL quota that may be getting distributed among the poor and non-poor alike due to lack of effective identification and implementation. The Expenditure Reforms Commission in its recent Report (July, 2000) observed, citing a major independent survey that "in rural India, 17 percent do not own ration cards" and that "18 percent of the below poverty households do not hold ration cards".

In the case of food subsidies, greater decentralisation can lead to efficiencies in carrying and transportation costs, and delivery and targeting mechanism. It will facilitate greater inter-state and inter-crop variation in the structure of support prices. A well-designed two-tier intervention can increase efficiencies and reduce subsidies. While satisfying the core objective, which is to make food available to BPL population at subsidized rates, food subsidies should be delinked from the target of supporting farmers. Buffer stocks may be maintained at the central and state levels. For any deficit state, there will be an option to purchase the required supply from its own stocks, central stocks, the stocks of other states, and the global market. All purchases and sales should be handled by open market operations – buying at times when prices are low and selling when market supply is less. States can decide their own mix of items for the buffer stocks. Central assistance to the states should be relative to the share of BPL population. In such an arrangement, the centre will be required to maintain a very small level of strategic buffer stocks.

As a first step, it would be appropriate to consider abolishing the Above Poverty Line (APL) category altogether as its subsidization is both undesirable and redundant in view of market prices often being lower than the economic cost of the FCI. At the same time, the benefit to Below Poverty Line (BPL) category should be increased both by increasing their entitlement and coverage of population. The latter may require undertaking a fresh survey where the poverty line is uplifted and exclusion errors of the previous survey are rectified. This will eliminate the more serious of the targeting errors, known as type I or exclusion error, where the deserving are missed out. The price for BPL category can also be reduced as percent of economic cost. Other measures in the short-run would include:

- The Minimum Support Price (MSP) for wheat and rice should be determined not just on a cost plus formula but also linking it to the position of existing stocks. The increase in MSP should be moderated according to the extent of excess of stocks over prescribed norms.
- The budget allocation by the central and the state governments for rural infrastructure construction, and other labour-intensive infrastructure should be increased, so that targets of reducing poverty and increasing the demand for food at the lowest income levels can be achieved simultaneously.
- Exports of foodgrains should be facilitated so that excess stock and the carrying costs can be reduced.

- MSP should be differentiated according to surplus and deficit states – lower MSP being offered in surplus states.

In the longer-run, a properly decentralized two-tier intervention for food subsidization should be developed. The centre should maintain minimum buffer stock for strategic market intervention and emergency purposes. The responsibility of procuring, storing, processing, and distribution should be largely handled by the state governments. This will eliminate the process of implicit inter-state transfer of resources to farmers of specific crops and eliminate operational inefficiencies arising from over-centralization. The centre can determine total amount of subsidy on the basis of the number of poor and the prevailing market prices and allocate to the states according to the number of poor and intensity of poverty. The centre can have a supervisory role and should ensure unfettered inter-state domestic trade in foodgrains. States on the other hand, should integrate the dimension of access to food within the context of an overall poverty reduction programme. The whole issue of supporting agricultural incomes should be tackled by a separate policy instrument.

10.19 Fertilizer Subsidies

A large part of fertilizer subsidies is used up in subsidizing the inefficiencies of the fertilizer industry. The present unit-wise retention price scheme implies that the more inefficient the industrial unit, the larger is the extent of its subsidization. Similarly, for the richer the farmer, the more he can provide for complementary inputs to fertilizer, the larger is his use of fertilizer and its subsidy. Overuse of urea, induced by the subsidies, also does long-term damage to the fertility of the soil and environmental degradation.

In this case also, subsidy reforms would require a short-run and medium-term perspective. In the short-run, both the unit-wise fixation of subsidy and the use of the Retention Price Scheme (RPS) should be given up. Instead of RPS, subsidy should be a specific nominal amount per metric tonne of output. Unit-wise differentials should be replaced by a group-wise scheme of concessions.

In a period of five years, fertilizer subsidies should be done away with in their present form. This would require setting up a proper exit policy for some of the inefficient units. These units should be facilitated to move to alternative technologies or to close down.

While the farmer would then be exposed to open market prices, greater efficiency would drive down the average cost. However, one segment of farmers may still need additional protection, *viz.*, the poor farmers with small landholdings. For all farmers, proper credit facilities would need to be developed, but for the poorer farmers, some subsidies can be administered linked to actual purchases through a reimbursement system subject to entitlement limits.

10.20 Irrigation Subsidies

While food and fertilizer subsidies emanate primarily from the central budget, irrigation and power subsidies are part of the state budgets. Irrigation claims a little more than 15 percent of the total subsidies implicit in the state budgets. A significant portion of this subsidy actually subsidizes only the excess staffing in the irrigation departments. The rest is due to extremely low user charges. Per capita subsidies are also large in the richer states like Gujarat, Maharashtra, and Punjab relative to those in Bihar or Uttar Pradesh. In almost all states, recoveries are extremely poor relative to costs. Apart from excess staffing, there is also considerable waste of water and water logging in many areas causing long-term damage to the soil. Staff is considerably in excess of requirements for maintenance and routine operations. Some of them can be utilized by increasing investment in the sector. The remaining staff would need to be redeployed or put through a properly designed retirement/redeployment scheme. It is important to induce discipline in water usage through better pricing, while bringing the costs down by eliminating inefficiencies.

Strategies for reducing irrigation subsidies should include: (i) re-deployment of staff to other sectors, (ii) introduction of Voluntary Retirement Scheme (VRS), and ensuring that when staff retires, vacant posts are not filled up and no new posts are created in this sector even on the plan side, (iii) fresh investment aimed at increasing irrigation coverage so that the ultimate irrigation potential is realized while average and marginal costs are reduced, and (iv) increase in user charges so as to recover at least the operation and maintenance costs (O&M). The O&M costs would be reduced after the excessive staffing costs are eliminated.

10.21 Power Subsidies

Power is subsidized for agricultural and domestic consumers through two sources: (i) state support to State Electricity Boards (SEBs) in the form of subventions or write off of loans or interest, etc., and (ii) cross-subsidization by charging higher prices from industrial and commercial consumers. Subsidies that remain unrecovered after these are carried forward as losses by the SEBs or remain as unpaid dues of the SEBs to central undertakings or state governments. Power subsidies largely subsidize inefficiencies. Two well known sources of inefficiency are: (i) transmission and distribution losses which include, apart from technical losses, a large portion of theft, and (ii) over-employment of personnel whose contribution at the margin in the provision of service may be zero. The power sector is characterized by shortages, poor quality and frequent breakdowns. Both industry and agriculture suffer on this account. Cross-subsidization makes power costlier for industry and commerce rendering them uncompetitive. Power subsidies are also highly regressive with higher per capita subsidies in richer states as compared to the poorer states.

The reform of power subsidies should be viewed in conjunction with the reform of the power sector both a short-run and long-run perspective. The new electricity Act does provide a framework for reforming the power sector. As long as the state electricity boards continue to be the major players in the power scenario, the following measures may help contain unwarranted power subsidies in the short-term:

- T&D losses should be reduced by meterisation of electricity supply up to bulk level consumers in rural areas and individual meterisation for farmers with large holdings. Energy audit should help to identify area wise pockets of losses in urban as well as rural areas.
- The power subsidy should be administered explicitly by making the farmers pay the regular tariff and claim the subsidy from State's Department of Agriculture. A change of this nature in Kerala has reduced not only the subsidy bill but also the wastage of power, as farmers become conscious of payments made by them to the Electricity Authority.
- Entry of private enterprises should be facilitated in all the segments.
- Staff strength of the Electricity Boards should be drastically pruned by introducing VRS and compulsory retirement scheme (CRS) after the SEB has identified its efficient workers.

In the long-run, average cost of supplying power has to be reduced by increasing the proportion of cheaper electricity from hydel sources in the overall mix of power supply. Costs will also be reduced when private enterprises are enabled to participate in all the activities, *viz.*, generation, transmission and distribution, and there is greater competition in the sector.

10.22 Subsidization of Agriculture

In reforming the subsidy regime, the issue of subsidizing agriculture should be considered as a whole. This issue was discussed at length in Srivastava and Sen (1997). Agriculture claims subsidies through the subsidization of inputs like fertilizers, power, and irrigation. In addition, it has a share in the food subsidies, where the minimum support price mechanism subsidizes the farmers of wheat and rice. Much of this subsidization leaks out to subsidize industrial inefficiencies as in the case of power and fertilizers, or inefficiencies of the government or public sector, as in the case of irrigation and power. Even in those subsidies that filter down to the farmers, it is the richer farmers who are able to take the larger benefits. These undesirable features arise because of the method of administering the subsidy through inputs.

The correct method for supporting agriculture is to identify the justifiable objectives of subsidization of agriculture and subsidize the potential beneficiary as directly as possible. The main objective of supporting agriculture, apart from making food available to BPL population at reasonable prices, should be to protect the farmers against excessive volatility in incomes, and to support the poorer farmers in terms of ensuring a minimum income, and credit support enabling the purchase of inputs at the right time. But subsidies should not be designed to support just a few selected crops, especially in times of sustained excess supply and availability of the global market to overcome any temporary shortages. The farmers should be allowed to respond to the market signals reflecting demand and supply imbalances, formulate short and medium term expectations, and accordingly select their cropping patterns. The best strategy is to achieve the two policy targets stated above by using no more than two policy instruments. The food subsidy for BPL population is best administered through a decentralized, limited and targeted PDS system. Volatility and income support to farmers should not be limited just to farmers of wheat and rice. This is best tackled by developing insurance and credit policies with support for selected crops. The selection of crops for support may be different for different periods and different states, depending on surplus/deficit profiles of outputs of different crops in different states.

Interventions through limited purchases/releases from strategic but small buffer stocks and imports designed to moderate excessive price/income fluctuations, but not meant for completely obliterating the market signals, would be helpful. These, supplemented by support to insurance services in the sector covering crop failures as well as excessive price crashes should protect farmers of all types against income fluctuations. The poorer farmers should be given subsidies and credit facilities for the purchase of inputs, without interfering with prices which should reflect economic and efficiency costs. The overall environment should be characterized by unfettered movement of produce throughout the country and access to global markets both for inputs and outputs. The input costs will be reduced through greater competition as well as by reducing inefficiencies in government operations. The only segment where government needs to invest is irrigation and new technology where the private sector is not likely to have a significant role. But here again resources can be released by drastically pruning the excess irrigation staff.

10.23 Social Sector Subsidies

Elementary education has been classified as a Merit I good deserving a high degree of subsidization. Further support may be needed in rural areas and small to medium towns and urban peripheries where private sector would not extensively participate in the provision of education. A distinction needs to be made between subsidization and participation by the government in actual production. Subsidization is possible even if children study in private schools, which are run under regulation. However, the subsidy is better administered to the identified child rather than to the school. But the fee structure in the schools should be regulated. However, in rural areas, remote areas, and urban peripheries, government may necessarily have to participate in running the schools. In these cases, even 95 to 100 percent subsidization may be justifiable but monitoring mechanisms are needed to ensure adequate quality and regular attendance.

Secondary and higher education have been classified as Merit II good deserving subsidization on an average to the extent of 60 percent. However, a much higher subsidy can be given to children from poorer families through scholarships. Loans should be made available to all categories of students through specialized institutions for educational loans. The degree of subsidization should be differentiated according to disciplines and types of institutions. Professional disciplines should be given much less subsidization and institutions should be asked to raise funds through professional fees and through consultancy and research services.

Primary and preventive health care has been categorized as Merit I service deserving of 90 to100 percent subsidization, and curative health services as non-merit good where full cost should be recovered. But in this case also partial subsidization could be provided to the BPL families. The entire sector should be served by extending insurance services so that unanticipated health care needs even for the better off can be taken care of.

Soil and water conservation may be taken as Merit I category but water supply in general should be taken as a service where costs should be recovered. But even in this case there could be partial subsidization for making water available to the poorer sections of the society. Sometimes due to lack of supply or poor quality of water, the poor may be made to pay much more in terms of medical costs. It would be better for the consumers to pay at least that cost of water supply which are calculated on the basis of cost norms and force the supply agencies to overcome inefficiencies and reduce average costs.

10.24 Subsidization of the Public Sector

Public sector enterprises with few exceptions are involved in providing a variety of goods and services that are clearly non-Merit goods. The public sector gets implicitly subsidized by the budgetary resources of the centre and the state governments because it does not give adequate return on the investments of these governments in the form of equity and loans. The difference between the opportunity cost of capital, i.e., the interest at which government borrows and the return that it gets on its investment from the public sector accounts for the implicit subsidization of the public sector. The average return on the public sector investments for states considered together is only 1.64 percent as against interest rates on their past debt ranging on average between 11-13 percent. Almost 90 percent of public enterprises in the states have become unviable and require be privatizing or closing down. Governments will be better off by supporting VRS/CRS programmes, which may otherwise be funded by the sale of assets of the enterprise including land. In many cases land may have sufficient value to fund the entire requisite VRS programme of a unit. Necessary changes in land related laws should be brought out by the state governments if this becomes a constraint in the disposal of land owned by public sector enterprises.

An important example of off-budgetary subsidies relates to guarantees extended by governments for borrowing by the public sector enterprises. These generate contingent liabilities for the budget, in case the concerned public sector enterprises default on servicing the debt which has been guaranteed by the government. Considering the performance of the public sector enterprises, the risk of defaults is very high, which makes servicing of debt a budgetary liability in the nature of subsidisation of the concerned enterprises, in case the guaranteed loans are defaulted.

10.25 Petroleum Subsidies: From Off-Budget to Budgetary Subsidies

Until recently an important example of off-budget subsidy pertained to the petroleum sector. This sector had an administered price regime which was coordinated by the Oil Coordination Committee (OCC) set up in July 1975. The OCC supervised a number of Oil Pool Accounts of which four main accounts are Crude Oil Price Equalization (COPE) Account, Cost and Freight Adjustment (C&F) Account, Freight Surcharge Pool (FSP), and Product Price Adjustment (PPA) Account. Important petroleum products categories are: Kerosene (SKO, domestic), LPG (domestic), High Speed Diesel (HSD), Naptha, Fertiliser (Fuel Oil), fertiliser, Light Sulphur Heavy Stock (LSHS), and Aviation Turbine Fuel (ATF).

The administrative price mechanism (APM) in the petroleum sector has been dismantled from April 1, 2002. During the APM regime, the producers were assured normative operating expenses plus a 15 percent post-tax return on their capital employed. The refineries were assured a norm-based acquisition cost of crude, normative operating costs, which include capacity utilization norms, and a 12 percent post-tax return on their net-worth. There were several components of the consumer prices comprising the ex-refinery price, marketing margins, surcharges, freight and excise duties, sales tax, and other local levies. Consumer prices were worked out through an ad-hoc Product Price Adjustment (PPA) mechanism, where selected products were subsidized. The price for the same product also varied depending on the end use. Differences between inflows and outflows in the Oil Pool Account led to surpluses or deficits.

The main items that were cross subsidized are kerosene and liquefied petroleum gas (LPG). The basic ceiling selling price of kerosene (domestic), is about 30 percent of its international price. It was also considerably lower than the domestic cost of production/supply. With inadequate targeting, much of subsidized kerosene leaks to unintended beneficiaries/uses. Estimates in 1996 indicated that only 70 percent of the kerosene (domestic) distributed through this mechanism reached to the poorer sections of society (Economic Survey, 2001). Kerosene is also widely used for adulteration of motor spirit (MS) and HSD, which has aggravated the problem of environmental pollution.

The subsidy regime worked on a cross-subsidy principle where some prices were kept at more than average cost, which then cross-subsidized others which were kept at less than average cost. However, when the two sides did not match, the difference spilled over into the oil pool account. If the oil pool account got into deficit, it meant that cross-subsidy is not enough to cover the subsidy being provided to selected oil products. The overall logic of cross-subsidisation was to use petrol, and aviation turbine fuel (used by the relatively rich) to subsidise the consumption of kerosene, cooking gas and fuels for fertiliser use, i.e., products meant for the vulnerable sections of society. The cross-subsidies therefore mitigate the extent of deficit on the oil pool account. However, to the extent that the increased cost of products like petrol and ATF feeds back into government expenditures, the cross-subsidisation simply replaced oil pool deficit by conventional budgetary deficit.

Maintaining a large differential, and for too long a period, between international prices/domestic costs and the prices paid by the users blunts the capacity of the economy to adjust to the market signals. These adjustments cannot be postponed indefinitely, and when such adjustments are eventually made, the element of shock to the economy is much larger. Further, maintaining large differential in the element of subsidy between different types of petroleum products also generates inefficient patterns of consumption.

The Oil Industry Restructuring Group, which was set up in 1995, was entrusted with drawing up a road map for the complete deregulation of the petroleum sector to overcome these inefficiencies. The following recommendations were made by the Group for complete dismantling of APM in a phased manner:

- Phase I (1996-98): Rationalisation of retention margin of refineries, deregulation of natural gas pricing, decanalisation of furnace oil and bitumen; partial deregulation of the marketing sector, with freedom to appoint dealers and distributors, removal of the subsidy on HSD and reduction of the subsidy on kerosene, LPG and input for fertiliser.
- Phase II (1998-2000): Pricing of indigenous crude on the basis of average f.o.b. price of imported crude; rationalisation of royalty and cess; further deregulation of the marketing sector, further reduction of subsidy on kerosene, LPG and input for fertiliser.
- Phase III (2000-02): Complete deregulation, including ATF, HSD and MS; and the subsidy on PDS kerosene and domestic LPG to be transferred to the general budget.

In a Resolution dated the 21st November, 1997, the Government of India had notified the details of a phased programme of dismantling of Administered Price Mechanism (APM) for petroleum products. Accordingly

- effective from 1st April, 1998, the consumer prices of all products (excepting motor spirit, high speed diesel, aviation turbine fuel, kerosene for public distribution system and LPG for domestic cooking) were decontrolled;
- from 1.4.2001 the prices of aviation turbine fuel were decontrolled; and
- from 1st April 2002, consumer prices of motor spirit and high-speed diesel will be market determined.

This left only kerosene for public distribution and LPG for domestic use, which needed to be subsidised. These are to be borne by the Consolidated Fund of India, thereby shifting the off-budget subsidies to the budget.

The Oil Pool account was wound up with effect from April 1, 2002. On the 30th March 2002, Government of India issued special bonds for the oil companies at 6.96 percent for a period of 7 years to partially take care of their outstanding dues. The total amount was Rs. 9000 crore. From April 1, 2002 subsidies on PDS (kerosene) and domestic LPG were provided on a flat rate basis and were explicitly financed and were explicitly shown in the budget. Consequent to these changes, subsidies for LPG and kerosene, amounted to Rs. 6265 crore in 2002-03

(RE) and Rs. 8116 in 2003-04 (BE). It has been stated that these subsidies will be withdrawn in a period of 3 to 5 years.

10.26 Reforming Subsidies

Budgetary subsidies provide the interface between the two sides of the budget, *viz.*, expenditures and non-tax revenues. Policy reforms affecting subsidies should address both these budgetary dimensions. The main objectives that should guide the formulation of a subsidy reform strategy should aim at lower volume, higher recoveries, better service focus, improved targeting, removal of inefficiencies, and promoting budgetary transparency.

Subsidization through budgetary support should be limited to Merit goods and services. Among these, the Merit I services like elementary education and primary health deserve a high degree of subsidization because of large positive externalities. Merit II services like secondary and higher education, other health services, and water supply and sanitation would also require budgetary subsidization albeit of a lower order. A significant portion of the present budgetary support for services is unwarranted as it does not pertain to services with high social benefits relative to private benefits, and therefore, pertains to the non-Merit category. Most of this unwarranted subsidization could also be harmful to the economy. It pre-empts budgetary resources which could be allocated to socially more relevant purposes like health and education. Such subsidization also distorts the structure of prices as in the case of power, thereby making domestic industry uncompetitive relative to the rest of world. The inter-state pattern of the budgetary subsidies also indicates that these are highly regressive. Subsidies often become detrimental to the environment damaging the fertility of the soil, as in the case of fertilizers where overuse of urea was induced by a high degree of subsidization. An important weakness of the present subsidy regime is that it ends up subsidizing inefficiencies – like the inefficiencies of the SEBs, State Irrigation Departments, the Food Corporation of India or the public sector at large, especially in the states.

Subsidy reforms should aim at

- reducing their volume relative to revenue receipts of the central and the state governments,
- limiting these to only Merit I and Merit II categories while eliminating the non-Merit subsidies,
- administering subsidies more directly to the targeted beneficiaries, thereby eliminating input-subsidies and focusing more on transfers as compared to price subsidies,

- making these subsidies transparent by showing them explicitly in the budget, and
- avoiding multiple subsidies to serve the same policy objective.

Costs of service provision and/or low negligible recoveries through user charges are the two critical sides of subsidization. Unit costs need to be reduced, wherever desirable and viable. Surplus employment and other operational inefficiencies must be reduced. Subsidy reforms, in the first instance, need to focus on selected sectors, which would yield maximum results and for those services for which there is considerable scope for higher recovery in the non-Merit category. In the case of centre, the immediate focus of reform should be on food and fertilizer subsidies, and for states, it is important to attend to power and irrigation subsidies, while reforming the overall subsidy regime.

Part IV: Fiscal Imbalance in India and Issues in Debt Management

11

Fiscal imbalance: Revenue, Fiscal and Primary Deficits

> Fiscal deficits are like obesity. You can see your weight rising on the scale and your clothing size increasing, but there is no sense of urgency in dealing with the problem.
>
> Martin Feldstein

In this chapter, we look at the basic problem of managing public finances, namely, the emergence of fiscal imbalance. Fiscal imbalance exhibits itself in different forms, although these are generally interrelated. We look at three indicators of fiscal imbalance: revenue deficit, fiscal deficit, and primary deficit. Revenue and fiscal deficits, under certain circumstances, can have deleterious effects on economic growth, although theoretical perspectives differ on this issue. We briefly review the literature on the impact of fiscal imbalance on the economy. We examine the fiscal profile of the centre, all-states, and individual states to look the extent of fiscal imbalance and the main causes that have led to the progressive deterioration in the fiscal profiles of the centre and the states.

11.1 Concepts: Revenue, Fiscal, and Primary Deficits

Revenue deficit measures the extent to which current, that is, revenue receipts are not able to cover revenue expenditures. The only way this gap can be met is by capital receipts, which are primarily in the form of borrowing. Thus, revenue deficit represents government consumption expenditure that is, current, not-asset building, expenditure, which is required to be financed by capital receipts. These capital receipts, apart from a small portion of non-debt capital receipts, consist of borrowing, which must be services by paying an interest from future budgetary receipts. The current borrowing by the government, net of repayments, amounts to fiscal deficit. The primary deficit is derived from fiscal deficit by deducting interest payments, and reflects the imbalance on the account of current receipts and expenditure leaving interest payments, which arise from the past imbalances. Primary deficits would accumulate into debt, unless growth overtakes the impact of the interest rate, which is discussed in chapter 12. This relationship is explained in the equation of dynamics of debt accumulation. The ratio of revenue deficit to fiscal deficit is also one useful measure as it indicates the extent to which borrowing is used for current expenditures. The concepts of fiscal imbalance are defined in terms of the budgetary aggregates below:

Revenue deficit = Revenue expenditure – Revenue receipts

Fiscal deficit = Total expenditure (revenue + capital) – revenue receipts – non-debt capital receipts

Fiscal deficit = Change in government liabilities = Liabilities at the current year – liabilities at the end of the previous year

These concepts of fiscal deficit relate to gross fiscal deficit. Sometimes, the concept of net fiscal deficit is also used, which is defined as below:

Net fiscal deficit = Gross fiscal deficit – Net lending

Primary deficit is defined as below:

Primary deficit = Fiscal deficit – Interest payments

11.2 Fiscal Imbalance: Impact on the Economy

There are three mainstream views regarding the potential impact of fiscal imbalance on the economy: Keynesian, Neo-Classical and Ricardian. In the neo-classical perspective, fiscal deficits are detrimental to investment and growth. In the Keynesian paradigm, fiscal deficit may be an important instrument of policy. Under Ricardian equivalence, fiscal deficits do not really matter except for smoothening the path of adjustment to expenditure or revenue shocks. While the neo-classical and Ricardian schools focus on the long run, the Keynesian view is more relevant in the short run. These are discussed in Rangarajan and Srivastava (2005).

11.3 The Neo-Classical View

Fiscal deficits imply a reduction in government saving or an increase in government dis-saving. In the neoclassical perspective, this will have a detrimental effect on growth if the reduction in government saving is not fully offset by a rise in private saving, thereby implying a fall in the overall saving rate. If there is a net fall in the saving rate, there will be pressure on the interest rate which will crowd out private investment, and therefore adversely affect growth. The neo-classical economists assume that markets clear so that full employment of resources is attained. In this paradigm, fiscal deficits raise lifetime consumption by shifting taxes to the future generations. If economic resources are fully employed, increased consumption necessarily implies decreased savings in a closed economy. In an open economy, real interest rates and investment may remain unaffected, but the fall in national saving is financed by higher external borrowing accompanied by an appreciation of the domestic currency and fall in exports. In both cases, net national saving falls and consumption rises accompanied by some combination of fall in investment and exports.

Gale and Orszag (2002) have looked at the US experience in detail and observe that 'a reasonable estimate is that a reduction in the projected budget surplus(or increase in the projected budget deficit) of one percent of GDP will raise long term interest rates by between 50 to 100 basis points'. Fiscal discipline, according to them, promotes long term growth primarily because budget surpluses are a form of national saving. The neo-classical paradigm does require the assumption that the consumption of each individual is determined as the solution to an inter temporal optimization problem where both borrowings and lending are permitted at the market rate of interest. It is also assumed that individuals have finite life spans where each consumer belongs to a specific generation and the life spans of successive generations overlap.

11.4 Keynesian View of Fiscal Deficits

The Keynesian view is relevant if there are unemployed resources. The focus of the analysis is the short run where fiscal deficit could serve as an instrument for raising aggregate demand in the system. It is argued that that an increase in autonomous government expenditure, whether investment or consumption, financed by borrowing would cause output to expand through a multiplier process. The traditional Keynesian framework does not distinguish between alternative uses of the fiscal deficit as between government consumption or investment expenditure. It also does not distinguish between alternative sources of financing the fiscal deficit, which could be borrowing from the domestic or external sources or from the central bank.

A budget constraint was not explicitly indicated in Keynes's own analysis although there have been modifications later. Subsequent elaborations of the Keynesian paradigm envisage that the multiplier-based expansion of output leads to a rise in the demand for money, and if money supply is fixed and deficit is bond financed, interest rates would rise partially offsetting the multiplier effect. However, the Keynesians argue that increased aggregate demand enhances the profitability of private investment and leads to higher investment at any given rate of interest. The effect of a rise in interest rate can therefore be more than neutralized by the increased profitability of investment. Keynesians argue that deficits may stimulate savings and investment even if interest rate rises, primarily because of the employment of hitherto unutilized resources. However, at full employment, deficits would lead to crowding out even in the Keynesian paradigm.

11.5 Fiscal Deficits and Ricardian Equivalence

The perspective of Ricardian equivalence on the issue of the impact of fiscal deficit on the economy has been developed by economists like Barro (1974, 1989). In the Ricardian equivalence perspective, fiscal deficits are viewed as neutral in terms of their impact on growth. The financing of budgets by deficits amounts only to postponement of taxes. The deficit in any current period is equal to the present value of future taxation that is required to pay off the increment to debt resulting from the deficit. In other words, government spending must be paid for, whether now or later, and the present value of spending must be equal to the present value of tax and non-tax revenues. Fiscal deficits are a useful device for smoothening the impact of revenue shocks or for meeting the requirements of lumpy expenditures, the financing of which through taxes may be spread over a period of time. However, fiscal deficits do not have an impact on aggregate demand if household spending decisions are based on the present value of their incomes that takes into account the present value of their future tax liabilities. Alternatively, a decrease in current government saving that is implied by the fiscal deficit is accompanied by an offsetting increase in private saving, leaving the national saving and, investment unchanged. There is no impact on the real interest rate.

Ricardian equivalence requires the assumption that individuals in the economy are foresighted, they have discount rates that are equal to governments' discount rates on spending and they have extremely long time horizons for evaluating the present value of future taxes. In particular, such a time horizon may well extend beyond their own lives in which case they save with a view to making altruistic transfers to take care of the tax liabilities of their future generations.

Rangarajan and Srivastava (2005) note that the economic universes of these alternative schools of thought are not comparable. These universes are characterized by individuals who differ in their behavioural responses in critical respects. The Keynesian world is inhabited by myopic, liquidity constrained individuals who behave under money illusion, and have a high propensity to consume out of current disposable income. The universe under the assumptions of Ricardian equivalence theorists consists of farsighted, fully informed, altruistic individuals. The neo-classical world is inhabited by rational individuals who respond to real changes in their wealth portfolios, and who are farsighted enough to plan consumption over their life-cycle. In real economies, there would be individual of all types, and the predictions of theory would prove to be more relevant than another depending on which type of individuals are represented more than others.

11.6 Revenue Deficit of Centre and States in India: Long Term History

In looking at the empirical patterns, it is useful to examine the profile of revenue deficit. The long term history of revenue deficits indicates a qualitative change in the eighties when revenue surplus got converted into revenue deficits. This happened first for the central government, then on the combined account, and lastly for the states. Among the states, first the less developed states and later the better-off states slid into revenue deficit. Only some of the special category states have remained in revenue account surplus. But this does not reflect any fiscal strength. It reflects the transmission of plan assistance where 90 per cent of assistance is given to them as grant. Although, this enters their budgets as revenue receipts, it is meant primarily for capital expenditure.

Chart 11.1 shows the time profile of revenue deficit of the centre, states, and on their combined account. It may be noted that revenue deficits are derived by simple addition, that is all-state revenue deficit is the summation of individual deficits and surplus. The combined revenue deficit is the sum of state revenue deficits and that of the centre.

Chart 11.1 Revenue Deficit Relative to GDP: Centre, States, and Combined

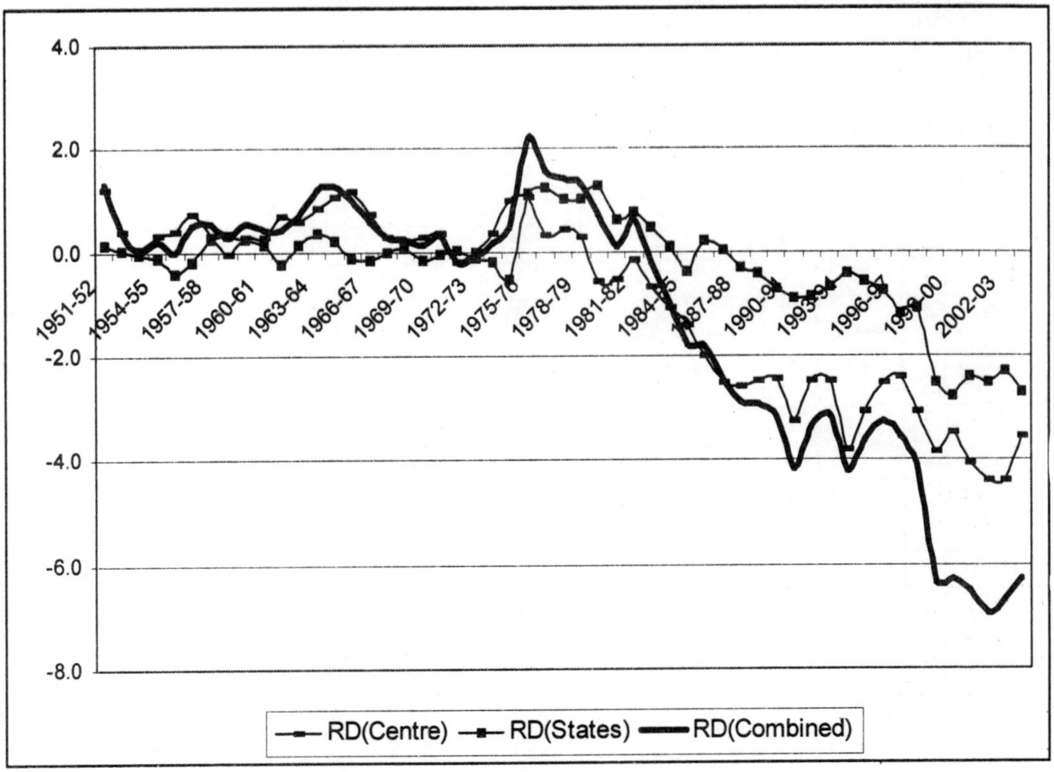

Table 11.1 covers the years of revenue surplus except for a few years. Table 11.2 shows the deficit years, first for the central account and later for the combined and the state accounts. It is evident that the central finances went into permanent revenue deficit in 1979-80. Since then, these have always remained in revenue deficit. Prior to this year, the central budget was in revenue deficit in only one year since 1951-52, which was 1971-72. The states were intermittently in revenue deficit for more than one year prior to 1988-89. But since then, their joint account has always been in revenue deficit. The combined account of the centre and the states went in permanent deficit in 1982-83.

Table 11.1: Revenue Account Balance: Centre, States, and Combined: The Surplus Years

Year	Amount (Rs. crore)			Per cent to GDP		
	Centre	States	Combined	Centre	States	Combined
1951-52	126.4	13.6	140.0	1.2	0.1	1.3
1952-53	38.9	3.4	42.3	0.4	0.0	0.4
1953-54	8.5	-3.8	4.7	0.1	0.0	0.0
1954-55	33.5	-11.6	21.9	0.3	-0.1	0.2
1955-56	41.7	-44.9	-3.2	0.4	-0.4	0.0
1956-57	93.3	-25.9	67.4	0.7	-0.2	0.5
1957-58	43.0	30.9	73.9	0.3	0.2	0.6
1958-59	-5.3	48.3	43.1	0.0	0.3	0.3
1959-60	42.6	39.6	82.1	0.3	0.3	0.5
1960-61	49.9	25.2	75.2	0.3	0.1	0.4
1961-62	124.9	-45.5	79.3	0.7	-0.3	0.4
1962-63	113.4	23.0	136.4	0.6	0.1	0.7
1963-64	187.5	83.6	271.1	0.8	0.4	1.2
1964-65	273.9	56.8	330.7	1.0	0.2	1.3
1965-66	319.8	-34.1	285.7	1.2	-0.1	1.0
1966-67	228.8	-52.8	175.9	0.7	-0.2	0.6
1967-68	104.3	-1.4	102.9	0.3	0.0	0.3
1968-69	81.0	20.0	101.0	0.2	0.1	0.3
1969-70	125.2	-65.9	59.3	0.3	-0.2	0.1
1970-71	163.0	-17.3	145.7	0.4	0.0	0.3
1971-72	-100.0	9.1	-90.9	-0.2	0.0	-0.2
1972-73	17.7	-69.6	-51.9	0.0	-0.1	-0.1
1973-74	236.8	-117.6	119.2	0.4	-0.2	0.2

1974-75	764.3	-401.9	362.4	1.0	-0.5	0.5
1975-76	886.9	952.9	1839.8	1.1	1.1	2.2
1976-77	298.5	1096.6	1395.1	0.3	1.2	1.6
1977-78	429.8	1019.1	1448.9	0.4	1.0	1.4
1978-79	292.3	1135.4	1427.7	0.3	1.0	1.3

Source (Basic Data): *Indian Public Finance Statistics.*

Table 11.2: Revenue Account Balance: Centre, States, and Combined: The Deficit Years

Year	Amount (Rs. crore)			Per cent to GDP		
	Centre	States	Combined	Centre	States	Combined
1979-80	-694.1	1,548.3	854.2	-0.6	1.3	0.7
1980-81	-776.8	900.4	123.6	-0.5	0.6	0.1
1981-82	-293.4	1,310.4	1,017.0	-0.2	0.8	0.6
1982-83	-1,254.3	888.8	-365.6	-0.7	0.5	-0.2
1983-84	-2,397.7	217.8	-2,179.9	-1.1	0.1	-1.0
1984-85	-3,497.6	-898.3	-4,395.9	-1.4	-0.4	-1.8
1985-86	-5,564.5	544.3	-5,020.3	-2.0	0.2	-1.8
1986-87	-7,776.0	21.5	-7,754.6	-2.5	0.0	-2.5
1987-88	-9,137.3	-1,038.3	-10,175.5	-2.6	-0.3	-2.9
1988-89	-10,514.4	-1,824.6	-12,339.0	-2.5	-0.4	-2.9
1989-90	-11,914.2	-3,507.2	-15,421.4	-2.5	-0.7	-3.2
1990-91	-18,561.4	-5,106.7	-23,668.1	-3.3	-0.9	-4.2
1991-92	-16,261.0	-5,652.0	-21,913.0	-2.5	-0.9	-3.4
1992-93	-18,574.5	-5,058.8	-23,633.4	-2.5	-0.7	-3.2
1993-94	-32,715.6	-3,475.2	-36,190.8	-3.8	-0.4	-4.2
1994-95	-31,028.8	-5,575.0	-36,603.8	-3.1	-0.6	-3.6
1995-96	-29,731.1	-8,734.2	-38,465.2	-2.5	-0.7	-3.2
1996-97	-32,654.0	-16,065.3	-48,719.3	-2.4	-1.2	-3.6
1997-98	-46,448.8	-16,701.9	-63,150.7	-3.1	-1.1	-4.1
1998-99	-66,976.3	-43,580.1	-1,10,556.4	-3.8	-2.5	-6.4
1999-00	-67,596.6	-53,763.1	-1,21,359.7	-3.5	-2.8	-6.3
2000-01	-85,233.9	-50,175.1	-1,35,409.0	-4.1	-2.4	-6.5
2001-02	-1,00,162.4	-56,942.1	-1,57,104.5	-4.4	-2.5	-6.9
2002-03	-1,07,879.0	-56,748.0	-1,64,627.0	-4.4	-2.3	-6.7
2003-04	-98,262.0	-74,439.0	-1,72,701.0	-3.6	-2.7	-6.3

Source: (Basic Data): *Indian Public Finance Statistics.*

11.7 Fiscal and Primary Deficits: Long Term History

Data on fiscal and primary deficits began to be compiled on a consistent basis only in the more recent years. For the combined account of the central and state government, a series on a consistent basis is available from the Indian Public Finance Statistics brought out by the Ministry of Finance since 1987-88. Indirectly, since fiscal deficit amounts to the change in government's liabilities, a series can be constructed from the series of government liabilities. The primary deficit figures can then be obtained by deducting interest payments from the fiscal deficit. The following analysis of fiscal and primary deficits is based on this methodology.

The time profile of fiscal deficit, as derived by deducting from the total liabilities at the end of the current year, the corresponding liabilities at the beginning of the current year may differ marginally from official data due to some borrowing that may be done off-budget. However, it seems to be a useful device to construct a long term series of fiscal and primary deficits on a consistent basis. It can be seen from Table 11.3 that fiscal deficit was low in the initial years until 1956-57 keeping below 3 per cent of GDP. This rose to as high as 9 per cent in 1966-67.

Table 11.3: Fiscal and Primary Deficit: Combined Account of Central and State Governments (per cent to GDP)

Year	Fiscal deficit (derived)	Interest payments	Primary deficit (derived)	Year	Fiscal deficit (derived)	Interest payments	Primary deficit (derived)
1951-52	1.12	0.644	0.477	1976-77	7.36	1.948	5.413
1952-53	0.64	0.724	-0.085	1977-78	7.12	1.723	5.395
1953-54	0.70	0.736	-0.035	1978-79	3.31	1.990	1.322
1954-55	2.58	1.040	1.542	1979-80	6.09	2.212	3.874
1955-56	2.77	1.140	1.631	1980-81	7.37	2.065	5.307
1956-57	2.93	0.957	1.971	1981-82	5.98	2.228	3.755
1957-58	4.91	0.989	3.924	1982-83	9.18	2.464	6.714
1958-59	6.31	0.988	5.324	1983-84	5.39	2.531	2.858
1959-60	5.78	1.142	4.643	1984-85	8.55	2.925	5.626
1960-61	3.51	1.270	2.236	1985-86	8.99	3.144	5.851
1961-62	2.93	1.341	1.587	1986-87	10.12	3.443	6.679
1962-63	3.99	1.467	2.520	1987-88	9.01	3.666	5.344

Contd...

1963-64	4.86	1.348	3.514	1988-89	9.09	3.901	5.187
1964-65	5.72	1.350	4.373	1989-90	8.99	4.217	4.774
1965-66	5.66	1.525	4.133	1990-91	9.38	4.397	4.985
1966-67	9.70	1.677	8.028	1991-92	7.16	4.746	2.417
1967-68	4.53	1.558	2.971	1992-93	7.24	4.792	2.447
1968-69	3.25	1.551	1.700	1993-94	9.82	4.953	4.871
1969-70	2.65	1.530	1.118	1994-95	6.94	5.128	1.817
1970-71	2.38	1.635	0.744	1995-96	6.78	4.962	1.816
1971-72	6.82	1.700	5.115	1996-97	6.08	5.111	0.970
1972-73	4.13	1.602	2.525	1997-98	7.63	5.159	2.471
1973-74	1.10	1.532	-0.431	1998-99	8.25	5.318	2.934
1974-75	3.04	1.508	1.529	1999-00	10.07	5.682	4.384
1975-76	2.09	1.394	0.695	2000-01	10.39	5.877	4.512
				2001-02	12.13	6.201	5.924
				2002-03	11.63	6.484	5.142

Source: (Basic Data): *Indian Public Finance Statistics.*

Thereafter it declined keeping in the range of below 5 per cent of GDP until 1975-76 with a few exceptions. Thereafter, the fiscal deficit reached levels as high as 9 per cent in 1982-83. However, it was only since 1986-87 that the combined fiscal deficit crossed 9 per cent on a persistent basis. There was a definite improvement in the mid-nineties after which the magnitude of fiscal deficit once again increased reaching levels close to or higher than 10 per cent of GDP.

Primary deficit indicates the part of borrowing that the governments get to use for its current expenditure that is in excess of current receipts. The level of primary deficit has also progressively increased. Its profile shows a clear cyclical pattern. The primary deficit levels relative to GDP were the highest in the mid-eighties, after which these fell only to increase once again since the latter part of the nineties. The level of interest payments relative to GDP depend on the debt-GDP ratio and the average interest rate. Interest payments to GDP ratio shows a steady rise over the years increasing from less than 1 per cent of GDP in the early fifties to more than 6 percent of GDP towards the end of the nineties. In the following sections, we examine the fiscal imbalance of central and state governments separately focusing on the recent period relating to fiscal reforms.

11.8 Central Government: Contours of Fiscal Imbalance

We examine below the profile of imbalance in the case of the central government. Table 11.4 provides the profile of different indicators of fiscal imbalance in respect of central finances from 1990-91. In comparing fiscal deficit since 1990-91, one adjustment requires to be made for figures prior to 1999-00, when lending to the states on account of small savings was not channelled through the public account of National Small Savings Fund (NSSF) and constituted part of centre's fiscal deficit. After this adjustment, the fiscal deficit of the centre, first declined from 6.6 per cent in 1990-91 to 4.1 per cent in 1996-97. It started rising from 1997-98 to reach a level of 6.2 per cent of GDP in 2001-02. After that, there is a fall in centre's fiscal deficit relative to GDP. A similar profile is observed in the case of revenue deficit, which, after declining from 3.3 per cent of GDP in 1990-91 to 2.4 per cent in 1996-97, rose steadily to 4.4 per cent in 2001-02. The year 2002-03 witnessed an improvement in fiscal deficit to 5.9 per cent of the GDP due to a reduction in primary deficit, although the revenue deficit continued almost at the same level as 2001-02. The situation seems to have improved in 2003-04 (RE), with the fiscal deficit and the revenue deficit declining to 4.8 and 3.6 per cent of GDP, respectively.

Table 11.4: Centre: Profile of Fiscal Imbalance (Per cent of GDP)

Year	Fiscal deficit	Revenue deficit	Primary deficit	Ratio of revenue to fiscal deficit (%)
1990-91	6.61	3.26	2.83	49.36
1991-92	4.72	2.49	0.65	52.72
1992-93	5.33	2.76	0.72	51.73
1993-94	6.43	3.81	2.15	59.21
1994-95	4.74	3.06	0.39	64.60
1995-96	4.23	2.50	0.02	59.16
1996-97	4.11	2.39	-0.24	58.06
1997-98	4.81	3.05	0.50	63.45
1998-99	5.14	3.85	0.67	74.78
1999-00	5.41	3.49	0.75	64.55
2000-01	5.69	4.08	0.93	71.74
2001-02	6.18	4.39	1.47	71.06
2002-03	5.87	4.37	1.10	74.36
2003-04 RE	4.77	3.60	0.27	75.59

Primary deficit is derived by netting interest payments from fiscal deficit.
Fiscal deficit figures exclude states' share against small savings.
Figures for 2003-04 are revised estimates.
Source: *Central Budget Documents* and *Indian Public Finance Statistics, 2002-03*.

The most persistent deterioration is observed in the ratio of revenue deficit to fiscal deficit, which, by indicating the extent to which borrowed resources are used for current expenditures, shows the 'quality' of fiscal deficit. In 1990-91, this ratio was about 50 per cent. It increased steadily to 75 per cent in 1998-99. Thereafter, there was some improvement, but the ratio again increased back to the level of 75.6 per cent in 2003-04, indicating that three-fourth of borrowing has been used for current consumption in some years.

The following are the main features of the profile of fiscal imbalance in the case of the centre:

(a) After declining in the mid-nineties, the fiscal deficit of the centre in 2001-02 was 6.2 per cent, only marginally lower than its level in 1990-91. In 2003-04 RE and 2004-05 BE, the fiscal deficit relative to GDP has shown a decline;

(b) Revenue deficit relative to GDP, having risen to a historical peak of 4.4 per cent comes down in 2004-05; and

(c) The ratio of revenue deficit to fiscal deficit has progressively deteriorated until 2003-04, when it amounted to 75.6 per cent.

11.9 All-States: Contours of Fiscal Imbalance

In the case of states also, the TFC has recently provided an overview of trends of three indicators of fiscal imbalance: revenue deficit, fiscal deficit, primary deficit. Table 11.5 shows that for the states considered together the revenue deficit as percentage of GDP, comparing the averages over 2000-03 and 1993-96 was higher by a margin of 1.9 percentage points, and the fiscal deficit, by a margin of 1.5 percentage points. The primary deficit relative to GDP had reached a peak in 1999-00, but has since showed a decline. In 1999-00, both revenue deficit and fiscal deficit of the states had reached a peak at 4.64 and 2.82 per cent of GDP.

11.10 Contours of Fiscal Imbalance: Inter-State Comparison

In this section, we look at fiscal imbalance in the states in a comparative perspective. This analysis is based on the data given by the Twelfth Finance Commission in their recent Report (2004). The aggregate account of the states went into persistent revenue deficit in1987-88. During the nineties, some of the individual states were still in revenue surplus. Among the general category states, Andhra Pradesh went into revenue deficit in 1994-95. Gujarat and Haryana went into permanent revenue deficit in 1995-96, and Goa, at the top end of income scale, also went into revenue deficit in 1997-98. As shown in Table 11.6, the largest revenue deficit on average during 1993-96 was that of Orissa at 2.0 per cent of GSDP. This was followed by that of Punjab, Uttar Pradesh, and West

Bengal. The deficits of these states rose persistently. In the three year period 2000-03, there were no states of the general category showing a revenue surplus. The magnitudes of their revenue deficits were higher and their relative position had also changed. The highest revenue deficit relative to GSDP was that of West Bengal at 5.5 per cent followed by Punjab, Orissa and Rajasthan. Among the special category states, Arunachal Pradesh, Meghalaya, and Sikkim continued to show a surplus. The deterioration in the case of general category states, comparing the 2000-03 average with that of 1993-96, was 2.33 percentage points of all-state GSDP of the general category states.

Table 11.5: Aggregate State Finances: Alternative Deficit Indicators

(per cent of GDP)

Year	Revenue deficit	Fiscal deficit	Primary deficit	Revenue deficit/ fiscal deficit	Debt./GDP
1993-94	0.45	2.35	0.52	19.05	21.79
1994-95	0.69	2.72	0.79	25.55	21.40
1995-96	0.73	2.59	0.76	28.06	21.00
1996-97	1.31	2.77	0.90	47.37	21.00
1997-98	1.23	2.94	0.93	42.01	21.73
1998-99	2.61	4.31	2.24	60.48	23.02
1999-00	2.82	4.64	2.34	60.87	25.20
2000-01	2.61	4.16	1.69	62.60	27.42
2001-02	2.68	4.09	1.41	65.49	29.37
2002-03	2.29	3.94	1.14	58.09	31.15
Averages					
1993-96 [A]	0.62	2.55	0.69	24.22	21.79
2000-03 [B]	2.53	4.07	1.41	62.06	31.15
[B]-[A]	1.90	1.51	0.72	37.84	9.36

Source: *Report of the Twelfth Finance Commission, 2004.*

The TFC notes that the difference between period averages of 1993-94 and 2000-03 shows that the largest deterioration in the revenue deficit to GSDP ratio was that for West Bengal followed by Orissa, Rajasthan, and Punjab. Thus, revenue deficit became high relative to GSDP for high income states like Punjab, middle income states like West Bengal, and low income states like Orissa. The states which did not show deterioration during this period were Bihar with an increase in the revenue deficit to GSDP ratio of only 0.04 percentage point and Haryana with an increase of 0.56 percentage point.

Table 11.6: Comparative Performance of States: Revenue and Fiscal Deficits

(Per cent of GSDP)

State	Revenue Account [Deficit(-)]			Fiscal Account [Deficit(-)]		
	1993-96 (A)	2000-03 (B)	[B-A]	1993-96 [C]	2000-03 [D]	[D-A]
Arunachal Pradesh	24.28	1.76	-22.51	1.48	-12.70	-14.18
Assam	-0.01	-1.90	-1.88	-2.38	-3.73	-1.34
Himachal Pradesh	-1.56	-7.28	-5.72	-6.70	-11.41	-4.71
Jammu & Kashmir	4.56	-1.82	-6.38	-3.85	-8.28	-4.44
Manipur	6.07	-2.46	-8.53	-3.02	-6.06	-3.04
Meghalaya	3.32	0.84	-2.48	-3.20	-5.28	-2.08
Mizoram	7.53	-9.07	-16.60	-5.82	-17.79	-11.96
Nagaland	-0.19	-2.12	-1.93	-5.26	-7.97	-2.71
Sikkim	8.10	11.30	3.20	-8.26	-3.42	4.84
Tripura	2.57	-0.61	-3.18	-4.04	-7.20	-3.15
Total: SCS	**1.96**	**-2.53**	**-4.49**	**-3.64**	**-7.04**	**-3.40**
Andhra Pradesh	-0.51	-2.03	-1.51	-3.16	-4.57	-1.41
Bihar	-1.83	-1.87	-0.04	-2.85	-4.52	-1.67
Goa	1.44	-2.44	-3.89	-2.30	-4.68	-2.38
Gujarat	0.10	-4.66	-4.75	-1.82	-5.74	-3.93
Haryana	-0.75	-1.32	-0.56	-2.50	-3.69	-1.19
Karnataka	-0.07	-2.21	-2.15	-2.71	-4.37	-1.65
Kerala	-1.18	-4.17	-2.99	-3.32	-5.13	-1.81
Madhya Pradesh	-0.61	-2.05	-1.44	-2.16	-3.94	-1.78
Maharashtra	-0.09	-3.09	-3.00	-2.16	-4.12	-1.96
Orissa	-2.00	-4.91	-2.91	-4.63	-7.84	-3.21
Punjab	-1.88	-4.53	-2.66	-4.37	-6.14	-1.77
Rajasthan	-1.09	-3.87	-2.78	-4.51	-6.05	-1.54
Tamil Nadu	-0.71	-2.50	-1.78	-1.99	-3.75	-1.77
Uttar Pradesh	-1.77	-2.98	-1.21	-4.04	-5.07	-1.03
West Bengal	-1.53	-5.47	-3.95	-3.18	-7.31	-4.13
Total: GCS	**-0.86**	**-3.19**	**-2.33**	**-2.93**	**-4.97**	**-2.04**
All States	**-0.72**	**-3.15**	**-2.43**	**-2.96**	**-5.08**	**-2.12**

Source: *Report of the Twelfth Finance Commission, 2004.*

Table 11.6 shows that the fiscal deficit among the general category states was the highest during 1993-96 in the case of Orissa, Rajasthan, Punjab, Uttar Pradesh, West Bengal, and Andhra Pradesh. During 2000-03, Orissa had become the highest fiscal deficit state among the general category states followed by West Bengal, Punjab, Rajasthan, Gujarat, and Uttar Pradesh. The average deterioration over these two periods was the largest in the case of West Bengal followed by Gujarat and Orissa.

11.11 Causes of Rising Fiscal Imbalance

Fiscal imbalance is always the outcome of expenditure growth outstripping the revenue growth starting from any position of fiscal imbalance. The early nineties witnessed several important changes with economic reforms being initiated in India. On the fiscal side, which constituted an important element of the economic reforms, significant changes in the regime of direct as well as indirect taxation were brought about. In the latter part of the nineties, following the recommendations of the Fifth Central Pay Commission, the salaries and pensions of the central government employees were revised. States also followed suit and accepted, one after another, comparable salary scales for their employees. Towards the latter half of the nineties, some of the nominal interest rates also increased inordinately. In the first three years of the new decade, the economy witnessed a severe recession. In 2002-03, a severe drought also occurred. The six years from 1997-98 to 2002-03 adversely affected government finances in a significant way. The first three years brought State finances under pressure because of the salary revision and high interest rates. The next three years suffered from low growth and severe drought.

Among others, three initiatives in recent years by the central government are quite important. These can play a significant role in reversing the fiscal deterioration witnessed since the late nineties. First, the central government enacted a Fiscal Responsibility and Budget Management Act, 2003 (FRBMA). This Act required the central government to take appropriate measures to reduce the fiscal deficit and revenue deficit, so as to eliminate the latter by 2007-08 and thereafter build up an adequate revenue surplus. The target date for this has since been modified to 31st March, 2009 through the Finance Act, 2004. In terms of the Rules made under the Act, the fiscal deficit is required to be reduced to 3 per cent of GDP by 31st March, 2009. The enactment of the FRBMA provides an institutional framework and binds the government to prudent fiscal policies. For this reason, it is important that the targets set for the various fiscal parameters in the Act and the Rules are not relaxed. This will set an example for the states also. Secondly, the central government has brought about pension reforms by introducing a new pension scheme meant for new entrants to government service. Although this scheme may initially increase the expenditure on pensions, as the centre will have to make contributions to the pension fund, it will prove to be beneficial in the long run. Thirdly, the central government brought out a debt swap scheme,, which has benefited the state governments and, to some extent, also the central government. The states have been able to swap their high cost debt to the centre with low cost market borrowings. These additional recoveries have enabled the centre to repay some of its own high cost debt to the NSSF.

State finances, in their aggregate account, had only occasionally shown small revenue deficits until1986-87. From 1987-88, state finances at the aggregate level have always been in revenue deficit. The magnitude of the deficit relative to GDP has also increased over the years. Since then, state after state, rich and poor, small and large, special category and general category, increasingly slid into revenue deficit. Only a few special category states showed surplus on revenue account, but this arose from the composition of plan assistance, being ninety percent in the form of grants, added to revenue receipts. As this was actually meant for capital expenditure, it does not signify any fiscal health.

As mentioned earlier, the six years from 1997-98 to 2002-03, have been the worst in the history of state finances. The first half of this period, saw one of the sharpest increases in the salary bill of state government employees, when as discussed in chapter 9, the average per employee salary increased by close to 60 per cent in a span of three years. This was also the period when central transfers, relative to GDP, fell and states were engaged in exemption-proiiferating tax competition. This resulted in a fall in the level of own tax revenue relative to GDP.

Unable to adjust their expenditure downwards, states depended more and more on borrowing to finance their revenue expenditures in a period when the nominal interest rates hit a peak. While the states finances smarted under these multiple pressures, the economy, as discussed in chapter 19, went into a recession, showing some of the lowest real and nominal growth rates in the first three years of the new decade. The TFC observes that the impact of these changes, in a short span of six years, was 'swift and debilitating'. In no other stretch of six years of the fiscal history of the states, has there been a rise of more than 10 percentage points in the debt-GDP ratio as the one which occurred in this period where the ratio of outstanding debt to GDP increased from 21 per cent in 1996-97 to 31 per cent in 2002-03.

Among the factors that have contributed to the deterioration of the state finances, a reference should be made to subsidies. The subsidies provided by the states are generally implicit rather than explicit. Implicit subsidies arise when services are provided at prices that do not recover costs. Low user charges have been a universal phenomenon. Budgetary support to the power sector in particular has been an important source of drain in states where explicit subsidy for this purpose has been provided for in the budgets.

The main trends relating to fiscal imbalance in the aggregate state finances, comparing the average over 1993-96 with that of 2000-03 may be summarized as follows:

- Revenue deficit of the states rose from 0.62 per cent of GDP in 1993-96 to 2.53 per cent in 2000-03. This amounted to an increase of 1.9 percentage points.
- Fiscal deficit of the states increased from 2.55 per cent during 1993-96 on average to about 4 per cent of GDP, implying a rise of about 1.5 percentage points.

11.12 Sustainability of Fiscal deficits

The question of sustainability of fiscal deficits, however, puts a limit on the borrowing, i.e. fiscal deficit that can be prudently undertaken by the two tiers of governments, considered separately as also together. Sustainable levels of fiscal deficits can be derived with reference to three key parameters: growth rate, ratio of revenue receipts to GDP/GSDP, and the interest rate. In fact, prudent levels of fiscal deficit may be determined in relation to growth and interest rates but growth may depend on fiscal deficit and interest rate. Much of this interdependence arises due to that fact that fiscal deficits affect the saving and investment rates of the economy, which in turn affect the growth and interest rates.

For fiscal sustainability, it is required that a rise in fiscal deficit is matched by a rise in the capacity to service the increased debt. It has been argued that from this angle, borrowing for generation of assets may be justified. However, for the large part, amounting to about 70 per cent of borrowing, is presently not being spent on capital assets. Even where there is capital expenditure, the return on assets is negligible. The more indirect return through higher growth to match the growing interest liabilities has also not been forthcoming. In fact, the high level of fiscal deficit combined with the rising debt-GDP ratio has led to a fall in the aggregate government demand net of transfer payments. Economists have argued that fiscal deficits relative GDP are equivalent to government dis-savings, which lead to a fall in the overall saving rate unless there is a corresponding rise in the private saving rate. Compared to the levels of domestic saving rate and investment rate in the mid-nineties, which ranged above 25 per cent in a few years, there was a clear fall in the rates in recent years where both have been languishing at around 22 per cent of GDP. There has been some improvement in recent years. Table 11.7 shows the saving, investment and growth rates since the early nineties.

There has been an interesting debate as to the right level of fiscal deficit and the debt that is sustainable in the Indian context. This issue is discussed further in the next chapter.

Table 11.7: Gross Domestic Saving and Investment Relative to GDP at Market Prices

Year	Gross domestic savings				Gross domestic capital formation			
	Household sector	Private corporate sector	Public sector	Total	Public sector	Private sector	Total	Adjusted Total
1990-91	19.33	2.67	1.10	23.10	9.34	14.73	24.07	26.30
1991-92	16.96	3.11	1.97	22.03	8.82	13.11	21.93	22.55
1992-93	17.51	2.67	1.59	21.77	8.55	15.24	23.79	23.61
1993-94	18.42	3.48	0.63	22.53	8.24	13.01	21.25	23.09
1994-95	19.68	3.48	1.66	24.83	8.71	14.67	23.38	26.00
1995-96	18.19	4.93	2.03	25.15	7.66	18.87	26.53	26.90
1996-97	17.05	4.47	1.67	23.19	7.03	14.74	21.77	24.48
1997-98	17.63	4.17	1.33	23.13	6.61	15.96	22.57	24.60
1998-99	18.77	3.74	-0.99	21.52	6.58	14.80	21.38	22.57
1999-00	20.88	4.35	-1.04	24.20	6.94	16.72	23.66	25.33
2000-01	21.93	4.12	-2.31	23.74	6.29	16.33	22.62	24.35
2001-02	22.74	3.46	-2.75	23.45	5.83	16.48	22.31	23.13
2002-03	22.65	3.41	-1.85	24.20	5.68	17.15	22.83	23.28

Data for 2001-02 and 2002-03 are provisional and quick estimates respectively.
Source: *Economic Survey*, 2003-04.

11.13 Controlling Fiscal Deficit

Recent institutional reforms can be classified into three broad groups: formal deficit and debt rules, expenditure limits, and transparency. The main examples of this approach are European countries bound by the Maastricht Treaty as supplemented by the Stability and Growth Pact. The UK since 1997 has operated a Golden Rule whereby borrowing is done only to finance capital spending and the limit on net debt is 40 per cent of GDP over a cycle. Several countries have deficit and debt rules at the sub national level. In the US, all but two states have laws requiring balanced budgets and limiting the states to raise debt. Nine provinces and territories of Canada have fiscal rules with balanced budgets requiring them to take on debt only for the purpose of financing investment projects. Canada has also focused on instituting a rigorous expenditure review process. Debt ceiling can serve as a useful adjunct to deficit rules. In practice, debt ceilings have been driven not by calculations based on theory, but run by the concern about reducing high debt levels and have thus generally been chosen on the basis of the experience of the individual countries. The main criticism of the deficit rules in general and balanced budget rules in particular is that they are invariant and therefore tend to be pro-cyclical. This is a more important consideration for national governments as compared to sub national governments. For this reason, the deficit rules in the national government have increasingly been defined in terms of cyclically adjusted deficit measures or as an average over the economic cycle. Thus, these rules allow the operation of domestic stabilizers and to some extent also provide room for discretionary policy within the cycle.

In the nineties, many countries around the world were able to achieve fiscal consolidation, attaining primary surpluses. Widespread reforms including debt ceilings and deficit targets have strengthened the fiscal frameworks. Expenditure rules and transparency in the fiscal management has also been emphasized in these fiscal frameworks. Evaluation of these fiscal consolidation efforts have identified certain factors that account for reliable and durable adjustments. Accordingly, fiscal consolidation is more likely to be successful when based on cuts in expenditure, particularly when undertaken by countries with high levels of debt. Widespread reforms in fiscal frameworks require institutional reforms aimed at achieving and maintaining fiscal consolidation, while leaving room for fiscal policy to respond to business cycles through automatic stabilizers and policy actions.

11.14 Role of Fiscal Responsibility Legislations

The central government has enacted a Fiscal Responsibility and Budget Management Act (FRBMA) with a view to controlling fiscal and revenue deficits through prescribing explicit targets. Clause 3 of the FRBMA provides that the Central Government shall lay in each financial year before both the Houses of Parliament, three statements relating to (i) Mid Term Financial Policy Statement (ii) Fiscal Policy Strategy Statement, and a (iii) Macroeconomic Framework Statement, which shall contain, an assessment regarding (a) growth in GDP (b) fiscal balance of the Union Government as reflected in the revenue balance and gross fiscal balance, and (c) external sector balance of the economy as reflected in the current account balance in the balance of payments. The 2004-05 budget estimates the central revenue deficit at 2.5 per cent and fiscal deficit at 4.3 per cent of GDP. As part of the requirement of the FRBMA, one set of forecasts covering the period up to 2006-07 has been presented to both the houses of Parliament as part of the medium term fiscal strategy statement. In the meanwhile, the central government appointed a Task Force for the implementation of the FRBMA to draw up the medium term fiscal framework to achieve the FRBMA objectives.

Box 11.1: The Fiscal Responsibility and Budget Management Rules, 2004

- Reduction of revenue deficit by an amount equivalent of 0.5 percent or more of the GDP at the end of each financial year, beginning with 2004-05.
- Reduction of fiscal deficit by an amount equivalent of 0.3 percent or more of the GDP at the end of each financial year, beginning with 2004-05.
- No assumption of additional liabilities (including external debt at current exchange rate) in excess of 9 percent of GDP for the financial year 2004-05 and progressive reduction of this limit by at least one percentage point of GDP in each subsequent year.
- No guarantees in excess of 0.5 percent of GDP in any financial year, beginning with 2004-05.
- Specifies four fiscal indicators to be projected in the medium-term fiscal policy statement. These are, revenue deficit as a percentage of GDP, fiscal deficit as a percentage of GDP, tax revenue as percentage of GDP and total outstanding liabilities as percentage of GDP.
- For greater transparency in the budgetary process, rules mandate the Central Government to disclose changes, if any, in accounting standards, policies and practices that have a bearing on the fiscal indicators. The Government is also mandated to submit statements of receivables and guarantees and a statement of assets, at the time of presenting the annual financial statement, latest by Budget 2006-07.
- The rules prescribe the form for the quarterly review of the trends of receipts and expenditures. The rules mandate the Central Government to take appropriate corrective action in case of revenue and fiscal deficits exceeding 45 percent of the budget estimates, or total non-debt receipts falling short of 40 percent of the budget estimates at the end of first half of the financial year.

Source: Economic Survey: 2004-05

Like the central government, many state governments have also enacted fiscal responsibility legislations. Important among these are Karnataka, Kerala, Punjab, Tamil Nadu, and Uttar Pradesh. The Twelfth Finance Commission has recommended rescheduling of the central debt to the states by consolidating and providing a new repayment period of 20 years with a rate of interest of 7.5 per cent. The states can avail of this facility subject to the condition that they should enact a fiscal responsibility legislation that aims at reducing the revenue deficit to zero by 2008-09 and fiscal deficit to a level of 3 per cent of GDP. The incentive for the fiscal responsibility legislation is strong, and it is expected that all states will find it beneficial for go ahead with a suitable responsibility legislation. The TFC has proposed two other changes that will help further in controlling state level fiscal deficits. One of these proposals is the establishment of a Loan Council, which can limit the overall borrowing of each state taking into account its borrowing from all sources including from the National Small Saving Fund. The second suggested change relates to discontinuation of central government's intermediation in state borrowing. Rather, states should be exposed fully to the discipline of the market. If the market assesses the finances of a state as well managed, it would be reflected in a lower risk premium. States with weak finances and chronic imbalances would have to a pay higher risk premia. The market message could bring considerable discipline by credit rating of the states.

12

Managing Government Debt: Issues of Sustainability

The growth of public debt has long been a hot issue in the debate over responsible fiscal policy

Musgrave and Musgrave

Government debt consists of central and state debt to domestic and external lenders. Centre's lending to the states requires to be netted out while calculating the combined debt of the central and state governments, since it represents inter-governmental debt. There are many theories relating to the use and management of debt. In the management of debt, the central government has to play a leading role in following a debt policy that is sustainable and conducive to growth. The increment in debt, that is, fiscal deficit is a potent instrument available to the government to address both the growth and macro economic stability objectives. In macro context, it is not just the central debt, but the management of the overall government debt that becomes important. The central government and individual state governments can exercise control on the growth of their respective debt relative to their GDP and GSDPs. However, a broader framework is required within which suitable debt management strategies can be evolved and guidelines framed. In this Chapter, we look at the growth and structure of central debt and combined debt of central and state governments in India. Various aspects of state debt are separately dealt with in the next Chapter.

12.1 Growth of Central Debt in India

According to available information, centre's debt at the end of 1950-51 was only about 28 per cent. The central government in those days was the primary borrower with state governments having only small liabilities. Over time, centre's debt increased steadily and is estimated in recent times at about 55 per cent of GDP. In measuring the volume of debt, certain clarifications are required as detailed below.

1. A certain proportion of centre's debt is external debt. This can be evaluated at historical exchange rates or current exchange rates. While both are possible, conventionally and in official records, external debt is evaluated at historical exchange rates.

2. The National Small Saving Fund (NSSF) was established with effect from 1.4.99 and is maintained in the Public Account of India. Prior to setting up of NSSF, centre used to put the small savings collection in the consolidated fund of India, and then states' share in these was passed on the states. The NSSF is a public account. Now states' share is passed on the basis of securities issued by the states. In effect, they borrow from the NSSF.
3. The central government created a Market Stabilization Fund in 2004-05. Although there is borrowing by the central government, it is not used by the government for expenditure. Rather, it is kept as an asset by the RBI.

The balance of collections into the NSSF over withdrawals is invested in special government securities issued by the Central as well as the State Governments, i.e. Central and the State Governments borrow from the NSSF on the basis of these special securities. Prior to 1998-99, small savings were shown as part of 'other liabilities' of India, where all net borrowings from the public account were shown, whether ultimately lent to the Central or the State Governments. Since 1999-2000, the central borrowings from the NSSF constitute part of Centre's 'internal debt'. However, one component of it continues to be shown as 'other liabilities' which primarily represents the borrowing from the NSSF by the State Governments. This component needs to be taken out while showing Centre's outstanding liabilities.

In the estimates given below, the external debt is evaluated at historical exchange rates, the NSSF based on-lending to the states are not counted as centre's liabilities, and the MSS liabilities are also excluded. Table 12.1 describes the profile of growth of centre's debt-GDP ratio.

In the initial phase, there was a steady increase in the debt-GDP ratio of the centre's, which went on increasing to a level of 44.4 per cent in 1972-73. Thereafter, there was a decline for a few years. The debt-GDP ratio fell to 32.9 per cent in 1975-76. The next peak was encountered in 1993-94 at 55.63 per cent. In fact, since 1987-88, the debt-GDP ratio was around 55 per cent with minor variations. There was some decline in the nineties. In the period from 1997-98 to 1999-00, it was around 51 per cent. By this time, the change of the NSSF had occurred. But even after the change of the definition, the debt-GDP ratio rose to about 55 per cent. If the NSSF on-lending to states is also counted the level of debt relative to GDP, which could be considered comparable would be seen to have risen to 68 per cent.

Debt in essence is an accumulation of borrowings net of repayments. While debt is a stock variable measured at a point of time, borrowing is a flow variable that adds to the stock. However, it is not the absolute amount of debt that is a cause of so much concern. What is important is whether debt relative to GDP is growing. Since the GDP itself grows, a corresponding growth in the absolute amount of debt will leave the debt-GDP ratio unchanged. It is only when debt grows faster than the growth of GDP that the debt-GDP ratio grows. This growth may become a problem when it gives rise to growing interest payments relative to GDP.

Table 12.1: Centre's Debt Relative to GDP: 1950-51 to 2003-04 (per cent)

Year	Debt-GDP Ratio	Year	Debt-GDP Ratio
1950-51	28.844	1977-78	39.542
1951-52	27.561	1978-79	39.481
1952-53	28.364	1979-80	41.554
1953-54	26.703	1980-81	41.560
1954-55	30.733	1981-82	40.442
1955-56	32.292	1982-83	45.082
1956-57	29.874	1983-84	43.400
1957-58	33.776	1984-85	46.205
1958-59	36.262	1985-86	49.456
1959-60	38.663	1986-87	53.521
1960-61	38.121	1987-88	55.190
1961-62	38.283	1988-89	54.504
1962-63	39.267	1989-90	55.163
1963-64	38.724	1990-91	55.314
1964-65	38.610	1991-92	54.303
1965-66	40.947	1992-93	53.707
1966-67	45.856	1993-94	55.628
1967-68	43.273	1994-95	53.182
1968-69	43.400	1995-96	51.029
1969-70	41.743	1996-97	49.384
1970-71	41.237	1997-98	51.118
1971-72	43.816	1998-99	51.224
1972-73	44.347	1999-00	51.189
1973-74	36.985	2000-01	53.310
1974-75	33.963	2001-02	55.801
1975-76	32.897	2002-03	56.156
1976-77	37.451	2003-04	54.482

Source: (Basic Data): *Indian Public Finance Statistics.*

Interest payments are committed liabilities and rising claims of interest payments may force reduction in primary expenditures that is, expenditures after excluding the interest payments. The interest payments can themselves rise because of two reasons: rise in debt and rise in the interest rate. Interest rates may rise as a result of the large borrowing requirements of the government sector. Thus, there are interrelationships in the size and cost of borrowing that require to be explored. The term 'derived fiscal deficit' is used for that increment of debt that is used for current expenditure

Using the following symbols, we can derive important relationships between debt, fiscal deficit and primary deficit.

Y_t = GDP at current prices in period t

F_t = Fiscal deficit in period t; f_t = fiscal deficit to GDP ratio in period t

P_t = Primary deficit in period t; p_t = primary deficit to GDP ratio in period t

B_t = Debt at the end of period t; b_t = ratio of debt (end-period) to GDP of period t

g_t = growth rate [= $(Y_t - Y_{t-1})/Y_{t-1}$]

I_t = interest payment.

i_t = effective interest rate [= I_t/D_{t-1}]

In general, we have

$B_t - B_{t-1} = F_t$

This equation applies when there is no change in the assets. However, some times, governments can liquidate their assets to reduce their liabilities. In that case,

$B_t - B_{t-1} = F_t + DA_t$,

Where the DA_t refers to change in assets where there is a corresponding change in the liabilities.

Thus, $b_t = D_t/Y_t$, and $p_t = P_t/Y_t$.

By definition, assuming change in liabilities due to change in assets to be zero,

$D_t - D_{t-1} = F_t$

or, $D_t - D_{t-1} = P_t + I_t$ ...(1)

We can write, $I_t = i\, D_{t-1}$, and $Y_t = Y_{t-1}(1 + g_t)$

Dividing (a) by Y_t, we have

$b_t - b_{t-1}[1/(1 + g_t)] = p_t + i_t b_{t-1}[1/(1 + g_t)]$

or, $b_t = p_t + b_{t-1}\, [(1 + i_t)/(1 + g_t)]$ ...(2)

or, $b_t - b_{t-1} = p_t - b_{t-1}[1 - (1 + i_t)/\,(1 + g_t)]$

or, $b_t - b_{t-1} = p_t - b_{t-1}[(g_t - i_t)/\,(1 + g_t)]$ ...(3)

In many analyses of accumulation of the debt, two factors contribute to the debt-GDP ratio: cumulated primary deficits and cumulated effect of the difference between growth rate and interest rate. The standard specification of the equation describing debt dynamics with discrete time periods is given by the following equation. Here, the decomposition proposed in Rangarajan and Srivastava (2003) is followed.

$$b_t = p_t + b_{t-1}\,[(1 + i_t)/(1 + g_t)] \qquad \ldots (4)$$

We can write, $z_t = b_t - b_{t-1}$, equation (1) can also be written as

$$z_t = p_t - b_{t-1}\left[\frac{(g_t - i_t)}{(1+g_t)}\right] \qquad \ldots (5)$$

The increment in debt can be cumulated over any relevant period t = 1 to T. Thus,

$$\sum_{t=1}^{T} z_t = \sum_{t=1}^{T} p_t - \sum_{t=1}^{T} b_{t-1}[((g_t - i_t)/(1+g_t)] \qquad \ldots (6)$$

Equation 6 helps in decomposing the change in the debt-GDP ratio between any two benchmark years $[\sum_{t=1}^{T} z_t = (b_T - b_O)]$ into the contribution of cumulated primary deficit relative to GDP and that of the cumulated effect of the weighted excess of growth over the interest rate. In the Indian case $\sum p_t$ has been much larger than $\sum z_t$ for long stretches of time, and the role of the growth/interest rate differential has been to absorb the impact of the cumulated primary deficits from getting translated into accretion to the debt-GDP ratio. It is, therefore, useful to write equation (6) as

$$\sum_{t=1}^{T} p_t = \sum_{t=1}^{T} z_t + \sum_{t=1}^{T} b_{t-1}[((g_t - i_t)/(1+g_t)] \qquad \ldots (7)$$

The part of cumulated primary deficit relative to GDP, which is absorbed by the differential of growth rate and interest rate is given by, say A1, where

$$A1 = \sum_{i=1}^{T} b_{t-1}[((g_t - i_t)/(1+g_t)] / \sum_{t=1}^{T} p_t \qquad \ldots (8)$$

The share of the cumulated primary deficit, which results in the accretion to the debt-GDP ratio (say A2) is given by

$$A2 = \sum_{t=1}^{T} z_t / \sum_{t=1}^{T} p_t \qquad \ldots (9)$$

Thus, A1 + A2 =1

Rangarajan and Srivastava (2003) have also proposed another decomposition of the term containing the effect of growth-interest rate differential between the effect of real growth-real interest rate differential and inflation. Writing g* and i* for real growth and real interest rates and π for the inflation rate, we have ($g_t - i_t =$

$g_t^* - i_t^*$) and $1 + g_t = 1 + g_t^* + \pi_t$. Using the expansion of the term and ignoring second order terms, with the assumption that $/g_t/<1$, the following can be written:

$$(1+g_t)^{-1} = (1 + g_t^* + \pi_t)^{-1} = 1 - g_t^* - \pi_t \quad \ldots(10)$$

$$\text{Thus, } \sum_{i=1}^{T} b_{t-1}(g_t - i_t)(1 + g_t)^{-1} = \sum_{i=1}^{T} b_{t-1}(g_t^* - i_t^*)(1 - g_t^*) - \sum_{i=1}^{T} b_{t-1}(g_t^* - i_t^*)\pi_t \quad \ldots(11)$$

This decomposition can help in identifying the impact of inflation on debt accumulation. The relative shares of the two terms on the right hand side in the factor giving the impact of the growth-interest rate differential can provide the relative contributions of the differential between real growth and interest rates and the inflation rate. The effect of inflation is in a direction opposite to that of the influence of the differential between real growth and real interest rate. Thus, when real growth rate exceeds the real interest rate, its beneficial effect in containing the process of debt accumulation is partly offset by the influence of the inflation rate.

The figures of derived fiscal deficit however differ from the official figures because certain securities issued by the Central Government are kept off-budget. This point was discussed in Rangarajan and Srivastava (2003). Important among these are securities issued to oil companies after the winding up of the Oil Pool Account as also securities issued to UTI, Industrial Investments Bank of India and the Kudremukh Iron Oil Project. The amount of these securities in some years is quite large.

It is seen that the cumulated primary deficit resulted in large cumulated increases in the debt-GDP ratio over some stretches of time and not in others. Table 12.2 shows the relative effects of the cumulated primary deficits and the factor reflecting the effect of growth-interest rate differential in the process of accumulation of debt of the central government since 1951-52. In the period from 1955-56 to 1999-00, it was the primary deficit that caused the increase in the debt-GDP ratio. Often a significant part of the pressure of primary deficit could be absorbed by the excess of growth over interest rates. Without this cushion the cumulated primary deficits through 1950-51 to 2001-02 would have resulted in a central debt to GDP ratio of about 146 percentage points.

In Rangarajan and Srivastava (2003), it is shown that in the case of the centre in the fifties, 52.2 per cent of the impact of cumulative primary deficit was absorbed by the growth-interest rate differential. Thus, only 47.8 per cent of the cumulated primary deficit of 20.5 percentage points resulted in an increase in the debt-GDP ratio of 9.8 percentage points. In the sixties, the pressure put by the cumulated primary deficit was relatively larger (29 percentage points). However, 89 percent of this was absorbed by the differential of growth over interest rate, resulting in only a small increase of 3.1 percentage points in the debt-GDP ratio. During the seventies and again during the nineties, nearly hundred percent of the impact of primary deficit was absorbed by the growth/interest rate differential leading to a negligible increase in the debt-GDP ratio during these two decades considered as a whole. In the eighties, only 72 per cent of the pressure of cumulated primary deficit could be absorbed by the (g-i) differential.

Table 12.2: Decade-wise Decomposition of Debt Accumulation Relative to GDP

Years	Cumulated changes in			Relative impact of cumulated primary deficit	
	Debt-GDP ratio	Primary Def-GDP ratio	Growth & interest rate differential	Increase in Debt-GDP ratio	Absorption by growth-interest differential
				D/p	w(g-i)/p
1951-52 to 1959-60	12.89	19.39	6.50	66.47	33.53
1960-61 to 1969-70	3.87	32.18	28.31	12.03	87.97
1970-71 to 1979-80	0.07	26.18	26.12	0.25	99.75
1980-81 to 1989-90	14.71	52.09	37.38	28.24	71.76
1990-91 to 2002-03	14.67	39.09	24.42	37.53	62.47
1951-52 to 2002-03	46.21	168.94	122.73	27.82	72.18
Memo:					
1996-97 to 2002-03	19.55	19.77	0.22	101.14	1.13
Debt-GDP ratio at the end of					
1950-51	29.6				
2002-03	75.8				

Source: (Basic Data): *Indian Public Finance Statistics*, Ministry of Finance, Government of India, and *National Income Accounts*, CSO.

The long term Indian experience is different in as much as for a stretch of 48 years, the single cause of the rise in debt was the cumulated primary deficit. The excess of growth rate over interest rate helped to mitigate the situation. In the case of the OECD countries, while both factors contributed to rise in the debt-GDP ratio, the growth-interest differential had become more important in recent years. In India over the period from 1951-52 to 2001-02, the central debt-GDP ratio rose by 26.5 percentage points. The increase occurred mainly in the fifties and the eighties. In the remaining period of thirty years, except for a small rise, all the pressure of cumulated primary deficit was absorbed by the excess of growth over interest rate

12.2 Growth of Combined Debt-GDP Ratio

We now look at the profile of growth of the combined debt of central and state governments. The combined debt of central and state governments consists of the sum of centre's debt and the states' debt minus states debt to the centre. This gives the liabilities of the governments sector to the rest of the world, domestic and external. Since the states do not borrow directly from external sources, the external debt is shown entirely on the centre's account. According to available information, the combined debt-GDP ratio of the central and state governments at the end of 1950-51 was 29.6 percent. During 1951-52 to 1959-60 a little less than 13 percentage points were added to the debt-GDP ratio. An additional accretion of about 4 percentage points took place in the sixties. In the seventies, there was hardly any change in the debt-GDP ratio. It was in the eighties and nineties (up to 2002-03) that there was an increase respectively of 14.7 percentage points for each period in the debt-GDP ratio. Table 12.2 shows the relative effects of the cumulated primary deficits and the factor reflecting the effect of growth-interest rate differential in the process of accumulation of combined debt of the central and state governments since 1951-52. It is shown that a significant part of the pressure of primary deficit could be absorbed by the excess of growth over interest rates. In particular, it was able to absorb nearly 72 percent of the cumulated primary deficits. Had this cushion been not available, cumulated primary deficits through 1951-52 to 2002-03 would have added about 169 percentage points to the combined debt to GDP ratio.

12.3 Primary Deficits and Excess of Growth over Interest Rates

The decade wise picture indicates that in the fifties, 33.5 per cent of the impact of cumulative primary deficit was absorbed by the growth-interest rate differential. The remaining 66.4 percent of the cumulated primary deficit of 19.4 percentage points resulted in an increase in the debt-GDP ratio of 12.9 percentage points. In the sixties, the pressure put by the cumulated primary deficit was relatively larger (32.2 percentage points). However, 88 per cent of this was absorbed by the differential of growth over interest rate, resulting in only a small increase of 3.9 percentage points in the debt-GDP ratio. During the seventies, nearly hundred per cent of the impact of cumulated primary deficit was absorbed by the growth/interest rate differential leading to a negligible increase in the debt-GDP ratio. In the eighties and the nineties (up to 2002-03), about 72 and 62 percent respectively of the pressure of cumulated primary deficit could be absorbed by the (g-i) differential.

However, for three consecutive years, *viz.*, 2000-01, 2001-02, and 2002-03, the nominal growth rate fell below the effective interest rate. In these years, instead of absorbing the impact of primary deficits, the growth-interest differential, being negative, worked in the reverse by adding to the debt-GDP ratio. Further, since this effect depends on the previous year's debt-GDP ratio, its impact became progressively larger for the same shortfall in the growth rate relative to the interest rate. At the end of 2002-03, the combined debt-GDP ratio stood at 76 percent when external debt is evaluated at historical exchange rates and, for the states, reserve funds and deposits are not included. If these adjustments are made, the combined debt-GDP ratio at the end of 2002-23 is estimated to be about 85 percent of GDP.

12.4 Profiles of Growth and Interest Rates

Effective interest rate is derived by dividing actual interest payments during a financial year by the outstanding liabilities at the beginning of that year. This means that the effective interest rate is the weighted average of past interest rates pertaining to debt that are currently being serviced. It implies that even if current interest rates fall, the effective rate will fall more slowly than the current interest rates. Conversely, it will also rise more slowly, in a period where nominal interest rates are rising. The steady rise of effective interest rate is observed until the end of the nineties after which it has started falling. Until 1959-60, the nominal interest rate was well below 2 per cent per annum. It generally remained in the range of 3.2 to 3.7 per cent up to 1973-74. Rising steadily since then, the peak was attained towards the end of the nineties with the average rate going above 10 percent. It is clear that over the long run, the nominal growth rate has been far more volatile than the nominal interest rate. As a result the intra-year variability in the debt accumulation process is largely due to the growth rate volatility.

The real average interest rate is derived by deducting from the effective nominal rate, the implicit price deflator of GDP at market prices. The real interest rate has been negative throughout the years during 1951-52 to 1994-95. The turning point seems to have occurred in 1995-96 when the real interest rate became positive. Concurrently, the excess of growth over interest rates, whether real or nominal, started falling in magnitude, becoming negative in 2000-01.

Historically, the real interest rates on government securities were kept low as the government was able to borrow from the domestic market at rates much below the market rates due to a variety of banking regulations including requirements for banks to maintain specified statutory liquidity requirements (SLR) and cash reserve ratio (CRR) and by controlling a number of financial institutions. With the liberalization of the financial sector, the government is borrowing at rates which are by and large market determined.

The six recent years from 1997-98 to 2002-03 require special attention. The 2002-03 figures are available as revised estimates. The recently announced revised estimates put growth of GDP at factor cost in 2002-03 at 4.3 per cent in real terms and 7.1 per cent at current prices. The effective interest rate on central government liabilities in 2002-03 is estimated to be in the vicinity of 9 per cent. Growth in GDP at market prices is likely to be marginally lower as the buoyancy of indirect taxes continues to be less than one. The central debt-GDP ratio at the end of 2002-03 is estimated to be 57.6 per cent. Thus, in 2002-03, the interest rate will again be higher than the growth rate. During 1997-98 to 2002-03 the central-debt GDP ratio has risen by 8.22 percentage points, at an average rate of 1.37 percentage points per year. This is a rate of growth in the accumulation of debt relative to GDP that is more than three times that of the average increment of 0.44 percentage points per year in the previous 46 years.

If the reversal in the sign of (g-i) is likely to be sustained, it is clear that rather than partially absorbing the impact of cumulated primary deficit, it will add to the accumulation of debt. With the prevailing debt-GDP ratio of around 57 per cent of GDP, every 1 percentage point differential in (i-g) will cause just a little less than 0.57 percentage points of increase in the debt-GDP ratio. Even if the (g-i) differential sometimes turns out to be positive, it is likely that the days of a large excess of growth rate over interest rate are over. Therefore, the likelihood of primary deficits getting converted into a rise in the debt-GDP ratio is stronger now. It may also be noted that the effective interest rate for the central government is lower than the corresponding effective rate for the states.

The primary deficit is the excess of primary expenditure i.e. total expenditure minus interest payments over revenue receipts. Its capacity to adjust to changes in the relativity of growth and interest rates is limited. The maximum build up of primary deficit was in the period from 1979-80 to 1993-94. During this period the primary deficit to GDP ratio remained above 3 percent except in three years. The peak was reached in 1982-83 when it exceeded 6.5 percent. However, throughout this period, a build up of the debt-GDP ratio could be contained because of the excess of growth rate over interest rate. The primary deficit to GDP ratio since 1993-94 remained below 2.5 percent of the GDP and the change in the debt-GDP ratio was modest till 1999-00 because the growth rate also exceeded the interest rate. The debt-GDP ratio has started rising from 2000-01 because of the combined effect of primary deficit and the negative difference between the growth rate and the interest rate.

12.5 Issues of Debt Sustainability

The issue of fiscal deficit assumed importance in India since the late eighties when the fiscal deficit to GDP ratio rose to levels above 7 per cent. In the early nineties, it was above 9 per cent, and after some improvement, it started rising again, crossing the threshold of 10 per cent of GDP in 2001-02. In the context of fiscal deficits in India, several distinct sets of issues have been examined from time to time. Some of the important issues that have been noted in the literature are listed in Rangarajan and Srivastava (2005) as follows:

1. Whether fiscal deficits of the central and state governments, considered together, and separately are sustainable;
2. Whether these governments are solvent, given their debt and deficit levels;
3. Whether the presence of high levels of structural fiscal deficits has constrained the usability of fiscal policy as a tool of stabilization in respect of output as well as prices;
4. Whether there is a meaningful asymmetry between accumulation of fiscal liabilities by the central and state governments;
5. Whether there is potential for additional seigniorage in the system for financing fiscal deficits;
6. Whether there is need to formulate rules and targets to stabilize debt and deficits, and how should these targets be derived;
7. Whether, apart from the size, the quality of fiscal deficit has progressively become more of a problem and, in particular, whether the rising share of revenue deficit in fiscal deficit, i.e. government dis-savings have resulted in a fall of the overall saving rate, thereby adversely affecting growth;
8. Whether fiscal deficits have crowded out private investment by putting pressure on interest rates, thereby adversely affecting growth;
9. Whether continued high levels of fiscal deficits, resulting in growing interest payments, have crowded out government capital expenditure; and
10. Whether public investment financed by fiscal deficits has the potential of crowding-in private investment, thereby positively affecting growth.

These issues are interdependent as the impact of fiscal deficits on growth affects its sustainability.

The link between fiscal deficit and growth, saving and investment rates, inflation and current account deficits have also been examined in many studies.

The relationship between fiscal deficit and interest rate and the existence of crowding out are important considerations in determining the advisability of deficit-financed expansionary fiscal policies. Authors like Sunderarajan and Thakur (1980), Pradhan et al (1990) and Parker (1995) had earlier examined the issue of crowding out in the Indian context. More recently, Chakraborty (2002) finds that fiscal deficit does not put upward pressure on the interest rate while Goyal (2004), using monthly data argues that there is a two-way causality between fiscal deficit and interest rates. In his view, interest rates did not rise in recent years in spite of high fiscal deficits because of larger liquidity available to the system. RBI (2002) has noted that raising public sector investment to boost aggregate demand in the economy crowds-out both private consumption and investment with no long-lasting impact on output. On the other hand, infrastructure investment by the public sector crowds-in private investment while public investment in manufacturing crowds out private investment. Rangarajan and Srivastava (2005) have given an overview of some of the major dimensions of the issue of sustainability as summarised below.

12.6 Solvency of the Public Sector

Buiter and Patel (1992) examined the issue of solvency of the Indian public sector by studying trends in debt, primary budget surplus, and seigniorage. In the accounting approach to public sector solvency, Buiter [1985, 1988] suggests that sustainable deficit levels can be financed without raising debt levels relative to GDP under feasible rates of growth, real interest and inflation. Following the neoclassical solvency approach, Buiter and Patel (1992) observe that the relevant criterion for the no-ponzi game condition on public debt is to judge it by comparing the rate of growth of public debt relative to GDP with the real interest rate. If the debt ratio systematically grows faster than the real interest rate, the public sector is insolvent.

Solvency requires that, with a finite time horizon, public debt in the last period becomes non- positive, i.e., no debt is left for further servicing. If the time horizon is infinity, the existing debt should be serviceable by current and future primary surpluses and future seigniorage. This implies that, at any time, the present value of future public debt becomes zero in the limit. If it becomes less than zero, it indicates a situation of 'super-solvency'. The requirement of present value of debt to be zero or less holds as long as the economy is not dynamically inefficient, i.e. it is not the case that interest rate is below growth rate forever. For a dynamically inefficient system (where growth rate is higher than the interest rate forever) Ponzi games can be viable. Buiter and Patel contend that while interest rate can be below the growth rate for extended finite periods of time, the

Indian economy is not dynamically inefficient over the long run, and that "there are no social free lunches to be earned by increasing the public debt". Calling the build up of public debt in India, 'this remarkable fiscal high wire act', they contend that continuation of existing patterns of behaviour will eventually threaten the solvency of the government. They also observe that solvency is a very weak criterion with which to evaluate the sustainability of fiscal and financial policy. They observe that a government can remain solvent even though its debt relative to GDP grows without bound, if the long run growth rate of the debt-GDP ratio, while positive, is less than the long run value of the excess of the interest rate over the growth rate. Thus, unbounded debt-GDP ratios can still be consistent with solvency.

12.7 Implications for Sustainability

Sustainability of debt and solvency of the borrowers should be considered distinct issues. Sustainability can be seen as the capacity to keep balance between costs of additional borrowing with returns from such borrowing, which could be in the from of higher growth that results in higher government revenues that can be used for servicing the additional borrowing. Sustainability issues should be viewed for combinations of debt and fiscal deficit, and not in isolation for either debt or fiscal deficit. Thus, a fiscal deficit of 10 per cent combined with say a debt-GDP ratio of 50 per cent will have sustainability implications that are quite different from when the debt-GDP ratio is 100 per cent. Thus, sustainability is not synonymous with stability of the debt-GDP ratio at whatever level it might have reached.

The level of debt in combination with interest rate determines the level of interest payments. Fiscal deficit net of interest payments determine primary deficit. Primary deficit represents the extent of borrowing used by the government for current expenditures, revenue and capital. The remaining part of fiscal deficit is claimed by interest payments, which are transfer payments that go back into the income-expenditure stream. In particular, government interest payments add to the disposable incomes in the private sector. This affects government revenues as well.

Interest payments add to government's revenue expenditures leaving less of current fiscal deficit for use for government capital expenditure. Increases in revenue expenditures, ceteris paribus, lead to a fall in government's net savings, which has an adverse impact on the overall savings and growth rate. However, private savings may be positively affected by a higher fiscal deficit because of a positive impact due to higher wealth in the private sector in the form of government bonds. As government capital expenditure on infrastructure is increased, the growth impulse is positively affected. The impact of fiscal deficit and level of debt on savings and investment as a result of the configuration of these variables determines the impact on growth as well as interest rate. These interrelationships are best dealt with in a macroeconomic model, which can bring together the monetary side influences on interest, growth rate, and inflation rates.

Given the configuration of growth and interest rates, debt would become unsustainable, if fiscal deficits follow a course that leads to a self-perpetuating rise in the debt-GDP ratio, which affects negatively the growth rate and positively the interest rate, such that the existing levels of primary government expenditures cannot be sustained. A sustainable debt-deficit combination would be stable in terms of debt-GDP ratio and fiscal-deficit GDP ratio consistent with the permissible levels of primary expenditures.

An alternative method by which the sustainability issues have been examined in the literature is to look at the growth and interest rates as stochastic processes. Although such an analytical framework does not help directly in designing fiscal policy, it helps ascertain whether debt and deficits show signs of unsustainability. In a recent contribution, Papadopoulos and Sidiropoulos (1999) show that a test for sustainability should check for the cointegartion of government expenditures and revenues. If these are cointegrated with the cointegrating vector of (1, -1), the necessary condition for sustainability of debt is satisfied. Jha and Sharma (2004) have carried out empirical tests to ascertain whether government expenditures and revenues are cointegarted in India using long time series data. They find, on the basis of a sample period starting in the early fifties, that if structural breaks are taken into account, government expenditures and revenues were cointegrated and, therefore growth in government debt in India has been consistent with the requirements of sustainability. An implication of the presence of cointegration is that adjustments in revenues and expenditures take place such that these move together. Thus, for example, if interest payments to GDP ratios increase, adjustments in other components of expenditure, notably government capital expenditure which, by itself, may not be desirable, would take place so that the co-movement of expenditure with revenues is maintained.

12.8 Financing Deficits by Alternative Channels

The relative merits of financing fiscal deficits by domestic borrowing, external borrowing, or borrowing from the central bank have also received attention in the literature. Financing by external debt would lead to pressure on the exchange rate. Financing domestic debt by monetization would put pressure on inflation and that by domestic borrowing, on interest rates. For example, Moorthy et.al. (2000), while examining the issue of bond-financing versus monetization, in the context of debt stabilization, conclude that the emphasis on market borrowing rather than borrowing from the RBI as part of economic reforms in India in the nineties has proved to be beneficial. In Rangarajan, Basu, and Jhadav (1989), the inter-temporal budget constraint was used to study the dynamic inter-linkages between government deficits and alternative modes of financing these. In particular, given the set of revenue and expenditure parameters, relevant for the late eighties, it was shown that the bond-financing scenario led to an explosive growth in the debt-GDP ratio, and the monetary-financing scenario led to an unacceptably high inflation rate within a short span of time.

12.9 Asymmetry in Central and Sub-National Debt

Another dimension that has received attention relates to the desirability of asymmetric treatment of central and sub-national debt and deficits on grounds of different degrees of endogeneity of interest, growth and other relevant variables. For example, Chelliah (2001) has argued that 'we must recognize that the state is borrowing largely from outsiders and paying interest to them' and that 'state governments do not have access to created credit'. In his view, the constraints on sub-national deficits must be stronger than those pertaining to the central government. The interest rates applicable to the borrowing by the states, both average rates and marginal rates are higher as compared to those for the centre, implying the need for more stringent norms for the same rates of growth of GDP.

12.10 Controlling Debt and Deficit: Rules and Targets

Borrowing by the government often appears to be a softer option than increasing taxes or reducing expenditures. That is why, as established by international experience also, it is important to provide exogenous limits on borrowing by governments, whether central or sub-national. Such limits can be exercised through fiscal responsibility legislations, or other institutional arrangements like the Australian Loan Council and the Maastricht Treaty for member countries of the European Economic Community. The Maastricht Treaty on Economic and Monetary Union, for example, has two convergence conditions for the members of the European Monetary Union: (i) Country's overall budget deficit for each fiscal year must be equal to or below 3 percent of the GDP and (ii) a country's stock of public debt must be equal to or less than 60 percent of the GDP. The 3 percent limit is not meant to be exceeded in 'normal' economic downturns.

There has been a discussion in the literature as to whether deficit targeting works in practice. The main institutional reforms for controlling the growth of debt and deficit relate to (a) formal deficit and debt rules, (b) expenditure limits, and (c) requirements of transparency.In regard to the first, apart from the Maastricht Treaty norms, the U.K. has operated a Golden Rule since 1997 whereby borrowing is done only to finance capital spending. Several countries have deficit and debt rules at the sub national level. In the US, all states except two have laws requiring balanced budgets and limiting the states to raise debt. The provinces and territories of Canada generally have fiscal rules with balanced budgets requiring them to take on debt only for the purpose of financing investment projects. Canada has also focused on instituting a rigorous expenditure review process. Debt ceiling can serve as a useful complement to deficit rules. The main criticism of the deficit rules in general and balanced budget rules in particular is that they are invariant and therefore tend to be pro-cyclical. This is particularly important for national governments. For this reason the deficit rules for the national government have increasingly been defined in terms of a cyclically adjusted deficit measure or as an average over the economic cycle so that the operation of domestic stabilizers and some room for discretionary policy within the cycle may be permitted.

Transparency in fiscal management has been emphasized by countries like New Zealand, Australia and the U K. Transparency is best served when there is an explicit legal provision for it requiring elaboration of the guiding principles of fiscal policy, clear statement of objectives of changes in fiscal policies, the need for a long term focus to fiscal policy, and requirements for providing fiscal information to the public. The UK, US, and New Zealand have enacted legislations for transparency, which require statements indicating the objectives for deficits and debt. International experience also suggests that expenditure rules have often proved to be effective. These rules typically emphasize ceilings on specific areas of expenditure like discretionary expenditure as opposed to non-discretionary expenditure and in some cases with respect to particular programmes.

In the Indian context, as far the central finances are concerned, a Fiscal Responsibility and Budget Management Act (FRBMA) was enacted in 2003. Some states have also enacted fiscal responsibility legislations. The central government has also framed Rules under the FRBMA. The Act and the Rules, as these presently stand, have provided for the elimination of the revenue deficit by 2008-09, with 0.5 percentage point of GDP as the minimum annual reduction target, and fiscal deficit to be brought to level of 3 percent of GDP, with 0.3 percentage point of GDP, as the minimum annual reduction target. The FRBMA has some built-in flexibility in achieving revenue and fiscal deficit reduction targets as there is a provision that the specified limits may be exceeded 'due to ground or grounds of national security or national calamity or such other exceptional grounds as the Central Government may specify'. The Act has also provided that 'Reserve Bank of India may subscribe to the primary issues to the Central Government Securities' for specified reasons.

12.11 Sustainability Analytics under the Canonical (Domar) Model

In Domar's analysis of the dynamics of debt accumulation, both interest rate and growth rate are taken as exogenous. Based on this assumption, results can be derived that can serve as useful benchmarks. In considering the dynamics of debt accumulation, the following notations will be used: b_t: debt-GDP ratio in period t; g_t: nominal growth rate in period t; i_t: nominal interest rate in period t; and p_t: primary deficit relative to GDP in period t. While the derivation of Domar's conditions can be shown in several ways, here the methodology used in Rangarajan and Srivastava (2005) is followed. The standard equation for debt accumulation is written as

$$b_t = p_t + b_{t-1}[(1+i_t)/(1+g_t)] \quad (1)$$

Equation 1 can be written as

$$b_t = p_t + x_t b_{t-1} \; [\text{where } x_t = (1+i_t)/(1+g_t)] \quad (2)$$

If $b_0 = p_0$,

We have, $b_1 = p_1 + x_1 p_0$

$b_2 = p_2 + x_2 p_1 + x_2 x_1 p_0$

Generalizing, we can write

$$b_t = p_t + (x_t)\, p_{t-1} + (x_t x_{t-1})\, p_{t-2} + \ldots + (x_t x_{t-1} \ldots x_1)\, p_0 \quad (3)$$

If it is assumed that x_t is constant, implying g and i are constant for all t,

We can write

$$b_t = p_t + x\, p_{t-1} + x^2 p_{t-2} + \ldots + x^{t-1} p_{t-1} + x^t p_0 \quad (4)$$

The canonical model (Domar, 1944) requires the additional assumption that p's are also constant for all t. Since $x_t = (1+i_t)/(1+g_t) = x$ for all t, three cases arise (1) when $g = i$, (2) when $g > i$, and (3) when $g < i$.

In the first case, we can write

$$b_t = p + \sum_{I=0}^{t-1} p = (t+1)\, p \quad (5)$$

This implies that if $g = i$, the debt-GDP ratio is the cumulated sum of the primary deficits in all the previous periods. In the second case, when $g>i$,

$$b_t = p\,\{1 + x + x^2 + \ldots + x^{t-1} + x^t\} \quad (6)$$

The term within parenthesis is a geometric series with common ratio $x<1$. As t tends to infinity, this sum tends to $x/(1-x)$. Then the long run value of the debt-GDP ratio can be written as

$b_t = p + p\ x/(1-x) = p/(1-x)$

$b_t = p\ (1+ g)/(g-i)$ as $t \rightarrow\infty$ (7)

In the third case, when $g<i$, $x>1$, and b_t will grow indefinitely.

Thus, a value of $p>0$, will eventually become unsustainable for both cases when $g = i$ and when $g<i$. In the case, when $g = i$, the debt-GDP ratio grows linearly by the size of the primary deficit, and when $g<i$, the debt-GDP ratios grows explosively if the primary deficit-GDP ratio is positive.

We will now focus on the case where $g>i$. From (7), the long run equilibrium value of $b_t = b^*$ is given by

$b^* = p\ (1+g)/(g-i)$ (8)

The fiscal deficit to GDP ratio (f^*) corresponding to a stable debt-GDP ratio (b^*) will be:

$f^* = p.g/(g-i)$ (9)

Equations (8) and (9) provide a system of two equations in three unknowns, *viz.*, b, f, and p, assuming values of g and i are given ($g>i$), and consistent with the a stable debt-GDP ratio. High values of p will be associated with high levels of b and f. However, these equations do not provide a unique solution as the unknowns are more than the number of the equations.

Using equations (8) and (9) together, the relationship between b^* and f^* can be written as:

$b^* = f^*(1+ g)/g$ (10)

12.12 Fiscal Deficit, Growth, and Stability

Fiscal deficit can stimulate growth if it can be used to generate demand for unemployed resources. This strategy can work, if the impact of fiscal deficit on growth rate is higher than interest rate. Then increases in fiscal deficit would not translate in to increases in the debt-GDP ratio, to the extent these are absorbed by higher growth rates. However, there are a number of factors that may constrain this process. In particular, additional borrowing can put pressure on the interest rate, particularly for the private sector, and thereby curb the growth rate because of reduced investment rate relative to GDP. Further, if governments' debt and interest liabilities rise, this strategy would be counterproductive as government's saving would fall or dis-saving would increase leading to a reduction in the overall saving rate.

An important use of borrowing is to reduce the amplitude of business cycles. All schools of economic thought approve of this rationale in using borrowing by the governments to temporarily augment aggregate demand. In using fiscal deficit for this objective, flexibility is greater when the debt-GDP ratio is low than when it is high. It is important to therefore recognize that existing debt-GDP levels can constrain stabilization effort under certain circumstances.

12.13 Structural and Cyclical Deficits

In this context, it is useful to distinguish between structural or cyclically neutral deficit and transitory deficit. The structural deficit should be determined within a sustainability framework aiming at maximizing trend growth rate. The short term component of fiscal deficit should be aimed at minimizing the impact of cyclical changes such that the economy is stimulated when it is below potential output and inflationary pressures are contained when prices are above trend levels.

Rangrajan and Srivastava (2005) discuss several methods for estimating structural and cyclical components of fiscal deficits. In the literature, three main methods have been used for this purpose:

- constant elasticities method, where the cyclical component is estimated first based on estimated of revenue and expenditure elasticities with respect to income,
- smoothed-ratio approach where the structural fiscal deficit is estimated first by smoothening the revenue and expenditure ratios to GDP, and
- structural time series approach where time-varying elasticities are used and the cyclical component is estimated first.

Rangarajan and Srivastava (2005) have used the smoothed-ratio approach, suggested by Cano and Kanutin (1996) for calculating the structural deficit in India. In this approach, revenues and expenditures are decomposed into a structural and residual component by using a Hodrick – Prescott (HP) filter.

Taking r_s and e_s to be the trend ratios of revenues and expenditures relative to GDP and r_c and e_c to be corresponding cyclical components, the structural deficit to GDP ratio can be derived as $f_s = (e_s - r_s)$. The cyclical deficit f_c is obtained as a residual. In their study, Rangarajan and Srivastava (2005) estimate the following: structural primary deficit by calculating the trend ratios of primary expenditure (pe_s) and interest payments relative to GDP (ip_s). Thus,

$$f_s = (pe)_s - r_s + (ip)_s \text{ and } f_c = f - f_s$$

Thus, $f = p_s + (ip)_s + f_c$ where $p_s = (pe)_s - r_s$

Thus fiscal deficit to GDP ratio has three components: primary structural deficit, structural interest payments relative to GDP, and cyclical fiscal deficit. Table 12.3 shows the structural and actual fiscal deficits since 1990-91 as estimated in the above cited study. Structural fiscal deficits account for a large part of actual fiscal deficit in the nineties. Structural interest payments to GDP ratio has increased continuously from 4.3 percent in 1990-91 to 5.9 percent in 2001-02, amounting to an increase of 2.6 percentage points. Structural primary deficit can be seen to have fallen from the peak of 4.14 percent in 1990-91 to 2.75 percent in 1997-98, before it started rising again. Although both factors have contributed to structural fiscal deficit, the impact of structural interest payments has been larger in the nineties and also more persistent.

Table 12.3: Combined Central and State Finances: Structural and Cyclical Deficits Relative to GDP (% to GDP)

Year	Actual fiscal deficit	Structural fiscal deficit	Cyclical fiscal deficit	Structural primary deficit	Debt-stabilizing primary deficit	Actual interest payments	Structural interest payments
1990-91	9.383	8.433	0.950	4.144	4.4757	4.397	4.288
1991-92	7.162	8.302	-1.140	3.822	3.2284	4.746	4.480
1992-93	7.240	8.171	-0.931	3.516	2.9542	4.792	4.656
1993-94	9.824	8.059	1.765	3.243	2.8343	4.953	4.816
1994-95	6.945	7.975	-1.030	3.012	4.3319	5.128	4.963
1995-96	6.778	7.947	-1.169	2.846	3.8711	4.962	5.101
1996-97	6.081	7.993	-1.912	2.757	2.5044	5.111	5.236
1997-98	7.660	8.118	-0.459	2.748	0.5467	5.159	5.370
1998-99	8.227	8.309	-0.083	2.801	1.9892	5.318	5.508
1999-00	9.002	8.548	0.453	2.899	0.3002	5.682	5.650
2000-01	8.792	8.816	-0.024	3.022	-1.1835	5.727	5.794
2001-02	10.557	9.099	1.458	3.159	-0.4902	6.098	5.939

Source: Rangarajan and Srivastava (2005).

A structural 'primary gap' is defined as the difference between actual structural primary deficit and the debt-stabilizing primary deficit (p^s) defined as $\{b_{t-1}*(1+g_t)/(g_t-i_t)\}$. Table 12.3 also shows that the primary deficit has been higher than the 'debt-stabilizing' primary deficit, in most of the years in the nineties except 1990-91, 1994-95, and 1995-96. The structural primary balance has been used in the literature to assess the medium-term fiscal stance. The large values of the structural primary balance since the late nineties clearly indicate that the current medium term fiscal stance is not sustainable.

The profile of structural and debt-stabilizing primary deficit is compared in Chart 12.1 since 1951-52. The structural primary deficit is shown by the bolder line. There are long stretches towards the end of the eighties and the latter part of the nineties that the structural primary deficit has been much higher than the debt-stabilizing primary deficit. These are the episodes in time where large accretion of debt relative to GDP took place. This led to larger structural interest payments relative to GDP. Together, structural primary deficit and structural interest payments have caused structural fiscal deficits to be large.

Chart 12.1: Comparison of Structural and Debt-Stabilizing Primary Deficit

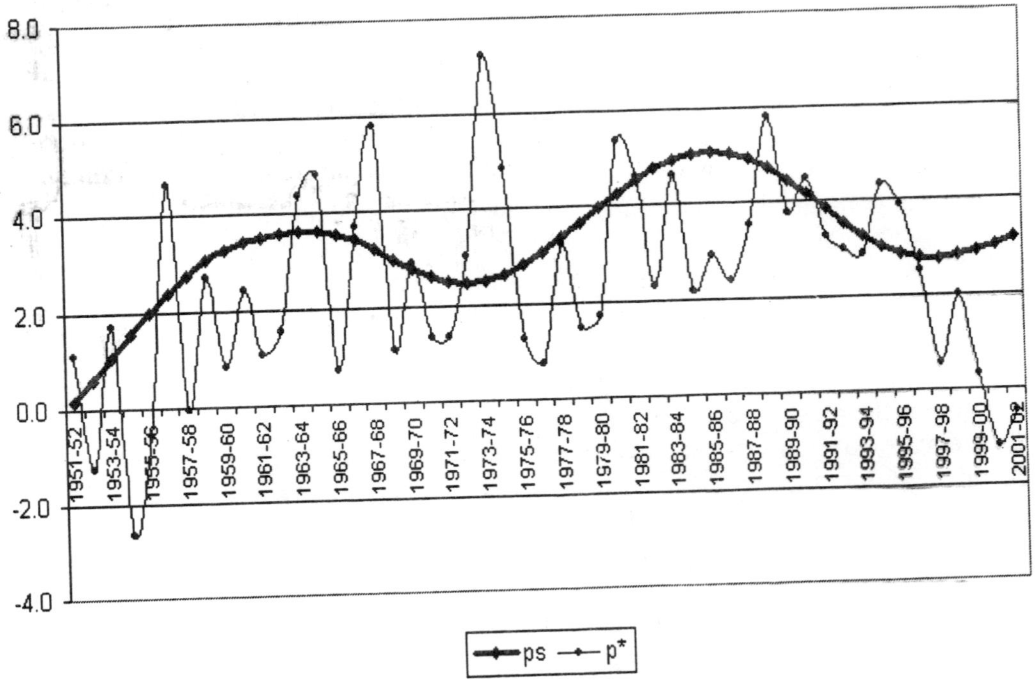

Rangarajan and Srivastava (2005) observe that in view of the large structural fiscal deficit, the role that cyclical deficit can play has become extremely limited in periods of recession. An appropriate short term fiscal stance should show opposite signs between cyclical deficit and departures of actual growth from trend growth, that is, when actual growth is below trend, the cyclical deficit should be positive and vice versa. It is seen that throughout the period from 1965-66 to 1987-88, the short-term stance was in the correct direction. It is in the period since 1988-89 that the short-term stance has not been robust except in the mid-nineties.

12.14 Summary and Concluding Observations

In this chapter, we have looked at the growth profile of central and combined debt-GDP ratio in India within the context of issues of sustainability. Fiscal deficit can prove to be detrimental to growth when they lead to or are accompanied by a rise in revenue deficits, which amount to reduction in government savings. This reduction may not be fully offset by a corresponding rise in the private savings, leading to a fall in the overall saving rate. The impact of fiscal deficit on investment arises both from its impact on private investment and government investment. The adverse effects on private investment occur if fiscal deficits put pressure on interest rates, and if private investment is sensitive to the interest rate. The effect on government capital expenditure is through committed interest payments, which rise if the debt-GDP ratio rises and/or interest rate rises.

In the context of debt accumulation in India, the main findings of the recent study by Rangarajan and Srivastava (2005) are summarized below.

1. Fiscal deficit and government debt in India have caused concern, particularly since the nineties, when in most years the combined fiscal deficit was higher than 9 percent of GDP.
2. Even if fiscal deficits may appear to be sustainable according to some studies, the critical issue relates to determining appropriate levels of debt and deficit relative to GDP at which these should be stabilized. This can be done by developing rules with given growth and interest rates and initial debt levels.
3. When fiscal deficits are high in magnitude relative to GDP and largely structural in nature, government's ability to mount counter-cyclical interventions is compromised, particularly when growth is below trend levels and intervention is needed. This was clearly experienced in the late nineties and the early part of the new decade.
4. In India, the household sector saves more than it invests, and the excess becomes available in the form of the financial savings of this sector to the private corporate sector and the government sector for their investment requirements that are not financed by their own savings. Although government dis-savings increased since the late nineties, the pressure on interest rates was not witnessed because of a fall in investment demand by the private corporate sector.
5. The overall growth rate depends on the overall savings rate and investment rate. There is reason to believe that when government saving falls, private saving rate increases as wealth held in the private sector in the form of government bonds increases. This compensatory rise in the private sector saving rate has been partial. On the investment side, government's own

investment demand also fell as its debt-GDP ratio and the ratio of interest payments to revenue receipts rose.

6. The centre's FRBMA has certain positive features, but it is not complete. It does not indicate a suitable level of debt-GDP ratio along with the specified fiscal deficit target. It also does not provide for a suitable strategy for coping with short term fluctuations.
7. It is important that centre's FRBMA is supplemented by state level fiscal responsibility legislations because, taken together, states' borrowing and debt contribute significantly to the overall fiscal deficit and debt relative to GDP and have significant macro implications.

The TFC Report as also Rangarajan and Srivastava (2005) argue that in the present situation there is a need to bring down the debt-GDP ratio from its present level, which is in excess of 80 per cent of GDP. The process of adjustment can be considered in two phases: adjustment phase and stabilization phase. In the adjustment phase, fiscal deficit will have to be reduced in each successive year to a level, which is less than the level of fiscal deficit relative to GDP that will stabilize the debt-GDP ratio at its previous year's level. This phase should be continued until the revenue deficit is eliminated. In the second phase, the fiscal deficit could be stabilized at 6 percent of GDP. In this phase, the debt-GDP ratio would fall for some more years and eventually stabilize at 56 percent. At this level of debt-GDP ratio, it is estimated that the interest payment to revenue receipts ratio, under given assumptions, would fall to 17 percent. As the ratio of interest payments to revenue receipts begins to fall, it will enable a progressively larger amount of primary revenue expenditure to be incurred on the social sectors.

13

State Debt: Aggregate and Comparative Perspective

> We must recognize that the state is borrowing largely from outsiders and paying interest to them...state governments do not have access to created credit.
>
> R.J. Chelliah

Growth of state level debt can be analyzed in terms of the aggregate level as well as in an inter-state comparative perspective. Issues of debt sustainability should be considered in the context, not just of the central debt, but also that of the states. Among individual states, some states are far more indebted than others. As in the case of central debt, the growth of indebtedness of the states can be analyzed in terms of the relative contributions of the primary deficits of the states and the differentials between the growth and the interest rates.

This Chapter looks at the growth of state debt relative to GDP since 1950-51. It also examines the comparative profile of debt of individual states. The debt-GDP ratio of the states remained around 19 per cent throughout the period of 1985-86 to 1997-98. Thus, for a period of about 22 years, it did not show any perceptible increase. It started increasing in 1998-99. By 2002-03 it has risen to a level of 27.4 per cent of the GDP, an increase of about 9 percentage points in five years. This does not include liabilities on account of reserve funds and deposits. If these are also included, state level debt exceeded 32 per cent of GDP in 2002-03. The effective interest rates for the states have also been higher than that for the centre. In spite of the higher interest rates, the pressure on debt-accumulation at the level of the states was lower than that at the centre due to the lower primary deficits.

Considering individual states, the incidence of debt varies widely in terms the debt-GSDP ratio as well as the per capita debt. The range of per capita debt, considering 2001-02 levels, varies from Rs. 33 for Bihar and Rs. 36 for Madhya Pradesh at the lower end to about Rs. 80 per person for Gujarat and Kerala and Rs. 120 for Punjab, among the general category states. The special category states have an extremely high debt-GDP ratio but lower interest payments to revenue receipts ratio. In their case, the revenue receipts contain plan grants, a large part of which comes to the other states as loan.

In the past, the Finance Commissions have by and large taken interest payments of the base year as actuals and justified committed liabilities. This left considerable adverse incentives in the system as states can finance current expenditures by additional borrowings and create liabilities to be underwritten by future Finance Commissions. Among federations that use a normative determination of debt charges, i.e. interest payments, an important example is that of Australia. However data requirements for their method may render its application in India extremely difficult. The panel estimation may provide a workable alternative.

Another aspect in managing state level debt is to recognize contingent liabilities for the states that are linked to loans taken by state level public enterprises on the basis of guarantees extended by the states. Sometimes, these guarantees and special purpose vehicles are used to borrow indirectly for meeting budgetary liabilities.

In this chapter, we look at the effective interest rate, profile of growth of state level debt, causes of differences in per capita debt of different states, and the problem of contingent liabilities.

13.1 Comparing Effective Interest Rates: Centre and States

Until the introduction of economic reforms in the nineties, governments, both at the Centre and of the States, borrowed from the market and elsewhere, on administered interest rates that were effectively determined by the central government. Further, states owed a large portion of their debt to the Central Government. States have had to pay higher interest rates than the centre primarily because the terms on which the centre borrows are modified, particularly by extending the maturity period, when the centre on-lends to the states. There is also a built-in premium for covering risk to the primary lenders like the small savers and the external agencies.

Table 13.1 gives a comparison of the effective interest rates of the Centre and the States. These are calculated as the ratio of interest payments in a given year to the outstanding liabilities at the beginning of the year respectively for the two tiers of governments. It is seen that the interest rate for the states was higher than that for the centre in all the years. Col 3 gives the excess of the state effective interest rate over that of the centre and column 4 looks at this difference as percentage of the central interest rates. There are two periods when this percentage difference is rather large. First during the years from 1968-69 to 1973-74, the effective state interest rate was higher than the centre's effective rate by a margin in the range of 37 to 51 per cent.

Table 13.1: Difference between Central and States' Effective Interest Rates

	Centre	States	Difference (State-centre)	Difference as % of Centre's int. rate		Centre	States	Difference (State-centre)	Difference as % of Centre's int. rate
1960-61	3.19	3.58	0.38	12.05	1981-82	5.35	6.08	0.74	13.76
1961-62	3.28	3.77	0.49	15.05	1982-83	5.77	6.23	0.46	7.93
1962-63	3.52	3.63	0.10	2.94	1983-84	5.65	6.13	0.48	8.43
1963-64	3.62	4.09	0.47	13.03	1984-85	6.27	6.61	0.34	5.47
1964-65	3.63	3.84	0.21	5.65	1985-86	6.62	6.79	0.17	2.52
1965-66	3.66	4.44	0.78	21.24	1986-87	6.73	7.73	1.00	14.92
1966-67	4.09	4.56	0.47	11.52	1987-88	6.76	8.17	1.41	20.92
1967-68	3.49	4.47	0.98	27.92	1988-89	7.30	8.60	1.30	17.74
1968-69	3.33	4.72	1.39	41.74	1989-90	7.73	9.01	1.28	16.53
1969-70	3.35	5.05	1.70	50.62	1990-91	8.02	9.50	1.48	18.50
1970-71	3.39	5.01	1.62	47.67	1991-92	8.45	9.94	1.49	17.58
1971-72	3.56	5.25	1.69	47.47	1992-93	8.76	10.00	1.24	14.11
1972-73	3.60	4.94	1.34	37.17	1993-94	9.14	10.81	1.67	18.26
1973-74	3.69	5.11	1.42	38.59	1994-95	9.22	11.90	2.69	29.14
1974-75	4.12	4.68	0.55	13.44	1995-96	9.29	11.87	2.58	27.74
1975-76	4.67	5.50	0.83	17.76	1996-97	9.81	12.07	2.26	23.02
1976-77	5.02	5.63	0.61	12.11	1997-98	9.71	12.48	2.76	28.45
1977-78	4.53	5.50	0.98	21.57	1998-99	10.01	12.78	2.78	27.76
1978-79	4.55	5.84	1.28	28.19	1999-00	10.61	13.23	2.62	24.74
1979-80	5.08	5.11	0.02	0.49	2000-01	10.40	11.24	0.84	8.05
1980-81	5.19	5.73	0.55	10.51	2001-02	10.24	12.12	1.88	18.33

Source: (Basic data): *Indian Public Finance Statistics*.

During the 20 year period from 1974-75 to 1993-94, in 6 years, this excess was less than 10 per cent of the corresponding central rate, 11 years in which it was between 10 and 20 percent and 3 years when it was more than 20%. Since 1994-95, again the difference has increased. For most years since then, it has been in the range of 27 to 29 percent. The margin has come down once again in 2000-01. As shown in the following section, in the process of accumulation of state debt the factor of excess of growth over interest rate, which absorbed the pressure of cumulated primary deficit, made a smaller contribution in the case of states, since the growth rate is the same but interest rate is higher for the states.

13.2 Debt-Accumulation: Role of Primary Deficits and the Growth-Interest Differential

An analysis of dynamics of debt accumulation for the Central Government was provided in Rangarajan and Srivastava (2003). A similar analysis can be done for analyzing the dynamics of debt accumulation for the state governments. In this chapter, we look at the relative contributions of accumulated primary deficit growth rate and interest rate in the process of accumulation of debt of state governments. For this part of analysis, liabilities on account of reserve funds and deposits are not included in debt as a suitably long time series is not available. Since in the case of state governments the effective interest rates is tangibly higher than that for the central government, the sign reversal between the growth rate and interest rate is visible for the first time in 1997-98 whereas it appeared for the first time in the central case in 2000-01.

The growth of indebtedness of the states over the period of 1950-51 to 2001-02 can be analyzed in terms of the relative contributions of the primary deficits of the states and the differentials between the growth and the interest rates. As shown in Rangarajan and Srivastava (2003), the relative contribution of the two terms can be shown by the following expression:

The increment in debt z_t can be cumulated over any relevant period t = 1 to T. Thus

$$\sum_{t=1}^{T} z_t = \sum_{t=1}^{T} p_t - \sum_{t=1}^{T} b_{t-1}\left[((g_t - i_t)/(1+g_t))\right] \qquad \ldots (1)$$

Equation 1 helps in decomposing the change in the debt-GDP ratio between any two benchmark years $[\sum_{t=1}^{T} z_t = (b_T - b_O)]$ into the contribution of cumulated primary deficit relative to GDP and that of the cumulated effect of the weighted excess of growth over the interest rate. In the case of state debt also $\sum p_t$ has been much larger than $\sum z_t$ for long stretches of time, and the role of the growth/interest rate differential has been to absorb the impact of the cumulated primary deficits from getting translated into accretion to the debt-GDP ratio. It is, therefore, useful to write equation (1) as

$$\sum_{t=1}^{T} p_t = \sum_{t=1}^{T} z_t + \sum_{t=1}^{T} b_{t-1}[((g_t - i_t)/(1+g_t)] \quad \text{... (2)}$$

A1, given below, shows that part of the cumulated primary deficit relative to GDP, which was absorbed by the differential of growth rate and interest rate.

$$A1 = \sum_{i=1}^{T} b_{t-1}[((g_t - i_t)/(1+g_t)]/\sum_{t=1}^{T} p_t \quad \text{... (3)}$$

Correspondingly, A2 shows the share of the cumulated primary deficit, which results in the accretion to the debt-GDP ratio:

$$A2 = \sum_{t=1}^{T} z_t / \sum_{t=1}^{T} p_t \quad \text{... (4)}$$

Table 13.2 shows that decade-wise picture of debt accumulation and the relative roles played by the cumulated primary deficits and the growth-interest differential. Considering the 90s as a whole, the increase in the debt GDP ratio amounted to 7 per cent overall at the end of the 2001-02 the states' debt relative to GDP stood at 25.8 per cent showing a rise of 22.2 per cent as compared to the debt GDP ratio at the end of 1950-51 which was 3.5 per cent. 21 percentage points of this increase is accounted for by accumulation in the 50s and the 90s.

Table 13.2: Decade-wise Decomposition of Debt Accumulation Relative to GDP

Years	Cumulated Changes in			Relative impact of Cumulated primary deficit	
	Debt-GDP ratio	Primary deficit GDP ratio	Growth & interest rate differential	Increase in Debt-GDP ratio D/p	Absorption by growth interest differential w(g-i)/p
1951-52 to 1959-60	11.99	15.78	3.80	75.94	24.06
1960-61 to 1969-70	3.20	13.65	10.45	23.46	76.54
1970-71 to 1979-80	-0.75	8.36	9.11	-8.95	108.95
1980-81 to 1989-90	0.87	13.05	12.17	6.70	93.30
1990-91 to 2001-02	6.86	11.14	4.27	61.63	38.37
1951-52 to 2001-02	22.18	61.98	39.80	34.78	65.22
Debt-GDP Ratio at the end of					
1950-51	3.48				
2001-02	25.66				

Sources: (Basic Data): *Indian Public Finance Statistics* and *National Income Accounts*.

Considering the period from 1951-52 to 2001-02, the accumulated primary deficit of the states accounted for about 62 percent of accumulation, of which 40 percentage points was absorbed by the growth and interest rate differential. In the case of the centre, the growth interest margin absorbed about 120 percentage points of the pressure of cumulated primary deficit of about 146 percentage points (see, Rangarajan and Srivastava, 2003 p. 4853). In that analysis, Centre's debt is inclusive of its lending to the states.

It is also possible to view debt accumulation in the states in terms selected episodes. There were only two significant stretches when the impact of the primary deficit relative to GDP was not observed by the positive differentials of growth over interest rates. The first period was in the 50s when debt GDP ratio increased by about 12 percentage point. Throughout the stretch from 1960-61 to almost mid 90s, the increment in the debt GDP ratio remain negligible. It is only since 1997-98 that once again the debt GDP ratio of the states has started rising.

Chart 13.1: Growth of State Debt Relative to GDP: Relative Roles of Cumulated Primary Deficits and Excess of Growth over Interest Rates

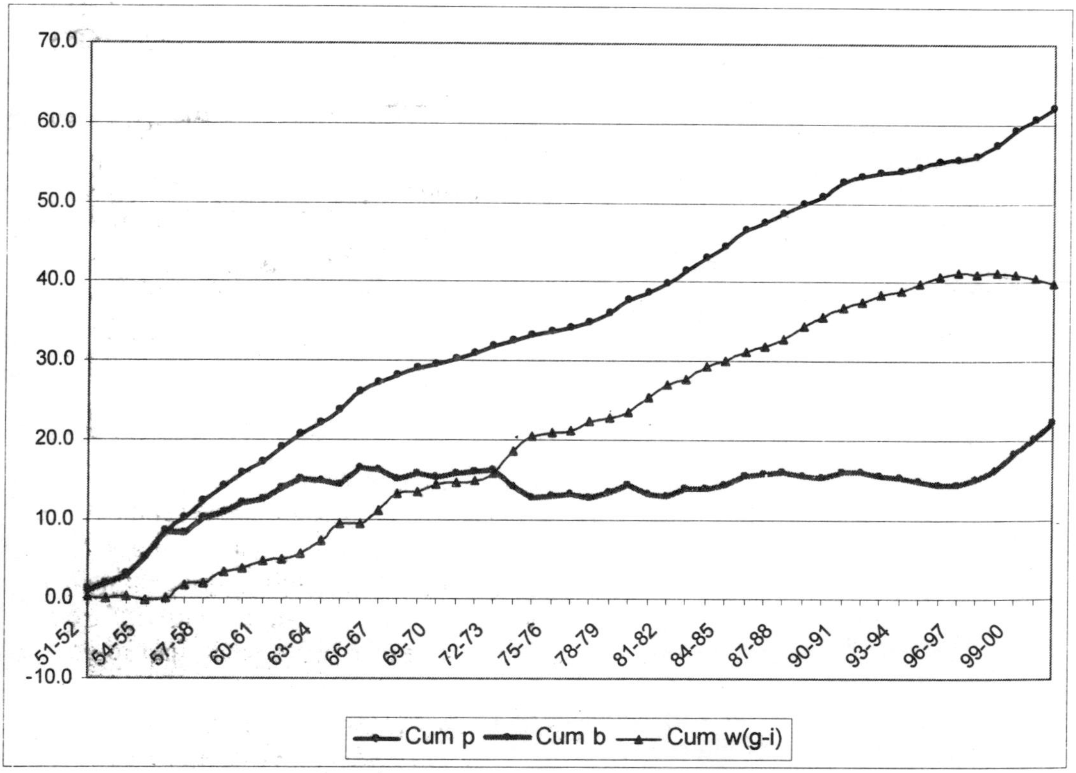

Chart 13.1 shows the profile of absorption of cumulated primary deficit by the excess of growth over interest rates. In 1961-62 the debt-GDP ratio was 17.4 per cent. In 1996-97, the debt GDP ratio was 17.8. It implies that throughout this stretch, the excess of growth rate over interest rate was able to absorb the impact of cumulated primary deficits.

Chart 13.2 shows the time profile of nominal growth and interest rates. The path of nominal interest rates show a steady upward trend up to 1999-2000 after which it dips but the growth rate decelerates even more sharply.

Chart 13.2: Time Profile of Nominal Growth and Interest Rates

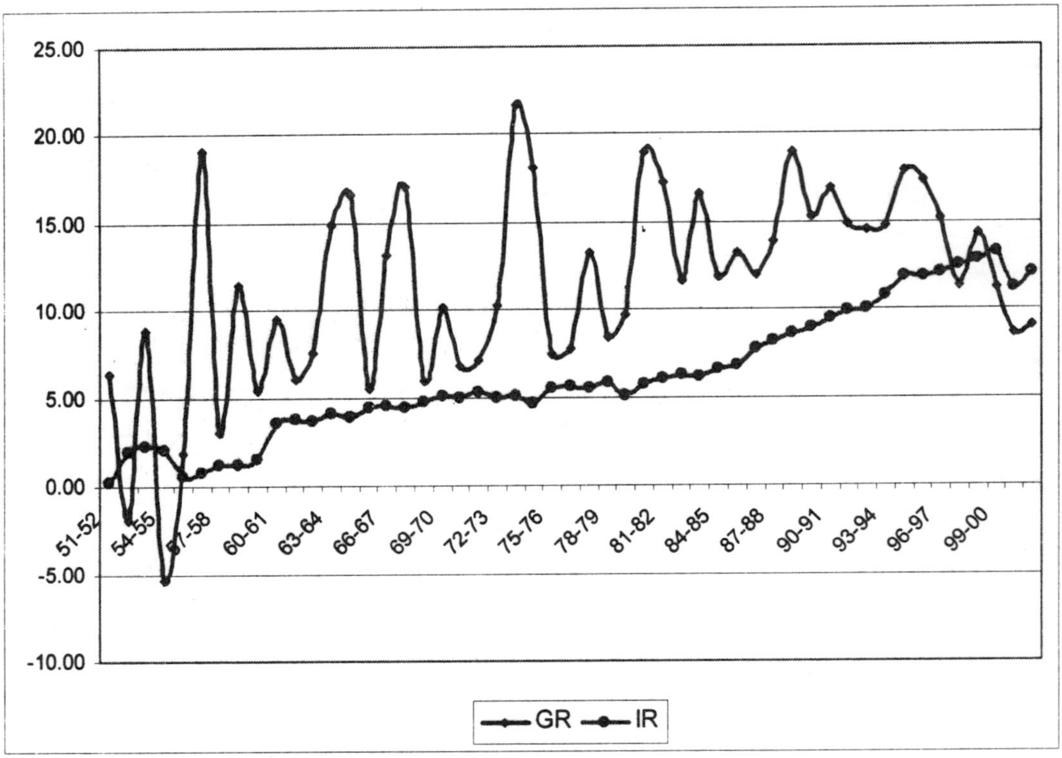

Chart 13.3 shows the inter-temporal comparison between the real growth rate and real average effective interest rates for the state debt. It is seen that except for a few years in the fifties, the real growth rate has been always above the real average interest rate except towards the latter part of the nineties. Chart 13.4 shows the profile of primary deficit relative to GDP. This may be compared to the excess of growth over interest rate.

Chart 13.3: Inflation and Real Growth and Interest Rates

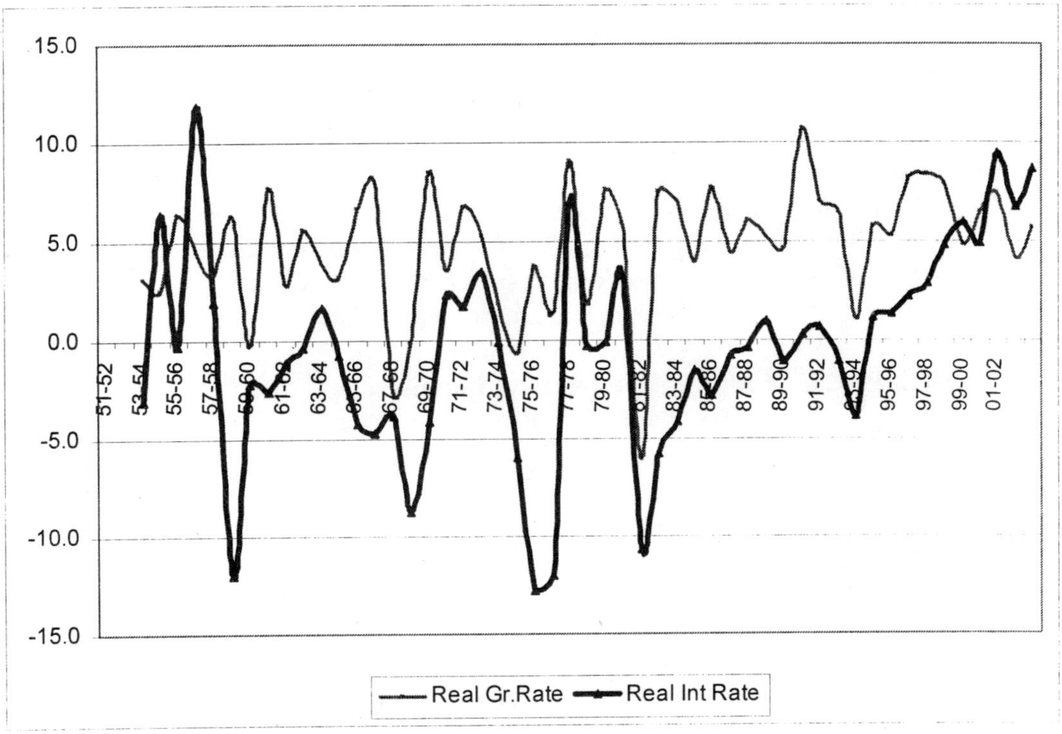

Chart 13.4: Primary Deficit to GDP Ratio and Excess of Growth over Interest Rates

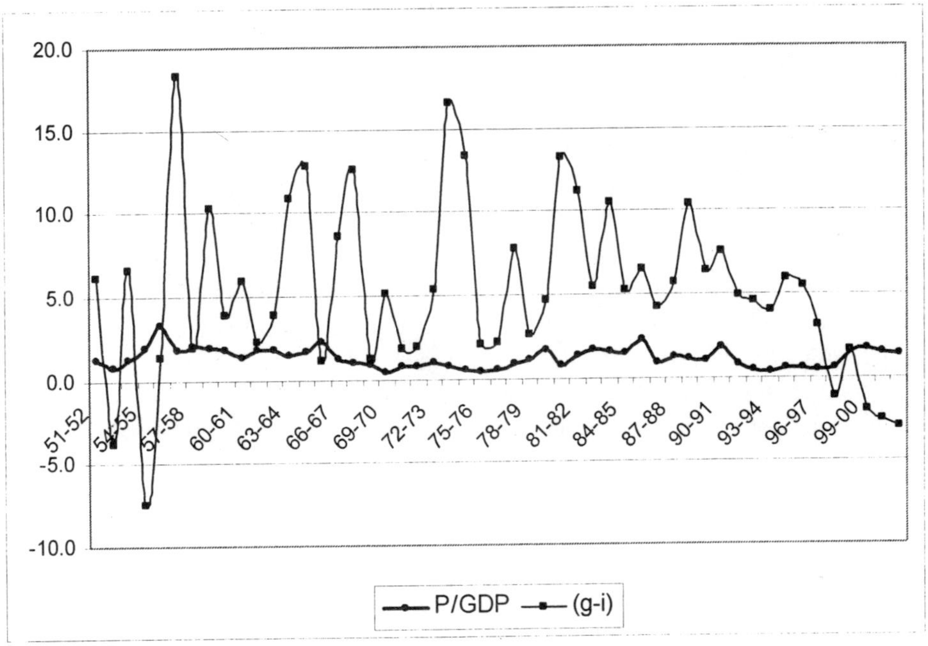

Since 1951-52, there were only 4 years when states primary deficit relative to GDP was above 2 per cent these years are 1955-56, 1957-58, 1965-66, and 1985-86. In the nineties, states' primary deficit did not cross the level of 2 percent of GDP in spite of the pressure brought on by the revision of salaries and payments. But primary deficit levels at 1.4 percent of GDP and above between 1998-99 to 2001-02 were much higher than its level during 1991-92 to 1997-98 when it kept well below 1 percent of GDP

However, growth rate was lower than interest rate in 1997-98 and for three years since 1999-00 to 2001-02. In 2002-03 also, interest rate exceeds the growth rate. Thus, for five years, growth-interest differential was in the in the negative, contributing to debt-accumulation in addition to the cumulated primary deficit

13.3 Debt Profile of States: Comparative Perspective

In the above analysis, state debt does not include liabilities on account of reserve funds and deposits maintained by the state governments. In the state-wise analysis given below, these are also included. The Twelfth Finance Commission has in its recent Report, analyzed state-debt in a comparative perspective. Relative to all-State GSDP, as shown in Table 13.3, the outstanding liabilities had increased by nearly 12 percentage points from 1993-96 average of 24.86 per cent to the 2000-03 average of 36.7 per cent. In the group of the general category states, Orissa had the highest debt-GSDP ratio during 2000-03 at 63.7 per cent followed by 47 per cent for Uttar Pradesh, and 46.7 per cent for Punjab. The debt-GSDP ratios at 44.9 per cent for Rajasthan, and 42.7 per cent for West Bengal are also quite high. In Table 13.3, the debt-GSDP ratios for two periods are compared: average over 1993-96 with that over 2000-2003. The highest deterioration during the period under review was that for Orissa at 27.5 percentage points followed by West Bengal at 19.5 percentage points, Gujarat at 16.9 percentage points, and Rajasthan at 16.6 percentage points.

The special category states had a high debt-GSDP ratio during 1993-96, the highest being that for J&K at 58 per cent, followed by 53.7 per cent for Sikkim. These ratios also increased sharply during the late 1990s. During 2000-03, the debt-GSDP ratio for Mizoram was as high as 85 per cent followed by 63.2 per cent for Sikkim, 61.8 per cent for Himachal Pradesh 56 per cent for J&K and 54.8 per cent for Arunachal Pradesh. A common pattern is noticeable. The level of the debt-GSDP ratio was higher for the special category states in both periods, but the deterioration in the case of the general category states was larger in percentage terms, if the 2000-03 average is compared with the 1993-96 average. The largest deterioration, comparing the two period averages, was for Mizoram at 32.3 percentage points of its GSDP, followed by 19.8 percentage points, for

Himachal Pradesh and 18.3 percentage points for Arunachal Pradesh, relative to their respective GSDPs. In the case of all-states comparison, debt-GDP ratios are lower than debt-GSDP ratios since the sum of GSDPs is lower than the GDP.

Table 13.3: Outstanding Debt Relative to GSDP: State-wise Position (per cent)

State	1993-96	2000-03	Col.[10-9]
Arunachal Pradesh	36.48	54.82	18.34
Assam	31.40	34.75	3.35
Himachal Pradesh	41.95	61.79	19.84
Jammu & Kashmir	58.01	55.99	-2.02
Manipur	38.16	47.88	9.72
Meghalaya	24.12	38.68	14.56
Mizoram	53.05	85.29	32.25
Nagaland	42.71	49.91	7.20
Sikkim	53.65	63.24	9.59
Tripura	38.77	38.11	-0.67
Total: SCS	**39.68**	**47.17**	**7.48**
Andhra Pradesh	21.86	29.93	8.07
Bihar	36.80	44.35	7.55
Goa	41.64	33.54	-8.10
Gujarat	21.07	37.92	16.85
Haryana	19.85	28.02	8.17
Karnataka	19.62	27.27	7.65
Kerala	27.27	37.58	10.32
Madhya Pradesh	19.95	30.42	10.47
Maharashtra	15.63	27.11	11.48
Orissa	36.21	63.68	27.47
Punjab	34.55	46.66	12.10
Rajasthan	28.28	44.88	16.60
Tamil Nadu	18.87	26.16	7.29
Uttar Pradesh	33.94	46.94	13.00
West Bengal	23.26	42.73	19.47
Total: GCS	**24.12**	**36.06**	**11.94**
All States	**24.86**	**36.65**	**11.79**

Source: (Basic Data): *Report of the Twelfth Finance Commission, 2004.*

13.4 Inter-State Debt: Why per Capita Debt Differs Across States

There is considerable variation in per capita debt across states. There are a set of capacity factors that may explain when some states commit to higher per capita debt. In this section an attempt is made to identify determinants of state per capita debt using data for the period 1993-94 to 2000-01. In a recent work, Srivastava and Das (2005) have looked at the issue in terms of a panel model. Table 13.4 summarises some of the results. Three capacity factors have been identified as per capita GSDP, per capita Central transfers, and share of tertiary sector in GSDP. The share of primary and secondary sectors were also tried separately and in combination but were not found to be statistically significant. A fixed effects model was selected. Variables are defined below:

LPL: Log to per capita debt real GSDP
LPGN: Log of per capita GDP
LPTR: Log of per capita central transfer
STER: Share of tertiary sector in GSDP
SHINT: Share of interest payments to revenue receipts
LPTR: Log of Per Capita Transfers
LPCSOTR: Log of Per Capita State Own task Revenues
DEF: Rate of Inflation
LEIR: Effective Rate of Interest lagged one year
SHCAP: Share of capital expenditure to total expenditure

The dependent variable is per capita debt as measured by the outstanding liabilities. The results of the estimation are summarized below.

It is observed that all the independent variables are statistically significant and have a positive impact on accumulation of state debt. Per capita real income has a positive impact. Across states, the higher the per capita income, the higher the per capita debt. Per capita own tax revenues and per capita transfers also have a positive impact and their response coefficients are much higher in their magnitude. Higher transfers induce higher debt level. The structure of GSDP also has a bearing on debt levels. States with higher share of the tertiary sector appear to have incurred more debt per capita.

Apart from these capacity variables which augment the capacity to borrow, these are the cost related variable. The effective interest rate is a cost variable. A positive response makes ‘Debt’ a Giffen good i.e. higher the cost, higher the debt. This is logged one year to avoid simultaneously with interest payments relative to revenue receipts. The implicit price deflator of GSDP also has a positive impact on debt. Higher the inflation, lower the real value of debt.

The effect of interest payments in revenue receipts is also positive. This variable captures the impact of committed debt-servicing factor. The higher the pre-emptive claim on borrowing, the greater is the need to borrow in order to meet unavoidable committed expenditures.

Table 13.4: Per Capita Debt of States: Determinants

Dependent Variable: Log of Per capita Debt of States(LPL)				
Method: GLS (Cross Section Weights)				
Sample: 1993-94 to 1999-00				
Total panel (balanced) observations: 120				
Variable	Coefficient	Std. Error	t-Statistic	Prob.
LPGR	0.7377	0.0908	8.1260	0.0000
SHINT	0.7239	0.0590	12.2745	0.0000
LEIR	0.0159	0.0048	3.3370	0.0012
LPTR	0.1666	0.0289	5.7620	0.0000
LPCSOTR	0.4522	0.0318	14.2266	0.0000
STER	2.2155	0.3202	6.9185	0.0000
DEF	0.1669	0.0400	4.1685	0.0001
RCAPEZP	-0.2100	0.1022	-2.0547	0.0426
Fizzed Effects				
Andhra Pradesh	-5.5672			
Assam	-5.1909			
Bihar	-4.9535			
Gujarat	-5.5635			
Haryana	-5.4649			
Karnataka	-5.7001			
Kerala	-5.6503			
Madhya Pradesh	-5.6026			
Maharashtra	-5.6609			
Orissa	-4.8254			
Punjab	-5.0552			
Rajasthan	-5.1775			
Tamil Nadu	-5.8911			
Uttar Pradesh	-4.9515			
West Bengal	-5.5067			
Weighted Statistics				
R-squared	1.000	Mean dependent var		5.3118
Adjusted R-squared	1.000	S.D. dependent var		3.7398
S.E. of regression	0.056	Sum squared resid		0.2988
F-statistic	77165.2	Durbin-Watson stat		1.7580

Contd...

Prob (F-statistic)	0		
Unweighted Statistics			
R-squared	0.9861	Mean dependent var	3.5501
Adjusted R-squared	0.9830	S.D. dependent var	0.4351
S.E. of regression	0.0567	Sum squared resid	0.3121
Durbin-Watson stat	1.5487		

13.5 Impact of Debt in Fiscal Transfers: Methods of Normative Assessment

There are not many examples, where a methodology of normative assessment of interest payments has been developed, in the context of determining fiscal transfers. One important exception is Australia, where such a methodology has been developed. We consider the assessment of debt charges (interest payments) as another example of the Australian expenditure assessment techniques because of its relevance to India. Interest payments constitute a significant portion of the so-called non-plan revenue expenditures of the state budgets in India and its normative assessment could provide the key to breaking away from the gap-filling approach that is followed in India.

The assessment of interest payments is complicated because present debt charges relate to past accumulations of debt. The Commonwealth Grants Commission in Australia uses an elaborate methodology for assessment of debt charges, i.e. interest payments. Their assessment technique of debt charges has been contested by the Australian states in the past. We consider here salient features of their assessment technique. In the 1999 Review, the debt charges were assessed on the basis of a private sector model that assumed that the states borrowed to finance deficits and capital expenditure on capital stock and financial assets. The 2004 Review has modified the technique of the 1999 Review after much discussion with the states. It starts with the position that unless it is demonstrated that there are disabilities, it is assumed that the states have the same per capita borrowing needs.

However, differences in borrowing needs arise due to current differences in the demand for and cost of non-replacement assets, recent population growth, and higher prices in recent years. Differences in the per capita level of capital specific purpose payments also influence borrowing needs. The CGC agreed with the states to make an assessment only of the borrowing need for non-financial assets. This was done by subtracting interest earnings from interest payments. There was a recognition that small states end up paying higher interest rates.

Standardization requires that standardized accumulated debt be worked out for each state and a standardized interest rate be applied to it to assess the standard debt charges in a year. Disability factors are applied on both the accumulated standardized debt and standardized interest rate to assess state-specific debt charges. Important considerations in this context are that only creation of non-replacement physical capital is considered. Borrowing for financial assets is not considered as this is policy driven. All states are supposed to have had equal per capita budget surpluses or deficits in the past. The composition of population and its size could give rise to valid disability factors. For example, a state with a greater proportion of aged people will need more hospital and fewer schools. Similarly, a smaller state may have to pay higher interest rate.

In the 2004 Review, debt accumulation on a normative basis was worked out since 1961-62 with a weight of 85 per cent. For debt accumulated prior to that an equal per capita amount was taken with a weight of 15 per cent Although an interest rate disability factor was used until the 1999 Review it was not used in the 2004 Review although the CGC recognized that smaller states may have to pay larger costs. This implies that once the quantity of borrowing was derived, debt charges were obtained by applying the standard interest rate to all states. There was also an adjustment to account for including the ACT as part of the equalization assessments. Appendix A13.1 describes the derivation of the quantity of borrowing.

Although a proper methodology for assessment of interest payments in India needs to be developed, several important differences may be noted in comparison to the Australian situation. In particular, borrowing has been extensively used for current expenditure as well as for financial assets. In the past, state debt has also been rescheduled from time to time based on the recommendations of some of the earlier Finance Commissions. Although for many years, borrowing was on administered interest rates, there are significant differences in the effective interest rates paid by the state governments because of the composition of debt.

13.6 Contingent Liabilities of State Governments

States frequently guarantee loans undertaken by their public enterprises or special purpose vehicles. These liabilities can become actual liabilities in the event of a default by the primary borrower. Since state liability is contingent upon such default, these are called contingent liabilities. Often, these liabilities become a source of indirect borrowing by the state government, when a normal budgetary function is sought to be performed off-budget through a special organization. In general, in guaranteeing loans, the state governments perform a service by reducing the risk of the lenders. As such they are entitled to a charge in the form of a guarantee fee, which the states can use to meet the liabilities arising from any default.

The outstanding guarantees of the state governments amounted to Rs. 168712 crore at the end of March 2002 amounting 7.2 per cent of GDP. In view of the rising volume of guarantees, many states have taken initiatives to subject guarantees to statutory ceilings. Some notable states, which have imposed statutory ceilings are: Goa, Gujarat, Karnataka, Sikkim, and West Bengal. Some other states like Assam, Orissa, and Rajasthan have imposed administrative ceilings on such guarantees.

13.7 Debt Relief to States: Recommendations of the Finance Commissions

Many Finance Commissions, taking into account, the difficult position of debt, have given debt relief to the states in various forms. We review below the recommendations of some of the recent Finance Commissions in this respect.

13.8 Eighth Finance Commission

The Eighth Finance Commission formulated its debt relief proposals in respect of central loans so as to grant relief on a progressive basis to all states. It recommended several debt relief measures as indicated below.

1. In respect of loans for relief and rehabilitation of displaced persons and repatriates, the Commission recommended that in respect of central loans, the outstanding amount against the States may be written off. In turn, the States should pass on this benefit to the displaced persons, repatriates.
2. Loans given under National Loans Scholarship Schemes to all States may continue to be recovered on the basis of the existing terms under which repayment to the Centre is limited to the recoveries effected by the States.
3. No change was recommended in the terms & conditions of the loans given to the States to clear overdrafts in respect of any State.
4. As regards the outstandings of the pre-1979 loans consolidated into 15 year loans and 30 year loans, such outstanding against Uttar Pradesh be consolidated into one new loan repayable in 25 equal annual instalments starting from 1984-85 and such outstandings against the States of Andhra Pradesh, Assam, Bihar, Himachal Pradesh, Jammu & Kashmir, Manipur, Meghalaya, Orissa, Rajasthan and Sikkim be consolidated into one new loan repayable in 30 equal annual instalments starting from 1984-85 and for Haryana, Gujarat, Karnataka, Kerala, Madhya Pradesh, Maharashtra, Nagaland, Punjab, Tamil Nadu, Tripura and West Bengal no change was made.
5. In respect of the outstandings of all the other loans received by the State Governments during 1979-84, they be consolidated into one loan for each State and repayable starting from 1984-85. For Gujarat, Maharashtra and

Tamil Nadu, it should be repayable in 15 equal annual instalments; 20 equal annual instalments for Karnataka, Punjab and Tripura; 25 equal annual instalments for Haryana, Kerala, Uttar Pradesh and West Bengal; 30 equal annual instalments for Andhra Pradesh, Assam, Bihar, Himachal Pradesh, Jammu & Kashmir, Madhya Pradesh, Manipur, Meghalaya, Nagaland, Orissa, Rajasthan and Sikkim.

13.9 Ninth Finance Commission

The Ninth Finance Commission (NFC) was asked in its TOR to suggest corrective measures with particular reference to investments in infrastructure projects and improvements in their performance. The NFC sought to link the extent of relief to the performance of the States in respect of their investments in two important sectors, viz., power and road transport. It worked out the rate of return on investments in these two sectors, i.e. defining the rate of return as equal to the gross operation surplus after depreciation as a percentage of total (cumulative) investments. On these bases, the States were divided into three categories:

1. Those where the rate of return was above 15 per cent [Andhra Pradesh, Karnataka, Madhya Pradesh, Maharashtra, Orissa and Tamil Nadu];
2. Those where the rate of return varied between 10 and 15 per cent [Gujarat, Rajasthan and Uttar Pradesh]; and
3. Those where the rate of return was below 10 per cent [Bihar, Haryana, Kerala, Punjab and West Bengal].

The NFC recommended that relief in repayment of 1984-89 State Plan loans due during the years 1990-95, to the extent of 10 per cent for the first category of States, 7.5 per cent for the second category of States and 5 per cent for the third category of States. A relief of 10 per cent was recommended uniformly for the special category States and Goa. Further, if loans remain outstanding after this relief, it should be made repayable in 10 equal instalments.

The NFC also gave some state-specific relief. The Central Government during the period 1984-89 granted loans to the Government of Madhya Pradesh to meet some of the immediate medical and rehabilitation needs of gas victims. The NFC recommended that all these loans may be written off and the payments already made by the State Government may be adjusted against other payments due from the Government. Additional relief measures were recommended in the second Report of the NFC. In particular, the following may be mentioned:

1. Central Government loans to the States for financing their plans from 1990-91 onwards should have a maturity period of 20 years i.e. 50 per cent of these loans should be granted a 5 year initial grace period, which would take care of

gestation period of capital projects, after which repayments should be spread over 15 years.

2. As far as assistance in relation to externally aided projects the following recommendations were made:

- The NFC recommended that 100 per cent of assistance should be passed on to the States as presently only 70 per cent of this assistance for such projects is passed on to the States except for assistance for socially oriented projects from 1989-90 and the States in effect get assistance for externally aided projects to the extent of 35 per cent to 42 per cent of the total cost of such projects but there is no logic in the Centre withholding a part of funds given exclusively for projects.
- The NFC felt that the World Bank assistance would remain same that is 30 per cent in the form of grant and 70 per cent in the form of loans. Also, the rate of interest charged be the same as applicable to other plan loans and the repayment period should be as prescribed by the World Bank.

3. Some States suffered heavily due to unprecedented droughts during 1986-87 to 1988-89. In lieu of this additional assistance was provided to them over and above 5 per cent of annual Plan outlays which is not adjusted against Plan assistance. 50 per cent of this additional assistance was given in the form of loans, but this burden of drought relief should not be cast upon the States. It was recommended that outstanding loans on account of drought be written off completely.

13.10 Tenth Finance Commission

The Tenth Finance Commission kept the following considerations in view, while recommending its debt relief measures:

1. the quantum of relief should be limited;
2. priority should be given to States under severe fiscal strain; and,
3. States with better fiscal management should be given an incentive. The recommended scheme of debt relief had two parts:

- A scheme for general debt relief for all States linked to fiscal performance;
- Special relief for States with high fiscal stress and special category States and States with debt problems warranting special attention.

With a view to inducing better fiscal management, the Tenth Finance Commission recommended a scheme of general debt relief for all States linked to fiscal performance. In this scheme, improvement of fiscal management was measured by comparing the ratio of revenue receipts (including devolution and grants from the Centre) to total revenue expenditure in a given year with the average of corresponding ratios in the three immediately preceding years. Thus, each State was to be measured against its own past performance.

In addition, specific relief was recommended for all special category States and three other States viz. Orissa, Bihar and Uttar Pradesh which are under high fiscal stress. For these states, a write off of 5 per cent of repayment was recommended with respect to fresh Central loans.

During 1996-97 to 1999-2000, 20 States have been able to avail the general debt relief recommended by the TFC by showing improvement on their revenue balance account.

13.11 Eleventh Finance Commission

While making a proposal for a debt relief scheme, the Eleventh Finance Commission (EFC) was guided by the objective of initiating corrective measures leading to sustainability of debt. The Commission opined that this can come about only when the state governments make persistent effort to raise additional revenue or by squeezing their expenditure. Fiscal reforms should focus on achieving revenue balance or reducing revenue imbalance to the minimum. The EFC followed the debt relief scheme introduced by Tenth Finance Commission with some modifications, introduced with a view to strengthening the scheme.

The EFC did not continue the scheme of debt relief based on disinvestment and fiscal stress as recommended by the Tenth Finance Commission. It focused only on debt relief linked to improvement in revenue balance. Improvement of fiscal management was measured by comparing the ratio of revenue receipts (including devolution and grants from the Centre) to total revenue expenditure in a given year (r) with the average of corresponding ratios (r*) in the three immediately preceding years. Thus, each State would be measured against its own past performance. Debt relief would be calculated as percentage of repayment falling due in each year of the period of recommendation. This percentage (R) will be five times the excess of (r) over (r*) as defined above. Thus, if the performance of a State improves by 2.5 percentage points, that is, (r-r*) = 2.5, the State government will become entitled to a relief equivalent to 12.5 per cent, that is, R = 12.5 (per cent). The maximum limit of R had been prescribed as 25 percent. This scheme of relief is dynamic because performance is to be evaluated every year.

It may be noted that for the calculation of relief in any one year, a reference to 6 years became relevant.

Thus, for relief in year t, the following years constituted important reference points:

Year in which relief is given : t

Year with reference to which relief : (t-1)
is determined
(repayments due will relate to this year)
Year for which latest actuals are available : (t-3)
(r is calculated for this year)
Years from which (r*) is calculated : (t-4), (t-5), (t-6)

The EFC was of a view to strengthen the incentives mainly for two reasons:

1. The EFC enhanced the relief factor from 2 to 5.
2. It also recommended that the maximum magnitude of the stipulated relief under the General Incentive Scheme be increased from 10 to 25 per cent.

13.12 Twelfth Finance Commission

The Twelfth Finance Commission (TFC) has recommended that all central loans to states contracted till 31.3.04 and outstanding on 31.3.05 (amounting to Rs. 1,28,795 crore) may be consolidated and rescheduled for a fresh term of 20 years (resulting in repayment in 20 equal instalments), at an interest rate of 7.5 percent. As a result of this rescheduling and lowering of interest rate, the debt relief during 2005-10 for all states was estimated by the TFC as Rs. 21,276 crore in interest payments and Rs. 11,929 crore in repayments.

The Commission also devised a scheme of debt write-off based on fiscal performance. In particular, the states are required, as a precondition, to enact respective fiscal responsibility legislations prescribing the fiscal adjustment path for reduction of the revenue deficit to zero by 2008-09. The extent of debt write-off scheme linked to the reduction of revenue deficit of states. Under the scheme, the repayments due on central loans from 2005-06 to 2009-10 after consolidation and rescheduling will be eligible for write-off. The quantum of write-off of repayment will be linked to the absolute amount by which the revenue deficit is reduced in each successive year during our award period. In effect, if the revenue deficit is brought down to zero, the entire repayments during the period will be written-off. The scheme of write-off shall be available for all states from the year they have qualified for the general debt relief by enacting the fiscal responsibility legislation.

The following steps have been specified for the operation of the scheme:

1. Fiscal performance will be measured with reference to the revenue deficit/revenue surplus, as worked out in absolute numbers by taking an average of three years, viz., 2001-02 (Actuals), 2002-03 (Actuals), and 2003-04 (RE). This average will be taken as the base year figure for 2003-04.
2. For states which were in revenue surplus, as per the base year figure (calculated in the manner indicated above), and continue to remain so in the

subsequent years till the end of our award period, the instalment of repayment due on the central loans (after consolidation and re-schedulement) may be written-off in each of the years from 2005-06 onwards so long as the revenue surplus of the states does not go below the base year level in absolute terms. In the year the revenue surplus is less than that in the base year figure, no write-off will be permitted.

3. As for the states which were in revenue deficit as per the base year figure, the revenue deficit is expected to be eliminated by 2008-09, i.e. over a five year period. Fiscal performance will be measured by the absolute amount by which the revenue deficit is reduced in each year compared to the deficit in the previous year starting from the base year figure. For the purpose of determining the scale at which the relief will be provided, the ratio of the repayment due by a state during the period 2005-10 (of central loans after consolidation and re-schedulement) to the base year revenue deficit figure has been worked out. This determines the amount of write-off of repayment that will be allowed to each state for the reduction of each rupee of revenue deficit. Annexure 12.8 of the TFC Report contains the ratios which will be applicable to the states for determining the quantum of write-off.
4. The actual reduction in the revenue deficit in each year over the immediately preceding one would determine the amount of write-off for the state in the repayment due in the immediately succeeding year. This is calculated by multiplying the above mentioned ratio by the amount of reduction of the revenue deficit. The total number of write-off in a year will, however, be restricted to the repayments due on the consolidated loans in that year. Further, the write-off will only be admissible if the state reduces the revenue deficit to a level lower than the base year figure.
5. It may be noted that, other things remaining the same, a reduction of revenue deficit is inherent from 2005-06 onwards as a result of the debt relief due to the lowering of the interest rate recommended in para 12.42 of the TFC Report. Reduction in revenue deficit which is at least equal to the interest rate relief shall be treated as an eligibility requirement. Each state will, therefore, be required to achieve, in each year of our award period, a reduction in the revenue deficit, which, compared to the base year figure, is cumulatively higher than the cumulative reduction attributable to the interest relief recommended by us. Details of the year-wise relief in interest payments and the cumulative reduction in revenue deficit arising out of lowering of interest rate for each state during 2005-10 are at annexure 12.9 of the TFC Report.
6. If the reduction in revenue deficit in a year is more than the minimum required for the write-off of the entire repayment due in that year, the excess

will be carried forward fully to the next year, provided the revenue deficit continued to follow a downward trend in the next year and is lower than the base year figure. On the other hand, if there is an increase in the revenue deficit in the next year, but the revenue deficit is still lower than the base year figure, the entitlement to write-off shall be determined on the basis of improvement from the minimum revenue deficit figure of the previous year that would have given full relief in the previous year.

7. If the performance of a state deteriorates in a year, with the revenue deficit registering a higher level over the previous year for which relief in repayment has been availed of, any improvement in the succeeding year will be measured, not with reference to that year, but the performance level in the previous year up to which relief has been availed of. If the revenue deficit reduction in that previous year was more than the minimum reduction required to qualify for 100 percent write-off of repayment, the revenue deficit in that year may be re-determined notionally keeping in view the minimum revenue deficit reduction that would have qualified the state for 100 percent relief in repayment.
8. One criticism against the debt relief scheme of the Tenth and Eleventh Commissions related to the time lag involved in granting the benefit. The TFC has therefore recommended that for the purpose of determining the write-off, the revenue deficit indicated in the revised estimates of the preceding year may be used provisionally, so that the relief in respect of a year is available in the immediately succeeding year.
9. Looking at the necessity of containing the fiscal deficit, it was further recommended that the benefit of write-off would be available only if the fiscal deficit of the state is contained to the level of 2004-05. If, in any year, the fiscal deficit exceeds this level, the benefit of write-off, even if eligible otherwise, would not be given.

13.13 Centre's Intermediation in Raising State Debt

In the context of the debt burden of states, the direction in which future lending policy of the centre should move was considered by us. While there might have been some justification for the centre to act as a banker to states when market rates of interest were high and in the process of on-lending to states, an indirect subsidy was granted to states by way of concessional interest, this is no longer valid in a low interest rates regime. In some ways, central lending to states, which is done at much higher rates of interest than the marginal cost of borrowing, results in a reverse subsidy from the states to the centre. In most federal countries, the federal government's loan intermediation role has been discontinued over the years, subjecting the states to market discipline. Such a dispensation allows the constituent units to borrow on terms that reflect their credit risk. While fiscally prudent states manage to borrow at rates lower than those offered by the federal government, the fiscally imprudent states would find their access to loan finance curtailed. The TFC felt that it would be appropriate for states to take advantage of the market rates and avoid the spread charged by the centre. The TFC has recommended that, in future, the central government should not act as an intermediary and allow the states to approach the market directly. If, however, some fiscally weak states are unable to raise funds from the market, the centre could resort to lending, but the interest rates should remain aligned to the marginal cost of borrowing for the centre.

13.14 External Assistance Loans: Terms and Conditions of Transfer

The TFC has also suggested reforms in the way external assistance is passed on to the states. External assistance to India is generally project based, except for structural adjustment assistance. The financing terms for externally aided projects and programmes vary according to projects and lending agencies. There are grants, soft loans and non-concessional loans, provided by lending agencies, depending upon the nature, the financial viability of the project. The external assistance received for states' projects is, however, passed on as 70 percent loan and 30 percent grant (10 per cent and 90 per cent respectively in case of special category states). Interest rates applied were those applicable to block loans.

While the external assistance from some sources and for some projects is highly concessional, in other cases it may be expensive. In the process of pooling and fixing a uniform interest rte in rupee terms, an element of cross-subsidization occurs at two levels: between centre and all states, and among the states. In the case of cross-subsidization between the centre and the states, the gain/loss to one side vis-à-vis another depends on the rate of depreciation of the Indian rupee against major foreign currencies. In the case of states, the cross-subsidization takes place, when states having a relatively larger share of grants and soft loans (which may offer relief to social welfare and long gestation, low return type of projects) in their assistance portfolio, are required to pay a higher rate of interest to help sustain the relatively larger share of high cost loans, which may often relate to commercial projects, used by some states.

The transfer of external assistance on back-to-back basis will enable states to participate on an equal footing in concessional external assistance. The TFC recommended that external assistance be transferred to states on the same terms and conditions as attached to such assistance by external funding agencies. States would get the same maturity, moratorium and amortization schedule, as the government of India gets from the external lender. Further, the Commission recommended that external assistance pass through to states should be managed through a separate fund in the public account. This fund could also be utilized for coping with foreign exchange risk.

Appendix A13.1: Derivation of Quantity of Borrowing in Debt Charges Assessment in Australia

(Based on Draft assessment Paper, CGC 2003/57 on Debt Charges)

Accumulated standard per capita non-replacement capital expenditure (A1) = Accumulated standard per capita expenditure on fixed assets and second hand assets – accumulated standard per capita depreciation

Accumulated per capita standardized non-replacement capital expenditure (**A2**) = A1* capital expenditure disability factor

Accumulated per capita standardized exp on non-replacement capital, land and other capital outlays (**A3**) = A2 + Accumulated per capita land purchases and other capital outlays

Borrowing gross of capital grants (A4) = A3 - Accumulated standard land sales and per capita other capital receipts – accumulated standard per capita recurrent budget result (including depreciation and included capital grants from 1998-99)

Per capita standardized net borrowings (**A5**) = A4 – accumulated per capita capital grants (APC before 1998-99, none thereafter)

Debt charges quantity of borrowing factor for 1961-62 onwards (**A6**) = A5/ standard net borrowings

Quantity of borrowing factor (**A7**) = .85 * A6 + .15* EPC factor to account for pre-existing gross debt at 30 June 1961

Part V: Issues in Fiscal Federalism

14

Finance Commission: Evolution of Terms of Reference

> The course of centre-state fiscal relations in India is both important and treacherous...treacherous because the complex political and economic situation possibly makes these, proper incentives, difficult both to foresee and to handle.
>
> George A. Akerlof

14.1 India's Federal Fiscal Structure

The federal ensemble in India comprises a central government, twenty-eight states (with three newly created ones), two Union Territories (UTs) with legislatures, and five Union Territories without own legislatures. There are also several autonomous regions within states. In addition, there is a three-tiered structure of rural local bodies, viz., gram panchayats, panchayat samities, and zila parishads. The urban local bodies are organized in terms of three levels, viz., municipal corporations, municipalities, and nagar panchayats. The system provides for an asymmetric constitutional treatment of the state of Jammu and Kashmir, and an asymmetric economic treatment of special category states (SCS). As per the classification of the Planning Commission, eleven states are categorized as special (SCS) while the remaining states are considered as non-special or general category states (GCS).

Some of the important institutions that oversee centre-state financial relations and intermediate between the central, state and local governments are the Finance Commission (FC), the Planning Commission, the Inter-State Council (ISC), and the National Development Council (NDC). In the context of state-local body relations, the constitution has provided for State Finance Commissions (SFCs), one for each state. While the Planning Commission is a permanent body, the central and state level FCs are set up with a normal periodicity of five years.

The three new States, Uttaranchal, Chhattisgarh, and Jharkhand, which came into existence in November 2000, have been carved out from the parent states of Uttar Pradesh, Madhya Pradesh and Bihar, respectively. The process of creation of new states, and demands from other regions in other states for separate statehood have gathered strength in the context of growing inter-regional disparities in the country. The organizational structure of the federation in terms of sub-national governments has remained in the process of evolution.

14.2 Indian States: Horizontal Disparity

The Indian states are different in terms of size of population, area, resources, geographical features, and cost constraints. This heterogeneity affects the size of government, the quantum and quality of publicly provided goods, and their needs for fiscal transfers. Table 14.1 describes the extent of disparity by looking at the per capita expenditure of individual states over the corresponding average for the group of states.

Table 14.1: Horizontal Imbalance in India: Per Capita Expenditure of States Relative to Average (Three Year averages) [in Rs.]

State	1987-88 to 1989-90	1990-91 to 1992-93	1993-94 to 1995-96	1996-97 to 1998-99	1999-00 to 2001-02
Andhra Pradesh	99.9	98.3	108.6	109.8	111.9
Assam	107.6	100.9	96.4	79.3	85.5
Bihar	67.7	62.9	52.7	50.7	50.1
Gujarat	139.1	136.9	130.1	143.7	152.7
Haryana	148.3	136.3	194.9	181.6	140.9
Karnataka	110.9	114.0	117.0	115.8	118.0
Kerala	108.4	109.2	121.1	134.2	127.3
Madhya Pradesh	88.6	84.1	81.5	83.0	75.4
Maharashtra	138.7	129.8	137.3	134.4	148.6
Orissa	90.3	90.8	89.2	89.2	91.6
Punjab	172.2	174.3	179.2	168.9	173.2
Rajasthan	100.1	104.2	112.5	104.2	96.0
Tamil Nadu	111.0	130.4	119.4	128.7	120.8
Uttar Pradesh	76.2	82.3	74.8	73.1	66.9
West Bengal	80.8	75.9	77.2	83.6	99.5
Total 15 States	100.0	100.0	100.0	100.0	100.0
Minimum	67.7	62.9	52.7	50.7	50.1
Maximum	172.2	174.3	194.9	181.6	173.2
Range	104.5	111.4	142.2	130.9	123.1
Coefficient of Variation	26.6	26.7	33.8	32.8	31.2

14.3 Finance Commissions in India

Role of Finance Commission: Fiscal transfers in India are overseen by two major institutions: Finance Commission (FC) and Planning Commission. The FC looks after the current account needs of the states while the Planning Commission is primarily concerned with the developmental needs of the states, which comprise both current and capital needs. The expenditure accounts of governments are further divided into non-plan and plan, and for the FCs with the exception of the first, second, and ninth, the ambit of concern has been limited to non-plan revenue (current) expenditures although there is no constitutional bar on their dealing with the full current account expenditures. In this chapter, we shall focus on the system of transfer brought into vogue by the FCs, while in Chapter 16, we shall consider the transfer system of the Planning Commission. So far, eleven Finance Commissions have been set up in India. There are two main channels of transfer: devolution of central taxes and grants.

14.4 Devolution of Taxes

Until the year 2000, sharing of central taxes was on a tax by tax basis. In particular, two important central taxes were shared with the states, *viz*., (personal) income tax and the Union excise duties. Two important central taxes were not shared with the states, *viz*. corporation tax and custom duties. The eightieth amendment to the constitution (May 2000, but effective from 1996-97) has put the sharing of central taxes with the states in an entirely new framework. With the amendment of the constitution, the net proceeds of all union taxes and duties except central sales tax and consignment tax, surcharges on central taxes and duties, and earmarked cesses, are distributable between the centre and the states. The amendment is based on the alternative scheme of devolution that was recommended by the Tenth Finance Commission, in its report submitted in November 1994. The amendment has been brought about to serve the following main objectives:

1. widening of the shareable revenue base for the states, thereby enabling them to share the aggregate buoyancy of central taxes including that of the corporation tax;
2. sharing of the burden of adjustment between the centre and the states in case of any temporary revenue erosion as a result of tax reforms;
3. reducing the overall volatility in the growth of shareable revenues implicit in a larger shareable base; and
4. providing an incentive for the exploitation of taxes mentioned in the existing Article 269 (except central sales tax and consignment tax) of the constitution by including these in the shareable pool.

With this amendment to the constitution, the share of the central taxes recommended for the states does not form part of the Consolidated Fund of India. It is implied in Article 270 that the same percentage share will apply to all central taxes that are to be shared. The sharing of central tax revenues with the states has both a vertical dimension, i.e. the aggregate share of the states in the central taxes, and a horizontal dimension, that is, the respective share of each state in the aggregate share of all states.

14.5 Constitutional Provisions

The duty of the Finance Commission as enunciated in Article 280(3), relates to:

"(a) the distribution between the Union and the States of the net proceeds of taxes which are to be, or may be, divided between them under this Chapter and the allocation between the States of the respective shares of such proceeds;

(b) the principles which should govern the grants-in-aid of the revenues of the States out of the Consolidated Fund of India;

(bb) the measures needed to augment the Consolidated Fund of a State to supplement the resources of the Panchayats in the State on the basis of the recommendations made by the Finance Commission of the State;

(c) the measures needed to augment the Consolidated Fund of a State to supplement the resources of the Municipalities in the State on the basis of the recommendations made by the Finance Commission of the State; and

(d) any other matter referred to the Commission by the President in the interests of sound finance.

Prior to the 80th Amendment to the Constitution, the term "are to be" made reference to income tax other than corporation tax under Article 270, and the term "may be" made reference to the Union excise duties under Article 272. After the 80th Amendment, there are no taxes that "may be" shared between the Centre and the States. The amended Article 270 provides for the sharing of all central taxes except taxes under Articles 268 and 269 and earmarked cesses, and surcharges under Article 271. Article 269 has also been amended and it contains only central sales tax and consignment tax. The latter has not been levied so far. Only "net proceeds" are to be shared, and as such 'cost of collection' has to be deducted to obtain the net proceeds as prescribed under Article 279. The proceeds are to be distributed among the States where the central taxes are "leviable" in "that year".

Article 275(2) provides that "after a Finance Commission has been constituted no order shall be made under this clause (i.e., Article 275) except after considering the recommendations of the Finance Commission". Article 275 provides that (i) these grants should be given to States which are in need of assistance, as Parliament may by law provide, and (ii) that different sums may be fixed for different States. Under constitutional provisions, only a Finance Commission can recommend grants under Article 275. Article 275 has two clauses. In the first clause, a distinction is made between its "substantive part" and the two "provisos". In the course of its work, the Second Finance Commission (1957) was confronted with the question as to whether their recommendations under Article 275(2) should cover not only the substantive portion of Clause (1) or these should also embrace the provisos appended thereto. The majority of the Members in the Commission held the view that Clause (2) of Article 275 covered not only the substantive part of Clause (1) but also the two provisos thereunder. The matter was, therefore, referred to the Ministry of Finance for clarification as to the interpretation, and the Ministry was requested that, if the interpretation of the Commission was acceptable to the President, or if the term of reference as it stood did not include the two provisos, as the case may be, the President be pleased to issue necessary orders to enable the Commission to make recommendations accordingly. The Ministry informed that the Commission's duty was to make recommendations only in respect of grants-in-aid as to which Parliament could make a law under Clause (1) of Article 275. Further, as the provisos constituted exceptions to the main provision, there was no provision for Parliament making any law in these cases. Therefore, the Ministry of Finance conveyed to the Commission the decision of the President that the power of the Commission to make recommendations under Clause (2) did not extend to the grants under the two provisos and remained limited to the substantive part of Para 1 of Article 275. With a view to avoiding any ambiguity in the matter, the TOR to subsequent Commissions made a specific reference to the grants under Article 275 by inserting the words 'for purposes other than those specified in the provisos to Clause (1) of that Article'. In the context of Article 275, another issue relates to whether the Finance commission can recommend grants for capital purpose also.

14.6 Finance Commissions in India

So far, twelve Finance Commissions have been constituted in India. The first Commission was constituted in 1951. The Twelfth Finance Commission was constituted in 2002. The Commission generally makes recommendations that apply for five years, although there have been some exceptions. Table 14.2 gives the period of award of different Finance Commissions. It also provides a comparison of these award periods with the period covered by different five year plans.

Table 14.2: Plan Periods and Finance Commission Award Periods

Finance Commissions			Plans		
No.	Period of award	No. of Years	No.	Period of award	No. of Years
First	1952-53 to 56-57	5	First	1951-52 to 55-56	5
Second	1957-58 to 61-62	5	Second	1956-57 to 60-61	5
Third	1962-63 to 65-66	4	Third	1961-62 to 65-66	5
Fourth	1966-67 to 68-69	3	APs	1966-67 to 68-69	3
Fifth	1969-70 to73-74	5	Fourth	1969-70 to 73-74	5
Sixth	1974-75 to 78-79	5	Fifth	1974-75 to 78-79	5
Seventh	1979-80 to 83-84	5	AP	1979-80	1
Eighth	1984-85 to 88-89	5	Sixth	1980-81 to 84-85	5
Ninth (1year Award)	1989-90	1	Seventh	1985-86 to 89-90	5
Ninth (main Award)	1990-91 to 94-95	5	Eighth	1990-91 to 91-92	2
Tenth	1995-96 to 99-00	5	Eighth (revised)	1992-93 to 96-97	5
Eleventh	2000-01 to 04-05	5	Ninth	1997-98 to 2001-02	5
Twelfth	2005-06 to 09-10	5	Tenth	2002-03 to 2006-07	5

Notes: AP refers to annual plan.
Source: Report of the Eighth Finance Commission (p.122) for periods up to the Seventh Plan and subsequent announcements.

14.7 Evolution of the Terms of Reference

Terms of Reference (TOR) to a Finance Commission have evolved over the last fifty years. Articles 270, 275, 280, and 281 of the Constitution have a direct bearing on the setting up and work of the Finance Commission. The TOR to the Commission are derived from Clause (3) of Article 280. While the reference relating to distribution of taxes and duties and grants-in-aid of revenues is built in Clause (3) (c) of Article 280, other matters are referred to the Commission 'in the interests of sound finance' under Article 280(3) (d) of the Constitution. It may be noted that the First Finance Commission, which was set up on the 22nd November, 1951 did not have any terms of reference, initially. A formal request from the President to make recommendations to him in regard to grants under Article 273(2) and under Article 275(2) was communicated to the Commission on the 6th of April, 1952.

Over time, the TOR have become elaborate and structured, and have often been the subject matter of wide ranging public and academic discussions, reflecting contemporary fiscal and economic concerns. The terms referred to some of the recent Finance Commissions could be studied as consisting of (i) core paragraphs making reference to the relevant constitutional provisions, (ii) para relating to the 'restructuring of public finances', as a reference in the 'interests of sound finance', (iii) para containing mandatory considerations and its sub-clauses, which reflect some current concerns and also have implications as to the scope of work and methodologies to be followed by the Commission, (iv) para relating to the debt position of the States, (v) para relating to calamity relief and disaster management, (vi) para relating to the 'State Fiscal Reforms Facility' (SFRF), and (vii) critical dates which provide guidelines as to the years that may be used as base and reference years with respect to the recommendation period. A separate para contains the directive mandating the use of 1971 population in the determination of tax shares and grants. Annexure 14.1 provides a comparison of the TOR of the last two Commissions, eleventh and twelfth, where the salient differences have been highlighted. Annexure 14.2 reproduces some of the important articles of the Constitution relevant for the working of the FC.

14.8 Core Tasks of the Finance Commissions

All the core tasks of the Commission are listed in Article 280(3). The core of the core consists of the task of determining the share of States in the central taxes and the *inter se* shares of individual States in the aggregate share of the States. Prior to the 80th constitutional amendment, two main central taxes were shareable with the States, *viz.* income tax other than corporation tax and the Union excise duties. The sharing of the income tax was mandatory as, under Article 270, it had to be shared with the States, while that of the Union excise duties was discretionary, as its sharing was subjected to the phrase "may be divided between the Union and the States" and could be shared if Parliament by law so provided. The share of income assignable to States did not become part of the Consolidated Fund of India (CFI). The States' share of Union excise duties went into the CFI first, and was then charged on the CFI. There were also two tax rental arrangements with the States, where the Union government collected the tax, as it were, on behalf of the States and then distributed the proceeds among the States on principles and shares recommended by the Finance Commission. These were additional excise duty in lieu of sales tax on textiles, tobacco, and sugar, and grant in lieu of the tax on railway passenger fares which was repealed in 1961. Reference in the TOR in respect of these two tax rental arrangements was also withdrawn after the 80th amendment in a modification of the TOR of the EFC vide Presidential Notification dated June 21, 2000.

Following the 80th Amendment of the Constitution, all central taxes have been brought into a pool and it is mandatory to assign a share from each central tax to the States. The share of the States does not go into the Consolidated Fund of India. Although, the amended Article 270 mandates that each tax has to shared, it does not necessarily mandate that the same share should be assigned for all taxes. However, the discussion preceding the 80th Constitution amendment and, in particular, the recommendations of the Tenth FC which had proposed this alternative scheme of devolution had envisaged that the same share should be assigned to the States in all the central taxes.

Two issues are critical for the consideration of the Finance Commission in this context. The first relates to the task of determining the vertical share, i.e., the respective shares of the Centre and the States in the central taxes. The second task pertains to the determination of the *inter se* shares of individual States from the share assigned to all States. This task is often referred to as the horizontal dimension of transfers. The vertical issue viz, the share of the states in Central taxes, has to be considered on the basis of objective criteria and in the context of the overall transfers from the centre to the states. The horizontal dimension has so far been addressed, prior to the Report of the EFC, on a tax by tax basis. The principle of 'return' was earlier given relatively greater weight in the distribution of income tax while developmental needs including adequacy of provision of essential general, social, and economic services was given greater attention in the sharing of Union excise duties. Over time, however, a convergence became visible in the factors determining both sets of shares. A full convergence was achieved with the recommendations of the EFC where three sets of factors reflecting needs, costs disabilities, and fiscal performance, were used.

In relation to grants, there are two duties cast upon the Finance Commission conjointly by Articles 280(3) (b) and 275. Article 280(3) (b) requires the Commission, to make recommendations as to the "principles" which should govern such grants-in-aid. Following from Article 275(1), specific "sums" are to be recommended to be paid to the States which are assessed to be in "need of assistance". It is significant to note that while Article 270 speaks of percentage share, Article 275 refers to specific 'sums'.

The Constitution prescribes that these grants are to be 'charged' on the Consolidated Fund of India, and have to be recommended by a Finance Commission.

Table 14.3: Chairpersons and Members of Finance Commissions

First (Nov.22, 1952)	**Fifth (February 29, 1969)**	**Ninth (June 17, 1987)**
K.C. Neogy	Mahavir Tyagi	N.K.P. Salve
V.P. Menon/V.L. Mehta	P.C. Bhattacharya/ G. Swaminathan	A.S. Qureshi (Justice)
R. Kaushalendra Rao (Justice)	M. Seshachalapathy	R.J. Chelliah
B.K. Madan	D.T. Lakdawala	Lalthanhawla/ S. Venkatiramnan/R. Keishing
M.V. Rangachari (Member-Secretary)	V.L. Gidwani (Member-Secretary)	Mahesh Prasad/K.V.R.Nair (Member-Secretary)
Second (June1, 1956)	**Sixth (June 28, 1972)**	**Tenth (June 15, 1992)**
K. Santhanam	K. Brahmananda Reddy	K.C. Pant
Ujjal Singh	S.S. Abal Masud (Justice)	D.B. Pal
L.S. Misra (Chief Justice)	B.S. Minhas	B.P.R. Vithal
M.V. Rangachari	I.S. Gulati	C. Rangarajan/M.R.Shroff
B.N. Ganguli	G. Ramchandran (Member-Secretary)	M.C. Gupta/Arun Sinha (Member- Secretaries)
H.B.Bhar (Secretary)		
Third (December 2, 1960)	**Seventh (June 22, 1977)**	**Eleventh (July 3, 1998)**
A.K. Chanda	J.M. Shelat	A.M. Khusro
P. Govinda Menon	Raj Krishna	N.C. Jain
D.N. Roy (Justice)	C.H. Hanumantha Rao	J.C. Jetly
M.V. Mathur	H.N. Ray	Amaresh Bagchi
G.R. Kamat (Member Secretary)	V.B. Eswaran (Member-Secretary)	T.N. Srivastava (Member-Secretary)
Fourth (May 5, 1964)	**Eighth (June 20, 1982)**	**Twelfth (November 1, 2002)**
P.V. Rajamannar	Y.B. Chavan	C. Rangarajan
M.L. Gautam	S. Mukerjee/T.P.S. Chawla (Justices)	Som Pal/S. Acharya
D.G. Karve	C.H. Hanumantha Rao	T.R. Prasad
Bhabatosh Datta	G.C. Baveja	D.K. Srivastava
P.C. Mathew (Member-Secretary)	A.R. Shirali	G.C. Srivastava (Member-Secretary)
	N.V. Krishnan (Secretary)	

The Seventh Finance Commission (1978), while recommending grants-in-aid for up-gradation of standards of administration, felt that grants should be made for meeting capital expenditure as well. The Commission noted that the grants made under revenue account did not make adequate provision for administrative and residential buildings. As this expenditure has to be on the capital account, the Commission felt that capital expenditure also should be provided for. Accordingly, the Seventh Finance Commission noted that it should recommend capital grants also, and found that there was an implicit and inherent provision for making capital grants, notwithstanding the fact that the proviso was specifically outside the reach of the Commission, under the terms of reference. The Commission stated:

"We have given careful consideration to the scope for grants-in-aid under Article 275 for meeting capital expenditure. The operative part of this article speaks of "sums". There is no restriction or bar in the article against making grants for capital expenditure. The first proviso of the article expressly speaks of grants of capital sums. This goes to show that the expression grants-in-aid of revenues do not limit grants to revenue expenditure only. We are fortified in this view by the Note of the Chairman of the Fourth Finance Commission appended to its Report on the interpretation of Article 275. Further, it seems unreasonable to hold that the operative part of the article enables the Commission to make grants for revenue expenditure only, while the proviso enables grants being made for revenue as well as capital nature. It is quite clear therefore that it is open to us to recommend grants for capital expenditure also, apart from grants for revenue expenditure under Article 275" (Para 8 of Chapter 10 of the Report).

The grants recommended by the Seventh Finance Commission for capital purposes amounted to Rs. 908.80 crore, while those for revenue purposes aggregated to Rs. 1490.65 crore for 15 States for the five years of its Report, i.e., a significant portion of total grants was for capital expenditures. These recommendations were accepted. It is important to mention that all the grants recommended by a Finance Commission are under the substantive portion of Article 275(1).

In principle, Article 275(1) makes no restriction as to whether needs should be considered only on revenue account, and further only on the non-plan revenue account. There has been a running debate for quite some time as to whether the whole revenue account or only the non-plan revenue account should be considered by the Finance Commission. There is no restriction in the constitutional provision in this regard. In fact, the term "grants-in-aid of the revenues" does not imply that consideration should only be of revenue expenditures, i.e., current expenditure. Revenues of the States are meant to be spent both on current and capital needs, and there is no constitutional restriction as to what needs should be considered and what should not be considered by the Finance Commission. Further, the distinction between plan and non-plan expenditures has not been made anywhere in the Constitution. Article 112 makes a reference to expenditure on 'revenue' account to be distinguished from 'other' expenditures. This issue is further discussed in this note in a subsequent section.

Para 4(iii) of the TOR derives from Article 280(3) (bb) and (3) (c), which was inserted in this article after the 73rd and 74th Amendments to the Constitution, relating respectively to the resources of panchayats (rural local bodies) and municipalities (urban local bodies). It is important to note that the Constitution requires the Finance Commission to make recommendations regarding the "measures" needed to augment the Consolidated Funds of States to supplement the resources of the panchayats and municipalities, respectively. These "measures" do not necessarily imply that grants should be provided, although such grants could be one of many such measures, and could also serve to induce other measures.

The second part of the clause under Para 4(iii) of the TOR provides that the Finance Commission should make its recommendations on the "basis of the recommendations by the Finance Commission of the State". The State Finance Commissions (SFCs) have had heterogeneous approaches, methodologies, and time periods. It wile be useful to develop a framework in which SFC reports can be considered in a comparable framework. The issue of local bodies is further discussed in a subsequent section. Some of the relevant issues in the context of Para 4 of the TOR are listed below.

In the context of resource transfers, three important issues for the consideration of the Commission relate to determining: (i) the size of overall transfers relative to Centre's gross revenue receipts, (ii) the appropriate ratio between tax devolution and grants in the overall transfers recommended by Finance Commission, and (iii) the relative shares of general purpose and conditional grants in total grants. It may be noted that determining the overall size of transfers relative to Centre's gross revenue receipts is not a constitutional requirement but becomes relevant in the context of restructuring of public finances and for benchmarking transfers through alternative channels viz, Finance Commission, Planning Commission and other discretionary transfers.

It was for the first time that the Eleventh Finance Commission (EFC) set out an indicative ceiling of total revenue transfers taking into account tax devolution, grants recommended by the Finance Commission, plan grants and other grants. This was considered useful in the context of their approach to restructuring public finances of the centre and the states. The EFC had postulated that 37.5 per cent of the Centre's gross revenue receipts comprising gross tax revenues and non tax revenues could be taken as the overall indicative limit on revenue transfers. In setting the ceiling, they took into account the levels of transfers relative to

Centre's revenue receipts in recent past. Given the overall ceiling, they then proceeded to determine the levels of tax devolution and grants-in-aid under their purview leaving the rest for resource transfers in the form of grants by the Planning Commission and other grants through Central Ministries. The TFC has raised the indicative benchmark to 38 per cent.

Given the overall ceiling, the share of aggregate transfers under the aegis of the Finance Commission, and within these, the relative shares of tax devolution and grants required to be determined. Grants are the more effective transfer instrument for state-specific and purpose specific targeting. On the other hand, tax devolution has a built-in responsiveness to buoyancies experienced in the central taxes as these are recommended as shares and not as absolute amounts. However, tax devolution is general purpose and unconditional, and for that reason, states often prefer this mode of transfer. Also, share in central taxes comes to the States as a matter of right under Article 270, whereas grants are more discretionary in nature. Tax devolution can also be targeted, but this is constrained by the limited scope of adjustments in the devolution formulae.

Within the domain of grants, another critical issue relates to the possibility and desirability of recommending conditional/specific purpose grants, and determining the appropriate proportion between the conditional and unconditional grants. For conditional grants the relevant purposes and associated conditions also need to be specified along with an effective monitoring mechanism.

The First Finance Commission had considered the 'principles' of determining grants at length and had opined that both unconditional and specific purpose grants can and should be considered by the Finance Commission under the Article 275 read with Article 280(3)(b). They had observed that the scope of these articles should not be limited solely to grants-in-aid which are completely unconditional and grants that could be directed to well defined purposes can also reasonably be considered as falling within the scope of the article 275. The First Finance Commission recommended specific purpose grants for primary education. The Second Commission had observed that grants-in-aid should be a residuary form of assistance given in the form of general and unconditional grants. However, they also agreed that grants for broad purposes may be given and in respect of these, States should be under obligation to spend the whole amount in furtherance of the broad purposes indicated. The Third Finance Commission gave specific purpose grants for improvement in communications.

Most of the subsequent Commissions had generally agreed to the principles listed by the First Commission but they had all proceeded to recommend unconditional revenue gap grants primarily. In addition, some earmarked grants were recommended for special problems, up-gradation of services and local bodies. However, as most resources are fungible and even if purposes are specified, States may continue to spend according to their own priorities by reducing normal allocations on the specified heads. In this context, it is important to ensure that for the selected services, States uplift allocations to the desired levels over and above the historical allocations, and that expenditures lead to verifiable improvement in services and outcomes.

14.9 Finances of Union and State Governments: Review and Restructuring

Para 5 of the TOR of the TFC asked for a 'review' of the state of finances of the Union and State governments and a 'plan' for a 'restructuring' of the public finances. Sub-clauses of Para 6 and Paras 5, 6(iv), and 9 of TFC's TOR were clearly inter linked and required consideration in an integral part of the restructuring plan. These are reproduced below:

Para 5: "The Commission shall review the state of the finances of the Union and the States and suggest a plan by which the Governments, collectively and severally, may bring about a restructuring of the public finances restoring budgetary balance, achieving macro-economic stability and debt reduction along with equitable growth".

Para 6(iv) "The objective of not only balancing the receipts and expenditure on revenue account of all the States and the Centre, but also generating surpluses for capital investment and reducing fiscal deficit".

Para 9: "The Commission may, after making an assessment of the debt position of the States as on the 31st March 2004, suggest such corrective measures, as are deemed necessary, consistent with macro-economic stability and debt sustainability. Such measures recommended will give weightage to the performance of the States in the fields of human development and investment climate".

The issue of review and restructuring of public finances was referred to the EFC for the first time in Para 4 of their TOR. There was a significant addition in the TOR of the TFC to the objectives enumerated with reference to which such a restructuring should be attempted. Apart from the objective of restoring budgetary balance and achieving macroeconomic stability, reference to "debt reduction along with equitable growth" was additional. The issue of debt was also referred to later in the TOR of the TFC in Para 9. But the reference to "equitable growth" was new and explicitly stated the concern with the growing inter-State disparities in growth and levels of per capita incomes.

One distinction in the TOR of the TFC vis-à-vis the corresponding reference to EFC in this context is that whereas in EFC's case, the Commission was asked to suggest 'ways and means', the TFC was asked to suggest a 'plan' by which such restructuring could be achieved. A plan would include ways and means to bring about restructuring. Among other considerations, a plan should clearly specify the 'sequence' of restructuring. Further, it should take into account in an explicit way the relevant inter-linkages within the fiscal sector, and of the fiscal sector with the rest of the economy.

The impact of public finances on "macroeconomic stability" requires to be analyzed in its various dimensions including the impact of fiscal imbalance on external balance, saving, investment, and growth. Given the interdependence of various sectors in the economy, particularly, the real, monetary, and external sectors, and the critical impact of government expenditure and the methods of their financing on growth, prices, savings, investment, and the balance of payments, this clause requires a study of the macro economy with a focus on the linkages with the fiscal sector.

The term 'restructuring' requires an analysis of the present 'structure' of public finances and identification of what may be wrong with it. The structure of public finances would need to be understood as a multi-dimensional construct comprising level and composition of government expenditure, level and composition of tax revenues including the rate structure of taxes and the exemption regimes, cost recoveries and non-tax revenues including returns on investment in departmental and public sector enterprises, borrowing, and the structure of debt. These require to be studied 'individually and severally' implying that not only the structure of public finances of the central and each State government will have to be analyzed but inter-linkages between these, transfers from the Centre to the States, and the public finance system as a whole will have to be considered.

In the macro context, the main issues relate to fiscal imbalance, which shows up in revenue account deficits, undesirable and unsustainable level of fiscal deficits and debt. These could cause instability in real, financial, and external sectors of the economy. Further, macroeconomic stability requires to be conceptualized in a growth context. The fiscal sector plays an important role in determining growth via public sector investment especially in infrastructure and human development. Government expenditure and its composition have a role to play both in the short and long run.

Achieving an equitable growth was an added consideration in the TOR to the TFC. This implied that growth was to be studied not only in the aggregate but also in terms of its inter-State composition. Determinants of growth and causes of variations in inter-State growth and the role of fiscal policies in this context have an important impact. The design of fiscal transfers has a critical bearing on achieving 'equitable growth'.

14.10 State Fiscal Reform Facility

The EFC was given an additional term of reference by a Presidential Notification dated April 28, 2000. This had extended paragraph 4 of the original TOR, by adding the following: "In particular, the Commission shall draw a monitorable fiscal reforms programme aimed at reduction of revenue deficit of the State and recommend the manner in which the grants to the States to cover the assessed deficits in their non-plan revenue account may be linked to progress in implementing the programme". In response to this additional TOR, the EFC recommended by a majority view the setting up of an Incentive Fund consisting of two parts, A and B. This facility came to be known as the State Fiscal Reform Facility (SFRF). Part A of the Fund consisted of 15 percent of the assessed non-plan revenue deficit grants, recommended in the main report of the EFC, which were withheld so as to be released, linked to progress in implementing the monitorable fiscal reforms programme. The total amount so withheld added to Rs. 5303.86 crore. This amount was available only to the revenue deficit States. Part B of the Fund consists of an equal amount. But this was to be made available to all States who could access an earmarked amount determined on the basis of their share in 1971 population. In both cases, the releases were to be linked to progress in the monitorable fiscal reforms programme. Unutilized amounts of up-gradation and special purpose grants would be added to the Incentive Fund in 2004-05. The balance left in the earmarked amounts on account of States not being able to qualify for the facility was also to become available for distribution among the qualifying States on a pro-rata basis in the last year.

The Ministry of Finance, Government of India brought out a paper entitled States' Fiscal Reform Facility 2000-01 to 2004-05. This paper specified that each State has to draw up a Medium-Term Fiscal Restructuring Policy (MTFRP), which should detail time bound action points on a variety of fiscal policy dimensions including taxation, pricing of publicly provided services, abolition of vacant posts, etc. Separate lists of action points on power sector reforms, public sector restructuring and budgetary reforms were also provided.

While the preparation of MTFRP by the States was to be a precondition, releases from the incentive fund were to be based on actual achievements, linked to a single monitorable index, *viz*., minimum improvement of 5 percentage points in revenue deficit relative to revenue receipts in each successive year with 1999-00 as the base year. A Monitoring Committee consisting of eight members including a Member-Secretary has also been set up. A Fiscal Reform Unit (FRU) has been set up in the Finance Commission Division of the Ministry of Finance to serve as the secretariat to the Facility. The FRU is also supposed to look after any other supplementary facility for the States including facilities from multilateral lending agencies.

The TFC, after an elaborate review, has recommended the abolition of the Fiscal Reform Facility. To achieve the objectives, it has suggested debt-relief measures and related incentives for the period 2005-10. More generally, proper incentives should be built into the overall scheme of transfers and separate incentive mechanisms should not be required. Other approaches to fiscal discipline include imposition of a hard budget constraint.

14.11 Para Containing "Considerations"

Evolution of Para Containing Considerations: Para 6 of the TOR of the TFC has several sub-clauses. This Para pertains to mandatory 'considerations', as the Commission was asked by the President that in making its recommendations, the Commission "shall" have regard to the considerations stated in the sub-clauses, among others. The use of the words, the Commission "shall" imparts this clause a 'directive' character. It has been argued by some that this violates the provision and spirit of Article 280(4), and of the Finance Commission (Miscellaneous Provisions) Act of 1951 as amended in 1955, whereby the Commission is to determine their own procedure. Article 280(4) clearly provides that "the Commission shall determine their procedure". It has been argued that since the central government is itself an interested party, it should submit a memorandum to the Finance Commission to make its views known rather than issue guidelines or give directives through the TOR. The duties of a Finance Commission are specified in the Constitution itself and analysts have said on earlier occasions that it should suffice that the terms of reference simply enumerate the matters on which the recommendations of a Finance Commission are sought, leaving the Commission free to determine the scope of their recommendations or the methodology on which these are based.

The use of the word "considerations" started with the TOR of the Second FC, where in Para 4(b), the phrase "having regard, among other considerations, to ..." was used. The same phrase continued in the TORs of Third and Fourth Finance Commissions. The phrase "shall have regard", appeared for the first time in the TOR of the Fifth Finance Commission in the context of resources and needs of the central government in Para 5 of their TOR, which read: "the Commission in making its recommendations on the various matters aforesaid *shall have regard* to the resources of the central government and the demands thereon on account of the expenditure on civil administration, defence, and border security, debt servicing and other committed expenditures or liabilities". This clause was repeated in the TOR of the Sixth Finance Commission. The practice of having a para containing several 'considerations' started with the Seventh Finance Commission where, for the first time, the phrase "in making its recommendations, the Commission *shall have regard, among other considerations*, to ..." was used. This para containing "considerations" has, since then been part of the TOR of all successive Finance Commissions. However, in the case of the Ninth FC, the TOR were converted fully into a directive by using the phrase in Para 4 of their TOR: "In making its recommendations, the Commission shall...". The tasks were enlisted but these were not mere considerations. The Chief Minister of Kerala had written to the Chairman of the Ninth Finance Commission articulating misgivings and apprehensions about the use of the word 'shall' in Para 4 of the Presidential Notification which appeared to be "mandatory almost amounting to a directive" (Para 1.7 of the First Report of the Ninth Finance Commission). Also, the suggestion to take account of all the committed liabilities in the case of the Centre and the absence of a similar suggestion for the States gave rise to misgivings that the 'guidelines' were loaded in favour of the Centre. Similar apprehensions were expressed by a number of participants in a seminar on Issues Before the Ninth Finance Commission. To dispel these, the Chairman of the Commission wrote to all the Chief Ministers (Para 1.7 of their First Report) setting out the Commission's perception of their role and obligations. He mentioned that it was the "Commission's prerogative" to adopt such approach and method as it considered fit and appropriate on subjects covered by (a) and (b) of Article 280(3) of the Constitution.

The phrase "The Commission shall have regard, among other considerations to ..." was reintroduced in the TOR of the Tenth FC and this practice has been continued since. A study of the sub-clauses of this para for the Tenth, Eleventh, and Twelfth Finance Commissions indicates that this has been utilised to refer to the following areas:

1. Resources and needs of the Centre;
2. Resources and needs of the States, particularly the consideration of the entire revenue account vis-à-vis only the non-plan revenue account;
3. Methodology to be followed by the Commission in determining transfers including choice of the base year;
4. Maintenance and upkeep of capital assets and maintenance in respect of plan schemes completed by a specified date;
5. Up-gradation of standards of services in general administration and non-developmental sectors;

6. Returns on government investments in specified sectors including irrigation and power projects; and
7. Fiscal management and economy in expenditure consistent with efficiency.

Para 6(i) and (ii) of the TOR of the TFC make reference, respectively, to the resources of the central government and the demands on those resources. Resources of the central government have to be assessed on the basis of "levels of taxation and non-tax revenues likely to be reached at the end of 2003-04". The 2003-04 tax and non-tax revenues can therefore serve as the base for assessment of resources for the period from 2005-06 to 2009-10. However, the phrase 'levels' of taxation and non-tax revenues requires to be analyzed further. Levels in absolute terms may not mean much in the present context. Levels in relation to respective tax and non-tax bases imply a certain relationship. If the tax and non-tax bases grow, tax and non-tax revenues would also grow, if this relationship is held constant. But, these would also grow because of additional revenue effort, modification of tax-rates, withdrawal of exemptions and other reforms. The para asking the Commission to suggest a plan for "restructuring of public finances" would require various measures to augment tax and non-tax revenues beyond levels reached in 2003-04, even when those levels are considered in relation to their bases.

Para 6(ii) of the TOR to the TFC makes reference to the demands on central resources by the central government. Particular reference has been made to expenditure on civil administration, defence, internal and border security, debt servicing and other committed expenditures and liabilities. A reference of this nature has been made to successive Finance Commissions since the Fifth Finance Commission. In relation to the previous references, the mention of the need on account of 'internal' security is new. The items listed for particular reference relate mainly to interest payments and pensions as committed liabilities and other general services including defence and border security. The structure and pattern of growth of central expenditure will have to be studied including that on social and economic services. This is also required in terms of the para on review and restructuring of finances of the Union and the States.

14.12 Assessment of States' Resources and Needs

In the case of States, a corresponding sub-clause, *viz*., Para 6(iii) of the TOR provides that the assessment of resources for the period 2005-06 to 2009-10 will need to be made on the basis of levels of taxation and non-tax revenues likely to be reached at the end of 2003-04. This is symmetrical to the corresponding consideration for the Centre, and gives rise to a similar set of issues.

In regard to the needs of States, particular reference to any specific needs was not made in the TOR of the TFC except to the non-salary component of maintenance and upkeep of capital assets and non-wage related maintenance expenditure on plan schemes. Clause 6(iv) specified the more general consideration in regard to 'the objective of not only balancing the receipts and expenditure on revenue account of *all the States and the Centre*, but also generating surplus for capital investment and reducing fiscal deficit'.

It is clear that this clause does not make reference to the entire 'revenue' account of the States and not just revenue expenditure on the 'non-plan' account. Both this clause and the para on review and restructuring of public finances required the TFC to study the entire revenue account. The para on restructuring of public finances and the reference to capital investment and fiscal deficit in Clause 6(iv) also implied that the financing of entire government expenditure, revenue and capital, was to be considered in an integrated framework.

The distinction between non-plan versus plan revenue expenditure became material with a minute of dissent given by the Member-Secretary of the Third Finance Commission (1961). The Third Finance Commission took into account the needs of the States for the 3rd Five Year Plan and recommended by a majority that the quantum of grants-in-aid should be fixed in such a way as to enable the States, along with any surplus out of devolution, to cover 75 percent of the revenue component of their plans. In determining the revenue component, the Commission deducted the amount of additional tax to be raised by each State as incorporated in the plan itself. The Commission also recommended special grants to 10 States for the improvement of road communications. The recommendations on the first item, were not accepted by the President but those on the second, were accepted. Asok Chanda, Chairman of Third FC, observed: "...the Planning Commission did not take kindly to the basic scheme or suggestions of the Commission. It was not unexpected therefore that the Member-Secretary of the Commission who was an official, should take the unusual step of appending a note of dissent, nor was it strange that government used this note for rejecting this particular recommendation" (Federalism in India: 1965, p. 222).

Later, the consideration of needs of revenue expenditure on the plan account was excluded from the purview of the Finance Commission by stipulations in the TOR. The Fourth FC was asked in their TOR to consider 'the requirements of those States to meet the committed expenditure on maintenance and upkeep of plan schemes completed during the Third Plan'. The TOR of Fifth FC provided that 'the requirements on revenue account of those States to meet expenditure on administration, interest charges in respect of their debt, maintenance and upkeep of plan schemes, transfer of funds to local bodies and aided institutions and other committed expenditure' should be a relevant consideration. A similar reference was made to the Sixth FC except that they were also asked to take into account provision for emoluments of Government employees, teachers and local body employees. The word 'non-plan' entered in the TOR of the Finance Commission for the first time in the TOR of the Seventh FC. Para 5(iv) of their TOR made reference to "the requirements on revenue account of those States to meet the expenditure on administration and other *non-plan commitments or liabilities* ..." A similar reference was there in the TOR of the Eighth FC. The TOR of Ninth FC were so framed that the option was open for the Commission to take the plan revenue requirements if the Commission so desired. The TOR of the Tenth FC again restricted the ambit of consideration to the non-plan account. In the case of the EFC, both non-plan and plan revenue requirements were referred to explicitly. However, the EFC considered the revenue requirement only on the non-plan account. For the Twelfth Finance Commission, reference was made to the entire 'revenue' account in Para 6(iv), which specified the 'objective of not only balancing the receipts and expenditure on **revenue account** of all the States and the Centre, but also generating surpluses for capital investment and reducing fiscal deficit'. This clause corresponded to the relevant clause in the TOR of the Ninth FC but not to comparable clauses in the TOR of the Tenth and the Eleventh FCs. The TFC still limited its assessment exercises to non-plan revenue expenditures of the states.

14.13 Assessment of Resources and Needs

Although most of the recent Commissions have made an attempt not to simply use historical growth rates of revenues or expenditures in their assessments, the assessments are still driven by a number of historical parameters, which are often subjected to modifications with a view to introducing an element of prescriptive benchmarks or norms. An explicit reference as to the use of a normative approach was made for the first time to the Ninth Finance Commission by including in their TOR the following:

"In making its recommendations, the Commission shall:

1. adopt a normative approach in assessing the receipts and expenditures on the revenue account of the States and the Centre and, in doing so, keep in view the special problems of each State, if any, and the special requirements of the Centre such as defence, security, debt servicing and other committed expenditure or liabilities;
2. have due regard to the need for providing adequate incentives for better resource mobilization and financial discipline as well as closer linking of expenditure and revenue raising decisions;

3. take into account the need for speed, efficiency and effectiveness of Government functioning and of delivery systems for Government programme; and
4. keep in view the objective of not only balancing the receipts and expenditure on revenue account of both the States and the Centre, but also generating surpluses for capital investment ..."

A direct reference to a normative approach in the TOR has not been made for the subsequent Commissions. Economists have frequently criticized the determination of transfers based on gaps derived from historical trends of expenditures and revenues due to their adverse incentives, where States find that it is to their advantage to maximize this gap by having a history of low revenue effort and profligate expenditures. Such an approach has been referred to as the 'Gap Filling Approach' (GFA). In this context, the Commission will have to deliberate on the general principles of assessment and the application of norms or prescriptive parameters and the considerations on which these may be based.

There were some important additions/alterations in the sub-clauses of Clause 6 of TFC's TOR, which had a bearing on the assessment exercise. One new sub-clause related to the taxation efforts of the central and each State government as against 'targets' and 'potential' in order to improve the tax-GDP and the tax-GSDP ratios respectively for the central and the State governments. Measurement of 'potential' tax revenue required a suitable methodology to ascertain the relevant tax bases and establish relationships between tax revenues and tax bases.

In the context of up-gradation of services, specific references were made to the earlier Finance Commissions starting with the Sixth, but with the exception of the Ninth because the Ninth Commission was required to adopt a normative approach. The following reference, for example, was contained in Para 4(iv) of the TOR of the Tenth FC:

"the requirements of States for modernization of administration, e.g., computerization of land records and providing faster channels of communication up to and above district level, and for upgrading the standards in non-developmental sectors and services, and the manner in which such expenditure can be monitored".

In the case of EFC, in Para 5(v) of their TOR, the following reference was made:

"the requirements of States for upgradation in non-developmental and social sectors and services particularly of States which are backward in general administration with a view to modernize and rationalize the administrative set up in the interest of speed, efficiency and sound fiscal management".

Although a similarly elaborate reference was not made on this account to the Ninth FC, it was asked to keep in view the special problems of each State. The Eighth FC was asked [Para 5(vi) of their TOR] to have regard to:

"the requirements of States for up-gradation of standards in non-developmental sectors and services particularly of States which are backward in general administration with a view to bringing them to the levels obtaining or likely to obtain in the more advanced States, the manner in which such expenditure could be monitored, being also indicated by the Commission".

As mentioned earlier, reference of this nature in the TOR of the Finance Commissions started with the Sixth Commission, although the need for up-gradation of selected services and making conditional grants for the purpose started with the First Finance Commission itself. The First Finance Commission had recommended, without being specifically asked to do so, grants for primary education to eight States. The Third Finance Commission had recommended grants for the development of communications.

Grants for 'special problems' are different from 'up-gradation' grants. A specific reference to special problems was made to the Ninth FC, which recommended such grants. The Tenth and Eleventh Finance Commissions also recommended grants for special problems. These grants were State-specific, recognizing special problems, which were different in different States. These grants were recommended not just for backward States but also the richer States. The Eighth FC also had recommended grants for 'special needs' to some States. The Twelfth Finance Commission has recommended a number of special purpose grants. These are discussed in detail in Chapter 17.

14.14 Para Relating to Local Bodies

Following the 73rd and 74th amendments to the Constitution relating respectively to the rural and urban local bodies, a stipulation was first made in the TOR of the EFC. First, under Article 280(bb) and (c), the Commission was asked to make recommendations as to "the measures needed to augment the Consolidated Fund of a State" to supplement the resources of the Panchayats and Municipalities on the basis of recommendations made by the Finance Commission of the State. In addition, a separate para in their TOR stipulated that:

"In the case of local bodies, the Commission shall take into account the recommendations of the State Finance Commissions; and where the State Finance Commissions have not been constituted as yet, or have not submitted their report giving recommendations, the Commission will make its own assessment about the manner and extent of augmentation of Consolidated Fund of the State to supplement the resources of the Panchayats and Municipalities in the State. While making such assessment, the Commission:

(i) shall take into account the provisions required to be made for the emoluments and terminal benefits of the employees of local bodies including those of teachers;

(ii) shall take into account the existing powers of the Panchayats and Municipalities to raise financial resources including those by way of raising additional taxes by the Panchayats and Municipalities; and

(iii) the powers, authority and responsibility transferred to Panchayats and Municipalities under Article 243(G) and 243(W) of the Constitution read with Schedules Eleven and Twelve".

The existing arrangements regarding assignment of functions and responsibilities as also sources of revenue are quite different in different States. The approach and the methodology followed by different State Finance Commissions are also quite heterogeneous. It has proved to be difficult to bring these different profiles in the State-Local division of responsibilities and resources and the variety of approaches followed by different SFCs to a common platform. In view of these difficulties, the EFC, which was the first Commission to which the provisions of Article 280 regarding the local bodies were referred to in their TOR, recommended as follows: "accordingly, we recommend that 'on the basis of the recommendations made by the Finance Commission of the State' appearing in sub-clause (bb) and (c) of Article 280(3) of the Constitution be deleted".

Although, the matter was not referred to the Tenth FC, since the Constitutional amendments had already been made in this regard, the Commission considered the provisions in Article 280(3) *suo moto*. This clearly demonstrates the fact that the Finance Commission need not confine itself to the TOR. Even the 'alternative scheme of devolution' recommended by the Tenth FC involved going beyond the TOR. In the context of the local bodies, the Tenth Commission analyzed the scope of the provisions in Article 280(3) (bb) and (c) as follows:

"(a) The need for augmentation of the Consolidated Funds of the States should first be ascertained and only thereafter the measures for such augmentation be recommended.

(b) Such measures need not necessarily involve transfer of resources from the Centre.

(c) Once the SFCs complete their task, the Finance Commission becomes duty bound to assess and build into the expenditure stream of the States the funding requirements for supplementing the resources of the panchayats and the municipalities. Measures needed for augmentation of the Consolidated Funds of the States may be determined accordingly.

(d) The responsibility for sharing and assigning taxes and providing grants to the local bodies rests with the States and does not stand transferred to the Centre.

(e) The transfer of duties and functions listed in the Eleventh and Twelfth Schedules of the Constitution would also involve concomitant transfer of staff and resources. Transfers of duties and functions to the local bodies should, therefore, not entail any extra financial burden".

The Tenth FC had recommended grants to rural and local bodies amounting to Rs. 5380.93 crore. The rural bodies were required to prepare suitable schemes and provide matching contributions. No amount was to be used for expenditure on salaries and wages. The EFC had examined the issue of local bodies in far greater detail. This followed partly from the fact that a separate reference was made in Para 6 of their TOR apart from the provisions of Article 280(3) (bb) and (c). They cited several measures which could augment the Consolidated Fund of the States including land taxes, surcharges on State taxes and profession tax, and a number of user charges. They expressed concern with the quality of maintenance of accounts and their audit at the level of local bodies and provided an elaborate set of guidelines to make accounting and auditing practices more robust. They also expressed concern with the non-availability of data on the finances of the Local Bodies in the absence of which more realistic assessment of the role of panchayats and municipalities for their basic, civil and developmental functions could not be made. They provided for the collection and compilation of a data base on the finances of the panchayats and municipalities which may be developed at the District, State and Central Government levels. They also provided grants earmarked for local bodies of an amount of Rs. 2000 crore per year for each of the five years during 2000-01 to 2004-05 as one among many measures to augment the Consolidated Funds of the States and used a five factor formula to determine inter-State shares of States in the amounts earmarked for rural and urban local bodies, respectively. The local body grants recommended by the TFC are reviewed in Chapter 18.

14.15 Financing Disaster Management

Para 10 of the TOR of the Twelfth Finance Commission refers to the issue of financing 'Disaster Management'. This para was considerably recast as compared to the corresponding para in the case of EFC. Whereas in their case, the Commission was asked to review the scheme of Calamity Relief Fund and make appropriate recommendations thereon, in the case of TFC, the review relates to the present arrangements as regards the financing of disaster management with reference to the National Calamity Contingency Fund (NCCF) and the Calamity Relief Fund. The term disaster management is new as part of the TOR. Also the NCCF has been set up on the basis of the recommendations of the EFC. Prior to this, there was a National Fund for Calamity Relief which was discontinued on the basis of the recommendations of the EFC and the National Calamity Contingency Fund was substituted for it. In addition, the EFC had also recommended the setting up of a National Centre for Calamity Management with the objective of the monitoring calamities that occurred on a regular basis and for assessing their impact on the area and population of a State.

Six varieties of calamities have been referred to as natural calamities namely, cyclone, drought, earthquake, fire, flood, and hailstorm. The proposed Centre was also to make recommendations as to whether a State is itself in a position to provide relief in a specific case of calamity of severe nature from the State's Calamity Relief Fund and its own resources. If in the assessment of this Centre, the State is unable to provide relief, it becomes eligible for assistance on the basis of recommendations of the National Centre for Calamity Management. The National Centre is also to take up studies on the recurrence of various types of natural calamities and to suggest short, medium, and long-term measures to prevent these.

Given that financing of disaster management has been referred to the TwFC, the Commission will have to review the working of the NCCF and the Calamity Relief Fund and also see whether the proposed Centre has been set up and with what responsibilities.

14.16 Para Mandating the Use of 1971 Population Data

Para 7 provides that "in making its recommendation on various matters, the Commission will take the base of population figures as of 1971, in all such cases where population is a factor for determination of devolution of taxes and duties and grants-in-aid. Such a direction has been given to all Finance Commissions since the Seventh. The only change in the case of TwFC's TOR is the substitution of the phrase "will take the base of population figures as of 1971" in place of "shall adopt the population figures of 1971". Although population figures are available for 1981, 1991 and 2001 from the relevant Census exercises, the Finance Commissions have been asked not to use these in matters relating to devolution. This implies that for the recommendation period of 2005-06 to 2009-10, the information base in respect of a key determinant will be 35 to 39 years out of date. While considering the TOR of the Ninth Finance Commission several analysts objected to the fact the Finance Commission was not left free to determine its own criterion and indicators in this matter. Some relevant considerations in this context are:

(i) A direction like this is not consistent with Article 280(4) and the Finance Commission's (Miscellaneous Provisions) Act, 1951 as amended in 1955 whereby the Commission is to determine their own procedure;

(ii) If the idea is to 'penalize' States for not effectively controlling population growth, this should apply only to unsatisfactory performance in controlling the birth rate. States should not be penalized for better performance in reducing death rates or in-migration of population. The method of providing the right incentives with appropriate indicators should have been left to the Finance Commission;

(iii) There is no constitutional sanction for this. The provisions regarding the use of 1971 population relate to election and reservation matters (e.g., Article 330).

There is no relationship between considerations for determining the number of seats for representation of population and determination of financial assistance to States for providing services to the entire population residing in their respective jurisdictions. In Articles 243(f) and 243 P (g), referring respectively to the panchayats and municipalities the term 'population' has been defined as follows: "population' means the population as ascertained at the last preceding census of which the relevant figures have been published".

Following the 'Family Welfare Programme: A Statement of Policy' resolution to adopt the 1971 population, the Constitution has been amended for limiting the number of members to the Lok Sabha and to the 'State Legislative Assemblies'. No specific amendment has been made in respect of Centre-State financial relations. The TFC has recommended that the practice of making reference to 1971 population in the TOR should be discontinued.

14.17 State Debt: Review and Relief Measures

It was the Sixth Finance Commission to which the assessment of States' debt position was first referred to. In their case, the relevant clause read as follows: "The Commission may make an assessment of the non-plan capital gap of the States on a uniform and comparable basis for the five years ending with 1978-79. In the light of such an assessment, the Commission may undertake a general review of the States' debt position with particular reference to the central loans advanced to them and likely to be outstanding as at the end of 1973-74 and suggest changes in the existing terms of repayment having regard inter-alia to the overall non-plan gap of the States, their relative position and the purposes for which the loans have been utilized, and the requirements of the Centre".

A similar reference was made to the Seventh and the Eighth Finance Commissions except for changing the reference years. For the Ninth Finance Commission, the relevant clause was substantively modified. Reference to the non-plan capital gap was dropped. There was no mention as to the purpose for which the loans have been utilized. The relevant clause read as follows: "The Commission may make an assessment of the debt position of the States as on the 31st day of March, 1989 and suggest such corrective measures as deemed necessary keeping in view the financial requirements of the Centre. The corrective measures will be with particular reference to investments made in infrastructure projects and shall have linkage with improvements in financial and managerial efficiency". This was further modified in the TOR of the Tenth Finance Commission. It now read as follows "the Commission may make an assessment of the debt position of the States as on 31st March 1994, and suggest such corrective measures as are deemed necessary also keeping in view the financial requirements of the Centre".

The Tenth Finance Commission recommended two debt relief measures, which were linked to (i) disinvestment undertaken by the State governments, and (ii) improvements in revenue balance. Whereas there were few takers of the benefit linked to disinvestment (as only Tamil Nadu could claim it) during the entire period of 1996-97 to 1999-00, twenty States were able to avail of the second debt relief scheme by showing improvement on their revenue account balance. The amount of relief claimed was Rs. 212 crore. Given the relative success of this scheme, the EFC increased the magnitude of relief linked to improvement in revenue balance and estimated that an amount of Rs. 600-700 crore is likely to be claimed by the States as relief in this scheme. The relevant clause in the TOR of the EFC was as follows: "the Commission may make an assessment of the debt position of the States as on 31st day of March 1999 and suggest such corrective measures as are deemed necessary, keeping in view the long-term sustainability for both Centre and States". The reference to long term sustainability was new.

The relevant clause referred to Twelfth Finance Commission made further changes. "The Commission may, after making an assessment of the debt position of the States as on the 31st March 2004, suggest such corrective measures, as are deemed necessary, consistent with macroeconomic stability and debt sustainability. Such measures recommended will give weightage to performance of the States in the fields of human development and investment climate". Instead of the term long-term sustainability, now the reference is to macroeconomic stability and debt sustainability. Further, it has been asked to ensure that the measures recommended give weightage to the performance of the States in the fields of human development and investment climate. The Commission will therefore need to consider indicators by which performance can be measured in relation to human development and investment climate.

In the context of debt, sustainability, relevant levels of fiscal deficit relative to GDP/GSDP would need to be determined for the Centre and the States that could stabilize debt relative to GDP/GSDP at desirable level taking into account relevant benchmarks such as the ratio of interest payments to revenue receipts. A path of adjustment specifying the required changes taking the current fiscal deficit ratios to the desired levels over the five year period up to 2009-10, and the measures by which these adjustments can be brought about has been indicated by the TFC, at an aggregate level.

Annexure 14.1: Terms of Reference: Twelfth and Eleventh Finance Commissions

	Twelfth Finance Commission		Eleventh Finance Commission
4.	The Commission shall make recommendations as to the following matters:-	3.	The Commission shall make recommendations as to the following matters:—
	(i) the distribution between the Union and the States of the net proceeds of taxes which are to be, or may be, divided between them under Chapter I Part XII of the Constitution and the allocation between the States of the respective shares of such proceeds;		(a) the distribution between the Union and the States of the net proceeds of taxes which are to be, or may be, divided between them under Chapter I Part XII of the Constitution and the allocation between the States of the respective shares of such proceeds;
	(ii) the principles which should govern the grants-in-aid of the revenues of the States out of the Consolidated Fund of India and the sums to be paid to the States which are in need of assistance by way of grants-in-aid of their revenues under Article 275 of the Constitution for purposes other than those specified in the provisions to clause (1) of that article; and		(b) the principles which should govern the grants-in-aid of the revenues of the States out of the Consolidated Fund of India and the sums to be paid to the States which are in need of assistance by way of grants-in-aid of their revenues under Article 275 of the Constitution for purposes other than those specified in the provisos to clause (1) of that article;
	(iii) the measures needed to augment the Consolidated Fund of a State to supplement the resources of the Panchayats and Municipalities in the State on the basis of the recommendations		(c) the measures needed to augment the Consolidated Fund of a State to supplement the resources of the Panchayats in the State on the basis of the recommendations

	made by the Finance Commission of the State.		made by the Finance Commission of the State;
	[(c) and (d) in the TOR of EFC are clubbed in one paragraph.]		(d) the measures needed to augment the Consolidated Fund of a State to supplement the resources of the Municipalities in the State on the basis of the recommendations made by the Finance Commission of the State.
	Twelfth Finance Commission		**Eleventh Finance Commission**
5.	The Commission shall review the state of the finances of the Union and the States and suggest a ***plan*** by which the Governments, collectively and severally, may bring about a restructuring of the public finances restoring budgetary balance, achieving macro-economic stability and ***debt reduction along with equitable growth.***	4.	The Commission shall review the State of the finances of the Union and the States and suggest ways and means by which the governments, collectively and severally, may bring about a restructuring of the public finances so as to restore budgetary balance and maintain macro economic stability. [in particular, the Commission shall draw a monitorable fiscal reforms programme aimed at reduction of revenue deficit of the State and recommend the manner in which the grants to the States to cover the assessed deficit in their non-plan revenue account may be linked to progress in implementing the programme] (Added by Presidential Notification dated April 28, 2000).

6.	In making its recommendations, the Commission shall have regard, among other considerations, to:-	5.	In making its recommendations, the Commission shall have regard, among other considerations, to:-
	(i) the resources, of the Central Government for five years commencing on 1st April 2005, on the basis of levels of taxation and non-tax revenues likely to be reached at the end of 2003-04;		(i) the resources of the Central Government and the demands thereon, in particular, on account of expenditure on civil administration, defence and border security, debt-servicing and other committed expenditure or liabilities;
	(ii) the demands on the resources of the Central Government, in particular, on account of expenditure on civil administration, defence, ***internal*** and border security, debt-servicing and other committed expenditure and liabilities;		
	(iii) the resources of the State Governments, for the five years commencing on 1st April 2005, on the basis of levels of taxation and non-tax revenues likely to be reached at the end of 2003-04;		(ii) *revenue* resources of the States for the five years commencing on 1st April, 2000, on the basis of the levels of taxation possible to be reached in 1998-99, targets set for additional resources mobilization for the Plan and the potential for raising additional taxes;
	(iv) the ***objective*** of not only balancing the receipts and expenditure on revenue account of all the States ***and the Centre***, but also generating surpluses for capital investment and reducing fiscal deficit;		(iii) the requirement of the States for meeting the Plan and non-Plan revenue expenditure; keeping in view the need for generating surplus for capital investment and reducing fiscal deficit;
	Twelfth Finance Commission		**Eleventh Finance Commission**

	(v) **taxation efforts of the Central Government and each State Government as against targets, if any, and the potential for additional resource mobilization in order to improve the tax-Gross Domestic Product (GDP) and tax-Gross State Domestic Product (GSDP) ratio, as the case may be;**		No corresponding clause
	(vi) the expenditure on the non-salary component of maintenance and upkeep of capital assets and the non-wage related maintenance expenditure on plan schemes to be completed by the 31st March 2005 and the norms on the basis of which specific amounts are recommended for the maintenance of the capital assets and the manner of monitoring such expenditure;		(iv) the maintenance and upkeep of capital assets and maintenance expenditure of plan schemes to be completed by 31st March, 2000 and the norms on the basis of which specified amounts are recommended for the maintenance of the capital assets and the manner of monitoring such expenditure;
	Dropped		(v) the requirements of States for up-gradation of standards in non-developmental and social sectors and services particularly of States which are backward in general administration with a view to modernize and rationalize the administrative set up in the interest of speed, efficiency and sound fiscal management;
	8. the need for ensuring the ***commercial viability*** of irrigation projects, power projects,		(vi) the need for ensuring reasonable returns on investment by the States in

	departmental undertakings, public sector enterprises etc. in the States through various means including adjustment of user charges and relinquishing of non-priority enterprises through privatization or disinvestment.		irrigation projects, power projects, State TransportUndertakings, departmental commercial undertakings, public sector enterprises etc;
	Twelfth Finance Commission		***Eleventh Finance Commission***
	Dropped		(vii) Such provisions for emoluments and terminal benefits of Government employees including teachers and other employees of aided institutions as obtaining on a specified date as the Commission deems it proper and with reference to appropriate objective criteria rather than in terms of actual increases that may have been given effect to;
	Dropped		(viii) the scope for better fiscal management consistent with efficiency and economy in expenditure including the incentives that need to be provided for better realizations of tax and non-tax revenue.
	Dropped	6.	In the case of local bodies—
			(a) the commission shall take into account the recommendations of the State Finance Commissions; and

			(b) where the State Finance Commissions have not been constituted as yet, or have not submitted their report giving recommendations, the Commission will make its own assessment about the manner and extent of augmentation of Consolidated Fund of the State to supplement the resources of the Panchayats and Municipalities in the State. While making such assessment, the Commission-
			(i) shall take into account the provisions required to be made for the emoluments and terminal benefits of the employees of local bodies including those of teachers;
	Twelfth Finance Commission		**Eleventh Finance Commission**
			(ii) shall take into account the existing powers of the Panchayats and Municipalities to raise financial resources including those by way of raising additional taxes by the Panchayats and Municipalities;
			(iii) the powers, authority and responsibility transferred to Panchayats and Municipalities under Article 243 G and 243 W of the constitution read with

			Schedules Eleven and Twelve.
	Dropped in amendment to TOR of EFC by Presidential Order dated June 19, 2000.	7.	The Commission may suggest changes, if any, to be made in the principles governing the distribution amongst the States of—
			(a) the net proceeds in any financial year of the additional duties of excise leviable under the Additional Duties of Excise (Goods of Special Importance) Act, 1957 (58 of 1957) in lieu of the sales tax levied formerly by the State Governments, and
			(b) the grants to be made available to the States in lieu of the tax under the repealed Railway Passenger Fares Tax Act, 1957 (25 of 1957).
7.	In making its recommendations on various matters, the Commission ***will take the base of population figures as of 1971***, in all such cases where population is a factor for determination of devolution of taxes and duties and grants-in-aid.	8.	In making its recommendations on the various matters aforesaid, the Commission shall adopt the population figures of 1971 in all cases where population is regarded as a factor for determination of devolution of taxes and duties and grants-in-aid.
8.	**The Commission shall review the Fiscal Reform Facility introduced by the Central Government on the basis of the recommendations of the Eleventh Finance Commission,**		No corresponding clause

	and suggest measures for effective achievement of its objectives.		
	Twelfth Finance Commission		**Eleventh Finance Commission**
9.	The Commission may, after making an assessment of the debt position of the States as on the 31st March 2004, suggest such corrective measures, as are deemed necessary, ***consistent with macro-economic stability and debt sustainability. Such measures recommended will give weightage to the performance of the States in the fields of human development and investment climate.***	9.	The Commission may make an assessment of the debt position of the States as on 31st day of March, 1999 and suggest such corrective measures as are deemed necessary, keeping in view the long term sustainability for both the Centre and the States.
10.	The Commission may review the present ***arrangements as regards financing of Disaster Management with reference to the National Calamity Contingency Fund and the Calamity Relief Fund and make appropriate recommendations thereon.***	10.	The Commission may review the present scheme of Calamity Relief Fund and may make appropriate recommendations thereon.
11.	The Commission shall indicate the basis on which it has arrived at its findings and make available the State-wise estimates of receipts and expenditure.	11	The Commission shall indicate the basis on which it has arrived at its report findings and make available the State-wise estimates of receipts and expenditure.

12.	The Commission shall make its report available by the 31st July, 2004, covering a period of five years commencing on the 1st April, 2005.	12.	The Commission shall indicate its report available by the 31st day of December, 1999 on each of the matters aforesaid, covering a period of five years commencing on the 1st day of April, 2000.

Annexure 14.2: Some Articles of the Constitution Having a Bearing on the Work of the Finance Commission

268. Taxes levied by the Union but collected and appropriated by the States.—(1) Such stamp duties and such duties of excise on medicinal and toilet preparations as are mentioned in the Union List shall be levied by the Government of India but shall be collected—

(a) in the case where such duties are leviable within any [1][Union territory], by the Government of India, and

(b) in other cases, by the States within which such duties are respectively leviable.

(2) The proceeds in any financial year of any such duty leviable within any State shall not form part of the Consolidated Fund of India, but shall be assigned to that State.

269. Taxes levied and collected by the Union but assigned to the States.—[2][(1) Taxes on the sales or purchase of goods and taxes on the consignment of goods shall be levied and collected by the Government of India but shall be assigned and shall be deemed to have been assigned to the States on or after the 1st day of April, 1996 in the matter provided in clause (2).

Explanation.—For the purposes of this clause,—

(a) the expression "taxes on the sale or purchase of goods" shall mean taxes on sale or purchase of goods other than newspapers, where such sale or purchase takes place in the course of inter-State trade or commerce;

(b) the expression "taxes on the consignment of goods" shall mean taxes on the consignment of goods (whether the consignment is to the person making it or to any other person), where such consignment takes place in the course of inter-State trade or commerce.

(2) The net proceeds in any financial year of any such tax, except in so far as those proceeds represent proceeds attributable to Union territories, shall not form part of the Consolidated Fund of India, but shall be assigned to the States within which that tax is leviable in that year, and shall be distributed among those States in accordance with such principles of distribution as may be formulated by Parliament by law.]

[3][(3) Parliament may by law formulate principles for determining when a [4][sale or purchase of, or consignment of, goods] takes place in the course of inter-State or commerce.

[5]**[270. Taxes levied and distributed between the Union and the States.**—(1) All taxes and duties referred to in the Union List, except the duties and taxes

referred to in articles 268 and 269, respectively, surcharge on taxes and duties referred to in article 271 and any cess levied for specific purposes under any law made by Parliament shall be levied and collected by the Government of India and shall be distributed between the Union and the States in the manner provided in clause (2).

(2) Such percentage, as may be prescribed, of the net proceeds of any such tax or duty in any financial year shall not form part of the Consolidated Fund of India, but shall be assigned to the States within which that tax or duty is leviable in that year, and shall be distributed among those States in such manner and from such time as may be prescribed in the manner provided in clause (3).

(3) In this article, "prescribed" means—

(a) until a Finance Commission has been constituted, prescribed by the President by order, and

(b) after a Finance Commission has been constituted, prescribed by the President by order after considering the recommendations of the Finance Commission;]

271. Surcharge on certain duties and taxes for purposes of the Union.— Notwithstanding anything in articles 269 and 270, Parliament may at any time increase any of the duties or taxes referred to in those articles by a surcharge for purposes of the Union and the whole proceeds of any such surcharge shall form part of the Consolidated Fund of India.

275. Grants from the Union to certain States.—(1) Such sums as Parliament may by law provide shall be charged on the Consolidated Fund of India in each year as grants-in-aid of the revenues of such States as Parliament may determine to be in need of assistance, and different sums may be fixed for different States:

Provided that there shall be paid out of the Consolidated Fund of India as grants-in-aid of the revenues of a State such capital and recurring sums as may be necessary to enable that State to meet the costs of such schemes of development as may be undertaken by the State with the approval of the Government of India for the purpose of promoting the welfare of the Scheduled Tribes in that State or raising the level of administration of the Scheduled Areas therein to that of the administration of the rest of the areas of that State:

Provided further that there shall be paid out of the Consolidated Fund of India as grants-in-aid of the revenues of the State of Assam sums, capital and recurring, equivalent to—

(a) the average excess of expenditure over the revenues during the two years immediately preceding the commencement of this Constitution in respect of the administration of the tribal areas specified in [6][Part I] of the table appended to paragraph 20 of the Sixth Scheduled; and

(b) the costs of such schemes of development as may be undertaken by that State with the approval of the Government of India for the purpose of raising the level of administration of the said areas to that of the administration of the rest of the areas of that State.

71, for "Part A" (w.e.f. 21-1-1972).

[7][(1A) On and from the formation of the autonomous State under article 244A,—

(i) any sums payable under clause (a) of the second proviso to clause (1) shall, if the autonomous State therein, be paid to the autonomous State, and, if the autonomous comprises only some of those tribal areas, be apportioned between the State of Assam and the autonomous State as the President may, by order, specify;

(ii) there shall be paid out of the Consolidated Fund of India as grants-in-aid of the revenues of the autonomous State sums, capital and recurring, equivalent to the costs of such schemes of development as may be undertaken by the autonomous State with the approval of the Government of India for the purpose of raising the level of administration of that State to that of the administration of the rest of the State of Assam.]

(2) Until provision is made by Parliament under clause (1), the powers conferred on Parliament under that clause shall be exercisable by the President by order and any order made by the President under this clause shall have effect subject to any provision so made by Parliament:

Provided that after a Finance Commission has been constituted no order shall be made under this clause by the President except after considering the recommendations of the Finance Commission.

279. Calculation of "net proceeds", *etc.*—(1) In the foregoing provisions of this Chapter, "net proceeds" means in relation to any tax or duty the proceeds thereof reduced by the cost of collection, and for the purposes of those provisions the net proceeds of any tax or duty, or of any part of any tax or duty, in or attributable to any area shall be ascertained and certified by the Comptroller and Auditor-General of India, whose certificate shall be final.

(2) Subject as aforesaid, and to any other express provision of this Chapter, a law made by Parliament or an order of the President may, in any case where under this Part the proceeds of any duty or tax are, or may be, assigned to any State, provide for the manner in which the proceeds are to be calculated, for the time from or at which and the manner in which any payments are to be made, for the making of adjustments between one financial year and another, and for any other incidental or ancillary matters.

280. Finance Commission.—(1) The President shall, within two years from the commencement of this Constitution and thereafter at the expiration of every fifth year or at such earlier time as the President considers necessary, by order constitute a Finance Commission which shall consist of a Chairman and four other members to be appointed by the President.

(2) Parliament may by law determine the qualifications which shall be requisite for appointment as members of the Commission and the manner in which they shall be selected.

(3) It shall be the duty of the Commission to make recommendations to the President as to—

(a) the distribution between the Union and the States of the net proceeds of taxes which are to be, or may be, divided between them under this Chapter and the allocation between the States of the respective shares of such proceeds;

(b) the principle which should govern the grants-in-aid of the revenues of the States out of the Consolidated Fund of India;

[8][(bb) the measures needed to augment the Consolidated Fund of a State to supplement the resources of the Panchayats in the State on the basis of the recommendations made by the Finance Commission of the State;]

[9][(c) the measures needed to augment the Consolidated Fund of a State to supplement the resources of the Municipalities in the State on the basis of the recommendations made by the Finance Commission of the State;]

[10][(d) any other matter referred to the Commission by the President in the interests of sound finance.

(4) The Commission shall determine their procedure and shall have such powers in the performance of their functions as Parliament may by law confer on them.

281. Recommendations of the Finance Commission.—The President shall cause every recommendation made by the Finance Commission under the provisions of this Constitution together with an explanatory memorandum as to the action taken thereon to be laid before each House of Parliament.

282. Expenditure defrayable by the Union or a State out of its revenues.—The Union or a State may make any grants for any public purpose, notwithstanding that the purpose is not one with respect to which Parliament or the Legislature of the State, as the case may be, may make laws.

Notes

1. Subs. by Constitution (Seventh Amendment) Act, 1956, sec. 29 and Sch. for "State specified in Part C of the First Schedule."

2. Subs. by the Constitution (Eightieth Amendment) Act, 2000, sec. 2, for clauses (1) and (2).

3. Ins. by the Constitution (Sixth Amendment) Act, 1956, sec. 3.

4. Subs. by the Constitution (Forty-sixth Amendment) Act 1982, sec. 2, for "sale or purchase of goods".

5. Subs. by the Constitution (Eightieth Amendment) Act, 2000 sec. 3 for article 270 (w.r.e.f. 1-4-1996).

6. Subs. by the North Eastern Areas (Reorganisation) Act, 171 (81 of 1971), sec.

7. Ins. by the Constitution (Twenty-second Amendment) Act, 1969, sec. 3.

8. Ins. by the Constitution (Seventy-third Amendment) Act, 1992, sec. 3 (w.e.f. 24-4-1993).

9. Ins. by the Constitution (Seventy-fourth Amendment) Act, 1992, sec. 3 (w.e.f. 1-6-1993).

10. Sub-clause (c) relettered as sub-clause (d) by sec. 3, *ibid.* (w.e.f. 1-6-1993).

15

Issues in Fiscal Transfers

The federal system was created with the intention of combining the different advantages which result from the magnitude and the littleness of nations.

Alexis de Togneville

15.1 Decentralization and Fiscal Federalism

There is a widespread acceptance of the view that decentralization of expenditure responsibilities to lower tier governments is efficiency augmenting. Sub-national governments are better informed and can more readily respond to the needs and preferences of the citizens living in their jurisdictions. The 'better information' argument can be traced back to Hayek (1945). A second reason, traceable to Tiebout (1956) links greater efficiency to competition among jurisdictions providing local public goods. Taxation responsibility, on the other hand, generally tends to be more centralized than the expenditure responsibilities, although whether or not taxation responsibilities should also be decentralized remains a controversial issue (see, Teresa Ter-Minassian, 1997 for a discussion). As long as taxes are less decentralized than expenditures, there will be an imbalance between resources and needs at different tiers of governments, with the central government having more resources than it needs and the sub-national governments having less than what they need. The system is then brought in balance by the mechanism of fiscal transfers which may take the form of revenue sharing and/or grants. The nature and extent of fiscal transfers can be decided upon in the context of incentives and allocation efficiency while taking into account vertical and horizontal fiscal imbalances which arise from needs relative to resources at different levels of governments.

Equity and efficiency are the main guiding principles in designing a system of fiscal transfers. An efficient fiscal transfer system should also be characterized by predictability and stability. Predictability of resource flows enables the sub-national governments to plan ahead, and stability ensures that there will not be sudden shocks in the transfer arrangements. In the consideration of the issue of equity, reference is often made to its vertical and horizontal dimensions. The main conceptual issues relate to the interdependence of the vertical and horizontal dimensions of equity and trade-off, if any, between equity and efficiency. The analysis has also take into account the implications of vertical and horizontal fiscal externalities.

15.2 Fiscal Imbalances and Role of Fiscal Transfers

In the context of fiscal transfers, three main imbalances arise: vertical fiscal imbalance, horizontal fiscal imbalance, and aggregate fiscal imbalance. These have been discussed in Srivastava (2002). The basic concepts are described below.

A. Vertical Fiscal Imbalance: Vertical fiscal imbalance refers to the simultaneous imbalance between means and responsibilities in two different tiers of governments. The vertical gap arises from the assignment of revenue sources and expenditure responsibilities. However, individual policy choices and the handling of these assignments by the governments in different tiers play a significant role in determining the actual gap that ultimately emerges. The imbalances may be mutually balancing in the sense that while in one tier, the means exceed the needs, and in the other, the needs exceed the means. The system is brought in balance by transfer of resources from the surplus tier (usually the central government) to the deficit tier (usually, the sub-national governments).

B. Aggregate Fiscal Imbalance: Aggregate fiscal imbalance exists if the surplus of one tier cannot wipe out the deficit of the other. It may arise because of an overall shortage of fiscal resources compared to fiscal needs, especially if fiscal needs are judged according to some exogenous targets, e.g. universalisation of elementary education.

C. Horizontal fiscal imbalance: Horizontal fiscal imbalance relates to the same level of governments, where the concerned tier comprises more than one government. It, therefore, necessarily refers to the lower, sub-national, tiers of governments. In particular, it refers to the differences in the fiscal capacity of the states to provide services at comparable levels to the citizens residing within its boundaries even while these governments make the same revenue effort to exploit their respective fiscal capacities. A process of redistribution can ameliorate horizontal imbalance. When explicit redistribution is not possible from one state to another due to legal or other constraints, both vertical and horizontal imbalances need to be attended to simultaneously in the process of resource transfers from the centre to the states.

The role of fiscal transfers is to redistribute resources between the central and the state governments in a manner such that vertical and horizontal imbalances are simultaneously removed with a view to maximizing the welfare of the citizens by promoting equity as well as efficiency. The task of designing a system of fiscal transfers becomes more difficult when the situation is that of aggregate fiscal imbalance where unless government resources are augmented, some of the governments/functions would face shortage of resources even after transfers. Augmentation of resources may require reassignment of revenue sources as between the central and state governments and/or greater revenue effort in respect of the already assigned resources. Equalization arrangements can be severely constrained by extreme vertical and/or horizontal imbalances prior to transfers. Full equalization may require large centre-state transfers or redistribution across states, which may be resisted by the richer states. Since vertical and horizontal fiscal balances are interdependent, failure to address the problem of vertical fiscal imbalance threatens efficacy of the horizontal fiscal equalization system as well.

15.3 Fiscal Equalization: Conceptual Issues

A fiscal transfer system may be constructed with the objective of ensuring that, through intergovernmental transfers, all states are able to provide comparable level of services if they also undertake comparable efforts for raising revenues. Fiscal capacity equalization and allocative efficiency may turn out to be mutually compatible and mutually supportive. Much depends on how the system of transfers is designed and implemented. A badly designed system may have distorting effects if it is not neutral with respect to state policies, especially if it permits states to influence the size of their grants through their own policies.

The philosophical foundation of fiscal equalization relates to the concept of equal rights and equal treatment of all citizens in all the states of a federation. This is to be complemented with greater responsiveness to the needs and preferences of citizens than would be possible in a unitary system of government. One of the earliest analyses advocating the case of equalization was put forward by Buchanan (1950, 1952). Buchanan sought an ethical justification for fiscal equalization not in terms of equality between states, but as fiscal justice between individuals. Horizontal equity calls for equal treatment of equals. Using the concept of fiscal residuum, defined as the difference between taxes paid by an individual and benefits received by that individual from public spending, Buchanan showed that differences in fiscal capacity between states necessarily result, in the absence of corrective action, in unequal fiscal treatment of equals; citizens in states with high fiscal capacity have higher fiscal residuums than comparable citizens (that is, citizens with the same incomes) in states with low fiscal capacity. An important means of bringing about fiscal equalization, i.e. equalization of the fiscal residuum, could be transfers between governments. Buchanan's linking of the case for fiscal equalization with the existence of economic union in a federation contained both efficiency and equity implications.

Scott (1950, 1952) provided a counter view. Scott showed concern with a different kind of efficiency, namely, the effects of fiscal equalization on the distribution of population among the states of a federation. Scott endeavoured to show that equalization transfers, by providing resources to poor people in resource-poor states, would be "inefficient" because: "...the maximum income for the whole country, and so the highest average personal income, is to be achieved only by maximizing national production" (p. 203). This requires labour to move from places where its marginal product is low to places where it is high. By discouraging labour mobility, fiscal equalization grants would result in allocative inefficiency. Scott recognized that equalization grants in a federation would merely treat individuals in low capacity areas in the same way as if they were in a unitary country. However, he argued that federalism without equalization provides through enhanced labour mobility, the opportunity to achieve greater efficiency, than is possible under a unitary system.

In 1971, Buchanan, with Richard E. Wagner as co-author, renewed the debate with a paper providing a justification for fiscal equalization grants purely on efficiency grounds. Their analysis drew on the concept of public goods and fiscal surplus. Public goods like defence are publicly provided goods and services that are supplied jointly in equal amounts to all citizens and are indivisible. Fiscal surpluses are the value citizen's place on public goods over and above the taxes they are required to pay to obtain the benefits of the public goods. These benefits arise because citizens value public goods at their average and not at their marginal values, and thus exist even when the conditions for public goods efficiency have been met (that is, when marginal tax prices are equal to the marginal evaluations by citizens of the public goods provided).

The rationale that Buchanan and Wagner provided rested on a distinction between pure public goods and "congestible" public goods. They showed that, because rich states can provide higher fiscal surpluses than poor states – taxes paid are lower for given benefits – there is an incentive for migration to occur from the latter to the former. In the case of the "congestible" public goods like roads, and facilities that are fixed in size, the addition of each person who shares in the public goods will partly reduce the amounts available for those in the existing population. This does not happen in the case of pure public goods, where the amounts available to individual citizens are not affected by the size of the population. As the population of the receiving state increases, congestion in the use of the publicly provided goods eventually occurs, and fiscal surpluses, fall.

In making their decisions to migrate, citizens are not likely to take into account the effects of their decisions on others. As such, too many people will migrate to states costing less for the same level of public goods. This will result in a loss of efficiency for the economy as a whole. Since the rich states cannot exclude migrants, another mechanism is needed to eliminate the fiscal surplus differentials. Buchanan and Wagner suggested that equalization grants from rich states to poor states could be used for this purpose. This serves as a mechanism of compensating citizens in poor states for not migrating and thereby equalizing fiscal surpluses as between states.

In contrast with Buchanan's 1950 paper, the emphasis now was that, even conceptually, equalization transfers must be between governments and not between individuals, because the source of the excessive migration lies in the provision of public goods. The corrective measures must work through the goods and services that are commonly shared.

In a later contribution, Boadway and Flatters (1982a and 1982b) made a distinction between two concepts of horizontal fiscal equity among individuals, which they suggested required alternative approaches to fiscal equalization. The first or broad concept postulated the equal treatment of equals in the federation, as a whole, while the second or narrow concept calls for equal treatment of equals only within each state. The reason why this distinction is important lies in the recognition of property rights and hence in the issue as to what state revenues should be brought into the equalization process.

Under the broad view of equity, the goal would be to equalize the net fiscal benefits (Buchanan's net fiscal residuums) of persons with equal incomes in all states. The application of the narrow concept would allow differences in net fiscal benefits to remain to the extent that they reflected property rights of states or citizens, revenues from which would not be subject to equalization. To help decide on the appropriate concept, Boadway and Flatters made a further distinction between two kinds of state taxes: those imposed on residents such as personal income and consumption taxes; and those imposed on the sources of income and wealth, such as company income taxes, land taxes and mining revenues or other taxes on resource rents.

Boadway and Flatters conclude that the application of the narrow concept would neither be equitable in the broad sense nor efficient. If resource were distributed only to the residents of a state, the allocation of labour and other factors would be inefficient across states, because the movement of factors would take place so as to equalize their average products (including their differential fiscal benefits) whereas efficiency would require the equalization of their marginal products (in the case of labour, wage rates). Wages would thus be lower in states with high resource rents.

They arrived at three main conclusions, namely:

1. In the absence of equalization, migration decisions by individuals are unlikely to lead to an efficient allocation of labour across states;
2. State governments, acting on behalf of their citizens, are likely to take budgetary actions that lead to inefficiencies and inequities in the federation as a whole; and
3. Faced with the inefficiencies and inequities resulting from individual and state behaviour, the central government is justified in using fiscal equalization to achieve nationwide equity and efficiency.

15.4 Alternative Approaches to Equalization: Musgrave

Musgrave (1961) undertook the pioneering work on theoretical models of fiscal equalization as an approach to a more general theory of political federalism. Musgrave was concerned with the distributional and state revenue effects of different kinds of equalization grants from federal to state governments. He distinguished between three approaches to fiscal equalization, described as (i) equalization of outlays or performance; (ii) equalization of differentials in need and capacity; and (iii) equalization of potentials for state finance.

Musgrave contended that intervention of the centre in the finances of the states, through fiscal transfers or otherwise can relate to two distinguishable sets of objectives: one, addressed to states, i.e. **groups** of individuals comprising the states; and two, individual citizens of the federations, whatever state they may be residing in. According to Musgrave (1961), the former approach is more federalist, and the latter, more centrist. In the former case, the individual citizen is subject to the policies of the state in which he is living, but the central government through its intervention may influence the terms at which public services are provided at the state level. In the second case, the central fisc may try to "equalise differentials in the position of federal citizens which arise from their respective citizenships in particular states. Thereby the central fisc attempts to isolate federal citizens from the fiscal consequences of their respective state citizenships".

Musgrave outlined several equalization plans with alternative objectives in the context of the first alternative, i.e. taking the states (groups of individuals) as a whole, rather than its citizens as individuals. In particular, he sets out alternative "equalization plans" aimed respectively at (i) equalization of actual outlay (or performance) (two variants); (ii) equalization of **differentials** in need and capacity; and (iii) equalization of potentials for state finance. As against pure equalization plans, he also considers "pure incentive plans". In all, he puts forward seven plans. Additional plans can be generated as composite plans targeted both at equalization and incentives. In developing these plans, various assumptions have been made. For example, possibilities of tax exporting, and spillover effects of expenditures have been ruled out. Borrowing as well as non-tax revenues through user charges for publicly provided services have also been assumed out. Relaxing these assumptions gives rise to additional equalization plans.

15.5 Fiscal Transfers in the Presence of Externalities

Externalities could be of two types: vertical fiscal externalities and horizontal fiscal externalities. They may arise from the side of taxation as well as expenditures. Horizontal externalities refer to jurisdictions at the same level of government. Here, the tax or expenditure decisions of one state government will affect the citizens of other states. In the case of vertical fiscal externality, it is the policy of the centre which will influence the states, or that of the states which will influence the centre. Externalities are direct when either tax bases overlap (fully or partially) and/or expenditure responsibilities are shared for the same function either fully or partially.

In several recent contributions, the implications of externalities in a federal system have been examined extensively. For example, Boadway and Flatters (1982) show that the existence of fiscal externality associated with the free mobility of individuals leads to an inefficient allocation of population among regions. They further show that equalization grants can be used to internalize this fiscal externality. Myers (1990) has argued that migration efficiency can be achieved through voluntary inter-regional transfers when local authorities can use such an instrument. In such a case, federal grants are not necessary.

In a simple, partial equilibrium framework, Dahlby (1994) shows that if a local government does not take into account the effect of its tax policy on the central government's tax revenue, the marginal cost of public fund (MCPF) is underestimated, which may lead to an excessive supply of local public goods. In Dahlby and Wilson (1994), this argument has been extended to a general equilibrium framework. Here, they have established that under conditions of the second best optimum, it is required that social MCPF's be equalized not only among tax bases in each local jurisdiction but also among regions. The explicit form of equalisation grants for achieving this objective has also been specified. The consequence of underestimation of MCPF by the local authorities is that they may raise local tax rates beyond the second best levels. In Dahlby (1996), it is recommended that matching grants could be used to internalize this tax externality.

Boadway and Keen (1996) raise the question as to what is the optimum level of fiscal gap between local and central governments. The kind of economy that they examined consists of homogenous regions in which a labour income tax is co-occupied by local and central governments and households are mobile. They conclude that the existence of the tax externality may make the optimal fiscal gap negative. In Sato (2000) some of these assumptions have been relaxed. Sato examines the second best policy at the federal level in the presence of both heterogeneous regions and imperfect individual mobility. He argues that in the presence either of perfect or imperfect mobility of households, the heterogeneity of the regions gives rise to different characteristics of the second best outcome. In partial modification to Dahlby and Wilson (1994), the second best does not generally require the equalization of the MCPF's between regions. He argues that a matching grant scheme as the function of the local tax rate or tax revenue needs to be employed to internalize the tax externalities which arise due to the misperception of the social MCPF's by the sub-national governments. The second best provision of the national public good and allocation of the population also require a lump sum transfer to equate the shadow prices of raising public funds among the governments. It is also shown that the optimal fiscal gap is indeterminate. This arises from the contention that federal tax policy is redundant as an instrument for the purpose of achieving the second best.

While several contributions have referred to tax and expenditure externalities, not many of them have treated them together. In Wrede (2000), an attempt is make to consider tax and expenditure externalities together under certain assumptions. On the tax side, a perfect tax base overlap is assumed. On the expenditure side, the case of shared expenditure is taken where the public goods provided by the two levels of government are perfect substitutes. It has been shown that the equilibrium is characterized by over-taxation and either under provision or overprovision of public goods depending on the degree of complementarity between public goods and tax base. He has argued that the recommendation by Brennan and Buchanan (1976) that public goods should be bound to tax bases which are highly complementary with them, might be misleading in a federal nation with tax base overlaps and shared expenditures. Some of the policy implications of Wrede's analysis are that overlapping of tax sources and expenditures need to be restricted by constitutional provisions and that vertical co-operation between governments might be beneficial under certain circumstances.

15.6 Instruments of Equalization

The instruments of equalization available in a system comprise all instruments whereby redistribution can be affected between states. These means can be both explicit instruments and implicit mechanisms. The main explicit instruments for redistribution are revenue sharing, general purpose grants, specific purpose grants, conditional grants, and matching grants. The implicit means of redistribution may relate to central policies/rules, and centrally administered prices which may differentially affect tax rates/bases in the states. The local incidence of central expenditures, especially, central investment would also be a means by which redistribution can be affected.

The sharing of central tax revenues, individually or globally, can be a potent means of redistribution among states. The extent of redistribution that can be affected through this means depends on the vertical shares of the centre and the states, and the horizontal shares pertaining to individual states. The horizontal shares will bring about redistribution depending on the weights attached to such criteria as can give higher shares to low revenue capacity states, and the total amount (vertical share) that is redistributed among states.

Grants, as an instrument of fiscal transfers, provide a range of options. First of all, grants may be conditional or unconditional. The justification of conditional grant is premised on the judgment that local decision making will fail to produce the socially optimum outcome, especially in the presence of inter-jurisdictional spillovers or externalities. Within the category of conditional grants, we may have matching grants where the sub-national governance may be required to contribute matching funds. The matching grants can be open ended or subject to caps. An open ended matching grant will encourage the local governments to internalize identified spillovers and provide the required level of services.

Unconditional grants are general purpose grants meant to augment the revenues of the low revenue capacity states without attaching any strings that may affect the preference pattern of spending in the concerned state. General purpose grants serve the same purpose as revenue sharing except that general purpose grants are specified in nominal terms, while in the case of revenue sharing, the amounts that actually flow to the states automatically respond to changes in the actual realizations of the central taxes.

Although approaches to fiscal capacity equalization differ in many respects among different countries that have attempted it, at first, a distinction may be made between revenue-side equalization, and two-sided equalization, i.e., equalization that looks at both the revenue capacities and expenditure needs. In the case of revenue-side equalization, the idea is that if revenue capacities are equalized for all the states, no further equalization is needed and the states may be left free to allocate their resources among various heads according to their own preferences. In the Canadian case, which may serve as an example of revenue capacity equalization, a representative tax system is utilized with a **Median standard**. The median standard refers to the average revenue capacity of the five median provinces. The richest province is left out of the equalization process and equalization is attempted for the seven provinces, which are assessed to be below standard capacity with reference to a detailed list of revenue sources comprising as many as 33 provincial and municipal revenue sources. The equalization entitlements are based on data on revenues and corresponding revenue bases. Attempts are now being made in Canada also to bring into the equalization programme, considerations of expenditure side equalization.

In Australia, fiscal capacity equalization has provided for equalizing revenues while taking into account specific cost disabilities so that provision of standard level of services can be ensured for all the states. Since cost disabilities differ across services, in practice different expenditure heads have to be considered in a disaggregated manner so that individual factors accounting for the cost differentials may be identified and their contribution to the cost may be quantified. In Australia, this approach has been referred to as the `Factor Assessment Method' for assessing expenditure needs. The determination of grants is based on both capacity equalization method and factor assessment method. As such, this process may be referred to as two-sided equalization.

In practice, it has been the Australian transfer system that has endeavoured to impart fiscal capacity equalization – taking into account not only resource differentials but also cost differentials. In a frequently quoted paper, which reviewed fiscal arrangements in Australia, for the Brookings Institution, Edward M. Gramlich (1985) argued that there is necessarily a conflict between fiscal equalization and efficiency. He argued that the Australian goal of equalizing tax prices of public services among the states, that is of allowing for differences in costs of providing services as well as differences in revenue capacity, removes any disincentives for citizens to move from high-cost to low-cost areas and therefore raises the overall cost of service provision. He concluded that no allowance should be made for these kinds of expenditure disabilities under fiscal equalization arrangements.

Mathews (1985) questioned Gramlich's argument that equalization for cost differences does in fact discourage migration from high-cost to low-cost areas, since the argument implicitly assumed that there are no valid and compelling economic and social reasons why people choose to live in high-cost areas. Mathews argued: "...the fiscal incentives for people to migrate from one jurisdiction to another have been very much exaggerated in the economic literature, and locational choice is usually influenced by private production and consumption activities (such as employment opportunities and housing) to a greater extent than by the fiscal and other activities of governments." (Mathews 1985, p. 24)

15.7 Representing an Equalization System

Both the Canadian and the Australian equalization systems can be described by the following general system.

$g_i = \theta\ [y_s - y_i] + e_s \,.\, c_i$

Here, all variables are in per capita terms. Therefore, total grant can be obtained by multiplying the per capita grant by the size of the population of the state. Thus

$G_i = N_i \,.\, g_i$

Subscript i refer ith state, and subscript s refers to the standard state. Other variables are defined as follows:

g = equalization grant,

y = revenue base

e = expenditure

[θ] = standard revenue effort (revenue per unit of revenue base)

c_i = differential cost of providing standard services in state i relative to the standard per capita cost.

If only revenue side equalization is attempted, the second term on the right hand side is implicitly set at zero. If, however, a two-sided equalization is attempted, the second term will have to be specified. The cost disability parameter (c_i) will be a function of economies of scale, dispersion or concentration of population, share of rural population, nature of terrain, climate and other special features of the population that is to be serviced. These factors may be different for different services and the disability factors may have to be calculated service by service.

In many federations, horizontal transfers from the above standard states to below standard states are not feasible, and the degree of equalization that can be achieved depends on the extent to which vertical transfers can be used to achieve equalization. This requires using the vertical transfers as not only the means for reducing the vertical imbalance, but also for achieving horizontal equity.

15.8 Constraints on Achieving Full Equalization

In practice, achieving full equalization of fiscal capacity among the states may become very difficult for one or more of the following reasons:

1. horizontal transfers are not possible between states because of constitutional or practical considerations;
2. the amounts of vertical transfers required are too large for the central government to afford; and

3. The degree of progressivity (with respect to revenue base) required for full equalization is extremely high.

These problems arise in cases where the differences in the revenue bases are large and growing, thereby requiring larger and larger amounts of equalization transfers. It is important, therefore, to also look at the determinants of differential growth in the revenue bases.

15.9 Equalizing Revenue Bases vs. Equalizing Revenue Capacities

If per capita revenue bases of all states are equal, and standard revenue effort is applied to estimate revenue capacities, all states will emerge with the standard or average revenue capacity and no equalization grant will be required, as far as revenue side equalization is concerned. At best, grants may be required to accommodate cost differentials. However, these amounts are likely to be small in per capita terms.

A dynamic perspective to the issue of equalization can be given by considering that the differences in the revenue bases between states are themselves the result of the standard of services provided by the states in the absence of full equalization. When, in the below - average states, services are provided at below average standards for long periods of time, differences in social and economic infrastructure may become so acute as to cause increasing disparities in the revenue bases, thereby calling for larger and larger per capita equalization transfers which happen to be constrained for the reasons listed above. This process gives rise to a vicious circle of causation such that equalization is not achieved and the extent of horizontal inequality left in the system continuously increases, being driven by a self-contained dynamics.

15.10 Reversing the Dynamics of Increasing Horizontal Inequities

In order to achieve a system of fiscal transfers for full two-sided equalization, one has to look at the determinants of differentials in revenue bases among the states, and introduce such policy intervention as can reduce these differentials. Important determinants of differentials in revenue bases may be listed as follows:

1. allocation of central government expenditure, particularly central investment between states;
2. level of services provided by different states as financed by the equalization transfers; and
3. Re-orientation of central policies so as to attract more private investment in the below average states.

Here, below average states may have to be provided per capita transfers even higher than what would be due in a static equalization exercise, so as to reduce disadvantages for initial levels of services.

Once the process of growing differentials in resource bases is reversed, a situation will arise where the residual differences in revenue bases will be due only to natural disadvantages or other structural causes. The amount of equalization transfers may also be within manageable limits.

15.11 The Vertical Dimension

Determining the aggregate share of states in the central taxes requires a comprehensive view of (i) the expenditure needs of the centre; (ii) the aggregate resources of the centre; (iii) the aggregate requirements of the states; and (iv) the resources of states from own sources. In the context of vertical devolution, the share of states and consequently that of the centre is supposed to be determined in a manner that provides both sides with adequate resources subject to the overall resource constraint. Furthermore, in the vertical share, there needs to be adequate predictability and stability. Stability in the vertical ratio would enable both the centre and the states to plan their expenditures in a longer-term perspective. The actual amount available to the states would increase automatically if the shareable central taxes increase, and decrease if the shareable central taxes decrease.

The vertical distribution in India requires an overall view of all the current resources of the centre. Since the transfers take place through three channels, *viz.*, Finance Commission, Planning Commission, and directly from the central government itself, these need to be put together in order to see the extent of vertical transfers. In Table 15.1, the aggregate transfer to the states through alternative channels has been indicated as percentage of the gross revenue receipts of the centre. Total transfers to states as percentage of centre's gross revenue receipts show considerable volatility – the range of variation extending from a minimum of 23.63 per cent to a maximum of 44.06 per cent. Transfers affected through sharing of taxes show a steady rise up to the annual plan following the Fifth Plan, after which it appears to stabilize at a level a little above 21 per cent of centre's gross revenue receipts.

Between the alternative modes of transfers, *viz.*, tax devolution and grants, the states show a preference for the former – as it represents constitutionally guaranteed transfers in which usually no conditionalities would be attached. In the case of grants, a distinction can be made between different types, *viz.*, statutory grants which are recommended by the FC, plan grants, and discretionary grants which are given directly by the centre. The EFC, with a view to imparting greater stability and predictability to central transfers to states, has set out an "indicative" limit of 37.5 per cent of centre's revenue resources for transfer to states through all modes of transfer.

Table 15.1: Central Transfers in India Relative to Centre's Gross Revenue Receipts and GDP

Year	Total transfers as % of			Year	Total transfers as % of		
	Centre's gross revenue receipts	GDP at market prices	CGRR as % of GDP mp		Centre's gross revenue receipts	GDP at market prices	CGRR as % of GDP Mp
1970-71	33.37	2.99	8.97	1986-87	37.96	5.21	13.73
1971-72	36.91	3.75	10.16	1987-88	39.18	5.31	13.55
1972-73	35.68	3.73	10.46	1988-89	37.23	4.92	13.22
1973-74	34.03	3.24	9.52	1989-90	32.66	4.51	13.82
1974-75	29.35	2.95	10.04	1990-91	38.97	4.89	12.56
1975-76	29.85	3.47	11.62	1991-92	38.62	5.05	13.08
1976-77	31.76	3.69	11.62	1992-93	39.62	5.14	12.97
1977-78	32.43	3.70	11.41	1993-94	42.84	5.03	11.74
1978-79	34.80	4.17	11.98	1994-95	37.86	4.46	11.77
1979-80	39.45	4.81	12.20	1995-96	35.55	4.28	12.04
1980-81	39.64	4.58	11.56	1996-97	35.40	4.28	12.10
1981-82	35.92	4.23	11.77	1997-98	38.90	4.86	12.49
1982-83	36.40	4.39	12.07	1998-99	32.25	3.73	11.57
1983-84	37.48	4.40	11.73	1999-00	30.23	3.79	12.52
1984-85	36.46	4.48	12.28	2000-01	34.93	4.26	12.19
1985-86	39.67	5.24	13.20	2000-01	34.93	4.26	12.19

Source: (Basic data): *Indian Public Finance Statistics.*

15.12 The Horizontal Dimension

In reviewing the *inter se* distribution of the aggregate share of states in central tax revenues, the approach of the FCs can be reviewed in terms of three distinct phases. Up to the Seventh Finance Commission, the distribution formulae used for determining the income tax shares were clearly distinct from those for the Union excise duties. This may be considered as Phase I. Since then, a process of convergence between the two sets of formulae began. But a full convergence has been arrived at only with the recommendations of the EFC, after a major amendment to the Constitution. The period from the Eighth to the Tenth Finance Commission may be considered as Phase II. In the case of TFC, 7.5 percent of the net proceeds of Union excise duties were kept outside of the general formula, for distribution according to assessed deficits. With the award of the EFC, a new phase has been started which is distinct from Phase II, in several important ways.

15.13 Phase I: Separate Criteria for Income Tax and Union Tax Duties

Population and collection/assessment were the only two criteria used for determining the *inter se* shares of the states in the case of income tax up to the Seventh Finance Commission. In respect of the Union excise duties, the criteria, as they evolved over time, had placed greater and greater emphasis on factors relating to economic backwardness and fiscal weakness of the states. However, population continued to be the largest determining factor up to the Sixth Commission, although its weight went down from 100 to 75 percent. The Seventh Commission further reduced this weight to 25 percent (a fall of 50 percentage points from the preceding Commission).

The changes in the relative weights to factors, as brought about by different Commissions, have been summarized in Tables 15.2 and 15.3. In respect of the Union excise duties, the importance of population went down with successive Finance Commissions while that of factors reflecting poor resource bases continued to increase.

Table 15.2: *Inter-Se* Sharing of Income Tax: Phase I

Finance Commission	Percentage Weight Assigned to	
	Population	Collection
1, 3, 4	80	20
2	90	10
	Population	Assessment
5, 6, 7	90	10

Source: Reports of successive Finance Commissions, Government of India.

15.14 Phase II: Towards Convergence: Eighth to Tenth Finance Commissions

Beginning with the Eighth Finance Commission, two changes occurred. First, there was a move towards unifying the formulae for the *inter se* distribution of both income tax and Union excise duties and, secondly, a portion of the Union excise duties was kept aside for distribution according to `assessed deficits'. The unified formulae used by the Eighth, Ninth and Tenth Commissions are given in Table 15.4.

Table 15.3: *Inter-Se* Sharing of Union Excise Duties: Phase I

Finance Commission	Relative Weights (%)		
	Population	Other Factors		
1	100	Discretionary Adjustments		
2	90	10		
3	Major Factor (Weight) Unspecified)	Financial Weakness and Economic Backwardness Weight Unspecified		
4	80	Social and Economic Backwardness 20		
5	80+16.66*	Index of Backwardness 3.33		
6	75	Distance 25		
7	25	Inverse-Income 25	Poverty Ratio 25	Revenue Equalization 25

*Among states with per capita income below the all states average.
Source: Reports of successive Finance Commissions, Government of India..

Table 15.4: *Inter-Se* Sharing of Union Taxes*: Phase II: Eighth, Ninth and Tenth Finance Commissions

Finance Commission	Criteria				
	Population	Distance	Inverse Income	Poverty Ratio	Index of Backwardness
8	25	50	25		
9(1)	25	50	12.5	12.5	
9(2)	25	50	12.5		12.5
	29.94	40.12	14.97		14.97
10	20	60	Area 5	Index of Infrastructure 5	Tax Effort 10

Note: * In the case of income tax, 90 percent of shareable proceeds were distributed according to criteria given in the table and the remaining 10 *were* to be distributed according to contribution. Similarly, the balance of the shareable amount in the case of Union excise duties was to be distributed according to assessed deficits.
Source: *Reports of Successive Finance Commissions,* Government of India.

The sharing of portions that were kept out of the unified formula was done as follows. In the case of income tax, ten percent of the share recommended for the states was to be shared on the basis of assessment of income tax as in the case of the Eighth and Ninth Commissions. In the case of Union excise duties, a portion of the shareable proceeds for devolution was kept apart for distribution among states on the basis of assessed deficits. The share kept aside for this purpose also gradually increased. It was five percent of the shareable proceeds of Union excise duties in the case of Eighth and the first report of the Ninth Commission. It was raised to 7.425 per cent in the case of the second report of the Ninth Commission and subsequently to 7.5 per cent by the Tenth Commission.

15.15 Phase III: Full Convergence: Eleventh Finance Commission

With the eightieth amendment to the Constitution, all shareable central taxes have to be treated at par, and full convergence of distributive criteria has emerged with the recommendations of the EFC. Apart from the two main taxes, *viz.*, income tax and the Union excise duties, two other arrangements for transfers were in vogue, *viz.* grant in lieu of tax on railway passenger fares and additional excise duties in lieu of sales tax on specified commodities (cotton textiles, tobacco and sugar). Both of these arrangements were tax rental arrangements in the sense that the original power to levy the tax was vested with the state governments but were transferred to the centre for the sake of uniformity across states among other reasons. With the amendment to the Constitution, the separate identity of these arrangements has been abolished. As a follow up, the power to levy sales tax on the selected commodities may be restored back to the states. However, as far as the *inter-se* shares are concerned now, with the EFC, only one set of shares prevail replacing four distinct sets in the case of TFC, relating respectively to (i) portions of income tax and Union excise duties subjected to common criteria; (ii) portion for devolution according to assessed deficits; (iii) grant in lieu of tax on railway passenger fares; and (iv) additional excise duties in lieu of sales tax on cotton textiles, tobacco and sugar. The criteria followed by the EFC for this generalized sharing reflect three considerations: (i) equity; (ii) incentives for efficiency; and (iii) cost disadvantages.

Two core criteria, which have been used by the previous FCs for providing higher per capita devolution to lower per capita income states, are distance and inverse-income formulae. In the case of the Eighth Finance Commission, the combined weight given to these two criteria was 75 percent. In the case of the Ninth Finance Commission, the combined weight was 62.5 percent for income tax and somewhat lower for the Union excise duties. The TFC had decided to use only one out of the two formulae, namely, the distance formula and gave it a weight of 60 per cent. However, the EFC has restored the weight to this criterion back to 62.5 per cent.

While computing distance-based shares of states, the EFC has introduced some changes. The practice followed by the Ninth and Tenth Finance Commissions was that of measuring the distance of the per capita income of a state from that of the highest per capita income. But for this purpose, Goa, being a very small state, was not considered a representative state, and distances were measured from the per capita income of Maharashtra. Maharashtra and Goa were exogenously given the same distance as for Punjab. As a result, three states, *viz.*, Punjab, Maharashtra, and Goa obtained the same distances, and consequently the same per capita shares. Instead of taking a single high income state as the `representative' highest income state, the EFC has taken the three-state average of Punjab, Maharashtra and Goa as the benchmark from which distances are measured. This is the weighted average of the per capita GSDPs of these states. The distances of these three states are then worked out as a fraction of the distance of Haryana from the representative benchmark. These fractions are obtained by taking the ratio of Haryana's per capita GSDP to the per capita GSDP of these states. The three-state average is taken as more `representative'; and their own per capita shares continue to fall as incomes increase, as a result of these changes.

The EFC has also endeavoured to evolve a suitable structure of incentives in the mechanism of fiscal transfer. The Tenth Finance Commission had utilized an index of tax effort made by the states. The EFC has utilized an index of tax effort and an index of fiscal discipline, and given these a combined weight of 12.5 percent. In the index of fiscal discipline, the improvement is measured by considering the ratio of the measure of fiscal discipline in a reference period in comparison to a base period. For the base period, the average for the three-year period from 1990-91 to 1992-93 was taken. For the reference period, the average of three years from 1996-97 to 1998-99 was taken. Higher own revenues or lower revenue expenditures or any combination of the two can bring about an improvement in fiscal self-reliance. Further, the state specific improvements are related to the corresponding all state improvement to neutralize factors that commonly affect all states. The comparison of the performance of a state with the all state performance reflects the consideration that if the revenue performance of states is deteriorating in general, the state that accomplishes a relatively lower deterioration is rewarded. Similarly, if all revenue balance profiles are improving, the state where improvement is relatively more than average is rewarded relatively more. The *inter-se* shares of the states in tax devolution as recommended by EFC and TFC utilize the following criteria and relative weights as given in Table 15.5.

Table 15.5: Criteria and Relative Weights for Determining *Inter-Se* Shares of States: Tenth, Eleventh, and Twelfth Finance Commissions

Criterion	Relative Weight (Percent)		
	Tenth	Eleventh	Twelfth
1. Population	20.0	10.0	25.0
2. Distance	60.0	62.5	50.0
3. Area	5.0	7.5	10.0
4. Index of Infrastructure	5.0	7.5	0.0
5. Tax Effort	10.0	5.0	7.5
6. Fiscal Discipline	-	7.5	7.5

Cost variations are brought into consideration through the criteria based on area and index of infrastructure: larger the area (per crore population) higher the per capita cost; similarly, lower is the index of infrastructure higher is the per capita cost. Thus, the three main considerations in the selection of criteria used by the TFC and EFC relate to: (i) resource deficiency; (ii) higher cost of providing services; and (iii) fiscal discipline, although the relative weights differ.

15.16 Distributive Criteria: Basic Principles

In conventional devolution in India, the principle of derivation was considered as an important guiding principle. This principle implicitly views the assignment of taxes to the central government as if they were tax rental arrangements. Thus, in the exercise of *inter-se* distribution, there is an attempt to `return' to the states what they would have raised had the taxing power of the shareable tax remained with them. It is in the context of this principle that collection/assessment was given some weight in the sharing of income tax. This principle was not, however, applied to the distribution of Union excise duties, which was a matter of `permissive' or `discretionary' sharing. As indicated earlier, there has been a gradual attempt in the dispensation of the FCs in India, to move away from conventional devolution towards revenue-sharing which is guided by three main principles, *viz.*, (i) capacity equalization; (ii) efficiency promoting incentives; and (iii) allowance for cost disabilities.

The principle of horizontal equity is the guiding principle in the consideration that as a result of revenue sharing, the fiscal resource deficiencies across states arising out of systemic and identifiable factors, and under normative revenue effort, are evened out. Thus, the revenue-sharing exercise is supposed to provide to the states resources complementary to their own, so that they may all be enabled to provide an agreed common set of public services at comparable standards in terms of quality and quantity to all citizens living in the different states. Thus, a citizen of India, no matter which state he resides in, becomes entitled to and is provided with, the same level of services (state level public goods and merit goods of high priority) throughout the country. This also calls for recognition of valid cost differentials in providing a service in different states. The principle of equity, however, is a compensatory principle as it makes up for resource deficiencies. As such, it also creates a vested interest in continuing with the resource deficiency, rather than making efforts to improve own revenue bases, thereby reducing the differences in revenue per unit of resource base across states. To neutralize this adverse incentive, it needs to be complemented by criteria that reward `efficiency', i.e. efforts to improve the resource bases and deliver services at minimum (efficient) costs.

In constructing a scheme of criteria-based devolution, certain basic features concerning the information base used for determining the respective shares may be considered desirable. Some of these features are listed below:

1. The information base for reflecting capacities/needs should be broad rather than narrow, so that fiscal performance can be properly estimated.
2. The data used should be comparable across states, and should have been compiled using common principles. That is why census data and income data on a comparable basis compiled by the Central Statistical Organization (CSO) have been used with much greater weight. In the case of tax effort, data provided by the Finance Accounts are preferable to budget data. However, reservations have been expressed by some state Governments (e.g., Tamil Nadu) on the reliability of the GSDP data from time to time.
3. Data should be as up-to-date as far as possible.

15.17 Core Revenue Sharing Criteria: Analytical Properties

A. Income-Based Formulae: Criteria Reflecting Fiscal Deficiency

The criteria that have received the highest weights in the dispensation exercises of recent FCs are the income-based criteria. Income, however, is proxied by per capita State Domestic Product (net or gross). In order to even out erratic changes, a three-year average is adopted. Two main criteria have been used in this context. One is based on the distance of per capita income of a state from the highest per capita income among all states. The other is based on the inverse of per capita income of a state [see, Srivastava and Aggarwal (1994) for a detailed analysis of the properties of these two criteria]. These criteria attempt to reduce post-transfer differences in the fiscal bases of the states through progressive dispensation. The difference between them is that while the distance criterion looks at the absolute resource gaps, the inverse income criterion looks at the relative gaps. Since, in the context of provision of services at equal standards across states, it is the absolute costs (and absolute gaps) that are relevant, successive FCs have (Eighth, Ninth and the Tenth) given more and more weight to the distance criterion. The inverse criterion was given a weight of 25 percent by the Seventh and Eighth Commissions. The Ninth Commission reduced this weight to 12.5 percent. The Tenth Commission dropped it altogether. In the case of Tenth, Eleventh and Twelfth Finance Commissions, the full weight of the income-based criterion was loaded on the distance criterion. Different Commissions have used the distance criterion with some variations. The term `distance' refers to the excess of the per capita income of a state (measured by per capita GSDP) of the highest per capita income among all states over that of an individual state. If per capita income (hereinafter referred to only as income), of the different states are indicated by y_i, and states are arranged in non-descending order of income, y_1 will refer to the per capita income of say, Bihar, and y_{25} will refer to the per capita income of Goa. In general,

$y_i \leq y_{i+1} \leq y_n$, $i = 1, 2, \ldots, (n-1)$

$n = 25$ (now, 28)

The distances can be defined as

$d_i = y_n - y_i$

The shares of states can be determined in the following alternative ways:

A1 Standard Distance Formula (SDF)

In this version, the share of the ith state can be written as:

$$\text{Share of State i} = \frac{\text{(Population X Distance) of State i}}{\text{Sum of (Population X Distance) for All States}}$$

In terms of symbols, this can be written as:

$s_i = N_i d_i / \Sigma N_i d_i$ $(i = 1, \ldots, 25)$

Since d_i for Goa will be zero ($d_i = y_n - y_n$), its share will be zero in this standard version. The per capita shares under the formula can be obtained by dividing s_i by N_i.

$$\text{Per Capita Share Under SDF} = \frac{\text{Distance of State i}}{\text{Sum of (Population X Distance) for All States}}$$

The SDF can be diagrammatically represented by a straight line falling to the right, where per capita share of a state is represented on the y-axis, and per capita incomes on the x-axis. States are arranged in ascending order of per capita income.

$s_i = N_i (y_n - y_i)/\Sigma N_i (y_n - y_i)$

or $s_i^* = \beta - \alpha y_i$

$s_i^* = \alpha y_n - \alpha y_i$

Suppose $\Sigma N_i (y_n - y_i) = 1/\alpha$

which is the equation of a straight line.

Then, $s_i = N_i [\alpha (y_n - y_i)]$

The distance formula provides higher per capita shares to lower income states. It attempts to bring in the principle of horizontal equity under the assumption of a normative (common) revenue effort. It can be interpreted as a fiscal capacity equalizing formula, where fiscal capacity (y_i) is measured by the (per capita) income (GSDP) of a state. If each state makes a revenue effort of the same degree (say, θ), its revenue capacity is given by θy_i. The revenue capacity of the highest income state is θy_n. The difference between these revenue capacities is $\theta(y_n - y_i)$. This gap is filled up, in the distance formula, as a result of which, the post-devolution fiscal capacities are equalized. However, the limiting assumption is that fiscal capacity is reflected in per capita income.

A2 Modified Distance Formula (MDF)

The standard version of the distance formula was modified by some of the FCs with two considerations in mind. First, in the SDF, the highest income state does not get any share, and secondly, a state other than Goa should be chosen as the highest income state for purposes of measuring distances. Goa has a small population and high income, and the Commissions have opined that this is not "representative" of a typical high income state. These two considerations were brought into the formula by measuring distances from Punjab rather than Goa, giving "notional distances to both Punjab and Goa equal to the distance between Punjab and Maharashtra". Thus three states get the same distance in the formula, *viz.*, Punjab, Maharashtra and Goa. The modified distance formula (MDF) provides shares according to the following dispensation:

$$s_i = \frac{N_i d_i^*}{\Sigma N_i d_i^*}$$

where $d_i^* = y_{24} - y_i \quad (i = 1, 2, 23)$

and $d_i^* = y_{24} - y_{23} \quad (i = 24, 25)$

In these formulae, the total number of states is taken to be n = 25 as an illustration. Corresponding formulae can be written when n = 28, which is the present situation in India. Dividing the shares can derive the per capita shares under MDF by the respective populations. The modified formula implies a "kink" in the dispensation line because the per capita shares of the three states at the higher income end become equal. It also implies a higher per capita income share for a few states at the low income end, as compared to the SDF.

The EFC has further modified this formula. Rather than measuring the distances from the per capita income of any single state, it has defined the benchmark income from which distances are to be measured as the weighted average of the per capita GSDPs of the three highest income states, *viz.*, Goa, Maharashtra and Punjab. Once the benchmark income is available (say, y^*), the distances of each state outside the highest income group are calculated as,

$d_i = y^* - y_i \qquad i - 1, \ldots, 22$

The distances of the three highest income states are fractions of the distance of the state with highest per capita GSDP after the top three states, calculated in the following way

$d_i = d_{22} \cdot (y_{22}/y_i) \qquad i = 23, \ldots, 25$

The shares of individual states are then given by

$s_i = N_i\, d_i / \Sigma N_i\, d_i \qquad i = 1, \ldots, 25$

A3 Augmented Distance Formula (ADF)

The consideration of giving a positive share to the highest income state can also be taken care of by measuring distances from a level higher than the y_n, the highest per capita income. Let this point of reference be $y_n + z$ where z is a positive amount. In this case, the `augmented' distances can be written as

$d_i = (y_n + z - y_i)$

and shares are given by

$$s_i = \frac{N_i\, d_i}{\Sigma N_i\, d_i} \qquad i = 1, 2, \ldots, 25$$

However, the ADF requires determination of the value of z. The EFC has used this criterion while determining shares of states in the context of grants for local bodies. The value of z has been taken as half the standard deviation of the per capita GSDP of states.

B. Inverse Income Formula (IIF)

The inverse income formula looks at `relative' fiscal deficiencies. If the revenue capacity on a common revenue effort is θy_n, relative to it, the revenue capacity of a state i, is θy_i, and the relative deficiency is given by $\theta y_n/\theta_i$ (= y_n/y_i). The share of a state under this formula is given by

$$\text{Share of State i} = \frac{\text{(Popopulation X Inverse of Income) of State i}}{\text{Sum of (Population X Inverse of Income) of All States}}$$

Correspondingly, per capita share is given by:

$$\text{Per Capita Share of State i} = \frac{\text{Inverse of Income of State i}}{\text{Sum of (Population X Inverse of Income) of All States}}$$

The inverse income formula can be represented in a diagram by a rectangular hyperbola where per capita share is represented on the y-axis and per capita incomes on the axis. This is indicated below.

$s_i = (N_i/y_i)/\Sigma(N_i/y_i)$ $\quad i = 1, \ldots, n$

Let $\Sigma(N_i/y_i) = 1/\beta$

Then, per capita shares can be written as

Under the inverse formula the per capita shares would be

$(s_i^* = s_i / N_i)$

$s_i^* = \beta / y_i$

or $\quad s_i^* y_i = \beta$

C. Population Formula: Criterion Providing Equal Per Capita Transfers

The population criterion provides equal per capita transfers to all states. A scheme of equal per capita transfers is a valid scheme if there are no resource and cost-differentials across states. It can be shown that the (standard) distance criterion will converge to the population criterion, as the per capita incomes of the states become more and more equal. Since the population criterion provides equal per capita transfers, it is indifferent (or neutral) to differences in the fiscal capacities of states. It is, therefore, useful as a benchmark for considering the departures from this neutrality in other criteria. For this reason, dispensation under the population criterion is often used for purposes of comparison.

As already indicated, the population formula gives equal per capita shares to all states, whatever may be their per capita income or fiscal capacity. Distribution according to population means that the share of a state in tax devolution would be equal to the share of the population of this state in the total population of all states.

Indicating population of a state i by N_i, where i varies from 1 to n where n is the number of states, the shares of individual states (s_i) in the population formula can be written as

$s_i = N_i/\Sigma N_i$.

Correspondingly, per capita shares are given by

$$s_i^* = \frac{1}{\Sigma N_i} = \text{Constant}$$

D. Criteria Reflecting Cost Disadvantages

Indices relating to area and infrastructure reflect cost disadvantages to state governments in providing services to its citizens. The larger the area of a state, the higher is the per capita cost of providing services. Similarly, the weaker the infrastructure of a state, the larger is the costs of providing services. This index is used to indicate relative deficiency in infrastructure. A state, which is, relatively more deficient in infrastructure is given a higher share in per capita terms. The deficiency in infrastructure indicates (i) extra costs in providing governmental services, and (ii) extra resource requirement to improve infrastructure and delivery systems. In the measurement of infrastructure, social infrastructure (e.g. health and education) expenditure has a large revenue component.

An index of infrastructure was especially constructed for the TFC by a commissioned study carried out by a team of experts (Anant, T.C.A. and K.L. Krishna). A similar study has now updated this index for the EFC and later for the TFC. In these studies, the aggregate infrastructure index (AII) is a weighted combination of economic and social infrastructure indices. In turn, economic infrastructure index (EII) and social infrastructure index (SII) are weighted combinations of a number of sub-indices. For EII, the main sectors are agriculture, communication, banking, electricity and transportation including roads. For SII, the main sectors are health and education. The sectoral indices are in turn constructed by weighted combinations of the sub-indices. Given the series of infrastructure index (I_i), the shares of states may be worked out from

$$s_i = \frac{N_i(I_h - I_i)}{\Sigma N_i(I_h - I_i)}$$

where I_h is the highest reading of index among the states, and I_i is the index value for state i. The EFC has used the weighted average of I_i's for the three highest index states and used the indices for deriving shares of individual states in a manner similar to one used for the distance formula. The TFC has not used the infrastructure in the allocation criteria.

E. Criteria for Performance/Incentives

The criterion of tax effort used by the TFC as well as EFC endeavours to reward, in a limited way, revenue performance of the states. It is intended to serve as an incentive for improving tax effort. In this scheme, a state, which shows higher tax revenue per unit of tax-base, gets a higher share in tax devolution. The basic conceptual issue is that of measurement of tax effort. Tax effort needs to be measured by relating tax revenues to tax potential. Measurement of tax potential (taxable capacity) usually requires an elaborate econometric exercise. Since many of the determinants of taxable capacity are not directly observable or adequate data regarding which are not readily available, often dummy variables and proxy measures are necessitated in such an exercise. As already noted, in criteria-based revenue sharing, criteria should be based on information compiled on a comparable basis. The approach of TFC and EFC was to let the tax base of states be proxied by GSDP. Using the ratio of per capita tax revenue (r) to per capita GSDP (y), as reflecting tax effort, the share of a state was defined as:

$$s_i = N_i \; w_i \; (r_i / y_i)/[\Sigma N_i w_i (\tfrac{r_i}{y_i})] \quad i = 1, \ldots, n$$

The weight w_i was set equal to $1/y_i$ by the Tenth Finance Commission, and $1/\sqrt{y_i}$ by EFC and TFC. Substituting these weights, the two formulae can be written as

$$s_i = [N_i \; r_i / y_i^2]/\Sigma(N_i \; r_i / y_i^2) \qquad (\text{TFC})$$

$$s_i = [N_i \; r_i / y_i^{1.5}]/\Sigma(N_i \; r_i / y_i^{1.5}) \qquad (\text{EFC})$$

The weights were set as related to inverse of income, arguing that if two states show the same tax-effort, the poorer state among the two, is the more constrained, and should get a relatively higher share. Factors which constitute genuine constraints in the exploitation of the tax-base can in general be used to set these weights. Such constraints could be below average level of development and distribution of income, which may favour consumption of a basket of necessities that bear low rates of taxes. In general, the weighting scheme can be a function of income and parameters reflecting distribution of income.

F. Criterion Related to Improvement in Fiscal Performance

The criterion on tax effort looks only at the tax revenues. However, in order to bring expenditures into analysis the EFC has constructed an index of fiscal discipline for use within the devolution formula. The index of improvement in fiscal performance was defined with reference to achieving improvement in revenue balance. The ratio of revenue receipts to revenue expenditure may be called z_i for the state i in the reference year. In the base year, this may be referred to as z_i^o. The corresponding ratios for the all state average may be called as Z_a and Z_a^o. The index of improvement in fiscal performance is given by

$$I_i = [Z_i / Z_i^o]/Z_a / Z_a^o$$

The better is the performance of a state in achieving revenue balance relative to others, the higher is its share in devolution. The respective shares are determined by

$$s_i = N_i \, I_i / \Sigma N_i \, I_i$$

The TFC has a similar formula.

15.18 General Purpose Grants by Finance Commission

Apart from revenue sharing, the main alternative channel of fiscal transfer available to the Finance Commission is grants-in-aid of revenues of the states under Article 275 of the Constitution. These grants are general purpose unconditional grants. The determination of these grants follows from two exercises carried out by the Finance Commissions: One, assessment of expenditures of each state on the non-plan revenue account, and two, assessment of own revenues. Once tax devolution to each state has been determined, grants-in-aid are devolved as a residual which is the difference between the assessed expenditure and the sum of the projected own revenues, and the projected amounts arising from their individual shares in central taxes. In other words, grants-in-aid under the Finance Commission are meant to fill up a 'gap' which represents expenditure not covered either by own revenues or share in central taxes. The main issue here is as to whether this gap should be projected on the basis of historical trends or by an assessment of expenditures and revenues on a normative basis. It is clear that if historical basis is followed it will give rise to strong adverse incentives where it will be to the benefit of each state to maximize their histories of expenditures and minimize their histories of raising revenues. On the other hand, if the gap where to be determined strictly on a normative bases, such an adverse incentive will not be present.

Although this problem has been discussed in the literature on fiscal federalism for a long time, the various Finance Commissions, subject to certain exceptions or qualifications, have followed only the gap filling approach. The Ninth Commission had attempted a normative approach, and the Tenth and Eleventh Commissions have attempted what may be described as a quasi normative approach.

The principles for grants-in-aid to the revenues of the states have evolved over the course of last half a century through recommendations of the various Finance Commissions. What came to be accepted is that the grants-in-aid may be given to the states to cover the assessed deficit on non-pan revenue account, after devolution of taxes and duties. The deficits are worked out after excluding any unusual or non-recurrent item of revenue or expenditure with the objective that the expenditure and revenues of the states should be comparable so that no state is allowed to take advantage by overstating its expenditure or understating its revenues. Secondly, grants-in-aid are also recommended for the up-gradation of the standards of administration of the states by the Finance Commission. This is because plan grants usually focus only on social and economic services and up-gradation of general administration is left unattended.

The approach of the Eleventh Finance Commission may be described as quasi-normative where an attempt was made, but not fully, to bring in normative elements in the assessment both of expenditures and revenues. Since these assessments were for a five year period from 2000-01 to 2004-05, two sets of norms were required, one to normatively determine the base year figures for assessment, and two, growth norms which affect the values of the relevant values during the whole period of reference. As far as growth norms used by EFC are concerned, there were some elements, which commonly affected expenditures. The approach of the TFC is discussed in Chapter 17.

16

Fiscal Transfers and the Planning Commission

> But political realities being what they are, we can expect to continue our collective life with much the same map in place.
>
> W.E. Oates

In this chapter, we shall consider the second main channel of resource transfer in India, viz., the Planning Commission. The Planning Commission works with a package of 'assistance' which comprises both grants and loans. While discussing these, we shall consider broadly the sources of capital grants. It is, in some sense, the responsibility of Planning Commission to look after the developmental needs of the states. Their resource bases get affected in an important way by the dispensation of these developmental funds.

16.1 Planning Commission: Initial objectives

The Planning Commission in India was set up in 1950 by an administrative order of the Government of India. The Prime Minister is the Chairman of the Planning Commission, which works under the overall guidance of the National Development Council. The Deputy Chairman and the full time Members of the Commission, as a composite body, provide advice and guidance to the subject Divisions for the formulation of Five Year Plans, Annual Plans, State Plans, Monitoring Plan Programmes, Projects and Schemes. The Commission was set up in an era, when planning was at the centre of the mechanism for allocating resources across sectors and regions within a framework of a mixed economy. The 1950 resolution setting up the Planning Commission outlined its functions as to:

1. Make an assessment of the material, capital and human resources of the country, including technical personnel, and investigate the possibilities of augmenting such of these resources as are found to be deficient in relation to the nation's requirement;
2. Formulate a Plan for the most effective and balanced utilization of country's resources;
3. On a determination of priorities, define the stages in which the Plan should be carried out and propose the allocation of resources for the due completion of each stage;

4. Indicate the factors which are tending to retard economic development, and determine the conditions which, in view of the current social and political situation, should be established for the successful execution of the Plan;
5. Determine the nature of the machinery which will be necessary for securing the successful implementation of each stage of the Plan in all its aspects;
6. Appraise from time to time the progress achieved in the execution of each stage of the Plan and recommend the adjustments of policy and measures that such appraisal may show to be necessary; and
7. Make such interim or ancillary recommendations as appear to it to be appropriate either for facilitating the discharge of the duties assigned to it, or on a consideration of prevailing economic conditions, current policies, measures and development programmes or on an examination of such specific problems as may be referred to it for advice by Central or State Governments.

It is notable that the original mandate did not envisage any direct role for the Planning Commission in determining either loans or grants to the states. Over time, this became its central role. So far ten five year plans and several annual plans have been prepared. The Tenth Five Year plan is currently in operation, its period running from 2002-03 to 2006-07. One of the critical questions is the way in which the Planning Commission should adjust its approach and functioning in the context of economic reforms and the growing market orientation and globalization of the Indian economy.

16.2 Infrastructure and Balanced Development

There is no doubt that disparities in the level of development and growth rates have varied widely across the Indian states, and the Plan interventions have not made any difference to increasing disparities across states. There is evidence, on the other hand, that disparities in per capita incomes and the levels of publicly provided services have increased over time.

Fiscal capacities of states depend on their resource bases which, in turn, depend on the incomes and economic activities in the states. Apart from other determinants of income and production in the states, an important role is played by the investment in infrastructure that takes place in the states. Sources of investment in infrastructure in the states may be (i) direct central investment, i.e., locational distribution of centre's investment in infrastructure; (ii) investment by the concerned state governments including projects financed by external assistance; and (iii) investment by the private sector including foreign direct investment.

There is now an extensive literature, which analyses the relationship between infrastructure and economic growth. Several studies (e.g., Aschauer, 1989, and Aschauer and Munnell, 1990) highlight that infrastructure investments are highly productive. They assert that new infrastructure investments may be potentially more productive than increases in labour or private capital. Further, better infrastructure itself becomes a source for attracting private capital to the states from the rest of the country as also from outside.

Growing disparities across states in India, calls for augmenting infrastructure investment in the relatively less developed regions. Since there is considerable disparity across states in infrastructure both in its social and economic components, resulting in disparities in GSDP (and resource bases), a distribution of resources meant for infrastructure investment favouring the poorer states/ regions may be considered important. Alternative sources of such investment, *viz.* central investment, grants for investment activities (developmental expenditure) given to states, and inter-state distribution of external assistance, need to take this into account in so far as the pattern of regional investment can be affected by policy intervention or by putting in place appropriate allocation criteria. The Planning Commission should have played a role in the inter-regional allocation of central investment, as also other investment allocations through the state governments and the markets in a manner that would have helped not only higher growth but a better balance in inter-regional distribution of that growth.

16.3 Trends in Plan Size

The size of the plan, as measured by the plan outlay of the public sector, which includes not only the central and state governments but also non-departmental public sector enterprises may be indicated by the volume of outlay relative to GDP at current prices. The time profile of plan outlay in India is shown in Chart 16.1 and Appendix Table A16.1. It is evident that initially the plan size was modest at 2-3 per cent of GDP. It steadily increased to reach a peak of more than 14 per cent of GDP in 1986-87. Thereafter, it started to fall. By 2002-03, the level of plan outlay has fallen to a little above 10 per cent of GDP.

It is not entirely coincidental that the plan size reached a peak at about the same period when the tax-GDP ratio was the highest in the late eighties. After that both the tax-GDP ratio and the plan size fell. In spite of the high levels of fiscal deficits of the nineties, it has not been possible to increase the plan size relative to GDP because of the pre-emptive claims of increasing interest payments.

16.4 Plan Assistance: Combining of Grants and Loans

The Planning Commission oversees allocation of resources in the form of loans and grants meant for developmental expenditures of the states. The Planning Commission provides developmental grants to states as part of an overall assistance package. This package is determined as a composite of loans and grants. The relative ratios of loans and grants are different for the special category states as compared to the general category. For the general category states, assistance is 30 percent grant and 70 percent loan. For the special category states, 90 percent of assistance is given as grant and 10 percent as loan.

Chart 16.1: Plan Outlay as percentage of GDP at Market Prices

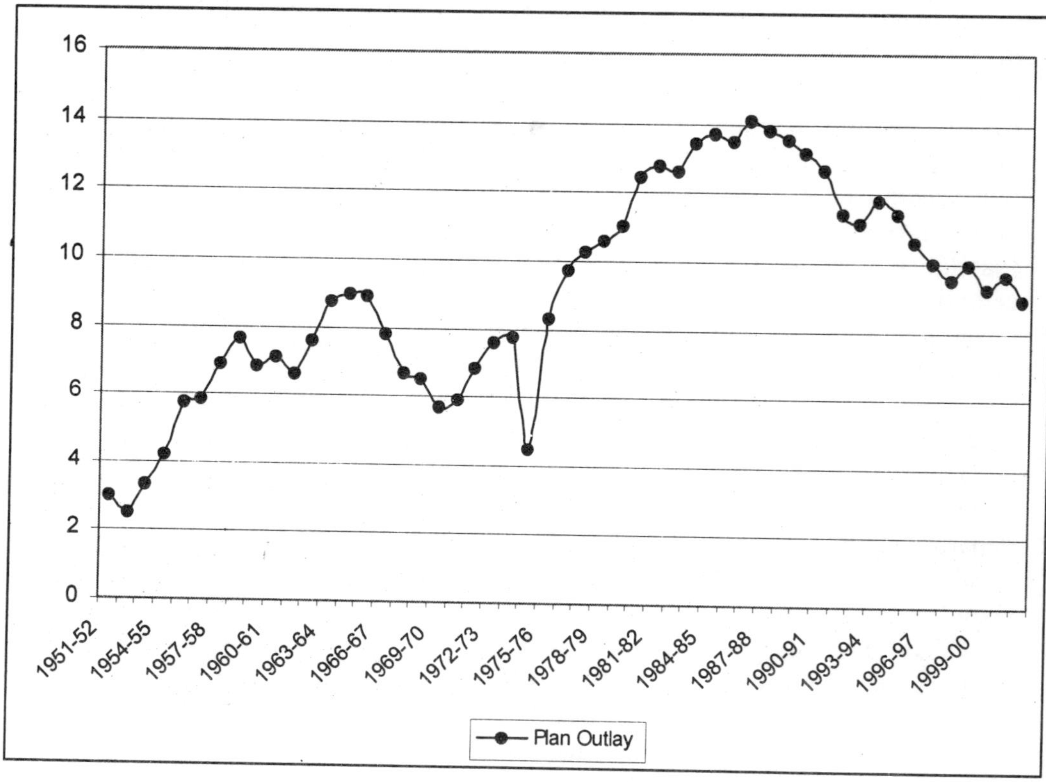

The expenditure side of the state budgets may be divided into four parts: non-plan revenue expenditure, plan revenue expenditure, plan capital expenditure, and non-plan capital expenditure. The first and second components combine to give the revenue account of a state, which pertains to recurrent (revenue) expenditures. Plan assistance is meant for the second and third components taken together. In the initial stages, when plan assistance was conceived of in terms of an overall package, the expectation was that nearly 30 percent of the plan would actually be in the nature of recurrent expenditures and 70 percent would pertain to capital expenditures. In accordance with such an expectation, the grant to loan ratio in plan assistance was fixed as 30 and 70 percent of total plan assistance. It was expected that all capital expenditures would be met by borrowing and by surpluses on revenue account. As such no capital grants were envisaged for the general category of states in plan assistance. Further, 30 per cent of the overall size of plan assistance was earmarked for the special category states.

The position of the special category states was different in the sense that from the 90 per cent that they were getting as grant, 30 per cent could be allocated for the revenue component of the plan, and the balance of 60 per cent could then emerge as a capital grant. In practice however the relative claim of recurrent expenditure continued to increase and has become on an average 70 per cent of plan outlay in the case of general category states. Borrowing thus began to be used progressively more for incurring revenue expenditure. The overall dispensation of (normal) plan assistance can be summarized according to special and non-special category states, and according to grants and loans as indicated in Table 16.1. Two other channels of plan assistance are additional central assistance (ACA) and external assistance. Both are given on the same terms and conditions as normal plan assistance.

Table 16.1: Dispensation of Plan Assistance: Normal State Plan (per cent)

States	Grants	Loans	Total
Special	27	3	30
General	21	49	70
Total	**48**	**52**	**100**

The planning Commission allocates aggregate (normal) plan assistance among states under a set of criteria called the Gadgil Formula. The original formula has been subjected to changes from time to time and the present version is referred to as the National Development Council (NDC) revised Gadgil Formula. The Gadgil Formula works in two stages. First, 30 percent of total assistance money is earmarked for the special category states. This is distributed among these states on the basis of their plan size and past plan expenditures, without using any explicit criteria. The remaining 70 percent are distributed among the general category states according to a set of criteria with relative weights. These criteria have been summarized in Table 16.2. A comparison can also be made between the alternative versions of the formula, as it has changed over time. The Planning Commission does not publish the actual shares of states either criteria-specific or aggregate as is done by the Finance Commission. The shares may change under each criterion, as more recent data on income, tax effort, etc., become available. However, as far as population is concerned, only 1971 population is used as in the case of the Finance Commission.

Table 16.2: Gadgil Formula: Alternative Versions

(Weights: per cent)

Criteria		Modified Gadgil Formula (1980)	NDC Revised Formula (1990)	NDC Revised Formula (1991)
A.	Special Category States (10)	30% share of 10 States excluding North Eastern Council	30% share of 10 States including North Eastern Council	30% share of 10 States excluding North Eastern Council
B.	Non-Special Category States (15)			
(i)	Population (1971)	60.0	55.0	60.0
(ii)	Per Capita Income	20.0	25.0	25.0
	Of which			
a.	According to the 'deviation' method covering only the states with per capita income below the national average	20.0	20.0	20.0
b.	According to the 'distance' method covering all the fifteen states	-	5.0	5.0
(iii)	Performance	10.0	5.0	7.5
	of which			
a.	Tax effort	10.0	-	2.5
b.	Fiscal management	-	5.0	2.5
c.	National objectives	-	-	2.5
d.	Special problems	10.0	15.0	7.5
	Total	**100.0**	**100.0**	**100.0**

Notes: 1. Fiscal management is assessed as the difference between states' own total plan resources estimated at the time of finalising Annual Plans and their actual performance, considering latest five years. 2. Under the criterion of the performance in respect of certain programmes of national priorities the approved formula covers four objectives, *viz*.: (i) population control; (ii) elimination of illiteracy; (iii) on-time completion of externally aided projects; and (iv) success in land reforms.

The important elements in this formula relate to factors of population, deviation of income from mean income, distance of income from highest income, and other factors reflecting fiscal discipline and achievement of national objectives. Due to the very high weight given to the population factor, which allocates equal per capita shares to all states, dispensations under the Gadgil Formula are only mildly progressive. As argued later, whatever little progressivity is there in the plan transfer, it gets disturbed by the inter-state distribution of external assistance.

16.5 Plan Assistance: Distribution of Funds

The profile of shares of plan grants across states for the period 1996-97 to 1998-99, indicates that more than 37 percent of plan grants have gone to the special category states (Table 16.3), whereas they account for less than 5 percent of population and only 3.3 percent of all state GSDP.

For the low income states like Bihar, Uttar Pradesh, Orissa, Madhya Pradesh, West Bengal and Rajasthan, the share of plan grants amounted to nearly 33 percent whereas they account for nearly 50 percent of the population and 38 percent of GDP. This pattern of dispensation of plan grants is both iniquitous and inefficient. Unless the allocation mechanism of plan grants is overhauled so as to augment equity as well as efficiency, ambitious growth targets cannot be attained.

When the original Gadgil Formula for the distribution of central assistance for State Plans was approved by the National Development Council in September 1968, it was agreed that the requirements of Assam, Jammu & Kashmir and Nagaland should first be met out of the total pool of central assistance. For the three annual plans immediately preceding the application of Gadgil Formula, the share of Assam, Jammu & Kashmir, and Nagaland in total plan assistance was 9.26 per cent. For the Fourth Plan (1969-74) when the Gadgil Formula was first applied, an amount was earmarked for these three states, but their share averaged to a little above 11 per cent.

For the Fifth Plan, the share of these states was a little 15 per cent. For two annual plans (1978-80), the share of these states became a little more than 16 percent. When the Fifth Plan was formulated, this list was extended to include Himachal Pradesh, Manipur, Meghalaya, Sikkim and Tripura, making eight states in all. It is only since 1980 that the share of SC states was predetermined at 30 per cent. In 1990, the number of special category states was increased to 10 with the inclusion of Arunachal Pradesh and Mizoram. Appendix 6 gives some historical details about the evolution of the system of earmarking for the special category states and the Gadgil Formula.

Table 16.3: Share of Plan Grants Across States

State	1996-97	1997-98	1998-99	Average 1996-99
Bihar	1.79	3.83	4.76	3.46
Uttar Pradesh	11.22	10.94	9.39	10.52
Orissa	3.60	3.55	3.82	3.66
Madhya Pradesh	7.29	4.82	4.83	5.65
West Bengal	5.42	4.82	6.12	5.45
Rajasthan	4.74	5.24	5.11	5.03
Andhra Pradesh	6.84	6.77	6.63	6.75
Karnataka	3.91	3.68	3.79	3.79
Kerala	2.39	2.04	2.39	2.27
Tamil Nadu	4.05	4.59	4.17	4.27
Gujarat	2.82	2.71	2.56	2.70
Haryana	1.87	1.81	1.62	1.77
Punjab	1.51	1.40	1.59	1.50
Maharashtra	7.54	5.67	4.60	5.94
Goa	0.23	0.21	0.18	0.21
GCS – Share	**65.22**	**62.08**	**61.56**	**62.95**
Assam	7.05	6.84	7.35	7.08
Tripura	2.45	2.47	3.11	2.68
Manipur	2.23	2.25	2.33	2.27
Meghalaya	1.55	1.41	1.88	1.61
Jammu & Kashmir	10.23	13.96	11.60	11.93
Arunachal Pradesh	2.62	2.60	2.79	2.67
Sikkim	1.07	1.20	1.33	1.20
Himachal Pradesh	3.92	3.56	3.85	3.78
Mizoram	1.75	1.80	1.95	1.83
Nagaland	1.90	1.84	2.23	1.99
SCS – Share	**34.77**	**37.93**	**38.42**	**37.04**

GCS = General Category States; SCS = Special Category States.
Source: (Basic Data): Finance Accounts of States.

Table 16.4 provides a comparison of per capita plan grants across general and special category states. In the case of the general category states' per capita plan grants increased from Rs. 139 in 1993-94 to Rs.189 in 2002-03 on average. But the pattern of distribution does not indicate any clear progressivity. States like

Bihar and Uttar Pradesh have obtained per capita plan grants that are less than many middle and high income states. The special category states have obtained on average, a much higher per capita plan grant. But in their case also, in per capita terms, poorer states like Assam and Tripura have obtained per capita grants that are much less in amount than their better-off counterparts.

Table 16.4: Per Capita Plan Grants: Selected Years (Rupees)

State	1993-94	1996-97	2000-01	2002-03
Andhra Pradesh	163.00	155.88	246.05	252.53
Bihar*	116.68	65.39	105.79	125.94
Goa	226.53	304.78	390.52	501.04
Gujarat	146.80	115.69	188.58	162.71
Haryana	134.06	164.64	186.97	199.46
Karnataka	142.11	146.25	248.05	231.11
Kerala	122.46	128.90	143.89	229.68
Madhya Pradesh*	135.64	147.86	186.00	243.08
Maharashtra	144.04	154.21	90.09	113.91
Orissa	166.17	168.70	246.07	358.30
Punjab	111.17	126.77	159.95	148.54
Rajasthan	232.50	202.31	223.77	236.66
Tamil Nadu	145.31	112.84	187.32	161.50
Uttar Pradesh*	125.08	101.59	115.95	180.87
West Bengal	100.96	119.12	160.90	156.94
Gen.Cat.States(Average)	139.12	128.41	163.44	189.01
Arunachal Pradesh	3,446.59	4,332.29	5,372.12	5,528.64
Assam	565.72	469.52	658.09	770.27
Himachal Pradesh	1,250.53	1,146.18	1,499.55	2,195.63
Jammu and Kashmir	1,288.83	1,883.13	1,630.34	2,156.14
Manipur	1,387.92	1,747.85	1,865.31	2,132.08
Meghalaya	1,277.02	1,246.12	1,937.66	1,975.62
Mizoram	2,879.21	3,589.05	5,701.38	5,899.14
Nagaland	1,995.40	1,985.03	2,522.10	3,107.97
Sikkim	2,823.56	3,778.82	5,395.42	6,547.34
Tripura	900.44	1,321.18	2,253.49	2,419.04
Sp.Cat.States (Average)	1,007.18	1,136.99	1,412.92	1,703.15

* Taken as undivided states.

Source: State Finance Accounts.

The main weaknesses in the application of the Gadgil Formula as complemented by other ad hoc mechanisms of plan assistance are summarised below:

1. There is no explicit basis for a 30 percent earmarking for the SC states; it is way beyond their capacity to productively absorb these funds, and has led to large debt-GSDP ratios even while only 10 percent of assistance is given as loan;
2. Shares determined on the basis of tax effort and fiscal discipline indexes are unscaled implying that if a large state like Maharashtra and a small state like Goa had the same tax effort ratio, they will get the same share regardless of their size. This would lead to a very large per capita share for Goa compared to that for Maharashtra, for example, for the same tax effort;
3. The link between plan schemes/projects and plan assistance has been lost, leading to a severing of a link between costs and benefits, and lack of effective project based monitoring; and
4. The 30:70 grant to loan ratio has long become irrelevant if the 30 percent grant ratio was meant to cover revenue expenditure on plans.
5. There are no objective criteria for the distribution of 30 percent earmarked share among the special category states.
6. Looked at in per capita terms, plan grants are characterized by lack of progessivity. These serve to increase rather than diminish disparities across states.

16.6 Finance and Planning Commissions: Dynamics of Inter-Dependence

The two main bodies that intermediate between the centre and the states in the matter of fiscal transfers, *viz.*, the Finance Commission and the Planning Commission follow approaches in a segmented way without any effective co-ordination. Especially important in this context is the impact of the dynamic linkage between the two major streams of resource transfers. In fact, the combination of the gap-filling approach followed by the Finance Commissions and provision of loans to the state almost by entitlement along with an emphasis on the size of the plan has led to major inefficiencies resulting in large debt burdens and corresponding burdens of interest payments and salary liabilities for the state governments.

The Plan generates three major liabilities for periods beyond the Plan: interest payments on funds borrowed for financing the Plan, maintenance of assets created during the Plan, and salaries of people employed in Plan schemes that remain in government employment after the plan has ended. For these liabilities, after the Plan period is over, state governments look to the Finance Commission for resource transfers. In making an assessment of the needs of state governments on the revenue non-Plan account, both interest payments and committed liabilities of the state governments have been taken into account by the Finance Commissions. Since the Plan is linked to a programme of borrowing, a larger Plan is typically linked with a larger borrowing programme and, therefore, leaves relatively larger future liabilities.

Interest liabilities as well as committed expenditures on Plan schemes of the past have been taken by the previous Finance Commissions as a first charge in making an assessment of the expenditure requirements. Given other things, the larger the interest and other committed liabilities, the larger would be the entitlement of a state in the form of tax devolution and grants. It is implicit in this approach that larger Plan outlays financed by larger borrowing, create larger state-specific liabilities which generate (i.e., after five years) larger claims for fiscal transfers.

The methods of working out transfers by the Planning Commission and the Finance Commission thus sets up a circuit of adverse incentives, because in both cases, a fragmented view is taken, without addressing the issue in its totality. The Finance Commission keeps looking only to the (non-Plan) revenue expenditures without paying much attention to the linkage of interest payments with past fiscal deficits and accumulated debt stock. The Planning Commission looks only at new schemes. It looks at the scope of borrowing in the Plan period without considering what future liabilities are being created and how they may be financed beyond the Plan period. Projects financed by external assistance, which is transmitted to the state on the same terms and conditions as normal Plan assistance, also create similar liabilities regarding interest payments and maintenance.

By mixing grants and loans, the Plan assistance mechanism combines two modes of resource transfer, which need to be governed by entirely different sets of principles. Grants should be given in consideration of resource deficiencies, and for projects with large social benefits but limited direct return like primary education and primary health. On the other hand, loans should be given taking into consideration the capacity of a state to absorb and service the loan, and in respect of projects which can give adequate returns, commensurate with the cost of the loan. By mixing the two together, the centre is burdening states with debt that they cannot service, but cannot afford to forego either, because with it the component of grant will also have to be foregone.

The artificial dichotomy between Plan and non-Plan expenditures generates a number of inefficiencies. There is an undue emphasis on taking up new schemes, while uncompleted projects of the past Plans and maintenance of assets acquired in the past get little attention. In effect, Plan schemes, as originally envisaged cannot be taken up fully, because the contemplated "balance from current revenues" (BCRs) do not come through, Plan finances are diverted to non-Plan items, and time overruns increase costs. As a result, many schemes remain incomplete. On the one hand, old assets degenerate due to inadequate maintenance, on the other, new assets are not ready to provide services as the schemes remain incomplete.

Apart from the Plan non-Plan, albeit the Finance Commission vis-à-vis the Planning Commission dichotomy, there are other channels through which resource transfers that take place between the centre and the states providing room for much adhocism. This includes resource transfers through central Plan schemes administered by states and centrally sponsored schemes. There are also departmental transfers like DRDA schemes. The dynamics of the linkage of Finance Commission and Planning Commission transfers has been depicted in

The incentive to increase borrowing as far as possible is inherent in the design of plan transfers. In order to get the 30 percent grant component, one has to take 70 percent loan. Further, the Planning Commission actually approves the borrowing programme of the states based on the plan size, and also its borrowing programme. But, while decisions may be taken with a five year perspective, plans create indefinite liabilities in terms additional interest payments, salaries and pensions which the Finance Commission is supposed to provide resources for after the plan period has ended.

Because of this dynamic linkage, a comprehensive view of the transfer programme should be taken rather than the segmented view as at present. It has earlier been argued that the transfers made to the special category states via the Planning Commission and subsequently via the Finance Commission entail considerable opportunity costs, and loss of development opportunities in the rest of the country. This is because, in the Gadgil Formula, 30 percent of total assistance is set aside for distribution amongst special category states only, whereas their share in population is only 5.3 percent. It was also indicated that the actual share of plan grants from all sources is even higher than 30 percent for the special category states, amounting to around 38 percent. Thus, the grants being given to special category states are more than 7 times their share in the population of the country. However, these massive grants do not generate any multiplier effects within the `special category states' because there is considerable leakage of expenditures. In the meanwhile, most of the plan expenditure is exhausted in creating more plan posts which after the end of the plan period will justify claims for additional Finance Commission grants. It is for this reason that these states have become the main recipients of the general purpose Finance Commission grants. In the meanwhile, in order to sustain a very large plan size, these states have also borrowed heavily even though out of total plan assistance, only 10 percent are given to them as loans. In spite of this large concessionality in plan assistance, the special category states are the most heavily indebted states among the Indian states relative to their respective GSDPs. These features have arisen because of lack of concern for proper scaling in the 30 percent share earmarked in the Gadgil Formula for the special category states. This was an ad-hoc figure, the rationale of which has not been explicitly stated.. Clearly, the Gadgil Formula needs to be recast.

16.7 Reforming Plan Transfers

At the beginning of the reform process there was some talk of redefining the role of plans and Planning Commission. But inertia has overtaken these discussions and the old practices have continued without much change. Since the Planning Commission oversees the dispensation of the development funds across states, the entire exercise of inter-state allocation of development funds requires careful review and redesigning.

As noted earlier, a segmented view of transfers taken in isolation by the two main bodies looking after these transfers sets up a circuit of adverse incentives. Emergence of revenue deficits in the government's budgets has resulted, to a considerable extent, from the manner of plan budgeting and financing. After the late eighties, the bulk of the requirements for the plans were met from borrowings from the domestic private sector or from external sources. On the other hand, while the focus of planning needed to be geared to investment expenditures, in practice, the revenue (current) expenditure emerged as the major component of plan outlay. This implied financing of current expenditures largely by borrowing.

In the context of plan transfers among the specific tasks, the following may be given priority.

1. The allocation of development funds for the special category states should be reconsidered taking into view their capacity to productively absorb these funds, since the opportunity cost of these funds to the system is extremely high.
2. The allocation of central expenditures including central investment has a significant impact on the profile of regional growth and these must be recast so as to serve the objectives of equity by stimulating growth in the poorer states.
3. The Gadgil Formula should be revised forthwith. The determination of grants and loans should be subject to separate criteria. Grants should be given according to resource deficiencies, and loans should be given or approved,

taking into account the capacity of the states to absorb and productively utilise the loans.

4. Since private capital flows both domestic and external are likely to favour the already prosperous states, devolution criteria for plan funds should favour the less prosperous states relatively more.

16.8 Reforming Transmission of External Assistance

External assistance is another major source for capital funds for the states. This comes from multilateral as well as bilateral sources. As discussed in the previous chapter, external assistance to states has been transmitted to the states not on the terms and conditions stipulated by the external creditors but on terms and conditions exactly similar to those for plan assistance. As such, external assistance became a perfect substitute for plan assistance. The allocation of external assistance among states depends however on the selection and approval of specific projects by the multilateral and bilateral creditors. Many of the developed states that have the technical capacities to prepare the relevant project proposals are able to get a relatively larger share of total external assistance that comes to the states.

Together, the allocation of plan assistance and external assistance does not provide a pattern of flow of funds among states for developmental purposes that may foster equitable interregional growth. Also, a large part of external assistance is used in central government projects, the location of which also has important implications for economic activities across states.

The system o` transmission of external assistance to the states in India is characterised by several deficiencies and needs to be reformed. The system gives wrong signals regarding the selection of projects by a state. Furthermore, external creditors are discouraged when they find that their grants or highly concessional loans, which suited the concerned projects, are being converted into highly costly loans. It is important, therefore, to maintain the basic character of the assistance programme. The exchange rate movements of recent years indicate that while in the pre-1991-92 years, there clearly was a subsidisation of the states by the centre, the situation is much closer to being that of unremitted concessionality in more recent years. To put the system on an even keel, two things are important: (i) the basic character of the external assistance programme should be maintained; and (ii) neither the centre nor the states should be a net beneficiary in the process of transmission. Both these objectives can be achieved by delinking the system from the terms and conditions of state plan assistance, and linking the interest rate to exchange rate movements. The TFC has recommended such delinking.

The regional allocation of external assistance, and the terms and conditions of its transfer to the states should also be redesigned. In particular, these terms and conditions should be delinked from the terms and conditions of state plan assistance as there is in fact no real nexus between them. In fact, external assistance should be passed on to the states on the same terms and conditions on which they are given, grants as grants and loans as loans. The only difference should be on the interest rate of loans where the states should be given the option either to bear the full exchange risk or pay a higher interest rate to the centre denominated in domestic currency terms. The difference between the original rate and this rate should be set equal to the anticipated long term rate of depreciation of the rupee.

16.9 Recommendations of the Twelfth Finance Commission

In this context, the recommendations of the Twelfth Finance Commission assume considerable relevance. The approach and recommendations of the TFC are discussed at length in Chapter 17. In the context of Plan assistance, the TFC has recommended that the link between grants and loans should be done away with. Loans should be given on principles that are different from those on which grants are given. Loans should not be given as a matter of entitlement. Loans should be determined for a particular state on the basis of sustainability. The TFC has recommended three mechanisms that can help bring state borrowing under control as well as make the use of borrowing more productive. First, is the suggestion regarding a Loan Council, which should look at borrowing by the states from all sources and approve an overall borrowing plan for each year. Second is the suggestion that the central government should discontinue inter-mediating so that states can be exposed to the market forces. The third is that each state government should manage its finances within the limits set out by a fiscal responsibility legislation.

While the overall borrowing may be regulated in this manner, there is a need to determine plan grants to the states in a manner that states with lower fiscal capacities are given higher grants. The principle of equalization advocated by the Finance commission should apply to Plan grants as well. Taking an overall view, the following steps need to be initiated for redesigning fiscal transfers in India:

1. Planning Commission should review its dispensation of development funds - leading to a reconsideration of magnitude of grants to special category states. The Gadgil Formula for general category states should be reviewed. The link between grants and loans should be discontinued as recommended by the TFC.
2. Also, as recommended by the TFC, steps should be taken to pass on external

assistance to the states on original terms and conditions except for augmentation of the interest rate to cover anticipated average rate of depreciation. With disintermediation, external borrowing meant to be passed on to the states should be handled through a public account.

3. Plan grants should complement the Finance Commission transfers in achieving the objective of equalisation by reducing disparities in fiscal capacities. However, if greater regional balance can be ensured by redesigning the transfer of development funds, the Finance Commission transfers would not need to be sharply progressive.
4. The inter-regional dispensation of development funds is governed by the handling of (a) central funds; (b) plan funds; and (c) external assistance. The regional allocation of these funds should be conducive to efficiency as well as equitable.
5. The strategy for the development of the special category states should be reconsidered taking into view their growth potential and their capacity to productively utilise large development funds placed at their disposal.
6. Both plan funds and external assistance need to focus on exploiting the growth potential of the low income general category states, while private sector flows both domestic and foreign, may serve more the already better off states.

Table A16.1: Plan Outlay of the Public Sector Relative to GDP at Market Prices

Year	Plan outlay of the public sector	GDP mp	Plan outlay as % of GDPmp	Year	Plan outlay of the public sector	GDP Mp	Plan outlay as % of GDPmp
	Rs. crore	Rs. crore	Per cent		Rs. crore	Rs.crore	Per cent
1951-52	296.6	9,934	2.986	1978-79	10,773.0	1,01,597	10.604
1952-53	267.6	10,566	2.533	1979-80	12,176.5	1,10,133	11.056
1953-54	343.0	10,366	3.309	1980-81	15,023.4	1,20,841	12.432
1954-55	475.9	11,282	4.218	1981-82	18,372.9	1,43,762	12.780
1955-56	613.9	10,678	5.749	1982-83	21,274.9	1,68,600	12.619
1956-57	635.0	10,873	5.840	1983-84	25,313.6	1,88,262	13.446
1957-58	890.0	12,951	6.872	1984-85	30,032.5	2,19,496	13.682
1958-59	1,018.0	13,349	7.626	1985-86	33,059.9	2,45,515	13.466
1959-60	1,012.0	14,874	6.804	1986-87	39,149.1	2,77,991	14.083
1960-61	1,117.0	15,675	7.126	1987-88	42,920.6	3,11,177	13.793
1961-62	1,130.3	17,167	6.584	1988-89	48,069.8	3,54,343	13.566
1962-63	1,385.5	18,196	7.614	1989-90	55,530.2	4,21,567	13.172
1963-64	1,713.6	19,566	8.758	1990-91	61,518.1	4,86,179	12.653
1964-65	2,014.8	22,482	8.962	1991-92	64,751.2	5,68,674	11.386
1965-66	2,332.3	26,220	8.895	1992-93	72,852.4	6,53,117	11.155
1966-67	2,164.5	27,668	7.823	1993-94	88,080.7	7,48,367	11.770
1967-68	2,084.9	31,305	6.660	1994-95	98,167.3	8,59,220	11.425
1968-69	2,376.0	36,649	6.483	1995-96	1,07,380.4	10,12,770	10.603
1969-70	2,209.9	38,823	5.692	1996-97	1,18,976.4	11,88,012	10.015
1970-71	2,523.5	42,750	5.903	1997-98	1,29,757.3	13,68,209	9.484
1971-72	3,130.3	45,677	6.853	1998-99	1,51,580.4	15,22,547	9.956
1972-73	3,727.3	48,932	7.617	1999-00	1,60,608.2	17,40,985	9.225
1973-74	4,187.8	53,947	7.763	2000-01	1,85,736.8	19,36,831	9.590
1974-75	2,928.4	65,613	4.463	2001-02	1,86,315.2	20,89,500	8.917
1975-76	6,416.9	77,479	8.282	2002-03 (RE)	2,33,732.7	22,71,984	10.288
1976-77	8,081.7	83,269	9.706	2003-04 (BE)	2,56,041.9	24,63,324	10.394
1977-78	9,226.2	89,739	10.281				

Note: Plan Outlay for 1974-75 to 1978-79 as originally envisaged.
Source: (Basic Data):*Indian Public Finance Statistics* and CSO.

17

Twelfth Finance Commission: Approach and Recommendations

The task is to devise a formula that redresses disadvantage but penalizes imprudence.

C. Rangarajan, Inaugural Address, Issues before the Eleventh Finance Commission, 2000

The Twelfth Finance Commission (TFC) considered that the scheme of transfers should be designed to serve the objectives both of equity and efficiency. Fiscal transfers should also be predictable and stable. These transfers should correct both the vertical and horizontal imbalances. The former relates to transfers from the central government to the States governments considered together, whereas the latter is concerned with allocation among the state governments. The TFC, apart from attending to the core duties of recommending transfers, also suggested a programme for restructuring government finances, and a set of incentive linked mechanisms for correcting fiscal imbalance particularly at the state level.

17.1 Vertical Imbalance

A vertical imbalance system exists in the system by design where revenues are more centralized and responsibilities more decentralized. The TFC notes that fiscal transfers to the states, through all channels, as percentage of the gross revenue receipts of the centre had increased from an average of 31.4 per cent in the period of the Sixth Finance Commission to 38.0 per cent for the Seventh. It increased further to 39.3 per cent for the period covered by the Ninth Commission before coming down to 35.2 per cent during the period of the Tenth Finance Commission. This ratio improved to 37.1 per cent considering the average of the first four years of the recommendation period of the Eleventh Finance Commission.

As percentage of GDP at market prices, fiscal transfers showed a decline, falling from the level of about 5 percent for the period covered by the Eighth Commission to 4.8 and 4.1 per cent respectively for the reference periods of the Ninth and Tenth Finance Commissions. In the first three years of the EFC period of recommendation, these have increased to well above 4 per cent of GDP on average. However, as percentage of GDP these remain below the levels close to 5 per cent of GDP in the early nineties. This fall is due partly to the fall in Centre's tax-GDP ratio. The TFC's approach to formulating a view on the vertical imbalance is based on the consideration of the availability of revenues and corresponding expenditures to the centre and the states after the transfers. Determining the aggregate share of states in the central taxes requires a comprehensive view of (i) the expenditure needs of the centre; (ii) the aggregate resources of the centre; (iii) the aggregate requirements of the states; and (iv) the resources of states from own sources. In the context of vertical devolution, the share of states and consequently that of the centre is supposed to be determined in a manner that provides both sides with adequate resources subject to the overall resource constraint.

Table 17.1 gives the share of the revenue receipts of the states in the combined revenue receipts of the Centre and the States, before and after transfers. It also gives the share of States in the combined revenue expenditure of Centre and States after netting out intergovernmental flows. It shows that in terms of access to revenue resources before and after transfers, the position of the Centre and States is completely reversed. In fact, the States get, after transfers, a share in the range of 62-64 per cent of the combined revenue receipts of the Centre and States and this share has remained remarkably stable.

Table 17.1: Share of States in Combined Revenue Receipts and Expenditures

Average*	Revenue Receipts Before and After Transfers		Revenue Expenditures
	Before	After	After Transfers
VII FC	35.3	61.4	58.0
VIII FC	34.6	62.0	55.7
IX FC	37.5	64.7	56.9
X FC	38.6	63.0	56.8
2000-01	38.6	63.9	56.0
2001-02	39.3	63.9	58.0
XI FC (Avg. 2 years)	39.0	63.9	57.1

*Average for years under recommendation period.
Source: (Basic Data): *Report of the Twelfth Finance Commission, 2004.*

Thus, as the TFC notes, the long term trends show larger share of states in the combined revenue receipts after transfers. A long-term stability of relative share of centre and states in the combined revenues is also indicated. More recently, central transfers to the states fell relative to GDP. The role of fiscal transfers is to redistribute resources between the central and the state governments in a manner such that vertical and horizontal imbalances are simultaneously removed with a view to maximizing the welfare of the citizens by promoting equity as well as efficiency. Considering the long term stability, the TFC considered that only a marginal increment may be required in the indicative benchmark of transfers as percentage of centre's gross revenue receipts. As such, it suggested that this benchmark may be raised from 37.5 per cent recommended by the EFC to 38 per cent. This threshold covers all transfers to the states, namely, transfers from the Finance Commission, Planning Commission, and other discretionary transfers.

17.2 Horizontal Imbalance

The horizontal imbalance has its roots in the differential capacities and needs of the states as also the differences in the costs of providing services. In India, not only the number of states is large, they differ widely in respect of area, size of population, incomes, tax bases, and mineral and forest resources. Resource gaps may arise because States have inadequate capacities as also because the revenue effort is deficient in relative terms. The former should be taken into account for correcting the horizontal imbalance, but the latter should not qualify for such correction.

The horizontal aspect of transfers relates to their *inter se* distribution among States. If, in per capita terms, all States were similar in fiscal capacities and cost conditions, equalization transfers would provide them with equal per capita transfers. The differences in per capita fiscal capacities and differential costs of providing services justify departures from an equal per capita transfer norm. Cost disabilities arise due to factors that are largely beyond the control of the state like large areas relative to population, hilly terrains, excessive rainfall, and proneness to droughts.

In combining these considerations into a suitable scheme of transfers, the TFC recognizes that there are both conceptual issues and practical problems. There are two major instruments of transfers: tax revenue sharing and grants. The latter can be unconditional and general purpose or conditional and purpose-specific. In the case of sharing tax revenues, two major considerations relate to selecting appropriate allocative criteria and the related indicators and determining their relative weights. The key determinant in this exercise is the relative revenue raising capacity of the States. Revenue capacity is often measured, as was done also by some of the previous Finance Commissions, by GSDP at factor cost even though it is recognized that GSDP is not a perfect correlate of income or fiscal capacity.

The principles that may be followed in determining the horizontal transfers also depend on the relative weights that may be given to the two principal modes of fiscal transfers, viz tax devolution and grants, which have certain distinguishing features. Tax devolution has a built-in flexibility as it can increase automatically if the central taxes are more buoyant. Conversely, there is risk if their buoyancy falls short of expectations. Grants are ensured as these are fixed in nominal terms. It is easier to target grants towards States or sectors. The flexibility in the case of devolution is limited by the criteria used. Yet States have often expressed a preference for devolution because by definition it is unconditional and comes to the States as a matter of right. Grants-in aid have been targeted more towards the horizontal aspect of the transfers. That is why many of the better-off States assessed to be in revenue surplus do not get the 'gap' grants. There has also been the question whether grants under article 275 can be given as conditional grants although these grants have generally been unconditional. We recognize that grants are the more effective transfer instrument for state-specific and purpose specific targeting.

Chart 17.1 shows, as percentage of GDP at market prices, the central and state tax revenues after tax devolution. The bold line indicates that States access to tax revenues after tax devolution was higher than what was left with the Centre as net tax revenues after transfers after the early eighties. The gap between the two has widened in recent years.

17.3 Tax Devolution

The sharing of central tax revenues, individually or globally, can be a potent means of redistribution among states because of its large weight in the complete scheme of transfers and redistribution. The extent of redistribution that can be affected through this means depends on the vertical shares of the centre and the states, and the horizontal shares pertaining to individual states. The horizontal shares will bring about redistribution depending on the weights attached to such criteria as can give higher shares to low revenue capacity states, and the total amount (vertical share) that is redistributed among states. The horizontal aspect of transfers relates to their *inter se* distribution among States.

Prior to the 80th constitutional amendment, two main central taxes were shared with the States, *viz.*, income tax other than corporation tax and the Union excise duties. The sharing of the income tax was mandatory as, under Article 270, it had to be shared with the States, while that of the Union excise duties was discretionary, as its sharing was subjected to the phrase "may be divided between the Union and the States" and could be shared if Parliament by law so provided. There were also two tax rental arrangements with the States, where the Union government collected the tax, as it were, on behalf of the States and then distributed the proceeds among the States on principles and shares recommended by the Finance Commission. These were additional excise duty in lieu of sales tax on textiles, tobacco, and sugar, and grant in lieu of the tax on railway passenger fares which was repealed in 1961.

Chart 17.1: Central and State Tax Revenues after Tax Devolution as % of GDP at Market Prices

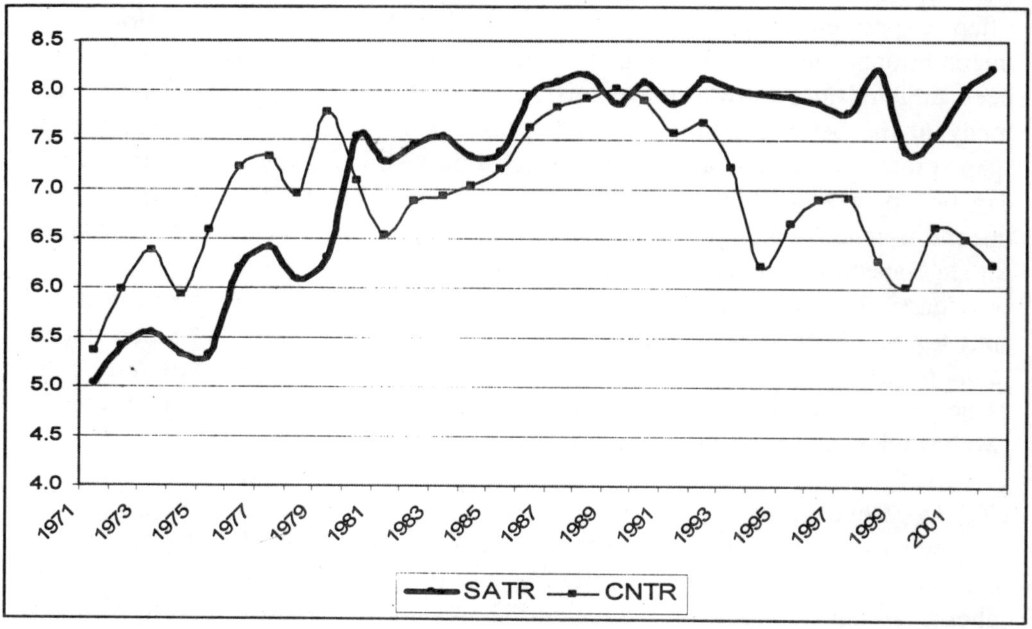

SATR= State tax revenues after tax devolution; CNTR= Central tax revenues after devolution

Following the 80th Amendment of the Constitution, all central taxes were brought into a shareable pool and it became mandatory to assign a share from each central tax to the States. The amended Article 270 provided for the sharing of all central taxes except taxes under Articles 268 and 269 and earmarked cesses, and surcharges under Article 271. Only "net proceeds" are to be shared, and as such 'cost of collection' has to be deducted to obtain the net proceeds as prescribed under Article 279. The proceeds are to be distributed among the States where the central taxes are "leviable" in "that year". Article 269 has also been amended and it contains only central sales tax and consignment tax, which is not levied. More recently, the constitution has been amended, and services have been added under the Union List in the Seventh Schedule of the Constitution. Taxation of services has been brought under the purview of article 268 A.

The taxation of services has a bearing on the size of the vertical transfers as it has the potential to impart additional buoyancy to tax revenues. With the 88th amendment to the constitution, article 268A provides that "Taxes of services shall be levied by the Government of India and such tax can be collected and appropriated by government of India and the States..." So far, the central government has been levying the service tax on specific services under its residual powers relating to subjects that are not specified in any of the three lists, services being an example. The sharing of this revenue has been on the basis of the recommendations of the Finance Commission, as applicable to other central taxes. However, revenue from taxation of services that are taxed by the Centre under article 268A rather than under Article 270 would be excluded from the purview of the Finance Commission. The Commission notes these developments with concern.

In its recommendations regarding tax devolution, the TFC has increased the aggregate share of states to 30.5 per cent from 29.5 per cent, as long the existing arrangements regarding the additional excise duties on textiles and tobacco continue. The TFC has also altered the weights on which the sharing of taxes is to be determined across states, as shown by Table 17.2. In particular, the weight of the distance formula was reduced to 50 per cent and the infrastructure index was dropped.

Table 17.2: Tax Devolution: Factors Determining Inter-se Shares

	Weights	
Factors	EFC	TFC
Population	10.0	25.0
Distance	62.5	50.0
Area	7.5	10.0
Infrastructure	7.5	0.0
Tax Effort	5.0	7.5
Fiscal Discipline	7.5	7.5
	100.0	100.0

Source: *Reports of Finance Commissions.*

On this basis, the shares of individual states as determined by the TFC and the difference from the corresponding shares under the recommendations of the EFC are given in Table 17.3. The shares of individual states can be compared with corresponding shares determined by the EFC.

Table 17.3: Shares in Central Taxes: Recommended by the EFC and TFC

State	(percent)		Percentage points	
	Twelfth	Eleventh	TFC-EFC	
Andhra Pradesh	7.356	7.701	-0.345	
Arunachal Pradesh	0.288	0.244		0.044
Assam	3.235	3.285	-0.05	
Bihar	11.028	11.589	-0.561	
Chattisgarh	2.654	2.385		0.269
Goa	0.259	0.206		0.053
Gujarat	3.569	2.821		0.748
Haryana	1.075	0.944		0.131
Himachal Pradesh	0.522	0.683	-0.161	
Jammu and Kashmir	1.297	1.29		0.007
Jharkhand	3.361	3.008		0.353
Karnataka	4.459	4.93	-0.471	
Kerala	2.665	3.057	-0.392	
Madhya Pradesh	6.711	6.453		0.258
Maharashtra	4.997	4.632		0.365
Manipur	0.362	0.366	-0.004	
Meghalaya	0.371	0.342		0.029
Mizoram	0.239	0.198		0.041
Nagaland	0.263	0.22		0.043
Orissa	5.161	5.056		0.105
Punjab	1.299	1.147		0.152
Rajasthan	5.609	5.473		0.136
Sikkim	0.227	0.184		0.043
Tamil Nadu	5.305	5.385	-0.08	
Tripura	0.428	0.487	-0.059	
Uttar Pradesh	19.264	19.137		0.127
Uttaranchal	0.939	0.661		0.278
West Bengal	7.057	8.116	-1.059	
	100.000	100.000	-3.182	3.182

Source: Derived from Finance Commission Reports.

Clearly a large number of states gained from these recommendations. Some of the states that lost out in comparison to the EFC shares were Andhra Pradesh,

Assam, Bihar, Tamil Nadu, Tripura, and West Bengal. In most of these cases, the redesigning of grants compensated to some extent. Table 17.4 gives the estimated year-wise amounts under devolution for the different states.

Table 17.4: Twelfth Finance Commission: Year-wise Estimated Amount of Devolution (Rs. crore)

State	2004-05	2005-06	2006-07	2007-08	2008-09	2009-10
Andhra Pradesh	6,137.70	6,721.62	7,695.11	8,829.33	10,153.27	11,701.19
Arunachal Pradesh	194.47	263.16	301.28	345.68	397.52	458.12
Assam	2,618.15	2,956.01	3,384.13	3,882.94	4,465.17	5,145.91
Bihar	9,236.43	10,076.95	11,536.39	13,236.80	15,221.62	17,542.24
Chattisgarh	1,900.85	2,425.12	2,776.35	3,185.57	3,663.24	4,221.72
Goa	164.18	236.66	270.94	310.88	357.49	411.99
Gujarat	2,248.34	3,261.21	3,733.53	4,283.84	4,926.18	5,677.21
Haryana	752.37	982.29	1,124.56	1,290.31	1,483.79	1,710.00
Himachal Pradesh	544.35	476.98	546.06	626.55	720.50	830.35
J&K	1,028.13	1,185.15	1,356.79	1,556.78	1,790.21	2,063.14
Jharkhand	2,397.38	3,071.15	3,515.94	4,034.17	4,639.09	5,346.34
Karnataka	3,929.21	4,074.46	4,664.56	5,352.09	6,154.62	7,092.93
Kerala	2,436.43	2,435.17	2,787.86	3,198.77	3,678.42	4,239.22
Madhya Pradesh	5,143.04	6,132.24	7,020.38	8,055.15	9,262.99	10,675.19
Maharashtra	3,691.70	4,566.06	5,227.36	5,997.85	6,897.21	7,948.73
Manipur	291.70	330.78	378.69	434.50	499.66	575.83
Meghalaya	272.57	339.00	388.10	445.31	512.08	590.15
Mizoram	157.81	218.39	250.02	286.87	329.88	380.18
Nagaland	175.34	240.32	275.12	315.68	363.01	418.35
Orissa	4,029.63	4,715.92	5,398.92	6,194.70	7,123.57	8,209.60
Punjab	914.16	1,186.97	1,358.88	1,559.18	1,792.97	2,066.32
Rajasthan	4,361.98	5,125.28	5,867.57	6,732.43	7,741.93	8,922.24
Sikkim	146.65	207.42	237.46	272.47	313.32	361.09
Tamil Nadu	4,291.85	4,847.50	5,549.56	6,367.54	7,322.33	8,438.66
Tripura	388.14	391.09	447.73	513.72	590.76	680.82
Uttar Pradesh	15,252.19	17,602.67	20,152.07	23,122.39	26,589.52	30,643.24
Uttaranchal	526.82	858.02	982.29	1,127.07	1,296.07	1493.67
West Bengal	6,468.45	6,448.40	7,382.33	8,470.45	9,740.57	11,225.57
Total Share in taxes	**79,700**	**91,376**	**1,04,610**	**1,20,029**	**1,38,027**	**1,59,070**

Source: *Report of the Twelfth Finance Commission, 2004.*

17.4 Determination of Grants

The main unconditional grant is the revenue gap grant. The grants-in-aid to cover non-plan revenue deficit have generally been the largest component of the Finance Commission grants. The objective has been to give grants to those states which are projected, on a normative basis, to have post devolution non-plan revenue deficit in any year, so that the normatively assessed deficit can be provided for. The normative approach is different from a pure gap filling approach. In the latter case, deficits are assessed without making any corrections for the fiscal behaviour of the states in the assessment exercise. The TFC like some of the previous commissions, followed the normative approach to a degree, which ensured that deficiency in fiscal capacity is corrected, but inadequate revenue effort or excessive expenditure is not encouraged. Under a normative approach, no state can obtain a larger share than what is warranted by the deficiency of its fiscal capacity. Similarly, a state should not expect expenditure not justified by normative considerations to be taken into account in the assessment.

The TFC acknowledges that it is not possible to apply fully the normative principle because of the heterogeneity of the states with respect to various dimensions affecting capacities and costs and problems related to the availability of relevant data. In the projections for the receipts and expenditure of the states made by the Commission, during the forecast period 2005-10, fiscal data for 1993-2003 as contained in the Finance Accounts, as well as on the revised and budget estimates for 2003-04 and 2004-05 were used. In the forecast period 2005-10, the annual nominal growth rate of GDP has been projected at 12 per cent. For the purpose of GSDP projections, the same growth rate (i.e., 12 per cent) was adopted for aggregate GSDP in order to achieve the overall goals for restructuring the states' finances but some adjustment was provided for by grouping states in different growth categories around the average rate.

For the purpose of normative assessment, at least partial adjustment for under-utilization of taxable capacity in the base year 2004-05, was considered reasonable for states where the ratio of OTR to GSDP was below the respective category average. For the purpose of normative base year estimation in respect of below average states, the TFC increased the initially estimated tax-GSDP ratios by 30 per cent of their distance from the respective group average of the special and general category states. This normatively determined OTR/GSDP ratio of each state was applied on the estimated GSDP level of 2004-05 to arrive at the base year adjusted level of OTR in nominal terms. This showed an adjusted own tax revenue aggregated for all states of 5.9 per cent to GDP in the base year.

The TFC envisaged an increase of a little less than 0.9 percentage point in the aggregate OTR as a percentage of GDP over the forecast period, i.e., from 5.91 per cent in the base year to 6.75 per cent in the terminal year. This was consistent with the suggested plan for restructuring government finances. The increase in OTR/GDP ratio implied that aggregate OTR should grow at an annual rate of 15 per cent in the forecast period. Keeping this in view, the TFC determined prescriptive buoyancy levels of 1.1, 1.2, 1.25, 1.3 and 1.35, which were assigned to individual states. While assigning prescriptive buoyancies to the individual states, the impact of the introduction of VAT was assumed to be revenue neutral, if not revenue augmenting. The assignment of prescriptive buoyancies was done keeping the following factors have been taken into consideration:

- Average OTR/GSDP ratio achieved in 2000-03.
- Improvement in OTR/GSDP ratio in 2000-03 over 1993-96.
- Average per capita GSDP for 1999- 2002.

A state was prescribed a higher buoyancy if its recent OTR/GSDP ratio as well as its improvement over time were relatively low, provided its per capita income was relatively high. The assigned buoyancy was multiplied by the projected state-specific GSDP annual growth rate to arrive at annual growth rate of OTR for each state, which was then applied on the base year estimates to generate OTR levels in the forecast period.

Normative adjustments were also required for expenditures. The non-plan revenue expenditures were considered under four broad categories viz., general services, social services, economic services, and compensation and assignment to local bodies. Within these categories, certain important items were been taken up individually for projection. These items included interest payments and pension payments under general services; education, health, and maintenance of buildings under social services, and maintenance of irrigation projects and roads under economic services.

After making separate projections for these items, the remaining items were clubbed under "Other General Services", "Other Social Services" and "Other Economic Services" on which specific norms were applied for projection. Compensation and assignment to local bodies was projected independently. In addition to these four broad categories, the expenditure relating to transfer of committed plan liabilities at the end of the Tenth Plan to the non-plan revenue expenditure side has also been projected.

The growth rate of interest payments for all states taken together was pegged at 7.5 per cent per annum. Using this level as the benchmark, general category states were assigned differential growth rates, namely 6.5 per cent, 7.5 per cent and 8.5 per cent for projecting their interest payments. States having IP/TRR ratio above 30 per cent in 2003-04 (RE) were assigned lower growth rate of 6.5 per cent, because these states have a very heavy burden of interest payment on account of excessive borrowings in the past, and this burden needs to be reduced relatively faster in the forecast period. States with IP/TRR ratio between 23 per cent and 30 per cent were assigned a growth rate of 7.5 per cent, and those below 23 per cent were assigned a growth rate of 8.5 per cent during the forecast period. All special category states were assigned a growth rate of 7.5 per cent, except one which was assigned a rate of 6.5 per cent due to its excessively high debt burden. Thereafter, state-specific growth rates have been applied on the base year estimates for projecting the interest payments during 2005-10. This was compared with the state's own projection, and the lower of the two adopted.

An annual growth rate of 10 per cent was applied on the base year estimates of each state to generate pension payment levels in the forecast period. It may be noted that this rate being higher than the rate of inflation, factors in the increase in the number of pensioners during 2005-10. On these considerations, among others, the TFC recommended, the following revenue-gap grants (Table 17.5).

Table 17.5: Revenue Gap Grants Recommended by TFC (Rs. crore)

State	2005-06	2006-07	2007-08	2008-09	2009-10	Total
Andhra Pradesh	0	0	0	0	0	0
Arunachal Pradesh	271.84	262.94	293.07	273.92	256.11	1357.88
Assam	305.67	0	0	0	0	305.67
Bihar	0	0	0	0	0	0
Chattisgarh	0	0	0	0	0	0
Goa	0	0	0	0	0	0
Gujarat	0	0	0	0	0	0
Haryana	0	0	0	0	0	0
Himachal Pradesh	2164.12	2107.14	2120.96	1991.64	1818.52	10202.38
Jammu and Kashmir	2458.56	2446.64	2552.18	2510.64	2385.44	12353.46
Jharkhand	0	0	0	0	0	0
Karnataka	0	0	0	0	0	0
Kerala	470.37	0	0	0	0	470.37
Madhya Pradesh	0	0	0	0	0	0

Contd...

Maharashtra	0	0	0	0	0	0
Manipur	808.39	841.17	889.1	918.5	934.82	4391.98
Meghalaya	376.67	359.02	393.24	355.78	312.15	1796.86
Mizoram	537.19	556.52	605.17	634	644.91	2977.79
Nagaland	993.65	1037.66	1124.44	1168.17	1212.58	5536.5
Orissa	488.04	0	0	0	0	488.04
Punjab	1556.83	922.64	653.2			3132.67
Rajasthan	0	0	0	0	0	0
Sikkim	66.81	47.06	52.86	21.94		188.67
Tamil Nadu	0	0	0	0	0	0
Tripura	1041.91	1064.3	1122.91	1131.9	1133.18	5494.2
Uttar Pradesh	0	0	0	0	0	0
Uttaranchal	1112.91	1064.3	1115.02	992.02	830.43	5114.68
West Bengal	2438.9	605.82	0	0	0	3044.72
Total	**15091.86**	**11315.21**	**10922.15**	**9998.51**	**9528.14**	**56855.87**

Source: *Report of the Twelfth Finance commission, 2004.*

17.5 Education and Health Sectors

It is seen that the formula used for horizontal distribution of sharable taxes among the states, by its nature, cannot take care of all dimensions of the fiscal needs of a state. It is, therefore, necessary to look at certain common as well as specific needs of the states. In the normative approach, as applied to the own tax revenues of the states, a correction was made in the case of states, where the tax-GSDP ratio was less than the group average. This is consistent with the equalisation approach, although only to a limited extent. There is a need to follow a similar approach on the expenditure side. Per capita expenditures of many states are much below the average per capita expenditure of the relevant group of states. While the amount of transfer required for a full application of the equalisation approach would be too large, we have decided to focus on two critical areas of deficiencies, namely, education and health. But, only a partial correction could be made, because of large disparity between the relevant group average and the actual per capita expenditure

The TFC methodology can be described in two steps:

- derivation of the average preference for allocation to health and education (say **a**)
- derivation of the gap from average all-state (separately for general and special category states) of the state-specific expenditure evaluated by applying the average preference to states aggregate expenditure.

Thus for, any service, suppose that the group average per capita expenditure is z and the notionally calculated state-specific expenditure for a state is z*. Here,

$z = \Sigma z_i N_i / \Sigma N_i$

The capacity of a state is given by r_I and the average capacity is given by

$r = \Sigma r_i N_i / \Sigma N_i$

The average budgetary allocation for this sector is given by

$a = \Sigma z_i N_i / \Sigma r_i N_i$

Thus, $z^*_i = a.r_i$ and $z=a.r$

Actual gap between a state and the average can be seen as the sum of two components: one due to deficiency in fiscal capacity and the other due to giving the concerned sector less than average preference. It is only the first part, that is deficiency in expenditure due to lack of capacity that is taken into account while deficiency that results from giving less than average preference in budgetary allocation although the resource may be equal to average is ignored. Thus, the actual gap may be written as:

$z-z_i = (z- ar_i)+ (ar_i - z_i)$

or, $z-z_i = a(r- r_i)+ (a- a_i)r_i$ [where $a_i = z_i / r_i$]

Thus, the relevant gap is reflected in the first term, which is due to the deficiency in the fiscal capacity, given the average allocation to the concerned sector. The second term is the difference due to allocating less than average share given the capacity of the state, and this difference does not require to be made up under the equalization principle.

In estimating the resources, r is proxied by resources devoted to expenditure excluding interest payments and pensions. Some other adjustments were also made to make inter-state revenue and expenditure data more comparable. Two services that are considered for the purpose are: Expenditure on education covers major head 2202 and that on health, major heads 2210 and 2211. The distance from the average after preference correction was made to the extent only of 15 per cent for education and 30 per cent for health. The resultant amounts are recommended as grants. The relevant amount is determined first for the year 2002-03. The next step was to bring it forward to the period 2005-10. A growth rate equal to the group's tgr over 1993-2003 was applied on the 2002-03 figure to come to 2004-05. Thereafter a growth rate of 9.5 per cent was applied during the forecast period. This is the rate allowed for in the overall assessment exercise. In the case of health, the growth rate applied for the forecast period is 11.5 per cent. A minimum amount for the qualifying state in any one year is Rs. 20 crore in the case of education and Rs.10 crore in the case of health (Table 17.6).

Table 17.6: Education: Equalization Grants (Rs. crore)

State	2005-06	2006-07	2007-08	2008-09	2009-10	**Total**
Assam	183.2	200.6	219.66	240.53	263.38	1,107.37
Bihar	443.99	486.17	532.36	582.93	638.31	2,683.76
Jharkhand	107.82	118.06	129.28	141.56	155.01	651.73
Madhya Pradesh	76.03	83.25	91.16	99.82	109.3	459.56
Orissa	53.49	58.57	64.13	70.22	76.89	323.3
Rajasthan	20	20	20	20	20	100
Uttar Pradesh	736.87	806.87	883.52	967.45	1059.36	4,454.07
West Bengal	64.83	70.99	77.73	85.11	93.2	391.86
Total	1,686.23	1,844.51	2,017.84	2,207.62	2,415.45	10,171.65

Source: *Report of the Twelfth Finance Commission.*

In the case of education, the total amount involved is Rs. 10,171.65 crore. Eight states out of twenty eight states were adjudged to be entitled for these grants. There is another channel available to all the states in the form of Sarva Shiksha Abhiyan for implementing the growth plans in respect of education. In the case of health, the state-wise recommended grants are given in Table 17.7.

Table 17.7: Health: Equalization Grants (Rs. crore)

State	2005-06	2006-07	2007-08	2008-09	2009-10	**Total**
Assam	153.58	171.24	190.93	212.89	237.38	966.02
Bihar	289.3	322.57	359.66	401.02	447.14	1,819.69
Jharkhand	57.39	63.99	71.35	79.55	88.70	360.98
Madhya Pradesh	28.88	32.20	35.90	40.03	44.63	181.64
Orissa	31.22	34.81	38.81	43.28	48.25	196.37
Uttar Pradesh	367.63	409.90	457.04	509.60	568.21	2,312.38
Uttaranchal	10.00	10.00	10.00	10.00	10.00	50.00
Total	938.00	1,044.71	1,163.69	1,296.37	1,444.31	5,887.08

Source: *Report of the Twelfth Finance Commission, 2005.*

17.6 Approach to Debt Relief

We have, therefore, followed a two-pronged approach to debt relief: firstly, a general scheme of debt relief applicable to all states and secondly, a write-off scheme linked to fiscal performance with a view to providing an incentive for the achievement of revenue balance by 2008- 09.

Keeping in view the fact that some premium in the form of transaction costs should be available to the centre, we recommend that the central loans to states contracted till 31.3.04 and outstanding on 31.3.05 (amounting to Rs. 128795 crore) may be consolidated and rescheduled for a fresh term of 20 years (resulting in repayment in 20 equal installments), and an interest rate of 7.5 per cent be charged on them. The consolidated loans include some loans which had been consolidated by earlier commissions at interest rates lower than 7.5 per cent. We have, however, included them in the present exercise so that management of loans becomes simpler for the central government. States would get benefit in repayment on account of reschedulement of these loans. In terms of these recommendations relating to consolidation, reschedulement and lowering of interest rate, the debt relief during the award period for all states put together, works out to Rs. 21276 crore in interest payments and Rs. 11929 crore in repayments. Thus, the proposed scheme provides benefit both in terms of interest rate reduction and a reschedulement of loans which will ease the liquidity position of states. The state-wise details of debt relief are indicated in annexure 12.7. In the debt consolidation exercise, we have not taken into account the fresh loans to be granted by the centre in the year 2004-05, as state-wise details of such loans were not available. The central government has, however, lowered the rate of interest on loans to states from 10.5 per cent to 9 per cent in 2004-05. This general debt relief comprising consolidation, reschedulement and lowering of interest rate to 7.5 per cent shall be available to all states with effect from the year they enact the fiscal responsibility legislation as recommended by us at para 12.36.

In addition to providing general debt relief by consolidating and rescheduling at substantially reduced rates of interest, the central loans granted to states before 31.3.04 and outstanding as on 31.3.05, the TFC devised a scheme of debt write-off based on fiscal performance.

The main recommendation regarding debt-relief may be summarized as follows:

1. Each state must enact a fiscal responsibility legislation prescribing specific annual targets with a view to eliminating the revenue deficit by 2008-09 and reducing fiscal deficits based on a path for reduction of borrowings and guarantees. Enacting the fiscal responsibility legislation is a necessary pre-condition for availing of debt relief.
2. The central loans to states contracted till 31.3.04 and outstanding on 31.3.05 (amounting to Rs. 128795 crore) may be consolidated and rescheduled for a

fresh term of 20 years (resulting in repayment in 20 equal installments), and an interest rate of 7.5 per cent be charged on them. This is, however, subject to the state enacting the fiscal responsibility legislation and will take effect prospectively from the year in which such legislation is enacted.

3. A debt write-off scheme linked to the reduction of revenue deficit of states is recommended under which the repayments due from 2005-06 to 2009-10 on central loans contracted up to 31.3.04 and recommended to be consolidated will be eligible for write off. The quantum of write off of repayment will be linked to the absolute amount by which the revenue deficit is reduced in each successive year during our award period. In effect, if the revenue deficit is brought down to zero, the entire repayments during the period will be written-off. The enactment of the fiscal responsibility legislation would be a necessary pre-condition for availing the debt relief under this scheme also with the benefit accruing prospectively.
4. In respect of future lending policy, the central government should not act as an intermediary and allow the states to approach the market directly. If, however, some fiscally weak states are unable to raise funds from the market, the centre could borrow for the purpose of on lending to such states, but the interest rates should remain aligned to the marginal cost of borrowing for the centre.
5. External assistance should be transferred to states on the same terms and conditions as attached to such assistance by external funding agencies, thereby making government of India a financial intermediary without any gain or loss. The transmission of external assistance to the states should be managed through a separate fund in the public account.
6. All states should set up sinking funds for amortization of all loans including loans from banks liabilities on account of NSSF etc. The fund should be maintained outside the consolidated fund of the states and the public account and should not be used for any other purpose, except for redemption of loans.
7. States should set up guarantee redemption funds through earmarked guarantee fees. This should be preceded by risk weighting of guarantees. The quantum of contribution to the fund should be decided accordingly.

17.7 Approach to Restructuring Public Finances

The TFC like its predecessor was asked under clause 5 of the TOR to "review the state of finances of the Union and the States and suggest a plan by which the Governments, collectively and severally, may bring about a restructuring of the public finances restoring budgetary balance, achieving macroeconomic stability and debt reduction along with equitable growth". As compared to the EFC, the reference to the objectives of debt reduction and equitable growth.

The Commission observed that restructuring public finances aimed at macroeconomic stabilization and achieving revenue account balance requires a broad analytical framework. The impact of the size and composition of government expenditure on growth, inflation, interest rate and the external account has to be considered in a framework that takes into account relevant interrelationships and feedbacks. Getting the right size of the government, and the right composition of government expenditure with a view to facilitating achievement of highest attainable growth rates, and meeting governments' social obligations including poverty reduction and provision of health and education should be considered integral to any plan for restructuring public finances. This requires increasing public spending in social and economic infrastructure for accelerating growth while reducing the overall fiscal imbalance.

In considering the issue of growth with stabilization, The TFC says that there is a need to examine (a) whether potential output along its growth path remains persistently below full employment levels and (b) whether actual output in any given year is above or below the growth path of potential output. In both cases, the structure of public finances and the management of fiscal policy have a role to play. When the long run growth path is below full employment levels, it is desirable to design public finances to remove the structural constraints such as supply bottlenecks and bring potential output closer to full employment levels. In this context, the structure of government expenditure, particularly the share of capital expenditure and its allocation becomes important. In regard to the second issue, in achieving stabilization, the management of aggregate government demand in response to the cyclical movements of potential output along its growth path becomes relevant.

It observes that the fiscal reform strategy envisaged by them 'centers on growth'. Growth depends, among other factors, on the rate of investment which, in turn, depends on the saving rate. The saving rate depends, among other factors, on government's revenue deficit, which amounts to government's net dis-saving. In other words, the aggregate saving rate, consisting of the saving rate of the household sector, the private corporate sector, and the government sector, remains less than what is potentially achievable as long as government is contributing negatively, i.e. drawing upon the saving of the private sector to finance consumption expenditure.

The TFC examines the saving-investment profile of the economy and summarises the main trends in recent years and highlights four main features as given below.

1. In the mid-nineties, the average growth of GDP at factor cost was 7.5 per cent

per annum, which fell to an average of 4.7 per cent during 2000-03;

2. The public sector saving rate fell during this period from an average level of 1.8 per cent to -2.3 percent of GDP, amounting to a fall of 4.1 percentage points;
3. The public sector investment fell by 1.9 percentage points from an average level of 7.8 percent of GDP to 5.9 per cent and the overall investment rate fell by 2.2 percentage points from an average level of 25.8 per cent to 23.6 per cent. The corporate investment fell from a high of 9.8 per cent of GDP in 1995-96 to 4.8 per cent in 2002-03;
4. The excess of gross domestic investment over gross domestic saving between the two periods, showing the extent of reliance on current account deficit, fell from 1.4 percentage points to -0.2 percentage points.

They argue that for increasing and sustaining the growth rate at 7 per cent, an aggregate investment rate of 28 percent is required on the assumption that the incremental capital-output ratio (ICOR) is 4.

Government debt is the outcome of accumulation of borrowing that is used to finance fiscal deficits. If the revenue account is balanced, the entire fiscal deficit would be spent on capital expenditures. Such investment can provide direct as well as indirect returns. The direct returns are in the form of interest receipts or dividends. The indirect returns arise when government investment stimulates growth, which results in higher revenue receipts. Debt becomes a problem when the increase in revenue receipts, whether direct or indirect, is not adequate to cover the interest liabilities that are required to service the debt. When large interest payments, remaining uncovered by an increase in revenue receipts, result in growing revenue deficits, the portion of fiscal deficit that is used for revenue expenditures becomes progressively larger and any revenue increases linked with increased expenditures remain small. Eventually, debt becomes unsustainable.

A review of the performance of different sectors in terms of the saving-investment balance provides evidence that in India, it is the household sector that has surplus savings that are absorbed by the private corporate and government sector. These surplus savings are their savings in the financial form. Table 17.8 gives a perspective on the surplus saving of the household sector that is available for use in other sectors. The financial savings of the household sector were roughly of the same order since 1993-94, being in the range of 10-11 per cent of GDP with small variations. Comparing the trend since 1995-96, it is apparent that the public sector has been absorbing a larger part of the financial savings of the household sector. The demand for this surplus by the private corporate sector came down from 4.65 per cent of GDP in 1995-96 to 1.4 per cent in 2002-03. That is why there was no pressure on the interest rates in the late nineties. Once the private sector demand picks up, a growth augmenting scenario would emerge only if the government is able to reduce its revenue deficit. This would also help in achieving a benign interest rate regime. If the government is able to eliminate its revenue deficit, and increase its savings and capital expenditures, demand for private investment would be strengthened. Studies have shown that government investment in infrastructure crowds-in private investment.

Table 17.8: Sector-wise Balance in Saving and Investment (per cent to GDP)

				(per cent points)
Year	Deficit Sectors		Surplus sector	Difference
	Pub sector	Private corporate sector	Saving of household sector in financial assets	Excess of investment over saving
	Ip-Sp	Ic-Sc	Sh-Ih	I-S
Average (1985-86 to 1989-90)	7.72	2.37	7.20	2.33
1990-91	8.23	1.47	8.73	3.20
1991-92	6.85	2.56	9.51	0.52
1992-93	6.97	3.79	8.73	1.85
1993-94	7.61	2.14	11.03	0.56
1994-95	7.05	3.43	11.92	1.17
1995-96	5.63	4.65	8.90	1.75
1996-97	5.36	3.58	10.35	1.30
1997-98	5.28	3.80	9.64	1.46
1998-99	7.57	2.65	10.36	1.05
1999-00	7.98	2.11	10.62	1.14
2000-01	8.61	0.94	10.66	0.61
2001-02	8.58	1.42	11.14	-0.32
2002-03	7.54	1.39	10.30	-0.92

Source: *Report of the Twelfth Finance Commission, 2004.*

The targets for revenue and fiscal deficits are essential ingredients of a restructuring program. Like the central government, similar targets would need to be fixed for the states, jointly and individually. These targets need to consider an underlying growth scenario along with levels of interest rates and other macroeconomic parameters. In fixing such targets, the TFC also took into account the determinants of debt dynamics. Growth in the debt-GDP ratio depends on two factors: (a) primary deficit to GDP ratio and (b) the excess of growth over interest rate. If growth rate is equal to interest rate, debt relative to GDP would be the outcome of accumulated primary deficits only. However, as long as growth rate is higher than interest rate, it absorbs some of primary deficits being translated into higher debt relative to GDP. On the other hand, if interest rate exceeds growth rate, the debt-GDP ratio would increase as a result of both factors. One critical limitation is that the nominal growth rate (g) and the nominal interest rate (i) cannot in reality be taken as exogenous. Although such assumption is made by the TFC, in particular, increasing levels of fiscal deficit, particularly when these are for investment, can increase the growth rate while high levels of fiscal deficit can put pressure on interest rates, particularly when the household savings in the financial form are not adequate to cover the demand for those savings from the government leaving enough for the private corporate sector. Using the equation of debt dynamics and assuming that the nominal growth rate (g) and the nominal effective interest rate are given and exogenous, the TFC states the following conditions.

- The debt-GDP ratio will be stabilized at a level b^* where $b^* = p\,(1+g)/\,(g-i)$.
- The fiscal deficit to GDP ratio will be stabilized at f^* where $f^* = p.g/\,(g-i)$.

These conditions can also be written in terms of ratios of interest payment to revenue receipts. The ratio of revenue receipts to GDP is indicated by (r) and the ratio of interest payments to revenue receipts is given by $(ip)^*$.

- The debt-GDP ratio will be stabilized at a level b^* where $b^* = (ip)^*r\,(1+g)/\,i$.
- The fiscal deficit to GDP ratio will be stabilized at f^* where $f^* = (ip)^*r.g/\,i$.

Using these conditions with growth rate of 5 per cent, the TFC suggests that fiscal deficit should be limited to 6 per cent of GDP, with 3 per cent each for the centre and states without any on-lending from the centre to the states. The corresponding stable debt-GDP ratio for the combined account, using the above relations is set at 56 per cent, with external debt measured at historical exchange rates, which is close to the actual level of combined debt relative to GDP at the end of 1996-97.

The TFC also emphasizes that there is a difference between stabilizing the debt-GDP ratio at the existing levels and stabilizing them at lower levels consistent with sustainability or desirable debt-GDP ratios derived from some considerations of optimality. In fiscal consolidation, two phases can be distinguished: adjustment phase and stabilization phase. In the adjustment phase, the debt-GDP ratio will steadily fall as primary deficit follows a path of adjustment so that the fiscal deficit target of 6 per cent is achieved. After the debt-GDP ratio has fallen to the desirable levels, primary deficit and fiscal deficit will be stabilized.

Keeping in view these considerations, The TFC has recommended that

1. The overall debt-GDP ratio on the combined account (with external debt measured at historical exchange rates) may be targeted to be brought down to 56 percent of GDP over a period of time. Since the level is estimated to be as high as 81 percent of GDP at the end of 2004-05, it should be brought down to at least 75 per cent by the end of 2009-10.
2. The level of combined interest payments relative to revenue receipts should be brought down from 34 per cent in 2004-05 to 22 per cent in 2009-10, and eventually to about 17 per cent.
3. The system of on-lending by the centre to the states should be phased out. The long term goal for the centre and state for the debt-GDP ratio should be 28 per cent each. Their fiscal deficit to GDP ratio targets should be 3 per cent each.

The fiscal adjustment plan of the TFC is based on the following assumptions regarding the macro economic scenario (Table 17.9).

Table 17.9: Macro Economic Scenario: Current and Forecast Period (per cent to GDP)

	2004-05 (estimates)	2009-10 (projections)
GDP Growth (constant prices) (per cent p.a.)	6.5	7.0
Inflation Rate (per cent p.a.)	6.0	5.0
Saving Rate	24.0	26.0
Investment Rate	24.5	27.5
Current Account Deficit	-0.5	1.5
Fiscal Deficit	8.9	6.0
Revenue Deficit	4.5	0.0
Government Capital Expenditure	5.6	6.6

Accordingly, the fiscal adjustment envisaged for the combined account of the central and state governments is given as summarized in Table 17.10

To achieve these changes, the TFC suggests a multi-dimensional restructuring as summarized below.

1. Taxation reforms aimed at building up non-distortionary and revenue-elastic system of taxation with tax rates that are low, limited in number of rate

categories, and stable;

2. Non-tax revenues where user charges, as a short term objective, ensure recoveries of current costs, and aim at full recovery of costs measured at acceptable efficiency levels in the longer run, in the case of services where there is no clear cut case for subsidization and ensure rates of return on investment that covers the average cost of borrowing;

Table 17.10: Summary of Suggested Restructuring: Combined Finances

Combined Finances	2004-05	2009-10	Adjustment 2009-10 minus 2004-05	Average Adjustment per year
Tax Revenue	15.6	17.6	2.0	0.40
Non tax Revenues	2.5	3.4	0.9	0.18
Total Revenue Receipts	18.1	21.0	2.9	0.58
Interest Payment	6.1	4.5	-1.6	-0.31
Total Revenue Expenditure	22.6	21.0	-1.7	-0.33
Capital Expenditure	5.6	6.6	1.0	0.20
Total Expenditure	28.3	27.6	-0.7	-0.13
Primary Expenditure	22.2	23.1	0.9	0.18
Revenue Deficit	4.5	0.0	-4.5	-0.90
Fiscal Deficit	8.9	6.0	-2.9	-0.57
Primary Deficit	2.8	1.5	-1.3	-0.26
Int. Payment/ Rev. Receipts	33.7	21.6	-12.1	-2.42
Outstanding Liabilities	80.8	74.5	-6.3	-1.26

3. Expenditure restructuring relating to both its size and sectoral allocations aimed at removing inefficiencies arising from misallocations, design and implementation of schemes, and delivery of services;
4. Rationalizing subsidies by reducing their overall volume, increasing their transparency by making them explicit, and improving their targeting;
5. Public sector restructuring where, apart from natural monopolies and strategic reasons, there is a strong case for reducing government's involvement;
6. Fiscal transfer system where equalizing transfers are given much greater weight and extended to local bodies;
7. Suggesting a reformed role for the plan process;

8. Strengthening the role of local bodies to become a more effective instrument in the delivery of local public goods;
9. Role of the central government in intermediating loans for the states including the need to specify annual ceiling of borrowing for each state and implementing a hard-budget constraint; and,
10. Suggesting institutional frameworks including ceiling on debt and deficits and mechanisms for their monitoring through state level fiscal responsibility legislation.

Part VI: Fiscal Policy and Macroeconomic Management

18

Fiscal Transfers to Local Bodies

Fiscal decentralization is in vogue.

W.E. Oates (1999)

Decentralization of governance is supposed to be efficiency augmenting. It is argued that the local bodies understand better the preferences of citizens of a locality in relation to local public goods. They also better understand the local cost conditions. Since they are large in number, competition among them for resources and skilled personnel is also a source of efficiency. In this chapter we look at the role of local bodies in India particularly after the 73rd and 74th amendments to the constitution, which have brought in to being the second tier of Finance Commissions in the form of state level Finance Commissions. We also look at the views and recommendations of the Tenth, Eleventh, and Twelfth Finance Commissions in this regard.

Although urban and rural local bodies have existed in India since long, two constitutional amendments, the 73rd for the rural bodies, and the 74th for the urban bodies, gave these bodies a constitutional recognition as institutions of 'self-governance'. In particular, the state governments were required to bring conformity legislations and clearly specify the responsibilities of the local bodies and the resources assigned to them. A provision was also made in the constitution requiring each state government to appoint a state level Finance Commission with a periodicity of five years. The Central Finance Commission was also required to look into the issues of the governance at the level of the third-tier and in particular suggest ways and means by which the resources of the states can be augmented with the explicit objective of strengthening the finances of their local bodies.

While the constitutional amendments made it mandatory for the state governments to bring forth conformity legislations for explicitly transferring functions and sources of resources from specified lists, states were given full freedom to specify as to what functions and/or resources were to be transferred from within the specified Lists.

A three tier structure for rural bodies comprising gram panchayat, block panchayat and nagar panchayat and three levels of municipal bodies viz. nagar panchayat, municipal council and municipal corporation provide the structure of the local bodies. According to information provided by the Twelfth Finance Commission, as given in Table 18.1, there are 2,43,685 rural local bodies and 3,723 urban local bodies in India.

Table 18.1: Number of Local Bodies in India

Rural		Urban	
Gram Panchayat	2,36,350	Municipal Corporation	109
Panchayat Samiti	6,795	Municipalities	1,432
Zila Parishad	531	Nagar Panchayats	2,182
Autonomous District Council	9		
	2,43,685		3,723

Source: Compiled from data in Report of the Twelfth Finance Commission.

The main issues in the context of local governance relate to whether the incorporation of the third-tier government involves an increase in the overall size of the government. The varied approaches and recommendations of the SFCs also generate problems of comparability. The role of the central Finance Commission in the context of the local bodies also requires careful consideration. The efficiency of delivery of finance to the third-tier in terms of time and impact is an important issue. Three types of transfers from the state to the local bodies have been envisaged – that of resources (funds), that of responsibilities (functions) and that of staff (functionaries). A critical issue is whether such a transfer of funds, functions, and functionaries is actually taking place in the states.

18.1 Constitution Provisions: Panchayats and Municipalities

On the constitution of the Panchayats and municipalities, the constitutional amendments have provided that "there shall be constituted in every state, Panchayats at the village, intermediate and district levels in accordance with the provisions of this Part. Panchayats at the intermediate level may not be constituted in a state having a population not exceeding 20 lakh." (Article 243 B). For the urban local bodies, it is provided that "There shall be constituted in every state-

1. a Nagar Panchayat for a transitional area, that is to say, an area in transition from a rural area to an urban area;
2. a Municipal Council for a smaller urban area; and
3. a Municipal Corporation for a larger urban area" (Article 243 Q)

The Constitution does not directly lay down any functional responsibility or fiscal powers for the panchayats and municipalities. It has provided in the seventh schedule, three lists, namely, a union list, a state list and a concurrent list. It is from the state list that state legislatures have to provide for the panchayats and municipalities, such powers and authority as they may consider necessary to enable them to function as institutions of self government, and such law may contain provisions for the devolution of powers upon panchayats and municipalities. The constitutional amendments contain two schedules, viz. schedule XI (243 G) and schedule XII (Article 243 W) that comprise a list of functions considered appropriate for devolution to panchayats and municipalities. The constitutional amendments have maintained the prerogative of the state in determining the functional responsibilities of the panchayats and municipalities.

In respect of tax assignment, the authority of the state legislature has not been fundamentally altered. But there is a recognition that the state-local fiscal relations in the country have historically been marked by ad-hocism and that these should be put on more certain and transparent grounds. The constitutional amendments have therefore provided for the setting up of a SFC in every state for the purpose of reviewing the financial positions of the panchayats and municipalities, and making recommendations covering areas like:

1. the determination of the taxes, duties, tolls and fees which may be assigned to, or appropriated by, the panchayats and municipalities;
2. the distribution between the state and the panchayats, and the state and municipalities, of the net proceeds of the taxes, duties, tolls and fees leviable by the state;
3. the grants-in-aid to the panchayats and municipalities from the consolidated fund of the state.

18.2 Local Governments in a Decentralized Framework

Local governments in India historically have been responsible for a variety of functions comprising in the main, public health (water supply), sewerage, sanitation and conservancy, and preventive health), public works (maintenance and repair of local roads and works) public safety (street lighting and fire fighting) public instruction (primary education and maintenance of libraries), management of common property, and a host of regulatory and developmental activities. The constitution amendments have visualized a larger role for the panchayats and municipalities. For this reason they have provided in the XI and XII schedules such functions as agriculture, including agricultural extension, rural electrification, non-conventional energy, and poverty alleviation.

For the urban bodies there is provision for such functions as urban planning, urban poverty alleviation, urban forestry, protection pf the environment and promotion of ecological aspects and slum improvement.

18.3 Approach of Tenth Finance Commission (TFC)

The TFC had taken a decision to consider PRIs and ULBs even though there was no specific reference in its terms of reference. However, in the absence of the reports of State Finance Commissions (SFCs), the TFC had made only an ad-hoc recommendation of granting Rs. 5,381 crore (4,381 crore for PRIs and 1,000 crore for ULBs) for a period of four years beginning from 1995-96. While recommending an ad hoc grant to local bodies, the TFC looked into the sources of information on the estimates of financial needs for operation of maintenance (O&M) of core municipal services in urban centers to assess the volume of transfers. The Ministry of Urban Development had requested for sources to supplement the finances of ULBs "to enable them to discharge at least their primary functions in an effective manner by improving the basic civil services as well as maintaining the existing assets." While providing an ad hoc grant of Rs.1,000 crore to ULBs, the Tenth Finance Commission had also decided to allocate the grant across states on the basis of the state-wise shares of slum population derived from the urban population, based on 1971 census. The Tenth Finance Commission also provided some guidelines for utilization of these grants stating that this grant was an 'additionality' over and above the amounts flowing to the ULBs from the state governments. The ULBs were required to provide suitable matching contributions by raising internal resources. The use of these grants for salaries and wages of municipal staff was not permitted.

18.4 Approach of the Eleventh Finance Commission

The process of decentralisation is likely to be made more effective by the Eleventh Finance Commission. The EFC constructed an index of decentralisation and linked a part of the grants to progress of decentralisation in each state. This is in conformity with some recent literature [e.g., see Smoke and Lewis (1996), Lewis and Smoke (1998)], which has emphasised the usefulness of rating of performance of local governments as a means of improving their performance. The decentralisation index constructed by the Eleventh Finance Commission utilised a set of ten indices to measure the commitment, the quality, and the content of decentralisation in the states in a comparative framework.

The experience, following the constitutional amendments in the early nineties, has been varied. While some state governments expeditiously brought forth the conformity legislations and appointed the State Finance Commission, others were slow. Often, even after receiving the recommendations of the State Finance Commissions, the state governments put those 'under consideration' for long years without either accepting or rejecting them.

On the issue of the recommendations of the central Finance Commission being based on the recommendations of the state Finance Commissions, the EFC had found itself unable to adopt the SFC reports as the basis for its recommendations because of:

- non-synchronization of the period of the recommendations of the SFCs and the central finance commission;
- lack of clarity in respect of the assignment of powers, authority and responsibilities of the local bodies;
- absence of a time frame within which the state governments are required to take action on the recommendations of the SFCs; and
- non-availability of the reports of the SFCs.

The EFC went so far as to recommend an amendment to the Constitution to delete the words "on the basis of the recommendations made by the Finance Commission of the State". It was expected as a result of EFC's recommendations regarding data collection and compilation for the local bodies, that there would be an effort to develop such a system of collection and compilation of such information at the state headquarters. This would serve to provide not only a basis for monitoring by the state government but also for the use of the SFCs and, therefore, the information would be updated and made available within a reasonable time.

The EFC had adopted the following factors and weights for working out the inter-se allocation of the grants-in-aid among the states:

Criterion Weight (per cent)

- Population 40
- Geographical area 10
- Distance from highest per capita income 20
- Index of decentralization 20
- Revenue effort 10

The EFC had selected the following10 parameters for the purpose of arriving at the index of decentralization:

1. enactment/amendment of the state/ panchayats/municipal legislation;
2. intervention/restriction in the functioning of the local bodies;
3. assignment of functions to the local bodies by state legislation;
4. actual transfer of functions to these bodies by way of rules, notification and orders;
5. assignment of power of taxation to the local bodies;
6. extent of exercise of taxation powers;

7. constitution of the SFCs and the submission of action taken on their reports;
8. action taken on the major recommendations of the SFC;
9. elections to the local bodies; and
10. constitution of the district planning committees as per the letter and spirit of article 243ZD.

In order to assess the 'revenue effort', the EFC had linked the ratio of own revenues of the local bodies to the state's own revenue and the GSDP separately and assigning a 5 per cent weight to each. While in the case of panchayats, the GSDP from primary sector excluding mining & quarrying was taken into account, in the case of municipalities the GSDP net of primary sector was taken as the basis. These were weighted by the rural and urban population.

18.5 Approach and Recommendations of the Twelfth Finance Commission

Para 4(iii) of the terms of reference asked the Twelfth Finance Commission to make recommendations as to: "the measures needed to augment the Consolidated Fund of a State to supplement the resources of the Panchayats and Municipalities in the State on the basis of the recommendations made by the Finance Commission of the State." This was consistent with the provisions contained in article 280(3)(bb) and (c) of the Constitution of India, as amended in 1993.

The TFC observed that the data furnished by the states did not facilitate quantification of the required augmentation of the consolidated fund on the basis of the SFC recommendations. Information could, however, be compiled regarding (a) the number of rural and urban local bodies at different tiers in each state, and (b) the details of own revenues and transfers from the states to their local bodies. The data that were compiled by the TFC show that the share of own revenues of the panchayats (all tiers) was 6.40 per cent of their total revenues for the period 1998-99 to 2002-03 which is a definite improvement over 4.17 percent estimated for the period 1990-91 to 1997-98 but is still low.

In terms of articles 243(I) and 243(Y) of the Constitution, the State Finance Commissions are to recommend

- the principles that should govern the distribution between the state on the one hand and the local bodies on the other of the net proceeds of taxes etc. leviable by the state and the inter-se allocation between different panchayats and municipalities;
- the determination of the taxes, duties, tolls and fees which may be assigned to, or appropriated by the local bodies; and
- grants in aid from the consolidated fund of the state to the local bodies.

The SFCs are also required to suggest measures needed to improve the financial position of the panchayats and the municipalities.

The TFC observed that the importance of the SFCs in the scheme of fiscal decentralization is that besides arbitrating on the claims to resources by the state government and the local bodies, their recommendations would impart greater stability and predictability to the transfer mechanism. The TFC observed that the convention established at the national level of accepting the principal recommendations of the Finance Commission without modification, however, is not being followed in the states. Often, even the accepted recommendations are not fully implemented, citing resource constraints and this defeats the very purpose of constituting the SFCs.

The TFC observed that while estimating the resource gap, the SFCs should follow a normative approach in the assessment of revenues and expenditure rather than make forecasts based on historical trends. Per capita norms for revenue generation must take into account the data relating to the tax bases and the avenues for raising non tax income by the municipalities and the panchayats, assuming reasonable buoyancies and the scope for additional resource mobilization. Per capita expenditure norms could be evolved on the basis of the average expenditure incurred by some of the best performing municipalities and panchayats in the provision of core services. The gap between the aggregate revenue and the aggregate expenditure calculated in this manner, after adjusting for the resource transfers recommended by the SFC, will provide the basis for the approach of the central finance commission.

In interpreting the role of the central Finance Commission in the context of the local bodies, the TFC observed that the purport of the relevant provision of the Constitution is two-fold:

- there may be a case to augment the consolidated fund of the state through additional grants from the centre keeping in view the special circumstances of the states, which may justify such assistance; and
- certain recommendations of the SFCs for augmenting the revenues of the state may require decision making by the central government as they may have centre-state and/or inter-state ramifications.

The central government may find the expert advice of the Central Finance Commission useful, while acting on the issues taken up by the state governments with the centre on the basis of such SFC recommendations. For example, the centre can act in respect of matters such as

1. revision of the rates of taxes/duties wherever the proceeds of such taxes/duties are to be appropriated by or assigned to the state; the stamp duty and duties of excise on medicinal and toilet preparations under article 268 and

the central sales tax under article 269 fall in this category;

2. revision of rates for certain categories of non-tax revenues, which are determined by the central government, such as the royalty from minerals wherever a part of such revenues have been recommended to be shared with the local bodies;
3. issues concerning central public sector undertakings, railways etc. including the property and other local taxes payable by them, return of land in their possession in excess of requirement etc.; and
4. upward revision of ceiling on profession tax requiring a constitutional amendment.

These according to the TFC provide only an illustrative list of issues, which do require central intervention and where the decisions of the central government would influence the flows into the consolidated fund of a state. Measures that a Central Finance Commission may choose to recommend on these and other issues of a similar nature after taking into account the views of the SFCs would, therefore, be a substantial fulfillment of its constitutional mandate. In view of this, the TFC recommended that the SFCs should clearly identify the issues which require action on the part of the central government to augment the consolidated fund of the state and list them out in a separate chapter for the consideration of the central finance commission.

The TFC, keeping in view the spirit of the 73rd and 74th amendments and the need to provide an impetus to the decentralization process, decided to recommend a sum of Rs. 25,000 crore for the period 2005-10 as grants-in-aid to augment the consolidated fund of the states to supplement the resources of the municipalities and the panchayats. This will be equivalent to 1.24 per cent of the sharable tax revenues and 0.9 per cent of the estimated gross revenue receipts of the centre during the period 2005-10.

In the case of grants for the PRIs, the TFC decided to introduce some conditionalities by providing that these grants should be utilized to improve the service delivery by the panchayats in respect of water supply and sanitation. The schemes being taken up under Swajaldhara are provided a grant of 10 per cent of capital costs as incentive for the O&M along with a matching contribution by the state government after it is run successfully for 12 months. There is no provision for O&M for the schemes completed previously. The panchayats need to be encouraged to take over and maintain all such schemes. Some of the existing schemes may require special repairs to make them fully functional. The PRIs may take over the assets and utilize these grants for repairs/rejuvenation and maintenance to make them fully operational. Even after this, the PRIs may not be able to bear the entire cost of O&M of water supply for an initial period of five years. They should, however, recover at least 50 per cent of the recurring costs in the form of user charges.

In the case of the urban local bodies, the TFC stressed the importance of public-private partnership to enhance the service delivery in respect of solid waste management. The municipalities in TFC's view should concentrate on collection, segregation and transportation of solid waste. State governments may require the municipalities of towns of population over 1,00,000 by 2001 census to prepare a comprehensive scheme including composting and waste to energy programmes to be undertaken in the private sector for appropriate funding from the grants in aid recommended by the Commission. Grants-in-aid should, however, be available to support the cost of collection, segregation and transportation only, as the activities to be taken up by the private sector should be commercially viable once the municipality is able to discharge its role effectively. The TFC therefore recommended that at least 50 per cent of the grants provided to each state for the urban local bodies should be earmarked for these schemes. The six mega cities of Delhi, Mumbai, Kolkata, Chennai, Bangalore and Hyderabad were excluded for the purpose of grants-in-aid.

In determining the *inter se* allocation of the grants in aid among the states, for the urban local bodies, the TFC used the average per capita GSDP excluding primary sector (at comparable prices) on the basis of the GSDP data supplied by the CSO and the population figures interpolated/projected for three years; viz. 1999-00, 2000-01 and 2001-02 based on 1991 and 2001 census data on urban population. The distance of each state was measured from the state with the highest average per capita GSDP, plus half of the standard deviation. The distances were then weighted by the urban population (2001) of the respective state to arrive at its share.

The TFC also constructed an index of deprivation to take into account intra–state disparities on the basis of data relating to certain minimum needs of the population. Drinking water and sanitation are the two core services performed by the local bodies, both rural and urban. State-wise census 2001 data are available with a break up between rural and urban areas regarding the number of households fetching water from a distance (over 100 metres in the case of urban and 500 metres in the case of rural households) households with no latrines within the house premises and households with no drainage facilities for flow of waste water. These have been used to construct this index. The formula used is $D.I=0.5x+0.25(y+z)$ where D.I is the Deprivation Index, x is the percentage of households fetching water from a distance, y is the percentage of households without latrines and z, the percentage of households without drainage. The distance from the minimum deprived state was then weighted by the census 2001 population for rural and urban areas to derive the state-wise share. A standard deviation of 0.5 has been allowed so as to enable the least deprived state also to get a share. We assign weight of 10 per cent to this criterion.

In order to assess the 'revenue effort', the EFC had linked the ratio of own revenues of the local bodies to the state's own revenue and the GSDP separately and assigning a 5 per cent weight to each. While in the case of panchayats, the GSDP from primary sector excluding mining & quarrying was taken into account, in the case of municipalities the GSDP net of primary sector was taken as the basis. These were suitably weighted by the rural and urban population as the case may be. The TFC decided to modify this criterion by including the mining and quarrying in case of panchayats, with a weight of 10 per cent to each of the elements. The period taken was 2000-01 to 2002-03 in the case of the own revenues of local bodies related to states own revenue and 1999-2000 to 2001-02 in case of own revenues of local bodies related to GSDP.

Table 18.2, based on the information given in the Report of the Twelfth Finance Commission gives the extent to which the rural local bodies depend on their own resources, tax and non-tax for selected states. At the aggregate level, the rural local bodies are able to raise less than 7 per cent of their expenditures. As such they are dependent very highly on transfers from the higher tiers.

Table 18.2: Rural Local Bodies: Ratio of Own Revenues to Total Expenditure (per cent)

State	1998-99	1999-00	2000-01	2001-02	2002-03
Andhra Pradesh	3.93	3.62	3.45	3.38	3.34
Bihar	20.15	10.23	25.88	2.37	21.76
Chhattisgarh	13.13	12.51	9.56	10.04	9.48
Goa	71.25	67.69	57.00	34.80	28.35
Gujarat	2.65	2.50	1.85	2.03	2.72
Haryana	45.35	20.26	32.85	21.83	20.82
Himachal Pradesh	8.86	12.43	14.82	16.01	16.11
Karnataka	1.67	1.37	1.48	1.25	1.45
Kerala	9.44	14.08	14.45	14.12	12.67
Madhya Pradesh	26.50	27.00	28.11	25.44	36.68
Maharashtra	7.88	7.98	8.57	9.16	9.98
Orissa	5.40	3.97	7.82	6.48	3.02
Punjab	66.33	59.69	58.94	59.10	55.32
Rajasthan	2.38	2.32	2.36	2.28	2.17

Tamil Nadu	14.56	10.97	9.95	12.09	12.39
Uttar Pradesh	11.60	9.18	9.52	13.68	10.62
Uttaranchal	8.69	8.21	15.64	10.50	20.46
West Bengal	16.89	10.36	5.26	7.30	17.64
All India	6.34	6.15	5.89	5.98	6.77

Source: (Basic Data): *Report of the Twelfth Finance Commission, 2004.*

In summary, it may be said that the experiment of decentralization brought about by the constitutional 73rd and 74th amendments is in an important phase of evolution. In almost all states, two rounds of State Finance Commissions have been constituted. The relevant conformity legislations have been brought about. What is now needed is for the State Finance Commissions to work under a minimum common framework so that timely and comparable information may become available to the Central Finance Commission. It is also necessary for the rural local bodies to reduce their dependence on transferred funds.

19

Fiscal Policy, Growth and Macroeconomic Stability

> It is increasingly recognized that sustained economic growth is possible only within a sound macroeconomic framework and that in such a framework fiscal policy plays a key role.
>
> Stanley Fischer and William Easterly, 1990

Government plays a key role in determining growth as well as in providing important social services like education and health. Government expenditure and the manner of its financing provides potent fiscal policy instruments through which the employment of resources could be uplifted to keep close to full employment levels and rate of inflation could also be kept at low and stable levels. Attaining an output growth rate consistent with full employment of resources and keeping output growth as well as inflation rate stable is part of macroeconomic stability.

In the sphere of economic activities, markets and governments are intertwined in a number of ways, acting sometimes in competition and, at others, as complements. In the competitive mode, governments attempt to take over the productive and allocative functions of the markets. In the complementary role, governments not only facilitate the working of the market, they also become endogenous to it by acting as a participant in the market processes. While competition is the essence of the market, governments are characterized by autonomy. More recently, scholars like Breton have pointed out that competition is also an attribute of governments. For example, within a country, sub-national governments may compete among themselves for attracting capital, both domestic and foreign, as also skilled labor. They may also compete with the central government for control over activities that are under concurrent jurisdiction as well as for resources that are shareable. Governments also compete, particularly in the mixed economies, with the private sector in activities that are open to both. While governments serve to guard against market failures, markets provide an antidote to government failures

By providing public and merit goods financed by taxation, governments succeed where markets fail. By internalizing externalities, promoting equity, reducing poverty, and achieving other social objectives, governments generate social utility. Governments help in reducing transaction costs by providing legal and institutional mechanisms for enforcing contracts as well as by indicating clear and explicit 'rules of the game' including protection of property rights, and modes of resolving disputes.

19.1 Assessing Fifty Years of Economic Growth

For an examination of potential of the future, it is useful to look into the mirror of growth experience of the past fifty years. This assessment requires an analysis of economic growth, and changes in the structure of output.

19.2 Trends in Growth

The initial years since 1950-51 were characterized by a low saving rate and a large share of agriculture in GDP. As a result the aggregate growth rate languished around 3 per cent for a period of about 35 years. This growth threshold came to be known as the Hindu Growth Rate. The saving rate, particularly of the household sector progressively increased, and the share of the agricultural sector became smaller.

These changes along with economic reforms initiated in the early nineties, led growth rates to even cross 7 per cent of GDP in the mid-nineties. Looking to the long period trends of growth rates after ironing out cyclical fluctuations, there was a fall in the growth rate from a little over 4 per cent in the early fifties to about 2.5 per cent in the mid-seventies. Thereafter, there is a sustained increase in the growth rate, which reached a level of 6 per cent on long term basis. It fell again to about five per cent at present on trend basis (Chart 19.1).

Similarly on trend basis, inflation rate as measured by the implicit price deflator steadily increased from a little less than 1 per cent in the early fifties to close to 10 per cent in the early nineties, after which it steadily fell to settle around 5 per cent on average at present (Chart 19.2).

19.3 Change in the Structure of Output

With higher growth, the structure of output also changed. Growth in agriculture was low but more volatile; growth in services was high and less volatile. With low average growth rates the share of the primary sector fell throughout the five decades.

It fell from 58 per cent to 27 per cent during this period. Agriculture considered by itself only accounts for about 23 per cent. The share of manufacturing together with electricity and construction increased from 13.5 per cent to 24.2 per cent of GDP.

Chart 19.1: Growth Rate and Trend Growth Rate

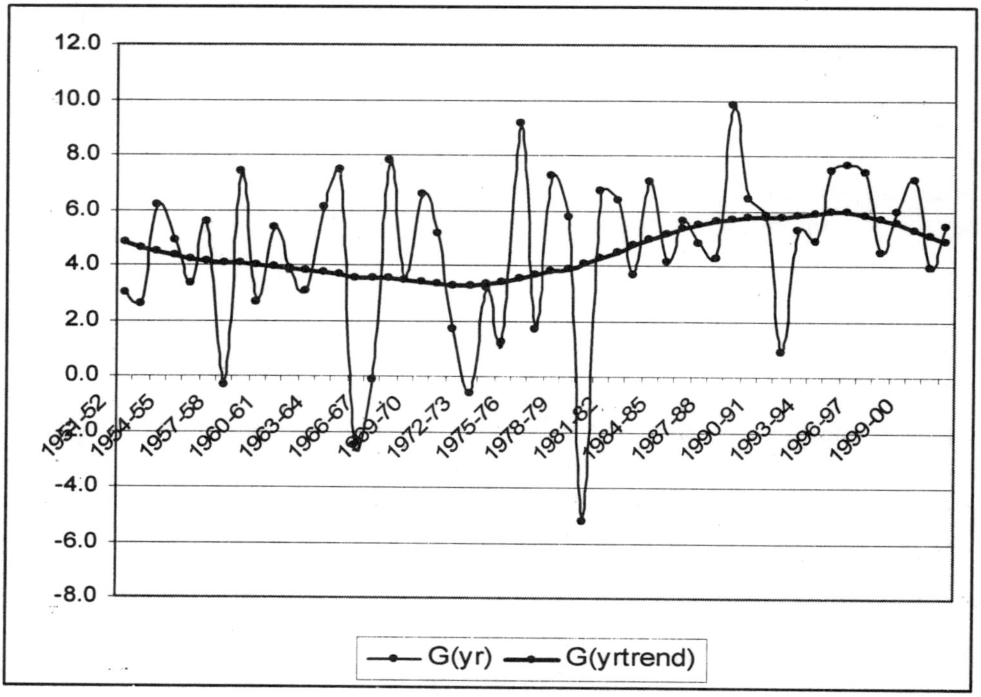

Chart 19.2: Inflation and Trend Rate of Growth in Prices

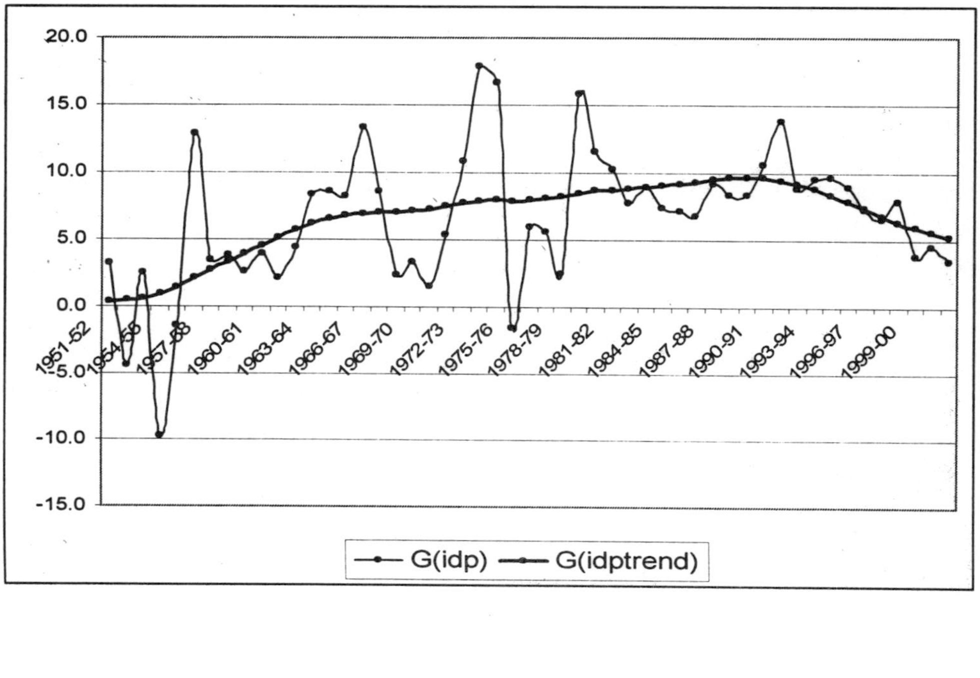

The three main groups under the services sector progressively increased their share, which rose from 28 per cent in 1950-51 to a little less than 50 per cent. The main increase came in trade, transport, and communications followed by public administration, defense, and other administrative services. In financial and business services, there was hardly any increase (Table 19.1).

Table 19.1: Changing Structure of Output: A Overview

Year	A	M	S1	S2	S3	S=S1+S2+S3
1950-51	57.66	13.51	9.68	10.30	8.85	28.83
1960-61	47.81	18.40	11.68	12.31	9.80	33.80
1970-71	47.15	19.58	12.72	10.36	10.20	33.27
1980-81	40.61	22.75	16.08	9.11	11.45	36.64
1990-91	34.01	24.89	18.39	10.39	12.31	41.10
2000-01	27.32	24.23	21.53	12.46	14.47	48.46

A=Agriculture, mining and quarrying.
M=Manufacturing, electricity, and construction.
S1=Trade, transport, and communication.
S2=Financial and business services.
S3=Public adm., defence, and oth. services.
Source: (Basic data): National Income Accounts.

Yet, India still nurses one of the largest populations of poor numbering more than 26 crore in absolute terms, with 27 per cent of rural population and 23 per cent of urban population being below the poverty line. India's agricultural sector has been characterized by low growth averaging below 3 per cent over the long run. Agricultural growth is not only low but also highly volatile making the rural population, which still accounts for more than 72 per cent of total population vulnerable to sharp economic fluctuations. Averaging around 23 per cent in recent years, India's saving rate could be counted as significantly lower than desired and necessary for stepping up the growth rate beyond 7 per cent on a sustained basis.

19.4 Agriculture: Low Growth and Dwindling Share

Chart 19.3 shows how agricultural growth has proved to be volatile around a trend path that is limited to only 2.6 per cent of growth. In fact agricultural growth was extremely sluggish in the first half of the eighties. Around 1996-97, with the start of the Green revolution, agricultural growth picked up steadily. With small variations in the trend, agricultural growth peaked at the end of the eighties. It is coincidental that in the nineties trend growth started to decline from a peak of 3.6 per cent reaching a low level of 2.6 per cent in 2000-01.

Chart 19.3: Agricultural Growth and Its Trend

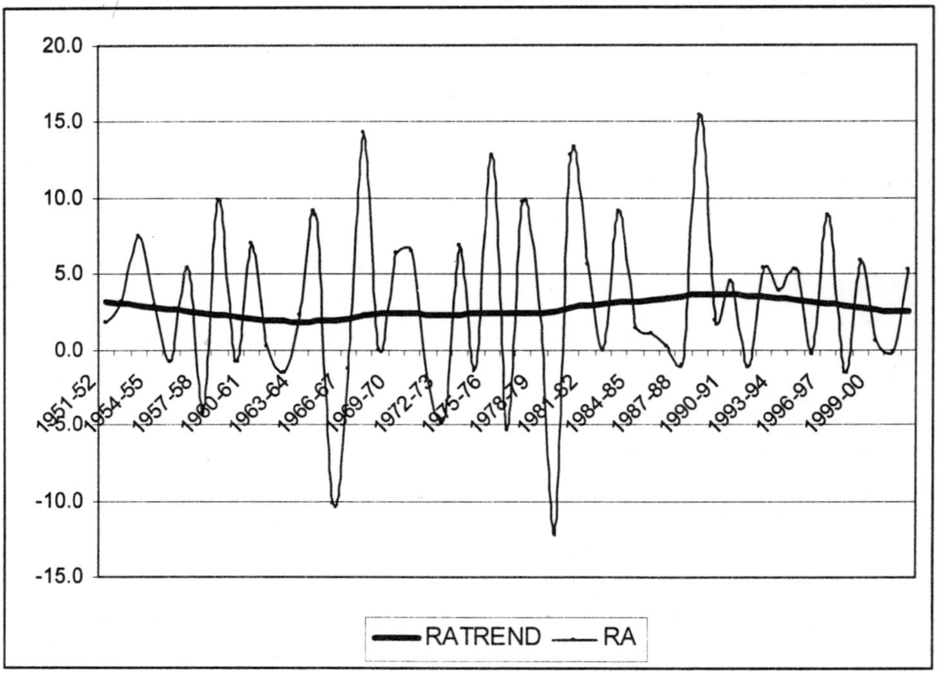

The volatility of annual growth rates in agriculture is also of some importance as it shows the vulnerability and risk to which the farmers are exposed. Annual growth rates show sharp fluctuations around the trend growth rate. The highest in any one year was 1967-68 at 14.3 per cent and later in 1987-88, the growth rate was 15.4 per cent. The worst year of negative growth was 1965-66 at -10.2 per cent and 1979-80 at -12.2 per cent.

In the context of overall growth, it may be noted that as events turned out, both growth and stability remained below par during 2000-01 to 2004-05, i.e. the period for which the recommendation of the EFC applied. The growth of output remained much below potential output. In fact, with stagnation in the investment rate around 22 per cent of GDP, even the potential output shows a downward trend. There has been considerable volatility around the trend line indicating potential output. The rate of inflation remained under check but in some years it fell well below trend levels. The nominal growth rates in the four years during 2000-01 to 2003-04 were 9.6, 8.4, 6.8 and 12.1 per cent (Table 19.2).

Table 19.2: Growth Rates in Agriculture: Actual and Trend

Year	Trend	Actual	Year	Trend	Actual
1951-52	3.216	1.763	1976-77	2.423	-5.379
1952-53	3.111	3.131	1977-78	2.452	9.713
1953-54	2.990	7.531	1978-79	2.486	2.320
1954-55	2.836	2.974	1979-80	2.571	-12.163
1955-56	2.678	-0.800	1980-81	2.749	12.853
1956-57	2.542	5.426	1981-82	2.909	5.705
1957-58	2.415	-4.198	1982-83	3.036	-0.023
1958-59	2.317	9.869	1983-84	3.144	9.141
1959-60	2.199	-0.835	1984-85	3.217	1.470
1960-61	2.086	6.980	1985-86	3.296	1.019
1961-62	1.971	0.265	1986-87	3.400	0.195
1962-63	1.893	-1.524	1987-88	3.523	-1.009
1963-64	1.875	2.363	1988-89	3.631	15.432
1964-65	1.899	8.926	1989-90	3.653	1.891
1965-66	1.958	-10.227	1990-91	3.629	4.591
1966-67	2.110	-1.254	1991-92	3.578	-1.140
1967-68	2.284	14.324	1992-93	3.526	5.414
1968-69	2.383	-0.034	1993-94	3.450	3.907
1969-70	2.425	6.364	1994-95	3.348	5.338
1970-71	2.402	6.504	1995-96	3.221	-0.325
1971-72	2.344	-1.711	1996-97	3.090	8.834
1972-73	2.319	-4.597	1997-98	2.939	-1.473
1973-74	2.349	6.948	1998-99	2.806	5.909
1974-75	2.384	-1.261	1999-00	2.682	0.566
1975-76	2.421	12.857	2000-01	2.588	-0.142

Source: (Basic Data): National Income Accounts.

19.5 Government Failures: Causes and Experience

Like market failures, there are also government failures. The literature on government failures, or more generally on non-market failures, is as extensive as that for market failures, although more recent. Governments are slow to respond to changes, bound as they are by laws, rules and regulations. In a hierarchical structure of decision-making in governments, there is also efficiency loss due to information loss in the process of its upward transmission. As in the case of markets, a critical source of government failure resides in the set of principal-agent problems. The principal in this case are the 'people' and agents are the elected representatives as well as the functionaries who have the responsibility of translating people's preferences into action. As the principal-agent theory says, there is no 'natural' reason for the agents not to substitute their own interests and preferences for those of their principals in their actions.

In the relationship between markets and governments, two aspects have been considered as the root causes for fostering inefficiency. One is what has been called by North, as the problem of 'state predation' whereby governments endeavor to persistently enlarge their share of and control over the economy. The second was identified by Kornai as the problem of absence of a hard budget constraint. State predation involves the attempt by governments to increase interventions in the economy by increasing taxes, regulations, assuming monopoly powers in specified production or distribution activities, or in appropriating property. There is a tendency at all levels of government to push for a larger involvement. However, history has demonstrated often enough that governments are inefficient as compared to the market in coordinating million upon million transactions to produce optimal outcomes. As Hayek had suggested several decades back, governments cannot match the ability of the market to process information including decentralized decisions of consumers and producers. Beyond a point, therefore, enlargement of government is likely to be inefficient. Carried to the extreme, state predation could be so inefficient as to be self-destructive, as evidenced in the case of the erstwhile USSR. The second problem, relating to the absence of a hard budget constraint, is also inefficiency inducing as, instead of economizing on the use of resources; agents operate under the impression that they can increase their share in resources.

Competition among governments can exhibit itself in a variety of forms. The famous 'race to bottom' among state governments exhibits itself in a competition for giving tax exemptions and concessions. Governments compete for all mobile resources, capital as well as human. Citizens are able to choose a different jurisdiction than where they reside for certain services, particularly health and education.

A threat to the working of the markets emanates from the existence of several tiers of governments if markets are fragmented by the construction of jurisdictional barriers with devices such as Octroi, toll and entry taxes or through other interventions in the unfettered movement of goods and services. In the Indian context, until very recently there were serious legislative restrictions in the movement of agricultural produce across states. At present, a high duty of sales taxes on inter-state sales, also called the central sales tax is a significant impediment in realizing a country wide integrated market allowing unfettered movements of inputs and final goods across state boundaries. The threat to markets is from government per se as well as its form, whether unitary or federal, and the nature of federalism whether cooperative or competitive.

19.6 Fiscal Imbalance and Growth

The deterioration in the revenue account balance of the centre, states and their combined accounts had started towards the end of the seventies. It was in 1979-80 that the central finances fell into revenue deficit after recording a surplus since 1950-51 in all but two years. The combined account of the centre and states went into revenue deficit in 1982-83, and that of all states in 1986-87 as noted by the EFC, almost all the states went through three-phase deterioration in the revenue account balance. In the first phase up to 1986-87, non plan account surplus was larger than the plan deficit and to that extent it yielded an overall revenue balance. During 1986-87 to 1991-92, the magnitude of plan revenue deficit increased sharply and it became larger than the non plan surplus. Since then, both the plan revenue account and the non plan revenue account have remained in deficit and the deficit has generally been growing in magnitude. Only some of the special category states continued to have a surplus on the plan revenue account. However, this was due solely to the special composition for plan assistance where they got ninety percent as grant credited to their revenue accounts. Not only has the revenue account remained in growing imbalance; fiscal deficits also grew steadily since the late 80s except for a period of small improvement in the early 90s.

Among the reasons generally given for this all round fiscal deterioration, some of the important ones are: revision of salaries and pensions in the wake of the recommendations of the Fifth Central Pay Commission, erosion in the buoyancy of central indirect taxes, and the unusually high nominal interest rates towards the end of the nineties. After the peak growth rate achieved in the mid-nineties, there was also a general slow down in growth towards the end of the nineties, which has continued till 2002-03. In the first three years of the new decade, the growth rates have been estimated at 4.0, 5.6 and 4.4 percent respectively, which are much less than the range of 7 to 7.5 percent envisaged by the Eleventh Finance Commission. In fact, in spite of the falling nominal interest rates, it has been noted that for these three years the growth rate has fallen short of the average interest rate on the outstanding liabilities. This has meant that the growth in the central debt relative to GDP has been due not only to the primary deficit but also to the sign reversal in the growth-interest rate differential (See Rangarajan and Srivastava, 2003). The situation is worse for the states as in their case the effective interest rate is even higher. In the context of macroeconomic stability at a reasonable level of growth, determination of sustainable levels of fiscal deficit and debt becomes important.

The combined debt-GDP ratio of the central and state governments at the end of 1950-51 was 29.6 percent. Rangarajan and Srivastava (2005) observe that during 1951-52 to 1959-60 a little less than 13 percentage points were added to the debt-GDP ratio. An additional accretion of about 4 percentage points took place in the sixties. In the seventies, there was hardly any change in the debt-GDP ratio. It was in the eighties and nineties that there was an increase respectively of 14.7 and 9.4 percentage points in the debt-GDP ratio. The Indian experience shows that throughout the period from 1955-56 to 1999-00 it was the primary deficit that caused the increase in the debt-GDP ratio. Often a significant part of the pressure of primary deficit could be absorbed by the excess of growth over interest rates. Had this cushion not been available, cumulated primary deficits through 1950-51 to 2001-02 would have added 165 percentage points to the combined debt to GDP ratio.

The major concern in macroeconomic stability is fiscal deficit, central as well as sub-national. The combined fiscal deficit of centre and states has remained above 10 per cent of GDP in 2001-02 and 2002-03. The combined fiscal deficit of the centre and states stood at 9.3 per cent of GDP in 1990-91. There was a clear improvement in the early nineties.

After falling to 6.26 per cent in 1996-97, the fiscal deficit to GDP ratio started rising again and exceeded 10 percent in 2001-02 and 2002-03. Although only marginally higher than that in 1990-91, this level of fiscal deficit is qualitatively much different because it is accompanied by much higher levels of the debt-GDP ratio, the ratio of interest payments to revenue receipts, and the share of revenue deficit in fiscal deficit.

The debt-GDP ratio has risen from 61.7 per cent in 1990-91 to about 79 per cent in 2002-03, when external debt is considered at historical exchange rates. Some six percentage points need to be added to this when external debt is evaluated at current exchange rates.

Fiscal deficit relative to GDP, when kept at high levels over long periods of time, Rangarajan and Srivastava (2005) observe, can adversely affect savings and investment, and consequently growth. The usability of fiscal policy as a tool of countercyclical intervention is also adversely affected when fiscal deficit is high and structural in nature.

19.7 Fiscal Deficit: Impact on Saving, Investment, and Growth

As an empirical and policy issue, the link between fiscal deficit and growth, saving and investment rates, inflation and current account deficits have been examined in the literature to provide results that may help determine the fiscal policy stance. The relationship between fiscal deficit and interest rate and the existence of crowding out are important considerations in determining the advisability of deficit-financed expansionary fiscal policies. Authors like Sunderrajan and Thakur (1980), Pradhan et al (1990) and Parker (1995) had earlier examined the issue of crowding out in the Indian context.

More recently, Chakraborty (2002) finds that fiscal deficit does not put upward pressure on the interest rate while Goyal (2004), using monthly data argues that there is a two-way causality between fiscal deficit and interest rates. In his view, interest rates did not rise in recent years in spite of high fiscal deficits because of larger liquidity available to the system. RBI (2002) has noted that raising public sector investment to boost aggregate demand in the economy crowds-out both private consumption and investment with no long-lasting impact on output. On the other hand, infrastructure investment by the public sector crowds-in private investment while public investment in manufacturing crowds out private investment.

19.8 Performance of Saving and Investment

The key to growth is capital accumulation, which depends on investment, which in turn depends on savings. An understanding of the behavior of saving and investment by the private and public sectors is also important for considering the impact of fiscal deficit. In India it has been the household sector, which proved to be the start performer in the context of savings. The government sector and to some extent the private corporate sector draw upon the unabsorbed household sector savings that are called financeable savings.

As long as the household sector is providing enough financeable savings, these may be absorbed by the public sector without putting pressure on the interest rates. Also, it has been argued that any reduction in public saving is a loss to the overall saving rate on a one to one basis. In this section, we look at the profile of the saving-GDP ratio since 1950-51 and the relative contribution of the household, private corporate, and public sectors.

We look at the saving-GDP ratio of the household, private corporate, and public sectors in India over the period 1950-51 to 2001-02, which is depicted in Chart 19.4.

Chart 19.4: Household, Private Corporate and Public Sector Saving Rates

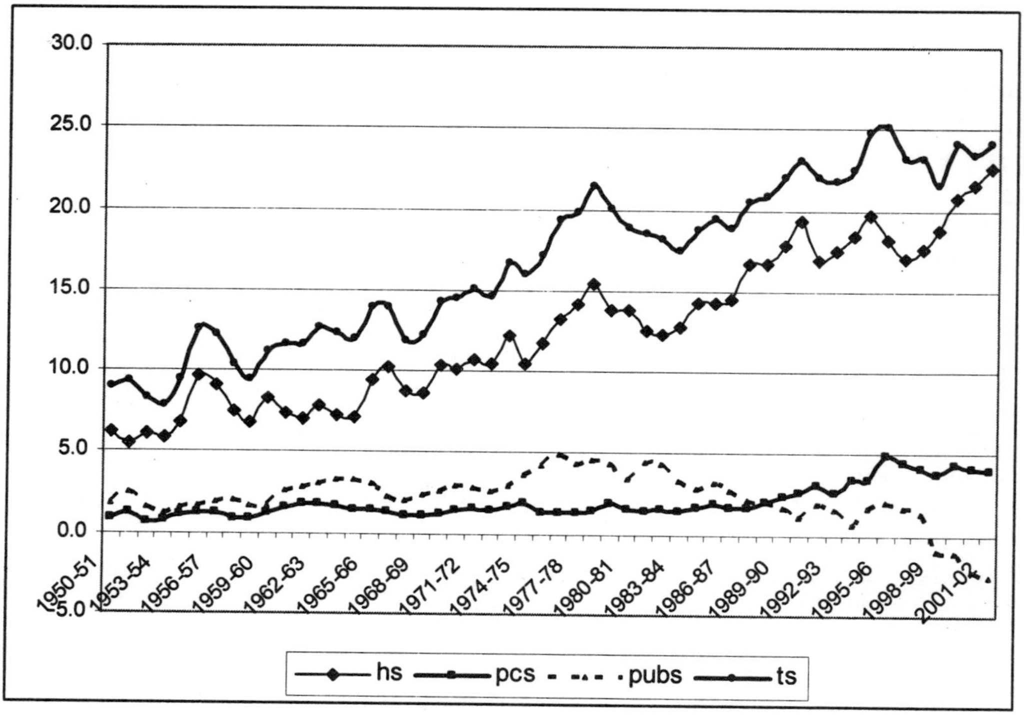

Starting from a level of just 6 per cent of GDP, the household sector saving ratio has shown a steady rise reaching levels of 22.6 per cent of GDP in 2001-02. The saving ratio of the private corporate sector has been somewhat stagnant at below 2 per cent of GDP until 1987-88 after which it steadily rose to cross 4 per cent of GDP in 1995-96. Since then it has generally been above 4 per cent but is not rising any further. The public sector savings, which reached a peak in 1976-77, have now become negative. The public sector savings relative to GDP had peaked in 1976-77 at 4.9 per cent. They fell marginally but had a local peak in 1981-82 at 4.5 per cent. Since then there has been a steady decline. The public sector saving to GDP ratio turned negative in 1998-99 and the dis-saving relative to GDP continued to increase in magnitude reaching a level of negative 2.5 per cent in 2001-02. This amounts to a fall of 7 percentage points from the level of 4.5 per cent achieved in 1981-82. If the public sector could achieve back this level the total saving-GDP ratio would increase to about 33 per cent of GDP. The growth achievable at that level would be significantly higher on a sustainable basis.

Chart 19.5 shows the time profile of public and private investment relative to GDP since 1950-51. Until 1988-89, both of these were rising along a trend path. Since then, while private investment has continued to rise along a trend path, public investment has nose-dived.

Chart 19.5: Private and Public Sector Investment Rates

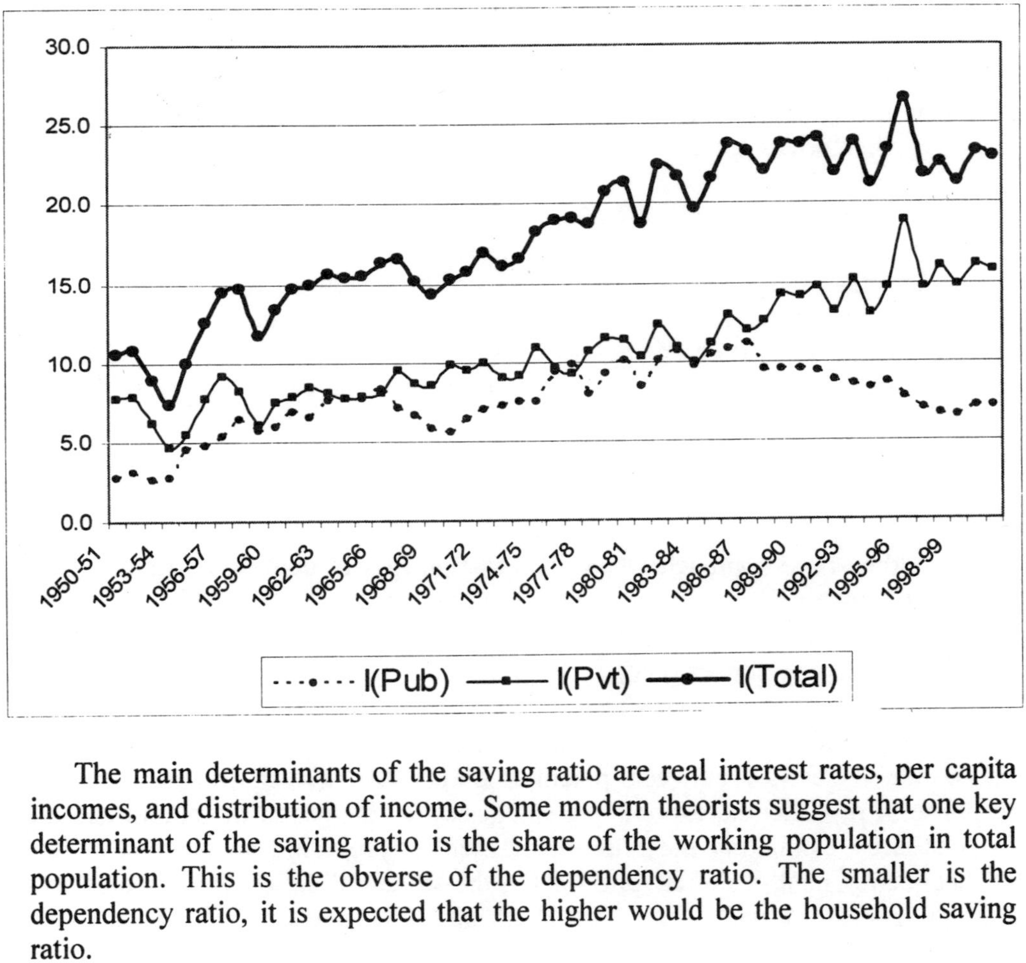

The main determinants of the saving ratio are real interest rates, per capita incomes, and distribution of income. Some modern theorists suggest that one key determinant of the saving ratio is the share of the working population in total population. This is the obverse of the dependency ratio. The smaller is the dependency ratio, it is expected that the higher would be the household saving ratio.

19.9 Fiscal Policy: Issues of Macroeconomic Stability

Economies are prone to go through business cycles. Fiscal policy is a potent instrument for moderating the amplitude of the cycle and the severity of its impact. This is done by supporting demand by borrowing in the case of recession, and controlling demand to curb inflationary tendencies in an expansionary phase. In using of fiscal deficit as a tool for temporary support to increase the government's demand, there is a need to distinguish between the long term or trend growth after adjusting for the cyclical component of growth and correspondingly between structural or cyclically neutral deficit and the transitory deficit.

The structural deficit should be managed to strengthen the growth impulse of the economy. The short term component of fiscal deficit should be used to minimize the impact of cyclical changes. The use of discretionary expenditure to stimulate the economy when it is below potential output and contain inflationary pressure when prices are above trend levels helps in macroeconomic stabilization.

19.10 Structural and Cyclical Deficit in India

In a recent study, Rangarajan and Srivastava (2005) review alternative methodologies to measure cyclical deficits with a view to applying a suitable method in the Indian case. Fiscal deficits can be seen as the sum of structural and cyclical components. If one component is estimated, the other can be derived as a residual. Methods for measuring the structural and cyclical components include the following.

- Constant elasticities method, where the cyclical component is estimated first based on estimated of revenue and expenditure elasticities with respect to income,
- Smoothed-ratio approach where the structural fiscal deficit is estimated first by smoothening the revenue and expenditure ratios to GDP, and
- Structural time series approach where time-varying elasticities are used and the cyclical component is estimated first.

The more traditional approach of constant elasticities used by OECD, among others, involves a three-step procedure. First, the output gap is calculated by taking the difference between potential output and actual output; secondly, response of revenue and expenditure categories to changes in the output gap are calculated by estimating the relevant elasticities, providing an estimate of the cyclical component of deficit; and finally, the structural deficit is calculated as a residual. Barrel, Morgan, Sefton and in't Veld (1994) and Bradner, Diebalk, and Schuberth (1998) show that estimates of structural balances are highly sensitive to the method of estimating trend output and uncertainty surrounding the output-elasticities of expenditure and revenue categories.

The structural time series approach has been suggested by Jaeger (1990). In this method, the variances of the parameters are not well defined. It has been shown by Harvey (1989) that in such models, the exogenous variables must be bounded from above and non-stochastic. Url (1997) has pointed out that nominal potential output cannot be regarded as bounded from above. The smoothed-ratio approach, suggested by Cano and Kanutin (1996) provides a direct and simpler method of calculating the structural deficit. In this approach, revenues and expenditures, expressed as ratios to GDP, are decomposed into a structural and residual component by using a Hodrick – Prescott (HP) filter.

Rangarajan and Srivastava (2005) have used the following methodology for distinguishing between structural and cyclical components of deficits. Taking r_s and e_s to be the trend ratios of revenues and expenditures relative to GDP and r_c and e_c to be corresponding cyclical components, the structural deficit to GDP ratio is derived directly as

$f_s = e_s - r_s$

The cyclical deficit is obtained as a residual. The trend levels are calculated by using the H-P filter. As a direct method, it is able to exclude transitory non-cyclical events. The linearity of the H-P filter also facilitates using a disaggregated approach since the disaggregated structural components add to 1. This method is also not very demanding in terms of data requirements. One disadvantage however, is that it cannot capture the impact of fiscal policy changes if these are located at the end-points of the sample.

19.11 Trends in Structural and Cyclical Deficits

In their analysis, Rangarajan and Srivastava (2005) make a distinction between structural fiscal deficit and structural primary deficit by calculating the trend ratios of primary expenditure and interest payments relative to GDP separately. Thus,

$f_s = (pe)_s - r_s + (ip)_s$ and $f_c = f - f_s$

The fiscal deficit to GDP ratio thus has three components: primary structural deficit, structural interest payments relative to GDP, and cyclical fiscal deficit. As shown by Table 19.3, structural fiscal deficits account for a large part of actual fiscal deficit in the nineties. Structural interest payments to GDP ratio has increased continuously from 4.3 per cent in 1990-91 to 5.9 per cent in 2001-02, amounting to an increase of 2.6 percentage points. Structural primary deficit can be seen to have fallen from the peak of 4.14 per cent in 1990-91 to 2.75 per cent in 1997-98, before it started rising again. Rangarajan and Srivastava (2005) observe that although both factors have contributed to structural fiscal deficit, the impact of structural interest payments has been larger in the nineties and also more persistent.

Table 19.3: Combined Central and State Finances: Structural and Cyclical Deficits Relative to GDP (Per cent to GDP)

Year	Actual Fiscal Deficit	Structural Fiscal Deficit	Cyclical Fiscal Deficit	Structural Primary Deficit	Debt-stabilizing primary deficit	Actual Interest Payments	Structural Interest Payments
1990-91	9.383	8.433	0.950	4.144	4.4757	4.397	4.288
1991-92	7.162	8.302	-1.140	3.822	3.2284	4.746	4.480
1992-93	7.240	8.171	-0.931	3.516	2.9542	4.792	4.656
1993-94	9.824	8.059	1.765	3.243	2.8343	4.953	4.816
1994-95	6.945	7.975	-1.030	3.012	4.3319	5.128	4.963
1995-96	6.778	7.947	-1.169	2.846	3.8711	4.962	5.101
1996-97	6.081	7.993	-1.912	2.757	2.5044	5.111	5.236
1997-98	7.660	8.118	-0.459	2.748	0.5467	5.159	5.370
1998-99	8.227	8.309	-0.083	2.801	1.9892	5.318	5.508
1999-00	9.002	8.548	0.453	2.899	0.3002	5.682	5.650
2000-01	8.792	8.816	-0.024	3.022	-1.1835	5.727	5.794
2001-02	10.557	9.099	1.458	3.159	-0.4902	6.098	5.939

Source: Rangarajan and Srivastava, 2005.

The structural 'primary gap' is defined in Rangarajan and Srivastava (2005) as the difference between actual structural primary deficit and the debt-stabilizing primary deficit (p^s). Table 19.3 also shows that the primary deficit has been higher than the 'debt-stabilizing' primary deficit defined as $\{b_{t-1}*(1+g_t)/(g_t-i_t)\}$, in most of the years in the nineties except 1990-91, 1994-95, and 1995-96. The structural primary balance has been used in the literature to assess the medium-term fiscal stance. The large values of the structural primary balance since the late nineties clearly indicate that the current medium term fiscal stance is not sustainable.

The profile of structural and debt-stabilizing primary deficit is compared in Chart 19.6 since 1951-52. The structural primary deficit is shown by the bolder line. There are long stretches towards the end of the eighties and the latter part of the nineties that the structural primary deficit has been much higher than the debt-stabilizing primary deficit. These are the episodes in time where large accretion of debt relative to GDP took place. This led to larger structural interest payments relative to GDP. Together, structural primary deficit and structural interest payments have caused structural fiscal deficits to be large.

Chart 19.6: Comparison of Structural and Debt-stabilizing Primary Deficit

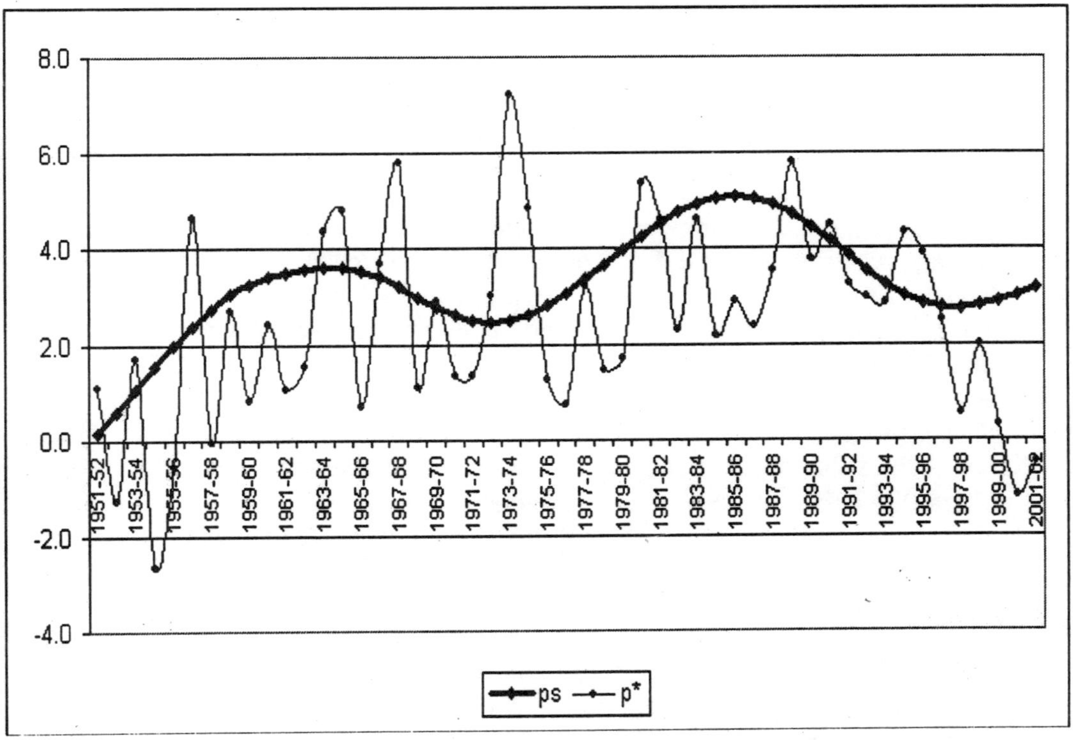

Rangarajan and Srivastava (2005) argue that in view of the large structural deficit, the role that cyclical deficit can play has become extremely limited in periods of recession in India. A suitable short term fiscal stance, they observe, would show opposite signs between cyclical deficit and departures of actual growth from trend growth, that is, when actual growth is below trend, the cyclical deficit should be positive and vice versa. In the period from 1965-66 to 1987-88, the short term stance was in the correct direction. It is in the period since 1988-89 that the short term stance has not been robust except in the mid-nineties.

19.12 Fiscal Reforms: Growth and Stability

The central government has enacted a Fiscal Responsibility and Budget Management Act (FRBMA) has been legislated after some amendments to the original Bill, following the recommendations of the Standing Committee on Finance. The FRBMA envisages that the revenue deficit would be eliminated by 2007-08 and adequate revenue surplus would be built up thereafter. However, the stipulation of reducing fiscal deficit to 2 per cent of GDP in five years contained in the original Bill was dropped. Instead, it has been provided that annual targets of fiscal deficit and revenue deficit during the period up to March 31, 2008 and also the annual targets for assuming contingent liabilities as percentage of GDP will be provided in the rules to be framed under clause 8 of the FRBMA. Clause III of the FRBMA provides that the Central Government shall lay in each financial year before both the Houses of Parliament, three statements relating to (i) Mid Term Financial Policy Statement (ii) Fiscal Policy Strategy Statement (iii) Macroeconomic Framework Statement, which shall contain an assessment regarding (a) growth in GDP (b) fiscal balance of the Union Government as reflected in the revenue balance and gross fiscal balance, and (c) External sector balance of the economy as reflected in the current account balance in the balance of payments.

Rangarajan and Srivastava (2005) observe that the Fiscal Responsibility and Budget Management Act enacted by the central government in 2003, read with its Rules, defines the target of achieving a fiscal deficit level of 3 per cent of GDP by 2008-09. This can be evaluated in relation to the Maastricht Treaty (MT) norms taking into account the potential of higher growth rate than what is implicit in the MT norms, where countries with nominal growth of about 5 per cent are supposed to maintain balance (zero fiscal deficit) under normal circumstances and up to 3 per cent of fiscal deficit, when faced with a down turn. The higher growth rate in India means that a higher fiscal deficit may be permitted. It should maintain the debt-GDP ratio at lower levels so that the burden of interest payments is lower enabling larger capital expenditures to promote medium term growth. The FRBMA does not spell out strategies that can cope with economic down turns. It has, however, defined a path of adjustment so as to reach a level of fiscal deficit that may be consistent with a medium term stance. The FRBMA is incomplete in two respects: one, it does not define a debt-GDP ratio that would be consistent with the need for keeping the economy on its potential growth path, and two, it does not define suitable limits of departure from the medium term stance to cope with cyclical fluctuations. It is also important that the centre's FRBMA is supplemented by state level fiscal responsibility legislations.

Since the state governments also borrow and have a large debt relative to GDP, no amount of central control would deliver a suitable fiscal policy stance by itself. It is imperative that mechanisms be set up for the state governments to run a fiscal deficit within an overall fiscal framework. For this purpose, the Twelfth Finance Commission has suggested the setting up of a Loan Council. It has also recommended that the states undertake their own fiscal responsibility legislations.

20

Fiscal Policy and Poverty Alleviation

> The policy literature on poverty removal has been deeply concerned with the perspective of income deprivation. I would even argue that it has been obsessed by one, undoubtedly important but partial, aspect of deprivation.
>
> Amartya Sen

Fiscal policy in a developing economy should keep poverty alleviation as one of its primary tasks. In this chapter, we consider briefly the trends in rural and urban poverty in India and the role that fiscal policy can play in further reducing the incidence of poverty in India. The role of fiscal policy becomes even stronger when poverty is considered not only in respect of nutritional threshold but also in respect of human development dimensions.

In conventional measures, poverty involves a deficiency with respect to income or nutritional thresholds. More comprehensively, poverty should encompass issues of access to services like education, health, water, and security. Poverty could be of many forms like chronic and transient poverty, and core and marginal poverty. It has been said that growth is the best antidote to poverty. Fiscal policy has a role to play in alleviating poverty by supporting sustained economic growth as well as by targeted and specific programs aimed at generating employment and income-generating assets for the poor. In addition, the government has a critical role in providing merit services, particularly education and health, which can create the necessary capabilities among the poor for combating poverty.

20.1 Measuring Poverty

Most measures of poverty in India, including the official measures, have viewed poverty as the shortfall in income that translates into to deficiency in food consumption below a prescribed nutritional threshold. However, for effective poverty alleviation a broader view of poverty should be taken. It needs to be visualized as a multi-dimensional deprivation encompassing health, education, access to water supply and sanitation, security and other relevant services. In a more comprehensive sense, as argued by Prof. Amartya Sen, poverty should be seen as an inadequacy of capabilities, which apart from other factors, is the outcome of lack of access to education and health services.

Measuring poverty requires defining a poverty line or threshold. Poverty lines can be defined both in absolute and relative terms. Any household or person below or on the poverty line can then be counted as poor, and any person above it can be counted as non-poor. Some of the frequently used measures of poverty include the head count ratio, the poverty gap ratio and the Foster-Greer-Thorbecke index. However, attempts have also been made to measure poverty as a multi-dimensional deprivation. Human poverty index is one such example.

20.2 Poverty Trends in India

The methodology of measuring poverty in India, particularly in terms of the Head Count Ratio (HCR), has evolved over time. Presently, a set of official poverty lines are available based on the recommendations of the Expert Group, headed by D.T. Lakdawala, whose report was presented in July 1993. The Expert Group had set out an alternative estimation methodology. Based on this methodology, the Expert Group had prepared estimates of poverty Head-Count Ratios using state-specific poverty lines. Using this methodology, a set of estimates of incidence of inter-state poverty are available for five reference points, *viz.*, 1973-74, 77-78, 1983, 1987-88, 1993-94 and 1999-00. These estimates utilize data from NSS quinquinniel surveys of consumer expenditure.

As shown in Table 20.1, estimates of HCRs of rural and urban poverty in India indicate that over the period 1973-74 to 1999-00, the rural poverty ratio has come down from 56 to 27 percent and the urban poverty ratio from 49 to 24 percent. The overall poverty head-count ratio shows a decline of about 29 percentage points over the 26 years' period. It amounts to an average per year reduction in the head-count ratio of a little more than 1 percentage point.

Table 20.1: Poverty Head Count Ratios and the Number of Poor in India

Years	Rural		Urban		Total	
	Head count ratio (%)	Number of poor (crore)	Head count ratio (%)	Number of poor (crore)	Head count ratio (%)	Number of poor (crore)
1973-74	56.44	26.13	49.01	6.00	54.88	32.13
1977-78	53.07	26.42	45.24	6.46	51.32	32.88
1983	45.65	25.20	40.79	7.09	44.48	32.29
1987-88	39.02	23.19	38.20	7.52	35.35	30.71
1993-94	37.27	24.40	32.36	7.63	35.97	32.03
1999-00	27.09	19.32	23.62	6.70	26.10	26.02

Source: (Basic Data): Government of India, Press Information Bureau, Poverty Estimates, Press Releases, Dated March 11, 1997 and Feb.22, 2001.

Even the absolute number of poor, which remained roughly the same between 1973-74 and 1993-94, has come down from 32.9 crore in 1977-78 to 26 crore in 1999-00. The poverty (head count) ratio for rural areas has remained higher than that for urban areas, but the decline in rural poverty has been sharper. The number of urban poor in 1999-00 is more than that in 1973-74, whereas in the case of rural areas, the absolute number of poor has fallen. Among the general category states, Orissa has the highest rural poverty ratio at 48 per cent followed by Bihar at 44.3 per cent, Madhya Pradesh at 37 percent and Uttar Pradesh at 31.22 percent. The number of rural poor in these four states considered together account for about 60 per cent of the total number of rural poor in the country.

Table 20.2: Number and Percentage of Population below Poverty Line: Selected States and All-India

by States-1999-2000 (30-day Recall period)						
	Rural		Urban		Combined	
States/UTs	No. of persons (lakh)	% of persons	No. of persons (lakh)	% of persons	No. of persons (lakh)	% of persons
Andhra Pradesh	58.13	11.05	60.88	26.63	119.01	15.77
Assam	92.17	40.04	2.38	7.47	94.55	36.09
Bihar	376.51	44.30	49.13	32.91	425.64	42.6
Goa	0.11	1.35	0.59	7.52	0.7	4.40
Gujarat	39.80	13.17	28.09	15.59	67.89	14.07
Haryana	11.94	8.27	5.39	9.99	17.33	8.74
Himachal Pradesh	4.84	7.94	0.29	4.63	5.13	7.63
Jammu & Kashmir	2.97	3.97	0.49	1.98	3.46	3.48
Karnataka	59.91	17.38	44.49	25.25	104.4	20.04
Kerala	20.97	9.38	20.07	20.27	41.04	12.72
Madhya Pradesh	217.32	37.06	81.22	38.44	298.54	37.43
Maharashtra	125.12	23.72	102.87	26.81	227.99	25.02
Orissa	143.69	48.01	25.40	42.83	169.09	47.15
Punjab	10.20	6.35	4.29	5.75	14.49	6.16
Rajasthan	55.06	13.74	26.78	19.85	81.84	15.28
Tamil Nadu	80.51	20.55	49.97	22.11	130.48	21.12
Uttar Pradesh	412.01	31.22	117.88	30.89	529.89	31.15
West Bengal	180.11	31.85	33.38	14.86	213.49	27.02
All India	1,932.43	27.09	670.07	23.62	2602.50	26.10

Source: As in Table 20.1.

The sharp reduction in the rural poverty HCR in 1999-00 was all the more remarkable because growth rate of agriculture in this year was negative at -0.11 percent although the aggregate GDP grew at a little above 6 percent. In contrast, 1977-78 was a high growth year with 12.5 percent growth over the previous year in real terms in agriculture, and 7.5 percent in GDP at factor cost. In 1983-84 also, the real growth rates in agriculture and aggregate GDP were 10.3 percent and 7.7 percent respectively. The year 1987-88 was a low growth year with growth rates of -1.4 percent for agriculture and 3.8 percent for aggregate GDP. Moderate growth was seen in 1993-94, with growth in agriculture at 4.1 percent and that in GDP at factor cost at 5.9 percent.

As shown by Table 20.2, the highest incidence of rural poverty is seen in the low income states like Orissa, Assam, Bihar, Madhya Pradesh and Uttar Pradesh. In respect of urban poverty, some of the better off states like Maharashtra also show a higher incidence of poverty. The highest urban poverty ratios among the general category states are seen in the case of Orissa, Maharashtra, Bihar, Andhra Pradesh and Uttar Pradesh. On the other hand, the lower urban poverty ratios among the general category states are seen in the case of Punjab, Goa, and Haryana.

Some authors like Deaton and Dreze and Sundaram and Tendulkar have written about certain difficulties with the estimation methods that were used in carrying out the consumer expenditure survey on which the poverty estimates are based. In the expenditure survey in 1999-00, most questions are canvassed on the basis of a 30 day recall period. There are some items, particularly relating to consumer durables where a 365 days recall period is also used. In some of the earlier surveys, some 7 days recall period questions were also canvassed instead of the 30 days recall periods. However, the samples of households were kept different where 7-day questions were canvassed. In the other case, for most questions, the recall period was 30 days, and for some of the infrequently used items, it was 365 days. While a clear distinction was made in the earlier rounds, for the 55th round, which produced results for 1999-00, in the 30-365 days version, there was a mix-up in the sense that for the same household for certain items, viz., food, pan, tobacco and intoxicants, information was canvassed for the 7-day and 30-day recall periods and recorded on two columns that were put side by side for the same set of households. It has been contended that in the 30-day recall answers were affected by the 7-day recall answers. Since the latter generally show higher consumption, expenditures in the 30 days, schedules were inflated, and showed a sharper decline in poverty than would have been the case if the 55th survey did not have this mix-up of recall periods. In the earlier rounds, the 7-day and 30-day reference periods were canvassed on two independent sets of sample households. Some analysts like Deaton and Dreze (2002 and 2003) have provided alternative estimates after correcting for this bias.

The main results following from their methodological revisions may be summarized as below.

1. The adjustment for the questionnaire design (i.e. using the 30-day recall period questions) imply that the rural head-count ratio for 1999-00 is higher by a little more than 3 percentage points (implying a lower decline rate in the nineties than officially claimed). However, revising the poverty line brings it a little lower than the official estimates.
2. For the urban head count ratio, the first adjustment (using the 30-day recall period questions) takes the estimates a little higher than the official estimate, but the revision of the poverty line brings down the urban estimates significantly lower than the official estimates. For 1999-00, the difference is of more than 12 percentage points.
3. Similar changes are noted in respect of the poverty gap index. With the revised poverty lines the urban poverty gap index is lower by 3.6 percentage points, becoming less than half of the official estimates.

20.3 Spatial Concentration of Poverty

Even as the poverty HCR has fallen over time, it has done so differently across state in a manner that poverty has become spatially more concentrated. As per the official estimates in 1999-00, as indicated by Table 20.3, nearly 74 percent of the rural poor were found to live in just six states *viz*., Orissa, Bihar, Assam, Madhya Pradesh, West Bengal and Uttar Pradesh. In the case of urban poverty, just eight states, *viz*., Orissa, Madhya Pradesh, Bihar, Uttar Pradesh, Maharashtra, Andhra Pradesh, Karnataka and Tamil Nadu accounted for a little less than 80 percent of the urban poor.

Table 20.4 shows the nature of spatial concentration in the case of the urban poor. It is indicated that eight states account for a little less than eighty per cent of the urban poor. However, four of these are middle to high income states. Five states, *viz*., Orissa, Madhya Pradesh, Bihar, Uttar Pradesh and Maharashtra account for 56 percent of the urban poor. Their individual poverty HCR ratios range from little above 26 percent (for Maharashtra to about 43 percent for Orissa).

The next four states accounting for a significant share in the total urban poor of the country are Andhra Pradesh, Karnataka, Tamil Nadu and Kerala and middle to high income states.

Table 20.3 States with Highest Rural Poverty Ratios

1999-2000 (30-day Recall period)			
General Category States and Assam			
No.	States/U.T.'s	No. of persons (lakh)	% of persons
States arranged in descending order of head-count ratio			
First six states			
1.	Orissa	143.69	48.01
2.	Bihar	376.51	44.30
3.	Assam	92.17	40.04
4.	Madhya Pradesh	217.32	37.06
5.	West Bengal	180.11	31.85
6.	Uttar Pradesh	412.01	31.22
Total number of poor		1,421.81	
Share of first six states in total rural poor (%)			73.6

Poverty Estimates, Press Releases, Dated March 11, 1997 and February 22, 2001.
Source: (Basic Data): Government of India, Press Information Bureau.

Table 20.4: States with Highest Urban Poverty Ratios

1999-2000 (30-day Recall period)			
No.	States/U.T.'s	No. of persons (lakh)	% of persons
First eight States in descending order of HCR			
1.	Orissa	25.40	42.83
2.	Madhya Pradesh	81.22	38.44
3.	Bihar	49.13	32.91
4.	Uttar Pradesh	117.88	30.89
5.	Maharashtra	102.87	26.81
6.	Andhra Pradesh	60.88	26.63
7.	Karnataka	44.49	25.25
8.	Tamil Nadu	49.97	22.11
Total number of poor		531.84	
Share of first 8 in total urban poor (%)			79.37

Poverty Estimates, Press Releases, Dated March 11, 1997 and February 22, 2001.
Source: (Basic Data): Government of India, Press Information Bureau.

Another noticeable trend is the growing urbanization of poverty in almost all states as indicated by the increasing ratio of urban poor to total poor in almost all states. Table 20.5 summarizes the pattern of growing urbanization of poverty. Thus for example, for Andhra Pradesh, in 1973-74, only 21 percent of the total poor resided in urban areas. This ratio steadily increased, until in 1999-00, 51.2 percent of total poor are reported to be urban poor in Andhra Pradesh. The general trend of urbanization of poverty is visible in states like Goa, where the share of urban poor in total poor increased from 24 percent in 1973-74 to 84 percent in 1999-2000. In Gujarat and Haryana, there is an increase of about 10 percentage points. In Karnataka, Kerala, and Maharashtra the increase is of a much larger order.

Table 20.5: Growing Urbanization of Poverty

Share of Urban Poor in Total Poor (%)						
State	1973-74	1977-78	1983	1987-88	1993-94	1999-00
Andhra Pradesh	21.0	24.5	30.5	39.9	48.4	51.2
Assam	6.7	5.6	5.5	2.9	2.1	2.5
Bihar	9.2	9.3	9.6	12.0	8.6	11.5
Goa	24.0	29.9	48.0	55.7	80.1	84.3
Gujarat	31.7	29.3	38.2	39.4	40.9	41.4
Haryana	21.5	25.5	25.6	25.7	16.7	31.1
Himachal Pradesh	3.6	4.3	4.6	3.3	2.9	5.7
Jammu & Kashmir	10.1	12.3	16.0	13.8	8.9	14.2
Karnataka	24.8	28.4	32.9	39.0	38.7	42.6
Kerala	17.8	19.2	23.6	30.3	26.8	48.9
Madhya Pradesh	16.3	18.0	22.5	24.3	27.6	27.2
Maharashtra	26.7	24.3	33.4	36.9	36.7	45.1
Orissa	7.9	7.8	9.2	9.6	12.3	15.0
Punjab	24.7	37.6	41.4	32.1	29.3	29.6
Rajasthan	21.1	23.5	23.7	26.5	26.3	32.7
Tamil Nadu	27.9	28.6	30.2	30.0	39.8	38.3
Uttar Pradesh	16.0	19.2	19.5	19.9	17.9	22.2
West Bengal	13.8	16.4	15.7	21.2	17.5	15.6
All India	18.7	19.7	22.0	24.5	23.8	25.7

Source: (Basic data): Planning Commission.

Considering, the all-India picture there has been an increase of 7 percentage points in the share of urban poor to the total poor. The trend of increasing urbanization of poverty is seen in all states except Assam. But in this case also, analysts have argued that 1999-00 estimates provided by the Planning Commission need to be revised because they are based on an urban poverty line, which is lower than the rural poverty line.

20.4 Human Poverty Index

The human poverty index is generally higher than the head count ratio for the lower income states, indicating that poverty is understated in respect of some critical dimensions for the lower income states. Estimates of human poverty index have been prepared by the Planning Commission for 1981 and 1991. Appendix Table A.20.1 gives state-wise estimates of the human poverty index, as prepared by the Planning Commission. The human poverty index captures three dimensions of deprivation: economic, educational and health. It consists of a weighted average of (i) proportion of population below poverty line, (ii) proportion of population without access to safe drinking water, sanitation, electricity, medical attention at birth, vaccination and proportion of population living in kutcha houses, (iii) proportion of illiterate population and children not enrolled in schools, and (iv) proportion of population not expected to survive beyond the age of 40. The 1991 estimates show that for the combined human poverty index for rural and urban areas among the states, the lowest poverty is seen in Himachal Pradesh at 20.9 and the highest at 50.5 percent in Bihar. In general, the value of the human poverty index is higher than the head count ratio (1991 compared with 1993-94). There are also considerable differences in the rural and urban values of index for the same state. With the urban index being significantly lower than the rural index, it is also noted that the human poverty index of Union territories has remained lower than the special and non-special category states.

Looking at the trends in poverty inter-state and all India, a recent study by Srivastava et al (2004) notes the following salient trends in the poverty profile of India:

1. All India, state-wise, rural as well as urban, poverty head count ratio shows a steady decline, the rate of the decline being the fastest in the nineties, i.e. during 1993-94 to 1999-00, a period characterized by some of the highest annual growth rates of income.
2. The 1999-00 estimates indicate average rural poverty head count ratio of about 27 percent for all India, with Bihar, Madhya Pradesh, Orissa, Uttar Pradesh, West Bengal, and Assam showing above average poverty levels.
3. In the context of urban poverty, the 1999-00 average head count ratio is 23.62 percent for all India, with Andhra Pradesh, Bihar, Karnataka, Madhya

Pradesh, Maharashtra, Orissa, and Uttar Pradesh and Assam showing more than average incidence of poverty. The inclusion of some of the higher income states in this list and the non-appearance of West Bengal in this list are the notable features.

4. The urban head count ratio is higher than the rural head count ratios in the following states: Andhra Pradesh, Gujarat, Haryana, Karnataka, Kerala, Maharashtra, and Rajasthan.
5. A visible general pattern is that the overall poverty ratio is higher for lower income states. This pattern is discernible more clearly for the rural incidence of poverty.
6. The incidence of poverty has steadily gone down both for rural and urban areas in all states.
7. Rural poverty has become more and more spatially concentrated.
8. Urban poverty has also been focused more and more in a limited number of states, but the list includes some of the better off states.
9. The concentration of poverty is higher in rural areas, and the spatial concentration has increased markedly over the years.
10. Human poverty index shows a higher incidence of poverty than the conventional measure. Although the broad inter-state pattern is the same as that for conventional poverty, human poverty index is relatively higher in the poorer states.

20.5 Poverty, Growth, and Human Development

Growth affects poverty and poverty in turn affects growth. There is considerable evidence that rapid growth has been associated with significant decline in poverty. However, the impact of growth on poverty reduction depends on a number of initial conditions including those relating to asset inequalities. Estimates indicate that the elasticity of income growth of the poor with respect to overall growth is well above 1. Initial inequalities in the distribution of land and of human capital have a clear negative effect on economic growth, and the effects are almost twice as large for the poor as for the population as a whole. An unequal distribution of assets, especially of human capital, affects overall growth, and it affects income growth of the poor disproportionately. A more equitable distribution of assets increases the incomes of the poor, reducing poverty directly. Also, by reducing the negative effect on growth of income inequality, it increases aggregate growth and further reduces poverty indirectly. Analysts argue that the more "connected" the poor are with the rest of the economy, the more effective will growth be in reducing poverty. Policy interventions that can improve credit and insurance market conditions for the poor and address issues of asset inequalities can also improve the impact of growth on poverty reduction.

An indication of the impact of growth on poverty in India can be seen by looking at how the poverty lines have changed relative to mean incomes, as measured by per capita NSDP at current prices. For example, the rural poverty line in Andhra Pradesh, which was 42.75 percent of NSDP in 1983 is only 20.55 percent in 1999-00. Correspondingly, the rural poverty head count ratio has fallen from 26 to 11 percent. In contrast, for Bihar at the other end, the rural poverty line as percentage of NSDP was 81 percent in 1983-84 and fell only to 67 percent in 1999-00. In consequence the rural poverty HCR, which was 64 percent in 1983, fell but remained at the high level of 44 percent. Clearly, states which have shown higher growth will show lower ratios of poverty line relative to NSDP and lower poverty head count ratios.

Empirical analysis in the Indian context indicates that enhancement of mean income is essential for poverty reduction. The results also show positive impact of better income distribution on the reduction of poverty. The structure of sectoral growth is also important, and under certain conditions non-farm growth can have a significant impact on poverty reduction. In a recent study, Dhongde (2003) examines the incidence of poverty of states in India in 1999-00 in relation to the all India poverty levels in order to measure as to how much of the total difference of poverty of a state and poverty at the all India level could be explained by the difference in the mean incomes as compared to extent to which it could be explained by the difference in the distribution of income. The study finds that the difference between state and national level poverty is largely explained by the difference in the mean incomes. Differences in state and all India distribution of income were less important in explaining differences in poverty levels. Similar findings are reported by Deaton (2002).

The structure of sectoral growth is also important, and under certain conditions non-farm growth can have a significant impact on poverty reduction. Ravallion estimates that while growth in agriculture as well as in non-agriculture helps to reduce poverty, the effect of the latter differs across states. Since the income and employment of the poor are closely related to rural poor, particularly the agricultural activities, much of the volatility in agricultural growth also makes the income profile of the poor highly volatile. Similar variability is also seen in agricultural prices relative to the implicit price deflator for the aggregate GDP. The range of annual percentage variation is between 22.84 percent in 1973-74 at the maximum and -17 percent in 1954-55 at the minimum. For the price deflator of aggregate GDP, this range is between 17.2 percent at the maximum and -10 percent at the minimum.

Clearly, farmers are exposed to large fluctuations in output as well as prices, which lead to variations in agricultural incomes. The element of uncertainty in agriculture is recognized to be far higher than that in other sectors. Analysts have also noted (Bhalla and Hazell, 2003) that there has been a steep deceleration in the rate of growth of in the crop sector from the 1990s compared with the 1980s. The growth rate of all crops taken together, the average growth in the 1990s is found to be only 2.38 percent per annum against 3.46 percent per annum during the 1980s. The decline in the growth rate of infrastructure investment in agriculture over a long period of time, declining efficiencies of input use, technological stagnation and surplus cereal production along with the falling prices have been noted as the main causes in the deceleration of agricultural growth in India in 90s. The second reason that has led to the decline in the employment in agriculture is the increasing capitalization of agriculture over time. As a result, the labour-intensity in agriculture has declined.

In Punjab, in the case of paddy, man-hours per hectare declined from 857.5 during 81-82 to only 450.4 in 1998-99. The corresponding reduction in Haryana was from 831.0 man hours to 584.1 in 1998-99. A similar fall was noted in the case of Wheat in Punjab and Haryana. The overall employment elasticity for the economy has fallen from 0.473 during 1973-74 to 1993-94 to 0.156 during 1993-94 to 1999-00. In agriculture, until recently, output growth was associated with high growth in employment, but there has been a steep decline in employment elasticity which has fallen from 0.49 during 1973-74 to 1993-94 to only 0.005 during 1993-94 to 1999-00. This pattern has been noted in most states and for most crops.

Deaton (2002) speaks of two areas of "regression" during the nineties: increase of economic inequality and the decline in female-male ratio among children from 945 girls per thousand boys in the 0-6 year's age-group in 1991 to 927 girls per thousand boys in 2001. He argues that economic growth may facilitate the spread of sex-selective determination by making use of the sex-determination technology more affordable. The largest declines of the female-male ratio among children between 1991 and 2001 occurred in some of the better-off states, *viz.*, Gujarat, Haryana, Himachal Pradesh, Punjab and Delhi. The fall in the female-male ratio, particularly in the case of children is strongly confirmed in the case of the four states surveyed in this study.

In a long-term perspective, emphasis on human development is even more important than growth per se. Human development is by itself an improvement in capability and it also sustains growth. Fiscal policies can be used both to support human development and growth in a manner that maximizes their impact on poverty reduction.

Investment in human development is the best long-term antidote to poverty.

First, lack of human development is itself a dimension of poverty. Illiteracy, poor health, and lack of education below a certain threshold are constituents of poverty. Secondly, with human development, i.e., through proper education and adequate health, choices regarding income opportunities widen, productivity is increased, and capacities are augmented. Thirdly, focus on human development is a potent means of fiscal intervention to reduce poverty in a country where provision of health and education is largely publicly provided. Public expenditure on education and health, especially elementary education and primary health can lead to sustained reduction in poverty levels.

Human development strikes at the root of chronic poverty. Education and health increase the capabilities of the individual to seek and sustain income earning opportunities. Restructuring public expenditure to support human development is critical fiscal intervention. Ranis and Stewart (2000) suggest that government's capability and stance in supporting human development can be looked at by examining three ratios:

1. share of public expenditure in GDP,
2. share of human development expenditure (on health and education) in public expenditure, and
3. share of priority human development expenditure (e.g. on elementary education and primary health) in total human development expenditure.

Discussion in the next section shows that in India the share of development expenditure has fallen in India over the last fifteen years, as also that on education and health.

20.6 Poverty Alleviation and Fiscal Policy

Since poverty encompasses not only income deficiency but also dimensions that relate to access to services like education, health, water supply and sanitation, and security, public provision of these services assumes critical importance. Budgetary policies play a significant role in terms of levels of expenditures, quality and delivery of service, cost of access, and volume and incidence of subsidization. Fiscal policies affect poverty directly through participation by the government in the provision of important social services including health and education and government's support of economic activities like agriculture and irrigation. Governments also undertake a number of direct poverty alleviation and social security programs. Indirectly, fiscal policies help by supporting overall growth and by catering to macroeconomic stability, which can protect the poor from vulnerabilities that come from economic fluctuations in the overall and sectoral growth rates.

An extensive policy regime in India provides for fiscal intervention with the objective, explicit or implicit, of poverty alleviation at the level of central, state, and local governments. All three tiers of the government, namely, central, state, and local are involved in poverty alleviation programs. The central and state governments sponsor a variety of programs and schemes aimed at these objectives while the local governments implement many of these programs. The Central government provides fiscal intervention by using a large number of central sector and centrally sponsored schemes. It also runs a large subsidy regime, particularly for food and fertilizers. The state governments also run large subsidy regimes supporting such economic sectors as agriculture, irrigation, power and transport.

Some empirical studies in the Indian context highlight the role of fiscal policy variables. For example, estimates provided by Ravallion and Datt (2001) show that an increase in real per capita state development expenditure, which represents a fiscal variable successfully reduces the incidence of poverty. An increase in per capita development expenditure by one percent leads to 0.14 percent fall in the head count ratio. Inflation, on the other hand, increases poverty. It is estimated that a one percent increase in the inflation rate leads to a 0.42 percent increase in the poverty.

20.7 Poverty Alleviation and Targeted Budgetary Subsidies

Most of this fiscal intervention is untargeted and general in nature. The volume of subsidy is large, but the pattern is regressive, and the benefits are appropriated to a large extent by the non-poor population. Alternative ways of measuring subsidies is discussed in Chapter 10. The discussion paper brought out by the Ministry of Finance, Government of India in 1997 had estimated the total explicit and implicit budgetary subsidies in India as accounting for more than 13.5 percent of GDP at market prices (Table 20.6).

These estimates, along with selected estimates pertaining to 1987-88, 1992-93, and 1994-95, which are roughly comparable in terms of approach and methodology, provide an idea as to the volume of continued subsidization in spite of fiscal reforms. Relative to GDP, the combined budgetary subsidies of the centre and states were at 13.51 percent in 1994-95 and 13.54 percent in 1998-99, although these were less than 13 percent for the earlier two years.

In order to segregate subsidies that may be considered desirable and justifiable vis-à-vis those that are not so, some studies, as discussed in Chapter 10, have divided services into three categories, namely, Merit I, Merit II, and Non-Merit categories. The Merit I group contains services like elementary education and primary and preventive health care deserving of a high degree of subsidization. As per the estimates for 1998-99, the non-merit services continue to claim relatively larger share of the overall subsidies being 56.5 percent of the total subsidies of the centre and states whereas Merit group had a share of 43.5 percent.

Table 20.6: Estimates of Budgetary Subsidies of Centre and States

Year	Subsidies (Rs. crore)	Subsidies as percentage of	
		GDPmp (%)	Revenue receipts (%)
1987-88 (M-R)	42,324	11.90	63.32
1992-93 (Tiwari)	95,373	12.74	70.43
1994-95 (NIPFP)	1,36,844	13.51	76.87
1998-99 (NIPFP)	23,5752	13.54*	85.80

*Estimates of income elasticity of subsidies (Srivastava and Sen, 1997) show a clear regressive pattern.
Source: Srivastava and Rao (2003).

Targeting of the implicit subsidies is difficult ab initio. Since subsidies constitute indirect fiscal intervention, no targeting can be done by definition. The benefits of subsidies are distributed according to the pattern of consumption of the subsidized goods (inputs/outputs). Since this pattern reflects the pattern of income distribution, the effect is likely to be highly regressive. Some evidence is provided in Srivastava and Sen, *et. al.* (1997) about the overall regressivity of the state subsidies. The higher per capita income of a state, the higher tends to be the per capita subsidy. This is especially noticeable in the case of non-merit subsidies. It is best to make subsidies explicit and progressive in their incidence.

In reforming the subsidy regime, the issue of subsiding agriculture should be considered as a whole. Agriculture claims subsidies through the subsidization of inputs like fertilizers, power, and irrigation. In addition, it has a share of the food subsidies which goes through the system of MSP to the farmers of wheat and rice. Much of this subsidization leaks out to subsidise industrial inefficiencies as in the case of power and fertilizers, or inefficiencies of the government or public sector, as in the case of irrigation and power. Even those subsidies that filter down to the farmers, it is the richer farmers who are able to take the larger benefits. These undesirable features arise because of the method of administering the subsidy through inputs. The correct method for supporting agriculture is to identify the justifiable objectives of subsidization of agriculture and subsidise the potential beneficiary as directly as possible. The main objective of support to agriculture, apart from making food available to BPL population at reasonable prices, should be to protect the farmers against excessive volatility in incomes, and to support the poorer farmers in terms of income or credit, enabling the purchase of inputs at the right time. But subsidies should not be designed to support selected crops against others, especially in times of sustained excess supply and availability of the global market to overcome any temporary shortages. The farmers should be allowed to respond to the market signals reflecting demand and supply imbalances, formulate short and medium term expectations, and accordingly select their cropping patterns. The poorer farmers should be given subsidies and credit facilities for the purchase of inputs, without interfering with prices, which should reflect economic and efficiency costs.

20.8 Central and Centrally Sponsored Schemes

The pattern of utilization of the grants for central and centrally sponsored schemes also indicates lack of adequate targeting. Considering average per capita grant for central and centrally sponsored schemes over the period 1999-00 to 2000-01, Bihar's per capita grant was only one-third of that of Goa and half of that of Andhra Pradesh or Tamil Nadu , and less than half of that of Karnataka. UP's per capita grant under central and centrally sponsored schemes was the lowest among all major states. In contrast, Rajasthan was able to avail of these grants, which in per capita magnitudes were nearly three times the per capita grants of UP, and has shown considerably lower HCRs in spite of continued droughts. This indicates that poverty ratios can be brought down by increasing grants on central and centrally sponsored schemes but making sure that the pattern of their distribution reflects the pattern of incidence of poverty across states.

There are other difficulties with the quality and implementation of policy aimed at social welfare and poverty reduction. Some of the main shortcomings arise from the fact that these are too numerous to effectively implement. The same design for all states is irrelevant in the context of centrally sponsored schemes. Further, the administration of schemes at the local level is characterized by considerable leakages and states, often due to lack of resources at their end, are unable to take full advantage of the central schemes as they often fail to provide the counterpart funds. Generally, untargeted programs waste a lot of resources. Table 20.7 shows that the distribution and utilization of the central and centrally sponsored schemes does not show a pattern that can be considered as related to the pattern of income levels or the pattern of incidence of poverty.

There are at least six institutional mechanisms looking at programmes that may have a bearing on poverty alleviation at the local level: the elected local body (Panchayat, Gram Sabha, Block and Zila Samiti), the District Rural (Urban) Development Agency which is a registered body and handles many central schemes bypassing the state government departments, the M.P. and M.L.A. local area development funds, the state government, and a number of autonomous user societies (like irrigation). There are many alternative centrally sponsored schemes virtually addressing the same subject. In some of the micro-credit schemes, commercial, and cooperative banks are involved. Given the involvement of a large number of agencies handling the same subject, there are considerable overlaps and coordination problems resulting into efficiency losses.

Table 20.7: Per Capita Grants for Central and Centrally Sponsored Schemes

State	Average: 1991-92 to 1992-93	Average: 1993-94 to 1995-96	Average: 1996-97 to 1998-99	Average: 1999-00 to 2000-01
Andhra Pradesh	68.21	84.58	87.70	105.98
Assam	59.57	92.74	67.87	91.24
Bihar [undivided]	54.10	65.72	15.65	57.05
Goa	98.08	129.15	118.22	151.83
Gujarat	35.81	71.75	50.73	57.41
Haryana	61.50	78.87	95.15	91.87
Karnataka	63.39	89.98	83.08	136.17
Kerala	56.20	84.14	73.90	72.73
Madhya Pradesh [undivided]	71.87	100.05	110.02	87.97
Maharashtra	61.88	67.64	56.37	63.28
Orissa	93.10	95.46	82.62	88.31
Punjab	52.74	67.22	63.05	87.24
Rajasthan	91.77	123.98	117.88	124.96
Tamil Nadu	61.28	68.74	69.23	94.63
Uttar Pradesh [undivided]	72.64	65.82	44.11	45.90
West Bengal	29.62	29.84	48.96	54.54

Source: (Basic Data): RBI Bulletin on State Finances.

20.9 Scale of Intervention

In a recent study by Srivastava et al (2004) on the role of fiscal policy in poverty alleviation in India, an attempt was made to estimate the magnitude of additional fiscal intervention, in terms of budgetary resources, translated into additional person-days of employment generation, which, if fully targeted, can help different states achieve near zero levels of poverty.

State-wise estimates for rural areas indicate, for example, that in Andhra Pradesh per poor household, 51 more person days of additional employment per year needs to be created whereas in Assam or Orissa a little more than 3 months of additional employment per poor household needs to be created. Corresponding estimates for urban areas show that as compared to the rural areas, where on average, considering the all-state position, 2.5 months additional employment per household needs to be created, in the case of urban poverty, 4 months of additional employment per poor household needs to be created.

Table 20.8: Additional Employment per Household Needed for Eliminating Poverty (With reference to 1999-00 Estimates)

(No. of Days per Household)

State	Rural	Urban
Andhra Pradesh	51.40	115.4
Assam	93.09	82.9
Bihar	78.49	92.8
Gujarat	63.93	87.6
Haryana	68.44	100.9
Himachal Pradesh	55.54	65.3
Jammu & Kashmir	59.41	50.9
Karnataka	57.71	136.1
Kerala	71.92	110.1
Madhya Pradesh	77.62	142.8
Maharashtra	70.93	161.9
Orissa	94.73	147.1
Punjab	54.83	48.6
Rajasthan	63.10	95.8
Tamil Nadu	68.26	123.9
Uttar Pradesh	75.10	106.7
West Bengal	85.76	82.6
All India	**75.45**	**120.0**

Source: Estimates are based on official poverty head count ratios for 1999-00; mean income of the poor derived from Deaton's estimates of the poverty gap ratio using official poverty line. Average size of the household is assumed to be 5 and average wage per day is assumed to be Rs. 50.

Table 20.8 shows that with reference to the undivided Uttar Pradesh and

Madhya Pradesh for rural areas, additional 75 days and 78 days per household, and for urban areas, additional 107 and 142 days of employment, will keep poverty at near zero levels. Results of a primary survey in these states (Srivastava et al, 2004) indicate that in the perception of the poor, the best schemes for tackling poverty are those that generate employment. The fiscal cost for creating additional person days of this order of employment comes to 0.76 per cent of GDP for rural areas and 0.42 per cent of GDP for the urban areas, adding to a total of 1.18 per cent of GDP. These estimates were made in respect of the 1999-00 estimates of poverty. As noted earlier, this was a year when agricultural growth was marginally negative at -0.11 per cent. In years in which agricultural growth is more buoyant, the requirement of creation of additional employment through government schemes would be less. However, to keep the additional fiscal burden at a minimum, the quality of targeting the poor households has to increase considerably.

20.10 Issues in Targeting

In India, a large part of fiscal intervention, even though often justified on the grounds of helping the poor, is very general in nature and untargeted. Consequently, a significant proportion of these benefits accrue to the non-poor. The impact of well-targeted interventions in reducing poverty could considerably increase the poverty reducing impact of fiscal policies, while reducing their costs. In principle, the finest of targeting can be done because a survey of 'Below Poverty Line' (BPL) households and within that, the sub-category of 'Antyodaya', which consists of the 'extreme' poor, is being compiled every five years. However, the BPL numbers indicate a poverty incidence ratio which is much higher than the conventionally measured poverty head count ratio, and is known to suffer from both exclusion and inclusion errors. While considering targeting strategies broadly, state-wise (area-wise) and group-wise (e.g., ST/SC population, landless agricultural labourers) targeting may be better and would involve lower administrative costs than very finely targeted interventions. In developing targeting strategies, incentive effects, and asymmetric importance of exclusion and inclusion errors need to be recognized. A greater weight should be attached to minimizing errors of exclusion of the poor rather than errors of inclusion of the non-poor.

20.11 Some Lessons from a Primary Survey

In the study by Srivastava et al (2004) mentioned above, a primary survey was canvassed in four poverty-incidence states, *viz.* Uttar Pradesh, Madhya Pradesh, Uttaranchal and Chhattisgarh on the basis of Village level as well as

Household level questionnaires. A total sample size of 9000 households was taken, split into two components: rural sector- 7000 households and urban sector- 2000 households. A three- stage design was adopted for the rural sector with district as the first stage unit, village as the second stage and household as the ultimate stage unit. Within the framework of the three-stage design in order to reach the poor, the selections of districts (first stage units) and villages (second stage units) within selected districts were done with probability proportional to size, size being indicated by female illiteracy rates as poverty is supposed to be associated with high illiteracy rates among females. In the selected village, the households were stratified into two strata. The poor judged on the basis of twin criteria of belonging to vulnerable group and below poverty line cardholders formed stratum 1 that is the main sample under study. The remaining households comprised the second stratum with a view to providing comparison.

In the urban sector the scope of the survey was limited to slum households in Class I towns of the four States. The allocation of a total of 2000 households to the four States was done on the basis of proportion of slum population. For Uttar Pradesh and Madhya Pradesh, towns were first stratified and then selected with probability proportional to size (pps), size being the proportion of slum population. For Chhattisgarh, two towns were selected with pps without stratification. In Uttaranchal, with smaller number of slums, two towns having more than a lakh of population were selected for the survey.

Some of the important characteristics of the poor households in the four states are brought together in Tables 20.9 to 20.14 to provide a comparative perspective. Table 20.9 shows, that the poor in Chhattisgarh are the poorest among the poor with a relatively larger family size and lower per capita income and expenditure levels. In almost all cases, a high proportion of expenditure is accounted for by food expenditure ranging from 56 percent in Uttaranchal to 71 percent in Madhya Pradesh. About 90 percent and above of households access the PDS for their food requirement. But they still need to access the market for food to a large extent indicating that PDS does not fully meet their requirements. An alarmingly large percentage of rural households in Chhattisgarh indicate that they do not have access to food throughout the year.

Table 20.10 indicates that male literacy rate for adults is highest in Uttaranchal and lowest in Uttar Pradesh. In all states, female literacy rates are lower than the male literacy rates of the state. In fact, the female literacy rates in the range of 25 to 37 percent in the four states are dismally low. It is a redeeming feature that male as well as the female literacy rates among children are considerably higher than the corresponding adult literacy rates. Further, although the female literacy rate among children is lower the male literacy rate, the difference is much narrower. In Uttar Pradesh, the literacy rate among the female children at 66.3 percent is the lowest among the four states.

Table 20.9: Key Characteristics of Focus Group

	Uttar Pradesh	Madhya Pradesh	Chhattis-garh	Uttara-nchal
Average Household Size	4.49	4.75	5.39	5.35
Per capita Annual Income	4,888.88	3,041.32	2,632.81	3650.92
Per capita Annual Expenditure	3,955.10	3,007.10	2,681.69	4081.23
% of food to total expenditure	62.13	71.02	68.57	56.30
% of HH Accessing food from the PDS	96.67	89.92	90.69	94.23
% of HH Accessing food from the Market	96.22	83.90	77.12	59.88
% of HH electrified	20.80	19.49	18.49	8.62
% of HH within drinking water facilities within premises	28.07	3.20	10.46	14.75
% of HH getting food throughout the year	94.42	86.12	52.77	87.59

HH is Households.

Source: Srivastava, D.K. et al (2004).

Table 20.10: Access to Public Service Delivery: Focus Group

	Uttar Pradesh	Madhya Pradesh	Chhatti-sgarh	Uttara-nchal
% of Literate Adult Male	47.68	50.95	55.16	64.87
% of Literate Adult Female	26.69	24.64	28.99	36.85
% of Literate Male Children	74.06	81.98	82.01	83.69
% of Literate Female Children	66.33	78.51	78.75	78.64
% of Children Receiving Benefits in School	132.37	151.22	95.13	173.59
% of Households Accessing PHC	68.18	75.38	69.96	86.6
% of Households Accessing Private Doctors	40.30	31.69	64.75	56.3
% of Health Expenditure in Total Expenditure	4.56	6.04	6.63	7.01
% Expenditure on travel in total expenditure	7.13	5.20	3.6	2.52
% of HH benefiting through Govt. Schemes	3.45	8.93	19.57	8.79

PHC is Primary Health Centre.

Source: Srivastava, D.K. et al (2004).

It was also found that access to electricity and to drinking water facility within the premises is extremely low. Households with electricity connections range from 8.6 percent in Uttaranchal to 20.8 percent in Uttar Pradesh among the total poor households (Table 20.11).

Table 20.11: Selected Public Services: Comparative Position of Benefits

(per cent)

	Madhya Pradesh	Chhatt-isgarh	Uttar Pradesh	Uttara-nchal
% of households benefiting from PHCs	75	69	0.68	0.86
% of households seeking services of the quacks	2	33	40	only 2%
Ante natal care: % of women who sought assistance from dais	74	41	55	7
Village Connectivity: % of villages not connected by road during certain seasons	1. 29	1. 32	1. 24	1. 26
Water supply: % of households having access to water within 100 meters of dwelling	66	74	63	68
% of poor households benefiting from government schemes	8	19	3	8

Source: Srivastava, D.K. et al (2004).

Table 20.12 shows the comparative perception about poverty across states. In all states, lack of employment is cited to be main cause of poverty. In Chhattisgarh, lack of housing is considered to be high in order of importance as indicative of poverty. In Uttar Pradesh and Chhattisgarh, lack of land possession is also associated with poverty by more than 13 percent of the poor households. Although a large percentage of the sample households access the primary health centres, their dependence on private doctors is very large. It is as high as about 65 percent in the case of Chhattisgarh.

Table 20.13 shows the perception of the sample households regarding the government schemes and other services. High percentage of households in Uttaranchal (66 percent) and Madhya Pradesh (60 percent) consider that government employment generating schemes were helpful. But only 25 percent of Chhattisgarh households considered it so. Almost all other services, *viz.*, electricity, irrigation, communication, housing, relief, PDS, education are rated very poorly by the households in terms of incidence of benefit.

Table 20.12: Perception of Poverty by Focus Group

	Uttar Pradesh	Madhya Pradesh	Chhattisgarh	Uttaranchal
Lack of Employment (%)	39.47	39.86	25.94	31.64
Lack of Land Possession (%)	13.10	4.44	13.84	2.86
Undernourishment (%)	5.73	3.49	9.33	6.32
Lack of Housing (%)	12.56	6.91	20.56	10.77
Lack of Wealth (%)	8.44	1.44	2.14	13.21
Lack of Education (%)	1.96	36.59	19.36	0.80
Others (%)	18.75	7.26	8.83	34.41
Total (%)	**100**	**100**	**100**	**100**

Source: Srivastava, D.K. et al (2004).

Table 20.13: Most helpful Government Schemes and Services Suggested by Focus Group

	Uttar Pradesh	Madhya Pradesh	Chhattisgarh	Uttaranchal
Employment Schemes (%)	43.84	59.54	24.86	65.91
Food for work programme (%)	0.24	0.30	1.84	0.70
Health facilities (%)	12.25	5.34	30.97	6.09
Provision of Electricity (%)	2.09	0.06	1.34	0.16
Provision of irrigation facilities (%)	0.22	3.12	6.83	0.49
Provision of communication facilities (%)	3.04	1.00	1.80	0.88
Provision of housing facilities (%)	12.87	3.86	3.59	8.44
Drought relief work (%)	-	0.35	2.53	
Public Distribution System (%)	0.09	0.16	1.70	0.13
Removal of Poverty (%)	1.91	4.26	0.32	0.21
Education (%)	3.56	0.95	4.85	1.60
Others (%)	19.89	21.07	19.36	15.40
Total	**100**	**100**	**100**	**100**

Source: Srivastava, D.K. et al (2004).

Table 20.14 shows the relative position of Panchayats in the four states along with some other critical features of rural poverty in the four states. Evidently, in terms of average expenditure, the Panchayats in U.P. have the least resources. In Chhattisgarh, although their own resources account for only 1.9 per cent of total revenue, their annual per capita expenditure is the highest. In the rural areas of Uttaranchal, the access to electricity is the minimum for the poor households. A very large percentage of households, i.e. close to 100 percent, in all the states indicate reliance on kerosene as fuel. Except in Chhattisgarh, percentage of poor, who emphasized employment creation as the primary means, was quite high ranging from 44 per cent in Uttar Pradesh to 66 per cent in Uttaranchal.

Table 20.14: Panchayats in Focus States: Some Parameters

	Madhya Pradesh	Chhattis-Garh	Uttar Pradesh	Uttaran-chal
Average Annual Expenditure of Panchayats	Rs. 67,047	Rs. 91,563	Rs. 29,130	Rs. 15,778
Own Revenue of Panchayats as % of Total Revenue	8.03	1.89	6.91	14.33
% of houses electrified	19.49	18.49	20.8	8.62
% of poor households using kerosene as a means of fuel	98.94	97.76	99.81	99.95
% of poor who emphasized employment generation for alleviating poverty	59.54	24.86	43.84	65.91

Source: Srivastava, D.K. et al (2004).

20.12 Poverty Alleviation: Micro and Macro Policies

While macro policies relate to growth of output and employment, monetary policies and inflation, and budgetary allocation to areas such as health, education, and other poverty related interventions, micro policies aim at individually targeted interventions. Two areas for micro interventions relate to micro credit and micro insurance. Micro credit schemes have succeeded in a significant way in many countries. In India also, these are showing signs of success although the progress may be different in different states. Micro credit is extended to the poor without the collateral, based more on his participation in the self-help groups. Many banks are now entering this market as it is a viable option rather than by compulsion under any regulations. The lowering of the interest rates in general has also helped because such micro credit directed to poor is also one aspect retail banking. The immediate success of the Kisan Credit Card scheme is also one dimension of micro credit. Extension of this scheme to the informal sector is now being undertaken.

One dimension of vulnerability of the poor is their exposure to risks in almost all walks of life. These relate to illness, disability, accident as well as income. This often generates a vicious cycle for them to remain in the poverty because for any such event they often borrow at high rate of interest and these sets up a cycle which they are unable to get out. Schemes of micro insurance therefore can be highly effective to protect the poor against risks. These will not only give them temporary relief but the effect would be the reduction of incidence in the poverty itself as they can avoid getting into the high interest induced poverty trap. However, unlike other life and non life insurance, neither insurance companies nor any other agency may take insurance for the poor as an attractive market proposition. The non government organizations, NGOs have shown initiatives on their own to provide insurance to the poor on a small scale. Examples often quoted are that of Sewagram Hospital, and ACCORD in Nilgiris. The difficulty in making this a marketable proposition arises from high risks, low premium and lack of organizational structure which can help in distributing the risk among participating agencies.

Analysts say that there are four key aspects to make micro insurance of the poor a viable business proposition. This relate to affordability, insurability, marketability and profitability. The insurance costs and the related premium need to be kept low in order to ensure affordability. This is one aspect where government subsidies have also been recommended, either directly to ensure poor or indirectly to the company/organization that provides insurance. The second aspect relates to risks in insurance. Predictability of the risks is an important aspect in determining its insurability as well as the corresponding premium. For any poor, most risks are high and relate to many aspects of his life. To reduce risks and make the proposition more insurable, it has often been recommended that a group based approach rather than an individual based approach may reduce the costs of insurance. Profitability should be compared with other insurance activities to attract the insurance conditions. Considering that some of the mainstream insurance companies may not be attracted for this sphere so either to direct them towards micro insurance for the poor under some regulation or to create a separate insurance organization exclusively for this purpose. This organization can serve as an intermediary between the poor, the NGOs and the insurance companies. Even at present, there are selected schemes being run by different departments, which aim at insuring a limited number of dimensions of the overall insurance requirements of the poor. One specialized insurance organisation can provide a platform where many of these individually run, and fragmented schemes can be brought together and integrated with the overall programme of insurance for the poor. Such an organization can also be supported though the budget, through subsidies as it will be easier to administer these through such an organization. This organization can also undertake other poverty related activities like social security premium for the poor, income generation, health care, maternity care, women & child welfare and so on. In fact, instead of having multiple schemes that run through various ministries and departments, it may be best to design and operate most of the required schemes though a single organization that can aim at combating poverty effectively.

20.13 Employment Guarantee Schemes

Based on the experience of some of the state governments, particularly Maharashtra, in successfully implementing an employment guarantee program for poverty alleviation, the central government had recently introduced a nation-wide employment guarantee program as the key policy intervention for combating poverty. The Government of India has brought out an Act in 2005 guaranteeing a minimum of 100 days of work for any adult in rural areas who volunteers to do unskilled manual work. The scheme will be implemented be the states. There is also a provision for making payment of an unemployment allowance under certain circumstances.

In regard to the costs, it is estimated on the basis of the available data on rural labour force and per capita consumption that some 35 to 40 per cent of the rural labour force would be the maximal number of those seeking such employment. If only one adult per household is provided with such work at the minimum wage, then the number of people eligible for such work would be between 35 and 40 million. At the minimum wage (which can be taken at a national average of around Rs. 60 per day) and with 2:1 ratio of wages to material costs, the cost per worker has been estimated at about Rs. 9,000 per year. This amounts to a total cost of about Rs. 31,000 crore. If half of the wage component is provided in food grains, the financial cost may come down further with some implicit public savings since this would reduce the food stock with the Food Corporation of India.

While providing for this amount of resources may itself cause some problems unless there is an increase in centre's tax-GDP ratio, a more serious practical difficulty will arise in regard to the implementation of the scheme on ground. There is also the need for a corresponding measure for relief to the urban poor.

20.14 Concluding Observations

There is overwhelming evidence showing that growth has a strong influence in reducing poverty, and its poverty reducing impact is larger, the better are the initial conditions regarding asset distribution, and the more connected are the poor with the rest of the economy. The positive impact of growth is strong enough to overtake any adverse effect of any worsening of income distribution. The combination of strong growth and a well targeted set of poverty alleviation programs would constitute the best antidotes to poverty. Fiscal policy has a role to play in both.

Fiscal policies can support growth by adequate investment in infrastructure, human as well as physical. They can improve the initial conditions by improving rural connectivity, and investing in education and health of the poor to prepare them to better partake in the growth processes. While such policies will attack at the root of chronic poverty, no poor can wait for it to take effect. For immediate and continuing relief, a well targeted poverty alleviation program is needed. In addition, safety net programs are needed to protect the poor from volatilities of economic growth, particularly agricultural, and other risks. This requires the participation of central, state, and local governments in designing, financing, and implementing these policies. It is not as if governments at all levels are not already involved in such participation. But the programs suffer from multiplicity, lack of targeting, minimal participation by the Panchayats and other local bodies, and inadequacy of resources. Successful interventions would depend, among other factors, on fiscal strength of the states.

On the part of the central government, a complete overhaul of the system of centrally sponsored schemes is needed. These schemes have been criticized as being too many with considerable duplication, being implemented by too many agencies, uniformly designed for attending to heterogeneous problems. There have been several rounds of rationalization and integration, but as on one end their numbers are reduced, new ones are created at the other. The solution to this problems lies in creating a framework in which the centrally sponsored schemes are made to *compete* with each other and the states are given the option to *choose* from among the available schemes the most suited to their requirements, subject to their entitlement of grants for this purpose, which are determined using criteria that use the existing incidence of poverty among states.

Appendix Table: A20.1: Human Poverty Index: 1991

State/UT	Rural		Urban		Combined	
	Value	Rank	Value	Rank	Value	Rank
Andhra Pradesh	45.04	19	24.78	26	39.78	19
Arunachal Pradesh	53.71	30	24.56	25	49.62	30
Assam	52.57	25	21.79	23	48.95	27
Bihar	55.85	32	28.04	30	52.34	32
Goa	24.04	4	14.48	5	37.71	18
Gujarat	33.59	12	20.29	18	29.46	13
Haryana	32.29	10	17.49	12	28.55	10
Himachal Pradesh	28.09	8	10.14	1	26.21	8
Jammu & Kashmir	39.34	16	17.81	13	34.19	16
Karnataka	37.54	15	20.69	20	32.70	15
Kerala	21.75	2	14.43	4	19.93	4
Madhya Pradesh	48.43	24	25.04	27	43.47	23
Maharashtra	36.53	14	16.20	8	29.25	11
Manipur	47.49	20	26.22	28	41.63	21
Meghalaya	56.45	31	18.05	14	49.19	28
Mizoram	45.96	18	17.39	11	32.20	14
Nagaland	46.83	21	21.70	22	42.07	22
Orissa	53.07	29	29.23	31	49.85	31
Punjab	27.95	6	18.26	15	25.06	7
Rajasthan	53.28	28	27.79	29	46.67	25
Sikkim	40.97	17	16.49	9	34.84	17
Tamil Nadu	33.98	13	18.71	16	29.29	12
Tripura	49.54	22	20.37	19	44.89	24
Uttar Pradesh	52.43	27	31.20	32	48.27	26
West Bengal	47.00	23	21.52	21	40.48	30
Andaman & Nicobar	31.53	9	15.41	6	27.09	9
Chandigarh	25.37	5	13.32	2	14.49	1
Dadra & Nagar Haveli	52.25	26	21.80	24	49.59	29
Daman & Diu	28.17	7	16.06	7	22.30	5
Delhi	20.90	3	16.60	10	17.01	3
Lakshadweep	19.04	1	13.88	3	15.88	2
Pondicherry	30.87	11	20.01	17	24.16	6
All India	**44.81**		**22.00**		**39.36**	

Contd...

Notes:

1. The HPI is a composite of variables capturing deprivation in three dimensions of human development viz. economic, educational and health. These have been captured by proportion of population below poverty line, proportion of population without access to safe drinking water/sanitation/electricity, medical attention at birth/vaccination and proportion living in Kutcha houses; proportion of illiterate population and children not enrolled in schools; and proportion of population not expected to survive beyond age 40.See the Technical Note for the estimation methodology and other details.

2. For sake of completeness, for some variables used in estimating the indices, the data for small States/UTs have been estimated/assumed following, in general , principles of physical contiguity or similarity in socio-economic or demographic profile. The details are available in the Technical Note.

Source: *Human Development Report*, Planning Commission.

Bibliography

Bibliography

Advisory Group (2001): Report of the Advisory Group on *Tax Policy and Tax Administration*, Planning Commission, Government of India.

Abel, Andrew B. N Gregory Mankiw, Lawrence H. Summers, and Richard J Zeckhauser (1989): "Assessing Dynamic Efficiency: Theory and Evidence", *Review of Economic Studies*, Vo. 56, 1989, 1-20.

Aschauer, David A. (1989): Is Public Expenditure Productive? *Journal of Monetary Economics*, 23(2), March.

Asha, P. (1986): Trends in Growth and Pattern of Subsidies in Budgetary Operations of Central Government, in *Occasional Papers*, Vol. 7, Reserve Bank of India, pp. 209-250, December, Bombay.

Australian Loan Council (1993): *Future Arrangements for Loan Council Monitoring and Reporting*. Canberra.

Bagchi, Amaresh (ed.) (2005): Readings in Public Finance, OUP, New Delhi.

Barro, Robert J. (1974): "Are Government Bonds Net Wealth?", *Journal of Political Economy*, November/December, 82, 1095-1117.

Barro, Robert (1976): "Reply to Feldstein and Buchanan", *Journal of Political Economy*, Vol. 84, No. 2, 1976, pp. 343-49.

Barro, Robert J. (1979): "On the Determination of the Public Debt," *Journal of Political Economy,* October 87, pp. 940-971.

Barro, Robert J. (1987): "Government Spending, Interest Rates, Prices, and Budget Deficits in the United Kingdom, 1701-1918," *Journal of Monetary Economics*, September 20, pp. 221-247.

Barro, Robert J. (1989): "The Ricardian Approach to Budget Deficit", *Journal of Economic Perspectives*, Vol. 3, No. 2, pp. 37-54.

Barrel, R., J. Morgan, J. Sefton, and J. in't Veld (1994): "The Cyclical Adjustment of Budget Balances, *Report Series No. 8*, National Institute of Economic and Social Research.

Barsky, Robert B., N. Gregory Mankiw, and Stephen P. Zeldes (1986): "Ricardian Consumers with Keynesian Propensities," *American Economic Review,* September 76, pp. 676-691.

Bernheim, B. Douglas and Kyle Bagwell, "Is Everything Neutral?" (1988): *Journal of Political Economy*, April 96, pp. 308-338.

Bernheim, Douglas B. (1989): "A Neoclassical Perspective on Budget Deficits", *Journal of Economic Perspectives,* Vol. 3, No. 2, pp. 55-72.

Beier, Christoph and Ferrazzi, Gabriele (1998): Fiscal Decentralization in Indonesia: A Comment on Smoke and Lewis, *World Development*, 26(12), pp. 2201-11, December.

Bird, Richard M. (1993): Threading the Fiscal Labyrinth: Some Issues in Fiscal Decentralization. *National Tax Journal*, June, 46(2), pp. 207-227.

Bird Richard M. and Pierre-Pascal Gendron (2000): *CVAT, VIVAT, and Dual VAT: Vertical "Sharing" and Interstate Trade*, International Tax and Public Finance (753-761).

Blejer, M.I. and T. Ter-Minassian (1997): *Macroeconomic Dimension of Public Finance: Essays in Honour of Vito Tanzi.*

Boadway, Robin and Frank Flatters (1982a): *Equalization in a Federal State: An Economic Analysis*, Economic Council of Canada, Ottawa.

Boadway, R and Flatters, F (1982): "Efficiency and Equalisation Payments in a Federal System of Government: A Synthesis and Extension of Recent Results", *Journal of Economics*, 15 (4), pp. 613-633.

Boadway, Robin (1992): *The Constitutional Division of Powers: An Economic Perspective,* Ottawa: Economic Council of Canada.

Boadway, Robin and M. Keen (1996): Efficiency and Optimal Direction of Federal-State Transfers, *Internal Tax and Public Finance*, Vol. 3.

Browning, Edgar K. (1976): The Marginal Cost of Public Funds, *Journal of Political Economy*, Vol. 84, April, pp. 283-98.

Buchanan, James M. (1950): Federalism and Equity, *The American Economic Review*, Vol. 40.

___ (1952): Federal Grants and Resource Allocation, *Journal of Political Economy*, Vol. 66.

___ (1965): An Economic Theory of Clubs, *Economica*, Vol. 32.

___ and R.E. Wagner (1971): An Efficiency Basis for Federal Fiscal Equalization, in J. R, Princeton.

Bradner, P., L.Diebalek, and H. Schuberth (1998): "Structural Budget Deficits and Sustainability of Fiscal Positions in the European Union", *Working Paper No. 26*, Oesterreichische National Bank.

Buchanan, James M. Musgrave Richard A (1999): "Public Finance and Public Choice: Two Contrasting Visions of the State", *MIT Press*, Cambridge, Massachusetts, p. 272.

Buiter, W.H. (1985): "Guide to Public Sector Deficit and Debt" Economic Policy, November 13-79.

Buiter, W.H. (1988): "Some Thoughts on the Role of Fiscal Policy in Stabilization and Structural Adjustment in Developing Countries", *Working Paper No. 2603*, NBER, May.

Buiter, Willem H. and Urjit R Patel (1992): "Debt, Deficits and Inflation: An Application to the Public Finances of India", *Journal of Public Economics*, Vol. 47, March 1992, pp. 172-305.

Charles E. McLure Jr. (2000): *Implementing Subnational Value Added Taxes on Internal Trade: The Compensating VAT (CVAT)*, International Tax and Public Finance (723-740).

Commonwealth Grants Commission (1995): *Equality in Diversity: History of the Commonwealth Grants Commission*, 2nd Edition, AGPS, Canberra.

Commonwealth Grants Commission (2004): Report on State Revenue Sharing Relativities, 2004 Review, Canberra.

Commonwealth Grants Commission (2004): Report on State Revenue Sharing Relativities, 2004 Review, Supporting Information, Canberra.

Collins, D.J. (2000): The Impact of the GST Package on Commonwealth State Financial Relations, Australian Tax Research Foundation, Research Study No. 34, Sydney.

Corden, W.M. (1997): T*he Road to Reform: Essays on Australian Economic Policy,* Addison-Wesley, Melbourne.

Commonwealth Grants Commission (1990): *Report on Issues in Fiscal Equalisation, Vols. I, II*, AGPS, Canberra.

Cano, L., and A. Kanutin (1996): "Estimation of Structural Deficits in EU Countries", *mimeo*, LSE.

Chakraborty, Lekha S. (2002): "Fiscal Deficit and Rate of Interest: An Econometric Analysis of the Deregulated Financial Regime", *Economic and Political Weekly*, Vol. 37, No, 19, May 11.

Chelliah, R J (1996): "The Meaning and Significance of the Fiscal Deficit" in *Towards Sustainable Growth*, Oxford University Press.

Chelliah, R.J. (2001): "The Nature of the Fiscal Crisis in Indian Federation and Calibrating Fiscal Policy", *Money and Finance*, ICRA Bulletin, Vol. 2, Nos. 4-5.

Chelliah, R.J. (2004): "Implementing FRBM Act, 2003: Evaluating Kelkar Task Force Report", Economic and Political Weekly, September.

Dahlby, B. (1994): The Distortionary Effect of Raising Taxes, in W.B.P. Robson and W.M. Scarth (eds.), *Deficit Reduction, What Pain, What Gain?*, C.H. Howe Institute.

___ (1996): Fiscal Externalities and the Design of Intergovernmental Grants, *International Tax and Public Finance*, Vol. 3.

Dahlby, B. and S. Wilson (1994): Fiscal Capacity Tax Effort, and Optimal Equalization Grants, *Canadian Journal of Economics*, Vol. 27.

Deacon, David A. (1990): Current State Aid Policy in the EC and the Implication of 1992, in Ronald Gerritse (ed.), *Producer Subsidies*, Pinter Publishers, pp. 64-75, London.

Dhawan, B.D. (1988): *Irrigation in India's Agricultural Development*, Sage Publications, New Delhi.

Domar, E. (1944): "The 'Burden' of Public Debt and National Income", American Economic Review, Vol. 34.

Eisner, Robert and Paul J Pieper, (1984): "A New View of the Federal Debt and Budget Deficit" *American Economic Review*, 74, March 11-29.

Eisner, Robert (1989): "Budget Deficits: Rhetoric and Reality", *Journal of Economic Perspectives,* Volume 3, Number 2, Spring, pp. 73-93.

Engle, R.F. and C.W.J.Granger (1987): "Cointegration and Error Correction: Representation, Estimation and Testing", Econometrica, 55, pp. 251-276.

Feldstein, Martin S. (1976): "Perceived Wealth in Bonds and Social Security: A Comment," *Journal of Political Economy*, April, pp. 331-336.

Fullerton, Don (1991): Reconciling Recent Estimates of the Marginal Welfare Cost of Taxation, *American Economic Review*, Vol. 81, March, pp. 302-08.

Gale William G. and Orszag Peter R. (2002): "The Economic Effects of Long-Term Fiscal Discipline," *Urban-Brookings Tax Policy Center Discussion Paper*, December 17.

George, P.S. (1988): in Per Pinstrup-Andersen and Alderman (eds.), *Food Subsidies in Developing Countries: Costs, Benefits and Policy Options*, John Hopkins University Press, Baltimore.

George, P.S. (1996): Public Distribution System, Food Subsidy and Production Incentives, *Economic and Political Weekly*, pp. A140-A144, September 28.

Government of India (1997): Government Subsidies in India, *Discussion Paper*, Ministry of Finance, Department of Economic Affairs, May, New Delhi.

Government of India (2000): *Expenditure Reforms Commission*, First and Second Reports, Ministry of Finance, November.

Government of India (2001): *Annual Report on the Working of the State Electricity Boards and Electricity Departments,* Planning Commission, June.

Government of India (Annual), *Finance Accounts of Union and State Governments.*

___ (1994): *Report of the Tenth Finance Commission*, December, New Delhi.

___ (2000): *Report of Eleventh Finance Commission*, June, New Delhi.

___ (2000): The Constitution of India, Ministry of Law, Justice and Company Affairs.

Goyal, Rajan (2004): Does Higher Fiscal Deficit Lead to Rise in Interest Rates? An Empirical Investigation, Economic and Political Weekly, Vol. 39, No. 21, May, pp. 2128-2133.

Gramlich, Edward H. (1985): Federal Fiscal Arrangements, in R. Cares and L.B. Krause, *The Australian Economy: A View from the North*, The Brookings Institution, Washington, D.C.

Guhan, S. (1992): State Finances in Tamil Nadu, 1960-90, in Amaresh Bagchi, J.L. Bajaj and William A. Byrd (eds.), *State Finances in India*, Vikas Publishing House, New Delhi.

Gulati, Ashok (1989): Food Subsidies: In Search of Cost-Effectiveness, *Economic and Political Weekly*, Vol. XXIV, No. 28, July 15, pp. 1584-1590.

Gulati, Ashok (1990): Fertiliser Subsidy: Is the Cultivator Net Subsidised?, *Indian Journal of Agricultural Economics*, January-March.

Gulati, Ashok and P.K. Sharma (1995): Subsidy Syndrome in Indian Agriculture, *Economic and Political Weekly*, Vol. 30, No. 39.

Gulati, Ashok and Sudha Narayanan (2000): Demystifying Fertiliser and Power Subsidies in India, *Economic and Political Weekly*, March 4, pp. 784-794.

Gramlich, Edward M. (1989): "Budget Deficits and National Saving: Are Politicians Exogenous", *Journal of Economic Perspectives,* Vol. 3, No. 2, pp. 23-35.

Garnaut, R. (2002): "Equity and Australian Development: Lessons from the First Century", Australian Economic Review, 35(3), pp. 227-243.

Garnaut, R. and Fitzgerald, V. (2002): "Issues in Commonwealth-State Funding", Australian Economic Review, 35 (3), pp. 290-300.

Garnaut, R. and Fitzgerald, V. (2002): Final Report of the Committee for the Review of Commonwealth-State Funding, Melbourne, Victoria.

Grewal, B.S. (1999): "Federalism and Fiscal Equalization: Should India Follow the Australian Path?" in I. Copland and J. Rickard (eds.) *Federalism: Comparative perspectives from India and Australia,* Manohar, New Delhi.

Harvey, A. (1989): Forecasting, Structural Time Series Models and the Kalman Filter, Cambridge.

Hsiao, C. (1997): "Co-integration and Dynamic Simultaneous Equation Model," *Econometrica*, 65(3), May, pp. 647-70.

Hsiao, C. (2001): "Identification and Dichotomization of Long- and Short- Run Relations of Co-integrated Vector Autoregressive Models, *Econometric Theory*, 17, pp. 889-912.

Hodrick, R. and Prescott, E. (1981): "Post-War U.S. Business Cycles: An Empirical Investigation", *Discussion Paper No. 451*, Carnegie-Mellon University, Pittsburgh.

Houthakker, Hendrik S. (1972): The Control of Special Benefit Programs, in U.S. Congress, Joint Economic Committee, *The Economics of Federal Subsidy Programs – A Compendium of Papers*, 92nd Congress, 2nd Session, Government Printing Office, Washington, pp. 7-12.

Howes, S. and Shikha Jha (1992): Urban Bias in the Indian Public Distribution System, *Economic and Political Weekly*, Vol. XXVII, May 9.

Hyman, David (1987): *Public Finance: A Contemporary Application of Theory to Policy*, The Dryden Press, New York.

Inter-Secretariat Working Group on National Accounts (1993): *System of National Accounts*, 1993 (Published jointly by the Commission of the European Communities, the IMF, the OECD, the United Nations, and the World Bank), Washington.

Inman, Robert P., (1996): "Do Balanced Budget Rules Work? US Experience and Possible Lessons for the EMU," *Working Paper 5838*, National Bureau of Economic Research, Cambridge, MA 02138, November.

Jaeger, A. (1990): "The Measurement and Interpretation of Structural Budget Balances", *Empirica*, Vol. 17, No. 2.

Jha, R. and A. Sharma (2004): "Structural Breaks, Unit Roots, and Co-integration: A Further Test of the Sustainability of the Indian Fiscal Deficit," Public Finance Review, 32, pp. 220-231.

Johansen, S. (1991): "Estimation and Hypothesis Testing of Co-integrated Vectors in Gaussian Vector Autoregressive Models," *Econometrica*, 59, pp. 1555-1580.

Johansen, S. and K. Juselius (1995): "Identification of the Long-run and Short Run Structure: An Application to the ISLM Model", *Journal of Econometrics*, 63, pp. 7-36.

Joshi Vijay and Little IMD (1994): "Fiscal Policy", in *Macroeconomics and Political Economy: 1964-1991*, World Bank, Washington, D.C.

Jha, Shikha (1991): *Consumer Subsidies in India: Is Targeting Effective?*, Discussion Paper No. 64, IGIDR, Bombay and in *Development and Change*, Vol. 23, No. 4, 1992.

Jha, Shikha (1994): *Foodgrains Price Distribution Policies in India: Performance, Problems and Prospects*, IGIDR, Research Reprint No. 134, Bombay and in *Asia Pacific Development Journal*, Vol. 2(1), June, 1995.

Keen, Michael (1998): Vertical Tax Externalities in the Theory of Fiscal Federalism. *International Monetary Fund Staff Papers*, September, 45(3), pp. 454-485.

Keen M. and Stephen Smith (2000): *Viva VIVAT!* , International Tax and Public Finance (741-752).

Kelkar, Vijay (2004), Report of the Taskforce on Medium Term Fiscal Policy, Ministry of Finance, Government of India.

Kopits, George (2001): Fiscal Policy Rules for India, *Economic and Political Weekly*, March 3, pp. 749-756.

Kotlikoff, Laurence J (1995): "Applying Generational Accounting to Developing Countries", *IED Discussion Paper Series*, No 67, Institute for Economic Development, Boston University, December, 1995.

Khatkhate, Deena (2001): "On Fiscal Deficits and Real Interest Rates" *Economic and political Weekly*, May 12.

Lahiri, A. and R. Kannan (2001): "India's Fiscal Deficits and Their Sustainability in Perspective" Paper presented at World Bank-NIPFP Seminar on Fiscal Policies for Growth, New Delhi.

Madden, J.R. (1993): "The Economics of Vertical Fiscal Imbalance", Australian Tax forum, 10(1), 75-90.

Madden, J.R. (2002): "Australian Fiscal Federalism, Global Integration and Economic Reform", Paper presented at Workshop on Federalism in a Global Environment, Stanford University, June 6-7, 2002.

Mathews, Russell (1972): "Horizontal Balance in the Australian Federation: The Reduction of Inequalities" in John Dixon (ed.), *The Public Sector*, Penguin, Sydney.

___ (1974): "Fiscal Equalization for Local Government", *The Economic Record,* Vol. 50, No. 131, September.

Mathews, Russell (1985): Fiscal Federalism in Australia, *Conference Discussion Paper on Edward M. Gramlich's Paper*, The Australian National University, Canberra.

Mazumdar, M.H. (1993): Fertilizer Subsidies in India: Who Benefits? in Vidya Sagar (ed.), *Fertilizer Pricing: Issues Related to Subsidies*, Classic Publishing House, Jaipur.

Munnell, A.H. (1990): How Does Pubic Infrastructure Affect Regional Economic Performance, *New England Economic Review*, September-October.

___ (1992): Infrastructure Investment and Economic Growth, *Journal of Economic Perspective*, 6(4), pp. 189-98.

Musgrave, Richard A. (1961): *Public Finance: Needs, Sources and Utilization*, NBER, Princeton.

Musgrave, Richard, Who Should Tax, Where, What? in Charles McLure, Jr. (1983): (ed.), *Tax Assignment in Federal Countries*. Canberra: Centre for Research on Federal Financial Relations, ANU.

Myers, N., et. al. (1998): *Perverse Subsidies: Their Nature, Scale and Impacts*, IISD, Canada.

Mundle, Sudipto and M. Govinda Rao (1991): *The Volume and Composition of Government Subsidies in India: 1987-88*, Current Policy Issue No. 13, December, National Institute of Public Finance and Policy, New Delhi and in *Economic and Political Weekly*, May 4, 1992.

Musgrave, P.B. (1972): *The Economics of Federal Subsidy Programs*, U.S. Joint Economic Committee, Part 2, p. 178.

Moorthy, Vivek, B. Singh, and S.C. Dhal, (2003): "Bond Financing and Debt Stability Theoretical Issues and Empirical Analysis for India", mimeo, RBI.

Niskanen, William (1992): The Case for a New Fiscal Constitution. *Journal of Economic Perspectives*, 6(2): 13-24.

Ng, Yew-Kwang (1980): Optimal Corrective Taxes or Subsidies when Revenue Raising Imposes an Excess Burden, *American Economic Review*, Vol. 70, September, pp. 744-51.

Oates, Wallace (1972): *Fiscal Federalism*. New York: Harcourt, Brace, Jovanovich.

Oates, Wallace E. (1991): *Studies in Fiscal Federalism. Economists of the Twentieth Century Series*, Aldershot, U.K. and Brookfield, Vt.: Elgar.

Organisation for Economic Co-operation and Development (1983): *Transparency for Positive Adjustment – Identifying and Evaluating Government Intervention*, OECD, Paris.

Organisation for Economic Co-operation and Development (1990): *Subsidies and Structural Adjustment; Industrial Support Policies in OECD Countries: Evolution by Policy Objectives and Financing Instruments 1982-1986*, OECD, Paris.

Pandey, Rita and D. K. Srivastava (2001): *Positive and Perverse Subsidies and Environmental Degradation: With Special Reference to Agriculture in India*, National Institute of Public Finance and Policy, New Delhi.

Parikh, K.S. (1993): *Who Gets How Much from PDS: How Effectively Does it Reach the Poor?*, Indira Gandhi Institute of Development Research, April, Bombay.

Pinstrup-Andersen, Per and Alderman (eds.) (1988): *Food Subsidies in Developing Countries: Costs, Benefits and Policy Options*, John Hopkins University Press, Baltimore.

Prest, A.R. (1974): How Much Subsidy?, *Institute of Economic Affairs Research Monograph No. 32*, London.

Prest, A.R. (1975): The Economic Rationale of Subsidies in Industry, in Alan Whiting (ed.), *The Economics of Industrial Subsidies*, U.K. Department of Industry, HMSO, pp. 65-76.

Prud'homme, Remy (1995): On the Dangers of Decentralization, *The World Bank Research Observer*, August, Vol. 10, pp. 201-220.

Papadopoulos, A. and M. Sidiropoulos (1999): "The Sustainability of Fiscal Deficit in the European Union," Advances in Economic Research, Vol. 5, No. 3, pp. 289-307.

Patnaik, Prabhat (2001): "Fiscal Deficits and Real Interest Rates", *Economic and Political Weekly*, April 12-20.

Pradhan, B K, D. K. Ratha and Atul Sarma (1990): "Complementarity between Public and Private Investment in India", *Journal of Development Economics*, Vol. 33, 1990.

Qian, Yingyi and Gerard Roland (1994): Regional Decentralization and the Soft Budget Constraint: The Case of China. *Centre for Economic Policy Research*, Discussion Paper: 1013, September 30.

___ and Barry Weingast (1997): Federalism as Commitment to Preserving Market Incentives, *Journal of Economic Perspectives*, Fall.

Quizon, J.B. and H.P. Binswanger (1984): Distributional Consequences of Alternative Food Policies in India, *World Bank – ARU–Discussion Paper No. 20*, The World Bank, Washington, D.C., August.

Rajaraman, Indira and Abhiroop Mukhopadhyay (2000): "Sustainability of Public Domestic Debt in India", in D.K. Srivastava (edited), "*Fiscal Federalism in India: Contemporary Challenges, Issues before the Eleventh Finance Commission*", Har Anand Publications Pvt Ltd., New Delhi.

Rajaraman, I., S. Bhide, and R.K. Pattnaik (2004): "A Study of Debt Sustainability at the State level in India", Reserve Bank of India, mimeo.

Rakshit, Mihir (2000): "On Correcting Fiscal Imbalances in the Indian Economy: Some Perspectives", Money and Finance, ICRA Bulletin, Vol.2, No.2.

Rangarajan, C., Anupam Basu and Narendra Jadhav (1989): "Dynamics of Interaction between Government Deficit and Domestic Debt in India", RBI Occasional Papers, reproduced in Amaresh Bagchi and Nicholas Stern (1994)(ed.), "*Tax Policy and Planning in Developing Countries*", Oxford University Press, Delhi, 1994, p. 135.

Rangarajan, C. and D.K. Srivastava (2003): "Dynamics of Debt Accumulation in India: Impact of Primary Deficit, Growth and Interest Rate, Economic and Political Weekly", Vol. 38, No. 46, November.

Rangarajan, C. and D.K. Srivastava (2004): Fiscal Transfers in Australia: Review and Relevance to India, Economic and Political weekly, Vol. 39, No.33, August 14, 2004 (with C. Rangarajan as co-author); Also published as NIPFP Working Paper No.20, 2004.

Rangarajan, C. and D.K. Srivastava (2004): Fiscal Transfers in Canada: Drawing Comparisons and Lessons, Economic and Political weekly, Vol. 39, No.19, May 8, 2004 (with C. Rangarajan as co-author); Also published as NIPFP Working Paper No.18, 2004.

Rangarajan, C. and D.K. Srivastava (2005): Fiscal Deficits and Government Debt in India: Implications for Growth and Stabilization, NIPFP Discussion Paper, Forthcoming.

Rao, C.H. Hanumantha (1998): *Fertiliser Pricing Policy Report of the High Powered Review Committee*, Department of Fertilisers, Ministry of Chemicals and Fertilisers, March.

Rao, M. Govinda and Sudipto Mundle (1992): An Analysis of Changes in State Government Subsidies: 1977-87, in Bagchi, A., J.L. Bajaj and W.A. Byrd (eds.), *State Finances in India*, NIPFP.

Ratha, D.K. and A. Sarma (1992): Price Subsidies and Irrigation Investment in India: Macro Implications, *Economic and Political Weekly*, September.

Reddy, K.N. and V. Selvaraju (1994): *Health Care Expenditure by Government in India: 1974-75 to 1990-91*, Seven Hills Publications, New Delhi.

Roberts, Donna and P. Trapido (eds.) (1991): Government Intervention in Latin American Agriculture, Agriculture and Trade Analysis Division, USDA, *Staff Report No. AGES 9152.*

Reserve Bank of India (2002): *Report on Currency and Finance*, 2000-01.

Reynolds, Patricia (2001): "Fiscal Adjustment and Growth Prospects in India", in Tim Callen, Patricia Reynolds, and Christopher Towe (edited): *"India at the Crossroads: Sustaining Growth and Reducing Poverty",* International Monetary Fund, Washington D.C.

Rye, C.R. and Searle, B. (1997): The Fiscal transfers System in Australia. In Ahmad, E. (Ed) *Financing Decentralized Expenditures - An International Comparison of Grants,* Edward Elgar, UK.

Sato, Motobiro (2000): Fiscal Externalities and Efficient Transfers in a Federation, *International Tax and Public Finance*, Vol. 7, March.

Scott, A.D. (1950): A Note on Grants in Federal Countries, *Economica*, Vol. 17.

___ (1952): Federal Grants and Resource Allocation, *Journal of Political Economy*, Vol. 60.

Shah, Anwar (1991): The New Fiscal Federalism in Brazil, *World Bank Discussion Papers,* No. 124, Washington, D.C.: World Bank.

___ (1992): Dynamics of Public Infrastructure, Industrial Productivity and Profitability, Review of Economics and Statistics, 74(1).

___ (1996): *A Fiscal Need Approach to Equalization.* Canadian Public Policy, XXII: 2, 99-115.

Smart, Michael (1998): Taxation Incentives and Dead Weight Loss in a System of Intergovernmental Transfers, *Canadian Journal of Economics*, pp. 189-206.

Smoke-Paul, Lewis, Blane D. (1986): Fiscal Decentralization in Indonesia: A New Approach to an Old Idea, *World Development*, 24(8), pp. 1281-99, August.

Srivastava, D.K., C. Bhujanga Rao et al (2002), *Budgetary Subsidies in India: Social and Economic Sectors*, NIPFP, mimeo.

Srivastava, D.K., S.K. Sanyal, Bhujanga, C. Rao, and Pinaki Chakraborty (2003), *India: Fiscal Reforms and Poverty Reduction, NIPFP, mimeo.*

Srivastava, D.K. and Surjit Das (2005), *State Government Debt in India*, mimeo.

Srivastava, D. K. and H. K. Amar Nath (2001): *Central Budgetary Subsidies in India*, National Institute of Public Finance and Policy, New Delhi.

Srivastava, D.K. and Pawan K. Aggarwal (1994): Revenue Sharing Criteria in Federal Fiscal Systems: Some Similarities and Differences, *Public Finance/Finances Publiques*, 49(3).

Srivastava, D.K., Tapas K. Sen, et. al. (1997): *Government Subsidies in India*, National Institute of Public Finance and Policy, August, New Delhi.

Srivastava, D.K., C. Bhujanga Rao and T.S. Rangamannar (2000): *External Assistance to India, Concessionality and Transmission to States*, National Institute of Public Finance and Policy, New Delhi.

Srivastava, D.K. (ed.) (2000): *Fiscal Federalism in India: Contemporary Challenges*, Har-Anand Publications Pvt. Ltd., New Delhi.

Strauss, Robert P. (1990): Fiscal Federalism and the Changing Global Economy, *National Tax Journal*, September, 43(3), pp. 315-20.

Sen, Abhijit (2002): *High Level Committee on Long-Term Foodgrain Policy*, Ministry of Consumer Affairs, Government of India, New Delhi, July.

Sidhu, D.S. and J.S. Sidhu (1991): *Paper presented at Seminar on Fertiliser Pricing held at The Institute of Development Studies at Jaipur*, September 30 - October 2.

Sihag, A. Rao and A. Sen (2001): Petroleum Sector Reforms: Progress and Prospects, The *Hindu Business Line*, 4th October.

Sirohi, A.S. (1984): Impact of Agricultural Subsidies and Procurement Prices in Production and Income Distribution, *Indian Journal of Agricultural Economics*, Vol. 38, No. 4, October-December, 1984, pp. 563-585.

Seshan, A (1987): "The Burden of Domestic Public Debt in India, *RBI Occasional Papers*, Vol. 8, No. 1, 1987.

Shigehara Kumiharu, "Commentary: Long Term Tendencies in Budget Deficits and Debt", in *Budget Deficits and Debt: Issues and Options*, Proceedings of a

Symposium (August 31-September 2), Federal Reserve Bank of Kansa City, US.

Sunderarajan, V and Subhash Thakur (1980): "Public Investment, Crowing Out, and Growth: A Dynamic Model Applied to India and Korea", *IMF Staff papers*, Vol. 27, No. 4, 1980.

Tiwari, A.C. (1996): *Volume and Composition of Subsidies in the Government - 1992-93*, ICRIER, New Delhi.

Tanzi, Vito (1996): *Fiscal Federalism and Decentralization: A Review of Some Efficiency and Macroeconomic Aspects,* Annual World Bank Conference on Development Economics, 1995, World Bank, Washington, D.C., pp. 295-316.

Teresa, Ter-Minassian (ed.) (1997): *Fiscal Federalism in Theory and Practice*, International Monetary Fund, Washington, D.C.

Url, Th. (1997): "How Serious is the Pact on Stability and Growth?, Working Paper No. 92, Austrian Institute of Economic Research.

United Nations (1992): *National Accounts Statistics: Main Aggregates and Detailed Tables*, United Nations (and previous issues), New York.

U.S. Congress, Joint Economic Committee (1972): *The Economics of Federal Subsidy Programs – A Staff Study*, 92nd Congress, 1st Session, Government Printing Office, January, Washington.

U.S. Congress, House Committee on Agriculture (1972): *Government Subsidy: Historical Review*, 92nd Congress, 2nd Session, Government Printing Office, April 3, Washington.

Vedder, R., L. Galloway, and C. Frenze (1987): "Federal Tax Increases and the Budget Deficit, 1947-86: Some Empirical Evidence, Joint Economic Committee Minority Staff Paper.

Virmani, Arvind (2002), Towards a Competitive Economy: VAT and Customs Duty Reforms, Working Paper, Planning Commission.

Von Furstenberg, George R Jeffery Green and Jin-Ho Jeong (1986): "Tax and Spend, or Spend and Tax, "The *Review of Economics and Statistics*, May, 68, pp. 179-188.

Webb, Alan J., Michael Lopez, and Renata Penn (1990): *Estimates of Producer and Consumer Subsidy Equivalents: Government Intervention in Agriculture, 1982-87*, Agriculture and Trade Analysis Division, Economic Research Service, U.S. Department of Agriculture (USDA), Statistical Bulletin No. 803, April, USDA, Washington.

Wildasin, David E., (ed.) (1997): *Fiscal Aspects of Evolving Federations,* Cambridge, New York and Melbourne: Cambridge University Press.

Wildasin, David E. (1997): Externalities and Bailouts, *World Bank Policy Research Working Paper No. 1843.*

Wrede, Mathias (2000): Shared Tax Sources and Public Expenditure, *International Tax and Public Finance*, Vol. 7, March.

Yellen Janet L. (1989): "Symposium on the Budget Deficit", *Journal of Economic Perspectives,* Vol. 3, No. 2, pp. 17-21.

Zhuravskayu, Ekaterina (2000): Incentives to Provide Local Public Goods: Fiscal Federalism, Russian Style, *Journal of Public Economics*, pp. 337-368.

Index

Index